International Handbook
of Holistic Education

Providing a comprehensive overview of holistic education's history, conceptions, practices, and research, this Handbook presents an up-to-date, global picture of the field. Organized in five sections, the Handbook lays out the field's theoretical and historical foundations; offers examples of holistic education in practice with regard to schools, programs, and pedagogies at all levels; presents research methods used in holistic education; outlines the growing effort among holistic educators to connect holistic teaching and learning with research practice; and examines present trends and future areas of interest in program development, inquiry, and research. This volume is a must-have resource for researchers and practitioners and serves as an essential foundational text for courses in the field.

John P. (Jack) Miller is a Professor in the Department of Curriculum, Teaching, and Learning at the Ontario Institute for Studies in Education at the University of Toronto, Canada.

Kelli Nigh is Sessional Faculty at the Ontario Institute for Studies in Education at the University of Toronto, Canada.

Marni J. Binder is an Associate Professor in the School of Early Childhood Studies in the Faculty of Community Services at Ryerson University, Canada.

Bruce Novak is Past Chair of the Holistic Education Special Interest Group of the American Educational Research Association and Co-Chair of the Assembly for Expanded Perspectives on Learning of the National Council of Teachers of English.

Sam Crowell is Professor Emeritus at California State University, San Bernardino; Affiliate Professor for UNESCO Chair for Education for Sustainable Development with the Earth Charter at University for Peace; and Faculty at Self-Design Graduate Institute, USA.

International Handbook of Holistic Education

Edited by
John P. Miller
Kelli Nigh
Marni J. Binder
Bruce Novak
Sam Crowell

NEW YORK AND LONDON

First published 2019
by Routledge
711 Third Avenue, New York, NY 10017

and by Routledge
2 Park Square, Milton Park, Abingdon, Oxon, OX14 4RN

Routledge is an imprint of the Taylor & Francis Group, an informa business

Library of Congress Cataloging-in-Publication Data
Names: Miller, John P., 1943- editor. | Nigh, Kelli, editor. | Binder, Marni J.,
    editor. | Novak, Bruce, 1956- editor. | Crowell, Sam, editor.
Title: International handbook of holistic education / edited by John P.
    Miller, Kelli Nigh, Marni Binder, Bruce Novak, Sam Crowell.
Description: New York : Routledge, 2019 | Includes bibliographical
    references and index.
Identifiers: LCCN 2018016589| ISBN 9781138082649 (hardback) | ISBN
    9781138082656 (pbk.) | ISBN 9781315112398 (ebook)
Subjects: LCSH: Holistic education. | Interdisciplinary approach in
    education.
Classification: LCC LC990 .I67 2019 | DDC 370.11/2—dc23
LC record available at https://lccn.loc.gov/2018016589

ISBN: 978-1-138-08264-9 (hbk)
ISBN: 978-1-138-08265-6 (pbk)
ISBN: 978-1-315-11239-8 (ebk)

Typeset in Bembo
by Swales & Willis Ltd, Exeter, Devon, UK

To the memory of Rachael Kessler, pioneering holistic educator

Contents

Contents

Contents

Acknowledgments

Compiling a Handbook is a mammoth task and inevitably includes many people. I would first like to thank my co-editors. I am grateful to Bruce Novak for initiating this project and then asking me to take the role of lead editor. I am grateful for this and the work he has done in editing the first section on Foundations. Sam Crowell has edited the last section and because of his work in Latin America he was able to obtain the chapter on the innovative doctoral program at Las Salle University in Costa Rica. The other editors live in Toronto and have met every month to keep the project on course. Marni Binder is one of those people and has edited the second section on Teaching, Learning, and Curriculum. Marni has also read chapters outside her section and provided very valuable feedback on these chapters and the Handbook as a whole. Kelli Nigh's contribution to the Handbook has been enormous. She has edited the section on research and has worked tirelessly on this manuscript. Her work has been invaluable to this project.

I am so grateful to my Graduate Assistant, Erica Killick. She has gone over every chapter and made sure it conformed to the Routledge guidelines. She also carefully cross-checked the references in every chapter. We could not have completed this project without her help. We would like to thank our colleague Mary Beattie for her valuable assistance with proof reading.

The editors are grateful for the staff at Routledge. First, I would like to thank Naomi Silverman, who conducted a review of our proposal and finalized the project with Routledge. I had worked with Naomi in the 1980s on a curriculum text and it was wonderful to connect with her again around the Handbook. Naomi retired and her successor, Karen Adler, has since provided valuable direction and support. We have also appreciated the assistance of Emmalee Ortega, who responded to so many of our inquiries about preparing the manuscript.

There are 57 contributors in this Handbook. We are grateful for the time and effort they have put into their chapters. We believe together they have given us the present state of holistic education as well as its promise. In some cases, we tested their patience with requests for revisions, but the authors always responded in a helpful and constructive manner. We recognize that there are people we were not able to include in the Handbook. We want to acknowledge all those working in this field who have inspired us to carry out this project.

I am very grateful for the support of my department, Curriculum, Teaching and Learning at the Ontario Institute for Studies in Education at the University of Toronto for space that has been created for holistic education. I have taught courses in holistic education and contemplative education since 1985 and supervised 40 doctoral students in the field.

At a personal level, we would like to thank our partners and families for supporting us throughout this project. At times it may not have been easy for them but their support has been invaluable.

John (Jack) Miller

Contributors

Heesoon Bai is Professor of Philosophy of Education in the Faculty of Education at Fraser University in Canada. She researches and writes in the intersections of ethics, ecological worldviews, contemplative ways, Asian philosophies, and psychotherapy. Her co-edited books include: *Fields of Green: Restorying Culture, Environment, Education* (2009); *Speaking of Teaching: Inclinations, Inspirations, and Innerworkings* (2012); *Speaking of Learning: Recollections, Revelations, and Realizations* (2014); *Contemplative Learning and Inquiry Across Disciplines* (2014); *The Intersubjective Turn in Contemplative Education: Shared Approaches for Contemplative Learning & Inquiry Across Disciplines* (forthcoming). She is a series editor, along with Professors Hongyu Wang, Jing Lin, and Xin Li, of the New Information Age Publishing book series: "Current Perspectives in Confucianism, Taoism, Buddhism and Education." She is a recipient of the Simon Fraser University Excellence in Teaching Award, and also Dean of Graduate Studies Award for Excellence in Supervision. She also received a Roger Hammill Award: Environmental Educators PSA Awards for Excellence in Environmental Education.

Mary Beattie is Professor Emeritus in The Department of Curriculum, Teaching and Learning at The Ontario Institute for Studies in Education at The University of Toronto. She has conducted narrative inquiry research for over two decades, and is the author of four books, *The Quest for Meaning: Narratives of Teaching, Learning and the Arts* (2009); *Narratives in the Making: Teaching and Learning at Corktown Community High School* (2004); *The Art of Learning to Teach: Creating Professional Narratives* (2001/2007); and *Constructing Professional Knowledge in Teaching: A Narrative of Change and Development* (1995). She has also written numerous journal articles, book chapters, reviews, essays, textbooks, and poetry.

Marni J. Binder is an associate professor in the School of Early Childhood Studies at Ryerson University, Toronto, Canada. Her scholarship of teaching and learning, artistic practice, research, and publications in the arts, literacy, multimodalities, and spirituality in the lives of young children are rooted in arts-based education research and a holistic philosophy. She teaches courses in the Creative Arts, Literacy and Transformative Literacy. Prior to Ryerson, she taught in the inner city schools of Toronto, Canada for 23 years. She is the co-editor, with Dr. Sylvia Kind, of *Drawing as Language: Celebrating the work of Bob Steele*, Sense Publications.

Jane Bone PhD, works at Monash University. Her research interests include: spirituality and holistic pedagogies, ethics and research with young children, different approaches to early childhood education including Reggio Emilia and Montessori, and innovative methodologies and theory, especially posthuman and post-qualitative approaches. Her current Australian Research Council (ARC) project is about the right of children in out-of-home care to their own records and documentation.

Edward J. Brantmeier is an educator, author, contemplative practitioner, and martial artist. As a peace scholar and educator, Ed co-edited the books *Spirituality, Religion, and Peace Education*,

Transforming Education for Peace, and *Re-Envisioning Higher Education: Embodied Paths to Wisdom and Social Transformation.* He co-wrote the book *147 Tips for Teaching Peace and Reconciliation* with colleagues. As a founding co-editor of a peace education book series with Information Age Publishing, Ed has advocated for practical, diverse, contemplative, and rigorous approaches to peace education. He enjoys organic gardening, forest bathing, music, and fishing with his family. Ed works at James Madison University in Virginia, U.S.A.

Brian Daniel Bresnihan (BS in Mathematics, MA and MEd in TESOL) is a devoted student of Waldorf education and anthroposophy. His life's path led him away from relying on his strengths to developing his weaknesses. After teaching mathematics in upstate New York and working as a computer systems analyst in California for relatively short periods of time, he began teaching English language in Hiroshima, and then in NYC and Tokyo. Now, he is a professor of English language in the School of Economics at University of Hyogo in Kobe, where he has been teaching for the past 25 years.

Gregory Cajete is a Tewa Indian from Santa Clara Pueblo, New Mexico. He has lectured at colleges and universities in the U.S., Canada, Mexico, New Zealand, Italy, Japan, Russia, Taiwan, Ecuador, Peru, Bolivia, the UK, France, and Germany. He worked at the Institute of American Indian Arts in Santa Fe, New Mexico for 21 years where he served as Dean of the Center for Research and Cultural Exchange, Chair of Native American Studies, and Professor of ethno-science. Currently, he is Director of Native American Studies and a Professor in the Division of Language, Literacy and Socio-cultural Studies in the College of Education at the University of New Mexico. Dr. Cajete has authored seven books and has chapters in 27 other books.

Jennie Caskey is an Upper Elementary Montessori guide at the NewGate School in Sarasota, FL. Jennie has a BA from the New College of Florida with a concentration in comparative cognitive psychology and received Elementary Montessori training through the Center for Guided Montessori Studies. Like many Montessorians, Jennie is a generalist with skills in dancing, music, and art. Jennie was raised as a modern-day gypsy, growing up on the North American carnival circuit. Jennie brings her diverse life experiences to her classroom, engaging her students with stories, philosophical conversations, and a wide span of knowledge.

Avraham Cohen is an author, educator, researcher, and psychotherapist, with 48 years of experience in the fields of psychotherapy and education. He is known for his ability to find and encourage the emergence of the "light in the darkness." As a lifelong learner, his path crossed many schools of thought, and he brings the resulting confluence into his own theorizing and practice. He has been particularly interested in the intersection of Eastern philosophy and practices and their applications within Western psychotherapeutic and educational modalities.

Dr. Cohen is the author of the book *Becoming Fully Human Within Educational Environments: Inner Life, Relationship, and Learning* (2015), and lead author of the books *Speaking of Teaching: Recollections, Revelations, and Realizations* (2014), *Speaking of Teaching: Inclinations, Inspirations, Innerworkings* (2012). He has also co-authored numerous articles and published in peer-reviewed journals and books. He is currently completing a funded research project on *The Human Dimension in Education.* Dr. Cohen teaches at Adler University in Vancouver BC, Canada. Contact him at: dr.avrahamcohen@gmail.com

Warren Lee Cohen MEd, BA Physics, is a practicing artist, educator, and scientist. Creativity and a striving for insight support his love of teaching others. He is the Director of Teacher Education at the Rudolf Steiner Centre Toronto and has been teaching adults and children through the insights of Waldorf pedagogy for the past 25 years. He was the director of Foundation Studies at Emerson

College in England. He is passionate about education that can foster healthy growth for body, mind, spirit, and community. His books include: *Baking Bread with Children* and *Raising the Soul: Practical Exercises for Personal Development*.

Sam Crowell is Professor Emeritus from California State University, San Bernardino where he was the recipient of the Outstanding Teaching Award and continues to serve as doctoral faculty. He founded the Masters Program in Holistic and Integrative Education at CSUSB and was a founding member of the Network for Spirituality and Education. He also serves as faculty of the UNESCO Chair for Education for Sustainable Development with the Earth Charter at the UN University for Peace, a faculty member at Self-Design Graduate Institute, and an invited adjunct faculty at St. Michael's College in Vermont. His writing includes topics of re-enchantment, emergence, holistic education, spirituality, and sustainability.

Tom Culham held a variety of senior business leadership roles, including managing director in an engineering consulting firm, vice president of a trade association, and forest products manufacturing executive. In 2007, he shifted his life focus to practicing, researching, and applying the contemplative aspects of ancient wisdom traditions in contemporary education. His Ph.D. thesis (2012), *Ethics Education of Business Leaders*, published as a book, draws on neuroscience, psychology, virtue ethics, Daoist contemplative practices, and leadership education, emphasizing emotional intelligence. Tom is currently Professor and Program Director, School of Management, City University of Seattle in Vancouver, Canada.

Vivian Darroch-Lozowski is Professor Emerita of the University of Toronto. Her writings and visual works cover different genres and media: scholarly, literary, creative non-fiction, artist books, painting/drawing, and film. She created, wrote, and co-directed the film *Black Earth*. Her books include *Interpretive Human Studies* (co-edited); *Voice of Hearing*; *Notebook of Stone*; *Antarctica Body*; *Blue Cloud*; *Surface of the Living World*; and *The Uncoded World: A Poetic Semiosis of the Wandered*. Her current project is returning 160 acres of agricultural land to prairie grassland with wetlands. Vivian lives in Moose Jaw, Saskatchewan.

Marian de Souza is an Honorary associate professor at Federation University, Ballarat, Australia. Marian was the Inaugural Chair, International Association for Children's Spirituality (IACS) from 2009–2016 and currently serves as an Honorary Member of the Executive Committee IACS. As well, she is the Chair of the Program Committee for the International Symposium for Religious Education and Values (ISREV). Marian has published extensively in the field of spirituality, well-being, and education.

Michael Dorer, Ed.D., is a senior consultant in the Montessori Foundation with a specialization in Montessori curriculum. His pedagogical interests include imagination, holism, classroom leadership, and storytelling in Montessori programs. He has authored seven Montessori textbooks, including *The Deep Well of Time: The Transformative Power of Storytelling in the Classroom*.

Susan M. Drake is a professor in Curriculum and Assessment at the Faculty of Education at Brock University, St. Catharines, Ontario, Canada. For almost 30 years, she has researched integrated curriculum approaches and how they have been implemented in practice. Author or co-author of several books and articles on such approaches, Susan has delivered talks and/or consulted around the world with a wide variety of jurisdictions. Although she has always been an advocate of this type of curriculum, she believes that the twenty-first century context is particularly ready for educators to adopt some form of curriculum integration.

Tony Eaude was headteacher of a primary school in Oxford, UK, for nine years before completing a doctorate. He has written extensively on young children's spiritual, moral, social, and cultural development and the implications for teachers. Much of his recent work has been related to professional development for primary teachers and teacher educators and campaigning for a more humane approach to young children's education. His latest book is titled "Developing the expertise of primary and elementary classroom teachers: professional learning for a changing world." Details of his work can be seen on www.edperspectives.org.uk

William L. Greene is an educational psychologist and professor in the School of Education at Southern Oregon University (USA). His research and scholarship focuses on holistic teaching and learning with an emphasis on self-development, human potential, and the spiritual nature of education. His teacher education courses include: Human Development, Social-Emotional Learning, Introduction to Core Reflection, and Philosophic Foundations of Education.

Yang Gyeltshen is a lead teacher of Lhomon Education at the Chokyi Gyatsho Institute, Dewathang, East Bhutan. Prior to his Ph.D. degree from the University of Massachusetts, Amherst, USA, in September 2016, he was a lecturer at one of the Teacher Education Colleges in Bhutan, heading Professional and Personal Development Studies. He earned his Master of Education in Curriculum from the University of New Brunswick, Fredericton, Canada in 1999. He believes in holistic learning—reflective and transformational, guided by the basic impulse for well-being and happiness. The purpose of education should be to create the necessary conditions that will help achieve this very fundamental goal.

Diana Harris works for the Open University, UK, as a doctoral supervisor and a lecturer on the Masters in Education Course. She has written widely on the subject of music education for Muslims and spirituality (in a non-religious sense) in the music classroom. Research in both these areas has led her to spend time doing fieldwork in Pakistan, Egypt, Turkey, and Nepal. She is the founder of the spirituality and music education group, which gives papers at conferences related to spirituality and holistic education, as well as running conferences every two years.

Tobin Hart, Ph.D. serves as Professor of Psychology at the University of West Georgia. He is co-founder of the ChildSpirit Institute, a nonprofit educational and research hub exploring and nurturing the spirituality of children and adults (www.childspirit.net). His work explores human consciousness, especially at the nexus of psychology, spirituality, and education. His recent books include: *The Four Virtues*; *The Integrative Mind: Transformative Education for a World on Fire*; *From Information to Transformation: Education for the Evolution of Consciousness*; *Transpersonal Knowing: Exploring the Horizon of Consciousness* (Ed.); and *The Secret Spiritual World of Children*.

Daniel Robinson Howe, III, EdD. "Robin" Howe is Co-Head of NewGate (the Lab School of The Montessori Foundation). Robin has AMS Early Childhood, Elementary I and II credentials, as well as an AMI Certificate in Adolescent Studies. Robin's qualifications include: BA in Religion and Spanish (Dickinson College); MA in Bioethics (University of South Florida), and Ed.D. (Argosy University). He is an IB CAS and DP Coordinator and works with AdvancED and the IMC as a school accreditor and consultant in the US and abroad. Robin is also an avid runner. This year marks his qualification for the Boston Marathon.

Jan Hurwitch directs the Visionary Ethics Foundation, an NGO based in Central America, focusing on the future of education, the environment, poverty, and injustice. She has degrees in organizational psychology, public administration, and is a candidate for the La Salle University doctorate in education with pedagogical mediation. She has applied innovative learning methods throughout Latin America and the Caribbean for over 30 years. Her areas of specialization include employment generation, non-formal education, scenario planning, ethical leadership, holistic and creative thinking, and ending existential poverty.

Four Arrows (Wahinkpe Topa), aka Don Trent Jacobs, Ph.D., Ed.D., is currently a professor in the School of Leadership Studies at Fielding Graduate University. He previously served as Director of Education at Oglala Lakota College on Pine Ridge Reservation where he fulfilled his Sun Dance vows. Author of 20 books and many articles and chapters relating to Indigenous worldview, he was selected by AERO as one of 27 "Visionaries in Education" and is a recipient of the Martin Springer Institute for Holocaust Studies Moral Courage Award. His hobbies include piano playing, surfing, handball, poetry, horse riding, and intuitive (no-spin) knife throwing.

Erica Killick is a Ph.D. candidate at the University of Toronto in the department of Applied Psychology and Human Development. Her research interests include yoga education for children and contemplative practices in childhood. Previously, Erica worked as both an early years educator and elementary school teacher in Taiwan, Hong Kong, and Canada. Erica combined her passion for yoga and meditation with her vocation for teaching young children by developing and teaching yoga and meditation to her students for over ten years. Erica is currently working on her dissertation, which examines how children in preschool experience yoga from the point of view of the child.

Bokyoung Kim is a professor of education at Incheon National University. He received his doctorate from the University of Connecticut-Storrs in 1991 and has authored numerous curriculum books in Korean and translated dozens of books into Korean, including *The Saber-Tooth Curriculum* by Abner J. Peddiwell (1939), *A Post-Modern Perspective on Curriculum* by William Doll, Jr. (1993), *Understanding Curriculum* by William Pinar and others (1995), *The Holistic Curriculum* by John P. Miller (1988), and *Exemplars of Curriculum Theory* by Arthur K. Ellis (2004). He also worked as a senior researcher at the Korea Educational Development Institute (KEDI) for three years and now serves two consecutive terms as president of the Korean Society for Holistic Education. He is currently a Big Data MBA student at Sejong University in Seoul to become a data scientist.

Younghee M. Kim is a child development specialist and professor in the School of Education at Southern Oregon University. Her scholarship includes holistic teaching and learning, core reflection approach to whole teacher development, human potential, presence, and contemplative education, and linking play to practice. She is a co-author of the book *Teaching and Learning from Within: A Core Reflection Approach to Quality and Inspiration in Education* (2013) and a co-editor of the book *Imagine a Place: Stories from Middle Grades Educators* (2017).

Fred A. J. Korthagen is the director of the Korthagen Institute for Professional Development in the Netherlands. He is a professor emeritus of Utrecht University, the Netherlands. His academic fields are the professional development of teachers and teacher educators, the pedagogy of teacher education, and, more particularly, reflection and coaching. He has published numerous articles and books, and given keynotes on conferences and workshops all over the world. His work on core reflection has influenced many working with holistic education. He received awards for his publications from the American Educational Research Association (AERA) and the Association of Teacher Educators (ATE). In 2015, he became Fellow of AERA. E-mail: fred@korthagen.nl

Frederik Leenknecht is an Education Officer at UNICEF Zambia. His research focuses on child development, early education, school readiness, social and emotional learning, and large-scale assessments of children's learning and development outcomes. He conducts educational research intended to increase access to quality education for children in developing countries such as Rwanda, India, and, currently, Zambia. He has designed, coordinated, and evaluated several large-scale education programs for national stakeholders, engaged in capacity building with educators in development contexts, and supported innovations in the collection, processing, and use of quality data to inform policy decisions and strategies to improve outcomes for children.

Carl Leggo is a poet and professor at the University of British Columbia. His books include: *Lifewriting as Literary Métissage and an Ethos for Our Times* (co-authored with Erika Hasebe-Ludt and Cynthia Chambers); *Creative Expression, Creative Education* (co-edited with Robert Kelly); *Poetic Inquiry: Vibrant Voices in the Social Sciences* (co-edited with Monica Prendergast and Pauline Sameshima); *Arresting Hope: Prisons That Heal* (co-edited with Ruth Martin, Mo Korchinski, and Lynn Fels); *Arts-based and Contemplative Practices in Research and Teaching: Honoring Presence* (co-edited with Susan Walsh and Barbara Bickel); *Hearing Echoes* (co-authored with Renee Norman); and *Sailing in a Concrete Boat*.

Jing Lin is Professor in International Education Policy, University of Maryland. Her extensive research concerns peace, environmental education, spirituality, religion, and transformative education. She published *Love, Peace and Wisdom in Education: Vision for Education in the 21st Century* (2006) and five books on Chinese education and society. She co-edited *Educators as Peace Makers: Transforming Education for Global Peace* (2008); *Spirituality, Religion, and Peace Education* (2010); *Transformative Eco-Education for Human and Planetary Survival* (2012); *Re-envisioning Higher Education: Embodied Pathways to Wisdom and Social Transformation* (2013); and *Toward a Spiritual Research Paradigm: Exploring New Ways of Knowing, Researching and Being* (2016).

Jamie Magnusson teaches in the Adult Education and Community Development program at OISE, University of Toronto. Her grass-roots organizing has involved developing community self-defence programs for LGBTQ+ and sex workers. She is interested in how urban spaces can be reclaimed from global financialized imaginaries, and her current chapter on queer holistic imaginaries builds on this idea. Interested in how cities can be reimagined as communities through prefigurative anarchist politics, she is inspired by spiritually and land based movements including the Zapatista's, Ghandians, Sri Lanka's Sarvodaya Shramadana, and Indigenous movements found globally. She believes that queer anti-capitalist politics begins with challenging white supremacy.

Aziza Mayo is a professor of education and the director of the research program Values and Value of Waldorf Education, at the University of Applied Sciences Leiden, the Netherlands. In this program, she closely collaborates with Waldorf educational practitioners and with teacher trainers to build knowledge and understanding of purposes and practices in contemporary Waldorf education. Previously, she worked at research universities in the Netherlands and the UK, studying the roles of parents and schools in children's educational experiences. She is a Waldorf school alumna.

John P. (Jack) Miller has been working in the field of holistic education for over 40 years. He is author/editor of 20 books on holistic learning and contemplative practices in education, which include *Whole Child Education, The Holistic Curriculum*, and, most recently, *Love and Compassion: Exploring their Role in Education*. His writing has been translated into nine languages. *The Holistic Curriculum* has provided the program framework for the Equinox Holistic Alternative School in Toronto, where Jack has been involved in an advisory role. Jack has worked extensively with holistic educators in Japan, Korea, and Hong Kong for the past 20 years and has been a visiting professor at universities in Japan and Hong Kong. In 2009, Jack was one of 24 educators invited to Bhutan to help that country develop their educational system so that it supports the country's goal of Gross National Happiness. Jack teaches courses on holistic education and spirituality education for graduate students and students in Initial Teacher Education Program at the Ontario Institute for Studies in Education at the University of Toronto, where he is Professor.

Jackie Mitchell has been an educator engaged in elementary teaching and curriculum development for 24 years. She recently completed her MA Ed in which her focus has been the development and application of sacred world outlook as an alternative educational worldview, integrating a holistic pedagogy with a culturally relevant and place-based approach. She was a founder of, and taught for 20 years at, the Shambhala School in Halifax, Nova Scotia, a Buddhist-inspired K-12 school. She has recently been invited to create curricula in Australia and Bhutan, integrating Buddhist and holistic principles into the curriculum.

Thomas Moore is the author of *Care of the Soul* and over 20 other books. He has been a monk, a teacher, and a psychotherapist and now is a full-time writer and lecturer. His work focuses mainly on soul in medicine, education, spirituality, and art. His most recent books include a four-volume translation of the New Testament Gospels; *A Religion of One's Own*; *The Soul of Christmas*; and *Ageless Soul*. He is a musician and writes fiction. He lives in New Hampshire and often works and relaxes in Ireland.

Patricia Morgan researches and teaches in contemplative inquiry and education. Currently, she is developing a course on compassion in the workplace and is an advisor on an ARC funded research project examining the impacts of ICT on work–life balance with the University of New South Wales (UNSW), Sydney, Australia. Patricia received an Australian government scholarship to complete her Ph.D., which is an applied philosophical study of contemplative consciousness in education, and the first of its kind in Australia and New Zealand. Her academic work evolved from an early interest in trance video art and use of contemplative practice in community development. Patricia has taught contemplative education, art, ethics, law, and academic studies at a number of universities in Sydney and has designed and facilitated a range of contemplative initiatives for the Office of Teaching and Learning, UNSW. She publishes in the areas of contemplative law, history, education, mathematics, and consciousness studies, is an invited lecturer at a number of universities in Australia and the US, and a workshop presenter, most recently at Project 30 Marina Abramović, Kaldor Public Art Event, Sydney, and the Embodied Research Lab, UC Berkeley, USA.

Ishmael I. Munene is a professor in the Department of Educational Leadership at Northern Arizona University. He has published widely on African higher education, higher education governance, education for the marginalized and educational technology. He has edited four books, and authored two. He has published numerous journal articles, book reviews, and newspaper commentaries on education and governance. He has also guest-edited a journal on African education. He is on the editorial advisory board of *Africa Education Review* and serves as an article reviewer for a number of journals. He has held visiting academic posts, and is a Carnegie African Diaspora Fellow. In 2008, he was honored by the African Studies and Research Forum with the Excellence in Research Award.

Yoshiharu Nakagawa is a professor at Doshisha University in Japan. He earned his PhD from the Ontario Institute for Studies in Education at the University of Toronto. His current interests include holistic education, Eastern philosophy, and contemplation. He is the author of *Education for Awakening: An Eastern Approach to Holistic Education* (2000), and the co-editor of *Nurturing Our Wholeness: Perspectives on Spirituality in Education* (2002). His contributions appeared in *Nurturing Child and Adolescent Spirituality* (2006), *Cross-Cultural Studies in Curriculum* (2008), *International*

Handbook of Education for Spirituality, Care and Wellbeing (2009), and *Global Perspectives on Spirituality and Education* (2014).

Kelli Nigh spent four years as an assistant and associate editor with the educational journal, *Curriculum Inquiry*. She is currently co-editor with John P. Miller for the series *Current Perspectives in Holistic Education* with Information Age Publishing. Kelli has recently authored *Nature and Learning: A Depth Perspective* (IAP). She has taught in public, private, and alternative educational settings and also has taught human development and holistic education in teacher education programs. Kelli is sessional faculty for the Department of Curriculum, Teaching and Learning at the Ontario Institute for Studies in Education, University of Toronto. Her research interests include nature and well-being, spirituality, holistic education, embodied learning, consciousness studies, and phenomenology.

Prapapat Niyom has a background in architecture and holds an honorary doctorate in education for local development from the Rajapat Phranakorn University, in Bangkok. She founded Roong Aroon School in 1997 and the Arsom Silp Institute in 2006, and is currently the President of the Arsom Silp Institute of the Arts in Bangkok. Her well-versed experiences are the applying of holistic education in schooling based on Buddhist principles. Most of her work involves running various extended supports and coaching to the wider network of Thai Buddhist approach public schools, including action research in verifying value-based lesson plan design for the mindful classroom, and teachers' reflection process. She has previously served as a member of the National Reform Council on Education and advisor to the Minister of Education, and has also served as the deputy governor for the Bangkok Metropolitan Authority.

Sarfaroz Niyozov is the Director of the Institute for Educational Development of the Aga Khan University in Karachi, and an associate professor of comparative curriculum studies and teacher development at the OISE, University of Toronto. His areas of research interest, in addition to Islamic education, include education reform and policy transfer in the developing world, specifically Central and South Asia.

Bruce Novak is currently writing *The Opening of the American Heart: The Great Educational Awakening on the Horizon of Democratic Life*, seeking to bring the democratic public to a definitive understanding of how the instituting of holistic education is integral to *bona fide* democracy. He is currently Immediate Past Chair of the Holistic Education SIG of AERA, on whose board he has served since 2006. Co-author of *Teaching Literacy for Love and Wisdom: Being the Book and Being the Change* (Teachers College, the National Writing Project, and the National Council of Teachers of English, 2011, and a press "bestseller"), he is also the author of many articles bridging the fields of philosophy, political theory, literacy, and literary theory, such as "Humanizing democracy," the lead article of the *American Educational Research Journal* in the Fall of 2002, and the winner of a 2013 University-Wide Teaching Excellence Award at Indiana University of Pennsylvania, where he taught English and English Education.

Ellen E. Nuijten is a senior trainer, coach, and consultant at the Korthagen Institute for Professional Development in the Netherlands. She works with individuals and teams on using their psychological capital. Her specialization is developing organizations, especially in education and social work. She holds a graduate degree in Human and Organizational Behavior, and was trained in various therapeutic approaches, such as constellation work (Hellinger), the contextual approach (based on Nagy), Gestalt therapy, psychosynthesis, and body work. In collaboration with Fred Korthagen, she has developed the core reflection approach. She regularly gives workshops and courses on this approach. E-mail: ellen@korthagen.nl

David Osher is vice president and Institute Fellow at the American Institutes for Research. Dr. Osher is an expert on violence prevention, school safety, supportive school discipline, conditions for learning and school climate, social and emotional learning, youth development, cultural competence, family engagement, collaboration, mental health services, and implementation science. He has led impact and qualitative evaluations of initiatives and programs, systematic reviews, and expert panels, as well as projects that have developed surveys, and supported schools, districts, and states to promote conditions for learning, including school safety, and to address disciplinary disparities.

Rebecca Oxford teaches with love and has received many teaching awards. She is Professor Emerita/ Distinguished Scholar–Teacher (University of Maryland) and teaches at the University of Alabama. She has published 260+ articles and 14 books. Topics include language learning (nine volumes); peace language and peace cultures (two volumes); and transforming higher education, transformative eco-education, and a spiritual research paradigm (these co-edited). She has presented her work in 43 countries. With Jing Lin, she edits the book series Transforming Education for the Future (IAP). With Jing and others, she edits the series Spirituality, Religion, and Education (Palgrave/Springer).

Antum Panjwani is the Academic Dean of Algonquin College, Kuwait. She completed her Doctoral Research at OISE, University of Toronto. Her research interests focus on Curriculum Studies, Muslim children's literature, teacher education, spiritually driven educational leadership, comparative education, and Canadian literature. She has been an education professional for 30 years in various parts of the world, including India, Canada, the UK, and the Middle East countries. With her major researches in both Humanities and Social Sciences, she has led educational programs for secondary, post-secondary, and adult education, particularly impacting women and the minorities.

Cruz Prado is the director of the Doctoral Program in Education with Pedagogical Mediation at the La Salle University in Costa Rica. She was in the first generation of Ph.D. graduates of this program. She participated in the creation of The Earth Charter, and has had vast experience working with educational programs in many Latin American countries, with a particular focus on pedagogical mediation and biopedagogy. She has been a co-creator with Francisco Gutierrez of the University De La Salle doctoral program since its formal conceptualization in 1999. Her areas of specialty include popular education, pedagogical mediation, eco-pedagogy, biopedagogy, political economy, and complexity theory.

Joanne L. Reid is an independent consultant and writer in Ontario, Canada. Her focus is on curriculum design and assessment, both classroom and large-scale. Dr. Reid has worked as an educator in high school classrooms, in the Brock University Faculty of Education, and with the Ministry of Education. She has co-authored articles and also a textbook that advocates for the interdependence of curriculum and assessment, and for curriculum integration.

Anne Robert is a member of the University De La Salle doctoral academic team. She has had a distinguished career as a consultant with many international organizations in various Latin American and African countries, focusing on different topics of specialty, such as migration, peace studies, systematization, scenario planning, training of facilitators in innovative techniques, and preparation of educational materials. Anne has a Master's degree in Linguistics and a Doctorate in Education. She has been instrumental in the design and continuous evolution of the University De La Salle doctorate in education with pedagogical mediation.

Susan A. Schiller Ph.D. is a professor of English at Central Michigan University. She is co-editor of *The Holistic Educator*, a bi-annual newsletter that serves an international audience of holistic educators. Her most recent publication, *Sustaining the Writing Spirit: Holistic Tools for School and Home* (2nd edn), is published by Rowman & Littlefield.

Charles Scott is Adjunct Professor in the Faculty of Education at Simon Fraser University and Associate Professor at City University of Seattle, in Vancouver. His research and teaching interests include contemplative inquiry and practices in education, and dialogue and its applications in education, particularly the applications of Martin Buber's work. His own contemplative practices are based in the Ra‾ja Yoga tradition. He is a co-editor, along with Heesoon Bai, Olen Gunnlaugson, and Ed Sarath, of a series published by SUNY Press on Contemplative Learning and Inquiry across Disciplines.

Tim Seldin is President of the Montessori Foundation and oversees its Lab School, the New Gate School here in Sarasota. He also chairs the International Montessori Council. He was the co-founder of the Institute for Advanced Montessori Studies and the Center for Guided Montessori Studies. Previously, he served as Headmaster of the Barrie School in Washington, DC, his own alma mater from age 2 through high school graduation. He earned a B.A. from Georgetown University, an M.Ed. from The American University, and Montessori certification from the American Montessori Society. He is the author of several books on Montessori Education.

Celeste Snowber is a dancer, writer, poet, and educator, who is an Associate Professor in the Faculty of Education at Simon Fraser University. Widely published, she is the author of *Embodied Prayer* and co-author of *Landscapes in Aesthetic Education*. Her most recent books are *Wild Tourist*, a collection of poetry, and *Embodied Inquiry: Writing, Living and Being through the Body*. She was the Artist in Residence in the UBC Botanical Garden from 2016–2018, creating site-specific performances of dance and poetry.

Elizabeth Spier is a Principal Researcher at American Institutes for Research. Her work focuses on child development, social and emotional learning, conditions in learning environments, and strengthening support systems for children and families. She has designed and managed large-scale, policy-relevant evaluations examining the effectiveness of programs and interventions designed to improve developmental and educational outcomes for children in over 20 countries. She provides technical assistance in early child development, social and emotional learning, and positive youth development, and has led the creation of monitoring systems and dashboards for comprehensive child and family supports, education, and early childhood development settings.

Julian Stern was a schoolteacher for 14 years, and has worked in universities for 25 years. Julian is widely published, with 15 books and over 30 articles, including *A Philosophy of Schooling: Care and Curiosity in Community* (2018); *Teaching Religious Education: Researchers in the Classroom*: 2nd edn (2018); *Can I Tell You About Loneliness?* (2017); *Virtuous Educational Research: Conversations on Ethical Practice* (2016); *Loneliness and Solitude in Schools: How to Value Individuality and Create an Enstatic School* (2014); *The Spirit of the School* (2009); *Schools and Religions: Imagining the Real* (2007); *and Involving Parents* (2003). He can be contacted by email on j.stern@yorksj.ac.uk, at Amazon on http://amzn. to/1g9cADN, and via @ISREV1978.

Njoki N. Wane, PhD, is a Professor at the University of Toronto. She is currently serving as Chair of Social Justice Education Department at the Ontario Institute for Studies in Education (OISE), University of Toronto. An accomplished educator, researcher and educational leader, Professor Wane's areas of research, writing and teaching are: African Indigenous education; Spirituality; Black Canadian feminist Thought; Women & leadership; Anti-Colonial thought and decolonization of education. From 2011 to 2014, Professor Wane served as Special Advisor on Status of Women Issues. She also served as Director, Center for Integrative Anti-Racism Studies (CIARS) at OISE from 2006 to 2014. An award winning professor, Dr Wane has received: African Women Achievement Award; Harry Jerome Professional Excellence Award; David E. Hunt Award, as well as the President Teaching Award at the University of Toronto for her tremendous contributions to teaching, learning and student supervision at the graduate level.

Wong Ping Ho is currently Adjunct Associate Professor in the Department of International Education and Lifelong Learning, The Education University of Hong Kong (formerly the Hong Kong Institute of Education). Before moving into teacher education, he had been a secondary school teacher for ten years. He was involved in the establishment of the Hong Kong Institute of Education's Centre for Religious and Spirituality Education in 2006, and was its Director prior to his retirement in 2016.

Preface

Educating the Whole Person

John P. Miller

In *The Coming Interspiritual Age*, Kurt Johnson and David Robert Ord (2012) argue that during the latter part of the twentieth century there was the unfolding of the Holistic Age. In their view, during this period an emerging holism developed that includes "a skilled understanding and synergy between our interior and exterior, subject and objective ways of knowing and working" (p. 163). Johnson and Ord refer to a number of developments, including various conferences, publications, and institutions that reflect this emerging holistic perspective. They cite books such as the integral work of Ken Wilber (2007), Paul Hawken's (2007) *Blessed Unrest*, which describes global grass roots change, and Beck and Cowan's (1996) *Spiral Dynamics*. Organizations and associations include The Charter for Compassion, California Institute for Integral Studies, Naropa University, Omega Institute for Holistic Studies, The Center for Contemplative Mind in Society, and The Garrison Institute.

Holistic education can be seen, then, as part of this unfolding of the Holistic Age. Holistic education as a term arose in the 1980s and in 1988 saw the publication of *The Holistic Education Review* and my book, *The Holistic Curriculum*. Since then seminal works in the field have included Ron Miller's *What Are Schools For?*, Rachael Kessler's *The Soul of Education*, Parker Palmer's *The Courage to Teach*, and Nel Noddings' books on care (1992) and happiness (2003). In recent years, there have been several important developments in the field of holistic education. For example, important conferences have taken place around the world. Under the leadership of Professor Yoshiharu Nagakawa, The Asia Pacific Holistic Education Network has held annual meetings in Japan, Korea, Thailand, and Malaysia where holistic educators have come together to present their work. In North America, conferences have been held at the Ontario Institute for Studies in Education at the University of Toronto, the University of Manitoba, and Southern Oregon University. Southern Oregon University has also established a Center for Holistic Education. There is also the Holistic Special Interest Group (SIG) at the American Educational Research Association (AERA), where research is presented on an annual basis. In response to growing interest in the field, Information Age Publishing has initiated a book series entitled Current Perspectives in Holistic Education. The American Institutes for Research has engaged in major research in whole child education that is described in the chapter by Spier and her associates at AIR.

This Handbook can also be seen in the context of the growth of Holistic Education as a field of inquiry and practice. The Handbook provides an up-to-date picture of the field, as it exists around the globe, its theories, practices, and research. The original proposal for the Handbook identified the following objectives:

- Describe the current state of the field of holistic education
- Examine the theoretical and historical foundations of holistic education
- Describe examples of holistic education with regard to schools, programs and pedagogies

- Present current research methods used in holistic education
- Outline new and emerging research in the field
- Examine potential areas for future program development and research

I believe we have met these objectives. Perhaps the greatest challenge has been in the area of empirical research, since this is an area that has not been developed as fully as the other areas. Recently, books such as *Toward a Spiritual Research Paradigm*, edited by Jing Lin, Rebecca Oxford, and Tom Culham (2016) have started to address the need for innovative research methods that could be used by holistic educators.

The overall purpose of this Handbook is to create a comprehensive resource for both researchers and practitioners, which we envision will be utilized as a foundational text. Notably, this Handbook is the first comprehensive overview of holistic education's history, conceptions, practices, and research. The Handbook will function as a valuable reference for practitioners and researchers, as well as for novices who are just learning about the field.

The Handbook has five sections. I am so grateful for the work of my co-editors, Kelli Nigh, Marni J. Binder, Bruce Novak, and Sam Crowell who have edited the different sections of the Handbook. Since each editor has written an introduction to his or her section, here I will just outline the overall structure of the Handbook. The first section, entitled Foundations of Holistic Education and edited by Bruce Novak, explores the history and theoretical foundations of holistic education. Marni Binder edits the second section of the Handbook that focuses on examples of teaching, learning, and curriculum in holistic education. I edit the third section that includes specific examples and programs in holistic education. The fourth section is edited by Kelli Nigh and explores research in holistic education. The last section is edited by Sam Crowell and is entitled Final Reflections: it focuses on future trends and possible areas for future program development and research.

The rest of this introduction will identify a few of the central themes of the book and cite certain chapters that are representative of these themes.

The Whole Child

Holistic education is about the education of the whole child—body, mind and spirit. The whole child is central to Montessori education and Waldorf education. Tim Seldin and his associates have contributed a chapter where they situate Montessori education within the context of holism. There are two chapters on Waldorf education; Warren Cohen and Brian Bresnihan describe life in a Waldorf school, while Aziza Mayo has written about research on Waldorf education in the Netherlands. There are also examples of educating the whole child in Bhutan, Thailand, and East Africa. Professor Prapapat Niyom in Thailand has written about how the incorporation of Buddhist principles in several schools nurtures the whole child, while Sarfaroz Niyozov and Antum Panjwani write about how Islamic education reaches the whole child in Madrasa schools in East Africa.

There are also examples of whole person education in higher education. Jamie Magnusson at the University of Toronto describes her graduate course that engages the whole person, while Cruz Prado at LaSalle University in Costa Rica writes about the holistic doctorate program there.

Nature

Another important theme in this book and in holistic education is the connection to nature. Holistic education seeks to be in harmony with nature and, thus, focuses on interdependence and connectedness to guide teaching and learning (Miller, 2007). This theme is central to Indigenous education and we are fortunate to have contributions from Four Arrows and Greg Cajete, leading indigenous scholars. One of the interesting developments in Korea and Japan is the planting of small forests on school grounds. Professor Kim describes how a large number of schools in Korea have planted these forests and how they encourage integrated learning. The forest can also be a place where children can meditate. Jane Bone, in her chapter, writes about how, in the Danish preschools, children walk into the forest on their own to "be at home in the pine trees".

Holistic Teaching and Learning

The Handbook explores many innovative approaches to teaching and learning that connect to the whole person. Fred Korthagen has developed a powerful model of learning that builds on one's core values. His approach has been adopted by faculty at Southern Oregon University. William Greene and Younghee Kim, Professors there, introduce the concept of *va*, which is the space or between-ness that connects and allows energy to flow in the classroom.

Several authors in the Handbook explore how various spiritual concepts like *va* are central to holistic teaching and learning. For example, Vivian Darroch-Lozowski introduces the concept of the *threshold body*, which allows the person to experience the world with a "wider and deeper inner wisdom". Ping Ho Wong explores how stillness and silence are critical to traditional Chinese spiritual practices which can lead to a state of *wuwei* or selfless, effortless action.

In conclusion, we are fortunate to have a contribution from Thomas Moore, whose writing about the soul helps us see how soul transcends religion and is crucial to our humanity. He offers his vision of the place of soul in holistic education:

> My final word on holism in education, therefore, is to suggest that educators might consider their deep work as taking care of the health of the students' souls, even as they focus on learning and knowledge. This Platonic or soul-based learning has roots in both the student' very being and in the culture. Certainly one of the goals in education is to improve the character of the culture at large by creating deeply educated persons.
>
> . . . if you are not concerned for your students' souls, you can easily do them harm. More than that you need to know what it takes to heal a wounded soul, because most if not all of your students come to you with such wounds. You come to them with your own wounds.
>
> Holistic education doesn't merely dispense knowledge; it does so in a way that both the teacher and the student's soul is engaged and benefits.

The contributors to this Handbook offer inspiring visions of holistic education. More than that, they have also described a variety of practices to enable teachers and schools to make holistic education a living reality. Holistic education is deep education that touches the whole human being. Through this education, it also offers the hope that the planet and all those who inhabit this wondrous globe can grow and thrive.

References

Beck, D. & Cowan, C. (1996). *Spiral dynamics: Mastering values, leadership and change.* Oxford, UK: Blackwell.

Hawken, P. (2007). *Blessed unrest: How the largest movement in the world came into being and no one saw it coming.* New York: Viking.

Johnson, K. & Ord, D.R. (2012). *The coming interspiritual age.* Vancouver, BC: Namaste.

Kessler, R. (2000). *The soul of education.* Alexandria, VA: ASCD.

Lin, J., Oxford, R., & Culham, T. (2016). *Toward a spiritual research paradigm.* Charlotte, NC: Information Age.

Miller, J.P. (1988/2007). *The holistic curriculum.* Toronto: OISE Press.

Miller, R. (1990). *What are schools for?* Brandon, VT: Holistic Education Press.

Noddings, N. (1992). *The challenge to care in schools.* New York: Teachers College Press.

Noddings, N. (2003). *Happiness and education.* New York: Cambridge University Press.

Palmer, Parker (1998). *The courage to teach: Exploring the inner landscape of a teacher's life.* San Francisco, CA: Jossey Bass.

Wilber, K. (2007). *Integral spirituality: A startling new role for religion in the modern and post modern world.* Boston, MA: Shambhala.

PART I
Foundations
Introduction

Bruce Novak

Almost from the outset of the founding of institutions of democratic public education, various movements of "progressive" education have been countered by those calling for a return to "the basics."

What perhaps most distinguishes the holistic education movement from other types of progressive education, though, is the effort to ground the education of human beings in what is most *truly* basic to our humanity.

The fact is that neither the popular construct of "the 3 R's" nor the idea that education has unspecified "social" foundations—upon which most progressive education has been based—provide adequate beginnings for the understanding of the depth of what can occur when teachers seek to raise learners to the fullest potentials of life that they are capable of attaining. And it is nothing less than the real foundations of that aliveness that holistic education has sought to arrive at.

Those foundations are plural—though irreducible to an alliterative list of mastered skills—because of the complex nature and history of our species. And holistic education can be understood as the attempt both to adequately define and to adequately intuit that complexity in order to bring our species into better harmony both with itself and with the world that we inhabit—and that we must now learn to better integrate ourselves within, to ensure, not just our flourishing, but our very survival.

What, then, *are* those real, true foundations? How shall we name and integrate them?

It has been one of the deep privileges of my life first to read each of these six uniquely marvelous pieces, and then to think about how they might be thought of together: brought to form a new, complex whole that might actually reflect the real complex wholeness of our humanity.

What I have found is that there are seven integrated dimensions of holistic education: three related to our organic nature; three related to the beginnings, middle, and prospective fulfillment of our being in the world; and a final, single overarching dimension.

The Gateway to Holism

Jack Miller's opening essay, "Holistic Education: A Brief History," shows how the intuitions that he and Ron Miller had in the 1980s in founding the holistic education movement[1]—I call them the "two bright angelic Millers" that life somehow conjured up to confront the Blakean "dark Satanic mills" of modern industrial schools—provided a new name that opened up whole realms of prior educational thought and practice as being much more than socially "progressive": actually psychically, socially, and spiritually "integrative." We are naturally integrative creatures, and can draw culturally and educatively on that nature to grow *more* integrated, and less *dis*integrated.

Natural Holism

1. The neurological dimension: Our brains are hardwired for holism. In an age in which our minds are mostly seen as machines in many ways inferior to mechanical computers, it is essential to notice that fully half—and evolutionarily the stronger half—of our brains is devoted to holistic imagination, not mechanical computation. Iain McGilchrist's revelatory *The Master and His Emissary: The Divided Brain and the Making of the Western World* (treated more fully in Hart's Section Five essay) first describes "the primacy of the right hemisphere" of imaginative, intuitive, holistic perception throughout most of the history of our species. Then it describes "the triumph of the left hemisphere" over it, and the active repression of holistic perception in the West, particularly since the "Enlightenment"—a deeply ironic term in this context, since it has actually proliferated a species-wide madness in which left-brained analysis has eclipsed intuitive, connective wisdom. Holistic education serves as nothing less than the healing of this historic neurological rift: a return of the human mind to sanity and health. It is *truly* "the change we need," the change that will *truly* heal our world.

2. The incarnated dimension: We think through our bodies. In all the reading I have done in the field of holistic education over the course of decades, no single essay has touched me more than Vivian Darroch-Lozowski's "Experiencing Nets of Holism through the Threshold Body." Describing quite personally, and with the utmost vividness, how the intimate experience of our own bodies brings us in active touch with the world around us, she movingly demonstrates, and holistically exemplifies, the psychic healing, and educative evocation of personal and interpersonal wisdom that McGilchrist points to the urgent need for. She shows us just what it is, just what it means, in Gandhi's phrase, "to *be* 'the change' we need to see in our world."[2]

3. The aesthetic dimension: Our first education comes through the feeling perception of beautiful things in the world. If Darroch-Lozowski's contribution to the foundations of holistic education is to articulate what it is like to be educated by our *own* bodies, Tobin Hart's gorgeous essay "Beauty and Learning" is about what it is like to be educated—literally "drawn out" of ourselves—by our perceptions of harmonious beauty in the world. These harmonious perceptions literally "tune us up," as Hart felicitously puts it. Darroch-Lozowski and Hart's contributions thus represent the two sides of the same foundational coin: the beauty we see in the world leads us to cultivate beautiful responses from our inmost selves when we encounter its imperfections. Together, this harmonious perfection and inward perfection constitute the natural, pure gold that can be converted into the holistic currency of general, *cultural* perfection that, as Hart maintains, literally *can* "save the world" from the murderous dissections to which we have subjected it. (For a fuller working out of these ideas see my "'National Standards' vs the Free Standards of Culture: Matthew Arnold's *Culture and Anarchy* and Contemporary Educational Philistinism," *Philosophy of Education*, 2003.)

Cultural Holism

As is beautifully traced in Miller's history, there have been three initiating eras, and hence three general cultural forms, of holistic education: the original Indigenous forms; the Axial forms, starting in the mid first millennium BCE; and the contemporary forms, starting in the mid eighteenth century. The actual term "holism" was first coined in the 1920s, first applied to education around the 1980s, and—as noted in Miller's General Introduction—is just now coming to be understood as the single most salient encompassing idea for the formation of a new ecological and empathic worldview that can take a newly united humanity beyond the materialism, egotism, and nationalism that are now rampantly burning up both the natural world and the human heart. It is becoming increasingly clear that we can escape this burnup only by, in Tobin Hart's words, educatively tuning *ourselves* up. And a large part of our capacity to do this lies in our acquiring a common understanding of the deep story of humanity, and how our species has alternately grown in and out of tune both with the world and with the depths of our own nature.

4. The anthropological dimension: Before "civilization" all human education was holistic. In his chapter, "A Much Deeper Place", Four Arrows, aka Don Trent Jacobs, introduces the reader to what he calls "Indigenous Worlding," and advocates for a return to a "non-anthropocentric worldview." He soulfully describes and demonstrates the deep connectedness our species lost by becoming "civilized," and can regain through holistic education's re-appropriation of that connectedness. From an Indigenous perspective this kind of connection leads to a communal relationship in which the natural world is a co-participant in our being and doing. Accessing its wisdom requires a different set of understandings and skills, a different mindset that lies at the foundation of all holistic education.

5. The historic dimension: Diverse wisdom traditions provide manifold educative resources for the recovery of our natural wholeness within "civilization." Across Eurasia, starting in the late second millennium B.C.E., new expansionary empires, fueled by the power of new military technologies, began to engulf the humanity of the ancient world. Eventually, though, and again all across Eurasia—in the time the philosopher Karl Jaspers first called "The Axial Age"— cultures of peace and what we can now recognize as holistic consciousness arose to stem the tides of violence, founded by individuals *still* recognized as among the greatest teachers in all history: the best known being Socrates and Jesus in the West, and Confucius and Buddha in the East. Yoshi Nakagawa's "Eastern Philosophy and Holistic Education" provides us with a deep and touching exploration of the "perennial philosophy" exemplified by the various branches of Eastern thought. Karen Armstrong's *The Great Transformation* (Knopf, 2006) is a powerful book-length treatment of all the Axial cultures and what they have to teach us.

6. The philosophical dimension: Bringing the left brain to know **what the right brain can** do. The largest part of Jack Miller's essay concerns an educational tradition, only recently named "holistic," stemming from the deeply *feeling* philosopher Jean-Jacques Rousseau. And in a recent conversation with the *other* "bright angelic Miller," Ron, who, along with Jack, founded the holistic education movement in the 1980s, I learned that his road to conceiving of the need for such a movement was paved by a deep engagement in the "*phenomenological* philosophy"—also stemming from Rousseau, as is detailed in my contribution to Section Five in this volume—that reconceives the hierarchical dualism of the modern *pseudo*-Enlightenment. Rather than being founded on the conquest of what is imagined as passive matter through the power of masterful minds, *this* tradition of both teaching and thought, which might be called "The Empathic and Ecological Enlightenment," seeks, at *its* foundation, to engage feeling and embodied minds in a lively and restorative dance with one another and the world. And it provides new left-brain conceptual support for a general holistic worldview in which the full intuitive power of the right brain is reinstated. Where the mottos of the left-brain *pseudo*-Enlightenment—"Knowledge is power" and "I think, therefore I am"—were ultimately divisive, the motto of this true, real, holistic Enlightenment might well be: "We empathically feel the world to holistically and soulfully heal both the world and the rifts we have created in and among ourselves through the false limitations of pseudo-enlightened *mis*education."

Bruce Novak

Holism and the Soul

7. The soulful dimension. Psyche and Eros as the fundamental matter and method of human education. What is it that is incarnated when we extend ourselves in holistic nets toward the world? What is it *in us* that is drawn to beauty? And what is the shared common core of Indigenous, Axial, and genuinely philosophical education? What else but the human soul? Thomas Moore reminds us in his profound contribution, "Care of the Soul in Education."[3] And when he says, "I would like to use the word 'erotic' instead of the word 'holistic,'" he reminds us of the ancient, intimate relation of Eros and Psyche you will find evident in every one of the essays in this volume: each encompassing the analytic left brain's attainment of knowledge and power with the erotic right brain's search for meaning and purpose. Moore quotes his own opening words from his classic *Care of the Soul* of a quarter century ago: "The great malady of the twentieth century, implicated in all our troubles and affecting us individual and socially, is 'loss of soul'." In seeking to place what he calls "intimate relations" between the soul and the world at the core of the nurturance of new generations of humanity, the holistic education movement bears the potential, as *this* century progresses, to mend that tremendous loss, by awakening each human being to the deep and soulful life that lies within and around us, waiting to be aroused. You will see, as you continue to read.

Notes

1 Ron Miller also notes the following as essential to understanding the historic intellectual origins of the field of holistic education: "A group of thinkers/therapists from the humanistic psychology and nascent New Age movements held two conferences under this banner in 1979 and 1980; among this group were Joseph Chilton Pearce, Jack Canfield, and Theodore Roszak. They formed a 'Holistic Education Network' which published two volumes by someone named Anastas Harris in 1980. Canfield co-authored an article in 'New Age Magazine' around that time, which is where I first encountered the term 'holistic education.' But then it faded out. Curiously, none of the folks involved in the 1979/80 events were still involved when we revitalized the movement around 1988/9."
2 Readers who would like *scientific* descriptions of the incarnated dimension of holistic experience that Darroch-Losowski so *humanly* describes can consult the writings of neurologists Antonio Damasio and Nicholas Humphrey. Readers who would like *philosophical* descriptions of it can consult the writings of Maurice Merleau-Ponty, Eugene Gendlin, and Mark Johnson.
3 The classic text on the pedagogy of the soul is Kessler's *The Soul of Education* (ASCD, 2000).

1

HOLISTIC EDUCATION

A Brief History

John P. Miller

The term "holistic education" arose during the 1980s. In 1988 the *Holistic Education Review* began and *The Holistic Curriculum* was published. Ron Miller (1988), founding editor of the *Holistic Education Review* defined holistic education in the first issue of the review.

> Holistic education, above all else, is an expression of profound respect for the deeper, largely unrealized powers of our human nature. Holistic educators see each child as a precious gift, as an embryo of untapped spiritual potential. This attitude is similar to the Quaker belief that there is "that of God in every one"—or at least an unfathomed depth of personality, contained in the soul of every person.
>
> *(p. 2)*

In the first edition of *The Holistic Curriculum* I presented this definition:

> The focus of holistic education is on relationships—the relationship between linear thinking and intuition, the relationship between mind and body, the relationships between various domains of knowledge, the relationship between the individual and community, and the relationship between self and Self. In the holistic curriculum the student examines these relationships so that he/she gains both an awareness of them and the skills necessary to transform the relationships where it is appropriate.
>
> *(1988, p. 3)*

In later editions (1996, 2007) the connection to the earth was included and soul replaced Self. Holistic education, then, is about educating the whole person—body, mind, and spirit—within the context of an interconnected world. Although the term is relatively new, as a practice holistic education has been going on for centuries.

Indigenous Education

Indigenous peoples were the first holistic educators. They saw the interconnectedness of life that is referred to as the "web of life". One of the best descriptions of Indigenous education comes from Gregory Cajete's book, *Look to the Mountain: An Ecology of Indigenous Education* (1994). He argues that "American education must move from a focus on specialization to holistic knowledge; from objective science to systemic science, and building to networking" (p. 27). Cajete identifies several characteristics of Indigenous education. Some of these are:

- A sacred view of Nature permeates its foundational process of teaching and learning.
- Integration and interconnectedness are universal traits of its contexts and processes.
- It unfolds within an authentic context of community and Nature.
- It recognizes that learning is about seeing the whole through the parts.
- We learn through our bodies and spirits as much as through our minds.

(pp. 29–31)

These characteristics are also fundamental to holistic education. I conducted a dialogue with Four Arrows about the relationship between Indigenous education and holistic education (Four Arrows & Miller, 2012). In our dialogue there was agreement around three principles—the first one is bringing to awareness the deep interconnectedness of life. Seeing how we are intimately connected to all life and the processes of the earth is shared by both Indigenous peoples and holistic educators. A second principle that is shared is a sense of the sacred. The cosmos, the earth and its inhabitants are viewed as sacred and imbued with wonder. No one has expressed reverence for the earth better than Indigenous peoples. Unfortunately, this has been lost today in the materialistic, consumerist mindset. We have forgotten how to be enchanted by looking at the stars, feeling the wind on our face, or smelling grass after it has rained. The third principle is educating the whole person, which includes body, mind, and spirit. Today, education focuses almost solely on the mind with some lip service to the body. The soul is almost completely ignored (Kessler, 2000; Miller, J., 2000).

Four Arrows, however, pointed out that Indigenous peoples have embodied these principles and thus have "walked the talk". It could be argued that although holistic educators are committed to these principles, they sometimes remain intellectual concepts rather than deeply embodied ways of being in the world. So holistic educators can look to Indigenous educators as guides on the path of holistic learning and teaching. Four Arrows' book, *Teaching Truly* (2013), is one guide for integrating an Indigenous perspective into the curriculum.

The Axial Age

Karl Jaspers (1947) coined the term Axial Age, which lasted approximately from 900 to 200 BCE. It was a time when great teachers appeared on the earth including the Buddha, Zoroaster, Lao-tzu, Confucius, Socrates, Plato, and the Israelite prophets. Karen Armstrong (2006) in her book, *The Great Transformation*, has given a wonderful description of this period and how these teachers embodied many principles of holistic teaching and learning. She writes that "As far as the axial sages were concerned, respect for the sacred rights of all beings—not orthodox belief—was religion. If people behaved with kindness and generosity to their fellows, they could save the world" (p. xiv).

A principle shared by most of the teachers during the Axial age was that within each person was a divine spark. Socrates called it the *daimon*, the Hindus named it the *Atman*, and in Asia it was called *Qi* and the "most concentrated form of qi was being itself, the "quintessence" (*jing*) of reality" (Armstrong, 2006, p. 292). The teachers of this time focused on spiritual and contemplative practices to realize this part of the human being. Plato and others believed that the divine spark "simply had to be awakened. Truth was not introduced into the mind from outside but had to be 're-collected' from a prenatal existence when each man or woman had enjoyed direct knowledge" (pp. 317–318). Armstrong states that in Plato's Academy, "Greek education became more spiritual" (p. 318).

Pierre Hadot, the French philosopher, makes the case that ancient philosophy was not just an intellectual exercise but was primarily a contemplative practice. He states that the Platonic dialogues were not just an intellectual exercise but were a form of spiritual practice, which demanded self-inquiry and self-transformation. Hadot (2002) states: "To live in a philosophical way meant, above all, to turn toward intellectual and spiritual life, carrying out a conversion which involved 'the whole soul'—which is to say the whole of moral life" (p. 65). Philosophy, then, could be called an education of the soul.

Education in the Axial age focused on textual study and engaging in spiritual practices. Armstrong (2006) writes:

> In India, education was never simply a matter of acquiring factual information. A pupil learning by doing things—chanting mantras, performing tasks, rituals or ascetical exercises that were just as important as textual study, and that over time transformed him, so that he saw the world differently.
>
> *(p. 121)*

By nurturing the divine spark, the person can also see this spark in others and this leads to a sense of connection and compassion. Armstrong believes that compassion was a central principle of all the great teachers of the Axial age. The teachers all had some form of the Golden Rule.

Rousseau–Pestalozzi–Froebel

These three educators lived in the eighteenth and nineteenth centuries. Rousseau (1712–1778) wrote *Emile*, which was published in 1762 and described his approach to education. Rousseau advocated a natural approach to child-rearing as he believed the natural soul of the child was good and must be protected from civilization. He said: "From the outset raise a wall round your child's soul," or it will be overcome by "the crushing force of social conventions" (1955, p. 6). This romantic view of the child has continued to inspire holistic and alternative school educators.

> In *Emile*, Rousseau describes four stages of development—infancy, childhood, youth, and adulthood. These stages are described in four parts of the book and in the last part Rousseau describes the education of a girl, Sophie. At the heart of his approach is negative education. Rousseau stated:
>   Nature provides for the child's growth in her own way and this should never be thwarted. Do not make him sit still when he wants to run about, nor run when he wants to be quiet. If we did not spoil our children's wills by our blunders their desires would be free from caprice.
>
> *(p. 50)*

> Give him no orders at all, absolutely none.
>
> *(p. 55)*

> Give your scholar no verbal lessons, he should be taught by experience alone; never punish him, for he does not know what it is to do wrong; never make him say, "Forgive me," for he does not know how to do you wrong. Wholly unmoral in his actions, he can do nothing morally wrong, and he deserves neither punishment nor reproof
>
> *(p. 56)*

> There the education of the earliest years should be merely negative. It consists, not in teaching virtue or truth, but in preserving the heart from vice and from the spirit of error.
>
> *(p. 57)*

Rousseau believed that the heart of the child was good and the soul of the child should be allowed to unfold according to its own natural pattern. The child, then, should be allowed to explore the world and make his or her own discoveries.

In a biography of Rousseau, Damrosch (2005) draws the following conclusion about *Emile*:

> . . . what was truly original was his claim that each person has a unique temperament that needs freedom to flourish. . . . His intention was to show how a person might prepare for life in society without sacrificing integrity, "seeing with his own eyes, feeling with his own heart, and governed by no authority except his own reason."
>
> *(pp. 333–334)*

Rousseau's phrase that the most useful rule in all of education is not "to gain time but to lose it" has inspired many holistic educators such as George Dennison (1970).

Johann Heinrich Pestalozzi (1746–1827), a Swiss educator, was influenced by Rousseau, and Comenius. He differs from Rousseau in that he taught most of his life and attempted to put his beliefs into practice. He cared about poor children and devoted much of his life to their education. A few of the major principles of Pestalozzi's approach to education reflect Rousseau's influence:

- Intuition is the basis of instruction.
- The time for learning is not the time for judgment and criticism.
- Teaching should aim at development and not dogmatic exposition.
- The educator should respect the individuality of the pupil
- The relations between the master and the pupil, especially as to discipline, should be based upon and ruled by love.

> *(Cited in de Guimps, 1889, pp. 154–155).*

Many educational historians (Bayles & Hood, 1966) have argued that the real genius of Pestalozzi was his empathy for children and how he could adjust his instructional methods to the unique needs of each student.

Friedrich Froebel (1782–1852), a German educator, was influenced by both Rousseau and Pestalozzi; however, he was more mystical in his conception of education. Froebel developed the kindergarten and focused on play as an important factor in the young child's development. He said:

> play is the first means of development of the human mind, its first effort to make acquaintance with the outward world, to collect original experiences from things and facts, and to exercise the powers of body and mind. The child indeed recognizes no purpose in it, and knows nothing, in the beginning, of any end which is to be reached when it imitates the play it sees around it, but it expresses its own nature, and that is human nature in its playful activity.
>
> *(as cited in Von Marenholz-Bulow, 1895, p. 67)*

Froebel, like Rousseau, believed in the inherent goodness of the child. Froebel (1887) claimed: "Therefore, a suppressed or perverted good quality—a good tendency, only repressed, misunderstood, or misguided—lies originally at the bottom of every shortcoming in man" (p. 121). The natural play of the child, then, allows this goodness to unfold.

Tolstoy

Leo Tolstoy, known for his novels *War and Peace* and *Anna Karenina*, was interested in education and ran a school on his estate. He also developed a Russian reading primer. Dan Moulin (2011) has written a book about Tolstoy's approach to education. Tolstoy read *Emile* and agreed with Rousseau's vision of the child as basically good. However, he felt Rousseau's theory was too abstract and not grounded in practice. He was aware of Pestalozzi and Froebel but he found their work too theoretical and not focused enough on the individual child.

In 1859 Tolstoy started a school on his estate, Yasnaya Polyana, for the children of the peasants working there. He also wrote about his ideas on education in a journal entitled *Yasnaya Polyana*. In reflecting back on his work at the school, Tolstoy considered teaching there one of the happiest periods in his life. His approach to teaching was to avoid theoretical approaches and focus as much as possible on the child. He believed in the goodness and wisdom of children and even encouraged his students to write their own stories. A few of these stories, which he helped with, were published. Tolstoy saw his school as a "pedagogical laboratory" where teachers could explore different approaches in working with children. He saw teaching and learning as an organic process that should avoid imposition and as much as possible arise from the interests of the children.

Tolstoy also developed a Russian reading primer, *Azbuka*, as he objected to teaching reading phonetically, which was the dominant approach at that time in Russia. The later version of *Azbuka* contained stories that he gathered from the peasants and other cultures. Moulin points out that "the stories are obviously intended to have educational value over and above that of basic literacy and true to Tolstoy's heuristic pedagogy, the moral of each is inductive, rather than didactic" (p. 98).

For Tolstoy, spirituality was inherent in education; the aim of education is to learn how to live. He felt that education should continually deal with the fundamental questions of life such as "Who am I" and "What is the purpose of my life?" The teacher and school do not offer answers to these eternal questions but help the student explore them. The teacher is crucial in this process and should "strive after perfection in love". If the student grasps this intention then "education will be good" (Moulin, p. 122). Teachers need to work constantly on their "moral and spiritual enlightenment", which Tolstoy saw as the foundation for education (p. 123).

Tolstoy traveled around Europe and Russia to visit schools. He was horrified by the rigid methodologies that were used and felt he was witnessing children drowning. Tolstoy wrote, "What is being drowned is that most precious thing, that spiritual something" (Moulin, p. 42). This is a powerful metaphor which could be applied to how "that spiritual something" is drowning in the world of No Child Left Behind and high stakes testing.

Tolstoy continued to write about education till the end of his life. His last essay on education, "On Upbringing" was written in 1909. Moulin writes that for Tolstoy "true education . . . is balanced, holistic and centered on the individual student's needs" (p. 128). During the 1960s, the free school movement grew and some schools such as the one described in George Dennison's book, *The Lives of Children*, were influenced by Tolstoy's ideas.

The Transcendentalists

In mid nineteenth-century America there was a group of individuals who lived mostly in Concord, Massachusetts and affirmed a belief in what Emerson called the "infinitude" of the individual. They include, among others, Ralph Waldo Emerson, Margaret Fuller, Henry Thoreau, Elizabeth Peabody, and Bronson Alcott. All of these individuals taught and wrote about education.

Ralph Waldo Emerson was the intellectual leader of the Transcendentalists and mentor to others in this group. His lectures and essays inspired many individuals connected with Transcendentalism. Buell (2006) comments that for the Transcendentalists it was more important to "inspire than explain" (p. xxiii). Emerson did not lay out a systematic philosophy but wrote and spoke in a manner that moved the reader and the listener. James Russell Lowell wrote, "I have heard some great speakers and some accomplished orators, but never any that so moved and persuaded me as he" (cited in McAleer, 1984, p. 493). Many of Emerson's ideas resonate with a holistic perspective. He wrote (1990), "Nothing is quite beautiful alone, nothing but is beautiful in the whole. A single object is only so far beautiful as it suggests this universal grace" (p. 26).

Henry David Thoreau lived in Concord and would stay in Emerson's home while Emerson was away lecturing. Thoreau was the earthy face of Transcendentalism. He loved nature and could be viewed as the father of the American environmental movement with his book, *Walden*, as one of its seminal texts. Thoreau was also a teacher; he and his brother, John, started and ran their own school that incorporated principles of holistic learning. He would take the students into surrounding country-side to study nature and could be considered one of the first environmental educators.

Margaret Fuller can be viewed not only as one the foremost Transcendentalists but as one of the most important women in nineteenth-century America. Her book, *Woman in the Nineteenth Century*, explored the intellectual and social position of women and argued against women's second-class status. She also was the first editor of the journal of Transcendentalism, *The Dial*. Fuller was also an elementary school teacher but is most known for the "Conversations" that she ran for women in Boston. She led discussions with women that covered a wide range of topics that were designed to intellectually engage the women who participated. Thus, she was an adult educator who worked on raising women's consciousness.

Bronson Alcott was interested in education throughout his life. He founded the Temple School in Boston where he engaged the students in discussions and inquiry that differed radically from the recitation and drill approach so common in most schools at that time. Alcott believed children held an inner wisdom that could be drawn out through Socratic questioning. Alcott, in the Temple School, also developed an approach to learning that was holistic. Martin Bickman (1999) comments: "The education was what we would now call 'holistic,' since skills like spelling, grammar, and vocabulary were integrated into larger lessons on ethical and spiritual matters" (p. xxiii). Alcott felt that all teaching and learning should be connected to the spiritual center, the soul. Alice Howell (1991), in commenting on Alcott's teaching, states:

> Alcott's secret, and I believe, his success consisted in his approach to children; he worked from his innermost center toward the same one he knew existed in each of them. A bond of trust, mutual respect, and affection was established at that level, so that the usual ego-to-ego tussle between teacher and student was avoided.
>
> *(p. xxxii)*

Like Bronson Alcott, Elizabeth Peabody devoted her life to education. Bruce Ronda (1999), in his biography of Peabody, states that "education was her great calling and her grand passion" (p. 7). She taught in several schools and helped Alcott in the Temple School, which she wrote about in *Record of a School* (1835). Her crowning achievement was being an advocate for kindergarten. Influenced by the work of Friedrich Froebel, Peabody argued that emphasis in kindergarten should be on play rather than academic work.

As a group, the Transcendentalists offer a redemptive vision of education that includes:

- educating the whole child—body, mind, and soul;
- happiness as a goal of education;
- educating students so they see the interconnectedness in nature;
- recognizing the inner wisdom of the child as something to be honored and nurtured;
- a blueprint for environmental education through the work of Thoreau;
- an inspiring vision for educating women of all ages through the work of Fuller;
- an experimental approach to pedagogy that continually seeks for more effective ways of educating children;
- a recognition of the importance of the presence of the teacher and encouraging teachers to be aware and conscious of their own behavior;
- a vision of multicultural and bilingual education through the work of Elizabeth Peabody.

(Miller, J., 2011, p. 6)

The Transcendentalists challenge us to provide an education that inspires, or, in Emerson's words, sets "the hearts of youth on flame". Transcendental education recognizes what Thoreau (2002) said, "Surely joy is the condition of life" (p. 5).

I have described the contribution of the Transcendentalists more fully in my book, *Transcendental Learning: The Educational Legacy of Alcott, Emerson, Fuller, Peabody and Thoreau*.

Summerhill/A. S. Neill

Holistic education can take many forms. Perhaps the most radical form was developed by A. S. Neill. Neill founded an alternative school in Germany in 1921, which was later moved to England to become the famous Summerhill School. Like Rousseau, Pestalozzi, and Froebel, Neill disliked moralizing or instilling guilt in children.

At Summerhill, children had the choice of going to class or staying away. Teachers tended to run their classes very informally. Croall (1983) comments that Neill "took virtually no interest in teaching methods, and gave no sort of guidance to his teachers as to what they should be doing" (p. 206). Neill was primarily concerned about the emotional life of the child. Parents often sent problem children to Summerhill and Neill excelled in responding to their needs. Because they were not forced to learn and because of Neill's caring presence, these children often overcame their difficulties to become healthy individuals. Croall (1983) in his biography of Neill, comments:

> Neill's greatest achievement, however, undoubtedly lay in his ability as "a curer of souls." A considerable number of adults now leading ordinary unexceptional lives, owe the fact that they do so to Neill. He himself in later life liked to argue that it was the environment of freedom rather than his individual work with problem children that was responsible for so many startling "cures." Many former Summerhill pupils thought otherwise as did several of the adults who worked alongside Neill over the years. To them, it was Neill's humanity and understanding which produced the results. As one former problem child said, looking back over his time at Summerhill: "I feel almost certain that, had it not been for Neill, I would have ended up in a mental hospital long ago."
>
> *(p. 407)*

Neill compared his approach to education with Bertrand Russell, who had established Beacon Hill School in 1927. Once he commented to Russell that if a child were with them, Russell would want the child to tell him about the stars while Neill would prefer to leave to the child with his own thoughts. Croall (1983) concludes that "while Neill aims to release the emotions, Russell wants to train the mind" (p. 159). Neill believed that if "the emotions were free, the intellect will look after itself" (cited in Croall, 1983, p. 219).

Neill was the benign authority at Summerhill. Although students did have a great deal of freedom, Neill drew limits in some areas such as the health and safety of the children and the hiring and firing of teaching staff. For example, he made rules about where the children could climb. Neill, like Rousseau and other romantics, was faced with the dilemma of where and how to intervene in children's lives.

Neill's influence beyond the school was immense. By 1969 his book, *Summerhill*, was selling at a rate of more than 200,000 copies a year. This book was a bible to many free school educators in the 1960s and 1970s as they attempted to set up their own versions of Summerhill. According to Graubard (1973), the number of free schools reached approximately 500 by 1972. Ron Miller (2002) has written an extensive analysis of the free school movement. He comments on the long-term legacy of the movement:

The free school movement, like all human endeavors, contained its own flaws, excesses, and blind spots, but it represented a serious effort to turn society away from the path of sprawling technocracy toward more democratic, holistic, person-centered values. More than opposition to public schools as such, free school ideology represented conscious deliberate resistance to the spread of technocracy, and this essential element of the 1960's radical education critique continues to resonate in the literature of alternative, progressive and holistic education.

(p. 179)

Today, the Sudbury Valley School in Framingham, Massachusetts runs on the same principles that operated at Summerhill. It has inspired approximately 50 other similar schools around the world.

Montessori Education/Waldorf Education

Montessori education and Waldorf education could be considered the most popular forms of holistic education in the twentieth century. There are other forms, such as Krishnamurti schools, Quaker schools, and Humanist schools, but Montessori schools and Waldorf schools continue to expand around the globe. Both are presented in the Handbook. Warren Cohen and Brian Bresnihan give detailed examples of Waldorf education in practice, including math and language arts. Aziza Mayo contributes a chapter that describes a study of Waldorf education in the Netherlands that looked at the effects of classroom practices there. Finally, Tim Seldin, Michael Dorer and colleagues write about how Montessori education engages the whole child as children learn through becoming a thing rather than simply learning about it. For example, the children may "become" the sun, a verb, a mathematical operation, or a famous person.

Humanistic Education/Transpersonal Education

In the 1960s and 1970s, humanistic education was an immediate forerunner of holistic education. Other terms that were used included affective education, psychological education, and confluent education. It arose out of humanistic psychology and particularly the work of Carl Rogers and Abraham Maslow. Rogers' book, *On Becoming a Person*, contained a chapter entitled "Personal Thoughts on Teaching" which included the following statements.

- My experience has been that I cannot teach another person how to teach.
- It seems to me that anything that can be taught to another is relatively inconsequential, and has little or no significant influence on behavior.
- I have come to feel that only learning, which significantly influences behavior is self-discovered, self-appropriated learning.
- I realize that I have lost interest in being a teacher.

(1961, p. 276)

These claims clearly challenged traditional conceptions of teaching. In 1969, Rogers expanded on his notions of education in *Freedom to Learn*, where he applied some of the assumptions of humanistic psychology to classroom practice and presented his vision for "self-directed change" in schools. Rogers develops the concept of "significant" or "experiential learning", which has

a quality of personal involvement—the whole person in both his feeling and cognitive aspects being in the learning event. It is self-initiated . . . It is pervasive. It makes a difference in the behavior, the attitudes, perhaps even the personality of the learner . . . Its essence is meaning.

(p. 5)

He cites a couple of examples of experiential learning. At the elementary level, he describes the work of one teacher, Miss Shiel, who used a contract system where students set their own goals. At the graduate level, Rogers describes an encounter group experience that was popular at that time but was rarely found in graduate education. Encounter groups aimed to facilitate communication and personal growth where participants could openly share their concerns and feelings. The emphasis was on affect and he states that there was little opportunity to discuss "cognitive learnings". He cited the positive comments from many of the students who participated in the group.

Rogers' "Plan for Self-Directed Change" includes an extensive system of encounter groups for enhancing the "openness of administrators, teachers, parents and students". The encounter group focused on personal growth and was inappropriate for system change. His proposal did not go anywhere as the encounter group movement died in the 1970s but his focus on the importance of self-directed learning did have an impact on humanistic educators.

Maslow (1968) argued for valuing the "peak experiences" of the child. These are experiences where we have direct experience of the world that often lead to awe and wonder.

> We must learn to treasure the "jags" of the child in school, his fascination, absorptions, his persistent wide-eyed wonderings, his Dionysian enthusiasms. At the very least, we can value his more diluted raptures, his "interests" and hobbies, etc. They can lead to much. Especially can they lead to hard work, persistent, absorbed, fruitful, educative.
>
> And conversely I think it is possible to think of the peak-experience, the experience of awe, mystery, wonder, or of perfect completion, as the goal and reward of learning as well, its end as well as its beginning. If this is true for the *great* historians, mathematicians, scientists, musicians, philosophers and all the rest, why should we not try to maximize these studies as sources of peak-experiences for the child as well?
>
> *(p. 695)*

Two leading humanistic educators were Gerry Weinstein and Mario Fantini, who were funded by the Ford Foundation to conduct a major project in developing curriculum materials that included the affect. They wrote about this work in *Toward Humanistic Education: A Curriculum of Affect*. One of the conclusions from their project was:

> "*Significant contact with pupils is most effectively established and maintained when the content and method of instruction have an affective base*" [original italics]. This is, if educators are able to discover the feelings, fears, and wishes that move pupils from any background, whether by adapting traditional content and procedures or by developing new materials and techniques.
>
> *(1970, p. 10)*

Weinstein and Fantini developed a "curriculum of concerns" that included student interests and concerns in the curriculum. These were integrated with the traditional curriculum of language, math, social studies, science, and the arts. They note that "concerns" go beyond feelings and sometimes involve an "inner uneasiness" (p. 37).

The book contains a number of activities that allowed students to express their concerns and feelings. The project was conducted with mostly Afro-American children in the inner city, so the concerns often focused on issues such as power and self-image.

Gerry Weinstein taught at the University of Massachusetts, which became a major center for humanistic education. Another major center was the University of California at Santa Barbara, which focused on confluent education. George Brown was one of the leaders of this approach and wrote *Human Teaching for Human Learning: An Introduction to Confluent Education*. He writes, "Confluent education is the term for the integration or flowing together of the affective and cognitive elements in individual and group learning-sometimes called humanistic or psychological education" (1971, p. 3). Brown was influenced by Fritz Perls, who was a practitioner of Gestalt therapy, which focused on being in touch with one's feelings in the present moment. Brown's books contain activities such as one for first grade children where students focus on body awareness. In one exercise the teacher, Gloria Castillo, who wrote her own book, *Left-Handed Teaching*, asked the children to walk outside on different surfaces—dewy grass, blacktop, concrete, and sand (1974, p. 134). Some of these activities are similar to mindfulness practices, which are being used in schools today.

Transpersonal Education appeared in the mid to late 1970s and grew out of transpersonal psychology, which included the spiritual dimension of experience. Much of the work was published in the *Journal of Transpersonal Psychology*. Gay Hendricks and Jim Fadiman (1976) wrote *Transpersonal Education: A Curriculum for Feeling and Being*, published by Prentice Hall as part of a series in Transpersonal Education. My book, *The Compassionate Teacher: How to Teach and Learn with Your Whole Self*, published in 1981, was included in this series. It contains the following quotation:

> Why transpersonal education? For many it has been natural development from humanism. For example, Abe Maslow, one of the founders of humanistic psychology, toward the end of his life wrote about self-transcendence as a stage beyond self-actualization. A transpersonal perspective allows us to see ourselves and our students not as isolated egos but as interdependent beings in a connected and dynamic universe. . . . Transpersonal education acknowledges our spiritual identity without sacrificing intellectual sensibilities. . . . the focus is on inner work, such as meditation, visualization, and movement so that we develop our "inner authority"
>
> *(p. ix)*

Transpersonal education never gained traction as the term was too esoteric for most practitioners. Holistic education as a term and movement arose in the 1980s and has continued to today. Some people originally connected holistic education to the New Age movement, but it has gained more credibility as a holistic perspective has been taken up in a variety of fields. More and more we hear individuals in business, health care, government, education, and other fields adopting a holistic perspective. Such a perspective is inclusive and recognizes interconnectedness as a fundamental reality.

Holistic/Wholistic

I have argued that holistic education includes the spiritual dimension while the term "wholistic education" focuses more on a biological and psychological holism (Miller, 2007, p. 6). This review has focused on holistic education. From this perspective, wholistic educators include John Dewey and Nel Noddings. For example, Ron Miller, in a detailed discussion of Dewey, argues that "Dewey's concept of aesthetic experience does not seem to encompass the meaning of spirituality represented by holistic thought" (p. 134). In my chapter "Atomism, Pragmatism, and Holism", Dewey's focus on problem solving and the scientific method place him within the pragmatic tradition (Miller, 1996, pp. 17–20). In *Experience and Education*, Dewey (1938/1963) wrote, "It means that the scientific method is the only authentic means at our command for getting at the significance of our everyday experiences" (p. 88).

Nel Nodding's writing on caring (1992) and happiness (2003) are very significant contributions but she mostly avoids including the spiritual. Her work has been beautifully celebrated in *Dear Nel: Opening the Circles of Care* (2012).

The work of Dewey, Noddings, and others is very important in that some educators cannot include spirituality in public education. Their work provides a bridge for teachers who are more comfortable with a wholistic perspective.

Holistic Education Today

Today there are holistic education initiatives around the world. For example, there is the Asia Pacific Network of Holistic Educators that conducts annual conferences in Asia. Meetings have been held in Thailand, Korea, Japan, and Malaysia. A comprehensive study of Whole Child Education conducted by the American Institutes of Research focuses on holistic education work in ten countries, including Ireland, Germany, France, Belgium, the Netherlands, Spain, Portugal, the UK, Canada (Ontario), and the USA.

This Handbook includes educators from Bhutan, Canada, Japan, Korea, the Netherlands, Pakistan, Thailand, United Arab Emirates, the UK, and the USA and, as stated in the introduction, it presents "visionary worlds" of holistic education. These educators share the belief in educating the whole child. Whole children and whole human beings are fundamental to building a world where all beings develop and thrive.

References

Armstrong, K. (2006). *The great transformation: The beginnings of our religious traditions*. New York: Alfred Knopf.

Bayles, E. E. & Hood, B. L. (1966). *Growth of American educational thought and practice*. New York: Harper & Row.

Bickman, M. (Ed.) (1999). *Uncommon learning: Henry David Thoreau on education*. Boston, MA: Houghton Mifflin.

Brown, G. I. (1971). *Human teaching for human learning: An introduction to confluent education*. New York: Viking.

Buell, L. (2006). Introduction. In L. Buell (Ed.), *The American transcendentalists: Essential writings* (pp. xi–xxlii). New York: Penguin.

Cajete, G. (1994). *Look to the Mountain: An ecology of Indigenous education*. Durango, CO: Kivaki Press.

Castillo, G. A. (1974). *Left-Handed Teaching: Lessons in Affective Education*. Santa Barbara, CA: Praeger.

Croall, J. (1983). *Neill of Summerhill: The permanent rebel*. London: Routledge.

Damrosch, L. (2005). *Jean-Jacques Rousseau: Restless giant*. New York: Houghton Mifflin.

de Guimps, R. (1889). *Pestalozzi: His aim and work*. Syracuse: C.W. Bardeen.

Dennison, G. (1970). *The lives of children*. New York: Vintage.

Dewey, J. (1938/1963). *Experience and education*. New York: Macmillan/Collier.

Emerson, R. W. (1990). *Selected essays, lectures and poems*. New York: Bantam.

Four Arrows (2013). *Teaching truly*. New York: Peter Lang.

Four Arrows & Miller, J. (2012). To name the world: A dialogue about holistic and Indigenous education. *Encounter, 25*(3), 1–11.

Froebel, F. (1887). *The education of man*. New York: Appleton-Century Crofts.

Fuller, M. (1999). *Woman in the nineteenth century*. Mineola, NY: Dover.

Hadot, P. (2002). *What is ancient philosophy?* Cambridge, MA: Belknap Press.

Graubard, A. (1973). *Free the children*. New York: Random House.

Hendricks, G. & Fadiman, J. (Eds.) (1976). *Transpersonal education: A curriculum of feeling and being*. Englewood Cliffs, NJ: Prentice Hall.

Howell, A. O. (1991). Introduction. In Alcott, A. B., *How like an angel came I down* (pp. xvii–xliv). Hudson, NY: Lindisfarne Press.

Jaspers, K. (1947). *The origin and goal of history*. London: Routledge and Kegan Paul.

Kessler, R. (2000). *The soul of education: Helping students find connection, compassion and character at school*. Alexandria, VA: ASCD.

Lake, R. (Ed.) (2012). *Dear Nel: Opening the circles of care*. New York: Teachers College Press.

Maslow, A. (1968). Some educational implications of humanistic psychologies. *Harvard Educational Review, 38*(4), 685–696.

McAleer, J. J. (1984). *Ralph Waldo Emerson: Days of encounter*. Boston, MA: Little, Brown.

Miller, J. (1981). *The compassionate teacher: How to teach and learn with your whole self*. Englewood Cliffs, NJ: Prentice Hall.

Miller, J. (1988, 1996, 2007). *The holistic curriculum*. Toronto: OISE Press.

Miller, J. (2000). *Education and the soul: Toward a spiritual curriculum*. Albany, NY: SUNY Press.

Miller, J. (2011). *Transcendental learning: The educational legacy of Alcott, Emerson, Fuller, Peabody and Thoreau*. Charlotte, NC: Information Age.

Miller, R. (1988). Holistic education: A radical perspective. *The Holistic Education Review, 1*(1), 2–3.

Miller, R. (2002). *Free schools, free people: Education and democracy after the 1960s.* Albany, NY: State University of New York Press.

Moulin, D. (2011). *Leo Tolstoy.* London: Continuum.

Noddings, N. (1992). *The challenge to care in schools: An alternative approach to education.* New York: Teachers College Press.

Noddings, N. (2003). *Happiness and education.* New York: Cambridge University Press.

Peabody, E. (1835). *Record of a school: Exemplifying the general principles of spiritual culture.* Boston, MA: James Munroe.

Rogers, C. (1961). *On becoming a person.* Boston, MA: Houghton Mifflin.

Rogers, C. (1969). *Freedom to learn.* Columbus, OH: Charles Merrill.

Ronda, B. A. (1999). *Elizabeth Palmer Peabody: A reformer on her own terms.* Cambridge, MA: Harvard University Press.

Rousseau, J.-J. (1955). *Emile.* New York: Everyman's Library.

Thoreau, H. D. (2002). *The essays of Henry D. Thoreau,* L. Hyde (Ed.). New York: North Point Press.

Von Marenholz-Bulow, B. (1895). *Reminiscences of Friedrich Froebel.* Boston, MA: Lee & Sheppard.

Weinstein, G. & Fantini, M. (1970). *Toward humanistic education: A curriculum of affect.* New York: Praeger.

2

EXPERIENCING NETS OF HOLISM THROUGH THE THRESHOLD BODY

Vivian Darroch-Lozowski

During my life I have been fortunate to travel widely to parts of our world that, at the time, were not fully open to what was then called the West. I traveled before the world became homogenized and in relation to my writing projects, not as a tourist, and rarely stayed in hotels. At first I did not understand why I was traveling with the existential necessity I was carrying. Nor did I know what that existential necessity was. As time passed, I came to realize I needed to witness how people and other life endure on our chaotic and beautiful planet, a world upon which all life is joined.

As I traveled, I learned that what I had been formally taught as truths often collided with what I was experiencing as I was involved with the life of others. The phenomenon of witnessing life itself while living in contexts physically unfamiliar to me overwhelmed my knowledge by other kinds of truth that issued from within me. Frequently, I needed to release understandings and beliefs that I held. My learning in others' life spaces became more important than all my academic learning. What I had learned in the different disciplines I studied were valuable mappings that allowed me to access the communities and cultures new to me, but it was only this. I use the word "mapping" and not "map" because I want to bring forward that holistic practice—writing, thinking, making, teaching, doing, being—requires an open-ended intelligence that is always transforming itself in the face of the mappings we learn and the ones we make ourselves.

I hope this chapter shall be a valuable mapping for readers. It cannot be more because what is crucial for the discipline of holism to recognize is that the foundational strength of holism arises from a deep subjectivity, as implied above. It is deep subjectivity that allows us continuously to be open to modifying our internal truths and beliefs; no external factor alone can confirm or disprove them. This places heavy responsibility upon our clarity and our honesty with ourselves in relation to the knowledge and truths in which we believe and out of which we practice. It also requires us to recognize and allow shifts from our certainty. My memory (I have rarely taken a photograph, and do not photograph now) includes thousands upon thousands of fragmented images of how humans endure their fates and these images of my life are imprinted forever with sensations of what humans have offered me of themselves: courage, dignity, hope, wisdom, mercy, compassion, laughter. It is these memories that permit me to write what is below and to confess that when I was a younger woman I did not fully understand at all what now I write.

In writing now I want to believe it is possible to live with more widespread daily sensitivity to each other, even nation unto nation, but how? I shall suggest that holism is a self-healing net, and that we live better when we attempt to approach the deep mystery within ourselves, within every one, all species, and the abundance of mystery on our planet and in our universe, too. Because I am taking this position, I shall suggest that complete holism is a relationship that depends upon the intimacy of our being together, a relationship that is awareness of how our outer and inner worlds associate with each other in our immediate existential reality. It is this, our experience of the "isness" of the present, rather than our psychic reality that is all-important. The reality of our psychological/cultural minds and emotions is the reality that places conceptual judgments on others and events. Our psychic reality is crucial for the continuity of our daily living, but it is living sensitively within our existential reality, enabled by what I call the threshold body, that allows our inner wisdom to enlarge and become deeper. Inner wisdom is not conceptual and any action it guides us to take (for the sake of justice, for instance) does not arise from judgment but, rather, from seeking a way to bring all into communion.

Visible and Invisible Nets

We live in a time when scientists, through evidential research, are coming to appreciate and understand the wisdom of the Indigenous peoples and of the ancients. The wisdom of Indigenous peoples depended upon recognizing the meetings of outer and inner worlds. Indigenous people in Australia practice *dadirri*. *Dadirri* is their word for a quiet listening that depends on a source of awareness within that leads to building of connections in community. In the Greenlandic language there is a word, *sila*. *Sila* simultaneously means weather, animal and human consciousness, and the power of nature. No distinction is made between human and animal minds within individuals who can "see" this way. In the third century, Indian philosophers developed a jeweled metaphoric "net of the world" in their attempts to teach about the interconnectedness of all things in the universe. At each point in this net where the threads connected was a pearl that reflected every other pearl, including all that had ever been reflected upon it. This continuous reflecting process of interconnection never ended. Similarly, in order to teach about the interpenetration of macrocosms and microcosms, ancient Chinese philosophers devised a metaphoric statue of a golden lion that, in each aspect of its anatomy, including each hair, was housed another golden lion. This evolution never ceased. In our time, it is common to use the idea of a net for the representation of the complex interconnectedness of various social, physical, and symbolic systems. Most obviously, in our daily life the internet of the world wide web (WWW) manifests for our use through invisible extremely low frequency (ELF) electromagnetic radiation and this enables us to connect with each other and with information.

In the past century, Carl Jung, the psychiatrist who founded analytical psychology, wrote extensively throughout his vast works about the collective unconscious, a non-material structure of the unconscious mind that is shared among humans. In this century, investigations of non-material science are becoming mainstream. A host of researchers show how human thought can influence the thoughts and images and physiology of other beings, including plants, cellular organisms, the molecules of water, machines, and so on. This non-material research is considered by many to be suspect because researchers have no theory to explain the data. By the deduction of science we yet do not know very much about the human consciousness and how its resonance influences the world. Readers may have their own stories of surprising conscious connections (telepathy, presentience) between themselves and loved ones, across species, or even specific world events. Through involuntary drawings, I recorded one of these events (Darroch-Lozowski, 2002). But where does consciousness come from? Where is it now as I write or as you read? We do not know. Further, while we acknowledge that electricity and electromagnetism is vital for life, we do not know how all the subtle energies of life and of the materials around us—electrical, electromagnetic, solar, seasonal, cosmic, and others that yet remain unnamed—affect us. These nets of being and of relation, for better or worse, affect us profoundly and we are scarcely aware of how the habits of our minds and the energies of our bodies are always changing as a consequence of their interconnections at a quantum level.

Today, one of the hardest problems for physicists and mathematicians studying quantum systems is that while knowing through their research that all particles in the universe do interconnect, they do not know how these complex connections are made.

Over the past century, in Euro-Western thought, ideational structures of the social sciences have contributed powerfully to the idea of holism as it exists in human communities. These structures (for example, the *ego*, the *id*, social class, active will, political alliance, the unconscious) are the foundations for our contemporary necessity of understanding each other and they have created their own nets. They came into being when persons believed that the laws of nature itself were structural and were fixed. At the same time, social and physical researchers were becoming aware that our descriptions of our structures of being and the material structures around us are always fluctuating, moving, and changing their forms. Today and every day, through how we recognize and respond to the streams of signs, messages, desires, and data through which we navigate, we experience these unceasing alterations. Especially data, information, are in the foreground of our lives today. Yet, all that these mappings carry are only intelligible or practicable when seen by a conscious observer and even then are only ways for indicating how we are interacting with reality. Notably, similar to scientific and social theories and religious precepts, data and its subsequent algorithms, sometimes described as "god" of the future, is not an experienced reality itself.

One scientist who continues to investigate the nets and fields of evolution in animals and humans is Rupert Sheldrake, who has proposed a theory of morphic resonance (Sheldrake, 1982, 2009). My summary that follows is retrieved from various posts on his website, www.sheldrake.org. His research is founded upon the concept of morphogenesis, the process by which a biological organism develops its shape. He reminds how, in psychology, we could consider the morphogenetic fields of the mind, developed from interacting with their context of daily living, as contributing to the developmental history of a child, influencing him or her to become what she or he is. Sheldrake's concept of morphic fields is defined by him as being essentially habits of the mind. They are not fixed, however. He describes how his research attempts to show that morphic fields are subject to natural selection, meaning the more times they are repeated, the more probable they become. It is morphic fields that underlie our mental activities, our perceptions and collective behavior. As well, through intention and attention, morphic fields extend beyond our minds, connecting members of social groups at a distance. Sheldrake hypothesizes that morphic fields at all complexity are self-organizing wholes and that they attract systems under their influence and interrelate morphic units within themselves. They also contain a built in memory given by self-resonance with their own past and by morphic resonance with all previous similar systems. Various morphic fields of thought and values within human history—past, present and emerging—can be identified. I suggest that so far, we, as practitioners in all fields, but especially political ones, are not recognizing the "invisible" net-like and recursive power of morphic fields in our attempts to bring further humane changes to societies.

The Threshold Body and Deep Subjectivity

In physics, what is called the world line is the unique path that an object has as it travels through space and time. Everyone and everything—a moving photon, a growing plant, a child's development, a living cell, and, yes, a thought, too—has a world line whose history, in theory, can be tracked. These moving world lines interact with each other, connect with each other, and weave through relationships that begin, last, and end. I have been emphasizing the outer and inner realities, the outer and inner nets, in which and by which we live. They all yield circumstances of relationship. Some of the relationships are damaged, while others are not. But their world lines of co-existence all connect and all are threads of the mysterious net of the world. Therefore, we are in relationship with every one and every thing all the time. It is our sensitivity to our felt experience of other world lines, to how we influence them, to how they influence us, that allows humanity and other species and the universe itself to evolve and expand. The depth of our awareness of our co-existence influences the kind of human beings each one of us becomes.

I devised the term "threshold body" as a metaphor around which to develop my thoughts (Darroch-Lozowski, 1999). A threshold is always a transitional space, a place occupying both sides of a boundary. Humanity stands in a politically and environmentally perilous space at the beginning of this century. We are disorientated as civilizations, too often fearful-at-large, yet live hourly with the hopeful potential to birth something new and humane. If we could fully accept this space–time in history as a threshold space and suspend our ideas and habits of difference (of status, race, gender, all differences between us), this space would be safer.

Our bodies are what markedly separate us from others, and from the world. Yet, each of us has the capacity to be aware of ourselves as a threshold body that can respond to others and the world in a way different from our usual ways. However, it is difficult to be a threshold body because the attributes of ourselves on a threshold are necessarily ambiguous: we are being influenced by what is on both sides of the threshold where we are. Therefore, the attributes of our being a threshold body can be described only by indirect reference. Our edges, or ourselves as a threshold body, are non-manifest because our body-ness is a pause of the entire whole/part of our normal existence. What does this mean? It means that with our attention on the resonance of things that surround us and by withdrawing from our limited boundaries of truths and beliefs, through its continuous reflecting of what is intuitively felt, the threshold body can allow the usual place, self, and inner substantiation of our body to be transgressed by other world lines for the sake of yielding spontaneous and new understanding and creativity. We shall sense, resonate with, this newness within ourselves and understand it, even without words.

A situation in which we all have experienced something akin to the sensations of the threshold body is the one in which we are "wandering" (Darroch-Lozowski, 1999). When we are wandering, we concentrate loosely on what we might pick up in our hand, on what we see. And then, usually, we open our hand or turn our gaze and let what we have found go—to be washed and encountered again by another wind, or sea, or memory, or being. When we wander, our focus is easeful on the detritus of thought and images, as they impinge upon us from what seems to be an infinite space–time. When we wander, our thoughts, perceptions, and sensations in-fold on our past and future memories. When we wander, our perceptual habit orients to *that all is*, rather than to what all is. Such perceptual reorientation shows that the awareness of the threshold body is different from our usual daily, psychological, social, and political awareness. It is an awareness that recognizes the world is unceasingly in flux, that what is loved in the world—a person, an animal, a mountain, a moon—will change. It is an awareness that carries us to understanding how our purpose to engage with each other is for the sake of our loss to each other. Out of such awareness flows a disposition toward things and toward self that involves a deeper responsiveness and sensitive responsibility. It is a disposition that is not encumbered with attempting to extend our influence and efficacy and possessions.

One day, long ago, when I was in rural People's Republic of China, I boarded a bus in which every seat was taken and dozens of persons were standing in the aisle. A place was made for me to stand. After a few miles, a young man stood. He had been sitting with a young woman who, it could be seen by all, was taken over by a silent anguish. With no word but with a serious gesture, he offered me his seat. I indicated no, thank you, because of my concern for the suffering young woman he was accompanying. I did not smile. Their situation was too grave. With gesture, he insisted (he said something but I did not know his language) and, finally, I sat beside her, saying nothing to him or to her as I did not wish to intrude upon their serious presences. When I sat beside her, she immediately clenched my hand and did not loosen this tight grip for the next almost two hours. During this time period, I felt my own hand tightening upon hers. Both of us sat quietly looking at our feet and the floor. I could not discern whether her great pain was issuing from her body or from her soul—are these separated? I did not think or imagine about the causes of her extremity. I did not speak. I only wanted to be aware of our hands grasping each other's. The resonance of her body was permeating me, as was my body's resonance permeating hers, and soon our resonance became unified. *This resonance allowed us to accompany something into itself. Neither of us knew what that was. Nor did it matter. We received the grace of it. That was enough.* When the woman stood to leave the bus, for the first time she and I looked at each other. Stricken, not speaking, we recognized that we did not want to lose each other. Yet we must. The woman's companion acknowledged our parting and I stayed on the bus because I was not yet at my destination. What was this linking between the woman and me?

I describe the above experience to show how the threshold body allows reaching essences of self, another, or even the other-than-human-world, that are not premeditated and that seem to situate our vision *in that which we are experiencing that is something larger than ourselves.* The effect of the threshold body on our experience is that the gap of being between mind and corporeal body disappears. This is to say our experience widens infinitely, and the boundary between our self's way of knowing and the coded world's way of being becomes less distinct. When we are resonant with an "other", we are not confined to being affected (and sometimes afflicted) from without through the historical, cultural, linguistic complexes in which we can so easily entangle ourselves.

Being in our threshold body allows for simultaneous unification of ourselves as living, subjective systems, for our body's capacity to understand its own fluctuating diversity, and for the fluctuating variety of our changing environments. We now know that experiential structures necessary for most of our abstract thinking are compelled and confined by our bodily functioning—that is, by our living selves. And it is our living selves that constitute ourselves as subjects of change, not the events in which we are participating or observing.

The threshold body is an intimate body, neither public nor private. The threshold body offers our self to a world without mediation. It represents a union of inner essence and outward phenomenon. It is a state of resonance that transcends the feelings of being or of non-being. All threshold phenomena, including the being of the threshold body, offer two possibilities—sacredness or blasphemy. Thresholdedness is an inherent inside the unique human condition of each of us: it is an inherent we deeply fear because it can endanger us. Elsewhere I have considered this (Darroch-Lozowski, 1990).

The sociologist of knowledge, Kurt H. Wolff, displaced from Germany and Auschwitz, wrote two important books of inquiry documenting his questioning of himself in his attempts to understand history and time (Wolff, 1976, 1989). Twice, years apart, I was privileged to share suppers and conversations with Kurt and, late in his life, we "co-existed" (his word) with each other, now and then, through paper correspondence. It is from him that I began to appreciate that the continuity of our "I-am" consists in our "I-am" beginning ever-again as we connect with other world lines and as we re-see ourselves. The threshold body is aware, instant by instant, of beginning again and again and again. In Kurt's thought, we must surrender to the world, and when we do there is always a catch. For Kurt, "surrender" meant touching the world. "'Everything' is everything within the surrenderer's awareness . . ." he wrote (Wolff, 1976, p. 201). By "catch", he meant its cognitive and existential results; in other words, our actions and cognitive love consequent upon our surrendering. I am suggesting that, from our threshold bodies, we may reach this.

In *O Loma!*, Kurt wrote, "Surrender is in touch with what happens. With the fully empty . . . to say this is to run naked through a half-crowded theatre so the spectators have space to stare and stone" (Wolff, 1989, p. 109). He muses how the touch of surrender has to do with the body, that the world becomes touchable in surrender: "And I say 'surrender'—*of course* I am naked, running naked through the human theatre—and the spectators stare and stone", he writes (Wolff, 1989, p. 109). Emerging from surrender, we are left with fragments of what we learned from being in touch with what happened. Afterward, what remains within ourselves of the experience and what we offer to others and to the community is the catch of that surrender. We can never know what surrendering can achieve in the world. We are not always able to discern the catch that is returned to the community by such profound surrendering as Wolff describes. Surrender and its catch form their own complex, intricate nets of cognition and feeling that cannot fairly be named or described. Certainly I do not and cannot live in and through the threshold body consciously all the time. But I try to be aware of where I am standing. Yes, even in coffee shops, walking down normal city streets, resting in a meadow, I try. Yes, I fail.

Historically, I began forming the metaphor "threshold body" long before humanity became immersed in our electronic virtual world. Obviously, the place of the threshold body in our world of virtual realities needs to be addressed. In their far-reaching studies that address the origin of humanness, Maturana Romesin and Verden-Zöller (2008) differentiate virtual reality from other experiences that we call "real" by stipulating that the only experiences that can be called real are those that we live understanding how they are coupled with the community in which we exist and how they are dependent upon the media that we use. They write,

> No matter whether we are aware or not of what kind of reality we live in in any instant, all the realities that we live affect us in the same way in the emotional dimensions of our psychic existence, because there is no virtual emotional life.
>
> *(Maturana Romesin & Verden-Zöller, 2008, p. 202)*

When they expand on this, they indicate that all that we live arises from our psychic existence whether or not this takes place in a virtual or a non-virtual reality. They remind that our nervous system is continuously changing "both in our conscious and unconscious, external and internal, relational psychic space" (Maturana Romesin & Verden-Zöller, 2008, p. 202), and that as we live and change congruently with others repeatedly through virtual media, "realities that were initially virtual progressively stop being virtual, and as features of our culture they become part of our biological manner of living and, hence, of the non-virtual reality that we live" (Maturana Romesin & Verden-Zöller, 2008, p. 202). They conclude that the problem is not virtual reality itself but, rather,

> whether we do or do not like the psychic manners of existence and cultural transformations that we generate through them. Virtual realities are never trivial, because we always become transformed as we live them according to the emotioning of the psychic space that they bring about in our living . . .
>
> *(Maturana Romesin & Verden-Zöller, 2008, p. 203)*

There is worldwide discussion now of what the electronic virtual reality has released in humanity and the question remains open with respect to how the communicative and moral habits and the bio-physical evolution of the entire larger morphic and netted field of humanity itself shall evolve.

When I began this essay, I emphasized that all we can know are mappings that give us access to reality, but that they are not reality itself. Yet, I am writing from within a reality, am I not—the reality of my own psychic space? Psychic space is the exceedingly significant reality that gives continuity to our lives, yet it is unceasingly being re-constructed by the routine, repetitive, and creative co-existence that we, as humans, have with everything else, as well as by our instincts and prejudices that usually lie below our consciousness. To assist us in receiving alterations of our psychic space as life proceeds, we need to be intentionally aware of the words we hear and the words we adopt and use. It is languaging, inadequate as so often it is, that allows us to bring meaning to the way the world touches us and reflects our touch upon us back to ourselves. I have written elsewhere about how the action of language and its touch on body makes its saying (Darroch-Lozowski, 1984, 1987).

Surrendering to Experience

On a subtle level, holistic practice requires a discovering within. Discovering within requires focusing and acting in a particular way when we are with another. I have used the threshold body as a metaphor to guide us toward this. Crucially, it requires recognizing the other as being representative of more than as might be identified as a "she" or a "he" or a trans-gendered person or a person of this skin color or that, of this culture or that, or under this stress or that. In other words, we need to accept and respond to another *only as a human being representative of a human here-and-now*. I was privileged to have Kurt review one of my works before I was acquainted with him and he articulated the above insight in that review. In this review, he also phrased what he considered to be the universal human question: "what must I do from sheer necessity since I am the human being I am"? (Wolff, 1991). We all, at one time or another, sight this question. Yet, we can easily let it fall away or suppress it entirely. We do so because answering it directly leads us to face the ambiguity and threat of being a threshold body. What must we do from sheer necessity, since we are the human beings we are?

Last, within everything, including ourselves, there is mystery. Every mystery, even the mystery of our own lives, holds an enigma. It is within our deep subjectivity and through attempting to live as a threshold body that we can approach the mystery of our own lives and, therefore, begin to understand and accept how our world line is weaving itself into the self-healing net of the world. The philosopher Gabriel Marcel (1950) wrote how the recognition of mystery occurs within ourselves as we interact with our outer world. He wrote:

> The recognition of mystery . . . is an essentially positive act of the mind. . . . In this sphere everything seems to go on as if I have found myself acting on an intuition which I possess without immediately knowing myself to possess it—an intuition which cannot be, strictly speaking, self-conscious and which can grasp itself only through the modes of experience in which its image is reflected, and which it lights up by being reflected in them.
>
> *(p. 212)*

If it were possible for us to be aware enough, would this not also be a beautiful description of the human-and-more-than-human net of our world?

Holism as a self-healing net is continuously evolving outside and within all of us, and everything, worldwide. And it is evolving within its own time. And some of its threads will always be damaged and torn. In closing this essay, I acknowledge the millions of earth's citizens who are working to make better each other's plight and our world's plight on all fronts of ethical concerns—local and non-local—fronts of war, environment, racism, health, food, equality—especially justice for women, aboriginal cultures, and the economically compromised. It is a gentle and undifferentiated joining and surrendering to our experience as we work and play with others that continuously reforms holism as a self-healing net.

Yesterday, on a narrow gravel road, I was driving home from the country at dusk. I passed a harvested field in which a large flock of Canada geese were standing, all in the same upright posture—all facing north—all absolutely still—none feeding. It was as if I had come upon an immense living still-life—charcoal-brown field, hundreds of greyish-brown birds, darkish surroundings, and earth-shadowed ambient air. Mesmerized, I stopped the car—lowered the window—silence, not a breath of air moving—and looked upon this scene. When I slowly began to move the car again, from the ditch on my left a female deer leaped in front of my vehicle—I braked in time—she paused and turned her face toward mine for a few seconds before leaping away. Looking upon each other, we touched each other, and in that instant tenderness filled my whole life.

Vivian Darroch-Lozowski

References

Darroch-Lozowski, V. (1984). *Voice of hearing*. Victoria, BC: Sono Nis Press.

Darroch-Lozowski, V. (1987). *Notebook of stone: From the Tibetan plateau and Berlin*. Kapukasing, ON: Penumbra Press.

Darroch-Lozowski, V. (1990). *Antarctica body*. Waterloo, ON: Penumbra Press.

Darroch-Lozowski, V. (1999). *The uncoded world: A poetic semiosis of the wandered*. New York: Peter Lang.

Darroch-Lozowski, V. (2002). *Surface of a living world*. Montreal, QC: Stéphane Huot.

Marcel, G. (1950). *Mystery of being: Reflection & mystery (Vol. 1)*. South Bend, IN: Gateway.

Maturana Romesin, H. & Verden-Zöller, G. (2008). *The origin of humanness in the biology of love*. Exeter, UK: Imprint Academic.

Sheldrake, R. (1982). *A new science of life: The hypothesis of formative causation*. Los Angeles, CA: J.P. Tarcher.

Sheldrake, R. (2009). *Morphic resonance: The nature of formative causation*. Rochester, VT: Park Street.

Wolff, K. H. (1976). *Surrender and catch: Experience and inquiry today*. Dordrecht: D. Reidel.

Wolff, K. H. (1989). *O Loma!: Constituting a self (1977–1984)*. North Hampton, MA: Hermes House.

Wolff, K. H. (1991). Review of the book *Notebook of stone*, by V. Darroch-Lozowski. *Human Studies*, 14, 99–104.

3

BEAUTY AND LEARNING[1]

Tobin Hart

The ancients knew that somehow value and virtue in life is not only about the good and the true, it is also beautiful. Through beauty we recognize qualities that make one thing more inviting and sometimes more valuable than another; this provides meaning and a kind of magnetism to our experience of life. We cannot necessarily measure it precisely or even explain it, and therefore it has been more difficult to incorporate into standardized modern curriculum. But somehow beauty sends a "ping" into our depths and we find ourselves drawn toward it.

The attention to beauty is so culturally and historically ubiquitous that it is surely natural to human existence. In human culture, beauty shows up in two important bookends (and lightning rods) that we have used to make sense of our existence: religion and evolution. Taking a moment to notice how beauty finds its way into these two very different realms helps to demonstrate just how significant and pervasive it is.

Religion has been a way of pointing to what is of highest value in human existence. Every religious tradition creates beauty to express or honor what is understood as most sacred. Creating and beholding beauty has served as both an act of devotion—an outpouring expressing our connection and commitment—and an invocation, designed to move us into reverence. From European cathedrals to Islamic mosques, from gospel hymns to Hindu chants, from Russian icons to Tibetan sand paintings, beauty is offered as a gift and a prayer to what is most sacred to us. It is a testament to the importance we place on the sacred, and testifies equally to how dear we hold beauty to be, as a bridge to the divine.

Beauty of a different sort shapes another way we have learned to think about creation: the process of evolution. Beauty long befuddled Darwin: "The sight of a feather in a peacock's tail, whenever I gaze at it, makes me sick!" (Darwin, 1887, p. 296). He first believed that only adaptations favoring stronger or more effective design of creatures would win the day and enable them to pass their traits along through natural selection. But he eventually discovered something else. Evolution was not only practical, for some reason it liked a kind of beauty. In time, Darwin came to understand that natural selection had a mate in sexual selection. And sexual selection leaned toward attributes that seemed aesthetically interesting—like the male peacock's feathers, the male baboon's rump, or the redness of the dot on a bird's beak. Evolution, so it seems, favors beauty.

"Beauty will save the world," writes Russian novelist Fyodor Dostoyevsky in *The Idiot*. Philosopher Alfred North Whitehead says the teleology of the universe is the production of beauty. Helen was said to have a face so beautiful that it launched a thousand ships. Even the face of an industrial era icon, the Chairman of General Motors Corporation at the time, said that his company's job was to produce "moving sculpture." This behemoth of the machine age defined even industrial corporate work as art. In fact, manufacturing has made a turn toward beauty. Apple, among others, has made products that are aesthetically pleasing in form and function and absolutely central to its great success. We can now buy toilet bowl brushes with attention to more than the stiffness of their bristles. While industrial design and marketing recognize the value in beauty, our contemporary education has yet to realize that beauty has even more "cred" in the human mind than it does on the street or in the marketplace.

Educators need to recognize that beauty is more than ornamentation. It cuts more deeply. There is something in beauty that touches our common humanity. We hunger for it; in and of itself beauty is nourishment and a necessity.

It is not simply the surface that makes the beautiful. Sometimes we confuse the shell with the nut. But beauty instead reflects some underlying quality that is revealed when form and perception meet and open to one another. In the beautiful object or act, we see what we want to join with. C. S. Lewis (1942) said it this way:

> We do not want merely to see beauty . . . We want something else that can hardly be put into words—to be united with the beauty we see, to pass into it, to receive it into ourselves, to bathe in it, to become part of it.
>
> *(p. 8)*

In the third century, Plotinus made similar sense of the strange gravitational pull of beauty, saying that our earthly embodiment means that you and I are splintered from the divine. Our soul carries its imprint and in beauty we get a glimpse of that divinity, our true home base. Whenever we get a sense of the perfection of that other world, our soul strives to reunite with it.

Said in a more contemporary way, we are "hardwired" for beauty. That ping, that magnetism, connects to something both deep within us and far beyond us. When we see yellow, it is not *just* somewhere; it is recognized inside and resonates universally. In this way, beauty brings knower and knowledge closer to one another and reveals a vibrant, holistic dimension of life toward which contemporary education can open.

Beauty in Science

While it is not hard to recognize the role of beauty in the arts and humanities—the arc of a dancer's movement or the turn of a phrase—it is more surprising that even the supposed detachment and objectivity of science seems to have beauty entwined in its roots.

Modernity split science from the arts. But the differences between them were turned into artificial division, absolutized as if they had nothing to do with one another and no way to relate. Resonance and reason, feeling and fact, were "officially" divorced from one another and our schooling, and we, ourselves, fragmented.

Bridging the supposed gulf between science and beauty, Robert Augros and George Stanciu, in *The New Story of Science* (1984), show "all of the most eminent physicists of the twentieth century agree that beauty is the primary standard for scientific truth" (p. 39). French mathematician and theoretical physicist Henri Poincaré (2003), for instance, understood the role of beauty in science in this way:

> The scientist does not study nature because it is useful to do so. He studies it because he takes pleasure in it; and he takes pleasure in it because it is beautiful. If nature were not beautiful, it would not be worth knowing and life would not be worth living. . . . I mean the intimate beauty which comes from the harmonious order of its parts and which a pure intelligence can grasp.
>
> *(p. 22)*

Plato long ago understood that one kind of beauty comes through the universality of the logic of mathematics. For Plato, it is particularly the qualities–harmony, balance, and proportion–within the object or act that we love, not the objects themselves.

Akin to Plato's sense of beauty, mathematician Steven Strogatz finds a hidden world during a schoolroom lesson involving graphing the swing of a pendulum, which formed a parabola:

> It was in that moment that I suddenly understood what people mean when they say there's a law of nature. There was this sort of veil over reality, a hidden universe that you couldn't see unless you knew math. It's a very intimate personal thing, this feeling of wonder of a sense of living in an incomprehensible and beautiful universe. But partly comprehensible, that's the beauty of it.
>
> *(Abumrad, 2008)*

This deep encounter at the edge of knowledge and mystery often comes with awe and reverence. I recall the feeling of mystery and intrigue each time I entered Mr. Simpson's sixth-grade science class. He was an environmentalist and naturalist ahead of his time, at least in my little rural town. I would see this tall, respectable-looking man walk home from school and pick up all the trash between his house and the school; he spoke of poison apples (pesticide laden) and the particularities of the coloring on birds; he developed a nature trail behind the school. His room always seemed to have layers and layers of fascinating real stuff, from a wasp's nest to a human skeleton, to rocks and minerals.

While I had some interest in science and the natural word, it was Mr. Simpson's fascination and slightly eccentric personality that drew in many of my classmates and me far enough to find what was beautiful. There was mystery and wonder here, not just facts to be picked up. Maybe the most important thing about his pedagogy was that he was still openly fascinated by the things and processes of the world and did not hide it. He might get "off track," speculating on the development of a particular rock or imagining the owner of some bone, just "thinking out loud," wondering beneath the surface.

Most significantly, this meant that we could be fascinated and wonder too. And amidst the growing concern to both find the one right answer and avoid being "uncool," we did not have to be afraid to show our fascination. He entered the mystery with us, led us in really, with a profound appreciation for the beauty of the thing. I suppose he had a curriculum to follow, but he wanted to show us stuff, and have us show him our little found treasures, a special rock or a piece of honeycomb. He helped us to see the world as treasure, as beautiful.

Bringing the object or idea to life was engendered by Mr. Simpson's simple and profound shift toward appreciation, curiosity, and beholding rather than simply categorizing or pinning the object or idea down like a dead bug to a mat.

Religionist Abraham Heschel (1972) recognized the significance and rarity of this way of seeing in schooling:

> Our systems of education stress the importance of enabling the student to exploit the power aspect of reality. . . . We teach the children how to measure, how to weigh. We fail to teach them how to revere, how to sense wonder and awe.
>
> *(p. 36)*

Beauty takes endless forms: a great work of art, a perfect lapis sky, but also a perfect pitch in baseball, a meal prepared with special attention to detail, the deep peace of an infant asleep in loving arms, an act of kindness or courage that somehow embodies immanence and transcendence all at once. We hunger for this depth. We are trying to capture something that speaks to excellence, or goodness or realness. Or maybe that splinter of the divine that Plotinus understood, or those laws of nature, or something we cannot quite put our finger on, but that we recognize nonetheless as awakening a vital aspect of our consciousness that ties somehow to the depth of the world.

Tobin Hart

Beauty as Catalyst in Teaching and Learning

First and foremost, beauty works through the emotions. It builds a closer link between feeling and thinking. It activates interest, even passion and wonder, and then raises questions. What makes this more beautiful than that? What draws me to this? Are a few sparse lines of Picasso's drawing of a bull "true," capturing some essence that is deeply satisfying, and if so, how is this so? How can I have more of this feeling I get in the presence of beauty: awe, love, inspiration, goodness, perfection, etc.? In this sense, beauty joins with considerations of quality, meaning, understanding, imagination, discernment, and self-reflection.

Educator Joe Winston (2011) argues that the likes of Shakespeare will not be understood by students or teachers and hence not valued until they experience the beauty of the writing. "Learning through beauty is here associated with joy, hope and fulfillment, as motivating a quest for understanding based upon our deepest desires" (p. 18).

> It is built on a tradition of ideas that explicitly does not confine beauty to the arts, but sees it as evident in human action, human character, in the natural world, in ideas, philosophy, and the foundational principles of science.
>
> *(pp. 18–19)*

In order to make learning an experience of beauty, our teaching must also be beautiful in some way. When asked to describe an influential teacher, Linda, now a successful teacher herself, told me that it was something about *being beauty*, that lived experience of being touched and immersed, that transformed a lesson into something extraordinary.

> It was an English class, an American mid-century poetry class. The way the guy read the poems, just to demonstrate. He was so completely into them. He was an older guy, looked like it was probably his last year of teaching . . . it was just sort of haunting. I felt *he was living this experience with the poem rather than just teaching it.* And I don't know if that's something I can try to bring in or not but sometimes I feel that in some of the texts I have students read, I can't have his passion but sometimes I still *feel* the experience at least. He was feeling it as he was teaching it.

Beauty activates desire and desire reaches for satisfaction, and in so doing provides intrinsic motivation. The modern world, claims Richard Sennett (2009) in his book *The Craftsman*, has two key methods for urging us to work hard and work well: competition against others, and a moral imperative to do work for the sake of the community. Both approaches are employed in educational practice and both have their difficulties. As an alternative or complement, the self-directed and deeply satisfying and fulfilling experience that comes from doing something with quality, with beauty—a well-crafted paragraph, painting, even a mathematical proof—provides self-sustaining motivation.

Beauty also tends to invite replication. That is, when we see something that is beautiful in some way we want to imitate it, capture it, to join with it. Exploring examples of quality and beauty can provide a magnetizing and catalyzing effect. We try to emulate the moves of our hero on the basketball court. We fall in love with a song and try to sing it or play it until we get it just right, or as right as we can. In such absorbed activity the process becomes more *autotelic*, meaning that the purpose is in doing itself. Self-consciousness recedes as we find ourselves immersed in the activity, and we are in "flow" (Csikszentmihalyi, 2008).

In many ways, contemporary schooling treats curriculum and the process of learning as if it were not substantial or sustaining on its own. Of course, it is not when we do not scratch beneath the surface and instead simply ask for recall for an examination and pledge allegiance to a test. When we have only a superficial meal prepared for a test, it is hard for the mind and heart to get engaged or nourished. And we know that ultimately carrots and sticks—extrinsic motivators—may actually spoil the opportunity for direct relevance and resonance.

In addition to the problem of superficial curricula, today's technology can so easily provide us a shell and not the nut. The quick flash of an image designed to grab our attention—sex, violence, and so forth—may activate an instinctual response to try to grab more, inviting titillation without ever moving past the initial reaction and into a full-bodied, full-minded experience. We know how to turn ourselves on (as do marketers), but that image does not quite satisfy and may lead to fixation on a narrow bandwidth of intense but shallow stimulation instead of an embodied experience of beauty.

Beauty can serve as medicine. Simply beholding beauty can be transformative; a bouquet of flowers brightens a day, time in nature seems to feed us, gorgeous surroundings or song brighten our senses and our mood. Beauty provides a bliss station, a restorative touchstone. And perhaps there is no more powerful and enduring source of healing and beauty than nature.

Nature serves as inspiration and nourishment. There is something about nature that resonates with us deeply and directly: "'Nature is on the inside,' says Cezanne. Quality, light, color, depth, which are there before us, are there only because they awaken an echo in our body and because the body welcomes them" (Merleau-Ponty, 1964, p. 164). In this sense, we are not just *on* the earth we are *of* it. Our name, *human*, reminds us of our origin. The word human comes from *humus*, which means *earth*. As naturalist John Muir (1979) understood: "The sun shines not on us but in us. The rivers flow not past, but through us" (p. 92).

Our thinking capacity enables us to imagine that we are separated from the world and permits us to live as if we are. Objectivism and reductionism help maintain this distance. The direct experience of nature helps us to reseat ourselves in the world and its beauty, our shared beauty.

There are plenty of wonderful examples that bring nature to schooling; the bottom line is to help bring ourselves and our charges into a direct personal connection with the natural world. It is in moments of communion and connection with nature that, as Thomas Berry said, "lays down the enduring value of beauty, wonder and intimacy. A sense of the sacred begins here" (Toben, 2011, p. 19). This experience is not only for students but also for educators: "Like other artists, educators rediscover spirit through turning to the physical world" (Richards, 1980, p. 79).

Beauty From the Inside Out

From where does beauty arise? Perhaps most profoundly, we find beauty not just in outward nature, but in our most inward constitution: within our own depths. We will not find a brain part responsible for beauty but we may be able to see something else. While our individual sense of beauty may sometimes be radically variable and individual ("You like this picture; I prefer that one"), the process of knowing that enables beauty may be somewhat more universal. Specifically, the interplay of *harmony* and *intensity* may constitute a dynamic process underlying both learning and beauty.

One primary way the mind develops is through an intertwined process of differentiation and integration. We make distinctions and then bring together parts advancing into a new patterned whole. We notice the difference between the sound and meaning of words: Dad and Dog, or give names to different shades of yellow: sunflower, saffron, butter, banana, and then find a way for them to coexist in our mental map or schema of the world. Beauty is so universal to our existence and so useful for learning because it may be fundamentally tied to this same process of knowing.

Philosopher Alfred North Whitehead argued that beauty emerges out of a process of differentiation or contrast on the one hand, and integration or harmony on the other. Light and shadow join with one another to produce a mood and image; various tones merge together and are contrasted with silence or gaps to form rhythm and melody; tension is built and released in a powerful story or a song. Contradictions become contrasts and contrasts elicit depth (Sherburne, 1966, p. 216). In a state of beauty, the contrast between parts brings everything into focus, so that "the parts contribute to the massive feeling of the whole, and the whole contributes to the intensity of feeling of the parts" (Whitehead, 1967, p. 252).

For Whitehead, the challenge of beauty is the dual aim of harmony and intensity, unity in diversity (or integration amidst differentiation). If the contrast is too great, there is a "painful clash" and the result can be a mess (p. 252). If the inclusion is too limited, the lack of diversity leads to tameness and monotony. Beauty rests on "not only the absence of conflict (harmony), but also the realization of new contrasts (intensity)" (Henning, 2010, p. 202) and "contrasts of contrasts" (Whitehead, 1978, p. 22). In Whitehead's conception, "Contrast is the opposite of incompatibility . . . *to set in contrast with* means *to put in a unity with*" (Sherburne, 1966, p. 216). This is not static but continues to expand as we come to recognize subtler or previously unseen contrasts as well as freshly perceived patterns or integrations.

Anticipating the emergent episteme, Whitehead says that value is achieved from "the vivid grasp of the interdependence of the one and the many" (Whitehead, 1968, p. 60). Essentially the whole point of existence, he contends, is the creation of beauty, this fusion of discord and harmony, of parts and wholes, of difference and integration.

In a learning situation, we can help students deepen understanding by directing their focus on differentiation and integration. We will use the word "beauty" here, but we could just as easily use other words that capture the particularities of experience such as: "better or worse," "more or less desirable," "quality," "colder," "fairer," "meaner", and so forth depending on the direction of the lesson. The point is just to draw out contrast and harmony. Here is a handful of the type of directions that may help to do so. Notice that everything depends on subjective experience in a dialogue between inner and outer that engages the whole person.

- Experiencing beauty: Think of something that is beautiful (or fair or wise or ugly or whatever might be useful to frame the particular topic) to you. What is your experience, the feeling, thoughts and sensations that are evoked?
- Quality and discernment: What makes this more beautiful (or better, worse, etc.) than that?
- Identity: When and how has beauty made an impact on you?
- Epistemology: How do you know something is beautiful? What makes it so?
- Values: When is beauty also good or true?
- Classical beauty: Notice harmony, balance, pattern, The Golden Mean, etc.
- Radical beauty: Notice something that has great intensity but that may not be appreciated by everyone.
- Natural beauty: What do you notice about the natural world and about your experience while in it?
- Transformation and paradox: When does beauty become ugly? (e.g., A great athlete does something dastardly—takes a cheap shot, for example.) By what means does something ugly become beautiful?
- Perception and projection: Has something grown more or less beautiful over time through your eyes or others'?

Beauty Through Presence

As a unique moment of harmony and intensity, every occasion is, to some degree, beautiful. Beauty reflects the quality of our knowing as much as it does the object before us. Beauty may indeed exist outside of the knower—a great work of art or a magnificent tree—but it is comprehended or covered over, enacted or ignored, by the human mind and heart. Perhaps the most important key of all to understanding the creation of beauty is that *we co*-create it through the quality of our presence: as when we open awareness—our feelings, thoughts, sensations—to the soul of something or someone, we can notice beneath the surface.

As we dive in, the world unfolds before us and within us. Like a great naturalist, we begin to see more depth, more subtlety and, ultimately, more beauty. The opening of awareness and perception can reveal the beauty in all things. William Blake, English poet and mystic, tells us, "If the doors of perception were cleansed, everything would appear to man as it is, infinite. For man has closed himself up, till he sees all things thro' narrow chinks of his cavern" (Blake, 1966, p. 154).

The beautiful depends on presence. There is a difference between racing through an art museum to see if you can see everything and instead *beholding*, and communing with a work of art. This is a shift from quantity to quality. In a classroom, there is always pressure to move on to the next demand of the curriculum. But there is also the opportunity to move into depth rather than on to the next surface. When we dive in we have a better chance of finding the whole story or pattern of the discipline rather than merely the facts that lie on the surface.

Are we awake to what is before us or are we just going through the motions? Whether a glimpse into history, the shape of geometry, the taste of our meal, or the turn of a phrase, the lesson from beauty is that depth, richness, and nourishment in learning requires our engagement, our presence.

Beauty is fundamental to human consciousness, yet essentially absent from most contemporary considerations of curriculum and pedagogy. In teaching and learning, beauty unites knowing and being and, in so doing, provides a means to bring depth and vitality to education.

Beauty activates and awakens something both within and between and reveals itself to the extent we open to it. When consciousness attunes to beauty, beauty has the potential to tune us up, opening to possibilities of discovery, awe, and nourishment.

Maybe beauty *will* save the world.

Note

1 Portions of this chapter have been excerpted from Hart, T. (2014). *The integrative mind: Transformative education for a world on fire.* Lanham, MD: Rowman and Littlefield.

References

Abumrad, J. (2008). "Yellow fluff and other curious encounters," audio podcast, *Radiolab.* Season 5, episode 5, December 12. www.radiolab.org/2009/jan/12/.

Augros, R. & Stanciu, G. (1984). *The new story of science: Mind and the universe.* Lake Bluff, IL: Regnery Gateway.

Blake, W. (1966). "The marriage of heaven and hell." In G. Keynes (Ed.), *Blake: Complete writings.* Oxford, UK: University Press.

Csikszentmihalyi, M. (2008). *Flow: The psychology of optimal experience.* New York: Harper.

Darwin, C. (1887). The publication of 'The Origin of the Species'. In F. Darwin (Ed.), *The life and letters of Charles Darwin.* London: John Murray.

Henning, B. (2010). Re-centering process thought: Recovering beauty in A. N. Whitehead's late work. In *Beyond metaphysics? Explorations in Alfred North Whitehead's late thought.* New York: Rodopi.

Heschel, A. J. (1972). *God in search of man.* New York: Octagon Books. Original work published 1955.

Lewis, C. S. (1942). *The weight of glory.* London: Society for promoting Christian values. (Preached originally as a sermon in the Church of St Mary the Virgin, Oxford, UK, on June 8, 1942.)

Merleau-Ponty, M. (1964). Eye and mind (Carleton Dallery, Trans.). In J. Edie (Ed.), *The primacy of perception: And other essays on phenomenological psychology, the philosophy of art, history and politics.* Evanston, IL: Northwestern University Press.

Muir, J. (1979). *John of the mountains: The unpublished journals of John Muir,* Linnie Marsh Wolfe (Ed.). Madison, WI: University of Wisconsin Press. Original work published 1938.

Poincaré, H. (2003). *Science and method.* Mineola, NY: Dover. Original work published 1914.

Richards, M. C. (1980). *Toward wholeness: Rudolf Steiner education in America.* Middleton, CT: Wesleyan University Press.

Sennett, R. (2009). *The craftsman.* New Haven: Yale University Press.

Sherburne, D. (1966). *A key to Whitehead's Process and Reality*. London: Macmillan.

Toben, C. (2011). A child awakens. In P. Whalen-Levit (Ed.), *Only the sacred: Transforming education in the 21st century*. Greensboro, NC: The Center for Education, Imagination, and the Natural World.

Whitehead, A. N. (1967). *Adventures of ideas*. New York: Penguin.

Whitehead, A. N. (1968). *Modes of thought*. New York: Simon & Schuster.

Whitehead, A. N. (1978). *Process and reality*. David Griffin and Donald Sherburne (Eds). New York: Simon & Schuster.

Winston, J. (2011). *Beauty and education*. New York: Routledge.

4

FROM A DEEPER PLACE

Indigenous Worlding as the Next Step in Holistic Education

Four Arrows, aka Don Trent Jacobs

Holistic education, grounded in a fundamentally different worldview, reflects very different assumptions about education and school.

(Ron Miller, 1997, p. 5)

Indigenous education embodies these principles more deeply . . . When Indigenous people speak about our relationship to earth and the universe, it does not come from the head but from a much deeper place.

(Four Arrows & Miller, J. P., 2012, p. 3)

The Need to Go Deeper

My goal in this chapter is to introduce ways to deepen present implementation and future research relating to principles shared by holistic and Indigenous education that can help us find ways to regain balance in our world before it is too late. Such principles are ultimately about "holding a sense of the sacred, valuing the web of life, and educating the whole human being" (Four Arrows & Miller, 2012, p. 9). Miller's words reflect his recognition of the connection between the Indigenous worldview and the field of holistic education.

The holistic ideal can be traced back to Indigenous cultures. In general, the Aboriginal or Indigenous person sees the earth and the universe as infused with meaning and purpose and not as cold and impersonal as in the modern worldview.

(Miller, 2009, p. 291)

Unfortunately, implementation of this holistic ideal has fallen short of what we need to achieve in education, with non-anthropocentric connections not matching those of the Indigenous worldview. In a review for this chapter, I've noted that most holistic education publications focus on body–mind–family–social community–art–pluralism–health without an authentic and consistent engagement with the other and often greater than human relations. When "web of life" concepts are mentioned, authors seem limited by hegemonic assumptions relating to financial and technological considerations for human benefit. Kopnina (2014) critiques this problem, writing, "Mainstream neoliberal discourse tends to maintain instrumental and essentially anthropocentric attitudes toward environment, subordinating 'natural resources' to economic and social objectives" (p. 6).

Kopnina's scholarship generally falls into the field of critical pedagogy. The problem with it is that it tends to address the problem of anthropocentrism with more of it, focusing on attacking oppression and fostering democratic orientations as opposed to an increased focus on the natural world *per se* for solutions. Such critical pedagogy is, in some ways, a cousin to holistic education, but misses the spiritual interconnectedness dimension (Jacobs, 1997). O'Sullivan (2005) complains about this when he writes, "My major criticism of critical pedagogy is the pre-eminent emphasis on inter-human problems frequently to the detriment of the relations of humans to the wider biotic community and the natural world" (p. 411). Gustauo, Stuchul, and Prakash (2005) are equally explicit about this problem when they say that critical pedagogy oriented interventions into Indigenous cultures often lack a deep understanding of their nature-based, holistic worldview.

We might forgive the field of critical pedagogy for this omission, but not holistic education. It is understandable perhaps that, to the degree that most holistic educators operate from a non-Indigenous worldview, they will fall into anthropocentrism. In fact, this may be why there are so few holistic education programs even being implemented in the world. I could not find statistics to verify this assumption but I did call Jerry Mintz, long time director of the Alternative Education Resource Organization, to find out. I recently asked him how many alternative schools actually do holistic education. After a long description of statistics, he concluded: "I might say that maybe 5–10% could be called holistic." An extensive study on interdisciplinary research in higher education (Van Noorden, 2015) shows a similar lack of integrated or holistic perspective when he writes that, worldwide, 9–13% of all the scholarly publications reviewed showed any reference to a journal outside of the particular field of study targeted. Interdisciplinary curricula is an aspect of holistic education because it encourages students to make connections between disciplines.

Thus I contend to move holistic education to its intended "deeper" orientation, we must return to our original non-anthropocentric worldview and begin to think and speak accordingly in the classroom. Mika (2017) refers to such languaging as "worlding" the Indigenous. Mika, a senior lecturer at the University of Waikato and author of a new book on Indigenous metaphysics and "worlding", also refers to the unfulfilled Indigenous realization of holistic education rhetoric.

> However, a second problem is the fact that Indigenous worldedness has not comprised much of the corpus of holistic literature. The authors of holistic education are still too human-derived and, alongside that, advocate too strongly that a thing is individually *there*. In that, it reflects the metaphysics of presence.
>
> *(p. 27)*

Mika is supportive of holistic education as a twenty-first century paradigm and he pushes it further toward the deeper goals of the Millers as expressed in the opening quotes using Indigenous Nature-centered perspectives. Students of Mika refer to such perspectives when they write in the journal, *International Education Studies*, "Holistic education seeks to connect the part with the whole and is founded upon a deep reverence for life and for the unknown (and never fully knowable) source of life" (Mahmoudi, Jafari, Nasrabadi, & Liaghatdar (2012, p. 185).

Mika (2017) goes deeper with his own description:

> Broadly I mean by *worlding* and its variations *worlded* and *worldedness* the following: one thing is never alone, and all things actively construct and compose it. As one thing presents itself to me others within it may appear and hide, but even if I cannot perceive them (which I cannot) we can be assured that they are there. An object that I perceive is therefore fundamentally unknowable. I can speculate on it and give it a name, but all I can be certain of is that it is mysterious precisely because it is "worlded." I can experience the thing in its full force without actually sensing that influence, but talk of knowledge is only minimally useful when we are

considering it. I am no more familiar with any one thing than if I had never encountered it. Indeed, I experience an aspect of the worlded thing and its mystery when I meet the limits of my ability to say much about it, or when I realize that I cannot fully know it. Perception is given rise by the formation of the self with the full force of all things in the world. Moreover, I can talk about the thing, or more precisely, I am discussing it as if I am a part of it.

(pp. 6–7)

Such worlding requires that we incorporate a worldview reflection into our holistic education classrooms. We must investigate the wisdom of our dominant worldview and its human-superiority assumptions to determine where and how it may impede the optimal utilization of holistic education. This is something that Greg Cajete, John Lee, and I did in looking at how the dominant worldview lens guides neuroscientific conclusions. We discovered that the dominant worldview deters even neuroscientists from realizing the truths of Indigenous wisdom via their "observations" and interpretations of laboratory experiments (Four Arrows, Cajete, & Jonmin, 2010). Looking at fundamental Indigenous worldview beliefs we found that much of Western science comes to faulty conclusions by looking at experiments through the Western lens. Such is the power of a worldview and why this worldview reflection is crucial for our holistic understanding of how we have managed to be on the verge of a mass extinction.

The English word, "worldview," comes from the German word, "*Weltanschauung*" that means "to see the world." It is not the best word to use when describing an Indigenous worldview that does not rely upon an understanding of the world by only what it can see. This does not align well with Indigenous ways of comprehending reality but it may be the best word available. I use it as per de Witt's (2013) definition:

The concept of worldview may appear to be similar or even interchangeable with concepts such as ideology, paradigm, religion, and discourse, and they indeed possess some degree of referential overlap. However, worldviews can nonetheless be clearly distinguished from these concepts.

(p. 19)

Robert Redfield, the first social anthropologist and a specialist in worldview studies at the University of Chicago in the 1950s, also believed that worldview describes the totality of ideas that people within a culture share about self, human society, natural and spiritual worlds (Redfield, 1953). He considered that since the Asian worldview had been mostly taken over by the Western one, that there remain only two worldviews for us to study—the primal or Indigenous one and the dominant one that continues to overshadow and destroy the original one.

With these ideas about worldview in mind, I believe going deeper with holistic education starts with seeking to find complementarity and understanding contradictions between the two worldviews. Then, with new awareness, educators must begin *worlding* the Indigenous perspective. We do this by actually participating in the world emotionally, physically, mentally, and spiritually, as if we are mysteriously inseparable from it and obligated to take action according to our highest potential for complementarity. It is a way of being in the world where distinctions between self and other disappear. I think of this as living fearlessly and, in so doing, embracing the full force of all things. By living the Indigenous worldview again, we cannot help but teach holistically.

So, our next step is to begin holistic education with worldview reflection, starting with ourselves. Before introducing how to begin Indigenous worlding, I offer two examples of what it is like to experience "the full force of all things," a simple one anyone can do, followed by a more difficult one I was forced into experiencing. The first requires only access to a plant; the second a near death experience.

Over the years I have started many conference workshops by asking the participants to step outside and touch a tree or plant and then to return to the conference room. I ask them to think about what they did, then ask them to go back outside and do it again, but this time I instruct them to ask permission of the plant or tree and *wait for a reply* before touching it. They often depart echoing skeptical, laughing attitudes but always return, no matter their age or culture, in silent awe. The stories they share about the experience seldom fail to bring tears to the story-teller or to others. One 14-year old Mexican child who was very skeptical about the exercise came back with a very different attitude for example. He told the class that a small palm tree wept about having lost relatives in a recent hurricane! He said it reluctantly and even embarrassingly at first, but then he became quite emotional in his efforts to describe something he could not quite fathom. There were few dry eyes around me and I was also moved by both his realization of another being in the tree and his understanding that he had missed such relationships until now. I conclude by asking them to imagine living under a worldview where this kind of relationship was continual.

The above experiment we can easily do but sometimes we can be forced into Indigenous worlding. This happened to me while kayaking the uncharted Rio Urique River in Mexico's Copper Canyon, I was sucked into a rock tunnel into which the entire river disappeared. As I submerged I felt an indescribable sense of peaceful oneness with the world. I felt a knowing that defies knowledge and a mysteriousing that was anything but mysterious. From that point on every rock, every water source and tree, every creature seemed to be an intimate relation or a teacher emerging at just the right time. Synchronicities and non-human teachings began popping up everywhere.

One of the more remarkable outcomes was my work with wild horses. Before the kayaking accident I was involved with 100-mile endurance racing and a sport called "Ride and Tie" that was a race whereby teams consisted of two people and a horse. Most of the mounts are Arabians who are known for their endurance prowess, but I wanted a mustang in honor of my Indigenous traditions. I had adopted one and brought it home just prior to my trip. I could not even approach it and when I used ropes for training, I lost every time. Frustrated with my failures, I left on the kayak trip to take on what I thought would be a more familiar adventure. However, when I came back a miraculous new rapport seemed to exist between the horse and me. The rest is history and I became well known as a horse-trainer, working for the Bureau of Land Management (BLM) to help people who had adopted mustangs but could not handle them or had young animals whose heads had grown into halters that no one could loosen until I arrived. Working with wild horses has given me many opportunities for Indigenous worlding as well. They are sophisticated bio-feedback entities that let you know when you are manifesting the kinds of virtues required for survival in the world, such as generosity, courage, patience, trustfulness, etc. The reader can get a good sense of this by watching a seven-minute TV segment about my working with a wild BLM mustang on Youtube.[1]

Stop for a moment and consider times in your own life, dramatic or otherwise, where you have had moments where ego was so melded into the "other thing" that you felt inseparably a part of it. If you did not remember such a time, start paying attention to your inherent relatedness to the life intelligence in all things and you will soon start to realize many such experiences. It will help to first let go of some dominant worldview assumptions and replace them with our original instructions, using what I refer to as the CAT-FAWN metacognitive worldview reflection tool.

The CAT-FAWN Connection

After the accident on the Rio Urique, I had a dream of two animals I came upon on my way out of the canyon, a mountain lion and a young deer. They turned into the letters, C-A-T and F-A-W-N. The words turned into a mnemonic for a metacognitive worldview reflection strategy for moving people toward a re-embracing of our Indigenous assumptions about how to best live with a truly holistic mindset. Rather than describe it myself, I defer to the excellent condensed description recently published by R. Michael Fisher (2017).

According to Four Arrows, CAT-FAWN is a metaphor, "a new theory of mind" and meta-cognitive mnemonic that tells of a predator (CAT) and its potential prey (FAWN) operating with the joint (dialectic) bonding of a hyphenated form; this indicates a basic integration of opposites in a complementarity—the latter, being a foundational principle of the Indigenous worldview (and harmony) as he has written about. The **CAT** portion stands literally for Concentration Activated Transformation. This refers to a heightened state of consciousness/awareness, which can be induced by many stimuli (situations), for e.g., meditation, dreaming, and/or a shock, etc.).

The problem, Four Arrows notes, is when we enter a **CAT** state without noticing or knowing we are so, and what is causing it. Thus, if largely unconscious to CAT we are highly susceptible to "inputs" from the environment that may condition us, that is hypnotize us and implant "messages" that are harmful to us. These trance-based learned messages, even if unconscious and subliminal, are deeply memorized and held in the nervous system, so goes the theory of hypnosis.

Let's move on to the other half of the "formula"—**FAWN**. Literally, F = Fear, A = Authority, W = Word(s) (and music) and N = Nature. This stands for what Indigenous Peoples of the 'old ways' always knew were "four major forces" that shape our lives, for good or ill (depending on our awareness and management of them). Fear is taken as very primal in both inducing CAT and joining with CAT (e.g., CAT-Fear) as a powerful two-some able to bring about "courage" as a virtue (for e.g.) or to bring about "panic" and "irrationality" as a vice (for e.g.). Great character/values are built on the former, and shabby destructive values built on the latter. To reach our highest human potential(s) one has to learn to manage CAT-Fear well—without doing so, this can undermine all the good ways of the other three major forces. Authority is very powerful because it can use Words (for e.g.) to hypnotize. Humans, as a social species, are particularly hard-wired through evolution to "follow" authority (dominant) individuals, groups, organizations, nations, ideologies. So, one has to be very aware when in CAT of their relationships going on via CAT-Authority and CAT-Word.

The last of the major forces of the de-hypnotizing technology is most foundational to the entire CAT-FAWN complex, and I prefer to write this formula (theory) as CAT-FAW/N. Which is saying that the common denominator and most influential factor is N = Nature [11]. It is the most benign of the forces. I won't go into all those reasons but many of us know how powerful it can be to connect with Nature when we are "off-center" or "hurting" and or "terrified" by the human world. The Natural world, in general, is our "Mother" (Source) for earthlings. Today some groups of modern people know this, as well as the Indigenous Peoples of this planet that have lived in relative harmony with Nature for 99% of human evolution, which is the basic premise of Four Arrows' theory and work overall.

How to Use CAT-FAWN to Access Indigenous Worlding[2]

Because CAT-FAWN uses five concepts for which Indigenous and dominant worldviews have significant contrast, it is the perfect tool for bringing Indigenous worlding into holistic education. These four concepts include:

Trance-based learning. Our original cultures and those still holding on to the old ways know that deep knowing and optimal action in the world requires alternative consciousness work. Most Olympic athletes today use TBL and use sports hypnosis to maximize their potential;

however, the rest of the population seldom uses self-hypnosis as do traditional Indigenous cultures. I realize the word "hypnosis" comes with lots of baggage and misunderstanding results. I use the concept here to describe what happens when we move from a normal beta brain-wave frequency into a lower one, like alpha or theta, and while in this altered state one focuses one's imaginative powers on a particular image of how one is being in the world, the image creates automatic transformations that allow or even cause a potentiation not otherwise likely to happen. I use "trance-based learning" or "concentration-activated transformation" and "hypnosis" as similar terms that describe this process.

Fear. In most dominant worldview cultures, fear itself is feared. We don't like it. We avoid it. Under the Indigenous worldview, fear is an opportunity to practice a virtue like courage, patience, humility, generosity or honesty.

Authority. The highest expression of authority under the Indigenous worldview is honest reflection on lived experience with the understanding that everything is related. Hierarchy did not exist as it is understood under the dominant worldview. During times of fear especially, people in the dominant cultures often become hyper-suggestible to the communication of a perceived trusted authority figure. I learned this from wild horses, so this may be true of all creatures as a survival mechanism. However, history shows us that when too much credibility is given to authority figures, especially in stressful situations, we can become hypnotized inappropriately. In the classroom, a child in this spontaneous hypnosis and with the hierarchy position of a teacher who says, "You are never going to amount to anything!", this child may have a long-term loss of self-esteem for many years.

Words. There was a time before deception, before the emergence of the dominant worldview around 9,000 years ago (Four Arrows, 2016). Certainly we can see that words are used far too often for deception today. Under the dominant worldview, deception is understood as a survival strategy whereas under the Indigenous worldview it is just the opposite (Four Arrows, Cajete, & Jonmin, 2010).

I conclude this piece with a brief overview of how to use CAT-FAWN to help change how we might hold on to the dominant worldview assumptions about these aforementioned concepts and move into ways that honor our original instructions. By making this transformation, I propose that we will then be able to go deeper into the implementation of holistic teaching and learning for the sake of future generations.

CAT. Concentration-activated transformation conveys the idea that most of our unconscious beliefs and actions stem from a previous hypnosis and that to change we must identify underlying assumptions and use trance-based learning to reverse or modify beliefs. Assume when you are out of balance, when anger lasts for more than a few minutes, when you behave or react in a way that seems to bring on stress, when you feel you are avoiding movements in behalf of your highest potential, when a relationship is not working, or when you feel separate from all our relations, etc., that there are unconscious belief systems operating, many, if not most, from early childhood "lessons" resulting from spontaneous hypnosis that is something that causes one to go into a different brain-wave frequency, thus increasing hypersuggestibility to words, whether self-uttered or from a perceived external authority figure. Using the four major forces in FAWN, learn if the dominant worldview perspective (fearing fear; overly depending on external authority; using words dishonestly; seeing nature as something separate) has maintained the hypnosis and if the Indigenous worldview can transform it by asking yourself the following questions relating to FAWN. Do this for yourself and guide students in the same way with the goal of implementing holistic perspectives.

FAWN

Fear. Ask what possible fear relates to the event, action, attitude or behavior. Note that the dominant worldview perspective is to avoid, dismiss or deny it. Move to the Indigenous perspective that sees Fear as a catalyst for practicing a virtue (courage, generosity, honesty, patience, fortitude, humility). Then, use a self-hypnosis technique (Four Arrows, 2016) to imagine yourself doing whatever makes sense to practice a virtue until by taking appropriate action via one or more of them you become fearless in that you are operating by fully trusting the universe and "worlding" a sense of complementarity into the situation.

Authority. Closely related to fear is the authority for it. Get in touch with the position, beliefs, feelings you have about the issue at hand. Ask yourself on whose authority did this position originate? As with the fear question, consider possibilities that some alternative state of consciousness might have been connected with it, though this is not necessary to know and you can assume probability. Now do the self-hypnosis and erase all forms of external authority from the picture, dismissing previous ones entirely and basing your new thoughts on only an honest reflection on your lived experience in light of a complementary attitude.

Words. Get in touch with all the words you use, especially self-talk, to describe the situation and analyze them for how accurate and truthful they really are. Consider what would happen if you understood them literally, as is done when in hypnosis. During hypnotic states of awareness we tend to image words relatively literally. A golfer imaging "I won't hit the ball in the sand trap" will likely hit it right into the sand trap because "sand trap" is more likely to create the image in this sentence. A proper hypnotic suggestion would be "I am hitting the ball into the fairway." A person who looks in the mirror and says "I am fat" would have to conclude that even if obese this would be an inaccurate use of words as opposed to "I am a beautiful person with temporarily too much adipose tissue around my belly." The English language is noun based and susceptible to inaccurate catagorizing. Find the best ways to honestly phrase the situation and use the self-hypnosis to process it. Then go the next step and realize that even the new words are insufficient to describe the unknown parts of the situation, including the potential complementarity between opposing energies and meditate on the beauty of the not needing to know.

Nature. Finally, find some other aspect of other-than-human or greater-than-human Nature. It could be a pet, an insect, a plant, a park, a river or a mountain, etc. Present the issue and consider metaphors that relate it to the other. Feel free to use the computer or ask others and come back to the other form of Nature with the new "information" and continue with the intuitive learning. Now allow yourself to continue to watch for other aspects of Nature as keys to a new realization as relates to the issue. Use ceremony with plants like pine, cedar, sage or sweetgrass to evoke images of other than, or greater than, human life forms. Only ceremony can truly continue to help you embrace the unknown. Balance it with discourse, knowing that discourse tends to remove the mysterious. All answers reside somewhere in what remains of the natural landscape in which you dwell. Nature is and always will be the ultimate teacher if we heed it accordingly.

Conclusion

I realize I have offered much new material in more or less abbreviated ways and hope it offers a sufficient introduction for readers. Perhaps this material will at least enhance awareness about how "worldview" has influenced the state of affairs in the world today and why it may be the missing ingredient for fulfilling holistic education. By better employing an "Indigenous worldview", we bring into play our original instructions that guided us for most of our time on Earth. We have both historical and present models for achieving relatively peaceful, joyful, and sustainable communities, a model that has for too long been ignored, dismissed, romanticized or ridiculed. This shift from an *Indigenous worldview* to what has become our *dominant worldview* may be the foundation for violence against all forms of diversity, that which is at the heart of what we call "holistic education"; it relates to the human mind, body, and spirit and how each of these is interdependent with the complex interactions of the seen and unseen world around us. Until we learn to understand, respect, and reclaim the worldview that operated for most of human history, whether comparing levels of warfare or numbers of fish in the ocean, social/ecological injustices and environmental degradation will continue unabated.

There will be those who resist the notion of replacing or finding complementarity with aspects of our Western or dominant worldview of course and I offer the words of two great non-Indian thinkers to help overcome such resistance to do worldview reflection or practice doing it with the transformational CAT-FAWN tool. Shephard (1992) contends that:

> [T]he legacy of History with respect to primitive peoples is threefold: (1) primitive life is devoid of admirable qualities (2) our circumstances render them inappropriate even if admirable, and (3) the matter is moot as "You cannot go back." This phrase shelters a number of corollaries. Most of these are physical rationalizations—too many people in the world, too much commitment to technology or its social and economic system, ethical and moral ideas that make up civilized sensibilities, and the unwillingness of people to surrender to a less interesting, cruder, or more toilsome life, from which time and progress delivered us.
>
> *(p. 44).*

David Abram's words in *Becoming Animal* offer a similar perspective:

> There are many intellectuals today who feel that any respectful reference to indigenous beliefs smacks of romanticism and a kind of backward-looking nostalgia. Oddly, these same persons often have no problem "looking backward" toward ancient Rome or ancient Greece for philosophical insight and guidance in the present day. What upsets these self-styled "defenders of civilization" is the implication that civilization might have something to learn from cultures that operate according to an entirely different set of assumptions, cultures that stand outside of historical time and the thrust of progress.
>
> *(2010, p. 267)*

In no way do I intend to "romanticize" the Indigenous with these quotes. All humans are subject to similar failures and susceptible to vices and loss of virtue. Moreover, many Indigenous People themselves, owing to years of genocide and culturecide, have lost touch with the traditional wisdom. This said, however, there are still many Indigenous Peoples who have resisted colonization of their hearts, minds, and bodies and, if we can support them, stop participating in their oppression, and attempt to learn from them, we can more readily recover our own ancient DNA in ways that can help us apply such wisdom in our own back yards before it is too late.

Notes

1 See "Four Arrows Wild Horse Hypnotist" at www.youtube.com/watch?v=vxzAm08731c
2 For more detail on CAT-FAWN, see *Primal Awareness: A True Story of Survival, Transformation and Awakening with the Raramuri Shamans of Mexico* (1998) and *Point of Departure: Returning to our More Authentic Worldview for Education and Survival* (2016) and Michael Fisher's text to be published by Peter Lang in 2018 entitled *Fearless Engagement in the Life and Work of Four Arrows: An Indigenous-based Social Transformer.*

References

Abram, D. (2010). *Becoming animal: An earthly cosmology*. New York: Pantheon.

de Witt, A. H. (2013). Worldviews and the transformation to sustainable societies (Doctoral dissertation), dare. ubvu.vu.nl/bitstream/handle/1871/48104/dissertation.pdf

Fisher, R. M. (2017). Dehypnotizing strategy technology of CAT-FAWN by Four Arrows. Fearless Movement Blog http://fearlessnessmovement.ning.com/blog/de-hypnotizing-technology-of-cat-fawn-by-four-arrows

Four Arrows (2016). *Point of departure: Returning to our more authentic worldview for education and survival*. New York: Information Age.

Four Arrows & Miller, J. P. (2012). To name the world: A dialogue about holistic and Indigenous education. *Encounter: Education for Meaning and Social Justice, 25*(3), 14–21.

Four Arrows, Cajete, G. J., & Jonmin, L. (2010). *Critical neurophilosophy and Indigenous wisdom*. Rotterdam, The Netherlands: Sense.

Gustauo E., Stuchul, D. L., & Prakash, M. S. (2005). From a pedagogy for liberation to liberation from pedagogy. In C. A. Bowers (Ed.), *Rethinking Freire: Globalization and the environmental crises* (pp. 44–51). Mahwah, NJ: Lawrence Erlbaum.

Jacobs, D. T. (1997). Critical pedagogy and spiritual dialogue: The missing partnership. Paper presented at Pedagogy of the Oppressed Conference. Omaha, NB: University of Nebraska, April 18.

Kopnina, H. (2014). Neoliberalism, pluralism, environment and education for sustainability. *Horizons of Holistic Education, 1*, 93–113.

Mahmoudi, S., Jafari, E., Nasrabadi, H. A., & Liaghatdar, M. (2012). Holistic education: An approach for the 21st century. *International Education Studies, 5*(2), 176–186.

Mika, C. (2017). *Indigenous education and the metaphysics of presence: A worlded philosophy*. London: Routledge.

Miller, J. P. (2009). Holistic education: Learning for an interconnected world. In R. V. Farrell & G. Papagiannis (Eds), *Education for sustainability Volume 1* (pp. 145–159). Encyclopedia of Life Support Systems, Oxford: UNESCO.

Miller, R. (1997, 2016). *What are schools for? Holistic education in American culture* (3rd edn). Brandon, VT: Holistic Education.

O'Sullivan, E. (2005). Education and the dilemmas of modernism: Toward an ecozoic vision. In D. E. Purpel & M. S. Shipiro (Eds), *Critical social issues in American education* (pp. 55–57). Mahwah, NJ: Lawrence Erlbaum.

Redfield, R. (1953). *The primitive world and its transformations*. Ithaca, NY: Cornell University Press.

Shepard, P. (1992). A post-historic primitivism. In M. Oelschlaeger (Ed.), *The wilderness condition: Essays on environment and civilization* (pp. 17–34). Washington, DC: Island Press.

Van Noorden, R. (2015). Interdisciplinary research by the numbers. *Nature, 525*(7569), 306–307.

5

EASTERN PHILOSOPHY AND HOLISTIC EDUCATION

Yoshiharu Nakagawa

Perennial Philosophy as a Foundation for Holistic Education

Holistic education has been concerned with providing a comprehensive worldview upon which the undertaking of education can be built, rather than just providing practical approaches. As the founding editor of *Holistic Education Review*, Ron Miller (1991) states that conventional education in an industrial-age culture has been based on a materialistic worldview, a reductionist attitude, an economic orientation, and the divisions between groups of people. By contrast, he regards a holistic worldview as promoting a reverence for life, an ecological perspective, a spiritual view of human beings, and a global perspective (pp. 1–3).

In his important work, *The Holistic Curriculum*, John Miller (2007) adopts "perennial philosophy" as a foundation of holistic education. "The 'perennial philosophy' (Huxley, 1968) provides the philosophic underpinnings of the holistic curriculum. The perennial philosophy holds that all life is connected in an interdependent universe. Stated differently, we experience relatedness through a fundamental ground of being" (p. 16). In this way, the perennial philosophy offers a valuable worldview to overcome fragmentary approaches in conventional education.

Authors in perennial philosophy have integrated the essential teachings of world wisdom traditions. According to Aldous Huxley (1968), who contributed to the expansion of this philosophy with his book, *Perennial Philosophy*, the perennial philosophy (*philosophia perennis*) explores "a divine Reality" or "the immanent and transcendent Ground of all being" (p. 1) to realize the eternal Self that is "identical with, or at least akin to, the divine Ground" (pp. 7–8). He writes, "The last end of man, the ultimate reason for human existence, is unitive knowledge of the divine Ground" (p. 29). It is important to note that Huxley (1975) in his last years developed a pioneering concept of holistic education called "nonverbal humanities" by introducing ideas of perennial philosophy (see Nakagawa, 2002).

Anna Lemkow (1990) states principles of perennial philosophy as follows: "the oneness and unity of all life; the all-pervasiveness of ultimate Reality or the Absolute; the multi-dimensionality or hierarchical character of existence" (p. 23). First of all, the ultimate reality is transcendent and immanent. "It is postulated that the Absolute transcends all apparent separateness; it is indescribable, ineffable and unknowable. Though it lies beyond all thought, it is not remote, but resides within the human heart, 'closer than hands and feet'" (pp. 23–24). The ultimate reality is boundless and beyond any description, yet simultaneously pervading and manifesting itself in everything.

Lemkow also emphasizes the multidimensionality as well as the nondual oneness of reality. "Thus the universe must be a unity. But it is also multi-dimensional, and so organized that each dimension or level of being produces the next, less inclusive level, from the most unitive to the most particular" (p. 38). The principle that the universe is a multidimensional manifestation of the ultimate reality is correspondingly reflected in the human being. A human is a microcosm of the macrocosm ("as above, so below"), and so he or she is, in fact, a multidimensional existence. Lemkow states, "Just as the universe is composed of a hierarchy of levels of being, so is man. Man is essentially one with the universe" (p. 36). Regarding this aspect, Huxley (1968) refers to three levels of body, psyche, and spirit:

> [M]an is a kind of trinity composed of body, psyche and spirit. Selfness or personality is a product of the first two elements. The third element . . . is akin to, or even identical with, the divine Spirit that is the Ground of all being.
>
> *(p. 48)*

Huston Smith (1976) describes a cosmology commonly accepted through ages that includes four levels of reality: the terrestrial plane, the intermediate plane, the celestial plane, and the "Infinite." Correspondingly, the levels of selfhood include body, mind, soul, and spirit. Compared to Huxley's model, the dimension of soul is added. The soul is defined as follows:

> The soul is the final locus of our individuality. . . . [I]t lies deeper than mind. If we equate mind with the stream of consciousness, the soul is the source of this stream; it is also its witness while never itself appearing within the stream as a datum to be observed. It underlies, in fact, not only the flux of mind but all the changes through which an individual passes.
>
> *(p. 74)*

While the soul is the inner self that observes and witnesses the body–mind, spirit is one with the Infinite as ultimate reality. "If soul is the element in man that relates to God, Spirit is the element that is identical with Him. . . . Spirit is the Atman that *is* Brahman, the aspect of man that *is* the Buddha-nature . . ." (p. 87).

Ken Wilber (1997) also regards the perennial philosophy as a multidimensional theory: "Central to the perennial philosophy is the notion of the *Great Chain of Being*. The idea itself is fairly simple. Reality, according to the perennial philosophy, is not one-dimensional" (p. 39). Wilber often describes five dimensions: matter, body, mind, soul, and spirit. Similar to Smith's view, he considers soul to be "the highest level of individual growth" as well as "the final barrier, the final knot, to complete enlightenment or supreme identity" (p. 47). The soul is "transcendental witness" that "stands back from everything it witnesses" (p. 47). Eventually, the soul turns into spirit. The spirit is pure awareness that is always universally present. Since pure awareness has no object to be witnessed, it becomes "nondual awareness" and turns out to be one with everything. Wilber writes, "Once we push through the witness position, then the soul or witness itself dissolves and there is only the play of nondual awareness, awareness that does not look at objects but is completely one with all objects" (p. 47). Everything arises in this nondual awareness, and so it is a manifestation of the spirit.

Izutsu's Reconstruction of Eastern Philosophy

Toshihiko Izutsu, a Japanese scholar of Eastern philosophy, explored core features across diverse trends of Eastern thought such as Vedanta, Mahayana Buddhism, Taoism, I-Ching, and Sufism in his attempt to reconstruct Eastern philosophy as postmodernist thought. What he brought about is a view of perennial philosophy based on Eastern perspectives (Izutsu, 2008a,b; see Nakagawa, 2008, 2010). Izutsu (1984) found that Eastern perspectives are identical in describing reality in terms of multidimensionality: "Existence or Reality as 'experienced' on supra-sensible levels reveals itself as of a multistratified structure" (p. 479).

For example, in *Tao Te Ching*, Lao-tzŭ (2001, translated by Izutsu) suggests such dimensions as the Way or Non-Being (the Nameless), One, Being (Heaven and Earth), and the ten thousand things. *Tao Te Ching* symbolically draws out the evolution of the universe: "The Way begets one. One begets two. Two begets three. And three begets the ten thousand things" (p. 108). As Izutsu (1984) explains, "From the Way as the metaphysical Absolute . . . there emerges the One. The One is . . . the metaphysical Unity of all things. . . . From this Unity there emerges 'two,' that is, the cosmic duality of Heaven and Earth" (pp. 400–401). Heaven and Earth imply *yang* (the active force) and *yin* (the passive force). Then, interaction between these two forces gives rise to the third "vital force of harmony," and the combination of them yields the ten thousand things.

According to Izutsu, a multistratified structure generally involves three major levels from the surface level through intermediate realms to the metaphysical depths of reality. Distinctions among things on the surface reality are produced by the "semantic articulation" of the mind (Izutsu, 2008b, p. 124). For Lao-tzŭ (2001), "The Named is the mother of ten thousand things" (p. 28). The middle realm contains symbolic and archetypical images that emerge into myths, cosmologies, celestial figures, sacred words, and other symbolic forms. To denote this dimension, Izutsu favors the concept of *mundus imaginalis* (Corbin, 1995), or an imaginative world of symbolic images. The *mundus imaginalis* is revealed only through the supra-sensory perception of the soul. Then, even symbolic articulation dissolves away, and the deepest dimension of reality is disclosed, which Izutsu (2008b) referred to as "the zero point" of consciousness and Being (p. 147). Eastern ways of contemplation in general aim at realizing the zero point.

Furthermore, Izutsu (2008b) emphasizes that once one attains the zero point the person must return to the surface reality. The zero point is a turning point from seeking to returning in the whole process of contemplation. In the returning path, each finite existence comes to reveal "the Unarticulated" (p. 149). This is the true ultimate reality viewed from Eastern perspectives. Izutsu (1984) writes, "The only 'reality' (in the true sense of the term) is the Absolute revealing itself as it really is in the sensible forms which are nothing but the loci of its self-manifestation" (p. 480). In this regard, Eastern philosophy is an attempt to reconstruct the entire world fundamentally by deconstructing it to the zero point. In doing so, a boundless immensity is being embodied in each existence.

Five Dimensions of Reality

Eastern philosophy contributes to holistic education particularly by incorporating such ideas as the zero point and its manifestation into the surface reality. Introducing these ideas into the discussion of holistic education, I have developed the concept of *five dimensions of reality* as a worldview of holistic education (Nakagawa, 2000). The five dimensions of reality include:

Objective reality: the phenomenal world of separate things;

Social reality: the semantic articulation of the objective reality;

Cosmic reality: the interconnection in nature and the universe;

Infinite reality: the deepest dimension or the zero point;

Universal reality: the nondual wholeness of all dimensions.

Objective reality is the phenomenal world composed of separate things arising in our ordinary perception. Since we are identified with this reality, we tend to take it as the only reality that exists. With such conditioning, we not only perceive things as objective entities separate from us but also ourselves as separate egos. However, objective reality comes into being through the "semantic articulation" of the mind to differentiate an immediate experience of "what is" into separate things. In this sense, objective reality consists of meanings that are semantically articulated. This semantic foundation is called *social reality*, because the semantic articulation of meanings is generated and maintained through our communicative actions.

Eastern thinkers fully recognized the mind's function to create distinctions among things; however, they concluded that this function is the primary cause of our delusive perception and false attachment. For example, the central thinker of Mahayana Buddhism, Nāgārjuna (1995), refers to "mental fabrication" (*prapañca*). In the *Middle Stanzas*, he states, "Action and misery come from conceptual thought. This comes from mental fabrication" (p. 48). *The Awakening of Faith*, a treatise on Mahayana philosophy attributed to Aśvaghosha (1967), maintains that "the deluded mind" gives rise to the phenomenal distinctions of things: "Since all things are, without exception, developed from the mind and produced under the condition of deluded thoughts, all differentiations are no other than the differentiations of one's mind itself" (p. 48). In a similar way, Advaita Vedanta holds that "ignorance" (*avidyā*) produces phenomenal differences among things. Ignorance means "superimposition," a function of the mind that imposes partial qualities upon absolute reality.

Cosmic reality is an all-embracing dimension of nature and the universe in which everything is interconnected to everything else. Faced with today's ecological crisis, holistic education has strongly introduced this dimension into the framework of education. Cosmic reality is not only comprehended by conceptual knowledge of ecology but also by direct connection with nature and the universe through contemplative awareness. Stated differently, the cosmic reality is experienced by the soul that goes beyond the differentiations of the mind.

Even a cosmic reality turns into *infinite reality*, or the zero point of reality. This dimension has been diversely called *nirvana, sunyata* (emptiness), and *wu* (nothingness) in Buddhism, *turiya* (the fourth state of consciousness) and *nirguna Brahman* (formless absolute) in Vedanta, *tao* (the way) in Taoism, and *li* (principle) in Neo-Confucianism. These concepts are describing something infinite beyond qualifications. Following Smith (1976), this is the dimension of the "Infinite" or the spirit. The fullest awakening to the infinite reality is called *moksha* (liberation) in Hinduism, *bodhi* (awakening) in Buddhism, *satori* (enlightenment) in Japanese Zen, and *fana* in Sufism.

Advaita Vedanta regards the infinite reality as pure awareness. For example, the legendary sage, Ashtavakra, states that the nature of reality is "pure awareness" (Byrom, 1990). Shankara (1978), the greatest philosopher of Advaita, remarks, "The Atman is the witness, infinite consciousness, revealer of all things but distinct from all" (p. 69). Sri Ramana Maharshi (1985), a modern Indian sage, says:

> You are awareness. Awareness is another name for you. Since you are awareness there is no need to attain or cultivate it. All that you have to do is to give up being aware of other things, that is of the not-Self. If one gives up being aware of them then pure awareness alone remains, and that is the Self.
>
> *(pp. 11–12)*

Sri Nisargadatta Maharaj (1982) makes the same point: "Awareness is primordial; it is the original state, beginningless, endless, uncaused, unsupported, without parts, without change" (p. 29).

Ch'an Buddhism is a way of awakening to one's true nature on this level. For example, Huang Po (1958) calls it the "One Mind" (*h'sin*): "All the Buddhas and all sentient beings are nothing but the One Mind, beside which nothing exists. This Mind, which is without beginning, is unborn and indestructible" (p. 29). The One Mind is ever-present as the deepest ground of our being.

It is important to recognize that Eastern thought does not see the infinite reality as the final phase. As Izutsu made it clear, there is a turning point in contemplation from the end of seeking to the returning path, for the infinite reality is not seen as a transcendental realm distanced from the ordinary world. Here, we come to experience this world as something identical with the infinite reality. The whole world is fundamentally transformed in a way that the infinite manifests itself through the finite world. This transformed reality is called *universal reality*, where all dimensions are unified in a nondual manner. In this way, the twofold movement of seeking and returning marks a dynamic character in the Eastern way of contemplation to restore the nondual wholeness of multidimensional reality.

Shankara (1978) states, "This universe is an effect of Brahman. It can never be anything else but Brahman. Apart from Brahman, it does not exist" (p. 70). Brahman appearing in the universe is called *saguna Brahman*. S. Radhakrishnan (1994) explains this as follows:

> Supra-cosmic transcendence and cosmic universality are both real phases of the one Supreme. In the former aspect the Spirit is in no way dependent on the cosmic manifold; in the latter the Spirit functions as the principle of the cosmic manifold. The supra-cosmic silence and the cosmic integration are both real. The two, *nirguna* and *saguna Brahman*, Absolute and God, are not different.
>
> *(p. 64)*

Nāgārjuna (1995) identifies *nirvana* with *samsara* (cyclic existence): "There is not the slightest difference / Between nirvāna and cyclic existence" (p. 75). Likewise, Huxley (1968) writes, "For the fully enlightened, totally liberated person, *samsara* and *nirvana*, time and eternity, the phenomenal and the Real, are essentially one" (p. 342). Seng-Ts'an (1993), the third patriarch of Ch'an, claims in his *On Trust in the Mind*: "Being—this is nonbeing, nonbeing—this is being. Any view at variance with this must not be held!" (p. 152). Mahayana philosophy maintains that the formless emptiness (*sunyata*) is one with the forms of the world.

Mahayana Buddhism uses the concept of *tathatā* (suchness) to imply the universal reality. According to D. T. Suzuki (1996), "*Tathatā* is the viewing of things as they are: it is an affirmation through and through. I see a tree, and I state that it is a tree" (p. 263). Absolute affirmation of suchness arises in the realization of emptiness; that is, an ordinary being is opened up to boundless depths and turns out into a wondrous being that manifests the infinite as it is. Suzuki continues to say:

> If *śūnyatā* denies or rejects everything, *tathatā* accepts and upholds everything; the two concepts may be considered as opposing each other, but it is the Buddhist idea that they are not contradictory. . . . In truth, *tathatā* is *śūnyatā*, and *śūnyatā* is *tathatā*; things are *tathatā* because of their being *śūnyatā*.
>
> *(p. 264)*

The Flower Ornament Scripture, the principal sutra of the Hua-yen school in Mahayana Buddhism, also conveys the universal reality, using the concept of "interpenetration" as follows: "One world system enters all, / And all completely enter one; / Their substances and characteristics remain as before, no different: / Incomparable, immeasurable, they all pervade everywhere" (Cleary, 1993, p. 215). Since everything is fundamentally empty and transparent, everything mutually interpenetrates everything else. Hua-yen philosophy calls this the *dharmadhatu of shih-shih*, or the realm of unobstructed interpenetration of all things.

Furthermore, the universal reality is a place where all-embracing compassion (*karunā*) flows out from clear wisdom (*prajñā*) that penetrates into emptiness and interpenetration of reality. Centered in emptiness, the agent of action no longer exists, and the action becomes what Lao-tzŭ (2001) calls "non-action" (*wu-wei*): "If one pursues the Way, (knowledge) decreases day by day. Decreasing, and ever more decreasing, one finally reaches the state of non-action. Once one has reached the state of non-action, nothing is left undone" (p. 117). Similarly, Ramana Maharshi (1985) states:

> As the activities of the wise man exist only in the eyes of others and not in his own, although he may be accomplishing immense tasks, he really does nothing. . . . For he knows the truth that all activities take place in his mere presence and that he does nothing. Hence he will remain as the silent witness of all the activities taking place.
>
> *(p. 137)*

The selfless action is really a compassionate action, because a fundamental unity is realized without intervention of the personal ego.

At last, the Zen Master Dōgen (1995) provides us with an important formulation to think on holistic education:

> To study the buddha way is to study the self. To study the self is to forget the self. To forget the self is to be actualized by myriad things. When actualized by myriad things, your body and mind as well as the bodies and minds of others drop away. No trace of realization remains, and this no-trace continues endlessly.
>
> *(p. 70)*

In forgetting the self, the self becomes *selfless*, dissolving into the interpenetration of myriad things. The primary aim of this cultivation is to empty the self toward the infinite reality. Then, the *selfless self* emerges on the universal reality with "no trace of realization" (see Nakagawa, 2014).

Within a framework outlined above, a definition of holistic education would be given as an attempt to explore and realize multiple dimensions in our existence. Even if the last two dimensions of infinite and universal realities appear to have little to do with education, these ideas become essential, seen from Eastern perspectives. Therefore, holistic education must involve such concepts as *awakening* and *enlightenment*, following the suggestion of Robert Thurman (1998) who celebrates an "enlightenment-oriented education system" (p. 119) in his analysis of the work of the Buddha. Thurman writes, "Education is the major tool of truth-conquest. . . . It promotes enlightenment as the flowering of the individual's own awareness, sensibility, and powers, and thereby develops a strong society" (p. 126).

Admittedly, an idea such as "enlightenment-oriented education" looks too lofty to be applied to everyday practice of education; however, as Lex Hixon (1989) points out, "Enlightenment is not a magical transcendence of the human condition but the full flowering of humanity. . . . Some taste of this Enlightenment which consciously touches the Ultimate is possible for each of us" (p. xi). Education needs to be much more concerned with enlightenment as a latent potentiality within our nature.

The Way of Awareness

Eastern wisdom traditions developed numerous approaches to contemplation for realizing enlightenment. Holistic education has been a foremost endeavor to integrate contemplation into education, considering it to be a basic practice of education. The way of enhancing awareness has been one of the most simple and elementary practices from ancient times. According to Charles Tart (1994), "To oversimplify, I can summarize the essence of the higher spiritual paths simply by saying, Be openly aware of everything, all the time. As a result of this constant and deepening mindfulness, everything else will follow" (pp. 25–26). Awareness is to notice what is really taking place at every moment without interpretation or judgment of the mind.

The Buddha values awareness or mindfulness (*sati*) as an essential path of liberating us from *samsara* to attain *nirvana*. In the *Dhammapada*, the Buddha says, "The path to the Deathless is awareness; / Unawareness, the path of death" (Carter & Palihawadana, 2000, p. 6). In addition, describing the path of mindfulness in the *Satipatthana Sutta*, the Buddha states, "That is why we said that this path . . . is *the most wonderful path*, which helps beings realize purification, transcend grief and sorrow, destroy pain and anxiety, travel the right path, and realize nirvana" (Nhat Hanh, 1990, p. 23). In his last novel, *Island*, Huxley (1972) writes, "Everybody's job—enlightenment. Which means, here and now, the preliminary job of practising all the yogas of increased awareness" (p. 236). The practice of awareness is for him "the only genuine yoga, the only spiritual exercise worth practising" (p. 40). Thus, all of them suggest that what is important is to establish "awareness" as such (see Nakagawa, 2008, 2009).

The practice of enhancing awareness has twofold implications because awareness has an intermediate position between the body–mind and pure awareness. On the one hand, since our surface consciousness is, at most times, occupied by the body–mind process, awareness serves as a way of dis-identification with the body–mind by witnessing what is going on in the body–mind. This brings about various benefits and improvements in the body–mind conditions. Jiddu Krishnamurti (1954) comments on this:

> When you are passively aware, you will see that out of that passivity . . . the problem has quite a different significance; which means there is no longer identification with the problem and therefore there is no judgement and hence the problem begins to reveal its content. If you are able to do that constantly, continuously, then every problem can be solved fundamentally, not superficially.
>
> (pp. 96–97)

On the other hand, awareness reveals pure awareness as the supreme identity of our existence. The continual practice of awareness may lead to the point where the observing self dissolves itself into pure awareness, and everything emerges in nondual awareness. Wilber (1997) writes:

> When I rest in the pure and simple Witness, I will even begin to notice that the Witness itself is not a separate thing or entity, set apart from what it witnesses. All things arise within the Witness, so much so that the Witness itself disappears into all things.
>
> (p. 292)

Nisargadatta Maharaj (1982) describes the state of pure and nondual awareness as follows: "I saw that in the ocean of pure awareness, on the surface of the universal consciousness, the numberless waves of the phenomenal worlds arise and subside beginninglessly and endlessly. As consciousness, they are all me" (p. 30). Since awareness no longer identifies exclusively with anything, as Roger Walsh and Frances Vaughan (1980) explain, "the me/not me dichotomy is transcended and such persons experience themselves as being both nothing and everything. They are both pure awareness (no thing) and the entire universe (every thing)" (pp. 58–59).

Holistic education needs to provide an enlarged picture of the education of awareness from the elementary to the highest levels. It is important to remember that Huxley (1978) suggested such a vision when he wrote on the Alexander Technique, a re-education technique of the use of the body–mind. He combined this technique with the mystic's technique of increasing awareness to build "a totally new type of education."

> Be that as it may, the fact remains that Alexander's technique for the conscious mastery of the primary control is now available, and that it can be combined in the most fruitful way with the technique of the mystics for transcending personality through increasing awareness of ultimate

reality. It is now possible to conceive of a totally new type of education affecting the entire range of human activity, from physiological, through the intellectual, moral, and practical, to the spiritual—an education which, by teaching them the proper use of the self, would preserve children and adults from most of the diseases and evil habits that now afflict them; an education whose training in inhibition and conscious control would provide men and women with the psychophysical means for behaving rationally and morally; an education which in its upper reaches, would make possible the experience of ultimate reality.

(p. 152; this article originally appeared in
The Saturday Review of Literature, *Oct. 25, 1941)*

The somatic approach, such as the Alexander Technique, cultivates elementary awareness on the physical plane by paying attention to immediate experiences of the bodily movements and senses, and it becomes a basis for further development of awareness. Moreover, awareness gives insight and understanding into the nature of the mind. Then, enhancing awareness may culminate in an awakening to ultimate reality. Holistic education acknowledges that awareness is, indeed, extremely relevant to the multiple dimensions of our existence.

References

Aśvaghosha (1967). *The awakening of faith* (Y. Hakeda, Trans.). New York: Columbia University Press.

Byrom, T. (1990). *The heart of awareness: A translation of the* Ashtavakra Gita. Boston, MA: Shambhala.

Carter, J. R. & Palihawadana, M. (Trans.) (2000). *The Dhammapada*. Oxford: Oxford University Press.

Cleary, T. (Trans.). (1993). *The flower ornament scripture: A translation of the* Avatamsaka Sutra. Boston, MA: Shambhala.

Corbin, H. (1995). *Swedenborg and esoteric Islam* (L. Fox, Trans.). West Chester, PA: Swedenborg Foundation.

Dōgen. (1995). *Moon in a dewdrop: Writings of Zen Master Dōgen* (K. Tanahashi, Ed.). New York: North Point Press.

Hixon, L. (1989). *Coming home: The experience of enlightenment in sacred traditions.* Los Angeles, CA: Jeremy P. Tarcher.

Huang, P. (1958). *The Zen teachings of Huang Po* (J. Blofeld, Trans.). New York: Grove Press.

Huxley, A. (1968). *The perennial philosophy*. London: Chatto & Windus.

Huxley, A. (1972). *Island*. London: Chatto & Windus.

Huxley, A. (1975). *Adonis and the alphabet*. London: Chatto & Windus.

Huxley, A. (1978). End-gaining and means-whereby. In W. Barlow (Ed.), *More talk of Alexander* (pp. 149–153). London: Victor Gollancz.

Izutsu, T. (1984). *Sufism and Taoism: A comparative study of key philosophical concepts.* Berkeley, CA: University of California Press.

Izutsu, T. (2008a). *The structure of Oriental philosophy: Collected papers of the Eranos conference. Vol. I.* Tokyo: Keio University Press.

Izutsu, T. (2008b). *The structure of Oriental philosophy: Collected papers of the Eranos conference. Vol. II.* Tokyo: Keio University Press.

Krishnamurti, J. (1954). *The first and last freedom.* New York: Harper & Row.

Lao-tzŭ (2001). *Lao-tzŭ: The way and its virtue* (T. Izutsu, Trans.). Tokyo: Keio University Press.

Lemkow, A. F. (1990). *The wholeness principle: Dynamics of unity within science, religion & society.* Wheaton, IL: Theosophical Publishing House.

Maharaj, N. (1982). *I am that: Talks with Sri Nisargadatta Maharaj* (S. S. Dikshit, Ed.; M. Frydman, Trans.). Durham, NC: Acorn Press.

Maharshi, R. (1985). *Be as you are: The teachings of Sri Ramana Maharshi* (D. Godman, Ed.). London: Penguin Books.

Miller, J. P. (2007). *The holistic curriculum* (2nd edn). Toronto: University of Toronto Press.

Miller, R. (1991). Introduction. In R. Miller (Ed.), *New directions in education: Selections from* Holistic Education Review (pp. 1–3). Brandon, VT: Holistic Education Press.

Nāgārjuna (1995). *The fundamental wisdom of the middle way* (J. L. Garfield, Trans.). New York: Oxford University Press.

Nakagawa, Y. (2000). *Education for awakening: An Eastern approach to holistic education.* Brandon, VT: Foundation for Educational Renewal.

Nakagawa, Y. (2002). Aldous Huxley: A quest for the perennial education. In J. Miller & Y. Nakagawa (Eds), *Nurturing our wholeness: Perspectives on spirituality in education* (pp. 140–163). Brandon, VT: Foundation for Educational Renewal.

Nakagawa, Y. (2008). Eastern wisdom and holistic education: Multidimensional reality and the way of awareness. In C. Eppert & H. Wang (Eds), *Cross-cultural studies in curriculum: Eastern thought, educational insights* (pp. 227–245). New York: Lawrence Erlbaum.

Nakagawa, Y. (2009). Awareness and compassion for the education of enlightenment. In M. de Souza et al. (Eds), *International handbook of education for spirituality, care and wellbeing* (pp. 593–609). Dordrecht: Springer.

Nakagawa, Y. (2010). Oriental philosophy and interreligious education: Inspired by Toshihiko Izutsu's reconstruction of "Oriental philosophy." In K. Engebreston et al. (Eds), *International handbook of inter-religious education* (pp. 325–339). Dordrecht: Springer.

Nakagawa, Y. (2014). The Japanese way of spiritual cultivation. In J. Watson, M. de Souza, & A. Trousdale (Eds), *Global perspectives on spirituality and education* (pp. 181–191). New York: Routledge.

Nhat Hanh, T. (1990). *Transformation & healing: The sutra on the four establishments of mindfulness.* Berkeley, CA: Parallax Press.

Radhakrishnan, S. (Ed. and Trans.) (1994). *The principal Upaniṣads.* New Delhi, India: HarperCollins.

Seng-Ts'an (1993). On trust in the mind (B. Watson, Trans.). In S. Bercholz & S. C. Kohn (Eds), *Entering the stream: An introduction to the Buddha and his teachings* (pp. 147–152). Boston, MA: Shambhala.

Shankara (1978). *Shankara's crest-jewel of discrimination* (S. Prabhavananda & C. Isherwood, Trans., 3rd edn). Hollywood, CA: Vedanta Press.

Smith, H. (1976). *Forgotten truth: The primordial tradition.* New York: Harper & Row.

Suzuki, D. T. (1996). *Zen Buddhism: Selected writings of D. T. Suzuki* (W. Barrett, Ed.). New York: Doubleday.

Tart, C. T. (1994). *Living the mindful life: A handbook for living in the present moment.* Boston, MA: Shambhala.

Thurman, R. (1998). *The inner revolution: Life, liberty, and the pursuit of real happiness.* New York: Riverhead Books.

Walsh, R. N. & Vaughan, F. (1980). What is a person? In R. N. Walsh & F. Vaughan (Eds), *Beyond ego: Transpersonal dimensions in psychology* (pp. 53–62). Los Angeles, CA: J. P. Tarcher.

Wilber, K. (1997). *The eye of spirit: An integral vision for a world gone slightly mad.* Boston, MA: Shambhala.

6

CARE OF THE SOUL IN EDUCATION

Thomas Moore

Over the years I have read and re-read a passage from Euripides's tragic play Hippolytos, about a young man who spurns the sensuous goddess Aphrodite and honors only the virginal Artemis. In punishment, Aphrodite causes his stepmother Phaedra to fall in love with him, and she becomes distressed to the point of lunacy. Seeing the frenzy she's in, her nurse asks the all-important question: Which god or goddess has she offended. Is it Pan's madness or Hekate's fury?

When things go awry the first question we can ask, with the Greek polytheistic imagination in mind, is which god are we neglecting? Years ago, I invited my class in mythology to sweep the college campus and decide which god was dominant, another way to pursue the same question. They reported back that Saturn ruled the campus with his love of hierarchies, authority, exclusive masculinity, order, testing, and tendency toward depression. I ask that question now about the state of education in the twenty-first century. Who have we neglected?

The answer is: nothing less than all the other gods with their rich, contributing spirits—Aphrodite's beauty and sensuality, Artemis's pristine naturalness, Hermes with his sense of fun and love of metaphor, Pan's love of play, and Zeus's strong spirit of family and community. One interesting way to imagine holistic education is to picture it mythologically, rooted in all the gods, not just one.

The dominance of one archetypal spirit, known in the Middle Ages as *monarchia*, is my definition of neurosis. Clearly, our way of education is highly neurotic and in need of a therapeutic intervention. If the *monarchia* of Saturn is the diagnosis, then we need a holism of the psyche in our educational methods and attitudes, a deepening that involves care of the educator's, the student's, and the system's soul.

Paideia

I first came across the idea of education as care of the soul in Werner Jaeger's richly nuanced, three-volume work, *Paideia*. There, he uses the phrase "care of the soul" many times. A person educates the soul "by reaching harmony with the nature of the universe, . . . through complete mastery over himself in accordance with the law he finds by searching his own soul." The goal is *arete*, excellence, which includes "courage, prudence, justice, piety—excellences of the soul just as health, strength and beauty are excellences of the body" (Jaeger, 1943, p. 44).

To live in harmony with the nature of the universe is a worthy goal of education even today. To live in harmony with your own nature is also part of the picture. It doesn't take much imagination to see how this goal could include science, philosophy, athletics, spirituality, and aesthetics. In each sphere, our objective is to be in tune with the world and with our deepest nature.

A holistic approach to science, for example, would not just offer information about the physical world, but also explore the spiritual powers of nature, such as the impact of a mountain climb on a person's sense of self and world, and on ethics. A school's scientific nature walk could include a pause to make sketches or paint watercolors, as a way of deepening and enriching a student's connection with the natural world. This approach would be holistic in so far as it aims at a complete experience of a lake or animals. The holism is about being as complete a person as possible in each learning experience.

Similarly, the study of psychology and philosophy, which can be done at any age, is not holistic and is seriously incomplete when it doesn't relate to our personal and social quest for peace of mind and good relationships. A statement from the ancient Greek philosopher Epicurus applies here: "Medicine is useless if it doesn't get rid of diseases of the body, and philosophy is useless if it doesn't get rid of diseases of the soul." We all need a deep appreciation for the ways of the psyche and how to deal with past traumas and difficult parents and abusive adults. We need ideas about being married and raising children; otherwise we do these things unconsciously and therefore badly. We all need a deep appreciation for reflection on the meaning of life in all its particulars so that we have a personal philosophy of life to live by.

This approach is not personalizing everything that is taught, but it does shine its light on everyday life. For example, many readers who have noticed my use of mythology as a means of taking many issues deeper tell me that the little mythology they learned in school had no relevance to their lives. But now they see how that subject could have helped them deal with many significant turning points in their lives. We could say the same about every subject. It isn't that the subject matter is not relevant to the student, it's that the teaching fails to connect the material of study with the people studying it.

Intimate Learning

The dictionary definition of "holistic" may help us go deeper into its relevance to education: "characterized by comprehension of the parts of something as intimately interconnected and explicable only by reference to the whole."

I want to focus on the phrase "intimately interconnected." The Greeks might use the word "eros" for this intimacy and connectedness. For them, gravity would be an example of eros in nature, as would the tendency of the planets to remain in their orbits. Therefore, I consider holistic education as necessarily erotic in this broad Greek sense of the word. It is intimate and connected.

I would like to use the word "erotic" instead of "holistic," but today it is impossible to avoid the strong connotation of sexuality. So, let's just say that in holistic education the various items studied are intimately connected to each other, and they are intimately connected to the one teaching and the one learning.

You can imagine that if someone wanted to learn about running a business, a good intimate way of learning would be to start a business, or at least apprentice to one and get "first-hand" knowledge. But learning intimacy doesn't have to be experiential. When I wanted to learn C. G. Jung's psychology, I read the eighteen volumes of his collected works three times. Now I keep those volumes right over my shoulder, next to my desk, as I write my books. That's a different sign of intimacy. When I go to Jung societies to speak and give workshops, even though I am not an official Jungian analyst, I feel intimately at home, and I'm received that way because of my knowledge and experience. Do you see how intimacy is a way of sustaining the learning process?

Much of modern education is at a distance. It is like learning about the people next door, instead of becoming friends with them. We sit in classrooms far from any action or materials or events that we are trying to learn about. We quantify all kinds of information that could be far more deeply studied if we were less abstract. We do all this because we are anxious about being correct. We don't want to make a mistake or trust our intuitions or make sensual observations.

Walt Whitman's celebrated poem "When I Heard the Learn'd Astronomer" may be too simple and romantic, but it makes a good point:

When I heard the learn'd astronomer,
When the proofs, the figures, were ranged in columns before me,
When I was shown the charts and diagrams, to add, divide, and measure them,
When I sitting heard the astronomer where he lectured with much applause in the lecture-room,
How soon unaccountable I became tired and sick,
Till rising and gliding out I wander'd off by myself,
In the mystical moist night-air, and from time to time,
Look'd up in perfect silence at the stars.

The Modern Distaste for Mysticism and Emotion

Our educational approach could indeed gain from a more mystical and moist quality. The problem is the anxiety-based emotion we bring to teaching and learning. We try too hard not to make a mistake, and in so doing we learn less than half of what is available. There is no reason why we could not blend the mystical, the emotionally moist, and the numerical into one impressive method.

It isn't just avoiding mistakes. We are a fact-oriented culture. We distrust anything else as fuzzy, sensational and unreliable. But people do pick up wisdom and knowledge from experience and reflection. Some are especially gifted in this way, and so we study novelists and philosophers who never use empirical methods. Often, it is more valuable to have a good insight than a load of facts.

Another mistake often made, in a similar vein, is to assume that new is good and old is bad. Many books have a clear bias against the past, thinking that we are always getting better and knowing more. But ancient texts and works of art are often exquisitely presented and insightful. You may have to allow for some lack of information that was discovered later, but still you can find insights that maybe were accessible only in that cultural situation.

Personally, I study the ancient Greek tragedians and philosophers because of their profundity and the European Renaissance magicians for their insights into power. Neither had the scientific and technological advantages we have, but neither were they blocked from exploring important issues that may be difficult for us to appreciate.

Education Takes Place Anywhere and Anytime

Another aspect of holism in education is using your entire environment and all your time as resources for learning. When I give workshops, I always ask the participants to think of the course as in process everywhere they go and at all times. The whole of life is a classroom. Therefore, for the younger person, his or her family is an important factor, offering support, information, guidance, creating a learning environment, and even offering some training. When I was a child, my father taught me how to use tools, the basic laws of physics, how to play sports, and how to show people respect. These lessons were easily as important as anything I learned in school.

Therefore, holism can refer to the entire environment of learning, not limiting it to school or to certain times. Our task as educators is to show a person how to learn, not just to offer information and training. A person leaving school after being with a holistic educator should be motivated and equipped to initiate learning on her own throughout her life. The full embrace of life is another significant aspect to the concept of holism.

Let me stop here to point out how these various descriptions of holism in learning stem from a sense of soul. Soul is that element in us that is our mysterious depth and makes us an individual while feeling connected to others and to the human community. It values the arts for the depth and layered presentation of experience they offer. Soul also overlaps powerfully with the spirit, which is our reach beyond ourselves, our appreciation for the sublime and the ineffable. In short, soul is our depth, connection, and reach.

Care of the soul entails attention to its needs of the natural world, the arts, home, friendship, intimacy, deep ethics, and work that contributes to our destiny and to the human community. From the soul viewpoint, a career is not so much about a job as about a life work that offers meaning. A soul-oriented education aims at making you a person of character, love, connection, and the creativity that comes from being a true individual.

We often ignore the soul, to our detriment, because its concerns and milieu are so much part of everyday life: home, family, work, local community, images, reflection and conversation, poetics, and the arts. In some ways it is the opposite of the focus in modern life, where we love facts, solutions to problems, technologies, and quantifications. The soul's tools are soft and subtle: intimate reflection and sharing, symbolic activities, poetics, and play.

When Soul is not Included in Learning

Neglect of soul leads to weak families, a desperate search for meaning, the feeling of being lost, not knowing your purpose or calling, the sense of not being at home, and being at the mercy of powerful emotions connected to the past or swirling autonomously in the present. As I wrote twenty-five years ago at the beginning of *Care of the Soul*, "The great malady of the twentieth century, implicated in all of our troubles and affecting us individually and socially, is 'loss of soul.'"

It may seem that formal psychotherapy is the main solution to soul loss, but as both an educator and a therapist I learned that, more than anything, bad ideas and faulty thinking prevent us from living more soulful lives. I am certain that holistic education, as I am presenting it here, could bring soul back into the life of individuals and culture, solving most of our problems and allowing us to live more just, free, and creative lives.

Remember that the Greeks sought *arete* in education: courage, prudence, justice, and piety—in general, excellence. Imagine if this *arete* were the main goal of education. Standardized tests would be inappropriate. Quantifying experience and focusing mainly on math and science, technology, and job skills would fall far short as worthy goals. Penalties and punishments would be absurd.

Another way to develop a focused and practical holistic education as care of the soul is to list several qualities associated with soul and consider their role in education. Let me offer ten examples of these basic elements:

1. *Home and Family*: The base of the soul's life. Qualities of home and family can be part of all learning—the setting and means of relating.
2. *Friendship*: Historically the basic way to relate with soul. The spirit of friendship could be in all contacts between teachers and learners.
3. *Poetics and Metaphor*: Go deeper into facts by perceiving the layers of meaning through an appreciation of narrative, poetics, and metaphor.
4. *Dream*: Dreams reveal the deep stories lived now at the level of soul. Regular, simple dream telling and discussing would deepen any form of education.
5. *Spirituality*: Every aspect of education has a spiritual dimension and relates to (holism) infinite mystery, the sublime, strong values, and an expansive sense of community.

6. *Nature*: In the ancient teaching of *anima mundi* (soul of the world) the natural world is alive with presence and metaphorical meaning. Experiences in nature are indispensable in a soul-oriented, holistic education.

7. *Art*: Both an appreciation of all arts as sources of meaning and fulfillment, as well as creative experiences in painting, music, building, dancing, photography, and all the arts make for an educated and sophisticated person.

8. *Service*: Essential to the soulful life is service to humanity—both local and in an increasingly larger sense. You learn some things only through the experience of service.

9. *Life Work*: Soul offers a strong individual identity that is not superficial but rises from deep currents and inspirations. A soul-based education is interested in a job as an element in the larger quest for a meaningful and contributing life work.

10. *Learning for Learning's Sake*: Holistic education is lifelong and may change in style over the course of a life. It reaches maturity when the person loves learning for its own sake.

The Teacher's Soul

For holistic education to work, the teacher has to be whole, not broken—at least not to the extent that his or her neurosis will negatively affect the learning experience. We are all neurotic to a degree, and we can't expect perfection. But we have to have dealt with basic personal issues that can interfere with good teaching. Of course, this is true for all kinds of teaching, but it applies especially to holistic learning that relies so heavily on the vision and character of the teacher.

The psychology of teaching is a vast topic, so let's look at some basics. Perhaps the most important issue in teaching is working out sado-masochistic tendencies in both teacher and learner. Sado-masochism is the display of power in every human relationship. The Sade side, from the Marquis de Sade, known for the extreme examples of domination in his fiction, includes strong influence over what one learns, the implied values, the strong impact of the teacher's point of view, and the dynamics in the teacher–student relationship.

Here is what I wrote about education in my book *Dark Eros*, published twenty-seven years ago:

> The presiders are 'principals' and 'masters.' One goes through many years of grades. . . . Educators pass children and fail them. We subject them to examinations. We take them away from the family and keep them against their wills. Education has a long tradition of physical and sexual abuse. Beating, incarceration after school hours, painful repetitious writing, threats of all kinds, ridicule in front of a class, ignorance paraded in public, strict curbs on walking, talking, eating, loving, thinking, imagining, daydreaming, and going to the bathroom—education teems with Sadeian methods.
>
> *(Moore, 1994, 174–175)*

Holistic educators are not immune to these sado-masochistic situations. It is archetypal, deeply buried in the process of teaching/learning itself. Medicine has a similar tendency toward inflicting fear and pain and ghoulish manipulations of the body. These may contribute to our health and are necessary. But their basic presence can lead to unnecessary exaggeration. The doctor can become Frankensteinian, and the educator can easily become an abuser.

A teacher has to deal with this inherent tendency to dominate the student, no matter how subtle that domination may be. One way is to help the student teach himself, become an independent learner and go off in his own directions. Then the teacher and student remain whole in themselves, not split into a single pattern of dominator–subject. A certain degree of strength and influence on the part of the teacher is necessary, but there is a line that should not be crossed, where the student loses his power and can no longer be an independent and free learner.

Thomas Moore

Splitting the Teacher–Student Pattern

The Swiss psychoanalyst Adolph Guggenbühl-Craig discusses this kind of split in medicine:

> The psychic process is blocked. A patient may no longer be concerned with his own cure. The doctor, the nurses, the hospital will heal him. The patient no longer has any responsibility. . . . There are no signs in patients of a will to health or what we might term a conscience of health. They are like school children who believe that only the teacher need be active in the process of learning.
>
> *(Guggenbühl-Craig, 1971)*

The situation is similar in education. We split the archetype of teaching/learning into two people. Then the student is passive, has no "conscience of learning." He leaves the responsibility of learning to the school and the teachers and is thus cut off from his own need to learn and his own tools for learning. But the split is not just the student's fault. Schools are set up to indulge in the split and teachers enforce it. Holism here means healing this split.

Here are a few more ways to avoid or heal the split:

1. Know that education has aggression and vulnerability built into it.
2. Promote and support any effort of students to learn on their own.
3. Be willing to disclose that you, the teacher, don't know everything.
4. Share power.
5. Plan lifelong learning.

The Teacher as Doctor of the Soul

Those many years ago, when I was so influenced by Jaeger's book *Paideia*, I found myself charmed by Plato's vision of a culture dedicated to the soul. In a footnote, Jaeger says plainly, speaking of Plato's teacher and the sage of his dialogues, "The purpose of all Socrates's educational activity can be described as 'caring for the soul'" (Jaeger, 1944, p. 304) In Plato's *Protagoras*, he speaks of knowledge as food for the soul and warns of those who go around selling their knowledge as often being unaware of the dangers of their wares for the souls of their students. They need to be "doctors of the soul," as well (*Protagoras*, 313d).

My final word on holism in education, therefore, is to suggest that educators might consider their deep work as taking care of the health of their students' souls, even as they focus on learning and knowledge. This Platonic or soul-based learning has roots in both the student's very being and in the culture. Certainly, one of the goals in education is to improve the character of the culture at large by creating deeply educated persons.

Don't confuse care of the soul with counseling or therapy in a formal sense. I am not suggesting that teachers be psychologists. However, they could understand, as Plato said so plainly, that if you are not concerned for your students' souls, you can easily do them harm. More than that, you need to know what it takes to heal a wounded soul, because most, if not all, of your students come to you with such wounds. You come to them with your own wounds. Holistic education does not merely dispense knowledge; it does so in a way that both the teacher and the student's souls are engaged and benefit.

References

Guggenbühl-Craig, A. (1971). *Power in the helping professions*. Dallas, TX: Spring.

Jaeger, W. (1943, 1944). *Paideia: The ideals of Greek culture: II. In search of the divine centre (Volume 2). III. The Ideals of Greek Culture (Volume 3)* New York: Oxford University Press.

Moore, T. (1994). *Dark eros: The imagination of sadism*. Woodstock, CT: Spring.

PART II

Teaching–Learning–Curriculum

Introduction

Marni J. Binder

In this section, the authors explain how holism informs and shapes curriculum and pedagogy. Each clearly demonstrates how holistic education is enacted in the classroom in relation to children, educators and teacher education students. The chapters offer a broad range of topics including whole child development, spirituality, core reflection, self-pedagogy, teacher education, contemplative education, holistic assessment, integrated curriculum and Indigenous education. Each of these is an important element of holistic education and represents areas where continued reflection and discourse can be fruitful for both practitioners and researchers.

Tony Eaude, in the UK, begins his chapter with a discussion on the child's spiritual, moral, social, and cultural development. He presents a number of current factors that affect the inner life of children: poverty, geographical mobility, and the omnipresent use of technology in our lives. Eaude reminds us of the need for holistic education and challenges us to continually ask: What is education for? Teachers need to develop a "relationship of mutual trust and respect" with children. Eudaimonia, "the well-doing and well-being" that allows children to thrive throughout their lives, should be nurtured in the classroom. Eaude presents many issues affecting education globally and describes what it means for children and educators to truly belong and learn to connect with others.

Integrating the holistic, creative and spiritual lives of young children, Jane Bone offers experiential examples of preschool pedagogy that nurture a child's spirit:

> A feature of early childhood education in Australia and Aoteaora New Zealand is the emphasis on holistic well-being as a key learning outcome. The vision for Te Whāriki, the curriculum for New Zealand, is that children will be "healthy in mind, body and spirit" (Ministry of Education, 2017).

Bone weaves a tapestry from various practices that pull together the threads of diverse instructional models. She provides examples of children's experiences with yoga and movement. Her description of children's experiences of "becoming animal" and her instruction on teaching yoga poses contribute to the applicability and relevance of her work to the classroom. Walking in nature as a mindfulness practice, the importance of aesthetics and art are explained as well as the influence of

Reggio Emelia's educational philosophy. Bone poignantly describes the work of Montessori, who "proposed the child as a spiritual embryo" and claimed that a calm and peaceful "environment soothed the soul of the child".

Imagine a world that embodies a sharing, caring, inclusive, interconnectedness with all living beings. Edward Brantmeier asks us to envision such an ideal world. Or is it so ideal? Brantmeier presents three "fellow travelers—holistic education, sustainability education, and peace education" as he takes the reader on a curricular journey that illustrates what a peaceful, holistic, sustainable world would look like in teaching and learning. These travelers can journey separately, as well as with each other. Brantmeier shares his "educational theory and practice in critical peace education for sustainability" and emphasizes the importance of critical pedagogy as a valuable framework. There are practical examples from teacher education and educational leadership preparation. Moving from the micro to the macro, he demonstrates how inner transformation can enact change through professional and societal connections.

Fred Korthagen's and Ellen Nuijten's chapter introduces their work on "core reflection", an approach which has been applied in both elementary and higher education. Drawing on positive psychology, this deep learning and coaching approach has provided student teachers and teachers, opportunities for profound shifts in personal growth. Positive insights in turn inspire positive change in the classroom. Focusing on core qualities such as courage, flexibility, and creativity, and "attention to inner obstacles" develop what they describe as "mindfulness-in-action". Through presence and a reflective process that encourages the teacher to remain in the moment, the complex layers of teaching and learning can be considered. Examples of coaching sessions show this change process through the "onion model". Korthagen and Nuijten connect theory to practice in ways that promote important change in teacher development, and, consequently, education in schools.

William Greene and Younghee Kim develop their work which builds upon Korthagen's "core reflection model." They expand on their ideas about self-development as pedagogy in teacher preparation programs. They acknowledge the vulnerabilities young adults may face when first entering into these programs, the repression of the imagination and the complex nature of education in the United States. Greene introduces us to "va", which is defined as "an energy of life drawn from Pacific cultures". Va is the breath, the life force and the primal energy that moves through this chapter. Kim shares reflection notes, and practical examples of rituals as she teaches her students. Soulful transformations occur from creative activities and being in nature. For Greene and Kim, it is "embodied" and "emergent wholeness" that instructors must explore *from within* so that they can be present, relational, and transformative with their students.

Heesoon Bai, Avraham Cohen, Patricia Morgan, and Charles Scott offer a collaborative chapter that illuminates the imperative of healing as an aim in education. The authors discuss the "absence of holism" in our lives and that through contemplative inquiry, healing can take place. Explored are many ways in which the disconnect from self, others, the planet, and the universe create trauma. It is from this disconnect that brain functions which privilege rational and analytical thinking are affirmed while holistic, or embodied learning remains optional. Offered are examples on how to "heal the wounds" from this disconnect. Shifting to healing solutions, such as engaging in the arts and contemplation, can place the educative process back in the hands of the educator. Intricate concepts and ideas are evoked to remind us about what is "blocking our ability to live holistically".

Susan Drake and Joanne Reid discuss the theory and practice of an integrated curriculum. They outline the varying degrees of integration currently conceptualized in education from a Canadian perspective. Drake and Reid argue for a curriculum "that addresses the whole child – the head (Know), hands (Do), and heart (Be)." A transdisciplinary model, supported by examples of practice for implementation, is presented. They also critically examine the challenges and opportunities for success. Drake and Reid make an important connection to The Truth and Reconciliation recommendations which calls for a curriculum revision that "include[s] respectful and accurate representations of Indigenous people and the history of assimilative government policies and laws targeted at Indigenous communities" in the province of Ontario's curriculum.

Readers are reminded of their own experiences in school as Julian Stern explores a topic not often critically explored in the holistic education literature—assessment. Stern maintains that the authenticity of assessment has been "corrupted" in education. He proposes holistic assessment through a dialogic approach and places this approach within mainstream education. The reader is invited to continually question "what are schools for?" Stern describes different types of assessments currently used in the UK. One would assume that these practices are echoed elsewhere in the Western world. While it is clear that assessment should not be removed from the system, Stern presents tangible examples of how it can be implemented from a holistic perspective, thereby interrupting the standardization of curriculum practice. Drawing on Martin Buber's idea of "genuine dialogue", Stern advocates for a dialogic where wholeness in the assessment experience is caring, relational, and engages the student and teacher in "curiosity".

This section closes with Gregory Cajete's explanation of Indigenous education and the power of art and vision. Cajete evokes ancient wisdom as it is experienced through art as ritual and art as ceremony. He positions an educational worldview which is not yet adequately evidenced in Western educational contexts. He has the reader "follow the tracks of the visionary/artist of Indigenous America". The power of dreams, visions, and art as alchemy are explained within a Tribal context. Poignant is his critical analysis of what he calls "cultural schizophrenia" which is now occurring with Indigenous youth. Cajete writes of the critical necessity for education to "reconnect American Indian youth with their dreaming creative selves".

In these chapters are pedagogical and curriculum practices of experienced educators who have advocated for holism in classroom teaching and learning. The authors are invitational, inspiring, practical and soulful in their efforts to engage the reader. We are reminded throughout many of these chapters how much Indigenous wisdom rings true with whole child education. Brantmeier's reflection resonates as he articulates a primary question: "how do we envision and live in a diverse world—as one?"

7

ADDRESSING THE NEEDS OF THE WHOLE CHILD

Implications for Young Children and Adults Who Care for Them

Tony Eaude

This chapter explores the needs of the "whole child" and how adults should address these, in a world characterized by diversity, fragmentation, and uncertainty and by constant change, the nature of which is hard to predict. The focus is on young children, up to the age of about 11 years old, though these vary to some extent within this age group, and on the whole range of their needs, not just those related to formal schooling. Much of my experience is in an English context, but the implications are similar in other industrialized countries with comparable challenges. While my background is as a teacher in primary schools, known in other systems as elementary schools, many of the implications apply to parents/carers and other adults.

The next section provides a definition of holistic education. This is followed by a consideration of the current social, cultural, and educational context and some challenges for holistic education which this presents. Different aspects of young children's development and needs are then discussed, recognizing that these are interlinked and must be treated as such in practice. The penultimate section considers the implications for adults with a role, formal or otherwise, in nurturing and educating young children. The conclusion summarizes the key points of the argument.

Holistic Education

Philosophically, the concept of holism presents a difficulty. Holism implies that a whole organism or system is seen as more than the sum of the component elements or parts. However, it is hard to describe an organism or system other than by considering its parts separately. I address this by discussing various aspects of children's development, in the section after next, bearing in mind the importance of not seeing these in isolation, and encouraging readers to do so. In doing so, some apparently conflicting needs, such as those for care and challenge, pace and space, and structure and freedom, may in practice become less problematic than they might appear.

While many definitions of holistic education highlight particular values, beliefs, and practices, I adopt a simpler definition that holistic education addresses every aspect of individual growth and development, recognizing that this must be understood and nurtured in relation to other people, societies and cultures, and the world around. As a result, holistic education involves far more than formal schooling and must be responsive to individual need and cultural norms.

Challenges in the Current Context

Young children grow up in a time of rapid social and cultural change, presenting different challenges from those of, say, thirty or forty years ago. As a result, there is a danger that they will be brought up, and educated in the more formal sense, for a world that no longer exists, rather than being able to cope confidently and thoughtfully with the challenges they face now and will face in the future. Some commonalities apply to all children, though the culture and contexts in which children live, and, therefore, their needs and adult expectations, may vary. Hence, creating an environment that is inclusive of all children is essential, but harder than it might seem.

Eaude (2016, p. 45) summarizes key aspects of recent social and cultural change in most industrialized societies, drawing on the Cambridge Primary Review (Alexander, 2010, especially pp. 53–55). Among these are:

- changing patterns in the immediate and extended family and communities;
- a higher level of disposable income and possessions for most but not all;
- a much improved level of physical health, though greater concern about mental health; and
- a rapid extension of the types, and availability, of technology.

The next four paragraphs highlight some implications, discussed more fully in Eaude (2016, pp. 44–52).

As a result of increased levels of family breakdown and greater geographical mobility, many children grow up in families and communities that provide less security and support. For instance, many of the structures and groups, such as extended families and faith communities, which provided support outside the immediate family are less available than previously. Many children have to live with difficult issues in their families and communities such as domestic violence, substance abuse, and crime and may have to shoulder responsibilities as carers from a young age, with relatively little support.

Despite recent concerns about obesity, often associated with a sedentary lifestyle and poor diet, most children are physically healthier, though this varies according to children's background and individual circumstances. However, there are increasing worries about children's unhappiness and mental health (Palmer, 2006; Unicef, 2007), not only in adolescence when symptoms may make a medical diagnosis appropriate, but in younger children; although, as Unicef (2013) indicates, there is a shortage of comparative data for young children.

Children have access to a wide range of technology and spend significant amounts of time playing computer games and involved with the internet and social media, especially as they approach adolescence. While technology may bring significant benefits, for instance in understanding other cultures, children have come to expect immediate responses and might be uncritical of what they see and hear without explicit guidance. Moreover, the media and advertising exert strong pressure with powerful messages about success, happiness and identity—and how these are achieved. As a result, children are encouraged to see themselves as consumers and have a tendency towards individualism and narcissism. Combined with the tendency of adults to see children as vulnerable and to overprotect them, many children find disappointment and difficulties overwhelming and become brittle rather than resilient (see Ecclestone and Hayes, 2009).

Primary schools increasingly offer a narrow curriculum, focused on discrete, decontextualized skills in literacy and numeracy, the aspects of English and mathematics which can be tested relatively easily. This reflects a strong, explicit emphasis in policy terms on cognitive development, attainment, and performativity (see Ball, 2003), although there is some recognition of the importance of social and emotional development. Despite the rhetoric which might suggest otherwise, little importance seems to be ascribed in practice by policy makers or inspection reports to what in England is called spiritual, moral, social, and cultural (SMSC) development, discussed in the next section. Such a view reflects an obsession with pace and what can be measured, whereas much of what is most important in life must be experienced slowly and cannot be measured meaningfully. Moreover, children's lives have become increasingly "scholarised" (see Mayall, 2010, pp. 61–62) with more demands on children, especially those in aspiring families, and fewer informal opportunities for play and being on their own, or with friends.

Schools, and society more generally, tend to place intense pressure on children, from a young age, to succeed, especially in terms of academic attainment. This is based on an individualized and competitive approach, which values other types of achievement less and so excludes some children, especially those from disadvantaged backgrounds or with aptitudes other than academic ones. A view of identity based on looks and possessions and a tendency to overprotect children encourage an emphasis on oneself and a lack of resilience. Many of the challenges and much of the stress that children face result from socio-economic deprivation, mostly obviously poverty, and those factors highlighted above. This is especially hard for those children for whom the possessions deemed to provide identity are not available. However, the pressure on children to be consumers and to succeed academically affects other, more affluent, children in different, but still challenging, ways. Holistic education should help counter many of these pressures and develop children's sense of agency and the qualities to enable them to thrive in a world of change.

Holistic Education: Nurturing the Parts While not Losing Sight of the Whole

This section considers different aspects of the whole child, remembering that holism implies that these are interconnected. One example is health, which is often considered largely in terms of physical health, or the avoidance of disease, resulting in concentration on aspects such as diet and cleanliness. However, as indicated, there are increasing worries about young children's unhappiness and mental health as a result of too much stress and lack of physical activity. Yet, increasingly, it is recognized that physical activity and exercise helps to improve both mental and physical health.

A second example relates to well-being and how this is achieved. With young children, the aim of education is often thought of in terms of just wanting children to be happy, with Noddings (2003) arguing that children's happiness should be one main aim of education. There is little doubt that children learn better when they are happy, though such happiness often results from relationships of trust and care and challenges overcome. However, children from a young age are increasingly encouraged, especially through the media and advertising, to believe that happiness is achieved largely through possessions and with little effort. Eaude (2016, p. 36) suggests that an emphasis on happiness is dangerous and that the idea of *eudaimonia*, as used in Ancient Greece, is a more appropriate goal. This entails well-doing and well-being, living flourishingly over time, a sustained, rather than an episodic, state, as opposed to being based on short-term pleasure, with happiness often a by-product rather than an explicit aim. Holistic education involves helping children to flourish over time, rather than simply seeking enjoyment through instant gratification.

Different aspects of the whole child's development can be characterized in various ways. However, I break this down into eight categories, remembering that such distinctions should be treated with caution and be seen as interlinked and overlapping, rather than treated as separate: spiritual, moral, cultural, mental, physical, social, emotional, and aesthetic.

The first five reflect the language used in the 1988 Education Reform Act (HMSO, 1988), in England, which amended the wording of the 1944 Education Act that "it shall be the duty of the local education authority for every area, so far as their powers extend, to contribute towards the spiritual, moral, mental and physical development of the community" (HMSO, 1944). Social and

Table 7.1 Questions associated with different aspects of spiritual, moral, social, and cultural development

Spiritual	Moral
Who am I? Where do I fit in? Why am I here?	How should I act?
	What sort of person do I want to become?
Social	Cultural
How should I interact with other people?	Where do I belong? What is my identity?

cultural were added to the 1988 revision, with mental and physical omitted, to complete the current combination of SMSC development. Neither emotional nor aesthetic development is mentioned explicitly, in legislation, but these are closely associated.

While there is not space to do full justice to these ideas, RSA (2014) provides a useful summary of what SMSC involves. In Eaude (2008, p. 56), I suggested that SMSC development involves exploring profound questions as outlined in Table 7.1.

Spiritual is not the same as religious development, recognising McLaughlin's distinction (as cited in Best, 2014, p. 12) between spirituality that is "tethered" or "untethered" to organized religion. In Eaude (2008), I presented spiritual development as involving the search for answers in relation to questions of meaning, identity, and purpose, including those which may be painful and hard to answer, and that such a search is universal, but can be explored within a religious or a non-religious framework. Hyde (2008) and other writers on children's spirituality, such as Hay with Nye (1998) and Hull (1998), emphasize relationships and connectedness with other people and the world around.

In Eaude (2016), I suggested that moral education should be seen in two interlinked ways—specifically in terms of explicitly moral decisions and more generally considering the ethical implications of one's actions and interactions throughout life. I argued, especially with young children, for an approach based on virtue ethics, emphasising qualities associated with character, such as empathy and thoughtfulness, and the importance of children belonging and being part of interdependent communities, rather than just individual will and effort.

Social is closely associated with emotional development, so that children learn to respond to emotions of different types and to interact with other people appropriately. For young children, this is often hard, given that neuroeducational research (see Eaude, 2016, pp. 75–79) indicates that emotion and cognition are closely linked and that the ability to self-regulate—executive function—is not well developed in very young children and reduced when people experience anxiety and stress.

Cultural development is associated with questions of belonging and identity and of extending children's horizons. The latter may be helped by their engaging with activities such as drama and the arts, but cultural development also involves children recognizing how they, and other people, are influenced by culture and background and being open to those of different cultures.

This emphasis on SMSC and associated areas does not overlook the importance of cognitive development, and children learning to read, write, and compute fluently and confidently, but to argue that education—and success—must be seen not solely in terms of cognitive attainment, but also relates to practical abilities and personal and interpersonal qualities. A holistic view involves education being seen more broadly than what can be measured, or school learning, and must address children's current needs and concerns, not just preparation for the future, or the skills deemed necessary for employment.

Implications for Young Children's Nurture and Education

This section discusses what young children require to flourish, both now and in a future the nature of which is hard to predict with confidence. While these needs will differ between different children and between older and younger children, there are some common threads.

Maslow (1970) emphasizes that basic physiological needs, such as those for food and warmth, must be met in order for children (and all of us) to able to face other challenges. Counter-intuitively, children must feel safe before they can be more adventurous and take risks. Young children tend to be engaged and motivated by active and meaningful learning, in a context of relationships with a trusted adult (see Donaldson, 1982, 1992), applying different types of knowledge rather than trying to memorize propositional knowledge or learn decontextualized skills. Relationships with trusted adults who care for them—and opportunities to care *for* others (Noddings, 2013)—are necessary if children are to thrive and become empathetic with other people. While young children need adult care, attention, and guidance, they also benefit from opportunities to be away from adults. For instance, in a world of constant stimulation, they benefit from chances to be calm and reflective, and to experience nature and the outdoors.

All children bring a greater depth and range of prior knowledge than adults tend to recognize. However, schools often ignore what Gonzales, Moll, and Amanti (2005) call "funds of knowledge" and their cultural capital. Funds of knowledge are the types of knowledge not valued in school, often of a practical nature. These may include interests and expertise as varied as geology and chess, photography and computer games. Children from many backgrounds find that the types of knowledge and activity, their cultural capital, valued previously or in different parts of their lives, is not valued in other contexts. For example, activities such as disco dancing, pigeon racing, and fishing might not be valued in school. Other, more profound, examples include the child's home language and religious and cultural practices where these are unfamiliar to the school or the teacher. A broad and balanced range of opportunities helps to reveal hidden interests and talents and to engage and motivate children, especially those from backgrounds where school learning and the norms of schooling are unfamiliar. However, this can present a dilemma for teachers, especially, of how to extend children's cultural horizons without devaluing the cultural capital that they bring.

In a world of diversity and difference, children need both of what Putnam (2000) calls bonding and bridging capital. The former is what enables people to bond with those similar to themselves, the latter to relate appropriately with those who are different. Bonding capital is easier to build up, but bridging capital matters particularly in a diverse world, in order to challenge stereotypes, such as those that lead to racism and misogyny. To do this, young children benefit from frequent opportunities to compare and contrast, particularly looking for similarities rather than differences, at least initially.

If children are to have some idea of what to do when they are unsure exactly what to do, they must develop qualities, the disposition and intrinsic motivation to manifest these, and a sense of agency. While any list of desirable qualities will vary somewhat between cultures, a world of change emphasizes those that enable children to be flexible and imaginative and work with other people. Many qualities, such as creativity, teamwork, and resilience are valued by employers (see CBI, 2012) though this is not the prime reason why they matter, but because they help children to be, and become, the types of people who can imagine new possibilities, interact with others, and overcome challenges. The instant access to information, sometimes of doubtful quality, emphasizes the importance of questioning and the skills and dispositions associated with critical thinking.

While young children need to be protected in some respects, they must be equipped increasingly to cope with challenges and difficulties themselves. Take the example of bullying. While children may require support to cope with bullying, sometimes a considerable amount, they also need strategies to enable them to avoid being bullied, including saying no forcefully, if they are to avoid overdependence on support which might not always be available. This is even more so in relation to cyberbullying, most of which occurs when children are unsupervised.

Bruner (1996, 2006) emphasizes that children, from a very young age, are active learners, trying to make sense of a complex and confusing range of experiences. In Pollard's (Pollard with Filer, 1996, p. 91) words, "it is essential that (children) exercise a significant degree of control of the (learning) process so that they can build on intrinsic motivation where that exists." Unless they have a sense of agency, of control over their learning and lives, children are likely to become passive, dependent, and disengaged.

Young children learn a great deal through play. In particular, play helps develop many social and emotional skills, such as understanding unspoken cues and turn taking, and a theory of mind—the recognition that other people see the world differently from oneself. Moreover, it is worth pondering Winnicott's (1980) words "it is in playing and only in playing that the individual child or adult is able to be creative and to use the whole personality. It is only in being creative that the individual discovers the self" (p. 63).

Bruner argues (2006, p. 23) that experience must be re-presented using one of three main modes: enactive, by doing, iconic, by observing and drawing, and symbolic, especially using language. Young children—up to the age of about 7 years—find it easier to process experience more through activity and visual modes than through language. This does not mean that adults should not use language, but that they should not rely on it as the main means of learning, and that young children, especially up to about 7 years old, but also subsequently, benefit from many different types of experience and ways of re-presenting it.

The humanities and the arts are not only enjoyable and engaging and help to develop skills that can be transferred to other subject areas, but offer opportunities to exercise and strengthen many desirable qualities. For instance, drama provides chances to be playful, to exercise imagination, and to manifest creativity. In Eaude (2017), I argue against seeing the humanities in terms of discrete subjects such as history, geography, and religious education—recognizing that in some countries such subjects may be grouped under broader areas of learning and that religious education might not be permitted. Rather, the humanities involve the study of human beings and the cultures in which they live, and the arts offer different ways of representing experience and expressing one's feelings.

Children, like adults, learn much of what is most important, especially beliefs and ways of working and interacting, by adult example and participation within communities of practice (Cox, 2017; Lave & Wenger, 1991) rather than direct instruction. For instance, respect and teamwork are best learned—and bridging capital built up—by cooperating with other people in a diverse range of situations and groups; thinking and working creatively is enhanced by adults who do so. This highlights the importance of the learning environment, as discussed in the next section.

Implications for Adults Working with Young Children

Many of the implications for adults follow logically from the previous discussion. For children to develop the qualities and dispositions highlighted requires adults to focus on how they act and interact reciprocally with children. In particular, the need for children to be engaged and to belong—and the danger of them otherwise being passive or belonging to groups which will not enable them to thrive—emphasizes the importance of adults creating a genuinely inclusive learning environment, with relationships of mutual trust and respect.

As Graham and Slee (2008, p. 278) write, "to include is not necessarily to *be* inclusive." In particular, inclusion requires a sensitivity, and responsiveness, to children's background and culture. The key, in terms of schools, is whether inclusion is understood as trying to adapt children to types of teaching that have typically served some children better than others, or as changing these (Thomson & Hall, 2015). In Eaude (2014), I explored the idea of hospitable space, where all children are welcomed, nurtured, and attended to and given a broad range of opportunities, and adults respect what children bring to the situation, even where this is not what is normally valued in formal school settings. However, one should note Nouwen's insight (Eaude, 2014, p. 245) that creating hospitable space is very hard in schools where individual success and competition with others are paramount.

To be inclusive, adults must try to:

- create environments in which children feel safe, but are challenged, especially setting their own challenges, and where there is a broad and engaging range of opportunities and space for reflection, as well as pace and energy;
- establish boundaries which help to contain anxiety but which are not restrictive, balancing structure and freedom;
- change the locus of control so that children develop a sense of agency and qualities such as resilience and intrinsic motivation;
- draw on children's "funds of knowledge" and cultural capital, seeing children as inexperienced rather than incompetent learners;
- encourage children to question and explore rather than adults always providing, and being expected to provide, answers;
- manifest qualities such as care, respect, and enthusiasm, given the importance of example and role modelling.

For teachers, if one is teaching the whole child, one must assess the whole child. However, this does not mean that one should measure everything, especially those aspects of the whole child (or people more generally) which are inherently not open to meaningful measurement. Such an approach suggests ending the current obsession with data and learning being seen as linear and hierarchical.

Holistic education requires adults to reassess the aims of education and the means to achieve these. An inclusive approach requires that adults challenge many of the assumptions of the current system of schooling and their own. For instance, adults must recognize, and help others to recognize, that:

- ability and intelligence are not fixed but can be enhanced by practice and hard work (see Dweck's (2000) work on growth mindset);
- knowledge is not just propositional, but procedural and personal/interpersonal (see Eaude, 2011, pp. 62–65);
- success is to be understood more broadly than in terms of academic attainment or possessions and celebrity.

The school curriculum currently offered to young children too often fails to meet many of their needs. However, education should not be equated with schooling. Adults must try to ensure that the needs of the whole child are met. In particular, adults must avoid scholarizing children's lives or overprotecting them, but see them as active, capable learners, though requiring support and guidance. This is helped where different adults—parents/carers, the extended family, professionals, and other significant adults—work together. This can be harder than it might seem. While parents/carers, teachers, and other influential adults, such as grandparents or leaders of voluntary groups, have distinctive roles, these must, as far as possible, be complementary, if young children are not to receive conflicting and potentially confusing messages. However, adults can also help to compensate when children get too much or too little from other sources. So, for instance, where children lack opportunities to play or engage in art or music at school, other adults can seek to provide these outside school, and schools can, obviously, offer opportunities that some children miss out on at home.

Conclusion

This chapter has argued that young children have distinctive needs and should not be seen as small, undeveloped adults. Adults should try to see young children as a whole, rather than just in relation to discrete aspects. This applies especially to parents/carers and teachers, because of their broad remit, but also to those with more specific roles, such as faith-based, or other, group leaders or sports coaches. The challenges of growing up in a world of diversity and constant change requires qualities such as respect, resilience, and empathy and the disposition and motivation to manifest these in different situations. Children must be equipped by being protected and interdependent as well as independent from a young age. Such an approach entails a radical change of priorities, especially in relation to formal schooling. In particular, children must be, and be seen as, active participants in their own learning and in their search for meaning, identity, and purpose rather than just vessels to be filled with propositional knowledge, which can then be measured and the child graded. A holistic approach highlights the importance of children belonging within inclusive environments, where diversity is welcomed and trusting relationships are created. Inclusive environments provide a range of opportunities that is broader and more enjoyable and meaningful than that currently offered in most schools, notably in terms of play, the humanities, and the arts. In such environments, adults encourage and set a good example, especially in terms of questioning, risk-taking, and learning from mistakes, and manifesting qualities such as respect, thoughtfulness, and enthusiasm. Such an approach entails adults challenging, and helping children increasingly to challenge, many current assumptions about ideas such as intelligence, ability, and success.

References

Alexander, R. (Ed.). (2010). *Children, their world, their education – Final report and recommendations of the Cambridge Primary Review*. Abingdon, UK: Routledge.

Ball, S. J. (2003). The teacher's soul and the terrors of performativity. *Journal of Education Policy*, *18*(2), 215–228.

Best, R. (2014). Spirituality, faith and education: some reflections from a UK perspective. In J. Watson, M. de Souza, & A. Trousdale (Eds), *Global perspectives on spirituality and education* (pp. 5–20). New York: Routledge.

Bruner, J. (1996). *The culture of education*. Cambridge, MA: Harvard University Press.

Bruner, J. (2006). *In search of pedagogy (Volume 11)*. Abingdon, UK: Routledge.

CBI (Confederation of British Industry) (2012). *First Steps: A new approach for our schools*. Retrieved from www.cbi.org.uk/insight-and-analysis/first-steps/

Cox, S. (2017). Developing values in primary classrooms and the place of the humanities. *Education 3–13*, *45*(3), 375–385.

Donaldson, M. (1982). *Children's minds*. Glasgow: Fontana.

Donaldson, M. (1992). *Human minds – An exploration*. London: Allen Lane.

Dweck, C. S. (2000). *Self theories: Their role in motivation, personality and development*. Philadelphia, PA: Psychology Press.

Eaude, T. (2008). *Children's spiritual, moral, social and cultural development: Primary and Early Years* (2nd edn). Exeter, UK: Learning Matters.

Eaude, T. (2011). *Thinking through pedagogy for primary and early years*. Exeter, UK: Learning Matters.

Eaude, T. (2014). Creating hospitable space to nurture children's spirituality: Possibilities and dilemmas associated with power. *International Journal of Children's Spirituality*, *19*(3/4), 236–248.

Eaude, T. (2016). *New perspectives on young children's moral education – Developing character through a virtue ethics approach*. London: Bloomsbury.

Eaude, T. (2017). Humanities in the primary school – philosophical considerations. *Education 3–13*, *45*(3), 343-353.

Ecclestone, K. & Hayes, D. (2009). *The dangerous rise of therapeutic education*. London: Routledge.

Gonzales, N., Moll, L., & Amanti, C. (2005). *Funds of knowledge*. Mahwah, NJ: Lawrence Erlbaum.

Graham, L. J. & Slee, R. (2008). An illusory interiority: Interrogating the discourse/s of inclusion. *Educational Philosophy and Theory*, *40*(2), 277–293.

HMSO (1944). *The 1944 Education Act*. London: HMSO.

HMSO (1988). *The 1988 Education Reform Act*. London: HMSO. Retrieved from www.legislation.gov.uk/ukpga/1988/40/contents

Hay, D. with Nye, R. (1998). *The spirit of the child*. London: Fount.

Hull, J. (1998). *Utopian whispers – Moral, religious and spiritual values in schools*. Norwich, UK: Religious and Moral Education Press.

Hyde, B. (2008). *Children and spirituality: Searching for meaning and connectedness*. London: Jessica Kingsley.

Lave, J. & Wenger, E. (1991). *Situated learning: Legitimate peripheral participation*. Cambridge: Cambridge University Press.

Maslow, A. (1970). *Motivation and personality*. New York: Harper and Row.

Mayall, B. (2010). Children's lives outside school and their educational impact. In R. Alexander (Ed.), *The Cambridge primary review research surveys* (pp. 49–82). Abingdon, UK: Routledge.

Noddings, N. (2003). *Happiness and education*. Cambridge: Cambridge University Press.

Noddings, N. (2013). *Caring: A relational approach to ethics and moral education*. Berkeley, CA: University of California Press.

Palmer, S. (2006). *Toxic childhood*. London: Orion Books.

Pollard, A. with Filer, A. (1996). *The social world of children's learning*. London: Continuum.

Putnam, R. D. (2000). *Bowling alone: The collapse and revival of American community*. New York: Simon & Schuster.

RSA (Royal Society of Arts) (2014). *Schools with soul: A new approach to spiritual, moral, social and cultural education*. Retrieved from www.thersa.org/discover/publications-and-articles/reports/schools-with-soul-a-new-approach-to-spiritual-moral-social-and-cultural-education

Thomson, P. & Hall, C. (2015). 'Everyone can imagine their own Gellert': The democratic artist and 'inclusion' in primary and nursery classrooms. *Education 3–13*, *43*(4), 420–432.

Unicef (2007). *Child poverty in perspective: An overview of child well-being in rich countries: A comparative assessment of the lives and well-being of children and adolescents in economically advanced nations*. Florence: Unicef Innocenti Centre (Innocenti Report Card 7). Retrieved from www.unicef.org/media/files/ChildPovertyReport.pdf

Unicef (2013). *Child well-being in rich countries: A comparative overview*. Florence: Unicef Office of Research (Innocenti Report Card 11). Retrieved from www.unicef-irc.org/publications/pdf/rc11_eng.pdf

Winnicott, D. W. (1980). *Playing and reality*. Harmondsworth: Penguin.

8

MOVING THE SPIRIT
Holistic Education and Young Children

Jane Bone

A feature of early childhood education in Australia and Aoteaora New Zealand is the emphasis on holistic well-being as a key learning outcome. The vision for Te Whāriki, the curriculum for New Zealand, is that children will be "healthy in mind, body and spirit" (Ministry of Education, 2017). *The Early Years Learning Framework* for Australia (EYLF) includes "good physical health, feelings of happiness, satisfaction and successful social functioning" (DEEWR, 2009, p. 30) in the learning outcome for well-being. In early years education generally, holistic approaches to learning are important, particularly given the amount of time children spend in a range of preschool environments. In both Australia and New Zealand, preschools and kindergartens are usually sessional and children attend for three-hour sessions or otherwise attend long day care on a daily basis. The provision for long day care can mean that children will spend a significant amount of their lives in that context and, therefore, attention to the whole child is essential. Who this whole child is, and what being holistic means, involves engaging with "our values, our aspirations for the next generation, our beliefs about child development, and more generally, our cultural perspective" (Nimmo, 1998, p. 296). Nimmo (1998) also points out that one of the factors to consider is whether the child is seen as an individual or as a child in community. In this chapter, I am looking at the spiritual dimension as an aspect of what it means to be holistic and will discuss programs that consider the education of children to be a complex enterprise.

To be holistic from my perspective is merely to recognize the connectedness of all things. My definition of spiritualty reflects this, as follows:

> Spirituality connects people to each other, to all living things, to nature and the universe. Spirituality is a way of appreciating the wonder and mystery of everyday life. It alerts me to the possibility for love, happiness, goodness, peace and compassion in the world.
>
> *(Bone, 2010, p. 403)*

From the spiritual and holistic viewpoint, it is impossible to focus on one area without influencing all aspects of the person. It may be considered an ethical imperative to realize that everything has meaning in the intra-activity (Lenz-Taguchi, 2010) that goes on in educational contexts, in and between people, animals, and things, the human and more than human. From this position, I look at some of the pedagogies and programs for young children that reflect this. There are always new and innovative possibilities available in early childhood education. In this chapter, consideration is given to the implications of the increasing popularity of yoga in preschools, the advances in walking and getting out and about in preschools in Australia and New Zealand (bush and beach 'kinder' or kindergarten), and, finally, the attention being paid to aesthetics in terms of a beautiful environment and the effect on the spirit. This chapter refers to 'moving the spirit' and in this discussion I hope to play with the idea of movement in both its literal and metaphorical sense, physical, social, spiritual, and affective.

Methodology as Assemblage

This chapter is not based on research in a traditional sense. Instead, evidence has been gathered from a variety of sources and forms an assemblage of information and connections (St. Pierre & Jackson, 2014) drawing on the following sources: previous research, personal narrative/author journals, information from websites, anecdotal evidence, the literature, early childhood policy documents, and sources of inspiration that drive innovative approaches to pedagogy. Some of the practices described here have their genesis in different situations other than early childhood settings. Yoga, for example, is a 'trickle down' activity; two million adults in Australia do yoga in one form or another and it is the fastest growing fitness activity in Australia (Roy Morgan, 2016). It is probably inevitable that children became involved. The growing popularity of walking in nature has been influenced by the Forest Schools of Denmark (Elliot & Chancellor, 2014). Scandinavian approaches to pedagogy are influential and, despite the different environments, walking was destined to become a part of educational practice in places that also value outdoor activity, such as Australia and New Zealand. The impetus to create beautiful environments is influenced by the preschools of Reggio Emilia, Italy, where the schools are carefully conceptualized and planned, are connected to an inspirational person (real or fictional), and are designed with the child in mind. These examples of initiatives that support holistic education are linked to well-being and spirituality.

Yoga: Body–Mind–Spirit

Yoga is one way that young children are encouraged to develop joy in movement. The emphasis on movement is a Western way of thinking about yoga. It is a word that means 'to join, yoke together' and this joining of body–mind–spirit is fundamental to yogic philosophy. According to B. K. S. Iyengar, who influenced yoga being popular in the West, the poses of yoga, or, more accurately, the āsanas, are holistic movements as "āsanas act as bridges to unite the body with the mind, and the mind with the soul" (Iyengar, 2002, p. 32). It is these movements, or postures, that programs with young children focus upon, rather than breathing or meditation and the more esoteric aspects of the practice.

In classical yoga, mindfulness and awareness are built through the practice of asana—and these postures are only one of the 'eight limbs' of yoga. The others include ethical principles and awareness of the breath. Iyengar (2002) interprets the yoga sutras of Patanjali as a guide for life and a way to "grow from life's afflictions towards freedom" (p. 290). There is a link to resilience, an aspect of education that is important in the early years (Roberts, 2010). Yoga encourages the thought that inner peace becomes something that is inside, not something dependent upon external rewards or material goods. Through the practice of āsana, "senses and mind are brought under control" (Iyengar, 2002, p. 290). While yoga may be fun in early childhood contexts, there is serious intent behind the practice of yoga.

In the West, yoga is usually thought of in terms of physical movements: for example, downward dog, or triangle pose, or tree. The stretches and postures that represent movements usually associated with animals are some of the more accessible ways that contemporary yoga programs connect with children. When researching with young children, I noticed that they engaged in the play of 'becoming animal' and suggested that this is "metamorphic play" (Bone, 2010). This play implies a spiritual aspect whereby the child can become Other in the moment and may suddenly wash her face like a cat or prance like a horse. These *becomings* are moments of intensity and children may no longer be present but in an imaginative world of their own as another creature entirely. Parents and educators also notice that children's imaginative play includes 'becoming animal'. Children not only relate to pets and soft toys that are part of their world but they also become animal, seemingly at will. I suggested in my article (Bone, 2010) that this spiritual aspect of play is very powerful and metamorphosis refers to the spiritual journey of change and the Pythagorean journey to the next world that could only be undertaken as a bird or animal. In Hindu mythology, the gods are often animal gods. For example, Hanuman, who embodies the monkey temperament and range of movement and facial expressions, and Ganesha, half man, half elephant, who embodies the strength of both. In shamanistic religions, becoming animal has a curative effect and it is the animal that gives the healers their power. In these spiritual perspectives, the animal spirit is channelled and used for good and this relates to emotional, physical, and spiritual well-being.

Becoming animal involves moving the body in certain ways, often ways that are associated with particular animals, such as trotting, pouncing, or waving a trunk, or turning the head in certain ways and this is the aspect that popular and successful yoga programs tune into. They access the intuitive world of play and the movements that children have observed. Danahy (nd, p. 9) describes a teacher of young children who used yoga to regulate the energy and emotions in her room "she reminds Joseph to go into his *turtle shell* to help him calm down. She does *monkey breaths* with Katherine as she works through her sillies" (original italics). Popular programs that include yoga are taught in a way that is less formal than the usual classes for adults. In recent research where pre-school children were asked, they said that they enjoyed yoga and they were positive about this activity and could also articulate why it supported their health and relaxation (Stapp & Wolff, 2017). In the adult world, yoga classes are ritualistic and the practice is commodified. It is considered essential to have mats and yoga clothing, to find an attractive setting, and the right teacher and yoga school. Yoga for children is presented in a way that is more fun (Engel, 2016). Early childhood teachers can use the internet or a book to teach poses. Even when not familiar with the animal or bird, children enjoy becoming the being that is celebrated in the āsana.

Through yoga, children experience connecting with animals and nature in their bodies as they move toward learning to be present in the moment (Iyengar, 2002). Being present and enjoying the moment is something that people who engage with spiritual practices spend much time and effort trying to achieve. In yoga, the positive effects of moving with mindfulness and awareness in a way that acknowledges the breath (pranayama) is a way of staying in the present. The individual works, even when part of a group, in a non-competitive and focused way. When becoming tree, for example, children are learning to balance but also to be strong and to pay attention and remain still and calm in order to maintain the position. Breathing and the gaze of the eyes are used to maintain focus and concentration. At the same time, falling or overbalancing is not seen as 'wrong', merely an opportunity to feel that life is never perfect and that one can always try again.

For some people, the reflection of our animal self in the āsana is problematic. It is thought that we need to grow up and in some way leave this behind, or the animal is seen as undesirable and inferior to the human. Contemporary posthuman theory proposes entanglements rather than binaries and hierarchies (Haraway, 2008). In the human struggle to become more intelligent, raise the IQ, be first in the class, and become an A grade student, it is easy to forget that the brain is part of the body and is nourished in physical movement and by movement of the breath.

I describe one āsana below, the cobra and give details of the instruction, the physical movement, and the symbolism that the movement represents. This is a movement that anyone with a back problem will have been urged to do.

The Cobra

Instruction:

Begin by lying full length on the floor, face down, with hands palms down flat on the floor under the shoulders, elbows raised. Start with the face down and, as you breathe in, raise your head slowly upward, passing forehead and nose lightly along the mat. Press the pelvis and legs into the floor. Start with the toes touching but if they come apart as you raise your head just allow this to happen. When at the highest point (this may well not be very high at all) work on dropping the shoulders, feel the neck lengthen and bring the head back like a cobra before it strikes. Let the gaze be upwards.

Commentary:

According to B.K.S. Iyengar "like a snake, the spine should be moved from end to end; when the head moves the movement is transmitted to the tail" (Iyengar, as cited in Radha, 1995, p. 149). "The symbol of the cobra can be found in twenty-two of the major countries of the world. Its deadly poison means instant death, yet its ability to shed its skin symbolizes renewal and resurrection . . . the paradox of the struggle of life" (Radha, 1995, p. 149).

Swami Sivananda Radha (1995, p. 149) recognizes that to start with, to be prone, facing down, "is a humbling and fearful position. . . ." Later in the movement she says, "I feel as if I am locked into position. What am I locked into?" and "I think of the snake, its eyes are always open, always seeing, always alert" (p. 149).

The lessons to be taken from the movement are truly holistic. There is also an element in yoga that is about taking the body back to positions that are relatively easy in childhood. The baby lies on its stomach and raises its head up and looks around. The movement is easy, a baby push-up, it enables the infant to see the world differently before he or she can sit up or stand unaided. The body loses flexibility and motion and, by working in this way, children are encouraged to keep this range of movement, and, in yogic philosophy, if the body is flexible so might the mind be. The infant who lifts up on his or her hands is curious and delights in this movement and is happy to repeat it over and over; holistic learning is happening, it is natural and joyful.

Movement is located in the body of the individual and as dance and joyful celebration of life also enriches the community.

At a community event recently the dancers, who were Aboriginal and Torres Strait Island people and from West Papua, suddenly 'became' kangaroo(s). They lay on the ground and held fingers behind their head like the upright ears of the kangaroo and reclined like kangaroos in the late afternoon sun. Later, they asked the children to become horse, making trotting movements and holding their hands as if holding reins; in this movement the children were both horse and rider. The children joined in and the community came together in appreciation of the artistry and the way that the young dancers inspired the children to dance, sing, and move. It is these events that preschools can organize and that change people's lives. As the Elder put on her possum skin cloak and began to speak, and as the digeridoo made the earth vibrate, the crowd of parents and visitors fell silent and were completely present in the moment. This is also 'yoga' – the joining, or 'yoking', of body and soul.

(Author notes)

Walking: Nature–Mindfulness–Belonging

Walking outside the preschool and walking in nature, on the beach or in a park, is increasingly part of the weekly program in preschools in Australia and New Zealand. In Aotearoa New Zealand, it is seen as important to know your local mountain (*te maunga*) and river (*te awa*) and in Māori culture this knowledge is part of knowing who you are and where you stand in the world. In a project that took children outside the gates of the preschool, the children mapped their locality and the project provided an opening for both them and the teachers to explore the history and natural features of the place where they lived and worked (Bone, 2014). Children showed that they were very knowledgeable about their locality. A side effect of the research is that the community felt invited into the preschool, boundaries were more permeable, and connections with the community increased. Ingold and Vergunst (2008, p. 2) note that walking is social and "lives are paced out in their mutual relations". Living beings find out who they are, what they know, and where they are going through walking and accessing physical, cognitive, and socio-emotional skills together with a spiritual sense of belonging. In the Australian Early Years Learning Framework, it is expected that children will "develop an increased understanding of the interdependence between land, people, plants and animals", "develop an awareness of the impact of human activity on environments", and respect their community (DEEWR, 2009, p. 29). In Australia, children learn to connect to country and this is encouraged in spaces like public parks and gardens, places of diversity and richness that collaborate with schools and provide resources for teachers (Royal Botanic Gardens Melbourne, 2013).

Walking connects to certain fields of study, for example, eco-psychology. In this regard, Trigwell, Francis, and Bagot (2014, p. 241) introduce the idea of 'eudaimonic well-being' as a connection to nature that is mediated by spirituality. From their perspective, mental health is enhanced through this relationship and "those who are highly nature-connected may find a sense of purpose or meaningful existence from their closeness with nature" (p. 243). This connection has a long tradition in early childhood, from Froebel's 'garden for children' to 'beach kinder' in Australia and programs such as Ngahere Tamariki—children of the forest (Schwalger, 2016) in Aotearoa New Zealand. It is a measure of the attention being paid to holistic aspects of well-being and education that research is coming forward that supports what is being carried out with young children.

The influence of Danish forest-schools has spread (Elliot & Chancellor, 2014) and is a pedagogical practice that is attractive in countries that have adequate outdoor spaces for children to explore and enjoy. Elliot & Chancellor (2014, p. 46) say that "the key underlying feature of the forest preschool approach is that children spend long and regular periods of time in unstructured play in natural forest or beach environments". In conjunction with environmental concerns and a changing image of the child as a redemptive agent in this time of climate change and extinctions, it is being increasingly seen as desirable for children to be in parks, bush, and on beaches, rather than confined within the boundaries of the preschool. Louv (2005) proposed 'nature-deficit' as a condition of disadvantage due to children being discouraged from being in wild places and his influential book encouraged early childhood educators to enlarge areas of play and exploration for children in their care and to ensure that children spend time outdoors. In their analysis of an Australian Bush Kinder program, Elliot & Chancellor (2014, p. 51) conclude that "children's health, wellbeing, learning and development" will drive, and enhance, children's interactions in nature.

In the Pacific region, recognizing that connections to nature will change attitudes has never been more important (Nunn et al., 2016). The way that children show their engagement in the world through walking has the potential to influence families and their decision-making about environmental issues. Nunn et al. (2016) argue that spiritual beliefs impact upon the ability of communities and individuals to adapt to environmental changes and when the threat is extreme this becomes important. Australia and New Zealand are countries in the Pacific and it is our neighbours, some 10 million people (Nunn et al., 2016), who are already suffering from rising temperatures and sea levels. It is sobering and inspiring to think that, as an early childhood educator, by taking a holistic approach to planning and by incorporating walking into a weekly program, this might eventually encourage rich countries to help their more vulnerable neighbours. This perspective acknowledges children as agents in the world.

Walking is movement and a way to be mindful in action. There is time to look around, to notice, to be distracted, and feel grounded. When I walk, there is so much to see and feel. I am also aware of the air, the atmosphere, the spirit of the place: noise and dust on city streets, the texture of sand on the beach, rain, the shape of trees. These things change my mood, and walking is an affective activity. Irwin (2006) proposes that walking offers "spiritual, sensory, and perceptual awareness" and she records and celebrates the movement, color, and variety that are offered her when walking. As an adult, I can walk as a deliberate spiritual activity, in mindfulness, or on a pilgrimage. Adults document their walks, taking photographs, keeping journals, noting the number of steps taken on fitness bracelets.

Children walk in different ways. On the walking project called "Our Place" (Bone, 2014), the children walked and talked, enjoying time in small groups with their teacher. In many preschools, the whole class goes out and walks with teachers, parents, and helpers. This involves educators in risk assessments and they carry First Aid equipment and sunscreen and insect repellent; the children have bags with play lunches and water.

> *I see a child walking with his father, they are holding hands, the parent takes long strides, the child runs beside him, feet barely touching the pavement, he chooses to walk and a family member pushes the buggy behind them; for a moment the wheels are rejected in favour of flying along the pavement. He is keeping up, learning to walk with purpose, learning that walking can be a serious business of getting from here to there.*
>
> *(Author notes)*

It is adults who can support or burden children when walking, giving too many rules and restrictions or letting them go free. In the Danish preschools, the children walk off into the forest and are gone from sight. They learn to be at home in the pine trees, a landscape that I find dark and slightly threatening. In this way, people find their place and develop a sense of attachment to it. This is something spiritual that continues through life, in the desert, by the sea, or on the street (Bone, 2016). Walking is something that, as Jung (2014) discovered, even when lost or challenging, is also "holistic, mindful, and adventurous" (p. 622). Jung suggests that there are layers of walking, and that mindful walking is something different, it is:

> an *interactive way of knowing*, allowing the entire *body*, and all of its *senses* to experience its surroundings, to trace, and connect different areas, to intuitively sense when and how to avoid potential dangers, and to live in the entangled social pathways.
>
> *(p. 625, original italics)*

Mindful walking, for an inspiring local educator whom I know, means to discover but not to take anything away from the place. Her program is based on connections to the local Boonwurrung people and the advice of the Elder is followed. Another innovative early childhood leader suggests that the point of walking with children is to let them wander off, so that they experience their surroundings and gain a sense of discovery, with only basic restrictions and boundaries. There is no right or wrong way of walking; it is a way of being in the world, being present, always in movement.

Beautiful Environments: Space–Peace–Aesthetics

Children respond to the beauty of nature and are also aware of the indoor environment. Binder (2016, p. 294) suggests that art forms and aesthetics are "a cohesive conscious joining of the creative to the everyday" and she finds that "balance and harmony" can be achieved through "lived aesthetic experience" (p. 293). This experience may be provided for children or it may be something they contribute to in the spaces where they live and learn. In the opinion of Curtis and Carter (2003), carefully designed and beautiful settings provoke wonder, curiosity, and intellectual engagement. They are aware of the joyful reactions and interactions of children in rich environments, full of magic and treasures "sparkles and shadows" (p. 121). Beautiful environments are not static. Curtis and Carter (2003) appreciate the way different people create beauty, and an example is given of an employee in an early childhood setting. They say:

> Mr Banks, the custodian, takes time to create a beautiful design in the sandbox with his tools. As the children arrive, they can't wait to see what he's done and talk eagerly about how they might add to it or change it during their sandbox play.
>
> *(p. 109)*

According to Curtis and Carter "children are intrigued with natural phenomena and the physical properties around them—things such as light, colour, reflection, sound motion" (p. 121). When materials and environments are aesthetically pleasing, children find it easier to explore spaces that are calm, soft, different, safe, and that provide sensory experiences. These elements can be healing for children; they feel welcomed into spaces that are attractive and inviting. Children who are invited find their sense of well-being enhanced because "the arrangements and provisions in the physical environment create the context for the socio-emotional climate and the quality of interactions among the people there" (Curtis & Carter, 2003, p. 24). Perhaps a shared and beautiful environment will bring out the best in people. Carlina Rinaldi (2006, p. 176), a key pedagogical influence in the preschools of Reggio Emilia, acknowledges this when she says that "beauty orients and attracts". People travel huge distances to see beautiful places that may be very old, or modern and contemporary, carved out of natural features or carefully constructed, finished or unfinished, like La Sagrada Familia in Barcelona, beautiful in its imperfection.

An early advocate for aesthetically pleasing and peaceful spaces for children was Maria Montessori. She felt that it was up to teachers to prepare environments for children that "encourage the natural tendency to investigate and theorise about things that provoke a sense of magic and wonder" (Montessori, 1970, p. 122). She always connected this to the spiritual aspect of the child, and proposed the child as a spiritual embryo, and, "like the physical embryo, the spiritual embryo must be protected by an external environment animated by the warmth of love and the richness of value" (p. 35). Her experiences setting up the Casa di Bambini in Rome meant that she noticed a difference in behavior and demeanor in children who lived in overcrowded conditions and who entered a school that was calm and peaceful. She felt that this kind of environment soothed the soul of the child and influenced everyone who worked there. Montessori deliberately created an environment intended to support "a sense of peace and well-being, of cleanliness and intimacy" (Montessori, 1967, p. 37). She felt that the environment should not have anything harmful, but instead encourage "ease and grace" and a sense of freedom (p. 48). The influence of Montessori is still obvious in preschools that operate with her philosophy in mind, because of her attention to the materials, furniture, and decorative features that she felt constructed the educational experience for children (Bone, 2017).

The Italian cultural sense of aesthetics is also evident in contemporary early childhood practice because of the attention given to design in the preschools of Reggio Emilia, the famous Italian preschools. Their influence has been felt globally and the Reggio discourse of documentation, dialogue, and design has impacted upon preschools in Australia and New Zealand. The beautiful environment from the Reggio Emilia perspective is a "relational space" and also holistic, consisting of "an environmental fabric rich in information, without formal rules. It is not the representation of a School, but a whole made up of many different identities, with a recognizable feel about it" (Ceppi & Zini, 1998). They go on to say that "the aesthetic quality depends [also] on the quality of the connections (the aesthetic of links)" (Ceppi & Zini, 1998, np). This is a spiritual aspect of these environments, the connectedness of all things made possible by the "aesthetic of links" (Ceppi & Zini, 1998, np).

Working with an eye to Reggio principles and aesthetic promptings has encouraged some pre-schools to use softer colors, to be aware of light, and to think about arrangements of spaces through a design aesthetic that focuses on the beautiful rather than the utilitarian. A preschool I enjoyed being in was remarkably peaceful, with small spaces for children as opposed to large brightly colored Macdonaldized spaces. Children could choose a place that suited their mood and what they wanted to do; they could be sociable or work on their own and the materials available were attractive and there was a sense of order. In this model of beautiful preschool design, the children moved carefully, had conversations, and were respectful; it was also a place full of laughter but without endless noise and distraction. The New Zealand curriculum for early childhood mentions that "the design of the physical environment" may present barriers to learning and participation (Ministry of Education, 2017, p. 13). The preschool I have described made learning and participation more likely.

There is not one pathway to beauty and Waldorf kindergartens have their own ideas of what is appropriate and beautiful, using specific soft colors, wood, and natural materials in the kindergarten. Some preschools only use sustainable or recycled materials and furniture so they have a different look. But both show that they are mindful and make careful decisions about these spaces. The pre-school in its entirety speaks to children and influences their lives. Rinaldi (2006) suggests that these kinds of decisions give what happens as a result special value, a value that, according to her view, is important because "you're choosing, you're taking responsibility" (p. 198). In this conceptualization of what is of value, the activity of making choices is reflected in the environment, and not just in the surroundings, but in the pedagogy. She says, "education is really about being passionate together. To have feelings together. To have emotions together" (p. 204). When this is a feature of the early childhood setting, then spaces may be beautiful because they reflect culture or are sustainable. It is unlikely that they will be conventional and bland. Holistic education is sensory and reflects a focus on well-being that may take many forms in the spaces where it operates.

Conclusion

Early childhood education has a holistic orientation and in the Early Years Framework for Australia attention is paid to holistic approaches to practice, a practice that will "recognise the connectedness of mind, body and spirit" (DEEWR, 2009, p. 14). This statement continues, "when early childhood educators take a holistic approach they pay attention to children's physical, personal, social, emotional and spiritual wellbeing as well as cognitive aspects of learning" (DEEWR, 2009, p. 24). These aspirations are shared by the New Zealand curriculum Te Whāriki, where holistic development, or kotahitanga, is a key principle (Ministry of Education, 2017). In this curriculum, the spiritual aspect is acknowledged as being a link between all other dimensions "across time and space" (p. 19).

In this chapter, yoga has been presented as an activity that moves the body and spirit; walking in nature is another holistic practice and, finally, attention is paid to beautiful environments as a way to move, and lift, the spirit. These three aspects of holistic education in early childhood are intended to acknowledge the work that has been done to respect the whole child in their communities. Influences from the past have been mentioned as well as contemporary initiatives and connections to community have been made. These programs are not specifically mentioned in policy documents, but they show the rich interpretations and creative responses possible when meeting requirements for the holistic education of young children.

References

Binder, M. (2016). Spirituality and the arts: Interwoven landscapes of identities and meaning. In M. de Souza, J. Bone, & J. Watson (Eds), *Spirituality across disciplines: Research and practice* (pp. 285–299). Switzerland: Springer International.

Bone, J. (2010). Play and metamorphosis: Spirituality in early childhood settings. *Contemporary Issues in Early Childhood*, 12(4), 420–417.

Bone, J. (2014). Through belonging: An early childhood perspective from a New Zealand preschool. In A. Alfrey, T. Brown, A. Cutter-Mackenzie, R. Jeanes, J. O'Connor, & B. Wattchow (Eds), *The socio-ecological educator: Connecting healthy, active and sustainable communities through health, physical, outdoor and environmental education* (pp. 125–137). New York: Springer Press.

Bone, J. (2016). Environmental issues and spirituality: Tracing the past and making contemporary connections. In M. de Souza, J. Bone, & J. Watson (Eds), *Spirituality across disciplines: Research and practice* (pp. 245–257). Switzerland: Springer International.

Bone, J. (2017). Maria Montessori as domestic goddess: Iconic early childhood educator and material girl. *Gender and Education*, https://doi.org/10.1080/09540253.2017.1396293

Ceppi, G. & Zini, M. (1998). *Children, spaces, relationships: Metaproject for an environment for young children*. Reggio Emilia: Reggio Children Domus Academy Research Centre.

Curtis, D. & Carter, M. (2003). *Designs for living and learning: Transforming early childhood environments*. St Paul, MN: Redleaf Press.

Danahy, L. (n.d.). Yoga poses for preschoolers. Good Guidance. *NAEYC, 8*(2), 9–10.

Department of Education, Employment and Workplace Relations (DEEWR) (2009). *Belonging, being and becoming: The Early Years Learning Framework for Australia*. Barton, ACT: Commonwealth of Australia.

Elliot, S. & Chancellor, B. (2014). From forest preschool to Bush Kinder: An inspirational approach to preschool provision in Australia. *Australasian Journal of Early Childhood, 39*(4), 45–53.

Engel, C. (2016). *ABC Yoga*. Lake Forest, CA: Quarto.

Haraway, D. J. (2008). *When species meet*. Minneapolis, MN: University of Minnesota Press.

Ingold, T. & Vergunst, J. L. (2008). *Ways of walking: Ethnography and practice on foot*. Aldershot, UK: Ashgate.

Irwin, R. L. (2006). Walking to create an aesthetic and spiritual *currere*. *Visual Arts Research, 32*(1), 75–82.

Iyengar, B. K. S. (2002). *Light on the Yoga Sutras of Patanjali*. London: Thorsons.

Jung, Y. (2014). Mindful walking: The serendipitous journey of community-based ethnography. *Qualitative Inquiry, 20*(5), 621–627.

Lenz-Taguchi, H. (2010). *Going beyond the theory/practice divide in early childhood education*. London: Routledge.

Louv, R. (2005). *Last child in the woods*. Chapel Hill: Algonquin.

Ministry of Education (2017). *Te Whāriki: He whāriki mātauranga mō ngā mokopuna o Aotearoa Early Childhood curriculum*. Wellington: Ministry of Education.

Montessori, M. (1967). *The discovery of the child*. New York: Ballantine Books.

Montessori, M. (1970). *The child in the family*. London: Pan.

Nimmo, J. (1998). The child in community. In C. Edwards, L. Gandini, & G. Forman (Eds), *The hundred languages of children* (pp. 295–313). Westport, CT: Ablex.

Nunn, P. D., Mulgrew, K., Scott-Parker, B., Hine, D. W., Marks, A. D. G., Mahar, D., & Maebuta, J. (2016). Spirituality and attitudes towards nature in the Pacific Islands: Insights towards enabling climate-change adaption. *Climate Change, 136*, 477–493.

Radha, Sivananda (1995). *Hatha Yoga: The hidden language symbols, secrets, and metaphor*. Spokane, WA: Timeless.

Rinaldi, C. (2006). *In dialogue with Reggio Emilia: Listening, researching and learning*. Abingdon, UK: Routledge.

Roberts, R. (2010). *Wellbeing from birth*. London: Sage.

Royal Botanic Gardens Melbourne (2013). Connecting to country: Teacher's kit. Retrieved from: www.rbg.vic.gov.au/learn/teacher-resources

Roy Morgan (2016). Strike a pose. www.roymorgan.com/findings/7004-yoga-is-the-fastest-growing-sport-or-fitness-activity-in-australia-june-2016-201610131055

Schwalger, M. (2016). Ngahere tamariki – children of the forest. Education Aotearoa. Retrieved from: http://ea.org.nz/ngahere-tamariki-children-forest/

St. Pierre, E. A. & Jackson, A. Y. (2014). Qualitative data analysis after coding. *Qualitative Inquiry, 20*(6), 715–719.

Stapp, A. C. & Wolff, K. (2017). Young children's experiences of yoga in an early childhood setting. *Early Child Development and Care* (online journal), 1–14.

Trigwell, J. L., Francis, A. J. P., & Bagot, K. L. (2014). Nature connectedness and eudaimonic well-being: Spirituality as a potential mediator. *Ecopsychology, 6*(4), 241–251.

9

SUSTAINABLE PEACE FOR THE PLANET

Edward J. Brantmeier

Imagine a world with minimal violent conflict and an abundant well-being of people and ecosystems, an integrated *Shangri-La* of sorts where people, animals, plants, and planet co-exist in a delicate yet vibrant interplay of ecological interdependence. Day to day norms of harmony and connection circumscribe thought, decision, and action and interactions typically result in happiness and the multiplication of well-being and positive relationships. People are intimately connected to the earth's rhythms and habitually make choices that are aligned with the long view in mind--the ability of the seventh generation of people to satisfy their basic sustenance and happiness needs. Imagine a world where physical and cultural boundaries were clear yet transparent, where biological and cultural diversity were revered as a strength and understood to be advantageous to the vitality and longevity of the whole of the planet. Imagine a world where the earth's abundant resources were carefully stewarded in ways that reflected a deep knowing that violence against nature is understood as violence against the self. Imagine a world where fair and just partnerships permeated relationships between people, communities, societies, and nations. Imagine a world where adults made decisions based on a long view of how current choices impact future generations not born yet. Imagine if our power needs came from renewable energy sources. Imagine if we significantly decreased our perceived need for consumption of the earth's finite resources; imagine if individuals and human communities practiced disciplined restraint out of care and reverence for the earth. Imagine a rich diversity of people and planet solving conflicts of need with mutually beneficial processes and mutually beneficial outcomes. Imagine if power in human relations and human–nature relations was wielded with courtesy, dignity, and respect for all living creatures. Imagine a world where sharing and caring are norms and where violence, domination, and exclusion were considered unimaginable. Reflecting on John Lennon's hopes and dreams in his quintessential song *Imagine* (Solt, Egan, & Ono, 1988), how do we envision and live in a diverse world--as one?

What kind of education would create such a world? What knowledge, values, behaviors, types of awareness, and sensitivities would be necessary to cultivate the conditions of a vibrant, sustainable peace? What would educational processes look and feel like? Where would education take place? How would learners relate to one another? What would the education of future teachers, educational leaders, and university faculty look like in such a world? This chapter focuses on the confluence of aims of fellow travellers--holistic education, sustainability education, and peace education; it also encourages more dialogue and cross-pollination among these important educational sub-fields.

Edward J. Brantmeier

Confluence of Aims: Holistic, Sustainability, and Peace Education

Holistic education addresses fragmentation and disconnection of modern, technologically mediated human life (Miller, 2007). Sustainability education addresses the threat to the planetary life support system for the human species (Nolet & Wheeler, 2010). Peace education addresses various forms of violence and provides solutions to alleviate those forms of violence (Harris & Morrison, 2003). Examining the aims of these subfields in education will shed light on their confluence and also reveal divergent approaches to ensuring quality of life for the human species during our tenure on earth and also for planetary well-being for the long haul.

Realities of climate disruption, mass migration, violent extremism, militarized aggression, and dominator leadership styles quickly sour an idyllic portrait of sustainable peace as a viable possibility for the future of humanity on planet earth. Yet hope remains for those who believe in the power of education to transform our world. Holistic education, sustainability education, and peace education seem to derive their strength and inspiration from a common source—the aim to create a connected, peaceful world where all—plants, animals, people—can live and prosper with relative health and well-being. These educational subfields have different branches, given that they address various challenges that we encounter as a human species, yet they grow from a common tree.

Holistic Education Aims

What are the aims of education, or, to say it differently, what are the aspirational purposes of education? An aim is "a purpose or intention; a desired outcome" (see Oxford English Living Dictionaries, n.d.). For example, holistic education is rooted in balance, inclusion, connection, and dynamism and has a spiritual quality that enhances integrated learning of the head, hand, and heart (Miller, 2010). The aims of holistic education are integration and connection--connection with self, other, community, the natural world, and the transrational. Ron Miller (2000) elaborates:

> Holistic education is based on the premise that each person finds identity, meaning, and purpose in life through connections to the community, to the natural world, and to spiritual values such as compassion and peace. Holistic education aims to call forth from people an intrinsic reverence for life and a passionate love of learning.
>
> *(Miller, 2000, para 2)*

Holistic education, then, aims to cultivate this reverence for life and it aims to kindle the flames of the love of learning. It attempts to heal fragmented, decontextualized, robotic forms of human learning that have threatened impassioned inquiry in our pursuits to make sense and meaning of an amazingly complex, simple, and elegant existence. Holistic education cultivates wisdom and equanimity—greatness of mind and kindness of heart.

Wisdom-based learning, rooted in systems thinking, seems imperative to move toward a sustainable future. Miller (2007) maintains "holistic education attempts to bring education into alignment with the fundamentals of nature. Nature at its core is interrelated and dynamic. We can see this dynamism and connectedness in the atom, organic systems, the biosphere, and the universe itself" (p. 3). Clearly, holistic education approaches were heavily influenced by systems thinking (Capra, 1996, as cited in Miller, 2007), rooted in new approaches in organistic biology, gestalt psychology, and ecology that examine networks, nodes, ". . . connectedness, relationships, [and] context" (as cited in Miller, 2007, p. 37). Holistic curriculum focuses on connections and relationship (Miller 2008). Miller (2010) further elaborates that students need ". . . to see their relationships to earth and its processes by reading Indigenous literature and by having direct earth experiences at school – such as gardening projects" (p. 266).

Holistic education draws on the power of direct connection and relationship. The simplicity and complexity of interdependence are radical and necessary concepts and embodied practices to teach in a compartmentalized world. Getting one's hands dirty is sometimes required. Holistic education can be considered an antidote to disconnection from place, fragmentation, violence, and unsustainability. An earth connections curriculum would focus on how our fate and the fate of planet are intimately tied, and how the self is intertwined with ecosystems and place.

My own work toward a critical peace education for sustainability draws from holistic education and the work of John P. Miller in efforts to design practical and deep learning experiences rooted in earth connections (Brantmeier, 2013). This work focuses on de-constructing domination in relationships—relationships people have with one another and relationships people have with planet earth. At its core, this critical peace education for sustainability approach aligns solidly with the aims of holistic education and has considerable confluence with sustainability education.

Sustainability Education Aims

Sustainability education aims to create positive outcomes through life-enhancing processes— process and outcome are critical. Sustainability education is education "about" sustainability. How can we do things differently as a species to promote current and future prosperity for people and the planet? Learning directly about unsustainable energy practices (think finite fossil fuels such as coal and gas) and renewable energy practices (think hydro, solar, and wind energy) could be the foci of sustainability education (Boyle, 2012; Shere, 2013). Current iterations of education for sustainable development focus on education about, and concern for, whether people of the future are able to meet their basic sustenance needs. Are we considering, with our present choices and actions, the health and well-being of people seven generations into the future and their ability to meet their material needs and to be happy? Education for sustainability focuses on the three E's: environment, the economy, and equity. According to the National Action Plan for Educating for Sustainability (2014), the outcomes are healthy ecosystems, vibrant economies, and equitable social systems.

When people (social equity), planet (healthy ecosystems), and profit (viable economies) are part of the process and content of transformative learning, ideal futures can be achieved—so the assumption goes. It is important to note that "deep sustainability" places priority on ecosystems first, then society, and last, economy (Ikerd, Gamble, & Cox, 2014). Deep sustainability is linked to "deep ecology," which is an approach that advocates a "widening of the self" in a radical, inclusive shift of human perception and behavior in collaboration with the natural world. Deep ecology assumes that ecosystems and the biological organisms within have an inherent right to live and prosper (Naess, 1995).

Focusing on the educational process is important. Education *for* sustainability focuses on educational process and the outcomes from those processes (Nolet & Wheeler, 2010). The Cloud Institute for Sustainability Education conveys: "Education for sustainability is defined as transformative learning processes that equips students, teachers, and school systems with new knowledge and responsible citizenship while restoring health and living systems upon which our lives depend" (see The Cloud Institute of Sustainability Education, n.d.). Education for Sustainable Development, a macro United Nations initiative aimed at promoting conscious, intentional development processes, ". . . empowers people to change the way they think and work towards a sustainable future" (see Education for Sustainable Development, n.d.). The purpose of sustainability education is a *process* of transformational change focused on knowledge and civic engagement in individuals and systems with an end goal in mind—healthy, living ecosystems. The important point to remember is that the process of education is just as important as the outcomes in this approach. Sustainable, transformative learning processes can result in sustainable outcomes—so the logic goes. Referred to by some as the "triple bottom line" of people, planet, and profit, the outcomes of education for sustainability would be vibrant economies, healthy environments, and equitable societies (Nolet & Wheeler, 2010).

Not dissimilar from the aims of holistic education, education for sustainability focuses on interdependence and real world challenges. Words that demonstrate the confluence are emphasized in the quote below:

> Education for Sustainability (EfS) is an approach to teaching and learning that addresses *interconnectedness*. It focuses particularly on the interdependence of ecological, social, and economic systems. . . . EfS implies learning that is focused on *authentic problems, personal behaviors, and decision-making* in complex, ill-structured problem spaces.
>
> *(Nolet & Wheeler, 2010, p. 1, my italics)*

Systems thinking, interdependence, and focusing on solutions to "wicked problems" (Rittel & Webber, 1973) become the heart of purposeful, relevant, and meaningful learning in education for sustainability. Movement toward connections, solutions to complex problems, and integrated learning experiences are part of the approach and aims.

Critical Approaches in Sustainability Education

In addition to defining education for sustainability with positive, generative definitions and approaches, critical approaches to sustainability and environmental education deconstruct the dynamics of power, oppression, and privilege by focusing on ecological and social justice. For example, Bowers (2001) urges for an ecological justice approach that aims to: understand domination and oppression, alleviate environmental racism, revitalize traditional ecological practices, and live sustainably with nature. This critical approach deconstructs dominant and subordinate relationships to expose injustice in all of its forms, including "cultural and structural violence"—though critical sustainability and environmental scholars typically do not draw on the these theoretical constructs from more rigorous forms of peace theory and peace education approaches (Galtung, 1969, 1988).

Critical scholars deconstruct existing realities for the purpose of transformative change, yet the difficult work of putting the pieces of critique back together and finding solutions remains a challenge. A new vision for the future is required, drawing on time-honored wisdom traditions and practices of the past. McNenny and Osborn (2015) provide a sustainable futures approach that deconstructs unsustainable practices and instills hope and gratitude:

> Replacing the dreams of endless affluence filled with non-stop consumption will be challenging. Imagining a sustainable future calls for a vision of ourselves in relationship to each other and the world in new ways—restrained in our consumption, respectful in our use of resources, taking on the role of steward but also of worshipper of the world's great gifts to us.
>
> *(pp. 20–21)*

In ideal form, education for sustainability would aim to question, transform, and actualize a positive future where both humans and natural world can "live and let live" through a "widening of the self" (Naess, 1995, p. 226).

Peace Education Aims

Peace education can be understood as education for the elimination of direct and indirect forms of violence (Harris & Morrison, 2003). The distinction between positive peace and negative peace are well known and used in the field of peace education and peace studies (Galtung, 1969). Negative peace is the absence of direct forms of violence such as war, racially motivated hate crime, or domestic violence. Positive peace is a condition where attitudes, dispositions, and behaviors are actively cultivated to sustain peace and prevent violence from occurring or re-occurring. Brantmeier and Lin (2008) maintain "Education for peace can generate new knowledge paradigms, connective relationships, institutional processes, and social structures" (p. xiv). This systems approach acknowledges that sustainable peace starts in the hearts and minds, permeates relationships, influences policy and procedures of institutions, and is woven in the fabric of social structures and how power operates within those structures. In a systems approach to sustainable peace, inner peace is paramount and the starting ground.

Clearly, cultivating inner peace is not enough; engaged action toward change is necessary. Brantmeier and Bajaj (2013) maintain:

> Peace education is generally defined as educational policy, planning, pedagogy, and practice that can provide learners—in any setting—with the skills and values to work towards comprehensive peace (Reardon, 1988). The areas of human rights education, development education, environmental education, disarmament education, and conflict resolution education are often included in a broader understanding of the multifaceted approaches to peace education.
>
> *(p. 139)*

An inclusive aim of peace education focuses on universal human rights and values (Brantmeier & Bajaj, 2013). So, peace education simultaneously focuses on human rights generally, and the various forms of violence within particular, historicized contexts. Critical approaches in peace education assume that without systemic analysis of power, oppression, and privilege at the local level, efforts toward actualizing sustainable peace are shallow in their transformative potential. Situating peace education efforts in the context of alleviating structural and cultural violence of a particular place, community, or society deepens theory and practice.

Johan Galtung (1969), a pioneer in the field of peace studies, explores the nuances of structural violence, "The violence is built into the structure and shows up as unequal power and consequently as unequal life chances . . . Above all, the power to decide over the distribution of resources is unevenly distributed" (p. 171). Chance, access, opportunity, and power are limited to some and readily available to others in conditions where structural and cultural violence permeate daily collective life. Galtung (1990) elaborates on how group norms can sustain conditions of violence, "Cultural violence makes direct and structural violence look, even feel, right – or at least not wrong" (p. 291). Cultural violence, put simply, is violence that is in the water or air of cultural groups; in time, this sort of violence becomes unquestioned, accepted, and saturates everyday experience and perception. For example, it is *Okay to* detain illegal immigrants in jails. It is *Okay* that people of color and people from low socio-economic backgrounds are disproportionately incarcerated and more often live in close proximity to U.S. Environmental Protection Agency designated toxic waste dumps. It is *Okay* to unnecessarily pollute the air or water for profit. Clearly, cultural violence is a tricky bit and requires questioning common group norms, cultural assumptions, and practices as well as deconstructing the legitimizing myths (Sidanius, Devereux, & Pratto, 1992) that justify inequality and social dominance.

Various theoretical strands and approaches in the field of peace education align well with the connective and integrative aims and practices of holistic education. For example, critical peace education aims to deconstruct power and find peaceable solutions within local contexts (Bajaj & Brantmeier, 2011). Bajaj (2015) elaborates:

> Critical peace educators emphasize that anchoring the learning process in local meanings and realities offers the best way of enabling student agency, democratic participation, and social action as a necessary outcome of the peace education endeavor. Further, critical peace educators hold that teachers must engage in critical self-reflection about their positionality and role in the educational process.
>
> *(p. 155)*

Critical peace education for sustainability aims to deconstruct and reconstruct power dynamics in learning processes and aims to reconnect people with the natural ecosystems from which they derive strength and sustenance (Brantmeier, 2013). This approach focuses on the economic, environmental, and social systems within a UNESCO education for sustainable development framework that comprises the opportunities and barriers to generating a fluid, vibrant, and sustainable peace. Related, The Earth Charter (2001), a foundational framework for integrating peace, ecology, and social justice is a visionary beacon of light and hope. Peace education for/as sustainability situates the planet and human survival at the fore of educational aims.

Inspired by Miller (2010) and Gruenewald (2003), I have focused my educational theory and practice in critical peace education for sustainability on examining power and connections to ecological place. In a "critical pedagogy of place," Gruenewald (2003) provides emancipatory solutions of reinhabitation and decolonization. Gruenewald elaborates:

> A critical pedagogy of place aims to (a) identify, recover, and create material spaces and places that teach us how to live well in our total environments (reinhabitation); and (b) identify and change ways of thinking that injure and exploit other people and places (decolonization).
>
> *(Gruenewald, 2003, p. 9)*

How do we connect our students and each other with our local ecological communities and with global planetary communities? How do we decolonize our minds and relationships and develop inner and relational sustainable energy? We create transformative learning opportunities.

Over the past few years, I have been developing a theory of sustainable peace that flows from my earlier academic work (Brantmeier, 2007). It begins with the cultivation of inner sustainable energy. The assumption in this theory is that we need to cultivate inner sustainable energy for the long haul in work that involves understanding and challenging human suffering, ignorance, and general shortcomings. How do we stay positive amid the daunting problems of our time: hatred, ignorance, greed, militarized aggression, climate change and denial, racially motivated hate crime, sexual violence, standardized knowledge and testing regime dominance, and consolidated wealth and power—to name only a few. Cultivating sustainable inner energy to endure the slings and arrows of time and present human–planetary realities requires commitment and practice. Contemplative practices are one way to cultivate inner sustainable energy and peace both at home and at work (Miller, 2014). Positive inner sustainable energy creates the potential for positive interpersonal relations—the

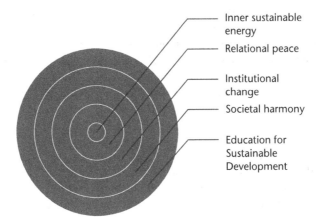

Figure 9.1 Theory of Sustainable Peace for the Planet

next layer of the theory of sustainable peace for the planet. When interpersonal relationships are harmonious, we gather the courage and foundation to promote institutional change in the context of our professional roles and relationships. Those of us in positions of power can influence the policy and procedures that promote violence (direct or indirect), fragmentation, isolation, exploitation, or abuse. Inner peace and sustainable energy, relational peace, and institutional change can help create conditions of societal harmony. Societal harmony is a condition of equity and equality among various individuals and groups of people within a broader social system. Circumscribing the individual and potentials for peace are economic, political, socio-cultural, and environmental systems that influence all layers of the theory of sustainable energy. In this sense, there should be lines radiating outward from inner peace and inward toward inner peace that represent the mutual and bi-directional influence of the layers of this theory of sustainable peace; inner peace is connected to macro-economic structures, for example.

Reflections on Teacher Education and Educational Leadership Preparation

The work of teacher education and educational leadership preparation is premised on the multiplier effect, that is, if we positively influence teacherleaders and administrators in K-12 schools, that influence, in turn, creates nourishing environments for children to learn and to grow. We multiply positive influence and impact by caring for, and working alongside, those who are direct practitioners in schools. Even teachers need teachers and co-teachers and even leaders need co-leaders and critical friends to help guide their work in a process of lifelong learning and discovery. Yet so many negative systems influence the impact, the aims and higher purposes of holism, sustainability, and peace in teacher education and in higher education in general.

Macro-economic, political, environmental, and socio-cultural influences create significant pressure and demand on schooling systems and this often results in stress, conformity, and the potential for dismal and robotic learning. Rather than discovery, emergent, elicitive, or holistic approaches to learning, the demands of progressively higher tests scores in the positivist, utility-focused areas of math and reading narrow the focus of learning in public K-12 schools.

It is within the context of outcomes-based learning that *higher* purposes of learning, such as holism, sustainability, and peace, battle for space within the scope and sequence of an already congested curriculum. Yet try we must. Fragmentation, environmental destruction, and violence in many forms threaten future generations of the human species' ability to meet basic sustenance needs, making the work toward holism, sustainability, and peace all the more important in our times.

In order to achieve the lofty United Nations Sustainable Development Goals, Nolet (2015) advocates for learner-centered pedagogies in teacher education programs, not content or teacher centered approaches. Within an "Education for Sustainable Development" framework, Nolet advocates for the aims of "all children [having] access to high quality, relevant, and equitable educational opportunities" and of "all learners [having] opportunities to develop and act a sustainability worldview" (pp. 56–57). He maintains that education that supports the development of a sustainability worldview ". . . is a thoughtful and skillful way of being in the world that is positive, life affirming, future oriented, and solutions-focused" (Nolet, 2015, p. 47). He continues, ". . . a sustainability worldview is a holistic phenomenon that involves a combination of values, knowledge, dispositions, and agency" (p. 47). I contend that integrating a sustainability worldview should be a priority writ large in higher education. Efforts at incorporating a sustainability worldview in content and pedagogy through university faculty development have shown promise and positive outcomes, especially when transformative and engaged approaches are actualized (Hurney, Nash, Hartman, & Brantmeier, 2016).

Sustainability big ideas are identified and these big ideas align nicely with the aims and purposes of holistic education and critical approaches to peace education: "equity and justice; peace and collaboration; universal responsibility; health and resiliency; respect for limits; connecting with nature; local and global; and interconnectedness" (Nolet, 2015, p. 49). The argument is made that teacher education programs should include these big ideas, and also in their courses and everyday practices in hopes that this knowledge and these values permeate global societies (Nolet, 2015). Lofty pursuits? Yes indeed. However, significant barriers exist.

In my own United States based work in Colleges of Education in Indiana, Missouri, Colorado, and Virginia over the past fifteen years, I have tried to actualize the aims of holism, sustainability, and peace in teacher education and educational leadership preparation. Over the years, I have additively included units of study on holistic education, sustainability education, and peace education in the context of teaching undergraduate and graduate level foundations courses. Deeper, more inclusive integration of holism and peace is more difficult. Yet, a significant number of my students have found meaning and direction from reading and applying core aims and approaches in articles or book chapters on holistic, sustainability, and peace education (Dalai Llama, 1999; Harris, 1999; Miller, 2010; Nolet, 2015; Reardon, 1988).

In talks on the topic of critical peace education for sustainability in the United States and the UK, I have argued for slowing down, humility, and aligning money with values. Slowing down is a revolutionary act. If we slow down, we can see the connections between and among seemingly fragmented needs, occurrences, and ways of being in the world. Consuming good, clean, fair food is one way (Slow Food, n.d.). Humility is a natural result of recognizing connections and the interdependence of all life. From this ontological position of interdependence, wonder, reverence for life, compassion, and nonviolence can be cultivated. Gandhi (1924) maintained, "The rock bottom foundation of the technique for achieving the power of nonviolence is belief in the essential oneness of all life" (p. 390). Nonviolence becomes the practice, process, and outcomes of learning if interdependence and connection are held in sacred trust. Finally, aligning our money with our values is necessary to curb unjust, unsustainable, and violent economic practices and systems and is an important everyday, revolutionary act. Klein (2014) maintains that the current economic model in place is at war with life, and, in particular, human life on planet earth. Mindful, everyday economic choices can help to alleviate destruction of the human species and the beautiful ecosystems on which our sustenance depends.

At times, holistic, sustainability, and peace education can seem counter-cultural in the United States and other countries elsewhere on the planet. Our everyday acts may seem insignificant amid larger political, economic, and socio-cultural forces that aim to create walls and amass fortresses of power and privilege in opposition to the majority of people and to the health of the planet. I grow depressed and weary some days—it's true. Yet, by cultivating inner sustainable energy through contemplative practice and rippling that peace, connection, and care outward into relationships, professional roles, society, and the wider world, there is hope. When I hold the hand of our five-year-old by a pond, listen to the wind amid the pines, or watch a sunset over the Appalachian Mountains and deeply listen to their enduring wisdom, I find hope and energy to continue the struggle toward healing and connection, for the seventh generation, the yet-to-be-born children of the future. I find hope and inspiration in contemplating and then trying to live the definition of sustainable peace generated by undergraduate students in my Inclusive Leadership for Sustainable Peace course in the spring of 2017:

> Sustainable peace is a state of global relationships where individuals, groups, and societies are enabled to be fully happy and well. A shared curiosity and understanding of diversity works to alleviate suffering by creating nonviolent and fair relations between and within communities of all sizes, the largest being the planetary community. Sustainable peace is both the process and the end goal.
>
> *(Brantmeier et al., 2017, para 4)*

References

Bajaj, M. (2015). Pedagogies of resistance' and critical peace education praxis. *Journal of Peace Education*, *12*(2), 154–166.

Bajaj, M. & Brantmeier, E. J. (Eds). (2011). The politics, praxis, and possibilities of critical peace education. *Journal of Peace Education*, *8*(3), 221–224.

Bowers, C. A. (2001). *Educating for eco-justice and community*. Athens: University of Georgia Press.

Boyle, G. (2012). *Renewable energy: Power for a sustainable future* (3rd edn). Oxford, UK: Oxford University Press.

Brantmeier, E. J. (2007). Connecting inner and outer peace: Buddhist meditation integrated with peace education. *Infactis Pax*, *1*(2), 120–157. Retrieved from www.infactispax.org/journal/.

Brantmeier, E. J. (2013). Toward critical peace education for sustainability. *Journal of Peace Education*, *10*(3), 242–258.

Brantmeier, E. J. (2017). Theory of sustainable energy. *Presented in interactive lecture entitled, Sustainable Peace Leaders*. February, 1. James Madison University.

Brantmeier, E. J. & Bajaj, M. (2013). Peace education praxis. In S. Totten & J. Pederson (Eds), *Educating about social issues in the 20th and 21st centuries* (pp. 139–159). Charlotte, NC: Information Age.

Brantmeier, E. J. & Lin, J. (2008). Introduction: Toward Forging a Positive, Transformative Paradigm for Peace Education. In J. Lin, E. Brantmeier, & C. Bruhn (Eds), *Transforming education for peace* (pp. xiii–xviii). Greenwich, CT: Information Age.

Brantmeier, E. J., Gormley, C. M., Gray, M., Minnick, A., Mirambel, J., Morrison, A. . . . Adhikari, B. (2017). Learning for inclusive leadership for sustainable peace. *Global Campaign for Peace Education Newsletter*, 3/1/2017. Retrieved from www.peace-ed-campaign.org/inclusive_leadership/.

Dalai Lama (1999). Education and the human heart. In S. Glazer (Ed.), *The heart of learning: Spirituality in education* (pp. 85–95). New York: Penguin.

Education for Sustainable Development. (n.d.). Retrieved from http://en.unesco.org/themes/educationsustainable-development.

Galtung, J. (1969). Violence, peace and peace research. *Journal of Peace Research*, *3*, 167–192.

Galtung, J. (1988). *Peace and social structure: Essays in peace research*. Copenhagen: Christian Eljers.

Galtung, J. (1990). Cultural violence. *Journal of Peace Research*, *27*(3), 291–305.

Gandhi, M. K. (1924). Young India. Collected works. Retrieved from www.gandhiashramsevagram.org/gandhi-literature/mahatma-gandhi-collected-works-volume-25.pdf.

Gruenewald, D. A. (2003). The best of both worlds: A critical pedagogy of place. *Educational Researcher*, *32*(4), 3–12.

Harris, I. M. (1999). Types of peace education. In A. Raviv, L. Oppenheimer, & D. Bar-Tal (Eds), *How children understand war & peace* (pp. 299–310). San Francisco, CA: Jossey-Bass.

Harris, I. M. & Morrison, M. L. (2003). *Peace education* (2nd edn). Jefferson, NC: McFarland.

Hurney, C. A., Nash, C. B., Hartman, C. J., & Brantmeier, E. J. (2016). Incorporating sustainability content and pedagogy through faculty development. *International Journal of Sustainability in Higher Education*, *17*(5), 582–586. 00. https://doi.org/10.1108/IJSHE-12–2 014–0 180.

Ikerd, J., Gamble, L., & Cox, T. (2014). Deep sustainability: The essentials. Retrived from https://saludos.sites.google.com/site/sustainabilitydeep/.

Klein, N. (2014). *This changes everything: Capitalism vs. the climate*. New York: Simon and Schuster.

McNenny, G. & Osborn, J. (2015). Discourses of hope in sustainability education: A critical analysis of sustainability advocacy. *Journal of Sustainability Education*, *10*, 1–27. Retrieved from www.jsedimensions.org/wordpress/content/discourses-of-hope-in-sustainability-education-a-critical-analysis-of-sustainability-advocacy_2015_12/, on 8/8/17.

Miller, J. P. (2007). *The holistic curriculum* (2nd edn). Toronto, Canada: University of Toronto Press.

Miller, J. P. (2010). Educating for wisdom. In E. J. Brantmeier, J. Lin, & J. Miller (Eds), *Spirituality, religion, and peace education* (pp. 261–275). Charlotte, NC: Information Age.

Miller, J. P. (2014). *The contemplative practitioner: Meditation in education and the workplace*. Toronto, Canada: University of Toronto Press.

Miller, R. (2000). A brief introduction to holistic education. *The encyclopedia of informal education*. Retrieved from http://infed.org/mobi/a-brief-introduction-to-holistic-education/.

Naess, A. (1995). Self realization: An ecological approach to being in the world. In G. Sessions (Ed.), *Deep ecology for the 21st century: Readings on the philosophy and practice of the new environmentalism* (pp. 225–239). Boston, MA: Shambhala.

National Action Plan for Educating for Sustainability (2014). Center for Green Schools. Retrieved from www.centerforgreenschools.org/sites/default/files/resource-files/National-ActionPlan-Educating-Sustainability.pdf, on 8/8/17.

Nolet, V. (2015). Powerful pedagogies that promote a sustainability worldview. The Third Asia Pacific Expert Meetings on Education for Sustainable Development. June 2–5.

Nolet, V. & Wheeler, G. (2010). Education for sustainability in Washington State: A whole systems approach. *Journal of Sustainability Education*, *1*(1), 321–326. Retrieved from www.susted.com/wordpress/content/edu cation-for-sustainability-in-washington-state-a-whole-systems-approach_2010_05/, on 8/8/17.

Oxford English Living Dictionaries (n.d.). Definition of aim. Retrieved from https://en.oxforddictionaries. com/definition/aim.

Reardon, B. R. (1988). *Comprehensive peace education: Education for global responsibility.* New York: Teachers College Press.

Rittel, H. W. J. & Webber, M. M. (1973). Dilemmas in a general theory of planning. *Policy Sciences*, *4*, 155–169.

Shere, J. (2013). *Renewable: The world-changing power of alternative energy.* New York: St. Martins Press.

Sidanius, J., Devereux, E., & Pratto, F. (1992). A comparison of symbolic racism theory and social dominance theory: Explanations for racial policy attitudes. *Journal of Social Psychology*, *132*, 377–395.

Slow Food USA (n.d.). Retrieved from www.slowfoodusa.org/publications.

Solt, A., Egan, S., & Ono, Y. (1988). *Imagine: John Lennon.* New York: Macmillan.

The Cloud Institute for Sustainability Education (n.d.). Brief history (n.d.). Retrieved from https://cloudinsti tute.org/brief-history.

The Earth Charter (2001). Retrieved from http://earthcharter.org/virtual-library2/the-earth-charter-text/.

Dedication

I dedicate this chapter to Estes David Brantmeier—may you live sustainably and enjoy life, my dear son. May you always find hope, sustenance, and abiding love in the rising and setting sun.

In addition, I dedicate this chapter to the future of MountainTop Learning Center near Sugar Grove, West Virginia—a place to connect, learn, live sustainably, and enjoy life. We all must dream, and then build a foundation under those dreams.

Acknowledgment

Deep gratitude for formatting work to Destin Webb—trusted research and teaching assistant. May your sustainability leadership capacities continue to grow and positively influence the planet.

10

CORE REFLECTION

Nurturing the Human Potential in Students and Teachers

Fred A. J. Korthagen and Ellen E. Nuijten

This chapter describes the core reflection approach, which is a practical approach to student and teacher learning, aiming at deep learning. The core reflection approach uses a holistic framework based on several theoretical foundations, such as positive psychology and theories on professional development. Greene described it beautifully in Kim and Greene (2011, p. 14):

> [Core reflection] is about the opportunity to be who you really are or really want to be. Some people might call it self-actualization. Some people might call it authenticity, some might call it flow, but I'm not sure it's any of those things exactly. I think it's about being human, being very natural in responses, and being very present.

The central goal of the core reflection approach is to overcome various habitual patterns in education that are counterproductive to deep learning and personal growth. The following example shows how small changes in habitual patterns in classrooms can make a significant difference:

> Peter is six years old. He loves making buildings with wooden blocks, and he is very interested in technical pictures that he sees in his encyclopedia for children. He looks forward to entering grade 1 in a Dutch school for primary education, as he expects that things will now really become interesting.
>
> However, during his first weeks in grade 1, Peter does not like what he has to do. He gets classroom handouts dealing with small words such as dog, bed, and so forth. This does not really interest him. After two weeks, he no longer wants to go to school, but, of course, he has to.
>
> After a month, Peter's parents receive a 'progress report' from the school. It describes many concerns about Peter, shows the word backlog three times, and does not contain any positive remarks. Peter's parents wonder if Peter may have an awareness of how the teacher perceives him and whether this might influence him. After a talk between the teacher and the parents, the teacher changes her behavior. She now starts to mention Peter's qualities to him and allows him to work more at his own level and pace.

The effect is surprising: within a week, Peter starts to like school again. He shows more self-assurance and more cooperative behavior in the classroom.

Three patterns surface in this example and can be observed in many traditional educational settings. We will now discuss these patterns.

The first pattern that often occurs in traditional education is *an emphasis on the cognitive side of learning* (Hoekstra, 2007). At all levels of education, academic standards promote a focus on cognitive abilities. Although there is nothing wrong with developing cognition, this one-sided focus tends to lead to a certain imbalance. It is often overlooked that including the affective and motivational dimensions in learning and professional growth leads to more positive outcomes, including academic outcomes (Durlak et al., 2011).

Second, relatively more *emphasis is put on what goes wrong* and on what should be improved than on what goes well. When we ask teachers or school principals whether they find it important to emphasize what goes well, they generally say that they give this much attention. However, reality is often different. A common situation is that a teacher says to a student: "Well done, but . . ." In such cases, it is not at all clear for the student *what* was done well. In addition, from psychology we know that there is a tendency in people to remember the part that comes after "but". This is the *negativity bias* (Cacioppo, Gardner, & Berntson, 1997). Therefore, as Voerman et al. (2014) emphasized, the "well done" type of feedback is not very beneficial to learning.

Third, if teachers or school principals do mention positive aspects, they tend to *focus on behavior* ("you did it well") and not on the person ("you are a creative person"). We call this a tendency to focus on the *outer side* of observable behavior instead of the *inner side* of personal strengths. We can see the same tendency when they coach people on problematic issues. In such situations, they will typically look for a solution in terms of a behavioral change (what to do) rather than for people's personal strengths and inner obstacles that block the enactment of these strengths. This means that the personal guidance of students and teachers generally remains somewhat superficial.

Core reflection is an approach that aims at changing these three patterns. This approach benefits teaching and learning situations in classrooms, as well as individual student learning. Core reflection makes a significant impact on the professional development of teachers.

Theoretical framework

In this section, we will discuss three underlying theoretical principles of core reflection.

Principle 1: Combining Thinking, Feeling, and Wanting

For deep learning that really influences behavior, the emotional and motivational aspects of learning need sufficient attention (Durlak et al., 2011). This view is supported by brain research showing the strong interconnection between the cognitive and affective processes in people (Immordino-Yang & Damasio, 2007). Attention to the motivational dimension of learning means taking the needs and ideals of learners into account, that is, what *they want* (Deci & Ryan, 2002). This is crucial for keeping the love for learning alive (Miller, 1997). Shifting the attention between thinking, feeling, and wanting generates more 'inner movement' and energy (*flow*) in the person (Korthagen, Attema-Noordewier, & Zwart, 2014).

The term we use for moving between these three dimensions of thinking, feeling, and wanting is *using the elevator*. This is a metaphorical way of looking at the three dimensions, namely as being located on three 'floors' of human functioning (see Figure 10.1).

Hence a concrete guideline for enhancing core reflection is to deepen learning using the elevator, which means focusing on thinking, feeling, and wanting.

Principle 2: A Focus on Qualities and Ideals

Generally, teaching or coaching situations lack depth if the focus remains primarily on a problem or on the search for a solution. Of course, problems that students and teachers experience should

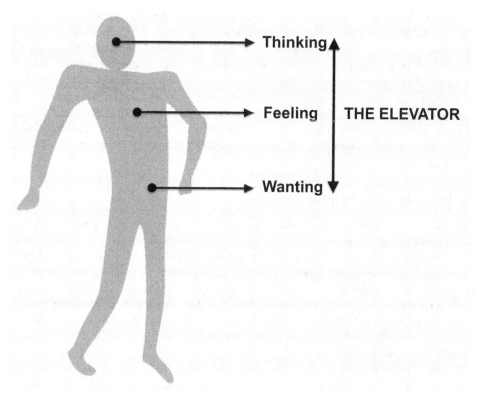

Figure 10.1   The elevator

be taken seriously, but a risk occurs when too strong of a focus on a problem creates negative feelings in them, which in turn narrow the cognitive and behavioral repertoire (Fredrickson, 2009). Moreover, someone experiencing a problem tends to think within the framework of this problem and does not develop a sense of strength. This often leads to a rather superficial solution to the problem, as it is not grounded in the person's inner potential. As a result, the problem will generally return (Scharmer, 2007).

Thus, positive psychology emphasizes the importance of building on positive experiences (Fredrickson, 2009). One way to do this is by shifting the attention from people's problems and deficiencies to their *strengths* (Seligman & Csikszentmihalyi, 2000). There is considerable research evidence that this makes people more creative, motivated, and effective (Fredrickson, 2009).

The implication is that a teacher or someone coaching a person (whether this person is a child or adult) should pay sufficient attention to what *went well* and less to what went wrong. More specifically, giving positive feedback is important, preferably by naming personal qualities, which we call *core qualities*. Examples of such core qualities are goal-directedness, clarity, courage, flexibility, preciseness, and creativity. Although researchers have defined certain categories of such qualities, the list of possible core qualities is almost endless. The notion of core qualities is closely connected to the classical concept of *virtues* (Peterson & Seligman, 2004). In Greek philosophy, a virtue was related to doing 'the good' and hence the term has a strong moral dimension. Aristotle, for example, related virtues to excellence at being human, which for him meant living life well and beautifully (Aristotle, 1975).

Giving feedback about core qualities ("you show the quality of preciseness, wonderful!") is fundamentally different from a compliment such as "well done" and more beneficial to learning (Voerman et al., 2014). Deep learning is promoted if the learner is stimulated to consciously use the core qualities in various circumstances (Seligman et al., 2005). Placing emphasis on *wanting* (and hence on *ideals*) is another way of creating positive feelings. Doing so brings people more into touch with their strengths than an orientation toward problems. In the end, the life-long process of building on one's ideals and developing one's core qualities is crucial for self-actualization.

Hence, a second concrete guideline is the following: Emphasize successes and devote less attention to what went wrong. Combine this with creating positive feelings by naming core qualities and building on ideals.

Principle 3: Attention to Inner Obstacles

Currently, there are various approaches that give attention to strengths, personal qualities, and talents; this is a development strongly enhanced by positive psychology. The focus shifts from deficiencies toward personal strengths, which generally creates positive feelings. However, this is often only a short-term effect. Therefore, it is important to also give attention to obstacles limiting the person's strength, specifically *inner obstacles*. This differs from a focus on the external problem. Inner obstacles are obstacles within the person that prevent core qualities and ideals from impacting behavior. A crucial aspect is to not only think about the obstacle, but most of all to *feel* its negative effect and to connect with the *will* to no longer go along with the limiting pattern (again the elevator movement). We call this *mindfulness-in-action*.

Therefore, the third concrete guideline is as follows: After core qualities and ideals have received attention and (most importantly!) have been felt, it is also important to focus on (an) internal obstacle(s) that are limiting the power of these core qualities and ideals in concrete situations. It is helpful if people become aware of an inner obstacle and its influence in the here and now.

The Core Reflection Process

Based on the three principles discussed above, a new perspective on learning and coaching emerges. The model in Figure 10.2 summarizes the core reflection approach by showing the intended process.

The three principles support this process. While the principles may seem evident, it is not always easy for people to use them, as this often requires changing habitual patterns that are common in our society. Such collective patterns are not easy to unlearn. In other words, for many people, the three principles require the expansion of one's comfort zone and some training under the guidance of an experienced coach.

The Onion Model

To work with the core reflection approach, it is important to understand the onion model (Korthagen, 2004). Figure 10.3 shows this model, describing various levels (layers) in the learning that play a role during core reflection.

The levels of the onion model are as follows:

1. *Environment.* This level refers to the context the person encounters.
2. *Behavior.* This refers to what the person does in relation to the environment, which is often determined by habitual patterns.
3. *Competencies.* This level is about what someone is competent to do. It encompasses knowledge and skills.

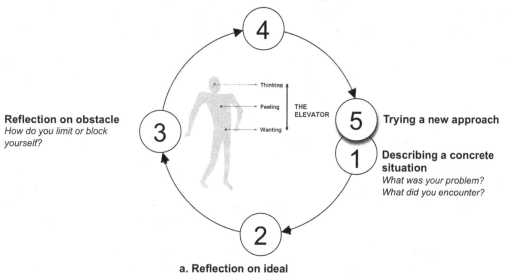

Figure 10.2 The five-step model of core reflection

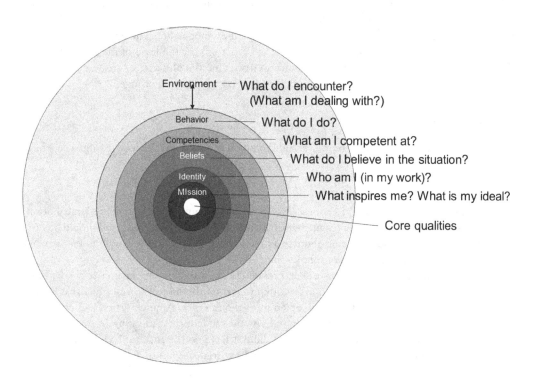

Figure 10.3 The model of levels in learning (onion model)

4. *Beliefs*. This level refers to beliefs or assumptions the person has about the situation and the environment, which are often unconscious.
5. *Identity*. This level refers to a person's assumptions or beliefs about themselves, their self-concept, and the role they see for themselves in the given environment. For teachers, this level concerns their professional identity.
6. *Mission*. This transpersonal level is about what inspires the person, what gives meaning and significance to life (or work). The level of mission is about *ideals* and important *values* and influences one's self-concept (identity).
7. *The core*. This final level concerns the person's core qualities.

A basic principle underlying core reflection is that if these levels are in harmony with each other (*alignment*), the person can act on the basis of the inner potential of core qualities and ideals. This has both a strong effect on the environment and leads to a sense of fulfillment and flow in the person. On the other hand, if someone encounters a problem, this means that there is friction between one or more levels of the onion model, creating an obstacle that limits the person's inner potential (Korthagen, 2017). For example, Peter's beliefs and self-concept influenced his feelings about school, which blocked his core qualities.

With the aid of the onion model, we can understand why a focus on a problematic situation and on what to do in this situation leads to a superficial type of reflection. In the onion model, such a focus corresponds with the outer levels, whereas for deep learning it is important to include the inner levels. This was confirmed in a study by Hoekstra (2007), who showed that teachers' reflection focusing on what to do in particular situations (i.e., the outer levels of the onion model) did not contribute much to these teachers' professional development. Hoekstra showed that it is necessary for long-term professional growth to focus on deeper, underlying meanings.

A focus on the inner onion levels, in particular on core qualities and ideals, creates a deeper connection with the person's potential and helps him or her become aware of the inner obstacle limiting that potential. Such obstacles can exist at all levels of the onion model, but generally an inner obstacle stems from the level of beliefs (i.e., a belief about the situation), or the level of identity (a limiting belief about oneself). A person's conscious choice to overcome the obstacle restores the connection between the inner potential and behavior and creates deep and enduring change.

The Case of Lisa

We now illustrate the core reflection process and the onion model with an example from a coaching session with a teacher.

An example of a coaching session

Secondary school teacher Lisa's ideal (*level of mission*) is to value each student's contribution. She views each human being as having personal qualities that deserve respect and should be nurtured, so that each person can contribute to a better world. She considers herself to be a teacher who models this view in the classroom (*identity level*).

In a coaching session with a colleague, Lisa describes an unpleasant experience she had that morning. Two students had handed in a written report on the subject of volcanoes that looked so perfect that Lisa suspected it to be copied from the internet. A quick search had confirmed her suspicion. She felt cheated and when she saw the students that morning (*environment*), she reacted furiously (*behavior*). In retrospect, she did not feel good about this. She felt she was not respectful toward the students, but did not know how to deal with such a situation in a better way (*competency*).

Her colleague mentions core qualities she notices in the here and now: openness, honesty, and commitment to her work. She asks whether Lisa can feel the strength of these qualities inside her (*core qualities*). Immediately Lisa starts to feel better. This is visible in her face. The colleague asks how she felt about the situation with the two students. Lisa says she felt sad and uncertain. Her colleague shows empathy for these feelings. Next, she asks for Lisa's ideal in this situation (her *wanting*). Lisa says that she values care for other people and respectful relationships, in particular in educational situations (*mission*).

Now her colleague says: "I notice many qualities in you: openness, honesty, commitment, respect, and care. Can you feel what a strong teacher you are?! Now, what happened inside you so that you lost touch with these qualities and with your ideal of respectful relationships?"

Lisa becomes aware of the strong impact of her *belief* "I am being cheated". As soon as this belief took hold, she became angry. This stopped her from acting in line with her ideal. Now she feels she has a choice: either she can let herself be taken away by the belief, or she can take charge of herself and not act upon the belief, but upon her ideal. She now knows what to do. She wants to go to the students and apologize for her furious reaction. But she also wants to start a respectful conversation and ask the students to have more respect for her value of honesty.

The case of Lisa illustrates that the essence of the core reflection approach is to elicit a deeper process than merely a reflection on a problem and a search for a solution in behavioral terms. The colleague does not give a suggestion for new behavior, but uses Lisa's inner potential (her core qualities and her ideal) for helping her develop a new perspective and approach to the situation.

Looking at Figure 10.2, this example shows that from phase 1, phase 2a can be easily reached by using 'the elevator'. This is even easier and more motivating when reflecting on a success experience. It is interesting that when a person is in touch with an ideal (phase 2a), immediately core qualities become visible (phase 2b). The person may recognize such core qualities and name them, but sometimes a teacher or coach is needed to make the person aware of core qualities that surface in the here-and-now. This may further enhance the person's awareness of his or her inner potential.

Only after the person strongly feels his or her inner potential, as shown in phase 2, and flow is visible in his or her body language, is it fruitful to look for inner obstacles limiting the flow, which is represented by phase 3 (see Figure 10.2). Now the focus is not on 'solving the problem', but on feeling how one tends to block the energy of the inner potential in oneself. The effect of this process is often a different way of relating to the situation under reflection. Scharmer (2007) named this process *presencing*: the person *senses* his or her inner potential and becomes more *present* with this potential and mindful about the inner obstacle. Often, the person then suddenly knows what to do. This comes from a formerly suppressed inner knowing, which is strongly connected to the person's whole being. Moreover, the will to act upon the inner knowing is evoked (see Figure 10.2, phase 4). The new behavior resulting from this process is completely different from the outcome of a rational analysis of the problem and the search for a practical solution. It is a process that brings one's consciousness to the deeper levels of the onion model and uses the power of these levels to change one's relationship with the outside world. This is what we call *learning from within*.

Practice and Research

We now look at the implementation of the core reflection approach in various educational contexts. We will give examples from practice and summarize research studies.

Primary and Secondary Education

In primary and secondary education, core reflection is being implemented for the individual coaching of students and teachers and for supporting learning in groups of students. Through the coaching of individual students, there is more awareness of personal strengths and talents, which creates more motivation and flow in the learning processes. It is noteworthy that the phases of the core reflection model (Figure 10.2) can be also used in the coaching of children as young as 7 or 8 years old. Coaching children is often easier than coaching adults, who tend to have more fixed and complex inner obstacles and an inclination to focus on external obstacles. In young children, such obstacles are still relatively simple, such as "I am not good at arithmetic." From our experience, children can relatively quickly understand how they themselves create a self-fulfilling prophecy through such a belief, which creates breakthroughs in their learning.

There have also been instances in which teachers taught principles of core reflection to students in grades 5 and 6, who then used these principles among themselves; for example, 'moving the elevator' during collaborative work and naming each other's core qualities. For many educationalists, it is surprising to learn that primary school children taught these principles to student teachers who came into their classroom. We have even seen a group of 12-year-olds give workshops on core reflection to teachers and teacher educators.

In secondary education, core reflection was also found to be helpful for preparing groups of students for a test. A teacher can support the students in their awareness of individual core qualities and the negative thoughts limiting their potential. Students then become more consciously aware of how they prepare for and take a test, and how they can use their core qualities more optimally while doing this.

The coaching of teachers based on core reflection can strongly push their professional development forward, as we have seen in hundreds of cases. This was also documented by two research studies. In the first study, Hoekstra and Korthagen (2011) investigated the learning process of an experienced teacher in secondary education, named Nicole, who struggled with a national educational development toward more self-directed learning. She was coached six times, based on core reflection. The researchers used quantitative instruments to show statistically significant changes in the teacher's educational beliefs, measured before and after the coaching, and in her behavior, as scored by her students, again before and after the coaching. This study yielded evidence that a deep learning process had taken place.

In particular, through the coaching, Nicole discovered that she tended to block her own development through the limiting belief that her students should not feel insecure during her lessons. As soon as her students struggled with working more independently, she herself also became insecure, returned to her traditional style of didactic teaching, and tended to conclude that her ideal could not be reached. The coaching helped her realize that this was a second limiting belief. Nicole gradually learned to be more aware of the relation between the cognitive, emotional, and motivational aspects in herself *while teaching* (core reflection in-action). She also became more aware of the dimensions of thinking, feeling, and wanting in her students, and even started to guide them in dealing with their emotions, for example by using their core qualities. In this way Nicole developed a different view of the role of a teacher, that is, of her professional identity.

Looking at the coaching process, it was interesting that the focus was not so much on Nicole's question of *what to do* in the classroom (i.e., the onion layer of behavior), but on the inner levels: the coach helped her explore her *ideal* of promoting self-directed learning in her students and helpful *core qualities* in herself, and he supported her awareness of her own *limiting beliefs*. Most importantly, he helped Nicole learn how to use the elevator in reflection on herself and in the coaching of her students. The significant change in her teaching behavior was a natural outcome of this core reflection process.

In the second study, Attema-Noordewier, Korthagen, and Zwart (2013) measured the outcomes of a core reflection training of teams of teachers. In six primary schools, quantitative and qualitative instruments were used to establish these outcomes for both the teachers and their students. At the teacher level, reported outcomes were increased feelings of autonomy, increased self-efficacy regarding the coaching of both students and colleagues, extended coaching skills, new insights about learning, and increased awareness of core qualities in students, colleagues, and themselves. The research showed that professional learning had taken place at all levels in the onion model. This is called *multi-level learning*, which is a noteworthy result of the core reflection approach. At the student level, a growth in communication skills and attitudes was reported, but these outcomes were based on observations by the teachers (see also Zwart, Attema-Noordewier, & Korthagen, 2015).

Quotes from teachers (translated from Dutch) may further illustrate what happens in schools when core reflection is implemented:

- Core reflection made us go beyond teaching subject matter. It makes you feel as though you are contributing to students' lives.
- This makes relationships with students more relaxed, we now have more fun and we experience real contact. The result is more depth, in a pleasant way.
- I changed my entire way of thinking about teaching. It is now more about stressing the good things instead of looking for mistakes, which is a habit in education. This creates more outcomes with less energy.
- Working on this together, as a team, brings a great value and is much appreciated by the parents.
- There is more cohesion among the teachers—more sharing, support, and care.
- This is it. This should be used in all schools! Our results have gone up, there are no longer any problems with keeping order in the classroom, and the problem of bullying has disappeared.

What 12-year-old students said about the application of core reflection in class is noteworthy:

- Our group has become a whole.
- Children who were not so much part of the group before, have now become part of it because we now see their qualities.
- Learning has become much more fun. The learning now comes from within.
- I would like many people to come here and see this.

Teacher Education

In several countries, especially in the Netherlands and the United States, core reflection is being used in the professional preparation of teachers. It is a strong means to connect the professional and personal aspects of teacher development. In particular, it appears to help student teachers to use their core qualities in their teaching and realize their ideals. Adams, Kim, and Greene (2013) showed this in their study on the role of core reflection in the professional development of six beginning teachers at Southern Oregon University. These students faced many problems in their teaching and often felt overwhelmed and disillusioned. The authors showed that core reflection enhanced the use of core qualities in these teachers and led to new insights, self-understandings, and behaviors. As one of them put it: "I feel like if I fall now, I can pull myself up." Another beginning teacher said: "The decisions that I'm making are from who I am—from my core."

Meijer, Korthagen, and Vasalos (2009) published an in-depth report of the learning process of a beginning teacher who struggled with her teaching and received core reflection coaching during seven one-hour sessions. Based on analyses of the audio-taped sessions and research interviews with this teacher, the study showed that the teacher developed more awareness of her core qualities and ideals, and reframed her initial negative self-concept and her educational beliefs. She started to act upon her core qualities and ideals, which helped her overcome her initial struggles. The essence for her was: "I am now more present while teaching!" This publication is very informative if one wishes to understand the details of the core reflection approach.

Teacher Educators

Core reflection can also be implemented to support professional growth in teacher educators. A three-year collaborative self-study by Kim and Greene (2011) described the impact of core reflection on their identities and work as teacher educators. The authors identified several core issues in their professional development process, such as more connection between the self as a teacher educator and as a person. Moreover, they found evidence of the beneficial influences of their own development on their student teachers. The authors conclude that core reflection served as a useful approach for aligning professional and personal identities with a sense of purpose, passion, and teaching ideals. The quote at the beginning of this chapter originates from this study.

Conclusion

In 2013, a book on core reflection was published (Korthagen, Kim, & Greene, 2013), which combines an overview of the basic principles of core reflection with detailed descriptions of research studies on the approach. This collection of studies shows the importance of addressing the whole person in learning and provides evidence that the core reflection approach can lead to a reframing of limiting beliefs and enduring effective behavior. The overall conclusion that can be drawn from the research on core reflection is that the approach leads to deep, transformative learning, that is, learning in which we experience "dramatic, fundamental change in the way we see ourselves and the world in which we live" (Mirriam, Caffarella, & Baumgartner, 2007, p. 130).

An important reason for this strong effect of the core reflection approach is that it makes people aware of both their potential and their inner obstacles. This gives them a sense of choice, and thus the freedom to align their behavior with their deepest qualities and ideals (Korthagen, Kim, & Greene, 2013). Therefore, as Miller (2013, p. x) stated, "core reflection offers real hope for significant change."

More information on core reflection, including research articles, can be found at www.korthagen.nl.

References

Adams, R., Kim, Y. M., & Greene, W. L. (2013). Actualizing core strengths in new teacher development. In F. A. J. Korthagen, Y. M. Kim, & W. L. Greene (Eds), *Teaching and learning from within: A core reflection approach to quality and inspiration in education* (pp. 61–75). New York: Routledge.

Aristotle (1975). *The Nicomachean ethics, Books I–X* (D. Ross, Trans.). London: Oxford University Press. Original work published in 1925.

Attema-Noordewier, S., Korthagen, F. A. J., & Zwart, R. C. (2013). Core reflection in primary schools: A new approach to educational innovation. In F. A. J. Korthagen, Y. M. Kim, & W. L. Greene (Eds), *Teaching and learning from within: A core reflection approach to quality and inspiration in education* (pp. 111–130). New York: Routledge.

Cacioppo, J. T., Gardner, W. L., & Berntson, G. G. (1997). Beyond bipolar conceptualizations and measures: The case of attitudes and evaluative space. *Personality and Social Psychological Review, 1*, 3–25.

Deci, E. L. & Ryan, R. M. (Eds). (2002). *Handbook of self-determination research*. Rochester, NY: University of Rochester Press.

Durlak, J. A., Weissberg, R. P., Dymnicki, A. B., Tyler, R. D., & Schellinger, K. B. (2011). The impact of enhancing students' social and emotional learning: A meta-analysis of school-based universal interventions. *Child Development, 82*(1), 405–432.

Fredrickson, B. (2009). *Positivity*. New York: Random House.

Hoekstra, A. (2007). *Experienced teachers' informal learning in the workplace*. Utrecht: IVLOS, Utrecht University.

Hoekstra, A. & Korthagen, F. (2011). Teacher learning in a context of educational change: Informal learning versus systematically supported learning. *Journal of Teacher Education, 62*, 76–92.

Immordino-Yang, M. H. & Damasio, A. (2007). We feel, therefore we learn: The relevance of affective and social neuroscience to education. *Mind, Brain and Education, 1*(1), 3–10.

Kim, Y. M. & Greene, W. L. (2011). Aligning professional and personal identities: Applying core reflection in teacher education practice. *Studying Teacher Education*, 7(2), 109–119.

Korthagen, F. A. J. (2004). In search of the essence of a good teacher: Towards a more holistic approach in teacher education. *Teaching and Teacher Education*, 20(1), 77–97.

Korthagen, F. A. J. (2017). Inconvenient truths about teacher learning: Towards professional development 3.0. *Teachers and Teaching: Theory and Practice*, 23(4), 387–405.

Korthagen, F. A. J., Attema-Noordewier, S., & Zwart, R. C. (2014). Teacher–student contact: Exploring a basic but complicated concept. *Teaching and Teacher Education*, 40, 22–32.

Korthagen, F. A. J., Kim, Y. M., & Greene, W. L. (Eds) (2013). *Teaching and learning from within: A core reflection approach to quality and inspiration in education*. New York: Routledge.

Meijer, P. C., Korthagen, F. A. J., & Vasalos, A. (2009). Supporting presence in teacher education: The connection between the personal and professional aspects of teaching. *Teaching and Teacher Education*, 25(2), 297–308.

Miller, J. P. (2013). Foreword. In F. A. J. Korthagen, Y. M. Kim, & W. L. Greene (Eds), *Teaching and learning from within: A core reflection approach to quality and inspiration in education* (pp. ix–x). New York: Routledge.

Miller, R. (1997). *What are schools for?* (3rd revised edn). Brandon, VT: Holistic Education Press.

Mirriam, S. B., Caffarella, R. S., & Baumgartner, L. S. (2007). *Learning in adulthood: A comprehensive guide*. San Francisco, CA: Jossey-Bass.

Peterson, C. & Seligman, M. E. P. (2004). *Character strengths and virtues: A handbook and classification*. Oxford: Oxford University Press.

Scharmer, O. (2007). *Theory U: Leading from the future as it emerges*. Cambridge, MA: The Society for Organizational Learning.

Seligman, M. E. P. & Csikszentmihalyi, M. (2000). Positive psychology: An introduction. *American Psychologist*, 55(1), 5–14.

Seligman, M. E. P., Steen, T., Park, N., & Peterson, C. (2005). Positive psychology progress: Empirical validation of interventions. *American Psychologist*, 60(5), 410–421.

Voerman, L., Korthagen, F. A. J., Meijer, P., & Simons, R. J. (2014). Feedback revisited: Adding perspectives based on positive psychology. Implications for theory and classroom practice. *Teaching and Teacher Education*, 43, 91–98.

Zwart, R. C., Attema-Noordewier, S., & Korthagen, F. A. J. (2015). A strength-based approach to teacher professional development. *Professional Development in Education*, 41(3), 579–596.

11

SELF-DEVELOPMENT AS PEDAGOGY IN TEACHER EDUCATION

William L. Greene and Younghee M. Kim

This chapter outlines a pedagogy that brings self-development to the forefront of teacher education. The ideas proposed here represent a radically untraditional orientation to the learner, classroom, and curriculum than is evident in most accredited teaching programs in the United States. The premise behind this approach is that teaching and learning reflect the inner condition of both teacher and student. With so much at stake in the preparation of new teachers, it is a wonder more focus is not aimed at supporting the internal phenomena of self-understanding. Content, methods, and skills are, of course, important, but new teachers also need opportunities to encounter their own human potential in the learning process. By facilitating such experiences, teacher educators can model a way of being with students that honors close contact with one's essential nature. The pedagogy described in this chapter provides a model for future teachers to develop and learn within an emotionally open and loving classroom, a context that invites forth the best qualities in one's self and each other.

There is a critical need to embrace the significant role for personal development in a holistic pedagogy of teacher education. To do so is to acknowledge that we teach—first and foremost—from within. Through a pedagogy of self-development, course curriculum is framed around the centrality of the whole *person* relative to theory, subject knowledge, and skills. This approach invokes the emotional and spiritual nature of who we are as whole human beings. These parts of us traditionally stay carefully tucked away and out of sight, especially in a professional and academic context. But college students regularly express pent-up desires to connect within themselves when they have the chance to experience vulnerability in a trusting and safe environment, to be truly seen and heard by others, and to be treated as whole individuals in their learning. The fears, doubts, longings, and life questions of new teachers remain largely unacknowledged. In fact, it is almost as if these aspects of who we are do not exist, at least while we are in school. Yet, the age of many students in undergraduate education courses—between 20 and 24—poses the question of when, if ever, have they had the chance to connect with the qualities that will empower them to teach from within and to bring out the highest learning potential in their students? Ready or not, many will receive their first contract upon graduating. The examples listed below are a few of the common *living questions* young adults who become teachers ask in our classes. Perhaps you recognize some of them?

Why do I so desperately need affection from others to feel okay about myself?
Why am I not good enough?

Am I the person I want to be?

What happens if my religion is wrong?

Am I worthy of love?

Am I really who I think I am?

When and why did I lose the ability to outwardly express my emotions?

Will I find my sense of purpose/belonging in this point of my life again?

Is teaching my true calling?

Making space in the curriculum for these heartfelt questions, doubts, and fears to emerge allows a class to consider the power of ambiguity and its potential for putting us (and our students) in closer touch with longings of the spirit in the context of teaching and learning. The big questions, mystery questions as Kessler (2000) called them, do not always need an answer to be instructive sources of self-knowledge. When students are given the opportunity to share their own vulnerabilities in a safe context, they can more clearly imagine a transformed notion of what it means to teach.

Teaching from Within

Scholars and educators in recent decades have drawn attention to the importance of cultivating a mindful presence in teaching. Zehm (1999), Danielewicz (2001), and Cullum (Gund & Sullivan, 2004) advocated for more emphasis on self-development in teacher preparation. Intrator and Kunzman (2006) argued that while professional development tends to focus on knowledge and skills, nurturing greater self-awareness is necessary to sustain a teacher's growth. Other writers have talked about educating with compassion and wisdom (Miller, 2006) and strategies for integrating contemplative practices across university disciplines (Barbezat & Bush, 2014).

In a three-year collaborative self-study, we explored the alignment of personal and professional identities in teacher education by applying the principles of core reflection to our own teaching practices (Kim & Greene, 2011). One of the principles in core reflection is that when we become aware of the connection to our essential nature, or core, we gain access to inner strengths like patience, compassion, courage, persistence, and love (e.g., Korthagen & Vasalos, 2005; Korthagen, Kim, & Greene, 2013). These core qualities, in turn, can help one access their personal capacities and potential in the moment. Using core reflection, our study sought better ways to support a perspective of wholeness and empowerment in ourselves and our students. We discovered four themes of core identity issues in the study that contributed to the emerging self-development pedagogy outlined in this chapter. These issues resulted in several significant implications in our work with students. Applying our own process from this study, we sought to build time into our teaching for students to realize and understand their emerging identities as teacher and self. Each class incorporated activities and discussions about personal development, and course assignments became more targeted to, and integrated with, issues of self-awareness. We still sought some of the same course and program outcomes, but the focus became much more strongly aimed at connecting with students' core strengths and aligning those to the outcomes of their course work. This study led to core reflection becoming an integral part of our pedagogy with students in teacher education and is described in more detail, among other contemplative practices we used, in a subsequent publication (Greene & Kim, 2018).

Key questions from the writings mentioned above explored what it means to discover a deeper connection with one's authentic self as a teacher, such as: Do you meet your students or yourself (Korthagen & Verkuyl, 2002)? Who is the self that teaches (Palmer, 1998)? How can we become more soulfully present in our classrooms (Greene & Kim, 2018)? These questions invite teachers to consider how their inner world is projected onto the perceptions, conditions, and relationships in their daily lessons. This body of work highlights a critical area of intersection in understanding the teacher's inner life; it is the area where one's identity and development as a human being intersects with one's identity and professional development as a teacher (e.g., Palmer, 1998; Danielewicz, 2001; Korthagen, Kim, & Greene, 2013).

The self-development as pedagogy approach presented here builds upon this work and shares a similar aim with Miller's (2010) description of transformative teaching; this is the kind of teaching that seeks to integrate "wisdom, compassion, and sense of purpose in one's life" to whatever subject or curriculum is being taught (p. 30). For us, this does not mean replacing discipline-based subject matter or skills with self-development, but rather that opportunities to encounter one's essential nature should be both prominent and common in teacher education programs.

The Pedagogy

Pedagogy is not just the act of teaching, or the content knowledge and curriculum, or the methods used, it is the relationship between teaching and learning and the relationship between teachers and learners (Loughran, 2006). Korthagen (2004) adds another significant relationship to understand the complexity of pedagogy: that is, the relationship of the teacher and the learner to themselves. This perspective underscores the relevance of self-awareness in defining the nature of all other relationships. Each of these relationships is changing constantly, creating a fluid stream of possibility and also challenges to the teaching and learning environment. This rather uncommon and somewhat postmodern depiction of *pedagogy* is inclusive enough to hold self-development as its overarching dimension.

Three Dimensions

There are three key dimensions to the pedagogy: self-development, content, and application. The overarching and most prominent dimension is self-development. This dimension can determine an individual's response to anything that is planned or that occurs in a class. It can affect what you bring of yourself to any given moment and to the potential of that moment. Self-development also encompasses our humanity, that is, all of those attributes, dispositions, thoughts, feelings, desires, and ideals that contribute to our human and spiritual nature. This dimension is where the expansion of one's ability to be present, mindful, and aware occurs. All of these aspects influence one's relationship with self and one's relationships with others, and together they create the classroom complexity that changes from moment to moment. For teachers, this dimension largely determines how each decision, each act, and each intention is conceived. The centrality of this dimension in the pedagogy poses a new challenge for professors and teachers to consider every part of their teaching through a new lens. The syllabus, the classroom layout, the daily lesson or agenda, and the electronically supported lecture all have a place. But it's the way we pay moment-to-moment attention to our constantly changing relationships that we can avoid losing our personal sense of wholeness behind the veil of a non-stop information flow.

The other two dimensions of the pedagogy are content and application. Elements of content can include discipline-based subject matter, theories, curricular standards, and benchmarks. Application refers to any form of practicing new skills and knowledge acquisition, including: scaffolded mentoring, internships, student teaching, and procedural training. The content and application dimensions both take into account characteristics of a more traditional view of pedagogy that considers, for instance: cognitive development, information processing, brain research on learning and memory, motivation, and individual accountability. Both content and application are linked ultimately and dependently to the momentary state of being that can be indicative of an individual's inner condition prompted by their level of self-development.

The Va

At the heart of our pedagogy and uniting all three dimensions is the *va*, a concept we have borrowed from the worldview of many Pacific cultures, including Samoan, Fijian, Maori, and Japanese. Wendt (1999) described the va as "the space between, the between-ness, not empty space, not space that separates but space that relates . . . the space that is context, giving meaning to things. The meanings change as the relationships and the contexts change" (p. 402).

The va is like the breath of life in a classroom; it animates all that happens among everyone present. In this pedagogy, the va is like an unseen entity floating in every lesson, in each activity, in each discussion, in each silence. One can feel or sense it if a pause is taken to become aware of it. In our classrooms, once students are introduced to this concept in the first class session, they can tell in an instant whether the va is satisfying and energizing or whether we have become disconnected from ourselves or each other and are counting the slow minutes until the end of class. In terms of the group, happy and caring relationships are vital signs of a healthy va. When relationships are suffering, for whatever reason, the va needs attention to restore caring connections among people. As instructors, being mindful of the va is one of the surest and quickest ways to situate the *person* at forefront of the content and application dimensions of pedagogy.

Being and Becoming

Finally, the state of *being* and process of *becoming* are considered simultaneous concepts that denote both a current state of development and, at the same time, a process of developing into something new. Considering all aspects of the pedagogy, the teacher and the student are each like the bud of a fruit tree as they come to any new learning experience. They are in a state of being, with their current level of self-development affecting both the relevancy of content and the perception of their ability to apply their learning. At the same time, like the bud slowly opening to a flower and the flower slowly transforming to fruit, they are in the process of becoming something new in the very next moment. This has been a powerful analogy for students who are learning to accept themselves and their future students with fewer perceived limitations, judgments, and labels. These terms give us permission to openly accept what we find in each other and in every new class and to let go of the idea that the content is somehow more important than the person.

Embodying the Pedagogy: A Teacher's Diary

Excerpts from Younghee's personal teaching diary illustrate how a few of the key ideas outlined above are implemented in practice. Her diary draws from a recent course on holistic education. Using Miller's (2007) *The Holistic Curriculum* as a text for the class to anchor content, and then applying the ideas through activities and practice, the va is an ever-present consideration as the relationships of self-to-self and self-to-others establish a context that promotes the emergence of transformative teaching and learning. Since the emergence of self happens for the teacher just as it does for her students, Younghee's own personal development becomes the thread for her reflection and gives the reader intimate insights from *inside* the pedagogy. The overarching dimension of self-development is evident as the primary factor in content relevancy and the ability to apply it in the class.

Creating the Va

It was a hectic weekend with the end of the school year and graduation happening on Saturday. As I was finishing grading final projects, exams, and papers from three undergraduate classes, I wasn't sure if I would be ready on Monday for the first day of the class. It is important to me to be fully present when I arrive—whole mind, heart, and spirit—for my classes and to prepare a safe and inviting space to welcome my students.

The classroom was prepared as a sacred place for the va to be naturally and organically created. Red buds of a flower plant on red striped cloth were placed in the center of the room next to red rose petals floating in a celadon bowl. Bright morning music was playing with gentle natural light streaming through large windows along one wall. Students were ready at the door anxiously waiting to enter the classroom. "The room is ready to welcome the students. Now I take a deep breath." My inner voice spoke to me with excitement and curiosity as I met the students one by one with smiles and handshakes at the door. "Good morning! Welcome to class!" I spoke as my heart filled with joy and anticipation for the beginning of my new class. This week was going to be full, intense, and demanding for a three-credit course to be completed in a week-long time frame. However, I wanted this class to allow for a slower pace with spaces for contemplating moments in life and gently connecting with the self and others. The va was being felt and sensed through acceptance and awareness in each activity, in each discussion, and in each silence. Most significant was connecting with our spiritual selves as singing souls while our spirits unfolded as flower buds slowly opening up to their unique beauty. The words of Miller (2007) were being embodied, "By working on ourselves, we hope to foster in our students a deep sense of connectedness within themselves and to other beings on this planet" (p. 199).

Content Relevancy

The week slowly unfolded with readings and activities including meditating, deep listening, looking into each other's eyes, honoring each other, and symbolic exercises such as finding our trees and transcending to 'become' a tree, observing and smelling the flowers, drawing insects, mindful walking in nature, hands-on art, dancing like dancers, doing yoga like acrobat yogis, and writing soul journals with each meditation in class and at home.

On Wednesday morning in the warmth of summer, the whole class was standing in a circle near the band shell area in a local park. Everyone was happily gathered to experience the day at the park with shining eyes and bright smiles. The class was about to embark on an hour-long mindful solo walk on the trails and engage in other contemplative exercises. As we stepped onto the trail, we became quickly immersed in the beauty and spaciousness the park had to offer. The solo, contemplative walk was to be a symbol of our life journeys. The morning hike was followed by watercolor painting in the raw beauty of nature of the Japanese garden and meditative soul journal writing where students described soulful encounters, honest and heartfelt reflections with themselves through recognizing their beings (embodied wholeness) and their becoming (emergent wholeness). Then, we shared our home-made foods in a family style meal appreciating fresh fruits and vegetables from the season at the picnic tables. Small group reading discussions on *The Holistic Curriculum* chapters and presentation planning followed. We concluded with a yoga class in a full circle along with nature observations of the eco-system of the park. Miller states, "Earth connections can reawaken us to the natural processes of life. The wind, the sun, the trees, and the grass can help us come alive and waken us from the treadmill we find ourselves on" (Miller, 2007, p. 163).

Application—Personal Efficacy

Seeing my students in nature outside the four walls of the university classroom, being happy while engaging in the tasks of the class confirmed my belief that anything that is done inside can also be done outside. This morning felt transcendental to me as well as to my students. Reflecting on my soul journal after watercolor painting, I thought, "Why not take all my classes to the park for soul-connected learning in nature for at least once each term?" Miller's words remind me, "By connecting mind and body, we facilitate human wholeness" (Miller, 2007, p. 128).

The week was unfolding to ignite our spirits and passions for cultivating a deep sense of purpose in our vocations. We were acutely aware of commitments to ourselves, to caring for nature and the earth, and to helping people who are not so equitably privileged. We asked the question: What can we do, as privileged individuals and teachers, to challenge ourselves and give of ourselves to humanity with compassion and sincerity? Together, we grappled with our deep concerns and commitment for our environment on the issue of ecological sustainability for both the earth and humanity. As Miller (2006) points out, one of the characteristics of timeless learning is "participatory," we realized that we are not just enjoying the nature's beauty but also actively committing ourselves to nurture and protecting the environment that we live in. We arrived to a deeper place together as a class.

Self-development

I thought back to how I started my career as a holistic teacher educator. I began as a traditional teacher educator adhering to standard institutional expectations. It was when I met Dr. Jack Miller, a prominent leader in holistic education, in one of the holistic teaching and learning sessions at the American Educational Research Association conference about ten years ago, that I was deeply moved by his examples of authenticity, presence, wisdom, and compassion in education. Little did I know that this encounter would shape and influence my own journey as a teacher educator. I found balance and became more grounded in my intentions. I have felt a constant and deep desire to grow and adapt my pedagogy to better blend intellectual, analytical approaches with self-development and heart-based learning approaches. Miller (2007) reminds us, "Change is interdependent and dynamic. The more we become attuned to this reality the deeper and more powerful the change that occurs" (p. 195).

Being—Embodied Wholenes

However, there are questions in my mind. What about course content? What about account-ability? Am I doing what I am supposed to be doing in teacher education? What does it mean to me to be a teacher educator with a thinking heart and quiet mind in this day and age of technological impulses? How could a university professor dare to teach from the heart and not from the head as licensing standards and benchmarks seem to require? How should I teach my students to pass their portfolio and performance assessments? While these are important topics to address in teacher education programs, they still focus on the traditional schooling values of cognitive or intellect-oriented teaching and testing. An educational system that solely teaches to the rational mind, but disregards the physical, emotional, and spiritual needs of the students is completely unbalanced. Miller (2007) provides simple yet profound advice: "Teachers should simply learn to be with students. In being with students, we are fully present" (p. 192).

My holistic education class presented a taste of transformation to all of us. Our analytical minds bowed to compassionate hearts, and it was incredible to experience this collectively. Despite my small physical stature, I feel I have grown tall and deep inside. My soul and spirit have grown. As I encourage my students to recognize and embrace their core qualities, I also find I have learned alongside them to bring to the surface my own strengths. I felt that I finally found my identity as a teacher educator according to my own beliefs and ideals. As this was only a new beginning of my deeper self-development, I embodied my wholeness to teach from my full authenticity, presence, and awareness.

Becoming—Emergent Wholeness

How can I move forward accordingly with this revelation? Perhaps the most intimate question to ask is not how much knowledge we have gained, but more importantly, have we experienced a deeper sense of self and outward compassion as teachers and learners? If I can create a space that nurtures my student's senses, creative minds, sense of wholeness, wonder and curiosity, and desire to explore and connect with themselves and nature, our souls can meet each other. If I can nourish the souls of my students and truly believe in and respect them, I can remind them of their talents and core qualities. If I see the innocence, beauty, and perfection in their spirits, and truly love and honor my students as who they are, I can invite them to rise to their potential.

Conclusion

As Younghee's diary suggests, teachers and professors need to attend to their own self-development if they expect their students to do the same; otherwise, how will they guide them toward their potential as learners until they have encountered this potential in themselves? While teachers may feel like they are swimming against a current of *status quo* pedagogy, there are important reasons for balancing the content and application of their pedagogy with self-development.

First, self-development matters. Just as we hope to remind our students who they are, they also can remind us who we are. During those moments of greatest weakness, confusion, or feelings of disconnection with our students or with our subjects, perhaps by paying deep attention to the va and to each other, we might reconnect to a quality or an ideal within ourselves that beckons us back to a place of strength or larger sense of purpose. In that state of presence and awareness, the *self* can more effectively integrate both subject content and its teaching application. Palmer (1998) said, "The connections made by good teachers are held not in their methods but in their hearts—the place where intellect and emotion and spirit and will converge in the human self" (p. 11). When teacher candidates encounter content and skills through a closer look at who they are in their learning, they begin to imagine how it might be to bring personal and holistic learning to their future classrooms. As Palmer suggested, incorporating more time for soulful connections and spaces for contemplation does not necessarily mean a sacrifice of content. However, opening their curriculum to the less common realm of self-exploration requires teachers to rethink their habits of pedagogy and to consider how each lesson might provide opportunities for students to experience expansive encounters with both the content and the self. O'Reilley (1998) beckoned us to consider framing the central questions of our disciplines as spiritual questions, to move past pedagogical practices that "crush the soul," and in doing so, create classrooms that allow students the "freedom to nourish an inner life" (p. 3).

Second, teachers and their students bring a diverse range of psychological conditioning to each new experience, and some will resist or be critical toward activities that invite open sharing of themselves with each other. There are inherent tensions and risks whenever we allow ourselves to be vulnerable in new or uncharted venues and with others who, for all we know, may be evaluating each other's professional worthiness, prompting guarded behaviors. Any new approach should be handled wisely and sensitively. Some of our experiences with these phenomena have been documented elsewhere (Greene & Kim, 2018; Kim & Greene, 2011). In spite of the uncertainties in facilitating self-development, many of our students are becoming teachers, and we hope they will build for themselves the kind of classroom culture where vulnerability can be seen as an asset, can be introduced safely, lovingly, and gradually, and where the learning environment can become a place of honesty and openness. In our classrooms, more often than not, poignant expressions of truth and emotional clarity emerge following activities that invited vulnerability and self-exploration. In these profoundly teachable yet delicate moments, we can glimpse what R. Miller (1999) called "the multifaceted mystery of human existence" (p. 194).

Finally, this pedagogy only works when it is genuine. Instructors must be open to the levels of self-discovery, vulnerability, and connectedness that they hope to engender in others. Students will sense the teacher's full presence and authenticity in modeling these attributes. When it works, it has the capability to draw the best from each person and relationship. It can transform each idea, feeling, and action in the classroom into something that expands the experience of learning for all.

This closing anecdote came from a diversity course we co-taught in our Master of Arts in Teaching program. After students had completed several activities on being fully present with someone else, one of the secondary math students raised his hand and said, "This makes me love my students before I even meet them." His comment silenced the class. He got it. They got it. He would be teaching math someday, but more importantly, he would be teaching his students. He would love them before he knew them by preparing himself to *see* them with his heart. He understood that his true power as a teacher would come from embracing his own wholeness and that he can meet his future students in a more soulful way than he might have imagined. When we honor *our* souls, we enlarge our capacity for honoring *others'* souls, too. This, truly, is what our students are really here for.

References

Barbezat, D. P. & Bush, M. (2014). *Contemplative practices in higher education*. San Francisco, CA: Jossey-Bass.

Danielewicz, J. (2001). *Teaching selves: Identity, pedagogy, and teacher education*. Albany, NY: SUNY Press.

Greene, W. L. & Kim, Y. M. (2018). Encounters with the soul in teacher preparation. In E. Dorman, K. Byrnes, & J. Dalton (Eds), *Impacting teaching and learning: Contemplative practices, pedagogy, and research in education* (pp. 7–16). Lanham, MD: Rowman & Littlefield.

Gund, C. (Producer) & Sullivan, L. (Director) (2004). *A touch of greatness* [Motion Picture]. USA: Aubin Pictures.

Intrator, S. & Kunzman, R. (2006). Starting with the soul. *Educational Leadership, 63*(6), 38–42.

Kessler, R. (2000). *The soul of education: Helping students find connection, compassion, and character at school*. Alexandria, VA: Association for Supervision and Curriculum Development.

Kim, Y. M. & Greene, W. L. (2011). Aligning professional and personal identities: Applying core reflection in teacher education practice. *Studying Teacher Education, 7*(2), 109–119.

Korthagen, F. A. J. (2004). In search of the essence of a good teacher: Towards a more holistic approach in teacher education. *Teaching and Teacher Education, 20*(1), 77–97.

Korthagen, F. & Vasalos, A. (2005). Levels in reflection: core reflection as a means to enhance professional growth. *Teachers and Teaching: Theory and Practice, 11*(1), 47–71.

Korthagen, F. & Verkuyl, H. (2002). Do you meet your students or yourself? Reflection on professional identity as an essential component of teacher education. In C. Kosnik, A. Freese, & A. P. Samaras (Eds), *Making a Difference in Teacher Education Through Self-Study (2)*. Proceedings of the Fourth International Conference on Self-Study of Teacher Education Practices, Herstmonceux Castle, East Sussex, England. Toronto, Canada: OISE, University of Toronto.

Korthagen, F. A. J., Kim, Y. M., & Greene, W. L. (Eds). (2013). *Teaching and learning from within: A core reflection approach to quality and inspiration in education*. New York: Routledge.

Loughran, J. J. (2006). *Developing a pedagogy of teacher education: Understanding teaching and learning about teaching*. New York: Routledge.

Miller, J. P. (2006). *Educating for wisdom and compassion: Creating conditions for timeless learning*. Thousand Oaks, CA: Corwin Press.

Miller, J. P. (2007). *The holistic curriculum* (2nd edn). Toronto, Canada: University of Toronto Press.

Miller, J. P. (2010). *Whole child education*. Toronto, Canada: University of Toronto Press.

Miller, R. (1999). Holistic education for an emerging culture. In S. Glazer (Ed.), *The heart of learning: Spirituality in education* (pp. 189–201). New York: Tarcher/Penguin.

Palmer, P. J. (1998). *The courage to teach: Exploring the inner landscape of a teacher's life*. San Francisco, CA: Jossey-Bass.

O'Reilley, M. R. (1998). *Radical presence: Teaching as contemplative practice*. Portsmouth, NH: Heinemann.

Wendt, A. (1999). Afterword: Tatauing the post-colonial body. In V. Hereniko & R. Wilson (Eds), *Inside out: Literature, cultural politics, and identity in the new Pacific* (pp. 399–412). Lanham, MD: Rowman & Littlefield.

Zehm, S. J. (1999). Deciding to teach: Implications of a self-development perspective. In R. P. Lipka & T. M. Brinthaupt (Eds), *The role of self in teacher development* (pp. 36–52). Albany, NY: SUNY Press.

12

HOLISTIC–CONTEMPLATIVE PEDAGOGY FOR TWENTY-FIRST CENTURY TEACHER EDUCATION

Education as Healing

*Heesoon Bai, Patricia Morgan,
Charles Scott, and Avraham Cohen*

Preamble

Holism has to do with the state of being whole. 'Whole' is derived from the Old English word, *hal*, meaning, whole in the sense of uninjured, intact, safe, and healthy.[1] This etymology takes us straight into the heart of the matter concerning holistic education: we of current civilization urgently need holistic pedagogy today in response to the hurt and damage that is experienced everywhere on this planet, to the point of threatening the very viability of sentient existence. A holistic paradigm of education including teacher education is for healing.

In this chapter, we aim to discuss holism and its absence, and a healing approach to education based on a conviction that healing should be an important aim of education, for both teacher and student. We will look to contemplative inquiry as a way of integrating the healing methodology into holistic education, and addressing the need for a critical approach to contemplative inquiry. We then turn to contemplative education itself and some of its contemporary challenges, and advocate for a holistic, integral approach that recognizes the importance of inner, first-person work, along with the second-person work of intersubjectivity. We end with suggestions for the inclusion of contemplative inquiry in teacher education as a means of offering an ontological focus, and outline how artistic practices can serve as an effective means of recovering holism in contemplative inquiry.

Holistic Education is for Healing

The understanding of how injury and damage occur, namely through breaking up and disconnecting what's whole in the first place, takes us to this question: what is it about human beings that disposes them to committing disconnection and damage? If wholeness and its functionality of interconnectivity and interpenetration is how the universe operates, then why wouldn't we humans be in a natural state of holism? Why do we drive our selves continuously to disconnect and consequent hurting and damaging? We can either deny that holism (empirically) holds true of reality, at least in human social reality, or else we need to show what's effectively preventing us from living and conducting ourselves holistically. We, the authors, choose the latter response. There are some clues as to what's preventing us from operating holistically.

The first clue we would like to consider comes from the British psychiatrist, Iain McGilchrist (2009), who wrote *The Master and His Emissary: The Divided Brain and the Making of the Western World*. According to his research, the left cerebral hemisphere specializes in perceiving and handling procedurally isolated details with precision. It sees the world in disembodied and static fragments. The right cerebral hemisphere specializes in holistic, hence, relational, perception of the world. It sees things and parts in relation to each other, and takes in the whole. McGilchrist notes that basically we have two separate brains packed into one cranium; however, they are connected by the corpus callosum—a 10-centimeter long flat bundle of commissural fibers—that enables communication between the two brains. Given this structural set-up, we humans seem to be at our holistic best when these two brains work collaboratively, neither one dominating the other.

What would happen if one brain's functionality dominates the other? It is McGilchrist's (2009) contention that such domination has been taking place throughout human history, particularly in certain cultures, namely, cultures falling under the large umbrella of Western civilization: the left brain over the right brain. The result is diminishment or erosion of holistic ways of perceiving and approaching the world. If wholeness is what heals, then, it stands to reason that educationally we need to address hemispheric domination and correct the imbalance. Imbalance hurts. This is not so much a call for discouraging and suppressing the left-brain functionality as a call for encouraging and promoting right-brain functionality so that we humans are holistically functioning. However, modern Western civilization has spread itself throughout the planet, and has emphasized approaches that emerge out of left-brain dominance: separation, lack of systems awareness, and individualized focus and gain. Not incidentally, these ways are central to the neo-liberal agendas that are increasingly pervading the whole planet. We now examine the role that education has played in this imbalance.

Schooling and Reproduction of Imbalance

Indeed—here is our second clue—when we examine our typical school curriculum and pedagogy, we see just how dominant the left-brain functionality is. We valorize analytic rationality, liable to become the instrumental rationality that Charles Taylor (1991) speaks of, that takes things apart into discrete, conceptual, hence disembodied, categories of words and numbers, and reduces the phenomenology of complex, dynamically relational, embodied processes into static and disembodied representations. By the same token, we neglect and dismiss ways of learning and knowing that rely on holistic–relational, embodied and affective perception, and manner of being and doing. We standardize both curricula and means of assessment in a one-size-fits-all model that is basically into measuring students' reception and retention of discrete bits and bytes of information downloaded to them, as if they are information processors. We further entrench this bias by associating the former (left-brain functionality) with power and efficacy of abstract, disembodied rationality, and the latter with the pejorative evaluations of 'soft, touchy, feely' for the heart and visceral qualities that are integral to our feeling and intuitively lived lives. We also see the valorization of the left and dismissal of the right being played out quite plainly in the way subject matters are valued hierarchically, with the so-called 'hard' subjects, such as math and science, at the top, and the so-called 'fluffy' subjects, such as arts and humanities at the bottom, often being relegated as 'non-academic' in K-12 and postsecondary education—unless the pursuits in the latter brings in 'big bucks,' by making them extremely competitive and creating a few winners and countless losers! Schooling, whether public or private, represents the mainstream views, norms, and values that drive modern Western—by now global—societies solely or primarily oriented to economic and analytic–rationalist principles. Such principles have not promoted healing for individuals, communities, or for the planet. We propose to re-orient ourselves to an education that heals.

Heesoon Bai, Patricia Morgan, Charles Scott, and Avraham Cohen

The Need for Education That Heals

From neurobiology and psychotherapy, we know how wounding and hurts come about and are typically handled by hurt people. Basically, when one's experience-based reality, or lived reality, is diminished, denied, invalidated, or assaulted, even if with good intentions, naturally one feels hurt, and if such practice continues, wounding becomes inevitable, calling for ways to cope with and manage damages. Examples abound in our schooling experience. Subtle ones are perhaps even more damaging than one-time blows. If a child wants to draw a lot, but is discouraged from doing so with such parental (or teacherly) advice as, "You won't be able to feed yourself if you become an artist. If you don't do math and science well, you will end up working in a coffee shop," the threatened child may respond in a few different typical ways (and in combination), depending on his/her temperament and learned coping patterns. The child may become defiant and continue to draw anyway, despite the disapproval of his/her parents. The child may continue to draw but in secrecy when his/her parents are not watching. Or, the child may stop drawing altogether, being frightened about his future viability, and worse, in fear of losing his parental support and love, in which case he is denying and suppressing his own desire. His autonomy is not supported to develop. All these ways correspond to the neurobiological terms of fight, flight, and freeze.

But to the extent that any of these adaptive moves (also known as defenses) create psychic division inside him or her in terms of parts or fragments (selves) that are in tension and conflict, and/or in hiding, the integrity of a person is broken, and is in need of healing and restoration. In severe instances of fragmentation, a person can be so fragmented that one part does not know what the other part is doing: a situation of dissociation and a clear illustration of how the integrity of a person, with its coherent and holistic consciousness, is seriously compromised.

There is a well-known saying in healing circles and communities: "Hurt people hurt people." We would amend it to read: "Hurt people, *when not healed*, hurt people." We invite our readers to reflect on the world around them, and see if this description applies to what they witness. Yet, we can be healed and regain wholeness and functional integrity. This is where we, the authors of this chapter, look to holistic and contemplative education as a source of solution rather than being part of the problem.

"But, Is Healing the Job of Educators?"

Healing has not generally been considered part of teaching in the modern context of schooling. However, the educational landscape has changed through the accelerating pace of life and constant connectivity through advances in information technology, leading to chronic stress and anxiety, time poverty, and frightening levels of fragmentation and dissociation for both students and teachers. We make the case here that healing has to be not only part, but an important and central part, of teaching in today's world that is sustaining significant suffering and damage. Indeed, it makes no sense to instruct our students solely in the technical details of subject matter, whether in Math, English, Physics, Spelling, or what have you, when they are, and the world is, hurt. The priority of attention should go to healing. This does not mean that teachers have to become psychotherapists or counsellors. The persistent argument mounted by some educators that it is not a teacher's job to be a therapist does miss the point. Being a therapist is a very specific job and requires skills and knowledge that are not, and need not be, part of teacher education. Likewise, becoming a professional chef is not the same as knowing how to cook. We are making the case here that educators who lack psychological and sociocultural understandings about, as well as knowing how to work with, hurt human beings will be handicapped in their ability to serve as holistic educators. The latter will know how to be with hurt students in empathically attuned ways, and about practicing ways of being that promote healing through supporting and nurturing them to (re)gain wholeness. As a holistic educator, a teacher is a wise leader and a compassionate healer in whose presence students are nourished

110

and nurtured, supported, guided, and healed, and learn to flourish while they are learning whatever subjects they are studying.

Contemplative Education

We turn now to an examination of contemplative education for its significant role as an integral part of holistic education. The recent re-emergence of an ancient educational orientation, contemplation, which can be traced back to prehistoric Indigenous rites of passage that used trance (Morgan, 2015), is said to have officially begun in 1995 with the opening of the Centre for Contemplative Mind in Society (CMind) and the associated Association for Contemplative Mind in Higher Education (ACMHE), in Northampton, Massachusetts. Just over 20 years later, nearly every disciplinary "area of higher and professional education from Poetry to Biology and from Medicine to Law is being taught with contemplative exercises" (Zajonc, 2013, p. 84). Contemplative education is described by Arthur Zajonc as the "quiet revolution," though its exponential growth has meant that this educational revolution is getting louder (Bush, 2010). Contemplative education's diversity is alive in the varied understandings of it, ranging from the psychologist Lea Waters and her colleagues' (2015) suggestion that it is a set of practices that heighten awareness, motivation and regulation of learning, to the contemplative educators David Keiser and Saratid Sakulkoo's (2014) definition of contemplative education as an educational approach based on: "individual transformation through the cultivation of inherent spiritual human qualities, including mindfulness, awareness, empathy, authenticity, and synchronized body, speech and mind" (p. 85).

There are four central ways that contemplative practice and theory is engaged pedagogically: first, in a remedial manner where, for example, a short breath-focusing exercise will be used to help students relax and orient their focus on class content. Second, contemplative experience is employed as a way of knowing and to support understanding and development of metacognition, intersubjective awareness, empathy, and values. Third, the physiological, psychological, philosophical, and religious foundations of the practices are taught. Lastly, a contemplative orientation is developed in classrooms or across entire institutions. Pedagogues may emphasize one of these approaches in their teaching or combine all four. Contemplative education that acknowledges these four aspects is defined by Robert Roeser and Stephen Peck (2009) as a "set of pedagogical practices designed to cultivate the potentials of mindful awareness and volition in an ethical–relational context in which the values of personal growth, learning, moral living and caring for others are also nurtured" (p. 127). As an aside, we mention that some of the best current examples we know of include Simon Fraser University's Master's Program in Contemplative Inquiry,[2] Lesley University's Mindfulness Master of Arts[3] program, Naropa University's undergraduate programs in contemplative inquiry[4] and their Contemplative Psychotherapy and Buddhist Psychology[5] Master's program, and Brown University's Concentration in Contemplative Studies program[6]. Additional postsecondary programs are listed by the Association of Contemplative Mind in Higher Education (ACMHE).[7]

What the foregoing descriptions about contemplative education show us is that it can be a methodological vehicle for implementing holistic education. We need skillful ways and means for restoring wholeness as a means of healing, and contemplative education offers an effective, well-integrated means of doing so.

Mindful Awareness Cultivation and its Challenges

Central to contemplative education is cultivating mindful awareness. But its cultivation is not something simple, as if all we have to do is just sit and meditate (as we see in all those usual alluring Zen-imaged advertisements), and through this process, this 'thing' called 'awareness' gets bigger and better. We may get that impression even when we hear contemplative theorists and practitioners talk about cultivating awareness. Harold Roth (2008), for example, states that contemplation includes practices designed to "concentrate, broaden, and deepen conscious awareness" (p. 19). In truth, however, for Roth, along with other serious theorists and long-term practitioners of meditation, contemplation is far more substantial, subtle, complex, and challenging than this. How so?

Carl Jung, the Swiss psychologist and progenitor of Jungian depth psychology, wrote an essay entitled, "Marriage as a psychological relationship" (Jung, 1954/1991). In this essay, Jung makes distinctions between the unconscious and the conscious experience as defining of relationship. Recall our earlier comments about holism and how it's all about relationality: parts that make up a whole are interconnected and interpenetrating. Our consciousness as a whole has the part that is conscious and the part that is unconscious, and the two are in deep relationship. The unconscious is, then, by definition, what we are not explicitly and consciously or reflectively aware of. Given this, deepening awareness would be challenged by the unconscious at work. Needless to say, we don't know about this work of the unconscious, except, typically, by seeing, after the fact, how this work resulted in our behaving in ways that we had no control of or handle on. Call this the psychology of the unconscious or, in the more recent languaging, of the pre-conceptual or pre-reflective. Here is an example, drawn from a real life story of one of the chapter authors, to illustrate our point regarding 'seeing after the fact':

> *I am an aikido student. I was having great trouble learning what seemed to be a simple aspect of a defensive move. I was told and shown how to place my hand in a certain position on my attacker's arm just above the wrist. Sensei (Teacher) watched. Each time he observed me grabbing my attacker's arm. Each time Sensei said, "Just place your palm on his arm. Don't grab!" Each time I said, "yes," and then proceeded to grab. I was astonished at my own inability to follow this seemingly simple instruction. What was at work here? My psychological knowledge (I'm a long-standing psychotherapist) and experience tell me that something is activated in my unconscious. Surely, remembering to not grab seems like a simple task; yet my hand seems to have a mind of its own. In fact, upon reflection, I would suggest that most human beingness and doings are of this sort. Even strong assertions of being liberated and independent, which we hear so often from people around us, represent this programmed and unconscious human characteristic.*

What applies to the unconscious also applies to the transcendent. Contemplation is the epistemological vehicle for apprehending what is transcendent, for what Wilber (1999) calls "transcendental inquiry." Contemplation makes possible the "direct, immediate, intuitive apprehension of Being" (p. 208). Contemplation is both the "tool and the territory" (p. 207) of such transcendent awareness.

Our contention is that all aspects of human interaction (with other humans and non-humans) and relationship have a deep and profound psychological basis in the unconscious, and that this psychological basis dictates strongly, consistently, and persistently what will take place. Those of us who have discovered and witnessed our unconscious patterns of being, thinking, feeling, and behaving, and who can witness these patterns being reenacted again and again, as we are in the grip of them, know only too well that working with awareness is difficult work (Ginot, 2015), precisely because we have to find ways of working with the unconscious. Sustained meditation practice, such as mindfulness, supports this difficult work. Over time, one comes to see the patterns of thinking, perceiving, and feeling that are laid down through familial and cultural conditioning and encoding, and have become automatic, meaning here, unconscious.

We are concerned with the work of the unconscious that results in ways that are not desirable and that we want to change. This is important to mention because we don't wish to give the reader an impression that human unconsciousness *per se* is a problem. The unconscious is an integral part of the ecology of human consciousness, and without it, no learning is possible. All that we are able to do, automatically and effortlessly, without having to explicitly cogitate or reflect, is the gift of the unconscious. As for the work of the unconscious that results in ways that are hurtful and hurting—our main concern in this chapter, we would simply perpetuate the hurting patterns or damaging *modus operandi*, unless we find a way to break through the pattern and come to change it. This reenactment can happen even in the name of contemplative education. Nowhere is this more apparent than in the current scene of mindfulness wherein mindfulness is used as a technique in education and in human services sectors to achieve objectives that are part and parcel of the exploitative social system.

Reproduction of the Unconscious in Contemplative Practice

Developing awareness takes place within context, which encompasses all dimensions of being, from the macro (socio-cultural–political-economic) to the micro (personal–familial) conditions. Herein lie challenges to awareness cultivation: what if the context within which we practice awareness contains constraining conditions that impair and impede awareness development? For instance, can one develop deep and expansive awareness, fit to heal our unwholesomeness (wounding), within the context of a situation that compels the person to exercise greed, hatred, exploitation, and violence, directly or indirectly? That is, such compulsion triggers the survival instinct, launching the afflicted into the fight–flight–freeze reaction pattern. More concretely speaking, what is it for a student to practice mindfulness within the context of schooling that encourages, if not compels, students to compete against each other, and to strive to be winners in a neoliberal socio-political–economic system that exploits humans and non-humans alike? In a situation like this, isn't it probable that mindfulness cultivation can actually feed unwholesomeness or at least be blind to the surrounding unwholesomeness? Isn't that what we are doing when we teach students to do five minute mindfulness before taking tests to "combat test anxiety"? And, are we not doing the same when we teach our stressed workers to do mindfulness so that they can continue their overworking for maintaining productivity for profit making?

What we are witnessing in the 'failure' or perversion of contemplative practices, as in "McMindfulness" and numerous other quick fix and context-free stand-alone programs and applications (Forbes, 2016; Hyland, 2015, 2016; Purser & Loy, 2013), is unconsciousness at work. These programs are often the cultural reproduction of the mindset of reductionism, instrumentalism, and addiction to greed and speed, which characterize capitalism and neoliberalism. Thus, contemplative practice, an important aspect of the major work to heal humanity and the planet (that has been seriously disturbed by hurt and hurting humans), has to be fortified by understanding human psychology (especially the unconscious), ontology, epistemology, ethics, sociology, politics, economics, and so on. Where the current mindfulness program has gone 'wrong' is that it is most often singled out of the context of a profound philosophy and a rich practice (such as Buddhism), and is taken up as a singular technique designed, and promised, to deliver a relatively quick fix for what is construed just as personal ills. Furthermore, corporate mindfulness, ignoring the importance of context, shifted the burden of responsibility back to the individual (worker, student, teacher), with stress being framed "as a personal problem, and mindfulness . . . offered as just the right medicine to help employees work more efficiently and calmly within toxic environments" (Purser & Loy, 2013, para 14). In contrast, we, the authors of this chapter, hold the view that every personal ill is (largely) an unconscious collaboration between the person and the environment. Knowing this may give us the chance, then, to undo the social and ecological ills within the self that has been constructed by such collaboration.

Not realizing and acknowledging the constructed nature of self (first-person experience, or subjectivity), and then prioritizing the work to do with objectivity (the order of things outside subjectivity) over that of subjectivity is a serious impediment to the kind of awareness cultivation we are recommending in this chapter. One of the reasons for the current lack of theoretical or pedagogical interaction with first-person experience in contemplative inquiry may be the dominance of natural science research and its objectifying and quantitative methods. Findings related to the benefits attributed to contemplative practice in education gained through the quantitative methods used by neuroscience and psychology are frequently quoted by contemplative theorists and pedagogues. While these findings have definitely played a huge role in validating the field, the overemphasis on these results from positivistic methods and sciences, and lack of engagement with first-person methods, has meant the marginalization of findings from the arts and humanities. In addition, the emphasis in quantitative methods on replicability, generalizability, and objectivity all fail to comprehensively engage either relevant contextual issues or the subtleties of the contemplative preconceptual (or what we previously called the unconscious) or transcendent experience.

Holistic, Integral Approaches to Contemplative Inquiry

Contemplation and contemplative inquiry can take many forms; we see this in examining contemplation, as it has existed in the wisdom traditions. The current overemphasis on secular mindfulness highlights the lack of holism in instances of contemplative education. In this context, we wish to note that contemporary adaptations of contemplative inquiry have taken a practice like mindfulness and stripped it away from the integrated Buddhist teaching, as expressed in the Eightfold Path that comprises teachings of right view, right speech, right conduct, right livelihood, for example, and we are left only with right mindfulness. While we may not wish to incorporate all the teachings of Buddhism into our adaptations of contemplative inquiry, especially in secular contexts, we do need to take an integral approach, incorporating considerations of ethics and right living. Simply put, programs of contemplative inquiry need to be located within a holistic framework that recognizes all lines of development: physical, aesthetic, intellectual, emotional, social/relational, moral, and existential/spiritual.[8]

Another possible consideration for applying contemplation, for both teacher and student, in a more holistic fashion lies in Lilburn's (1999) observation, similar to that of Wilber's (1999), that "Contemplation is inquiry into the nature of being" (p. 27). As Arthur Zajonc (2013) suggests, we need a "more robust and complete ontology, investigated by a broad range of methods, and a more inclusive ethics that gets beyond cost benefit" (p. 93). Lilburn is pointing in the same direction: ontology. Some of us have used the language of spirituality to point to the same. Ergas (2016) designates contemplation as a spiritual research paradigm that works with 'inwardness' (first- and third-persons) and connectedness (second-person). In previous work (Bai, Morgan, Scott, & Cohen (2016), we have pointed to a pluralistic, integral conception of spirituality that includes meaning making; realization of, and engagement with, the sacred or transcendent; a sense of awe and wonder; that which is sensorially or perceptually extraordinary; a sense of wholeness, connectedness, integration, and harmony; compassion, love, kindness, joy; intuitive clarity and insight; and creativity and vitality. Thus, contemplation can serve as a spiritual research paradigm, if we adopt such an integral conception of spirituality.

Varieties of Contemplative Inquiry in Teacher Education

If we are to bring contemplation into schools, we need to redirect focus in teacher education. We may not need to add more content material, necessarily; rather, we need to change the focus. Jack Miller (2014) has pointed to the significance of the presence of the teacher, claiming it to be of primary importance in learning. We concur. We have Parker Palmer's (2007) famous line from the first page of his classic *The Courage to Teach*: "We teach who we are" (p. 1). Trite, assuredly, but just as assuredly true.

However, as we articulated in previous sections, if the teacher is both hurt and is hurtful, and working with students who are suffering in the same way, then teacher presence in such cases can be damaging. Avraham Cohen, one of this chapter's authors, added to Parker Palmer's statement a line: "We teach who we are and that is the problem" (2015, p. 25). If we are not aware of our unconscious, of our own ruptures and hurts, we are liable to hurt others. Hence, it is important that we teachers engage in our own healing. It is our proposal that we create teacher education that is optimally designed to support student teachers' healing and growth and development. Such programs would include, besides contemplative practices, a knowledge base that is both theoretical and practice-oriented about being human, and that is essential for educators. To list a few here: psychological knowledge that includes developmental process, developmental trauma and arrest, self-cultivation, such as inner work (Cohen, 2015) that facilitates an ongoing process of development of relationship to self, to human others, and to nonhuman others; practice-based psychological knowledge of attuned communication, empathy, and compassion; and group leadership and facilitation in the service of developing a felt sense of community within the classroom environment. This list can be expanded well beyond what we have included here, such as cultural factors, socio-economic class issues, race, gender, and all manner of fear of otherness. Integration of contemplative practices with the above knowledge and skill bases would create an optimal learning focus and environment to support student teachers in their personal and professional growth and development.

And, finally, we wish to highlight the importance and power of contemplative art as a method or vehicle that bypasses the left-brain discursivity, and takes us to the ineffability of the contemplative interior (Morgan & Abrahamson, 2016). It is possible, through contemplative art, to enter realms of feeling and knowing beyond dianoetic consciousness and duality where the practitioner is taken to a "subtle beyond" (Barthes, in Bai et al., 2009). It is in this finely textured space that practitioners can experience direct immersion in their elemental or primordial ground. As the educational philosopher Mary Richards (1996) affirms "[a]rt integrates also the verbal and non-verbal worlds, showing the work of the hands to be soul language, and the energies of speech to be translations of non-verbal impulses" (pp. 7–8). Contemplative art, as pedagogy, provides entry to, and a means congruent with, the pre-conceptual state both Richards and Barthes describe.

As contemplative art, ranging across all arts genres, engages the pre-conceptual or pre-reflective, somatic, affective, intersubjective, and cognitive, it offers pedagogues the chance to know the wholeness of themselves and their students. Alluding to this in their description of transpersonal art therapy, Franklin and his colleagues (2011) describe it as phenomenological, humanizing practice—one that avoids the "clinification syndrome," which, in the current educational climate, could be translated as the "commodification syndrome."

Through focused, contemplative practice in the arts, one learns how to pay close attention, through the body and its senses, to the external, to our immediate or even distant context, and connect those worlds intimately with that contemplative, phenomenological interior; this becomes both a subjective, first-person contemplation and an intersubjective, second-person one. The body itself is, if we contemplatively allow it to be, "an active and open form, continually improvising its relation to things and to the world" (Abram, 1996, p. 49); there is an "improvised duet between my animal body and the fluid, breathing landscapes that it inhabits" (p. 53). It is this increased capacity for intimate engagement with others and the world that allows contemplation to serve holistically. In the artistic engagement, there is what Barthes (1981) called the "punctum," the "element which rises from the scene, shoots out of it like an arrow, and pierces me" (p. 26). One is pierced, touched, wounded, pricked, and there is the potential for a sympathetic, loving response.

Concluding Thoughts

We propose contemplative inquiry as an integral part of holistic approaches in education designed to promote healing in a fractured, disconnected world. Contemplation in its many forms allows us to address the pre-conceptual, creative and spiritual dimensions of our being, thus allowing for an education as healing from the disconnected, instrumentalist, and materialistic ethos of our times. In turn, the application of contemplative inquiry in educational settings and in pre-service teacher education will benefit from a holistic, integral perspective: such inquiry can serve not as a means of 'waking up' to greater awareness but of 'growing up' along all lines of development (Wilber, 2016, 2017). Contemplative inquiry can serve effectively as a means of educational healing when it is based on the principles of holistic education and, at the same time, is housed within holistic educational programs or approaches. We need to apply what Miller (2014) refers to as a "holistic vision" to contemplative inquiry while also recognizing that contemplative practices themselves can nurture holism and healing.

Notes

1 Source: online etymology dictionary www.etymonline.com/index.php?term=whole
2 This Master's program in Contemplative Inquiry has the objective of building the foundational capacity through dialogic cohort community building, individual and collective cultivation of contemplative dispositions and skills, and enactment-based knowledge building in educational subject matters ranging over curriculum design, pedagogy, educational programming, assessment, leadership, embodiment, Indigenous knowledge, arts-based inquiry, and social and moral philosophy/ethics.
3 www.lesley.edu/academics/graduate/mindfulness-studies-masters
4 www.naropa.edu/academics/bachelors/index.php
5 www.naropa.edu/academics/masters/clinical-mental-health-counseling/contemplative-psychotherapy-buddhist-psychology/index.php
6 www.brown.edu/academics/contemplative-studies/concentrating-contemplative-studies/formal-concentration
7 www.contemplativemind.org/resources/study
8 See Wilber 2006, 2016, 2017 for further discussions of these points.

References

Abram, D. (1996). *The spell of the sensuous: Perception and language in a more-than-human world*. New York: Vintage.
Bai, H., Morgan, P., Scott, C., & Cohen, A. (2016). Prolegomena to a spiritual research paradigm: Importance of attending to the emotional and the subtle. In J. Lin, R. Oxford, & T. Culham (Eds), *Toward a spiritual research paradigm: Exploring new ways of knowing, researching, and being* (pp. 77–96). Charlotte, NC: Information Age.
Bai, H., Scott, C., & Donald, B. (2009). Contemplative pedagogy and revitalization of teacher education. *The Alberta Journal of Educational Research*, 55(3), 319–334.
Barthes, R. (1981). *Camera lucida: Reflections on photography*. New York: Macmillan.
Bush, M. (2010). Contemplative higher education in contemporary America. In *Contemplation nation: How ancient practices are changing the way we live* (pp. 221–236). Kalamazoo, MI: Fetzer Institute.
Cohen, A. (2015). *Becoming fully human within educational environments: Inner life, relationship, and learning*. Burnaby, BC: Write Room Press.
Ergas, O. (2016). Knowing the unknown: Transcending the educational narrative of the Kantian paradigm through contemplative inquiry. In J. Lin, R. Oxford, & T. Culham (Eds.), *Toward a spiritual research paradigm: Exploring new ways of knowing, researching, and being* (pp. 1–24). Charlotte, NC: Information Age.
Forbes, D. (2016). Modes of mindfulness: Prophetic critique and integral emergence. *Mindfulness*, 7(6), 1256–1270.
Franklin, M., Farrelly-Hansen, M., Marek, B., Swan-Foster, N., & Wallingford, S. (2011). Transpersonal art therapy education. *Art Therapy Journal of the American Art Therapy Association*, 17(3), 101–110.
Ginot, E. (2015). *The neuropsychology of the unconscious: Integrating brain and mind in psychotherapy*. New York: W. W. Norton.
Hyland, T. (2015). McMindfulness in the workplace: Vocational learning and the commodification of the present moment. *Journal of Vocational Education & Training*, 67(2), 219–234.
Hyland, T. (2016). The limits of mindfulness: Emerging issues for education. *British Journal of Educational Studies*, 64(1), 97–117.
Jung, C. G. (1954/1991). Marriage as a psychological relationship. In *The collected works of C. G. Jung* (Ch. 17). Princeton, NJ: Princeton University Press.
Keiser, D. L. & Sakulkoo, S. (2014). Fitting in breath hunting: Thai and U.S. perspectives on contemplative pedagogy. In O. Gunnlaugson, E. W. Sarath, C. Scott, & H. Bai (Eds), *Contemplative learning and inquiry across disciplines* (pp. 81–96). State University of New York Press.
Lilburn, T. (1999). *Living in the world as if it were home*. Dunvegan, ON: Cormorant Books.
McGilchrist, I. (2009). *The master and his emissary: The divided brain and the making of the western world*. New Haven, CT: Yale University Press.

Miller, J. (2014). *The contemplative practitioner: Meditation in education and the workplace.* Toronto, Canada: University of Toronto Press.

Morgan, P. (2015). A brief history of the current reemergence of contemplative education. *Journal of Transformative Education, 13*(3), 197–218.

Morgan, P. & Abrahamson, D. (2016). Cultivating the ineffable: The role of contemplative practice in enactivist learning. *For the Learning of Mathematics, 36*(3), 31–37.

Palmer, P. J. (2007). *The courage to teach: Exploring the inner landscape of a teacher's life.* San Francisco, CA: Jossey-Bass.

Purser, R. & Loy, D. (2013). Beyond McMindfulness. *Huffington Post, 1*(7), 13.

Richards, M. C. (1996). The public school and the education of the whole person. In D. Haynes (Ed.), *Opening our moral eye: Essays, talks, and poems, embracing creativity and community* (pp. 77–112). Hudson, NY: Lindisfarne Press.

Roeser, R. & Peck, S. (2009). An education in awareness: Self, motivation, and self-regulated learning in contemplative perspective. *Educational Psychologist, 44*(2), 119–136.

Roth, H. (2008). Against cognitive imperialism: A call for a non-ethnocentric approach to cognitive science and religious studies. *Religion East and West, 8*, 1–26.

Taylor, C. (1991) *The malaise of modernity.* Toronto, Canada: House of Anansi Press.

Waters, L., Barsky, A., Ridd, A., & Allen, K. (2015). Contemplative education: A systematic, evidence-based review of the effect of meditation interventions in schools. *Educational Psychology Review, 27*, 103–134.

Wilber, K. (1999). *The collected works of Ken Wilber: A sociable God; Eye to eye.* Boston, MA: Shambhala.

Wilber, K. (2006). *Integral spirituality: A startling new role for religion in the modern and postmodern world.* Boston, MA: Shambhala.

Wilber, K. (2016). *Integral meditation: Mindfulness as a way to grow up, wake up, and show up in your life.* Boston, MA: Shambhala.

Wilber, K. (2017). *The religion of tomorrow: A vision for the future of the great traditions–more inclusive, more comprehensive, more complete.* Boulder, CO: Shambhala.

Zajonc, A. (2013). Contemplative pedagogy: A quiet revolution in higher education. *New Directions for Teaching and Learning, 134*, 83–94.

13

INTEGRATED CURRICULUM FOR THE TWENTY-FIRST CENTURY

Susan M. Drake and Joanne L. Reid

We are two Canadian educators with decades of experience in public education. Susan has worked in schools on a variety of integrated projects and has researched curriculum as a teacher educator. Joanne became an advocate of interdisciplinary curriculum (IC) when she was teaching many different subjects at the same time and saw the connections among them. We write this chapter from an Ontario, Canada perspective. But we also present evidence that adoption of IC is a global phenomenon that connects to an international shift of emphasis from achievement accountability measures to a more fulsome view of education and the whole child.

In this chapter, we argue that the time is right for an integrated curriculum (IC) in education. There are many reasons why IC makes sense. One is greater efficiency in curriculum coverage and assessment through reduced duplication. Another is increased relevance for students because IC is often situated in complex, real-world contexts that reflect an organic, interdependent view of knowledge. But the twenty-first century context makes an integrated approach even more appropriate, perhaps even urgently needed.

We can see that IC fits into a holistic perspective (Miller, 2007) when we deconstruct curriculum into component parts —content (Know), skills (Do), and values, attitudes, and ways of being in the world (Be)—while always understanding them as an interconnected holistic system. Although knowledge and skills remain important, they are balanced by the increasing recognition that social, emotional, and spiritual well-being are equally important. Today, there is a renewed appreciation for a holistic approach that addresses the whole child—the head (Know), hands (Do), and heart (Be) (see, for example, The Association for Supervision and Curriculum Development Whole Child Initiative[1]). We will explore the relationship of integration and a holistic approach later in this chapter.

What is Integrated Curriculum (IC)?

For theorists, finding a common definition of IC has been frustrating. Cross-disciplinary, intradisciplinary, fusion, multidisciplinary, interdisciplinary, transdisciplinary, and integrated are all used to describe integrated approaches that vary from one context to another (we use the terms interdisciplinary and integrated interchangeably). Such contexts may also include project-based, problem-based, place-based, and passion-based learning.

IC has a long history and is connected to the progressive movement that began in the late nineteenth century in the United States. Its tenets, including subject integration, are still in existence. In the 1930s, IC was recommended to improve schools and make learning more relevant (Aikin, 1942). This movement was grounded in constructivism and the ideas of John Dewey (1916/1966, 1938/1969): democracy, learn by doing, experiential learning, and systematic inquiry. Dewey's ideas continue to influence how and why we integrate curriculum today.

A continuum of increasing degrees of integration (Figure 13.1) is a way to conceptualize integration (see, for example, Daly, Brown, & McGowan, 2012; Fogarty & Pete, 2009; Jacobs, 1989). In a multidisciplinary model, each discipline and its assessment is distinct, but the disciplinary learning activities revolve around a common theme, issue or project (Brough, 2012; Dowden, 2007). In another form of multi-disciplinary curriculum, the activities are developed separately but the culminating activity and its assessment bring all the subjects together. As an example, Susan was involved in a multidisciplinary project involving the arts and language arts. One cohort of Grade 9 students wrote a script, created the sets, and composed the music for a play. These activities were all done in separate classrooms with three different teachers, but subjects were integrated into the culminating activity—the actual drama performance—which was assessed.

In an interdisciplinary model, subject boundaries are present but blurred by a shared focus. In Joanne's history class, students explored the Know (causes and effects of various wars), the Do (inquiry and research), and the Be (global citizenship). Students read and interpreted poetry and stories, analyzed primary source documents, and explored art related to war. In the end, they put on a multimedia presentation at the school's Remembrance Day assembly. The common theme for all these activities was "war and peace". Students reflected on ways to contribute to peace in their homes and community, and in the world (Be).

Transdisciplinarity is the most integrated model and the most transformative. Disciplines, although present if looked for, are seamlessly blended and their particularities are not central to the planning. The Alpha school, a school within a school in Shelburne, Vermont, has operated since 1972. It offers a good example of what a transdisciplinary model can be (Drake & Burns, 2004; Kuntz, 2005). Multi-aged student teams design their own transdisciplinary curriculum using state standards. Students generate three or four major questions a year based on personal or social/world issues. For example, in 2016–2017, one of the inquiry questions was "How does perspective influence the way individuals and groups of people deal with conflict?" Then the students decide on the theme (e.g., Conflict and Change), the standards to meet, methods of instruction, and assessment.

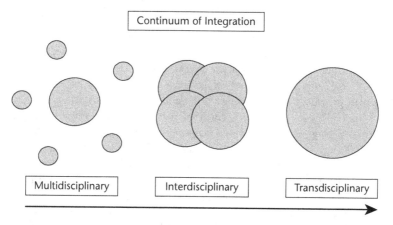

Figure 13.1 A continuum of increasing disciplinary integration

IC and the Holistic Approach

For Miller (2007), the holistic curriculum is connected to the earth, the inner self, body–mind, intuition, and inquiry. He sees curriculum as a continuum of increasing connections. He outlines three different levels to curriculum that roughly parallel the continuum of interdisciplinarity we have presented in Figure 13.1. In the transmission level there are few connections. The teacher is the expert, the student is a passive learner who learns in isolation (traditional method). The transactional level features interaction between teacher and student. Rational problem solving or inquiry is at the heart of this model. The next level is transdisciplinary or holistic, where the student moves beyond the cognitive to connect to others, and to feelings, intuition, and ways of being. In this orientation, the student's awareness of connections makes learning personally and socially meaningful.

> We want to let students see how subjects relate to one another and to the students themselves . . . We care about the students' being. We realize that the final contribution that they make to this planet will be from the deepest part of their being, not just from the skills we teach them.
>
> *(Miller, 2007, pp. 198–199)*

An integrated curriculum can find the most comfortable home at the transdisciplinary level.

IC supports an Indigenous way of teaching and learning because of its natural fit with a holistic view of the world. Storytelling and a culturally responsive curriculum are particularly important aspects (Archibald, 2008; Kanu, 2011). For example, the Medicine Wheel is one way to represent the fundamental philosophical principles of this holistic worldview. (We note that non-Indigenous use of the Medicine Wheel without deep grounded knowledge is inappropriate.) While there is similarity among First Nations' use of the Medicine Wheel, there are some differences in what the four directions can represent. For some, the four directions in the Medicine Wheel represent the self as comprising four interconnected components: spiritual, physical, emotional–mental, and intellectual. The circular shape of the Medicine Wheel represents interconnectedness, equality, balance, continuity, and inclusiveness: a completeness that can be seen in the cycles of life, in the changing seasons, in the migrations of animals, and in the movement of the sun and stars. As Cajete (1996) wrote, "the active focus on maintaining and/or striving for a harmony between one's self and one's natural environment was the most essential principle for applying knowledge" (p. 138). An integrated curriculum also complements the values common to many Indigenous societies such as the Ojibwe Good Life Teachings (also known as the Seven Grandfather/Grandmother Teachings): respect, love, bravery, wisdom, humility, honesty, and truth (Battiste, 2002; Toulouse, 2008).

In response to the Truth and Reconciliation Commission of Canada's Final Report, which calls for a revision of the Canadian educational curriculum to include respectful and accurate representations of Indigenous people and the history of assimilative government policies and laws targeted at Indigenous communities, there is a movement across Canada to revise the K-12 curriculum (See Calls to Action # 62, 63 and 64, *Truth and Reconciliation Commission of Canada Calls to Action*, 2012, pp. 7–8). Canadian provinces are addressing the lack of recognition of these cultures by integrating Indigenous knowledge and infusing Indigenous perspectives into the curriculum. Indigenous education strategies are suggested in *Aboriginal Perspectives: The Teacher's Toolkit* (Ontario Ministry of Education, 2011). This is a collection of specific instructional strategies that connect to existing curriculum and insure representation of Indigenous cultures and pedagogical methods.

Another good example of IC and a holistic curriculum is the the work from the Reggio Emilia community in Italy. The philosophy of the *Hundred Languages of Children* embodies the multiple ways that children interpret the world and represent their ideas and theories (Thornton & Brunton, 2015). Originally, the Reggio Emilia approach was used in early childhood education but today it is implemented around the world and is expanding into higher grades. A Reggio-inspired (as it is often referred to) curriculum focuses on exploration and discovery. Using a project approach framework (Moran, 1998), student knowledge is expressed through creating with local or found materials materials, using the arts, collaborating with others, and reflecting on their learning. Play is the basis of learning: painting, sculpting, and drama are common activities. Consideration of child development includes physical–motor, language, cognitive, social–personal and emotional, sensorial, and creative and aesthetic appreciation development (Mohanty, 2014).

Designing an Integrated Curriculum

In this section, we outline the components we have found to be important to designing an integrated curriculum (Drake & Reid, 2010; Drake, Reid, & Kolohon, 2014). We present this process in a linear fashion, but the actual experience is iterative; the designer often goes back and forth among components.

We favour a backwards design approach (Wiggins & McTighe, 2005) because it helps create a curriculum that is accountable to curriculum mandates. In the backwards design approach, teachers plan by first establishing the end goal connecting to the curriculum standards/outcomes of a unit or course. Second, they design a summative task that will assess students' demonstrated achievement of those standards. Last, they plan instructional activities and formative assessments that scaffold to the summative task. This process ensures that all learning activities and assessments are aligned and cohesive. We have expanded the Wiggins and McTighe model to make it more holistic (see Figure 13.2). We have written this section with the educator in mind, but it is important to remember that students can and should play an active role as co-designers in their own curriculum.

Know your students. Who are your students? What experiences are they bringing to a classroom? What is relevant to them? What are their questions? What strategies/methods will be needed to meet their individual interests and needs?

Know your curriculum. Given that most jurisdictions have curriculum mandates, curriculum designers need to know them in order to align the curriculum to them. It is easier to integrate across subjects if you look at the standards from a big picture perspective rather than looking at specific standards. We have found that three or four broad-based standards are enough to begin the process. Use students' questions and interests as a lens to look at the standards and next steps.

Create a concept map. After reviewing the standards for a selected grade level, it is a good idea to sketch out a concept map or mind map. This is brainstorming only, meant to give you an idea of where authentic, natural connections can be made. Figure 13.3 is an example for a Grade 5 unit. The teacher is looking for ways to integrate disciplinary knowledge, interdisciplinary skills, and the Be. The question marks show that the concept map is a work in progress.

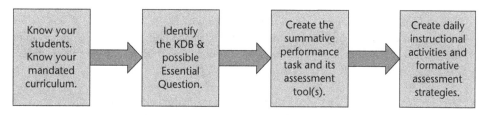

Figure 13.2 Designing a holistic integrated curriculum

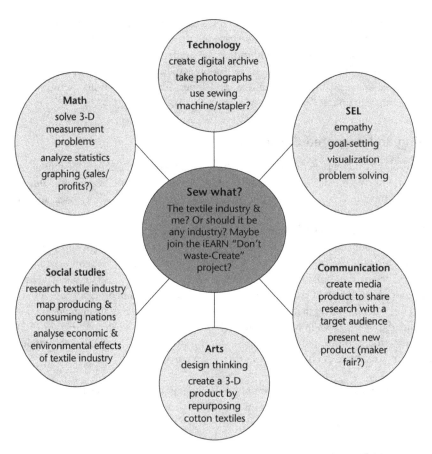

Figure 13.3 Exploratory web for a Grade 5 interdisciplinary unit

Construct the Know-Do-Be (KDB) organizer. The overarching KDB umbrella shown in Figure 13.4 is created when looking at the curricula through the widest lens to discover what is most important for students to know, do, and be across the disciplines. The Know involves content and concepts that are cross-disciplinary when defined as Big Ideas or Enduring Understandings. Examples of Big Ideas are sustainability, conflict, patterns, and systems. These concepts apply to more than one subject area and act as a connecting bridge. An Enduring Understanding is also universal and interdisciplinary. An example is "Individual consumer choices affect people everywhere, and the global environment".

The Do refers to competencies that are described above. The Asia Society (2013) defines competencies in three broad categories:

- Cognitive: Academic mastery, critical thinking, creativity.
- Interpersonal Competencies: Communication and collaboration, leadership, global awareness.
- Intrapersonal Competencies: Growth mindset, learning how to learn, intrinsic motivation, grit.

(p. 4)

The Be refers to attributes that contribute to inner personal development (connection to inner self, well-being, mental health, socio-emotional learning, metacognition, self-actualization, and ethical behaviour) and learning how to be in community (collaboration, inclusiveness, respect for our planet).

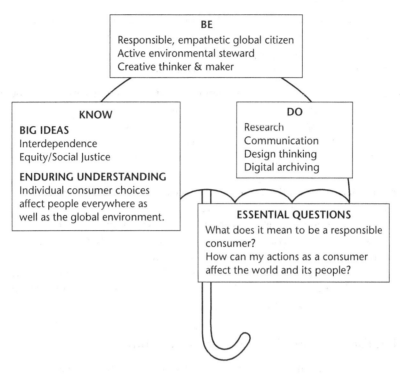

Figure 13.4   The KDB umbrella for a unit

The Know, Do, and Be are interconnected. The twenty-first century competencies are a Do, but often involve the Know and Be as well. To be able to *do* inquiry, the student must *know* the procedural steps of inquiry. Once inquiry has become a way of thinking/acting, the student has *become* an inquirer.

Determine the essential question(s). A powerful question can insure inquiry and can shape the unit planning (Wiggins & McTighe, 2013). These questions are sometimes called driving questions. They are usually interdisciplinary in nature, and are generated from the Know in the KDB Umbrella. Here are two examples: What is love? How does art affect culture and culture affect art?

Create a rich performance assessment task (RPAT). You will need to design a performance task that allows students to demonstrate that they have acquired the knowledge, skills, and personal attributes of your designed curriculum. The RPAT is a summative assessment that is extremely important to creating a rich and coherent integrated unit. Designing the RPAT is done *after* you have decided the KDB and *before* you determine daily activities. Including students as designers of the RPAT is an excellent opportunity for them to exercise voice and choice. Certainly, flexibility and choice are important ingredients of any RPAT.

This is the stage where the RPAT's assessment tool(s), such as a rubric, should be designed and given to the students so that expectations are transparent. An example of the RPAT could be outlined like this through creating a maker faire.

You will choose a common object (e.g., blue jeans, chocolate bar). You will research and evaluate the social, environmental, and economic effects of the process to manufacture that object. You will keep an ongoing journal that records your personal thoughts and actions in response to your research. You will create a new product using design thinking to repurpose a discarded or no longer useful object. Throughout the process you will digitally archive how you made your new product and why. You will participate in a Maker Faire (perhaps a charity fundraising?) where the community is invited. At the faire, you will do two things:

- Share your research through a communication/media product (brochure, public service video, poster) to be displayed at the Maker Faire.
- Present your repurposed product. Be prepared to answer questions on the design thinking procedure you used, and how your product fits into an interdependent world where there is greater equality and respect for the environment.

Determine the daily instructional activities/ embedded assessments. From the holistic perspective, it is important that curriculum, instructional strategies, and assessment are seamlessly interwoven. This is done last so that all instruction will align with both the KDB on the umbrella and the requirements of the RPAT. Assessment of daily activities is largely formative, with the teacher and/or peers giving constructive feedback, and also with student self-reflection. For example, students could annotate a template that outlines the steps of design thinking by adding notes about their own actions. Thus, the teacher and/or student can see how well the student understands the design thinking process while it is under way.

Factors that Facilitate and Challenge Implementation

We hope the steps outlined above will support your move towards implementation of IC. Those who have implemented IC say they would never go back to a traditional subject-based curriculum despite the big investment of time and energy (Clark, 2011). Their experiences light the way for your own positive implementation (Adler & Flihan, 1997; Applebee, Adler, & Flihan, 2007; Fenwick, Minty, & Priestley, 2013; Virtue, Wilson, & Ingram, 2009).

While not all IC programs involve teaching partnerships, diversity of content expertise and perspective can enrich the experience. However, team teaching requires interpersonal skills, and a willingness to collaborate, compromise, take risks, and learn. Teacher attributes are important. Teachers need to be deeply committed to student learning in an interdisciplinary context. Their passion needs to override the additional demands of time for meeting with others. Leadership and administrative support are needed to provide professional development, to fund time and resources, to schedule appropriately, and to maintain staff continuity.

Despite our enthusiasm for IC, we are not naive. There are challenges to implementing IC. According to the literature, these challenges include scheduling, protectiveness of disciplinary terrain, interpersonal conflict with collaborators, lack of confidence when teaching outside one's comfort zone, among other obstacles (Brand & Triplett, 2012; Hargreaves & Moore, 2000; James, Lamb, Householder, & Bailey, 2000; Lam, Alviar-Martin, Adler, & Sim, 2013; Venville, Sheffield, Rennie, & Wallace, 2008; Weinberg & Sample McMeeking, 2017). However, the effort is worthwhile (Fenwick et al., 2013; Russell & Burton, 2000), especially in the twenty-first century.

IC and the Twenty-first Century Context

The traditional model of education is out of step with the twenty-first century context (Brooks & Holmes, 2014; Fullan, 2013; Huber & Hutchings, 2004). The longer students remain in school, the more engagement declines, according to American, Australian, and Canadian studies (Gallup, 2014; Jasperson, 2014; Willms, Friesen, & Milton, 2009). Students find IC more appealing than the traditional model that is based on isolated subjects (Hinde, 2005; McNaughton, 2014; Russell & Burton, 2000; Venville et al., 2008). Research shows that student engagement links to academic achievement and a host of factors related to healthy youth development (Finn, 1991; Fredericks, Blumenfeld, & Paris, 2004; Lee, 2014; Li & Lerner, 2011; Li et al., 2014). Stronger motivation, better attendance, and fewer dropouts are some of the positive factors associated with IC (McNaughton, 2014; Pushpanadham, 2013; Sill, 2001; Smithrin & Upitis, 2005; Vega, 2012). To increase student engagement is one reason, among many, why educators should consider an integrated approach. As well, integrated curriculum is engaging for teachers, especially those inclined to "child-centered", "problem-centered", constructivist, and holistic views of learning (Drake et al., 2014; Lieberman & Hoody, 1998). Academically, students in interdisciplinary programs do as well as, or better than, their counterparts in traditional classrooms (see, for example, Aikin, 1942; Drake, Savage, Reid, Bernard, & Beres, 2015; Vars & Beane, 2001).

The twenty-first century student is likely comfortable with technology, having had access to it from a young age. Ubiquitous technology can present both positive and negative opportunities. On the one hand, students can be distracted by constant and superficial interruptions, and fall victim to unkind (e.g., bullying) and unreliable uses (e.g., fake news). On the other hand, researching with the internet can break down disciplinary and cultural/geographic boundaries. Students can see for themselves that knowledge does not have disciplinary boundaries.

The twenty-first century classroom is connected to the world; students can share their work and connect with resources including experts anywhere. With global outreach comes an awareness of, and responsibility for, global issues. Students discover a sense of social justice and how to be local, national, and global citizens. This goes far beyond disciplinary thinking, and taps into the democratic philosophy that can ground IC (Beane, 1997; Dewey, 1916/1966). iEARN[2] is a non-profit organization that connects teachers and students with global counterparts for work in disciplinary and integrated projects. iEarn is an impressive organization involving 140 countries, 30 languages, 50,000 educators and two million youths. In the "One day in the life" project (iEarn, n.d.), students from 66 countries have so far recorded and shared videos of their everyday activities. Another project tracks garbage around the world. Students become activists in sharing ideas for reduction, reuse, and recycling.

Although literacy and numeracy are still at the core of education, and traditional subjects persist, new literacies are claiming space in the twenty-first century learning landscape (Lankshear & Knobel, 2011; Rowsell, 2013). Curriculum documents in Ontario and elsewhere call for technological, critical, financial, media, spatial, visual, scientific, and movement literacies. These literacies are interdisciplinary. For example, environmental literacy is infused into every subject (Ontario Ministry of Education, 2017a,b).

Significantly different countries have revised their policies to include such IC approaches (Drake & Savage, 2016). South Korea and Quebec, Canada favour an integrated approach and Finland has shifted from subject-based to phenomenon-based education. These policy shifts are a response to twenty-first century life. Today, we inhabit a world of "wicked problems" (Camillus, 2008, p. 1), problems so global and complex that they are rarely solvable within a single discipline. Some wicked problems of our times are environmental destruction, widespread poverty, and the migration of people. Tackling these wicked problems requires diverse perspectives and the interdisciplinary skills that educational experts are calling for (Lederman, 2008). These skills are referred to variously as the twenty-first century skills/competencies/capacities. Some examples are multi-modal communication, inquiry and research, creative and critical thinking, collaboration, global awareness and citizenship, and learning how to learn (Ontario Ministry of Education, 2016).

As well, a twenty-first century vision of education explicitly articulates the values and personal character traits that education should foster, such as empathy, character, citizenship, respect, responsibility, resilience, social awareness, and relationship management. Since these competencies are applicable in many subjects, and are more like life skills, it seems efficient to teach and assess them in a holistic, interdisciplinary curriculum (Rennie, Venville, & Wallace, 2012). Singapore (for example, see Singteach, 2012) is focusing on values as well as knowledge and skills in a student-centered, values-driven curriculum; character comes first and this focus will help shape students into holistic individuals who will contribute to society.

As a holistic educator, you will want to keep the Be at the forefront. How can this be done, given the sometimes excessive emphasis on test scores of content knowledge? Consider the International Baccalaureate (IB) program with over a million students. The IB curriculum is integrated, particularly up to Grade 5. An umbrella over its entire curriculum is the Learner Profile (International Baccalaureate Learner Profile) which describes what students are expected to be: knowledgeable, thinkers, inquirers, principled, open-minded, caring, balanced, risk-takers, communicators, and reflective.

Considering the Future

Now is the right time for IC. It will require a shift in thinking about students and their world, and about teacher identity and role. Perhaps, in the twenty-first century context, we should reconsider the way we organize curriculum content. Rather than by subjects, we could organize curriculum according to themes or big questions/wicked problems. We could create teaching teams in which teacher identity is not determined by subject or even by grade, but rather by theme, problem, or topic. Personal goal setting and formative assessment (assessment for learning) would be organizing principles to facilitate self-regulation or self-directed learning and intrinsic motivation. The twenty-first century competencies would be explicitly taught and consistently assessed as well as content. There would be a focus on a deep understanding of concepts. But most importantly, the Be would be highlighted throughout the day and recognized as central to the education of the whole human being.

Notes

1 See The Association for Supervision & Culture's (ASCD) website for further information about the Whole Child Approach (www.ascd.org).
2 See the iEARN website for further information on the One Day in a Life Project (https://iearn.org/cc/space-2/group-6).

References

Adler, M. & Flihan, S. (1997). *The interdisciplinary continuum: Reconciling theory, research and practice*. Report Series 2.36. Albany, NY: National Research Center on English Learning and Achievement.

Aikin, W. (1942). *The Story of the eight-year study*. New York: Harper.

Applebee, A. N., Adler, M., & Flihan, S. (2007). Interdisciplinary curricula in middle and high school classrooms: Case studies of approaches to curriculum and instruction. *American Educational Research Journal, 44*(4), 1002–1039.

Archibald, J. (2008). *Indigenous storywork; Educating the heart, mind, body, and spirit*. Vancouver, B.C.: UBC Press.

Asia Society. (2013). *Measuring 21st century competencies: Guidance for educators*. United States: Rand Corporation.

Battiste, M. (2002). *Indigenous knowledge and pedagogy in First Nations education: A literature review with recommendations*. Ottawa. National Working Group on Education and the Minister of Native Affairs Indian and Northern Affairs Canada.

Beane, J. (1997). *Curriculum integration: Designing the core of democratic education*. New York: Teachers College Press.

Brand, B. R. & Triplett, C. F. (2012). Interdisciplinary curriculum: an abandoned concept? *Teachers and Teaching: Theory and Practice, 18*(3), 381–393.

Brooks, M. & Holmes, B. (2014). *Equinox blueprint for learning 2030*. Waterloo, ON: University of Waterloo and Perimeter Institute for Theoretical Physics. www.wgsi.org/sites/wgsilive.pi.local/files/Learning%20 2030%20Equinox%20Blueprint.pdf.

Brough, C. J. (2012). Implementing the democratic principles and practices of student-centred curriculum integration in primary schools. *The Curriculum Journal, 23*, 345–369.

Cajete, G. (1996). An education for harmony and place: American Indian expressions of environmentally literate citizenship. *International Research in Geographic and Environmental Education, 5*, 2, 136–139.

Camillus, J. (2008, May). Strategy as a wicked problem. *Harvard Business Review.* https://hbr.org/2008/05/strategy-as-a-wicked-problem.

Clark, E. T. (2011). Implementing an integrated curriculum. *Encounter: Education for Meaning and Social Justice*, *24*(4), 34–45.

Daly, K., Brown, G., & McGowan, C. (2012). *Curriculum integration in the International Baccalaureate Middle Years Programme: Literature review.* Report prepared for the International Baccalaureate organization. www.ibo.org/globalassets/publications/recognition/dpguideforuniversities-en.pdf.

Dewey, J. (1916, 1966). *Democracy and education.* New York: Macmillan/Free Press.

Dewey, J. (1938, 1969). *Experience and education.* New York: Macmillan/Free Press.

Dowden, T. (2007). Relevant, challenging, integrative and exploratory curriculum design: Perspectives from theory and practice for middle level schooling in Australia. *The Australian Educational Researcher, 34*, 51–71.

Drake, S. M. & Burns, R. (2004). *Meeting standards through integrated curriculum.* Alexandria, WV: ASCD.

Drake, S. M. & Reid, J. (2010). Integrated curriculum: Increasing relevance while maintaining accountability. *What Works? Research into Practice*, Sept. Toronto, ON: Ontario Ministry of Education.

Drake, S. M. & Savage, M. (2016). Negotiating accountability and integrated curriculum from a global perspective, *International Journal of Learning, Teaching and Educational Research, 15*(6), 127–144.

Drake, S. M., Reid, J. L., & Kolohon, W. (2014). *Interweaving curriculum and class assessment: Engaging the 21st Century learner.* Toronto, ON: Oxford University Press.

Drake, S. M., Savage, M., Reid, J. L., Bernard, M., & Beres, J. (2015, June). *An Exploration of the Policy and Practice of Transdisciplinarity in the IB PYP Programme.* www.ibo.org/globalassets/publications/ib-research/pyp/an-exploration-of-the-policy-and-practice-of-transdisciplinarity-in-the-pyp-final-report.pdf.

Fenwick, A. J. J., Minty, S., & Priestley, M. (2013). Swimming against the tide: A case study of an integrated social studies department. *The Curriculum Journal, 24*(3), 454–474.

Finn, B. (1991). Young people's participation in post-compulsory education and training: Report of the Australian Education Council Review Committee. www.voced.edu.au/content/ngv%3A42925.

Fogarty, R. & Pete, B. M. (2009). *How to integrate curricula* (3rd edn). Thousand Oaks, CA: Corwin.

Fredericks, J. A., Blumenfeld, P. C., & Paris, A. H. (2004). School engagement: Potential of the concept, state of the evidence. *Review of Educational Research, 74*, 59–109.

Fullan, M. (2013). *Stratosphere.* Toronto, ON: Pearson.

Gallup (2014). *The state of America's schools: The path to winning again in education.* Available at www.gallup.com.

Hargreaves, A. & Moore, S. (2000). Curriculum integration and classroom relevance: A study of teachers' practice. *Journal of Curriculum and Supervision, 15*(2), 89–112.

Hinde, E. R. (2005). Revisiting curriculum integration: A fresh look at an old idea. *Social Studies, 96*, 105–111.

Huber, M. T. & Hutchings, P. (2004). *Integrative learning: Mapping the terrain.* Washington, DC: Association of American Colleges and Universities.

International Baccalaureate Learner Profile. www.ibo.org/contentassets/fd82f70643ef4086b7d3f292cc214962/learner-profile-en.pdf.

iEARN: One Day in the Life Project (n.d.). Retrieved from https://iearn.org/cc/space-2/group-6.

Jacobs, H. H. (1989). *Interdisciplinary curriculum: Design and implementation.* Alexandria, VA: ASCD.

James, R. K., Lamb, C. E., Householder, D. L., & Bailey, M. A. (2000). Integrating science, mathematics, and technology in middle school technology-rich environments: A study of implementation and change. *School Science and Mathematics, 100*, 27–35.

Jasperson, P. (2014). *In Australia, student engagement dips with each year in school.* The Gallup Blog, September 24. Retrieved from www.gallup.com/opinion/gallup/175085/australia-student-engagement-dips-year-school.aspx.

Kanu, Y. (2011). *Integrating aboriginal perspectives into the curriculum.* Toronto, ON: University of Toronto Press.

Kuntz, S. (2005). *The story of Alpha: A multiage, student-centered team, 33 years and counting.* Westerville, OH: National Middle School Association.

Lam, C. C., Alviar-Martin, T., Adler, S. A., & Sim, J. B.-Y. (2013). Curriculum integration in Singapore: Teachers' perspectives and practice. *Teaching and Teacher Education, 31*, 23–34.

Lankshear, C. & Knobel, M. (2011). *New literacies* (3rd edn). Maidenhead, UK: Open University Press.

Lederman, L. M. (2008). On the threshold of the 21st century: Comments on science education. *Yearbook of The National Society for The Study Of Education* (Wiley-Blackwell), *107*(2), 100–106. Doi:10.1111/j.1744–7984.2008.00174.x.

Lee, J. (2014). The relationship between student engagement and academic performance: Is it a myth or reality? *Journal of Educational Research, 107*, 177–185.

Li, Y. & Lerner, R. M. (2011). Trajectories of school engagement across adolescence: Implications for academic achievement, substance use, depression, and delinquency. *Developmental Psychology, 47*(1), 237–247.

Li, Y., Agans, J. P., Chase, P. A., Arbeit, M. R., Weiner, M. B., & Lerner, R. M. (2014). School engagement and positive youth development: A relational developmental systems perspective. *Teachers College Record*, *116*(13), 37–57. Retrieved from www.tcrecord.org/library/abstract.asp?contentid=18288.

Lieberman, G. A. & Hoody, L. L. (1998). Closing the achievement gap: Using the environment as an integrating context for learning. Paper presented at the State Education and Environmental Roundtable, San Diego, CA.

McNaughton, M. (2014). From acting to action: Developing global citizenship through Global Storylines drama. *The Journal of Environmental Education*, *45*(1), 16–36.

Miller, J. P. (2007). *The holistic curriculum*. Toronto, ON: University of Toronto Press.

Mohanty, S. P. (2014). A holistic curricular and pedagogical approach to early childhood care and education. *Pedagogy of Learning*, *2*(1), 53–61.

Moran, M. J. (1998). The project approach framework for teacher education: A case for collaborative learning and reflective practice. In C. Edwards, L. Gandini, & G. Forman (Eds), *The hundred languages of children* (2nd edn) (pp. 405–417). Westport, CT: Ablex.

Ontario Ministry of Education (2011). *Aboriginal Perspectives: A Guide to the Teacher's Toolkit*. www.edu.gov.on.ca/eng/aboriginal/toolkit.html.

Ontario Ministry of Education (2016). *21st Century Competencies: Foundation document for discussion*. www.edugains.ca/resources21CL/About21stCentury/21CL_21stCenturyCompeten.

Ontario Ministry of Education (2017a). Environmental Education: Scope and sequence of expectations. *The Ontario Curriculum Grades 1 to 8 and The Kindergarten program*. www.edu.gov.on.ca/eng/curriculum/elementary/environmental_ed_kto8_eng.pdf.

Ontario Ministry of Education (2017b). Environmental Education: Scope and sequence of expectations. *The Ontario Curriculum Grades 9 to 12*. www.edu.gov.on.ca/eng/curriculum/secondary/environmental_ed_9to12_eng.pdf.

Pushpanadham, K. (2013). *A critical analysis of the International Baccalaureate Primary Years Program in India*. Research report prepared for the International Baccalaureate Organization.

Rennie, L., Venville, G., & Wallace, J. (2012). *Knowledge that counts in a global community: Exploring the contribution of integrated curriculum*. New York: Routledge.

Rowsell, J. (2013). *Working with multimodality: Rethinking literacy in a digital age*. New York: Routledge.

Russell, C. & Burton, J. (2000). A report on an Ontario secondary school integrated environmental studies program. *Canadian Journal of Environmental Education*, *5*, 287–303.

Sill, D. J. (2001). Integrative thinking, synthesis and creativity in interdisciplinary studies. *The Journal of General Education*, *50*(4), 288–311.

Singteach (2012, May/June). Values come first, *36*. http://singteach.nie.edu.sg/issue36-scienceed/.

Smithrin, K. & Upitis, R. (2005). Learning through the arts: Lessons of engagement. *Canadian Journal of Education*, *28*(1 and 2), 109–127.

Thornton, L. & Brunton, P. (2015). *Understanding the Reggio Approach: Early years education in practice* (3rd edn). New York: Routledge.

Toulouse, P. R. (2008, March). Integrating aboriginal teachings and values into the classroom. *What works? Research into practice, Research monograph # 11*. Toronto, ON: Ontario Ministry of Education.

Truth and Reconciliation Commission of Canada Calls to Action. (2012). Truth and Reconciliation Commission of Canada. Winnipeg, Manitoba. www.trc.ca/websites/trcinstitution/File/2015/Findings/Calls_to_Action_English2.pdf.

Vars, G. & Beane, J. (2001). *Integrative curriculum in a standards-based world*. Eric Digest. www.ericdigests.org/2001-1/curriculum.html.

Vega, V. (2012, August 29). *A Research-Based Approach to Arts Integration*. www.edutopia.org/stw-arts-integration-research.

Venville, G., Sheffield, R., Rennie, L., & Wallace, J. (2008). The writing on the wall: Classroom context, curriculum implementation, and student learning in integrated, community-based science projects. *Journal of Research in Science Teaching*, *45*(8), 857–880.

Virtue, D., Wilson, J., & Ingram, N. (2009). In overcoming obstacles to curriculum integration, L.E.S.S. can be more! *Middle School Journal*, *40*(3), 4–11.

Weinberg, E. & Sample McMeeking, L. B. (2017). Toward meaningful interdisciplinary education: High school teachers' views of mathematics and science integration. *Meaningful Interdisciplinary Education*, *117*(5), 204–213.

Wiggins, G. & McTighe, J. (2005). *Understanding by design*. Alexandria, VA: ASCD.

Wiggins, G. & McTighe, G. (2013). *Essential questions*. Alexandria, VA: ASCD.

Willms, D., Friesen, S., & Milton, P. (2009). What did you do in school today? Transforming classrooms through social, academic and intellectual engagement. *Canadian Education Association*. www.ccl-cca.ca/pdfs/otherreports/WDYDIST_National_Report_EN.pdf.

14

HOLISTIC ASSESSMENT
Assessing Dialogically, Personally, Individually

Julian Stern

Assessment in school-based education is often seen as an entirely *additional* activity, added to the 'real' education that goes on within schools. Assessment is seen as being completed for outsiders (auditors, inspectors, school managers, exam boards) and, therefore, as helping create a performative culture, a culture where the whole child, and the whole teacher, are reduced to a standardized number. This is a popular and dangerous idea, dangerous in itself, and dangerous in its disparaging of assessment. There is another account of assessment, though: as a dialogic process in which adults and children treat each other as persons, not merely as performers "for the English to see" (www.phrases.org.uk/bulletin_board/37/messages/200.html, explained further in this chapter). It is an account of holistic assessment, in which assessment promotes individuality, community, and the spirit of the school. This chapter explains why both accounts of assessment are alive and well in schools and, to a certain extent, in scholarly literature. It argues for holistic assessment as entirely possible within conventional mainstream education. Not just possible, but necessary: necessary even for those under pressure to gain the very highest grades.

Well-intentioned and carefully organized holistic education can be undermined if assessment is not considered as integral to the system. And avoiding assessment altogether is not an option, as learning of all kinds is completed in dialogue: it is in dialogue that the value of learning, and learning of value, takes place. This chapter, therefore, begins with the corruption of assessment.

The Corruption of Assessment

Educational assessment has a history as long as formal education, and perhaps longer. The word *assessment* derives from the Latin meaning of *sitting beside* someone (OED, 2005). Etymology is not the best guide to current meaning, but the idea of sitting beside someone in order to understand what they know, understand, and can do, and what will help with further learning, is a refreshing 'new' idea that is carried in the very history of assessment. Sadly, the history of assessment practices in schools has been more problematic. Some of the intentions of assessment have been distorted or corrupted by educational policies, and assessment itself is sometimes used to distort or corrupt other aspects of education. However, understanding assessment starts with understanding its forms and its many purposes. All assessment involves making a judgment or determining a value of someone or something. In education, forms of assessment include criterion-referenced (assessing according to an independent set of criteria), norm-referenced (assessing performance according to the performance of other people, whether it is better or worse or the same as the 'norm'), summative (assessing the value of a whole set of work or study), formative (assessing something in order to influence the next period of learning), ipsative (assessing a person or a person's work according to that person's previous performance, is it improving, worsening, or just the same?). These forms also imply some purposes, the purpose of ipsative assessment includes judging improvement (or worsening) of performance, and so on. But there are always other possible purposes. Assessment may be used to judge a *person*, or to judge a person's *work*. It may be used to judge a teacher (as a person), or to judge teaching (and its effectiveness). Increasingly, assessment is used to judge schools, or groups of schools, or national education systems.

None of the various forms or purposes of assessment is inherently appropriate or inappropriate, ethical or unethical. The first decision, then, in the assessment of assessment, is what the purpose of schooling is: what are schools primarily *for*? Many would say that schools are primarily intended to help children learn, but even that relatively uncontroversial statement poses further questions. If schools are intended to help children learn to be "better people" (Noddings, in Stern, 2016, p. 29), then assessment can be judged according to its contribution to this aim. If schools are intended help children learn that life is a battle for survival in which only the strongest thrive, then assessment can be judged quite differently. For this chapter, given that it is within a handbook of holistic education, the first of those two purposes of schooling will be followed (see Stern, 2009, 2018). School-based assessment will be judged according to its contribution to the holistic development of children, attempts to "nurture the development of the whole person", including "the intellectual, emotional, physical, social, aesthetic, and spiritual" aspects of the person (Miller, in Miller et al., 2005, p. 2).

Once this assumption is made (that schooling is primarily intended to help children learn to be 'better people', across all dimensions of personhood), then there are various ways in which assessment can corrupt or be corrupted. Criterion-referenced assessment can and usually does involve criteria that assess only a narrow range of children's knowledge, understanding, and skills. If such assessment is treated as though it were a comprehensive assessment of the 'whole child', rather than an assessment of only some aspects, then the pupils and teachers alike will be downplaying or ignoring significant qualities. Schools may be expected to promote social skills, and moral and spiritual development (which is a statutory requirement in UK schools, Education Act 1944, section 7, p. 4, although it has never been systematically assessed), but if these qualities are not assessed, there is a danger that other qualities (more easily 'testable' qualities) will take precedence (Gipps, 1994; see also Gipps & Murphy, 1994; Stobart & Gipps, 1997). This is not to say that it would be easy to assess social, moral, and spiritual qualities.

Norm-referenced assessment presents a different range of challenges and possible corruptions. Comparing children to other children, and placing them at, above, or below a 'norm' is problematic in a number of ways. There is a tendency for such assessment to label children, that is, to give children the sense that they, not just their work at this moment, have been judged. 'Sub-normal' judgments can give children the sense that they are 'sub-normal' and that this is a permanent condition. Harm can be done if children are labeled as 'super-normal', too; this may be the basis for distorted feelings of superiority towards other children, with dangerous consequences. Additional problems include the lack of substance in norm-referenced assessment; it judges performance according to other performance, not according to any absolute criteria. In a class full of composers, if Chopin, say, were in a class in between Mozart and Beethoven, Chopin might get a sense of being 'sub-normal.' This is likely to make him believe (wrongly) that his achievements are of little or no value. That is an implausible example, of course, but in school systems that group pupils by achievement, there is a tendency for most of those in the highest group to judge themselves as inadequate because they fall behind the very 'top' achievements in that group. Norm-referencing makes for people always feeling compared, rather than feeling valued in themselves. There are some absurdities in norm-referenced assessment, too. Moss reports a recent discussion of school inspection at the UK parliament's education select committee, involving the then secretary of state for education, Michael Gove:

Chair: if 'good' requires pupil performance to exceed the national average, and if all
                  schools must be good, how is this mathematically possible?
Michael Gove: by getting better all the time.

(Moss, 2016, p. 937)

That was not an isolated comment. A previous UK secretary of state for education, John Patten, complained publicly that too many schools and too many pupils were "below average" (www.tes.com/news/school-news/breaking-views/student-self-esteem-sacrificed-for-standards), and introduced 'league tables' of schools to address this mathematically absurd 'problem.' The league tables were real, of course, and they continue to corrupt education in the UK.

Summative assessment involves judging a whole set of work or study, and this is often completed at the end of a stage of learning. Problems arising from 'fixing' an achievement at one point in time derive from the fact that people are constantly learning and developing. Any summative assessment that leads to significant effects on a person's life chances will be problematic because it assumes a single judgment is valid across time. End-of-school summative assessments in particular are likely to affect progression to work or further study, with impacts on earnings and other life chances for many years to come, along with profound effects on the self-worth and psychological well-being of those receiving the judgments. Notwithstanding the common view that teenage years are a time when people are poor at long-term planning, summative assessment during those years can affect the rest of those teenagers' lives. This is a distorting impact of summative assessment as it is currently used. It is worth noting, again, that there is nothing inherently damaging in summative assessment, or of any other form of assessment; it is how the assessment is managed and used that can be corrupting.

The explicit development of 'formative' assessment was intended in large part to counter the potentially harmful effects of summative assessment. Of course, formative assessment (explaining how a child is doing in order to guide future learning) is as old as any form of assessment, and harkens back to the etymological origin of the word assessment as 'sitting beside' someone. The Assessment Reform Group (ARG) of the mid-1990s onwards was particularly influential on formative assessment, redescribing it as 'assessment for learning' and combining formative with ipsative assessment, centered on pupil progression. Studying the detailed practice of assessment, "inside the black box" (ARG, 1999; Black & Wiliam, 1998a,b; see also Brookhart, 2013; Moss & Brookhart, 2009, 2012), this group provided research evidence that if teachers wanted their pupils to maximize their performance, then formative assessment could be one of the most important teaching tools. "The value that assessment can have in the process of learning as well as for grading work and recording achievement has been widely recognised" (ARG, 1999, p. 2), they said, but there has been "insufficient use made of assessment and national testing as a means of evaluating learning and teaching and of matching work to pupils' needs" and "[t]he use of assessment information for discussing progress with pupils. . . was not widespread" (ARG, 1999, p. 3). Harmful uses of assessment were listed as:

- a tendency for teachers to assess quantity of work and presentation rather than the quality of learning;
- greater attention given to marking and grading, much of it tending to lower the self-esteem of pupils, rather than to providing advice for improvement;
- a strong emphasis on comparing pupils with each other [i.e. 'normative assessment'] which demoralises the less successful learners;
- teachers' feedback to pupils often serves social and managerial purposes rather than helping them to learn more effectively;
- teachers not knowing enough about their pupils' learning needs.

(ARG, 1999, p. 4)

Instead, to improve learning, teachers should concentrate on these 'deceptively simple' factors:

- the provision of effective feedback to pupils;
- the active involvement of pupils in their own learning;
- adjusting teaching to take account of the results of assessment;
- a recognition of the profound influence assessment has on the motivation and self-esteem of pupils, both of which are crucial influences on learning;
- the need for pupils to be able to assess themselves and understand how to improve.

(ARG, 1999, p. 4)

Influential as this group of researchers is, formative and ipsative assessment do not ameliorate all the damage that can be done by other forms of assessment. In the first place, it says nothing of the criteria used for assessment, and so it is as open as any other form of assessment is to partiality in the choice of criteria. A second problem is that formative feedback and summative feedback are not necessarily complementary. If schools are still required to grade pupils (perhaps for the sake of school targets or external auditors, whether or not this is beneficial to pupils), then no amount of ungraded feedback (as recommended by the research on formative assessment) will ungrade schooling. In the US, Kohn (2010) has written of moving from 'degrading' schooling to 'de-grading' schooling, with the same concerns and the same hopes as those in the Assessment Reform Group. This concern over the potential damage done by some forms of assessment, the damage done even to the final summative grades of the pupils, has been described for a number of years. In 1964, the Scottish educational philosopher Macmurray wrote of the time he was concerned about the effects of examinations on schools, and the reason why reform of assessment was so difficult.

> I took every opportunity to consult with teachers. 'Don't you find,' I would ask, 'that the examination system frustrates your efforts to educate your pupils?' Mostly I got an affirmative answer. Where upon I would go on: 'Then let's get rid of it.' Astonishingly often the reply was, 'Oh! but you can't do that!'
>
> Why not? If examinations frustrate education, why can't we stop them? . . . The only answer that I can find is that we are afraid to. Fear has been, from the beginning, one of the major forces in human society.
>
> *(Macmurray, 1979, p. 13)*

The fear described by Macmurray is the fear of staff not being able to show what they have been doing, the fear of being judged poorly because they refuse to judge others. Fear besets assessment. As Boud says, "assessment hurts, it is uncomfortable and most of us have been deeply touched by it" (quoted in Stobart, 2008, p. 185), and something as uncomfortable as this all too easily creates fear. Fear is not a necessary corollary of assessment, but it is common, especially where *people* are judged rather than *work*, and where the consequences of the assessment of performance overshadow the learning itself. "When the classroom culture focuses on rewards, 'gold stars,' grades, or class ranking", according to Black and Wiliam, "pupils look for ways to obtain the best marks rather than to improve their learning" (Black & Wiliam, 1998b, p. 143, see also Clarke, 2001 on the damage done to the 'learning culture' of the school by external rewards). A pupil who values learning history, say, may find an assessment process somewhat fearful, but if the learning of history is itself the main purpose of history lessons, then the fear of assessment will be much smaller than if history lessons are entirely directed towards successful grades. A US middle school teaching pupils aged 11 to 14 currently (at the time of writing) has on its website "[o]ur number one priority . . . is to help our students gain essential skills to master all Standardized Assessment tests." (The name of the school has been withheld, even though the statement was on a public website: there is such pressure on schools to focus to this degree on test results, that a Principal honest enough to put this on the school website should not be labeled for having done so.) In such conditions, assessment is more than likely to induce fear in the school staff and, in consequence, in the pupils, too. Noddings is one of many writers who "argue[s] against an education system that put too much emphasis on academic achievement defined in terms of test scores" (Noddings, 2005, p. xiii).

Assessment can, therefore, corrupt, by distorting the views of pupils and teachers, and can be corrupted, in turn, by external targets and performativity (Ball, 2003). Performativity moves pupils and teachers away from being concerned with the learning itself, and towards thinking only of the extrinsic rewards or punishments arising from the assessment systems. Learning is merely performed 'for the English to see', a Portuguese phrase ('só para inglês ver', www.phrases.org.uk/bulletin_board/37/messages/200.html) originating in the nineteenth century when English boats policed the Atlantic to stop the slave trade. The English were not particularly interested in stopping the trade, but colluded with other vessels (including Portuguese vessels) to pretend that there was no trade being carried out. So, 'for the English to see' refers to a performance that is not sincere and does not reflect the real situation, but allows the continuation of a corrupt system. For those interested in holistic education and concerned with such corrupting influences of assessment, is there an approach to assessment that can overcome some, if not all, of these negative qualities? Is the only option to abolish assessment? The following section attempts to answer those questions.

Holistic Assessment

This section can begin with a quick answer to the question about whether assessment in schools should be abolished. The answer is 'no': avoiding assessment altogether is not an option. Recognising the distinctive forms of learning that take place in schools with professional teaching and formal learning, this is a process that will inevitably involve some kind of assessment. It is certainly possible to learn informally without any recognisable assessment. Many young children learn their first language without such assessment: although some adults regularly correct their children's developing language and provide informal assessment ('you shouldn't say that!'), much of the time, most children listen, copy, learn, make mistakes, listen, copy, learn, make fewer mistakes, and so on, in a gradually widening circle of language users. Most learn to make friends, and learn, later in life, to make love, unassessed, one hopes. It is not that language and friendship cannot be assessed. Even levels of spiritual development can be assessed: such assessment is regularly done in the appointment of religious ministers and, more rarely, the nomination of gurus and saints. But schooling, with its professionalised teaching and learning processes, has always involved assessment, even if it is the formative and ipsative assessment carried out by sitting beside pupils, encouraging and guiding successful learning, and providing alternatives to misguided or blocked learning. Such assessment, at the very least, is of the very character of professional teaching. But can assessment in school avoid or overcome the corrupting influence of assessment described in the previous section?

Barrow provides one response: "It is not perhaps that we need to do away with assessment, so much as that we need to become less hypnotised by the results of assessment" (Barrow, 1981, p. 197). Those committed to holistic education can do more than this. They can develop holistic approaches to assessment, and can thereby, at least to a degree, ameliorate the negative influence of other forms of assessment. The starting point is how teachers can sit beside, rather than 'loom over', their pupils. This is a matter of *dialogue*. The philosopher Buber describes three types of dialogue: there is

> genuine dialogue – no matter whether spoken or silent – where each of the participants really has in mind the other or others in their present and particular being and turns to them with the intention of establishing a living mutual relation between himself and them;

There is "technical dialogue, which is prompted solely by the need of objective understanding"; and there is

> monologue disguised as dialogue, in which two or more men, meeting in space, speak each with himself in strangely tortuous and circuitous ways and yet imagine they have escaped the torment of being thrown back on their own resources.
>
> *(Buber, 2002, p. 22)*

All three types of dialogue can be spoken or written, and can be expressed in smiles and frowns as well as in language; and all three types have a part to play in the process of assessment. Technical dialogue is vital: the exchange of information that is needed by learners and teachers, the accurate correction of errors, the information about how further progress might be made, the accounts of useful sources to be used. All are important to learning. However, if assessment is restricted to technical matters, teachers and pupils will not be using the full range of dialogue opportunities, and the discussions will not engage them as 'whole' people. Genuine dialogue, also referred to by Buber as 'real' dialogue (Buber, 2002, p. 22), engages the whole person, it involves an imaginative leap to the reality of the other person, what Buber calls "imagining the real" or *Realphantasie* (Buber, 1998, p. 71).

In assessment talk (including written 'talk'), pupils recognise the difference between teachers who are really in dialogue with them, and those who have *only* technical information to give. (Pupils want and need technical information, but they need more than *just* this.) And pupils recognize, too, those teachers who are not in dialogue at all, in their assessment communication: those who are going through the motions, who are not engaging at all, those who exhibit monologue disguised, sometimes very thinly disguised, as dialogue. It is in dialogue that the value of learning, and learning of value, takes place, and here I want to provide some examples from research in the USA, UK, and Sweden to illustrate the possibility and value of assessment dialogue that is really dialogic. The first account is from the research of Geiger, which took place in three Episcopal high schools (for pupils aged 14–18) in the USA (Geiger, 2015, 2016a,b, 2018). Based on earlier research (e.g., Stern, 2007; Stern & Backhouse, 2011), Geiger wanted to create a consciously dialogic process of "notebooking", in which teachers and pupils continued a written conversation about an initial piece of work by the pupils. The process was described as a "safe relational space for developing self-conscious agency" (Geiger, 2018, p. 20), and Geiger interviewed both pupils and teachers to explore their views on the notebooking project. What he found was that "[n]umerous students . . . spoke of putting forward a *persona*, a mask, in school in order to get a good grade", while "their teachers did not realize the students were putting forth an insincere self-expression and engaging with course content inauthentically" (Geiger, 2016b, pp. 506–507). One teacher within Geiger's project "said that he felt 'privileged' to be privy to the students' personal appropriation of RE content", and yet one of his pupils "state[d] bluntly in an interview that she and her classmates were 'faking it'" because they did not believe the teacher was genuinely interested in what they said (Geiger, 2016b, p. 507). This highlights the importance of dialogue itself, and not just a pedagogic approach that involves teachers and pupils communicating with each other. Pupils can recognize the difference between genuine dialogue and monologue disguised as dialogue. Positive feedback from another pupil was in this form:

> He . . . wrote basically a page back, and it's very personal. He talks about his own religion, and how he follows God. That he had his own falling out with religion, too. So I think it's nice to hear that feedback and how "I can identify," or "I agree with you in some ways," and in other ways he says, "I feel this way, you might feel this way." But its nice to know that you have that, sort of . . . he's not like, "oh, good job!"
>
> *(Geiger, 2015, original ellipses)*

It is worth noting that the teacher was *not* agreeing with the pupil: he was admired for being in dialogue about the work, not simply saying 'good job.' Some schools may think that the only way to help pupils is to indiscriminately praise them, while this pupil notes that disagreement is one of the signs of dialogue. Geiger said that his approach did not work with all teachers or with all pupils, but that when it worked, it worked because of the recognition of real dialogue.

> I am not proposing that the reflective and relational practice of notebooking is a fool-proof way to get students to engage in RE non-deceptively. The research suggested, however, that when teachers invited students into reflection through relational feedback, students ruminated on course content and personal spiritual/religious identity matters more thoroughly than when teachers lacked relationality.
>
> *(Geiger, 2016b, p. 516.)*

Within the UK, research with pupils aged 9–10 (along with teachers, university student teachers, and university tutors) asked them to evaluate examples of written assessment feedback, using analytical categories of how the teacher feedback brought (other) people into the conversation, how it involved treating people as individuals (as ends in themselves), how it involved magnanimity, how it enabled friendship to thrive, how it promoted real dialogue, and how it helped create meanings, things, and people (Stern & Backhouse, 2011, p. 332). One pupil said "nice comments i am proud of this work" and another said "I feel proud of this comment", while another said "the things that the teacher said makes the child want to improve." In contrast, some felt 'left out' by comments: "I thought it was a good piece of work and she [the teacher] hasn't marked anything (both pages)." A pupil said that the teacher's comments were "shamed/upsetting", another said "the teacher is very harsh and upsetting the pupil" (Stern & Backhouse, 2011, p. 341). "All she has done", said one pupil, "is marked mistakes agine!!!", while another said that "Pointing out moor spellings mistakes makes me feel very bad inside" (Stern & Backhouse, 2011, p. 342). "Please say why you like it!" was the plaintive comment from another pupil (Stern & Backhouse, 2011, p. 343). What this research indicated is that the 'ordinary' written feedback on pupil work, in contrast to the distinctive set-up of Geiger's 'notebooking' practice, was recognized as more or less dialogic, and this was recognized by pupils, students, and teachers. Improved written feedback can, the research concluded, help in "making a greater contribution to creative learning and the communal nature of learning through dialogue", and this "is not necessarily related to the quantity of feedback" as "[s]ome of the most 'spirited' comments were very short, and some longer comments were dismissed as exasperating" (Stern & Backhouse, 2011, p. 344). Written assessment feedback could, it was suggested, be more 'spirited', in the sense of contributing to the holistic–spiritual development of pupils.

A second UK example is based on my visits to Kingstone School, a secondary school for pupils aged 11 to 16 in the Northern English city of Barnsley. (The school no longer exists, having merged in 2012 with another school and reopened with a different name on a different campus.) Traditionally, towards the end of each school year, pupils would take tests in most or all subjects, reports would be written by teachers (based on performance through the year and the end-of-year tests), and meetings would be held with the parents or carers of each pupil to discuss performance and progress. The traditional processes are time-consuming, stressful for many of the pupils and teachers, and were not felt, in this school, to contribute a great deal to pupils' learning. They changed to a viva system, which, at the time of my visits (in 2009), included all pupils in Year 7 (aged 11–12). Pupils were given six weeks to prepare a 1500-word essay about a subject of their own choosing, along with a presentation on what they had learned that year and an electronic portfolio demonstrating achievement in terms of their personal learning and thinking skills. (These skills were promoted, briefly, in English education, see QCA, 2008.) Each child led an hour-long discussion about their progress at school, and reflected on what they needed to do next to improve further. The discussants included other children from the same class, the class teacher (who chaired the meeting), an adult significant to the child (such as a parent), and another professional adult not known to the child. Assessment depended on how pupils performed in the interview, with the emphasis on *performing learning* as individuals rather than *performing to/for grades*. Such a transformation from a conformist to a creative approach to assessment is evidence of how assessment can be more holistic, even within a conventional school with all the external pressures experienced by UK schools. It also recovers performance of learning from the corruption of performativity directed at those beyond the school.

Not all external accountability is corrupting, and it is reasonable that some assessment should help assure external bodies that worthwhile learning is taking place. As Reiss and White describe it, "[a]ssessment of students' attainments can serve a number of functions, but is used principally for reasons of accountability and in order to help students in their learning", and "[o]n the first of these, citizens have to be assured that schools are doing a good job, and part of this depends on evidence that their students are progressing satisfactorily" (Reiss & White, 2013, p. 55). In Sweden, moral and ethical education is established in the national curriculum (Skolverket, 2011), and research has been completed on how this element of the curriculum can and should be assessed. Inevitably, there are challenges in not only teaching but assessing ethics (Stern, 2017), but the reason for including this project is that it highlights some opportunities, and some risks, in assessment that goes beyond the more easily assessible criteria, such as knowledge. Lilja reported how teachers experienced the teaching and assessing of ethics, and one teacher reported:

> You can see it as normative, but I do not think it has to be normative. It is up to the teacher to open up and make the pupils aware of what is what. You do not have to use the word normative, you can use questioning. 'Does it have to be like this?', and have a discussion about it too.
> *(Teacher quoted in Lilja, 2017, p. 77)*

The same teacher later said, "I think ethics is about how to treat others, not only about right and wrong, but how you actually act in practice", so "ethical competence", which is being assessed, "is then about being able to relate to other people in a good way" (Lilja, 2017, p. 77). Another teacher, however, found the practice harder to assess: "In one way it is more important that they are good human beings, of course it is more important, but I cannot grade that" (Lilja, 2017, p. 80). The Swedish curriculum and its assessment attempts to move to a more holistic approach; attempting, that is, to assess a much wider range of pupil qualities, including their 'ethical competence.' Yet, there are challenges in such assessment, including, for example, the use of grades, and the idea that it is much more straightforward to assess written eloquence than it is to assess ethical practice.

In the research of the Assessment Reform Group (ARG), assessment that best supports pupil learning (whatever they are learning) will have the following characteristics:

- it is embedded in a view of teaching and learning of which it is an essential part;
- it involves sharing learning goals with pupils;
- it aims to help pupils to know and to recognise the standards they are aiming for;
- it involves pupils in self-assessment;
- it provides feedback which leads to pupils recognising their next steps and how to take them;
- it is underpinned by confidence that every student can improve;
- it involves both teacher and pupils reviewing and reflecting on assessment data.
> *(ARG, 1999, pp. 5–6.)*

One element in this list that is not explored in this chapter is peer assessment. Having peers as well as teachers involved in assessment is clearly a more holistic and communal approach (see Topping, 2009, focusing on schools, and Buchanan & Stern, 2012, focusing on student teachers). So the ARG list is tremendously helpful, and it has the research support indicating it is helpful precisely in raising pupil grades. It is an advantage that it is not tied to particular educational approaches, but is suggested as appropriate for all approaches. And yet, for holistic education, there is a narrower range of appropriate educational approaches. The examples given in this section from the USA, UK, and Sweden indicate that the personal intentions of teachers and pupils, and how they are perceived by the pupils, are central to the meaning of assessment in holistic education. Those willing to engage in dialogic assessment (whatever detailed assessment processes are used, with or without grades, whether summative, formative, ipsative, criterion-referenced or norm-referenced), if the engagement between teachers and pupils is genuinely dialogic, it will be more likely to be engaging and personally affecting.

Conclusion

Buber's description of genuine dialogue is one that is characterized by *surprise*. Dialogue is surprising in a "real conversation", a "real embrace", a "real duel", and a "real lesson." A real lesson is "neither a routine repetition nor a lesson whose findings the teacher knows before he starts, but one which develops in mutual surprises" (Buber, 2002, p. 241). Teachers should be surprised by pupils, their insights and creative responses to their work, and, in assessing work, teachers should admit their surprise. Pupils, too, should find their teachers surprising, even in assessment feedback. Assessment systems can all too easily destroy surprise, making everything predictable (according to pre-set criteria) and only measuring that which is easily measurable. However, assessment can be made more holistic, and can, therefore, celebrate surprise and uncertainty. In a real dialogue, there are surprises and uncertainties, and some issues remain unresolved. Such surprise and uncertainty is characteristic, also, of research and scholarship, so school learning that is meaningful and assessed holistically will also be preparing pupils for higher levels of learning.

Holistic schooling is characterized by care (of/for individual people) and curiosity (of/for that which is studied) (see Stern, 2018). Holistic assessment can contribute to holistic schooling by being itself dialogic, open to surprise and uncertainty, and thereby being caring and promoting curiosity.

References

Assessment Reform Group (ARG) (1999). *Assessment for learning: Beyond the black box*. Cambridge: University of Cambridge School of Education.

Ball, S. J. (2003). The teacher's soul and the terrors of performativity. *Journal of Education Policy, 18*(2), 215–228.

Barrow, R. (1981). *The philosophy of schooling*. Brighton: Wheatsheaf.

Black, P. & Wiliam, D. (1998a). Assessment and classroom learning. *Assessment in Education: Principles, Policy & Practice, 5*(1), 7–74.

Black, P. & Wiliam, D. (1998b). Inside the black box: Raising standards through classroom assessment. *Phi Delta Kappan, 89*(2), 139–148.

Brookhart, S. M. (2013). *How to create and use rubrics for formative assessment and grading*. Alexandria, VA: ASCD.

Buber, M. (1998)[1965]. *The knowledge of man: Selected essays*. New York: Humanity Books.

Buber, M. (2002)[1965]. *Between man and man*. London: Routledge.

Buchanan, M. T. & Stern, L. J. (2012). Pre-service teachers: Perceptions of the benefits of peer review. *Journal of Education for Teaching, 38*(1), 37–49.

Clarke, S. (2001). *Unlocking formative assessment: Practical strategies for enhancing pupils' learning in the primary classroom*. London: Hodder.

Education Act (1944). Retrieved from www.legislation.gov.uk/ukpga/Geo6/7–8/31/contents/enacted.

Geiger, M. W. (2015). Religious education person to person: Attending to relationality. *Religious Education, 110*(2), 162–180.

Geiger, M. W. (2016a). Emerging responsibilities, emerging persons: Reflective and relational religious education in three Episcopal high schools. *Religious Education, 111*(1), 10–29.

Geiger, M. W. (2016b). Personae, persons, and intersubjectivity: A relief for understanding roles, deception, and communion in religious education. *Religious Education, 111*(5), 504–520.

Geiger, M. W. (2018). Locating intersubjectivity in religious education praxis: A safe relational space for developing self-conscious agency. *British Journal of Religious Education*, 40(1), 20–30.

Gipps, C. (1994). *Beyond testing: Towards a theory of educational assessment*. London: RoutledgeFalmer.

Gipps, C. & Murphy, P. (1994). *A fair test? Assessment, achievement and equity*. Milton Keynes, UK: Open University Press.

Kohn, A. (2010). 'From degrading to de-grading', *Alfie Kohn*, Retrieved from www.alfiekohn.org/topics/degrading-de-grading-2/ (accessed 1 August 2017).

Lilja, A. (2017). Teachers' experiences of ethics in religious education. In O. Franck (Ed.), *Assessment in ethics education: A case of national tests in religious education* (pp. 69–86). Cham, Switzerland: Springer.

Macmurray, J. (1979)[1964]. *Ye are my friends and to save from fear*. London: Quaker Home Service.

Miller, J. P., Karsten, S., Denton, D., Orr, D., & Kates, I. C. (Eds) (2005). *Holistic learning and spirituality in education: Breaking new ground*. Albany, NY: SUNY Press.

Moss, C. M. & Brookhart, S. M. (2009). *Advancing formative assessment in every classroom: A guide for instructional leaders*. Alexandria, VA: ASCD.

Moss, C. M. & Brookhart, S. M. (2012). *Learning targets: Helping students aim for understanding in today's lesson*. Alexandria, VA: ASCD.

Moss, G. (2016). Knowledge, education and research: Making common cause across communities of practice. *British Educational Research Journal*, 42(6), 927–944.

Noddings, N. (2005). *The challenge to care in schools: An alternative approach to education* (2nd edn). New York: Teachers College Press.

Oxford English Dictionary (OED). (2005). *The Oxford English Dictionary* (3rd edn). Oxford: Oxford University Press.

Qualifications and Curriculum Authority (QCA) (2008). *A framework of personal, learning and thinking skills*. London: QCA.

Reiss, M. J. & White, J. (2013). *An aims-based curriculum: The significance of human flourishing for schools*. London: Institute of Education Press.

Skolverket [Swedish National Agency for Education] (2011). *Curriculum for the compulsory school, preschool class and the recreation centre 2011*. Stockholm: Ordförrådet AB.

Stern, L. J. (2007). *Schools and religions: Imagining the real*. London: Continuum.

Stern, L. J. (2009). *The Spirit of the School*. London: Continuum.

Stern, L. J. (2016). *Virtuous educational research: Conversations on ethical practice*. Oxford: Peter Lang.

Stern, L. J. (2017). The assessment of ethics and the ethics of assessment. In O. Franck (Ed.), *Assessment in ethics education: A case of national tests in religious education* (pp. 177–191). Cham, Switzerland: Springer.

Stern, L. J. (2018). *A philosophy of schooling: Care and curiosity in community*. London: Palgrave.

Stern, L. J. & Backhouse, A. (2011). Dialogic feedback for children and teachers: Evaluating the spirit of assessment. *International Journal of Children's Spirituality*, 16(4), 331–346.

Stobart, G. (2008). *Testing times: The uses and abuses of assessment*. Abingdon, UK: Routledge.

Stobart, G. & Gipps, C. (1997). *Assessment: A teachers' guide to the issues* (3rd edn). London: Hodder and Stoughton.

Topping, K. J. (2009). Peer assessment. *Theory Into Practice*, 48(1), 20–27.

15

TRANSFORMATION THROUGH ART AND VISION[1]

An Indigenous Perspective

Gregory Cajete

In the unfolding of Indigenous Tribal[2] education, the visionary and artistic contexts share a mutually reciprocal relationship. Indeed, they interpenetrate one another in their sharing and elaboration of dream, image, and creative response. Their forms of expression may differ but their meanings always stem from the same sources—the spiritual and cultural roots of a Tribe. Both contexts reflect and honor an inner alchemy of the visionary/artist whose task becomes that of representing, sharing, and celebrating a "dream". It is the dream and the representation of its essence, spirit, thought, or action through symbolic images that *transforms* both visionary/artist and *user* in some significant way and communicates some significant meaning. Vision and art structure and bring to completion a *transformative* natural process of learning and development. Vision and art reflect the reality of humans as imaginative and fully creative beings.

The tracks of vision and art can be traced back to the realm of dream and myth that are the origin and motivation for creative expression. The first visionary, the first artist, was none other than the First Shaman, who sanctified and legitimized his/her vision through dream and myth.

> The Blackfoot Indians tell us that it was Old Man who showed them how to make everything they needed. "Always at bottom there is a divine revelation, a divine act, and man has only the bright idea of copying it". . . The first god-begotten hero-king of all nations and races—like Osiris in Egypt and Quetzalcoatl in Mexico, was the one who taught the arts and showed people how to make tools.
>
> *(Dooling, 1978, p. 24)*

Indeed, it is to the First Shaman that the guiding visions, the sacred arts, the knowledge of medicine, hunting, building, learning, and living in one's environment are usually ascribed. The shaman was the first dream keeper, the first artist, the first poet, the first hunter, the first doctor, the first dancer, singer, and teacher. And, while the shaman personified the archetypal visionary and artist, the visionary and artist are potentials that abide in each and every one of us, every man, every woman, and every child. Tribal people understood and honored this "potential," this "calling" as an integral part of learning, being, and becoming complete. Through encouragement, through ritual, through training and practice, Tribal people formed and guided this reflection of the divine in each other.

This chapter follows the tracks of the visionary/artist of Indigenous America. The *first track* reveals the nature of dream and vision as viewed through the eyes and words of American Indian visionaries and artists, both past and present. The *second track* explores the central role of vision in the context of

Tribal educative endeavors. The *third track* reflects on the alchemy of the creative process from the perspective of transformation and orientation. From each of the aforementioned tracks radiate concentric rings which overlap not only the other tracks but the previous foundation of myth. The triad of myth, vision, and art echo the other foundations of the environment, affective, and communal. The integrated whole of Indigenous education becomes more apparent as we explore this dimension of that place that Indigenous people talk about, that place of dream and vision.

Creating Through Dream and Vision in Native America

Dream and vision are an integral dimension of artistic creation. For Indigenous peoples there exists a huge body of belief regarding the nature of dreams and visioning. This body of belief is itself very ancient, with its roots first being reflected thousands of years ago during the creative explosion of the upper Paleolithic, when both Neanderthals and Cro-Magnons first began imaging their "dreams" on cave walls and in clay, wood, and stone. Of this diverse and extensive body of belief, the belief that dreams represent the life of our spirit is the most commonly held and represented among American Indians. A foundation of Lakota spiritual belief, expressed in the Sun Dance, is that seeking a vision through the execution of proper rituals, fasting, and sacrifice brings one into contact with the dream world and the spiritual energy contained therein.

Among the Lakota, the elders tell that everything consists of four unique, yet wholly integrated, spiritual counterparts. These counterparts are similar to what Western theologians call "souls". The *first* of these souls is called "*Niya*" (or life breath) and is the essence that animates all beings and entities. The *second* counterpart is called the "*Nagi*" and is similar to the unique personality exhibited by each person or entity, be it plant, animal, or other material forms. The *third* soul is called "*Sicun*" and is that special property, power, or way of being which sets it apart as a group or family. For example, Grizzly Bear, White-Tailed Deer, Blue Spruce Tree, Sweet Grass, or Obsidian Flint would characterize distinct groups or entities with special traits and properties. The *fourth* soul, the "*Nagila*" is the universal base energy which courses through all things; it is the ground energy of the Universe, the breath of the Great Mystery, the "*Takuskan Skan*" in all things (Amiotte, 1982, p. 30).

During the Lakota Sundance, the "*Hanbleceya*" (crying for a dream) is the time, after extensive fasting and physical sacrifice, that the four souls of the sun dancers may be activated to interact with the souls of other spirits and entities of the world through a vision. If the sun dancer is of "good heart" and has prepared properly, he may enter a visionary state of dream. The interactions which occur between "souls" therein imparts important knowledge and understandings which the sun dancer becomes obliged to share with others for the good and the "life of the People." As Arthur Amiotte (1982), Lakota artist and educator, states: "One is more than mere physical being, the possibility for interaction, transaction, and intercourse within other dimensions of time, place and being is what the dream experience is to the Lakota: an alternative avenue of knowing" (p. 32).

As an alternative avenue of knowing and learning, dreaming has served Indian people in substantial ways. As with the Lakota, dreaming was recognized by all American Indian societies as a way of creating and understanding the essential nature of relationship within and outside one's self. The use and context of dreaming, of course, varied widely from Tribe to Tribe and region to region. But in every case, dreams and its more ritualized and structured form of visioning, were an integral part of American Indian ritual, ceremony, and religious philosophy. Dreams were both a source and catalyst for transformation. Among some Tribes, dreams and their Tribal structuring through visioning were important enough to warrant a special status in the social organization of a Tribe, with special roles and designation given to the dream interpreter or the dream societies that choreographed visioning ceremonies.

Dreams were deemed as important avenues for glimpsing the future, finding that which had been lost, understanding the cause of psychological disharmony, and the origin of needs and wishes which needed to be honored. Throughout Indian America, dreams and dreaming were considered essential to success and happiness in life. This orientation and valuing of dreams set the psychological and social context necessary for receiving, remembering, and incorporating dreams into the reality of everyday living.

Indeed, American Indian dreamers, within such a social context that valued dreams, developed extensive abilities to plan and manipulate the content of their dreams toward desired outcomes. In every Tribe there were cultural and social rewards for dreams that helped "the people". And through rewarding "culturally significant dreams", American Indians reinforced the role of dreaming in the fabric of their social/cultural being. With such incentives, American Indian dreamers actively sought to catch hold of any dream song or dream object that might symbolize an aspect of the deepest sense of themselves or of "the people", their Tribe or clan. It was through such dreams and visions that American Indians created meaningful personal and/or group rituals, ceremonies or customs, many of which continue to be enacted today. American Indians also gave their dreams creative waking form through art, song, dance, story, poetry, ritual, or ceremony. And it is through art that Indian people continue to communicate their dreams today (Garfield, 1974).

Taken as a whole, American Indians used dreams effectively in a variety of problem-solving and learning situations that required them to come to know their inner selves. To achieve this required the development of a direct and practiced understanding of a kind of "ecology" of the mind and spirit seldom equaled in these contemporary times. From the earliest ages, children were conditioned not only to honor their dreams, but also to learn how to manipulate them toward desired outcomes. In short, many American Indians learned how to "dream for effect". By coming to terms with their fears, their hopes, their ambitions, and their shortcomings through honoring their dreams and learning from them, many American Indians developed a discernible steadfast and self-reliant nature which enabled them to cope with stressful situations and face the trials and tribulations of their lives with a high level of integrity.

That legacy of dreaming, which at the time of the first contact with Europeans was so noticeably apparent, must be revitalized in a contemporized reassertion of the Indigenous education process. The enabling power of understanding and honoring the dream process within the context of a "new" form of Indigenous education is, as yet, largely an untapped domain. Today, Indigenous people everywhere suffer, in varying degrees, from a kind of cultural schizophrenia. Being constantly faced with having to adapt themselves to two very different worlds of being has caused untold confusion, misery, social and personal dysfunction among Indian people.

The educational process must again reconnect American Indian youth with their dreaming creative selves. Through the process of art making and the realization of the visioning process as a part of the educative process, great strides are possible in addressing the personal, social, and cultural disintegration that has become too much a part of the lives of many Indian people today. Denying the spiritual and psychological importance of dreaming, and not honoring its place in the educative process, leads not only to a stunting of an elemental process of human learning, but it ensures that a kind of cultural–social schizophrenia will continue to plague American Indians and take its toll on their lifeblood, be they young or old, reservation or urban, blue or white collar, full blood or mixed blood.

The key to this "existential" dilemma lies, in part, in learning and then understanding how to apply the creative process of visioning in a meaningful and direct way within a contemporary Indian educational setting. Visions are essential: they are integral to individual and communal success and they are the foundation of conscious evolution and human development.

The Role of Vision in Indigenous Education

Visioning embodies and focuses our creative power to visualize and bring to reality new entities in communion with others and with our own spirit. Visions always mirror what we deem as sacred and intimately important to us. Also, visions always relate and act to integrate all aspects of our lives.

Gregory Cajete

Visions are always about our individual movement toward wholeness. Whether the visions are for and about ourselves, our work, our community, or the whole world, they affect us at our deepest level of being. Honoring and living through vision is a quintessential learning process. Living through vision engenders living for a purpose and, as such, significantly enhances the meaning and quality we find in living. Vision also forms a contextual frame of reference through which we can measure, relate, and act on during the course of our daily lives. As a whole, visions are the source of the important motivation of our lives and the straightest path to fulfilling our innate human potential (Marks, 1989).

It is no wonder that visions held, and continue to hold, such an important place in many Indian societies. The process of visioning is indeed a basic creative response to make meaning of life. Visions are, indeed, for "life's sake".

The elaborations of visioning through ritual and ceremony by Indian people are pregnant with spiritual and psychological meanings. These elaborations in and of themselves model the integration of myth, dream, art, ecological philosophy, communality, and spirit. In the Lakota Sun dance, myth, art, ritual, depth psychology, and human community combine with dream to produce a complete and fully integrated sphere of education toward the goal of developing a complete and fully potentiated human life. The Vision quest, among the Lakota, is to "find life" in one's being, in one's world, and in one's community of relationships.

As Linda Marks (1989) so beautifully states in her book, *Living with Vision*:

> To develop a visionary process means to develop the ability to see the way things are; to see how things can be; to know what needs to be done from where we are to where we are going; to know what part we are to play in partnership with others; to feel the inspiration and call to act; and to be able to know and take appropriate action to live a life with purpose.
>
> *(p. 8)*

The essential dilemma of many Indian young people is how to live purposefully. That is, Indian youth need to learn how to see the relationships between Indian cultural values, finding a purpose for their lives, understanding the kind of work they need to do to act on purpose, and their development of a vision which guides them toward the basic fulfillment of themselves as complete human beings.

This is exactly what the context and process of dreaming and visioning was able to accomplish for Indian people in the past. Visioning continues to do this today for those Tribes and those individuals who have the remnants of this once great and highly effective educative process. Will Indian people, Tribal leaders, Indian professionals, and Indian educators heed such a call? This question is yet to be answered and it is a question that only Indian people themselves can answer.

Art and Alchemy

Art was a monumental evolution in the development of human learning. Art, which is the transformation of raw materials into a form that reflects meaning to both artist and user, is equally a reflection of a kind of elemental transformation. Indeed Art, in its highest forms of expression, *is* a kind of magic. And in this "magic" of creation, the artist becomes immersed within his media and the "mind" of creation.

In order to honor this intimate and sacred relationship, the artist must understand and master his own creative center through patient and exercised discipline. That is, the artist must work with clarity of purpose; an understanding and true appreciation of his materials and his "tools"; maintain an inner harmony and vitality of spirit, mind, and body; and work with a focused meditative attention which exercises his full intelligence in a prayerful act of bringing an entity, a form which lives, into being.

142

The creation of art is an alchemy of process in which the artist "becomes" more himself through each act of true creation, as he transfers his life in a dance of relationship with the life inherent in the material which he transforms into an artistic creation. In each process of creation, there must be an initiation, purification, death, and rebirth of the artist through focused creative work. For in working, reworking, and the suffering into being of a work of art, the artist is, in reality, creating and recreating himself. It is, in a metaphoric sense, "a matter of life, death, and rebirth".

This is the beautiful essence of artistic creation that the master Indigenous artist knows so well. This is the "age-old ceremony of art" whose aim is the making of one's self, the celebrating and symbolizing of an aspect of life deemed important to the artist, and the reality which he sees and shares with his Tribe, his people, and himself.

Yet, the master Indigenous artist was set apart from others of his Tribe only by his relative level of practice and skill in a particular art form. All Tribal people engaged in the creation of artistically crafted forms. Young and old, men and women, each in their own measure participated in the "making" of things. Whether songs, ceremonies, dances, pottery, baskets, dwellings, boats, or bows, Indigenous people were one and all engaged in creating the "utilities" of their lives. Art was an integral expression of life, not something separate; it rarely had a specialized name. The modern perception of "art for art's sake", as it is defined and expressed in modern and usually egocentric terms, had little meaning in Indigenous society. Everyone was an "artist", a maker of things, and the things made always had their proper form and use as well as inherent symbolic meaning. In each case, the traditional art form reflected the mythos of the Tribe, that is, the way a people viewed and understood themselves. The Indigenous artist vested meaning in every work he created. He made the "divine", as he and his people defined it, visible through his art. Art was a way of expressing his whole being in relationship with his Tribe and the spiritual essences that moved his world. Therefore, Indigenous art was functional and meaningful at the same time. There was no separation between craft and fine art as exists today in modern Western society. As Coomaraswamy (1991), suggested:

> Primitive man, despite the pressure of his struggle for existence, knew nothing of such merely functional arts. . . He could not have thought of meaning as something that might or might not be added to useful objects at will. Primitive man made no real distinction of sacred from secular: his weapons, clothing, vehicles, and house were all of them imitations of divine prototypes, and were to him even more what they meant than what they were in themselves; he made them this 'more' by incantation and by rites. . . to have seen in his artifacts nothing but the things themselves, and in the mythos a mere anecdote, would have been a mortal sin, for this would have been the same as to see in oneself nothing but the 'reasoning and mortal animal', to recognize only 'this man', and never the 'form of humanity'.

(pp. 7–8)

Indigenous Art: Mandalas of Creative Transformation

Traditional American Indian art forms are created for a specific purpose and/or activity and have been handed down from teacher to pupil through a symbolic initiatory process that significantly transforms the pupil. It also reflects the mythos of the Tribe *and* has meaning and value for the Tribe a number of generations after its creation. The educative foundation of traditional art forms is inherent in the ceremony of its process of creation. For the Indigenous artist, traditional art influenced the form and expression of life as well as provided a pathway to commune with the Great Mystery. The creation of art was actually a "mandala" of process for the re-creation of not only the Tribal artist, but also a way to evoke and focus the creative and healing power of the foundational guiding myths and traditional knowledge of a Tribe.

The outcome of this approach to art-making was a restoring or reforming of both artist and participants to a higher level of completion. Art, viewed in this way, becomes a series of acts for developing and perpetuating a process of life-enhancing relationships. In this context, the process and ceremony of "making" becomes far more than the product; the product becoming only a "kind of symbolic documentation" of the creative and spiritual process which gave it form. However, because such forms were created with a specific intention, many were used to evoke the original creative magic through ritual and ceremony. Artifacts created in this way were used and reused as needed, while others, such as the Navajo ceremonial Sand Painting, were destroyed after they had served their curative re-harmonizing purposes.

The concept of the mandala is useful in understanding the inherent wholeness of this way of "arting" and how the transformation and rejuvenation occurs. The word *mandala* comes from the Sanskrit root phrase meaning "center" or "to circle" or "in the middle place". In every respect, the mandala represents a structural metaphor for wholeness or completion. The mandala is an archetypal structure whose variations can be found in sacred art traditions, ranging from architecture to iconography to weaving to sand painting.

Wherever the mandala structure is found, it conforms to four basic characteristics. It has a center, reflects a basic symmetrical pattern, has a boundary defined by cardinal points, and its specialized construction provides a "tool" for concentration and meditation toward a pre-defined purpose. As a whole, the creation of a mandala embodies a therapeutic ritual which honors our basic impulse to strive toward wholeness through an active engagement of processes leading toward centering, healing, health, and transformative growth and development.

A primary function of creating a mandala is to engender a process which recognizes the relatedness of elements in a specific context, situation, or spiritual process to a person, place or group. Mandalas show the relationships of elements to "problems" which are being addressed. In the reflection of relationships, mandalas also mirror the nature of "self-relatedness" to the creator or participants.

Indeed, it may be said that each person is a "living mandala" at the physical–mental–social and spiritual levels. The mandala is an elemental learning tool, in that, through its construction, each person must learn how to concentrate their various levels of being, understand their basic orientations, and come to know their "center", in order to release the creative energy stored therein. The creation of art by Indigenous artists mirrors the creation of mandalas. In fact, some Tribal art, such as the Navajo Sand Painting, *are* mandalas. In the creation of a mandala, distinct stages of development are readily apparent. For instance, the creation of a mandala always begins with a stage of cleansing one's being in which there is a process of *purification* through prayer, fasting or meditation, the purpose of which is to increase the receptivity of the artist to his/her creative task.

This is followed by an activity that helps to *center* the artist's mind, body, and soul through concentrating one's energy inward, thereby energizing the creative spirit. Then there is an *orienting* of one's self to the creative task by ordering preliminary activities, preparing tools, testing patterns, and an overall immersion in preparatory actions and research of pertinent knowledge and gathering of necessary materials.

The next step, which is *construction* of the actual artifact, comprises the creation or "putting together of the parts". This making of the artifact, dancing of the dance, or singing of the songs is the direct expression of the activity completed in prior stages. But in a mandala process, the creation or performance is not the end, but rather the middle, point.

To complete the whole of a mandala process, there must be a complementary side to that of production. This complement might best be termed the "making of meaning" or reflection. For in the making of a mandala, there must be a stage of *absorbing* or internalizing the implied or inherent message of the mandala by the maker, the audience, or user. This is the point where all who have participated in the mandala process identify with its essence, its spirit. Once this identification has occurred, which is very profound and transformative, there is the need for a gradual detachment from emotional states which usually characterize the identification stage. This is a stage of "letting go" which flows into the next two stages of *reintegration* into a more basic level of being and the *actualization* of what has been learned about oneself and the purpose of the mandala into everyday life. This is exactly what happens in the whole making process of the Navajo Sand Painting (Argelles, 1972).

A mandala process almost always characterizes the making of sacred or ceremonial forms among Indigenous peoples. Traditional art forms among Indigenous people, regardless of their mode of expression, integrate and reflect the very essence of "the people". The mandala process structurally articulates the "sacred" play between creativity and entropy for all those who participate in its unfolding.

Art as a Way of Wholeness, Creativity, and Orientation

The making of art in Indigenous societies provided a pathway to wholeness for both the artist and those who utilized the artist's creations. Indigenous art provided a vehicle for approaching wholeness in that it required the artist to honor four basic orienting roles in the creation of a traditional art form, especially those created for ceremonial or spiritually empowering purposes. Applying the Indigenous metaphor of sacred directions, and the expression of dual yet complementary natures, these basic roles can be characterized as follows.

In the East, which represents for many Tribal peoples of North America the place of new beginnings (heralded by the first light of dawn), there are the orientations of the Shaman–Priest. The pairing of shaman and priest in the East is metaphorically appropriate in that both archetypes preside over the visionary and spiritually transforming foundation, which provides the basic impetus for the making of Indigenous art, and the centering process, which prepares and guides the artist in the creative process. This is the "seeing" of what needs to be done.

In the North are the orientations of the Hunter–Warrior, which represent the tracking, finding, and holding of the manifestations and symbols of both spirit and vision. These orientations are primarily concerned with the application of one's innate intuition in the finding of those "things" which are needed to create the kind of art that properly addresses the essential elements of the vision and presents the spirit of that which is to be created. Through these orientations, the creator develops the courage and self-confidence to follow that which has been seen. In these orientations, there is a process of centering, developing the "heart", and strategy to carry through the creative act.

In the twilight orientation of the West are the Artist–Poet. These archetypes creatively represent the unfolding of events, beginning in the visionary–spiritual orientation of the East, through the metaphoric use of images, words, forms, music, songs, and dance. In the roles as creative "presenters" of the Sun's illuminating light, Artist and Poet mirror or represent the images or forms or thoughts or sounds or actions that document and illuminate the path toward wholeness.

In the South are the orientations of the Philosopher–Teacher. These archetypes represent the quest for understanding and organizing the metaphorically coded messages inherent in the art that has been made. The creative play between understanding, which is the domain of the philosopher, and communicating, the domain of the teacher, form the infrastructure for the formal and informal transmission of knowledge and meaning of that which has been created. This is the "knowing" of what has been made.

In some Indigenous orientations, the South is the source of the fertile, creative winds and the monsoon rains, which warm and nourish the arid lands of the Southwest. The philosophical and educational orientations associated with the South provide a poetic and natural frame of reference to reflect on the creative process of learning through the art.

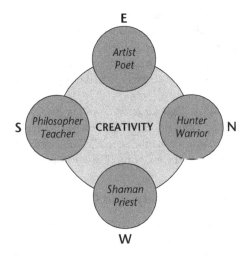

Figure 15.1   The cardinal orientations of Indigenous creativity

Cajete, G. (1994). *Look to the Mountain.* Skyland: Kivaki Press, p. 161

These orientations run parallel to contemporary understandings of the creative process. In essence, each of the orientations mentioned thus far mirror the generally accepted stages of the creative process. Viewed from this perspective, *First Insight*, the first stage of creation, might be associated with the Artist–Poet. In this stage, creative thought begins with dreams, intuitions, exploring archetypes, forms and images within the individual or group unconscious. The process then evolves to a "perceptive" play with Visual/Verbal/Special/Tactile or Auditory symbols and forms. Next comes a period of searching, introspection, and intellectualization, which develops the artist–poet's level of sensitivity and empathy for the creative work. Finally, the creator enters into the realm of macro vision, which is characterized by metaphoric thinking and transformative vision, which dwells upon the metaphysics and spirituality of that which is to be created.

The second stage of *Preparation/Immersion* is closely akin to the orientation of the Philosopher–Teacher. This stage begins with a process of making meaning, addressing contingencies, and exploring key relationships relative to planning an approach to developing an artistic work. There is a learning of "tools," research, and application of strategy and logic to finding the best way to make what needs to be made. The process then moves to more reasoning, symbolization, responding, and searching, combined with establishing the proper emotional and intellectual context for the making of the artistic work. At the macro level, this stage is marked by inquiry, scholarship, accumulation of knowledge, and further reflection on the metaphysics of the work to be done. Through this stage and the preceding one of First Insight, the form of the creative work gradually begins to take a tangible prototypical form.

The third stage of *Incubation* closely resembles the orientation of the Shaman–Priest and is similar to the beginning stage of "First Insight." The difference between the two lies in the relative depth each stage submerges into the unconscious. While "First Insight" is more perceptual, "Incubation" is more primal and alchemically transformative. The learning that is characteristic of First Insight and Preparation moves to the deeper unconscious realms of dreams, drives, archetypes, intuitions, and pre-concepts based on life–death symbols. Incubation, at its deepest levels of expression, gives rise to metamorphic processes and mythological thinking revolving around transformation and rebirth. These processes and thoughts are, in turn, expressed through forms of initiation, ritual, and ceremony. At the macro level, Incubation engenders hologizing (whole making), healing, and expressions of spirituality including those that are characteristic of various kinds of religious rites and practices. This stage "cooks" or "fires" the forms being created in the deep kilns of the unconscious.

The fourth and final stage of *Evaluation* is similar to the orientation of the Hunter–Warrior in that evaluation is like finding your "prey" or producing the work, and taking a stand in defense of what you have done. Evaluation primarily involves developing a strategy for presenting a "work" and addressing one's critics and one's shortcomings with courage. As a whole, this stage engenders self-confidence through boldly taking risks and a defense of the principles and integrity of the creative process that has led to the "art" which has resulted. At the macro level, the realization of this stage results in a state of completion. A relative state of spiritual centeredness and holistic perspective, which is expressive of the "good heart" engendered by the completion of a creative work, characterizes this last stage of creativity.

Indigenous arts provided, and continues to provide, a foundational way to express and nourish the soul of the instinctual human need to learn and create. Art is an essential part of human learning and plays a pivotal role in the development of the inherent potentials of every person regardless of social, cultural, or political status.

Conclusion

The place of the arts in Indigenous educational philosophy is without question. What is questionable is the reliance upon Western European concepts of art and the ego-centered, capitalistic, "schooling" for art which underpins the tacit infrastructure of the education of Indians in the arts. There is a *Way* of Indian art that is distinctly non-Western, non-European in its orientation, philosophy, aesthetic criteria, and aims. To understand this difference, it is important to understand the ceremony of art as it is practiced by Tribal people in the creation of ceremonial artifacts. For, historically, Indigenous artists created for *Life's Sake. Be with Life!*

Notes

1 Portions of this chapter have been adapted from a previously published work: Cajete, G. A. (1994). *Look to the mountain: An ecology of Indigenous education.* Skyland: Kivaki Press, pp. 142–164.
2 The terms *Indigenous, Tribal, Tribe* are capitalized to add emphasis and to convey an active and evolving identity. (The term *Indigenous* is used as the larger inclusive group term while *Tribal* refers to specific contexts, both terms are capitalized as an honorific designation. American Indian is used when referring specifically to a Tribe that resides in the United States.)

  Quotation marks, italics and capitalized letters are used with some words and phrases to add emphasis to those terms, thoughts or processes.

References

Amiotte, A. (1982). Our other selves, the Lakota dream experience. *Parabola*, 7(2), 29–33.
Argelles, J. (1972). *Mandala.* Boston, MA: Shambala.
Cajete, G. A. (1994). *Look to the mountain: An ecology of Indigenous education.* Skyland: Kivaki Press
Coomaraswamy, A. K. (1991). The use of art. *Parabola*, 16(2), 6–10.
Dooling, D. M. (1978). Alchemy and craft. *Parabola*, 3(3), 24–29.
Garfield, P. (1974). *Creative dreaming.* New York: Simon and Schuster.
Marks, L. (1989). *Living with vision.* Indianapolis, IN: Knowledge Systems.

PART III
Examples of Holistic Education, Practices
Introduction

John P. Miller

The one principle that almost all holistic educators agree on is the importance of teaching the whole child, that is, body, mind, and spirit. The forms for doing this can vary widely but the vision of human wholeness remains at the core of holistic teaching and learning. The contributors to this section demonstrate this with examples from around the world.

The section begins with chapters on Waldorf education and Montessori education perhaps the most well-known examples of holistic education. Although these approaches started in Europe, Montessori and Waldorf schools can now be found around the world.

In the first chapter in the section, Warren Cohen and Brian Bresnihan write that "Waldorf schools and pedagogy are designed to gently stimulate children's head, hearts, and hands, including all their senses and to promote their healthy development". The "head, hearts, and hands" encapsulate the vision for the whole child in Waldorf education. Spirituality is emphasized as the authors describe 'beautiful' lessons that are "soul-massages that help children to step more fully into life". Cohen and Bresnihan describe lessons in math, Greek history, and science in grades 4, 5, and 7. They also show how the Main Lesson, which takes up the first part of the morning, focuses on integration of subjects around a theme. Students create their own books that are filled with drawings and writing rather than using textbooks. All of this is to develop individuals who are free. By freedom, Cohen and Bresnihan mean the person sees the world clearly beyond personal preferences, cares about others, and develops the will to act using one's thinking as well one's feelings.

Michael Dorer, Tim Seldin, Robin Howe, and Jennie Caskey also stress the importance of reaching the whole child, which they identify as the first principle of Montessori education. The other three major principles of Montessori education that they discuss in their chapter include structuring education principles from the whole to part, an emphasis on inclusion with integration of diverse ages and learning styles and a responsiveness to cultural contexts within the principle of universality. The Cosmic Curriculum is presented as one of the central features of Montessori education and presents the unfolding of the universe through story, starting with the Big Bang and eventually coming to the Story of Language and the Story of Numbers. One of the central principles of holistic education is connectedness and this principle is also found throughout the curriculum. Maria Montessori wrote, "We shall walk together on this path of life, for all things are part of the universe and are connected with each other to form one whole unity". This chapter demonstrates how Montessori education is deeply holistic and why it continues to be one of the most popular forms of holistic education.

Tom Culham, Rebecca Oxford, and Jing Lin have explored the role of love in holistic education. They write about how a pedagogy of love encompasses the whole person:

> The pedagogy of love helps cultivate the abilities of the heart, the first aspect of the person in holistic education. Heart-cultivation through the pedagogy of love necessarily ties into the other three aspects of holistic education: the body (e.g., embodied learning), the mind (e.g., mindfulness and mindful learning), and the spirit (e.g., spiritual learning).

They begin the chapter by identifying the theoretical foundations of love and then describe how each of the authors includes love in their teaching. Readers will be inspired by how the authors brought a pedagogy of love into different educational environments.

The other chapters in this section describe programs in Asia and Africa and show how the whole person is at the center of their programs in holistic education. In 2009, I had the privilege of going to Bhutan to help that country orient their education system to the goal of Gross National Happiness (GNH). GNH is also at the heart of a school in Bhutan that Jackie Mitchell and Yang Gyeltshen describe in their chapter. Lhomon education (LME) is part of a school within a monastery in Bhutan that serves as a laboratory for innovative education in Bhutan. They write, "LME is holistic in its pedagogical practice, seeking to educate and nurture the whole child, body, heart, mind, and spirit". LME focuses on the interconnectedness of nature and employs the following principles: contemplative practice, ecological perspectives, and compassionate action. Such an approach brings an education that is "relevant, joyful, and effective" and has universal applicability.

Professor Bokyoung Kim from Korea describes the school forest movement in South Korea. Similar to Lohomon education, there is a strong emphasis on interconnectedness as an organizing principle. The school forest movement involves schools planting a small forest on the school grounds. A small forest provides an opportunity for inquiry learning into nature as well as a place where students can rest and meditate. The idea for the movement was inspired by the work of Giichiro Yamanouchi, now a retired principal, who initiated several forest schools in Niigata, Japan. There are now 762 forest schools in Korea. Other environmental agencies and government groups have contributed to the project and Professor Kim discusses the challenges for the movement as it expands.

The *Madrasa* schools in East Africa are the focus of Antum Pajwani and Sarfaroz Niyozov in their chapter. Using Miller's framework from *Whole Child Education*, they show how these schools reach the whole child. The *Madrasa* schools in Kenya have been developed with the support of the Aga Khan Foundation and present a curriculum that goes beyond religious teaching. "The curriculum draws from global educational best practices, is modified to be culturally appropriate, and incorporates Islamic teaching and practices". Community is another important feature of the schools, as the curriculum integrates learning activities with the town or village. The authors write, "In providing education that involves parents, communities and children, the *Madrasa* schools are civil societies that bring about change through community empowerment".

The most challenging environment for teaching holistically is the university. Jamie Magnusson, in her chapter, demonstrates how it is possible to teach the whole person at this level. Working in the department of Adult Education at the Ontario Institute for Studies in Education at the University of Toronto, she teaches a course entitled "Embodied Learning and Alternative Models of Community Development". Jamie also works in the community, particularly with people from the LGBTQ+ community including queer/trans youth who have been beaten and thrown out of their family homes. In working with these youth she introduces them to Qi Gong and breath work and also employs these in her course as many of the students are also doing work in the community. Professor Magnusson introduces various art forms that can be used for community work, including theatre of the oppressed, slam poetry, dance, singing, drumming, and dub poetry, so that students can incorporate these forms into their course projects. Her chapter gives a dynamic picture of holistic teaching and learning in a graduate school classroom.

Professor Wong has written a chapter on traditional practices in China that are used to cultivate spiritual development. These include such arts as zither (*qin* in Chinese) playing, calligraphy, poetry, and reading Buddhist scriptures. He writes how "life in its totality is an art". Daily activities such as walking, sleeping, traveling, and meditation are seen in the context of spiritual practice as well. Central to these practices is stillness, which refers to a state of mind rather than an absence of motion. Silence supports the stillness of mind and deep, spiritual listening. The process allows the practitioner to "break out of one's ego and connect spiritually with both one's deep self and the world (and the deep self and the world are actually one)".

The chapters in this section demonstrate how holistic education can be conducted in a variety of settings and yet maintain a focus on reaching the whole child/person. The practices described in this section actively engage the person's whole being. The chapters by Magnusson and Wong also show how holistic education is a life-long process and how it can go beyond the classroom and become part of one's whole existence.

16

WALDORF EDUCATION
Freeing the Human Being

Warren Lee Cohen and Brian Daniel Bresnihan

One week before the first Free Waldorf School opened in Stuttgart, Germany on September 7, 1919, Rudolf Steiner said to an audience of prospective parents, "A real education takes care that body, soul and spirit will be intrinsically free and independent. A real education takes care to put people into life" (Steiner, 1995, p. 63).

You step into a Waldorf school classroom and see colorful, hand-drawn pictures on the chalkboard. The gently painted, lazured walls have a sampling of student paintings and Celtic knot drawings displayed on them. An arrangement of flowers, autumn leaves, and pinecones is near the door. And, what is this grade 4 teacher saying?

"I understand that most of you like pizza. Is that correct?"—to which it seems all of the lively children answer, "Yes!" The teacher continues. "Well, we can have pizza next week, but it would be helpful to know the answer to this question first: Would you prefer one eighth of a pizza or one sixth?" A few students answer immediately, "One eighth," and a few others say, "One sixth." However, they do not all seem sure. "Well, let's see if we can figure this out," the teacher continues.

So begins the study of fractions for these inquisitive 4th graders. As there is no more effective place to start than with food, the teacher takes out a few cutting boards, knives, and a bag of apples. Soon they are eagerly cutting the apples into equal pieces in as many different ways as possible: into halves, quarters, eighths. . . . This gives the students an immediate and delicious experience that will help them to step with confidence into this new theme. Before class ends, the students draw apples split into even pieces and labeled in their main lesson books. These are their self-made reference books in which they record of all their work.

In the following days, the students do more dividing by separating groups of objects and cutting paper. They learn the roles of numerator and denominator. Soon, they see how common and useful fractions are, not only with food but also in many other areas of human endeavour, from building a house, to designing a book, to planting a field. Fractions are everywhere.

Of course, most children have already encountered the idea of fractions earlier when trying to divide things fairly or while working with recipes. This kind of preconscious exposure is a common and important part of all learning. However, Waldorf teachers know that the 'formal' study of fractions is most effective if it comes after the children have an inner experience of themselves being 'a distinctive part of a whole.' Each child is a fraction of the class and of her/his family. As 4th graders, they have an inner sense of their own individuality as separate from their parents that they did not have in their younger years. This inner feeling of being a part of a whole lays a strong foundation for the understanding and relevance of fractions. With it, learning how to manipulate them is filled with both meaning and purpose.

Yes, fractions could be taught earlier. However, bringing them to consciousness at this point in children's lives makes fractions not only useful tools for working in the outer world but also deeply resonant with their inner awakening. Fractions become so much more than just something else to be learned. They affirm children's inner reality. After this four-week introduction to fractions, my 4th grade daughter proudly said, "Fractions are not nearly as hard as regular math. They're fun!"

If you then step into other classrooms, you will see teachers standing before their students reciting poetry, or telling a story by heart; perhaps leading students in singing songs from around the world, or stamping out rhythmical patterns with their feet. You may see a teacher carrying out a science experiment or demonstrating how to create a certain mood in a painting. Eager children with bright eyes and rosy cheeks will be working individually and in unison. And, if you are lucky, you may notice the delicious smells of baking bread or of beeswax being modeled. Whatever the class, it will be a rich sensory experience with a focus on holistic learning, harmony, and beauty.

The aesthetics of Waldorf schools are distinctive, calm, and nurturing. Waldorf schools and pedagogy are designed to gently stimulate children's heads, hearts, and hands, including all of their senses, and to promote their healthy development. But, aesthetics alone do not make a Waldorf school. Above and beyond the aesthetics is the empowerment of the teachers as the decision makers in all aspects of their classes, the understanding of children as physically, emotionally, and spiritually developing human beings, the conscious inclusion of the arts as an essential feature in the learning process, the deliberate identification and removal of hindrances to the children's development from their environment, and the envisioned future goal of each child's individual freedom.

Every day, Waldorf teachers bring their students to laughter and sadness, to new understanding and intense interest, to caring and empathy for others. These 'beautiful' lessons are soul-massages that help children to step more fully into life. They work to slowly awaken their intellectual abilities in harmony with their social, emotional, and physical development. These essential human capacities will enable them to achieve their fullest potential and to find inner freedom as adults. Waldorf teachers are granted a great deal of freedom in their work. With this freedom also comes a tremendous responsibility to make this a rigorous and artistic education that meets the children's growing needs.

Children yearn to become adults, and therefore they look up to the people around them. Thus, teachers lead children most powerfully through the examples they set. It is essential that elementary school teachers are loved and admired by their students. With feelings of love and respect, children drink in what their teachers say, follow what their teachers ask, and learn from what their teachers do. They imitate their teachers. The capacity for freedom in adulthood is born from these forces of love, respect, and imitation that are best fostered in childhood. Waldorf teachers understand this responsibility and know they must lead their students with reverence and enthusiasm and in as artistic a manner as they can.

Children usually act based on their feelings instead of their thinking. This is more accurately characterized as impulsiveness rather than freedom. If children are often permitted to do whatever they like when they expect to be directed by their teachers, parents, or guardians, they will not be able to think or act out of inner freedom as adults. Instead, they will be controlled by the onslaught of advertisements, the media, entertainment, and by their emotions. They will be indulgent rather than free.

On the other hand, children also need breaks between periods of concentration and study, and they need time to act freely out of their own inspirations. Healthy 'breathing' in education has periods of focused teacher led activity followed by free play. This supports children's balanced development, supports digestion and integration of the lessons they have been learning, and helps them form their own moral compasses.

Waldorf teachers plan their classes to meet the natural rhythms of their students. They structure their lessons so as to foster healthy inbreathing, with activities that require concentration and focus, and healthy outbreathing, which allows for the expression of feelings and thoughts and the release of energy. They work sympathetically with the students' major circadian rhythms (their daily cycle of waking and sleeping). They take into consideration the cycles of the day, week, month, season, and year when planning their classes and other school activities. Following these rhythms lessens some of the hard work of learning and teaching. 'Rhythm replaces strength!' is a very helpful Waldorf teacher motto.

Art and the Artistic: Carrying out Waldorf Education

Pondering all this, you enter the grade 5 classroom and immediately notice a detailed map of Ancient Greece drawn on the chalkboard. Students' versions of Greek artwork adorn the lazured walls. A display of flowers and driftwood is behind the teacher, who is standing telling the class a story.

> . . . Zeus was sitting by Lake Triton suffering from a terrible headache. His head pounded, and the pain was unbearable. He had eaten Metis, the goddess of cleverness, to avoid a prophecy. Nevertheless, the headache became so bad that he begged the blacksmith, Hephaestus, to split open his head with his ax. When he did so, the Goddess Athena leapt out, fully grown and in full armour. Athena quickly won the heart of Zeus and became his most beloved daughter, the goddess of wisdom. . . .

Ancient Greek history, a cultural flowering that lasted little more than 150 years and yet has had profound impact on culture up to this day, is taught in Waldorf schools when the students are in the golden age of childhood, just before the advent of puberty. Their bodies are in a wonderfully balanced proportion and harmony. Their minds are not yet distracted by all the inner and outer changes that are soon to come. They love listening to stories from mythology and history as they are told to them by heart. They drink in accounts such as this, and how democracy was born in the small city-state named after Athena, Athens, and how, every four years, all battles were put on hold so that athletes could travel to Olympia to pay homage to the gods through their competitions. These tales enthral the students and inspire in them their growing sense of self and of the value of the shared ideals of humanity.

In this 5th grade year, Waldorf students come together with students from other regional schools to create their own Olympic Pentathlons, in which grace and teamwork are valued every bit as much as speed and strength. Dressed in togas they have designed and often sewn themselves, they come together for a weekend of sharing, competition, and friendship. These are remarkable gatherings in which they are all encouraged to shine and make new friends. It enables them to live more deeply into this rich curriculum they have been working with in their classrooms.

The event begins with each class making an offering of a poem, song, or play the students have learned. Then, the students are divided across classes into city-states to compete in the five events of the classic Greek Pentathlon: wrestling, long jump, javelin, discus, and running. Everyone has opportunities to excel as their classroom curriculum comes to life through their own efforts. Here, the best of Ancient Greece is celebrated. They experience this while making new friends and working together on the athletic field. By coming together and creating a community, they see how this process enlivens them in return.

Waldorf education is filled with artistic work created and being created by both students and teachers. Students sing and recite poetry. They draw and paint. They perform dramas and eurythmy. They model with clay and learn how to knit. "[I]f children are being educated only intellectually, their inborn capacities and their human potentials become seriously impaired and wither away" (Steiner, 1986, p. 17).

Art is the gateway to the soul. Waldorf teachers make use of every opportunity to engage the students in this way as they teach them what they need to learn to become adults who are both self-fulfilled and ready to contribute their gifts to society. However, this alone is not all that is meant by teaching artistically. It also refers to the artistic ways in which the teachers conceive of and present their lessons, how they interact with their students and colleagues, and how they imagine and structure their school as a creative learning community. Flexibility and spontaneity based on the needs of the students in the moment take precedence over the details of predetermined lesson plans. This artistic ideal is imbued in all facets of how Waldorf schools function.

Careful Observation: A First Step toward Understanding and Truth

You decide to visit one more class, grade 7. When you enter, you see the windows have been completely blacked out. You take a seat in the back of the room, and notice that the cracks around the door have also been covered. The teacher begins. "Our world is filled with light. It makes it possible for us to see. It helps plants to grow. It reveals the colors. Where does this light come from?"

There are a number of enthusiastic answers. "The sun." "Light bulbs." "Stars."

"Yes," responds the teacher. "There are a number of sources of light. But, what is its nature? What is light? Can we see light itself? Before we try to answer these questions, let's have an experience of the absence of light, complete darkness, and try to notice all that we can. This may make it easier for us to understand light itself. It is important that we are silent so that we can observe without distractions, using all of our senses." With that, the teacher turns off the lights.

The room falls into complete darkness and silence. As you adjust to this darkness you notice many things: that your eyes are adjusting, that the space feels larger. You may see dots of light, or feel scared or nervous. . . . You come to notice that your eyes can no longer see anything, not even your hand in front of your face. Then the teacher, using a rheostat and a hidden light source, gradually brings light into the room and asks the students to observe what is happening both in the room and in themselves. "What are the first things you notice? What comes next?" A rich discussion follows.

After this, the students are asked to write a poem about darkness and light. These are shared over subsequent days and are added to their main lesson books. More experiments revealing the mysterious nature of light are carried out. Through this rigorous phenomenological process, the teacher leads the students to ever-deeper levels of insight into, questions about, and interest in the physical world.

Waldorf teachers "want to learn from the nature of the developing child how children want to develop themselves as human beings, that is, how their nature, their essence should develop to become truly human." (Steiner, 1995, p. 55) They know that their students want to be led—to be shown what is worthy to do and to know—and they are expected to discover how to best do this for their particular students. Out of a deep knowledge of the stages and progression of child development and of love for their students, they try to make what they teach relevant and come alive for their students. They try to identify their students' strengths so that they can work through them to help their students overcome their weaknesses. They support their students in the unfolding of their inherent capacities. Through following their teacher's guidance at this age, students will gain the possibility of attaining the capacity for free initiative as adults.

Main Lessons: Depth Rather Than Fragmentation

The first two hours of a Waldorf school day begin with an intensive block of study called Main Lesson.[1] This is the heart of the school day, led by the main teacher, who teaches the same class of students over many years; ideally from 1st through 8th grade. As Waldorf schools are founded on the ideal of individual striving in the context of long-term supportive relationships, teachers go through many years with their students. They grow apace with them and, thus, provide a model of a life being lived working towards mastery.

Figure 16.1   Three interconnecting aspects of the human physical body, soul, and spirit

Main lesson blocks focus on one subject for three to four consecutive weeks, after which this subject is allowed to rest and a new subject taken up. Focusing on one subject (i.e., math, science, history, or language arts) intensively facilitates a deep level of engagement. These highly integrated, teacher-led lessons build upon each other from day to day, enabling students to strengthen their thinking (head), feeling (heart), and willing (hands). Such immersion fosters interest and allows time for effective and efficient learning.

Waldorf teachers introduce a new main lesson block with an oral story and/or an experiment. Listening to a story allows students to exercise their creative imagination. Observing an experiment allows students to take notice of something carefully, from which they then describe all that their senses experienced in detail. Both strengthen sense perception and concentration.

Teachers begin main lessons with a variety of awakening activities that include movement, recitation, singing, math skills practice, discussion, and recorder playing. These focus the students' attention, harmonize the class, and prepare them for work on the theme. There then follow academic and artistic activities to deepen student engagement, including writing essays, drawing sketches, painting pictures, modeling clay sculptures, solving problems, and doing further experiments.

Waldorf students create their own textbooks.[2] They are given blank notebooks, into which they write essays, poems, and explanations, do calculations and measurements, and paint and draw pictures. They often add colourful borders to enhance the beauty of their books. They turn these blank notebooks into much cherished treasures. Each page reveals how well the student is connecting with the materials and themes being studied as well as how the student's abilities to express herself/himself are developing. These are tangible, reliable expressions of each student's capabilities, weaknesses, and progress. This is *their* work.

Curricula: Integrated Rather Than Disconnected

Let us now take a look in detail at Grade 7 Astronomy, an exciting block in the Waldorf science curriculum, to see how it fits into the overall Waldorf approach to pedagogy. The Waldorf science curriculum builds from kindergarten onwards, giving the students as many direct experiences of natural phenomena as possible. In the younger grades, science is not so much taught as it is directly experienced. More formal science education begins in grade 4 (the same year as fractions), when the children are waking up to their separateness from others. Here begins the study of zoology, followed by botany in grade 5, and geology in grade 6. The study of Astronomy begins in grade 7, when students are ready and interested to learn about the 'fixed' and 'wandering' lights of the sky. They have learned about the world around them (in botany and zoology) and the world beneath them (in geology). Now, it is time to encourage them to look up. They have observed the sun, moon, stars, and planets for years, but do not really know much about them or their movements. It is an opportunity for students to begin to discern assumption from observation as well as theory from fact.

Waldorf teachers begin with a geocentric (earth-centered) perspective and later look from a heliocentric (sun-centered) perspective. It is vital that the students first understand how the night sky appears from the earth, from their own human perspective. This affirms their place on earth, their earth citizenship, and their own capacities to learn about the world through their own efforts. The movements of the sun, moon, stars, and planets are complex. They stretch the students' ability to observe with care and think with patience before leaping to conclusions.

While the students wrestle to understand the connections between how the heavens move and what they see, they learn about the work of astronomers since ancient times. The lives of Ptolemy, Copernicus, Tycho de Brahe, and Galileo, for example, offer fascinating pictures of human striving for understanding and the many impediments that stand in its way. Their knowledge was hard won, as were the moral struggles that came along with it. Did they have the convictions and the courage to believe, and to tell others, what they saw with their very own eyes?

Once students have penetrated this earth-based perspective and strengthened their capacities for detailed observation and reflection, they are ready to experience the leap in understanding that comes with the heliocentric perspective. What was complex and beautiful now seems simpler and easier to understand, but where has man, the observer, placed himself in order to gain this perspective? The students soon realize that the observer is no longer on the earth. They soon realize that they can think this heliocentric model even if they have never actually seen it. They are consciously being led from sensory-based knowledge towards abstraction.

After studying the movements of the starry world for a few weeks, the teacher organizes a night observation. What might this be like?

It is a cold winter night. The eager students and teacher are dressed in multiple warm layers. Talking in whispers, they walk to the middle of an open field and lay back in the snow. Silence. There are some clouds in the western sky, but not many. Orion's belt is spotted quickly to the east, and then the whole of the hunter's constellation appears. The big dipper is found nearly directly overhead, and Polaris is identified in the north. "Oh, I found Taurus' horns," one student softly cries out. The students had learned about the constellations they might see in class and what to look for. But, as the clouds pass by, what is this very bright star in the western sky so close to the thin crescent moon? And look, there's another bright star near the moon that seems to be reddish, not white. These are things to research the next day in the warm classroom.

This is one of many ways students can enter fully into the subject of astronomy. It is important to be mindful of their awakening capacities for logical thinking at this age and to use these to harness their interest in the outer world. As they enter puberty, teenagers' inner world, as well as their ever-fluid status in their social groups, may become compelling. This can consume their thinking, feelings, and will if teachers, and other adults, do not support them to draw their attention back into the outer world.

It is equally important to connect the astronomy block with other themes in the 7th grade year so that the curriculum unfolds as a coherent, interwoven tapestry. It is planned in the context of the expanding worldview of the Renaissance. The students have journeyed from the graceful ideals of Ancient Greece in grade 5 through the raw power of the Roman Empire and into the dark ages that descended upon Western culture with the collapse of Rome in grade 6. The students have gone through a similar journey in their inner lives from harmony, to power, to disunion. Now, in grade 7, new capacities are waiting to be born, and the many-faceted discoveries in the arts, sciences, and ideals of the Renaissance resonate deeply with the students. Their growing body of knowledge, insight, and interest matter to them as they try to understand the world and their place in it.

Leading Toward Freedom: The Final Goal

In addition to being based on an understanding of children's physical, emotional, and psychological development as unfolding in a sequence of predetermined stages, Waldorf education is founded on a holistic understanding of the human being as comprising body, soul, and spirit. The physical body is enlivened by the capacities of the person's soul for thinking, feeling, and willing. The body and soul are, in turn, guided in life through inspirations from the person's eternal spirit and by divine grace. Waldorf pedagogy stands as an antidote to the pervasive materialism and the malaise of meaninglessness that plague our world. It emerges from a deep study of body, soul, and spirit as expounded in the work of anthroposophy. If we take the notion of a spiritual aspect of human existence seriously (not just as a matter of blind faith), then the implications for this in life and education are profound. Each human being matters. In each relationship, we meet an element of the divine in the other. All of life's experiences are meaning-filled and form part of a larger meaning-filled whole. This spiritual perspective reveals deeper layers of holism that inform Waldorf education. These explorations are central to the work of Waldorf teachers and faculties.

Educators can only aim at 'freedom' obliquely. If they try to teach it directly, they will miss the mark every time. All true education is self-education. Educators may teach lessons, but "it is really the children who educate themselves through [the teacher]" (Steiner, 2007a, p. 126). Waldorf teachers know that their teaching can only be effective if it connects with their students' feelings, engages their will, and sparks their thinking. This is why they teach directly out of themselves, from what they have made their own, not out of textbooks. It is also why flexibility and the artistic element are so central to the way Waldorf education is carried out. Teaching must stir the students' hearts and souls for them to learn, not solely address their intellect, which is still mostly dormant.

The long-term goal of Waldorf education is to help students become free individuals in adulthood. This informs every teacher's preparations, presentations, and interactions with students. Being free means the ability to view and consider things objectively and not to be swayed by personal preferences or prejudices; the ability to care about others as well as oneself and to put one's will into action based on one's objective judgments; the ability to base one's actions on one's thinking instead of only one's feelings. Waldorf teachers are not teaching freedom, nor are they allowing children to do freely whatever they want. They are creating safety, warmth, and rhythm to best offer students engaging activities that will enable them to become free in their inner beings as adults.

Beginnings: The First 'Free' Waldorf School

The school was called 'free' for a number of reasons. It was not bound by pedagogical regulations set by the state. There was no outside body controlling the curriculum, the teaching schedule or methods, the hiring of the teachers, or the enrollment of students. It was revolutionary in that teachers were free to decide what and how to teach. Classes were not divided by gender, as was common at the time. Although the first students were factory workers' children, it was planned that the students would eventually come from all social, religious, and economic strata. This was soon the case. Religious beliefs and ability to pay tuition were also not considerations in admission. Most importantly, the teachers and the whole school would "work for the [children's] freedom, in the truest sense of the word" (Steiner, 2007b, p. 124).

In the wake of the massive destruction and social upheaval caused by the First World War, Rudolf Steiner founded the Waldorf School to counter the continuing worldwide tendencies towards

159

nationalism. The school offered a comprehensive, holistic education, featuring the arts and crafts integrated with academic studies. The aim was to foster each child's tolerance of others, abilities to engage in life's tasks in practical ways, and creativity. Central to achieving this was a well-balanced curriculum, motivation through the arts, and deep respect for individuality. As Steiner said,

> We can be certain that, if we respect human freedom, our teaching will place people in the world as free beings. We can be certain that the root of education can develop freely if we do not enslave children to a dogmatic curriculum. Later in life, under the most varied circumstances, children can develop appropriately as free human beings.
>
> *(Steiner, 1996, pp. 41–42)*

Enrollment in the first Waldorf school increased dramatically (from 300 to 1,200 students in five years) as did interest in the school by other cities and countries. By 1928, it was the largest non-denominational school in Germany, and other Waldorf schools soon opened in Germany, Switzerland, Holland, Norway, Austria, Hungary, England, and the United States.

Now, nearly 100 years on, Waldorf education is still at the forefront of holistic pedagogical practices and educational research, with over 2,000 independent Waldorf schools and early childhood centers in over 60 countries around the world (Waldorf World List, 2016). Most of these are privately funded. Others are government funded, and all are modeled after the holistic intentions established by the first. Each school is founded by the communities it will serve. The cultural and geographic contexts and socio-economic needs and opportunities are central considerations in its subject offerings, festival life, and structures. Each school is a unique expression of Waldorf education in its local context while maintaining connections with the original founding intentions of the first school. This can be seen in the motto of the Waldorf school movement:

> Accept the children with reverence,
>
> Educate them with love,
>
> Send them forth in freedom.
>
> *(Petrash, 2002, p. 16)*

Notes

1 The vignettes included are of Main Lesson classes. See Cohen & Bresnihan (2017) and Petrash (2002) for others.
2 For examples of pages and details from main lesson books, see Carlgren (1976).

References

Carlgren, F. (1976). *Education towards freedom*. West Sussex, UK: Lanthorn Press.
Cohen, W. & Bresnihan, B. (2017). The art of education: Waldorf education in practice. In J. Miller & K. Nigh (Eds), *Holistic education and embodied learning* (pp. 77–101). Charlotte, NC: Information Age.
Petrash, J. (2002). *Understanding Waldorf education: Teaching from the inside out*. Bletsville, MD: Gryphon House.
Steiner, R. (1986). *Soul economy and Waldorf education*. Spring Valley, NY: Anthroposophic Press.
Steiner, R. (1995). *The spirit of the Waldorf School*. Hudson, NY: Anthroposophic Press.
Steiner, R. (1996). *Waldorf education and anthroposophy vol. 2*. Hudson, NY: Anthroposophic Press.
Steiner, R. (2007a). *Becoming the Archangel Michael's companions*. Great Barrington, MA: Anthroposophic Press.
Steiner, R. (2007b). *Education, teaching, and practical life*. Chatham, NY: Association of Waldorf School in North America.
Waldorf World List (2016). *Freunde der Erziehungskunst, Rudolf Steiners e.V.* Retrieved from www.freunde-waldorf.de/fileadmin/user_upload/images/Waldorf_World_List/Waldorf_World_List.pdf.

17

HOLISM IN MONTESSORI

Michael Dorer, Tim Seldin,
Robin Howe, and Jennie Caskey

This chapter will focus on holism in Montessori as a pedagogy that emphasizes the fundamental principles of interconnectedness, the relationship of the whole to its parts, and inclusion. In Montessori education, these topics pertain not only to the intellect but also to the physical, emotional, and spiritual aspects of child development—as well as the philosophical stance that the fundamental purpose of education is to nurture human potential (Miller, 2009).

Holistic education is called a "curriculum of connections" (Miller, 2009, p. 291); that is, it is based on the premise that each person finds identity, meaning, and purpose in life through connections to the community and the natural world, while incorporating a spiritual dimension which acknowledges the "unknowable and irreducible within the human psyche" (Miller, 2009, p. 290).

Holistic education aims to call forth from people an intrinsic reverence for life and a passionate love of learning. There is no one best way to accomplish this goal. Instead, holistic education suggests there are many paths of learning; what is appropriate for some children and adults, in some historical and social contexts, may not be best for others. The art of holistic education lies in its responsiveness to the diverse learning styles and needs of evolving human beings (Montessori, 1989). This is done not solely through an academic curriculum that condenses the world into isolated subjects or instructional packages, but rather through direct engagement with the learning environment. Holistic education nurtures a sense of wonder and the natural curiosity of children.

What is Montessori Education?

Montessori pedagogy is regarded as a pioneering example of constructivist theory in education. Founded on principles of concrete, hands-on experiences, it allows students to draw conclusions about the world around them from the bottom up while providing them an overarching context for their learning. Its founder, Dr. Maria Montessori (1870–1952), was an Italian physician with a deep personal investment in child development, human nature, peacemaking, and equal rights. Montessori developed a radical educational approach for the time. Today, Montessori education is one of the largest organized forms of holistic education in the world. It is estimated that there are more than 4,500 Montessori schools in the United States alone and as many as 20,000 schools around the globe. Many Montessori schools offer programs from infancy all the way through to high school graduation (AMS, 2017b; NAMTA, 2017).

The *Montessori Method* was first conceptualized by Dr. Maria Montessori in 1907. In that year, she founded the first of her schools in the impoverished San Lorenzo district of Rome. The school provided an early day-care program for preschool children aged three to six years. Montessori called this first school and others after it, *Casa dei Bambini*—in English, *Children's Houses* (Hendriksen & Pelgrom, 2014).

Montessori was trained as a medical doctor, specializing in psychiatry at the University of Rome (AMS, 2017a). In those days, psychiatry was not akin to psychotherapy as we know it today, but rather resembled what is now called neuroscience, or the study of the human brain (Whitescarver, 2010). Montessori was an early pioneer in the effort to understand how human beings develop from birth to adulthood. Her early work with children with disabilities and children from low-income families led to the initial development of an organized approach to education and the establishment of thousands of schools in the early years of the twentieth century (Whitescarver, 2010).

It is important to note that Montessori did not intend to have her name associated with what evolved into a school reform movement. Instead, she titled her first book, *Il Metodo della Pedagogia Scientifica Applicato All'Educazione Infantile Nelle Case Dei Bambini*, or *A Scientific Method of Pedagogy as Applied to Child Education in the Children's Houses*. The book detailed the first early childhood schools designed with her methodology in mind, in Rome, Italy (Montessori, 2012, p. 7). Montessori focused on student observation and a prepared environment designed to facilitate students' independence, sense of order, concentration, and hand–eye coordination. Her philosophy of teaching was not, at first, what she considered to be of her own design at all; rather, she saw it as the application of a scientific method of providing stimulus to a subject and recording the results.

Over time, Montessori's curriculum and philosophy were deeply influenced not only by her early work with the young children in the first Children's House but also through her observations of human spirituality while living in India. Of course, her personal experience as one of the first female scientists to gain renown in her field influenced many of her key principles (Montessori, 2004). San Lorenzo Children's House exposed her to children with significant developmental challenges and families from cultural contexts of poverty and struggle.

After several years in India, unable to return home due to Italy's involvement in the Second World War, Montessori was exposed to a culture deeply infused with reverence for the interconnectedness of all living things. In India, Montessori was exposed to a new ideology wherein all aspects of life are connected. Living in this culture gave birth to a deeper, more profound understanding of the experience of being human and existing in the world. This appreciation of the interconnected nature of human experience had a profound influence on the evolution of Montessori's approach (Standing, 1957).

Montessori may never have had these experiences had she not been one of the first female medical doctors in Italy. As such, she was subjected to the prejudices of men who came before her—and worked alongside her. The ongoing challenges that she faced as a woman of medicine and science offered her a new perspective that fundamentally shaped her worldview and committed her to a mission of peace and education, with a deep reverence for the potential she saw in every child.

Today, Montessori programs have been developed for students of all age ranges, spanning from newborn infants through to age 18, or the completion of high school in preparation for the university. All Montessori programs are intended to be multi-aged, corresponding to patterns of child development that Montessori identified as *Planes of Development* (McKenzie & Zascavage, 2012). In addition to their traditional application in mainstream schools, Montessori strategies have been successfully used with other populations, including children with physical and cognitive handicaps and in elder care for patients with dementia.

Key elements of Montessori's theory of Planes of Development align with the theories of Piaget, Erikson, Vygotsky, and other psychosocial scientists of the era. Montessori and her contemporaries influenced each other's work significantly. Her theories identified patterns of student need and described the features of four distinct planes. Each developmental plane lasts approximately six years and is characterized by distinct physiological and intellectual markers. These markers are:

infancy (birth to age 6), childhood (ages 6 to 12), adolescence (ages 12 to 18), and maturity (ages 18 through 24). After age 24, Montessori considered the individual to be adult (Dorer & Grant-Miller, 2011). The needs and characteristics of the student at each plane were then used in the design of the prepared environment and the Montessori educational curriculum.

There are many guiding concepts of Montessori pedagogy, but they can be briefly summarized by Dorer's (2017) statement of ten core principles, which are respect, creativity, freedom of movement, freedom of choice, freedom to repeat, the prepared environment, the planes of development, mixed age groups, independence, and holism. To bring each of these principles together in the classroom environment, Dorer (2017) states that the catalyst of Montessori education is the Montessori teacher who directs the classroom and activities within it; it is relevant to note that Montessori teachers are not titled as such, but instead, called *Guides*[1] (Epstein & Seldin, 2003).

Several Montessori organizations work to support the Montessori movement around the world, including the Association Montessori International, which was established by Dr. Montessori herself, the American Montessori Society, the Pan American Montessori Society, and the International Montessori Council. Hundreds of additional Montessori organizations also operate at national and regional levels around the world. The organizations foster formal processes of teacher preparation and certification. Each of the major Montessori societies issues teaching diplomas, and there are still other accredited programs unaffiliated with the mentioned organizations. The Montessori Accreditation Council for Teacher Education (MACTE) is the accrediting body for Montessori teacher education recognized by the United States Department of Education and is becoming increasingly recognized throughout the world. Because of this, many international organizations require that their teacher education programs maintain MACTE accreditation along with their own affiliation standards.

It is important to understand that because the name Montessori was never copyrighted and there is no single central authority governing the establishment and operation of individual schools, there has been confusion regarding authentic Montessori practices leading to diverse public perception about Montessori schools and the Montessori method (Howe, 2017). The variations in everyday practices can be confusing to parents and others attempting to understand exactly what Montessori does and does not do. Still, even though some aspects of their everyday operation or general school culture may differ, the following aspects of Montessori pedagogy should be found in any school that represents itself as one offering a Montessori program; these characteristics all strongly support the principles of holistic education.

The Cosmic Curriculum

Montessori described in her written observations children's natural interest in the world around them. She called the educational program that was aimed to nurture this interest, Cosmic Education (Montessori, 1989). The purpose of Cosmic Education is to help the child understand the unity of the universe: acknowledge the long path of universal history that has led to the present; recognize their own role within not only that history but also the evolution of the earth. Through such a macro-experience, Montessori envisioned learning that is naturally enchanting and inviting.

Based on its fundamental principles of holism, Montessori pedagogy is holistic:

1. Its focus on the whole child.
2. Its structuring educational experiences from whole to part, fostering a view that ". . . the universe is harmonious and interconnected" (Miller, 1996, p. 21).
3. Its emphasis on inclusion, the integration of diverse ages, learning styles and individuality.
4. Its responsiveness to the cultural contexts of students and the Montessori perspectives on universality, or the universal potential of the child.

Michael Dorer, Tim Seldin, Robin Howe, and Jennie Caskey

The Focus on the Whole Child

While many educational approaches, such as mastery learning (Miller, 1996) focus on a student's ability to demonstrate command of independent skills, such as math or language, the Montessori approach recognizes the importance of the whole child, including academic success as well as the child's social, emotional, physical, and spiritual development. In fact, the Montessori curriculum has a specifically designed curriculum to meet the needs of the children in these non-academic areas. A Montessori education is meant to provide a thorough preparation not only for future academic or professional growth, but also for success in their everyday lives.

Montessori recognized that a student's academic success and emotional health were not mutually exclusive. A student who was emotionally unhealthy would not be able to reach the highest level of academic potential. The correlation between these two concepts was first observed in the early years of the first Children's Houses. While working with the children in San Lorenzo, Montessori observed that students who were hungry or emotionally neglected were not able to achieve academic success. Instead, it was clear that students needed their fundamental needs met first; they needed to feel comfortable, safe, and cared for—both physically and emotionally—before they were able to learn.

This deeper understanding of child psychology and developmental needs formed the basis for what is referred to in Montessori as the *prepared environment*. The prepared environment is one that is deliberately designed to meet the child's needs—a literal house for children, with furniture sized to their bodies, materials accessible and encouraging of independent exploration, all the accommodations of a comfortable home. Here, children's unique planes of development are recognized through adult Montessori guides who create and maintain the environments and provide rich academic experiences.

The environments include Montessori learning materials designed to be beautiful and enticing— usually carefully constructed of natural materials. These are placed in an attractive display on beautifully constructed shelves and are done so sparely, in an uncrowded array to facilitate their selection by the children. Children access these shelves and choose their own materials freely.

The Montessori curriculum includes not only academic subjects typical to most educational systems, but also life skills and emotional education. As part of the Practical Life curriculum,[2] Montessori weaves in lessons in *Grace and Courtesy*, which incorporate skills of etiquette, communication, care of self, and care of the environment, as well as emphasizing spiritual, cultural, and civic awareness.

Montessori's Practical Life curriculum can be misunderstood because it serves several purposes. In a Montessori classroom, students can be seen washing tables or wiping floors, preparing food, dusting, or learning and practicing other common skills. There is no doubt that these skills contribute to the good of the community, help children develop self-reliance, give children the experience of success, and they imbue children with the self-regard of being able to do something that adults usually do

It is, however, important to note that these exercises have an even more profound purpose. Their deeper aim is to help children develop a sense of order, concentration, coordination of movement, and independence. Many tasks involve several steps, and Montessori programs are designed to help young children learn the skills of sequencing; that is, organizing complex tasks into organized units in order to achieve complex or long-term goals (Montessori, 2004). Sequencing practice at this level prepares students for future academic pursuits, such as advanced arithmetic, as well as other endeavors that involve executive functioning and problem-solving skills.

The Montessori learning environment is built to not only provide for the students' fundamental needs, but also to enable a curriculum which gives them the skills and tools to provide for themselves and care for others, while at the same time, offering them an inspiring vision of the entire universe and their place within it. In this way, the Montessori pedagogy brings together the body, the mind, and the spirit of the child to prepare all three for learning and achievement at the highest level.

From Whole to Parts

Montessori education uses what is referred to as an integrated, spiral curriculum. In most educational modalities, curriculum is taught is small segmented pieces, or silos, which, when completed, contribute to a collective whole. This approach is sometimes referred to as *Atomism* (Miller, 1996) as it metaphorically builds up knowledge and understanding in the same way that atoms build up elements, compounds, and increasingly complex structures.

In contrast, Montessori introduces whole concepts before introducing the smaller pieces. The emphasis on teaching or exposing children to the whole before the more specified components or parts exists at all levels of Montessori. As children progress through the curriculum and advance in age, they become able to conceptualize more complex holisms.

The Montessori approach is based on a few fundamental principles: first, Montessori believed that in order to develop a deep understanding of something, a student had to have a conceptual, or impressionistic, understanding of it. Second, she believed that in order to help children develop an intrinsic desire to understand, concepts have to be contextually relevant. To achieve this, students are given an overarching, impressionistic, *big picture* idea through stories and lessons that provide a preview of what they are to be learning about throughout the year (and years). This creates relevance as students integrate more focused, in-depth lessons and experiences into their existing constructs.

Montessori education differs from some other alternative education pedagogies with holistic elements, such as immersion learning, in that it has an extremely well established structure of thought, culture, and curriculum. Although all Montessori guides are encouraged to be polymaths and prepared to follow the children's natural interests and pursuits, the Montessori curriculum also has a backbone which allows all spontaneous or planned lessons and activities to fall into one of five general themes: the universe, life, people, language, and math. In the Elementary Montessori curriculum, those themes are explicitly introduced through what are called the *Five Great Lessons* (Dorer, 2016).

The Great Lessons begin with three stories that examine a progression commencing with *The Story of the Universe* or Big Bang. The next story, the *Coming of Life on Earth*, explores the beginnings of life, and the third, the *Coming of Humans*, examines human evolution and development. These three story-based lessons emphasize change over time and focus on how those changes resulted in what we see around us today. The last two stories, *The Story of Language* and *The Story of Numbers*, describe how humans developed systems of communication and calculation that allowed for the rapid progression of our species in the most recent era.

Each of the Great Lessons is presented to Montessori students every year along with supplementary lessons that examine the topics in more detail and allow for increasingly complex engagement with the overarching concepts of each passage. The stories spark students' imaginations, providing the base and framework for them to discover their own questions and theories that form the basis of the initial exploration of the prepared environment.

All lessons and materials in the Elementary Montessori classroom connect back to these five core themes and allow the students to break down overarching concepts into smaller parts. Montessori materials are specifically designed to isolate skills and allow students to draw conclusions for themselves, with direction and support from their guides, about the many smaller facets of curriculum. Using self-exploration, not only can students apply new-found concepts to the context of the Great Lessons, but in a contrasting, nearly Atomistic (Miller, 1996) way, they are then able to build up their knowledge from the bottom up through observation and discovery, finally reaching the whole once again. In fact, the ideal Montessori environment is carefully constructed to provide students ample opportunities for dramatic epiphanies and moments of discovery.

Although the Great Lessons are presented to all Montessori students every year, the organized academic curriculum does not hold an obviously prominent role in students' lives before the Elementary years. In the Children's House or Early Childhood program, Montessori focuses most on individual human development and assisting children in understanding how to interact with the world around them. However, these early lessons provide the groundwork for later connections between experiences both practical and academic.

Inclusion and Integration of Diversity

Since its genesis, Montessori education has been grounded in addressing the needs of the individual. Montessori herself was not an educator but a scientist; she felt deeply that the way to provide the most effective education for children was to respond to their apparent needs, interests, and planes of development. This could only be done by observing those aspects of the children on a daily basis. In fact, when the practice was first implemented, Montessori recommended that every classroom have, at all times, some adults whose sole role was to observe silently, without influencing the children. This practice later led to the differentiation between the role of a Montessori *guide* as opposed to a traditional school teacher, the Montessorian both observing the students and aiding them in their explorations of their environments. Montessori wrote: "Children reach the goal of self-fulfillment and self-control by different roads, indirectly prepared by the perceptive adult" (Montessori, 1965, p. 18). In this way, the Montessori education system consistently adapts to the changing needs and learning styles of its students and provides constant feedback for teachers to reflect upon the efficacy of their work.

Like fingerprints, all children are different. The Montessori approach and the Montessori teacher's ability to modify instruction to meet a wide variety of students' needs and academic abilities are meant to serve every individual. For this reason, the mixed-age classroom not only provides opportunities for younger students to learn from their elders but also for the elder students to be leaders in their class. Furthermore, because traditional Montessori programs have three-year cycles, these opportunities repeat at each stage.

Students who are ready to progress beyond what, in conventional schools, is identified as their grade level can, therefore, forge ahead in unique ways. A Montessori guide supports this by offering increasingly creative enrichment opportunities for the students to expand the breadth and depth of their knowledge and understanding. At the same time, those students who are identified as below grade level in one or more areas can work alongside their more confident peers on the same topics, while receiving focused, personalized support. While each student engages with the same topics in their own distinct ways and various skill levels, they also interact with their peers above, at, and below grade level, creating an enriching learning experience for everyone.

The inclusive and integrative nature of Montessori is even yet more personalized, as students are able to progress within different areas of the curriculum while exploring applications of particular interest to them. For example, a student who is above grade level in math but has challenges in reading need not be subjected, as she might in a traditional school, to being labeled as requiring remediation. Instead, she will be encouraged to find personal applications in math that expand the depth and breadth of her learning in conjunction with age-mates,[3] while at the same time continuing to work with other age-mates in language arts, again finding personal applications. No being held back from her potential or stigmatized where she struggles. This is why this approach is called personalized rather than individualized.

The ability of the Montessori class to meet the spectrum of needs of many different learners also lends itself to the philosophy and pedagogy of addressing the needs of students of varied cultures and social status in a classroom. Paradoxically, the understanding that all children are different and Montessori education's ability to meet these different needs demonstrates the universality of the children: the belief that children, despite differences in background such as gender, religion, or wealth, are born with the same innate skills and capable of great things when provided a fertile environment for growth. Thus, Montessori schools around the world consciously welcome and seek out a wide range of children and families in terms of social, ethnic, religious, and socio-economic backgrounds, as well as learning styles. Maria Montessori celebrated diversity as an opportunity for children to experience the differences among the world's people. When describing the role of the Cosmic Curriculum and its role in helping students understand the interconnectedness of the world and their place in it, she wrote: "We shall walk together on this path of life, for all things are part of the universe, and are connected with each other to form one whole unity" (Montessori, 1989, p. 6). Montessori emphasized the interconnected nature of all things, including people. Based on this philosophical reverence, a platform for inclusivity, not only of individuals but also of diversity on a larger scale, was created.

In part, Montessori was inspired to incorporate religious, spiritual, and cultural diversity, and education about each, into her curriculum because of the patterns of history to which she bore witness during her lifetime. Discrimination-based politics, scientific fascination with eugenics, industrial development, and technological advancements in weapons, communications, and transportation were leading to widespread social inequality, world wars, and environmental pollution. Montessori grew convinced that the only long-term solution to the problems facing humanity was to focus on the future by educating children on these topics. Therefore, Montessori encouraged children and families to celebrate diversity in her classrooms. Her rationale was her understanding of the fundamental and common needs of human beings and the universality of children's innate developmental pathways. This fundamental principle continues to be one of the globally revered characteristics of Montessori, widely recognized as an educational movement of peace and inclusion.

Universality of the Child

Montessori described how human beings do not, like other animals, have a precise instinct to perform certain behaviors; instead, humans have continuously shifted throughout history, changing and adapting, exploring and reacting. She explains that the diversity of human work requires special adaptation, a different kind of *cosmic task*. The "great power of man," according to Montessori,

> is that he adapts to the environment and modifies the environment. For this reason, every man that is born must prepare his personality anew . . . We must see this vision of man in correlation with the environment and his adaptation to it.
>
> *(Montessori, 2012, p. 92)*

In her 1946 lectures, Montessori (2012) addresses a fundamental characteristic of man, that he distinguishes himself from all other living life forms. She writes about the human ability not only to adapt to the environment but also to adapt the environment to meet our own human needs. Of significance, she notes that these inherent abilities are perceptible throughout human existence and not limited to a certain generation or demographic.

Montessori recognized that, universally, typical child development follows a general pattern through which all children exhibit common characteristics and interests. Based on her observations, Montessori designed both a curriculum and environment that would meet these common patterns, needs, and characteristics as a validation of her understanding of the universality, or universal potential of children.

The Montessori Method is, therefore, based on the idea that children, regardless of external factors, have shared common interests and needs at certain times during normal development. One key concept of Montessori's universalism lies in her identification of specific sensitivities, or periods, in which a child is most interested in, or able to integrate, new information about certain experiences or ideas. Because these occur regularly during specified times in typical development, she called these *sensitive periods* and created child-focused, concrete materials to fulfill each period's particular developmental sensitivities or needs. The Montessori Children's House, for example, is deliberately designed to meet the needs of the child in the second half of the first plane of development, or, roughly, the years between ages 3 and 6. During this period, children continue to absorb information and stimulation from their experiences, construct internal concepts about reality, and begin to use language, allowing them to participate in their larger group's culture (Montessori, 2004). The Montessori environment of the 3- to 6-year-old, therefore, is designed with materials that meet these needs, sequentially, in a scaffolded curriculum that presents new information based on the demonstrated mastery of preceding skills. Students in this environment will learn phonetic sounds and their corresponding written characters. As they master these, they will begin to construct simple phonetic words that initiate the introduction of writing and, later, reading.

Montessori theorized that all children of the world, if provided the right environment (including the trained guide), would be able to absorb information and develop in these areas at a rate that, if missed, would never be attainable again. A most apparent example is the sensitive period of language, with which we all have experience. A child who is exposed to language (even multiple languages!) can not only acquire fluency with ease but can learn intonation and grammar without needing to be explicitly taught. An adult trying to learn a new language will almost certainly have to work diligently and will likely never achieve the same proficiency as someone exposed to a language naturally, during their sensitive period for it.

Montessori suggested that, like language, all developmental sensitivities need to be met in the prepared environment to maximize a child's potential. Since her original publications, modern child development studies support these theories of sensitive periods. Usually they are referred to as "critical periods" (Scott, 1962), with strong supporting evidence from studies of language development in feral children, in particular. Because of the integrated nature of Montessori education, it is difficult to isolate students' various experiences during each sensitive period, and, thus, hard to compare the impact of exposure during these times to other environments constructed without such deliberate emphasis on developmental stages. However, it is this exact feature of Montessori that makes it a strong, practical example of holistic education.

Conclusion

Montessori education represents a sizable percentage of the educational pedagogies or methods that honor holism throughout the world, and it shares with its holistic kin a child-centered, unified nature, designed and operating with the ultimate goal of helping to create a future world of thoughtful and insightful peacemakers. Montessori teachers and students focus on relationships in their studies and among people, the interconnected role of humans in the universe, personal and collective making of meaning, and the importance of being present in their own existence.

Notes

1 The word "guide" is often used in Montessori schools rather than "teacher" or Montessori's own chosen title, "directress." The reason is that the function of the adult in the classroom is less to instruct than to act as a catalyst or inspirer. The concept of a guide suggests some combination of a spiritual guide and a tour guide, guiding the students on a learning tour that is not only curricular, but spiritual in its unifying approach (Dorer, 2017).

2 Practical Life is one of four traditional areas of the Montessori Children's House. The others are Sensorial (aimed at sensory growth and development), Mathematics, and Language Arts. The Practical Life area emphasizes Montessori activities to develop the children's sense of order, their coordination of movement, their concentration, and their independence. It also includes activities of politeness, social grace, manners, and etiquette. These are called activities of Grace and Courtesy.

3 The term, *age-mates*, means other children of the same age or grade.

References

American Montessori Society (AMS) (2017a). *Maria Montessori Biography*. Retrieved September 30, 2017 from https://amshq.org/Montessori-Education/History-of-Montessori-Education/Biography-of-Maria-Montessori.

American Montessori Society (AMS) (2017b). *Montessori schools*. Retrieved October 2, 2017 from https://amshq.org/Montessori-Education/Introduction-to-Montessori/Montessori-Schools.

Dorer, M. (2016). *The deep well of time: The transformative power of storytelling in the classroom*. Santa Rosa, CA: Parent Child Press.

Dorer, M. (2017). Ten essential Montessori principles (plus one). *Tomorrow's Child Magazine*, *25*(1), 15–19.

Dorer, M. & Grant-Miller, J. (2011). *Planes of development*. St. Paul, MN: Privately Published.

Epstein, P. & Seldin, T. (2003). *The Montessori Way*. Sarasota, FL: The Montessori Foundation.

Hendriksen, J. & Pelgrom, E. (2014). *And now: Montessori!* Heino, Netherlands: Sonodruk.

Howe, D. R. (2017). An examination of Montessori practices in American elementary schools (Doctoral dissertation). Retrieved from Argosy University Dissertation Library.

McKenzie, G. K. & Zascavage, V. S. (2012). Montessori instruction: A model for inclusion in early childhood classrooms and beyond. *Montessori Life*, *24*(1), 32–38. Retrieved September 22, 2017 from http://origin-search.proquest.com/docview/1009924821?accountid=34899.

Miller, J. (1996). *The holistic curriculum*. Toronto, ON: OISE Press.

Miller, J. (2009). Holistic education: Learning for an interconnected world. Education for Sustainability. In *Encylopedia of Life Support Systems (EOLSS)*. Retrieved from www.eolss.net/EolssAllChapter.aspx.

Montessori, M. (1965). *Dr. Montessori's own handbook: A short guide to her ideas and materials*. New York: Schocken Books.

Montessori, M. (1989). *To educate the human potential*. Oxford, UK: Clio.

Montessori, M. (2004). *The Montessori method: The origins of an educational innovation*. Lanham: Rowman & Littlefield.

Montessori, M. (2012). *The 1946 London Lectures*. Amsterdam: Montessori–Pierson.

North American Montessori Teachers' Association (NAMTA) (2017). *How many Montessori schools are there?* Retrieved December 17, 2017 from www.montessori-namta.org/FAQ/Montessori-Education/How-many-Montessori-schools-are-there.

Scott, J. (1962). Critical periods in behavioral development. *Science*, *138*(3544), 949–958. Retrieved September 30, 2017 from www.jstor.org/stable/1709580.

Standing, E. M. (1957). *Maria Montessori: Her life and work*. London: Hollis & Carter.

Whitescarver, K. (2010, July–September). Montessori in America: The first 100 years. *Montessori International*, *96*, 18–19.

18

Cultivating the Abilities of the Heart

Educating through a Pedagogy of Love

Tom Culham, Rebecca Oxford, and Jing Lin

Fourteenth century poet and Sufi master Hafiz (2003) suggests that love is the best topic, now and forever. Two young teachers of today, Jennifer and Brian, would agree. They commented sincerely on love, soul, and caring while becoming teachers of English as a foreign language.[1] According to Jennifer, who loved Hafiz's poems and the pedagogy of love when encountering them in a graduate course, "Positive emotions are essential to learning; emotions are from the mind and felt in the body, which is experienced in the spirit. The most positive part of teaching and learning occurs *when love is involved*" (Keith, 2016, emphasis added). Brian's passionate words also reflect the pedagogy of love: "Students are not breathing robots that will produce output if you give them enough input. *The human soul needs to be fed* as much as the brain. Teachers need to *create caring environments*" (Rice, 2015, emphasis added).

The pedagogy of love, already understood by these young teachers, cultivates the abilities of the heart, such as wisdom, compassion, caring, and understanding. Part A below focuses on the theoretical foundations for the pedagogy of love. Part B offers multiple examples of the pedagogy of love in action. Part C offers further thoughts, including ties between the pedagogy of love and holistic education.

Part A. Theoretical Foundations for the Pedagogy of Love

This part presents five foundations of the pedagogy of love: a general theory of love, the heart as an electromagnetic energy field, the opening of the heart, uniting reason and intuition, and contemplative keys.

1. A General Theory of Love: Child and Adult Development

Love begins with the beginning of our lives. Lewis, Amini, and Lannon (2000) state in their book, *A General Theory of Love*, that the love between caregiver and child is the foundation of human survival and brain development. The nature of the relationship is critically important, though it might be largely unconscious.

Before a child's development of language and conscious memory, a loving mind-to-mind relationship is vital to brain development and lifelong social well-being. If a fully attentive and loving relationship is not present in the early years, the child's brain will not be fully developed, causing relational problems later in life. Mind-to-mind communication occurs between the limbic (emotional) part of the brain of mother and child. The limbic part of the brain holds our mainly unconscious knowledge of how to relate to others. It has been found that healing of emotional wounds and learning in adult life can be enabled by an adult-to-adult loving relationship like that of the mother-child relationship. The limbic part of the brain can heal, grow, and learn in later life under these conditions. This part of the brain not only affects our relational skills but also has amazing problem-solving skills. Scientific experiments have illustrated that the limbic part of the brain can outperform some problem-solving skills of the conscious, rational part of the brain.

2. The Heart as an Electromagnetic Energy Field

The heart is an electromagnetic energy field, in which positive energies can emerge for the benefit of humans, all other creatures, our planet, and the cosmos. Sustained by the electromagnetic field that is the heart, the pedagogy of love involves teaching love, embodying love, and teaching through love. Einstein, Gandhi, and Martin Luther King, Jr. described the nature and power of love as a force in the world. In the heart are many abilities that can be cultivated, and the greatest is love, which infuses all others.

The Chinese character for mind, or more appropriately translated as heart-mind, is an image of the heart: 心 symbolizing a unitary concept of mind and body. Taoists think of the heart as an electromagnetic field originating in the Tao that coordinates and regulates the energy, physiological, and emotional function of all the other organs. It is through cultivation and adjustment of one's heart that one achieves internal and external harmony with other. The idea that the heart is an energetic source that connects to and influences other people has been confirmed through scientific investigation (McCraty, 2004, 2015). The Tao is the primordial energy field that is integrated with spirit, information and matter, that propels life and connects, and that is love, compassion, yielding, softness, and giving. In Taoist thinking, the self is viewed as in a process of exchange of powerful, life-nurturing energies with others and the cosmos (Roth, 1999). This view has similarities with quantum understanding, which holds that all phenomena are interrelated and that they exchange information and energy (Capra, 1991).

As Zhang (1999) explains, Chinese medical philosophy unites emotions and energy. The heart generates fire energy, which is united with love and loving kindness. The heart enables the whole body to circulate qi (prana in Hindu, Ki in Japanese) and oxygen, propelling blood and qi to all the organs and various parts of the body. The loving heart is a force that can pull people together, and a heart that lacks love pushes people away. That is one reason why humans are so negatively affected by violence, that is, the lack of love.

Because the heart is an electromagnetic field, cultivating the abilities of the heart is to open ourselves to others and to cultivate reciprocal relationships. Information about a person's emotional state is encoded in the heart's electromagnetic field and is communicated throughout the body and into the external environment. Psycho-physiological information can be encoded into the electromagnetic fields produced by the heart. There is a direct relationship between the heart-rhythm patterns and the frequency spectra of the magnetic field radiated by the heart. Thus, information about a person's emotional state is encoded in the heart's electromagnetic field and is communicated throughout the body and into the external environment. Interactions between and among humans are affected by subtle yet influential electromagnetic communication systems.

The Heart Math Institute has found that the emotional state of people is reflected in their heartbeats, and this is unconsciously perceived by others through the electromagnetic field generated by the heart (McCraty, 2015). Therefore, before we can teach love we need to practice love. We can cultivate love for ourselves by practicing self-compassion (self-love) and self-awareness; admitting mistakes; meditating; engaging in counseling; doing yoga, qigong, tai qi, or dance; and journaling or doing other forms of writing. We can foster compassion toward others and know ourselves better by being vulnerable; deepening relationships; listening non-judgmentally and speaking without expectation; practicing humility; participating in dialogue, group discussions, group therapy, and healing circles; and contributing to supportive, compassionate teamwork toward a single goal.

Schwartz (2007) argues that "everything is ultimately energy" (p. 45). He contends that the heart and mind are linked, and our emotions and cognitions produce electromagnetic forces, albeit subtle. He found that one person's heart energy registers in another person's brain. He discovered that the degree of people's experience of having been loved and cared for by a parent predicted their ability to receive others' heart energy.

Given the hatred and conflicts that have built up in society over time, we need the courage to love unconditionally, like a parent with a newborn, and teach with the pedagogy of love. Our challenge is to drop our expectations and judgments of others and to care and love unconditionally. It is said that our historical time is ready for a shift to deep inner learning and an approach to life that, compared to today's approach, is slower, softer, nuanced, insightful, intuitive, patient, empathetic, and spirit-based. We hope that the shift will come. Our energy of love can help the educational paradigm to shift from domination, competition, hierarchy, and control to cooperation, interdependence, care, and reconciliation.

3. The Opening of the Heart

The pedagogy of love enables the opening of the heart-mind. The Taoist Wuwei opens the heart-mind, releases the universal love deeply embedded in our collective unconscious mind, and strengthens the heart's ability to feel and give love. Opening the heart and cultivating relationships necessarily involve compassion, which is among the "three treasures" of Taoism (see, e.g., Mair, 1990). Similarly, in Buddhism, meditative practices, interpersonal generosity, and compassion help the heart to open. The opening of the heart metaphorically requires the caring encouragement of light, which reduces fear, according to Hafiz (1999), the poet we met earlier.

Palmer (2009) says that a broken heart can become a truly open heart. Using a magnificent image, he says, "Imagine that small, clenched fist of a heart 'broken open' into largeness of life, into greater capacity to hold one's own and the world's pain and joy" (Palmer, 2009, p. 6). To hold another person's pain and joy involves empathy, which is a necessary capability of a teacher using the pedagogy of love. Empathy is an other-oriented response containing a constellation of caring emotions tied to the perceived welfare of someone else. Empathy involves feeling the other person's emotions, sensing his or her needs, and in some instances non-judgmentally understanding the person's strengths and weaknesses. To have empathy with others, teachers optimally must have enough courage and self-understanding to recognize their own emotions, needs, strengths, and weaknesses (Brown, 2010).

Empathy can be deepened when the individual has developed emotional intelligence (EI). EI, like empathy, is related to an open heart. EI is the "ability to understand feelings in the self and others and to use these feelings as informational guides for thinking and action" (Salovey, Mayer, Caruso, & Yoo, 2011, p. 238). Research shows that EI can reduce anxiety and conflict, improve relationships, and increase harmony, achievement, and motivation (Goleman, 2005). The best teachers, those who teach with the pedagogy of love, are empathetic and emotionally intelligent, and they have become that way through the opening of the heart.

Yet what if a broken heart refuses to open and remains caked with hatred? What if the heart is dominated by violence and hate? True example: A bitter young man seeking to be a teacher says loudly, "If minorities can't learn in my classroom, *they can get THE F*** out.* Minorities are worthless, and *they should die*" (verbatim).[2] The antidote to this is love. "Hatred paralyzes life; love releases it. Hatred confuses life; love harmonizes it. Hatred darkens life; love illuminates it" (King, 1963, in Couch, 2011, p. 4). Brown and Miller (in progress) describe ongoing group campus meditation and refer to Eros[3] as a heartfelt connection and a heart space, where a loving momentum thrives. If facilitated well, such meditation might cultivate a heart space for all, even a bitter person. Individual, ongoing work with a compassionate therapist or teacher might also help. Sooner or later, working on projects with people from minority groups might be valuable. These processes might eventually build a heart space marked by openness, acceptance, and even love and empathy.

4. Uniting Reason and Intuition

According to Einstein (1918/2017),

> There is no logical path to these laws [of the universe]; only intuition, resting on sympathetic understanding of experience, can reach them. . . . The state of mind that enables a man to do work of this kind is akin to that of the religious worshipper or the lover; the daily effort comes from no deliberate intention or program, but straight from the heart.
>
> *(p. 2)*

Thus, Einstein, the icon of Western science, credits the discoveries of science to the heart, to intuition, and to something akin to worshipping and loving, rather than to Enlightenment-born reason, logic, analysis, reductionism, detachment, materialism, critical thinking, objectivism, and measurement, which are favored in much of modern education (Palmer, Zajonc, with Scribner, 2014; Zajonc, 2006). However, it is not necessary to forsake science. Zajonc (2006) calls for resituating science "within a greater vision" of knowing and living (p. 2), a perspective that includes reason but also encompasses intuition and all other abilities of the heart.

5. Contemplative Keys to the Pedagogy of Love

The pedagogy of love can foster peak experiences (Maslow, 1971), which come from experiencing something ordinary as extraordinary. A peak experience is

> a great and mystical experience, a religious experience if you wish – an illumination, a revelation, an insight. . . [leading to] "the cognition of being,". . . the cognition that Plato and Socrates were talking about; almost, you could say, a technology of happiness, of pure excellence, pure truth, pure goodness.
>
> *(p. 169)*

Peak experiences are especially joyous, exciting, ego-transcending moments involving sudden feelings of intense love, empathy, awe, happiness, ecstasy, creativity, well-being, wonder, and timelessness. Peak experiences can happen in the classroom, in nature (seeing a sunset, brilliant autumn leaves, or a sparkling river), at home, or with friends, when dancing or listening to music, and in countless other circumstances. Rebecca and her graduate students have had peak experiences through art, telling stories of our transformative learning (see later), and reading poetry together.

Matthew Fox's (2014) concept of "deep education" echoes many of the ideas of the pedagogy of love, and is actively contemplative. Deep education is aimed at wisdom, which involves love, compassion, creativity, intuition, imagination, and engagement, and is linked with wonder and awe ("radical amazement"). The emphasis on wisdom in Fox's deep education comes from Meister Eckhart's Wisdom Schools in the thirteenth and fourteenth centuries. Eckhart combined education, wisdom, and spiritual psychology (Oxford, 2016). Deep education involves both sides of the brain, the logical and rational left hemisphere and the artistic and intuitive right hemisphere. Similarly, contemplative inquiry is a key to what Zajonc (2006) calls the "epistemology of love," which includes the stages of respect, caring, gentleness, intimacy, vulnerability, transformation (containing insight, which can be great enough to be an epiphany), and peace.[4]

We have discussed five foundations of the pedagogy of love. Now we turn to concrete illustrations of the pedagogy of love in action.

Part B. Diverse Examples of the Pedagogy of Love in Action

Here we offer authentic examples of the pedagogy of love. First, Tom leads meditations in his business ethics courses. Second, he develops self-compassion and admits mistakes. Third, Jing teaches with mindfulness. Fourth, Rebecca's students discuss transformative learning.

1. Tom Leads Meditations in Business Ethics Courses

In my instruction of business ethics, I utilize a class of attentional meditations that train mental processes related to the regulation of attention to assist students to know themselves better, a foundation of ethics. This includes two types of meditation: focused attention and open monitoring (Dahl, Lutz, & Davidson, 2015). Focused attention involves narrowing attention to a single object, while open monitoring involves expanding attention to one's internal flow of perceptions, thoughts, emotional content, and/or subjective awareness. The key attribute of this class is the "systematic training of the ability to intentionally, initiate, direct, and/or sustain these attentional processes while strengthening the capacity to be aware of the processes of thinking, feeling, and perceiving" (p. 3). While apparently a very self-oriented activity meditation, this paradoxically has the effect of transforming one's relationship with others and potentially broadening one's worldview.

Relationships are transformed because, according to neuroscience research, people who meditate 15 minutes a day or more are better able to regulate their emotions. Rather than impulsively acting on emotions, they are able to know how they feel and choose how to respond, which can have a powerfully positive effect on relationships with other people. According to ancient Taoist texts, those who meditate gain access to universal knowledge that resides within each person. This influences the person to take a broader, less self-centered, and perhaps more other-caring perspective. When students are engaged in meditation focusing on a positive emotional experience of the past several weeks, they commonly report feeling lighter, more open, and expansive. Instead of rushing to get a coffee after arriving at the university, one student mentioned they now stop and simply breathe in the morning fresh air.

2. Tom Learns Self-Compassion and Admits Mistakes

The gift of self-compassion is part of the pedagogy of love. This gift comes when one recognizes that all human beings have strengths and weaknesses and that we ourselves are not perfect (Brown, 2010). Acceptance of ourselves as we are lets us admit mistakes without feeling like failures and reduces the power of others over us because we cannot be shamed into actions we might later regret. We can admit mistakes if we know we do not have to be perfect. The best way to teach self-compassion and admitting mistakes is to serve as a role model.

I can attest to this experience. I was brought up with the message that making mistakes shows that I can't be counted on, that I am not good enough, and probably worse. Thus, admitting mistakes in life or to a class was something I had great difficulty doing, and when I made a mistake I felt very embarrassed and deflated. These emotions have lessened, but to some extent they still have a hold on me. Now, however, I can and do admit my mistakes or failings in class settings and have found it to be liberating for me. Modeling of this kind of vulnerability is also helpful to my students. It has helped me to be able to provide positive feedback to students and support their efforts to experiment and learn through trial and error in class interactions. The feedback I get from students is that they feel comfortable saying what they think and believe in my classes rather than saying what they think I want to hear.

3. Jing Teaches with Mindfulness

I designed my summer class to incorporate the concepts of Roth (2006): third-person inquiry, laboratory or inner work, and critical first-person reflection. Roth also calls for opening the heart and freeing the intuition through meditation, music, dance, and other means. We used some of these modes. I emphasized mindfulness and presence, involving being attentive to students' questions and being present when students share their problems. A body scan exercise helped students connect with the baby and the body. Students participated in a forgiveness exercise; a peace dance for transforming violence; a compassion exercise; yoga and tai chi for uniting the body, mind, and energy; and an experience of education as healing. One student walked the Labyrinth, thus stimulating compassion, understanding, and reconciliation.

4. Rebecca's Students Discuss Transformative Learning

In a setting of love, I teach the course "Adult Learning" to pre-service and in-service teachers. They are especially interested in exploring their own transformative learning (Merriam & Bierema, 2014). One class member, L., a kindergarten teacher in a small Alabama town, said that before her transformative learning experience, she accepted local beliefs about undocumented workers: that they steal American jobs and are stupid, disrespectful, uncivilized, socially ignorant, dirty, and possibly dangerous. However, transformative learning opened her heart toward these new neighbors and demolished stereotypes. Transformation occurred gradually through taking diversity courses, meeting undocumented workers, teaching their children, helping them with food and clothing, and inviting them over for holiday festivities. L. is now a caring advocate who, along with her church, strengthens the town's newfound commitment to social justice. Sharing individual transformative learning experiences both echoes and enhances the pedagogy of love pervading the graduate class.

Part C. Further Thoughts

This chapter has explained the pedagogy of love in terms of cultivating the abilities of the heart. We addressed five foundations: (a) a general theory of love, (b) the heart as an electromagnetic field of energy, (c) the opening of the heart, (d) the uniting of reason and intuition, and (e) contemplative keys to the pedagogy of love. In the process, we revealed that love is the language of the emotional limbic system. Love powers transformative learning for different ages. Treating students with humility and respect and guiding them to treat others similarly are important to the pedagogy of love. The pedagogy of love shows students as equal souls, the purposes of which can be fostered by at education. To teach with love, we must love ourselves and embody the pedagogy of love. "We teach who we are" (Palmer with Scribner, 2017, p. 102).

The question arises: How is holistic education related to the pedagogy of love? Denton and Ashton (2004) call readers to explore the loving heart of holistic education. Denton (2005) refers to being "in the flame," where teaching, spirituality, and compassion co-occur in holistic education. Holistic education aims for the integration of four aspects of the person: heart, body, mind, and spirit. As we have seen, the pedagogy of love helps cultivate the abilities of the heart. Heart-cultivation through the pedagogy of love[5] necessarily relates to the other three aspects of holistic education: the body (e.g., embodied learning), the mind (e.g., mindfulness and mindful learning), and the spirit (e.g., spiritual learning). The pedagogy of love and holistic education have so much in common that it is difficult to separate them, and for that we are very glad.

Notes

1 When they made the comments in this paragraph, Jennifer and Brian were students in Rebecca's graduate teacher education courses. Jennifer now teaches in China, and Brian teaches for the Peace Corps in South America.
2 This occurred in a nearly all-white state university in the American Midwest. The student's professor shared the story with one of us and asked what to do.
3 Also see Miller (2009, in press) for wonderful ideas about education and Eros.
4 Another stage, formation or *Bildung*, is no longer in the model (Palmer & Zajonc with Scribner, 2014).
5 In addition to this chapter, see also Almaas and Johnson (2013), Bache (2008), Kessler (2000), Lin (2006), Lin and Wang (2010), Palmer (2003), and Zajonc (2003). See Oxford (2014), including Wang's (2014) chapter.

References

Almaas, A. H. & Johnson, K. (2013). *The power of divine love: Illuminating force of love in everyday life*. Boston, MA: Shambhala.
Bache, C. M. (2008). *The living classroom: Teaching and collective consciousness*. Albany, NY: SUNY Press.
Brown, C. B. (2010). *The power of vulnerability*. Presented at TEDExHouston. Retrieved from www.ted.com/talks/brene_brown_on_vulnerability.
Brown, K. & Miller, J. P. (in progress). Cultivating a heart space: The role of Eros in facilitating campus group meditation. In J. Lin, S. Edwards & T. Culham (Eds), *Contemplative pedagogies in K-12, university, and community settings: Transformation from within*. Charlotte, NC: Information Age.
Capra, F. (1991). *The Tao of physics: An exploration of the parallels between modern physics and Eastern mysticism*. Boulder, CO: Shambhala.
Couch, A. (2011, Jan. 27). Martin Luther King Day: 10 memorable MLK quotes. *Christian Science Monitor*, p. 4. Retrieved February 12, 2018 from www.csmonitor.com/USA/2011/0117/Martin-Luther-King-Day-10-memorable-MLK-quotes/Hatred-paralyzes-life.
Dahl, C. J., Lutz, A., & Davidson, R. J. (2015). Reconstructing and deconstructing the self: Cognitive mechanisms in meditation practice. *Trends in Cognitive Sciences, 19*(9), 515–523.
Denton, D. (2005). In the flame of the heart: Toward a pedagogy of compassion. In J. P. Miller, S. Karsten, D. Denton, D. Orr, & I. Colalillo Kates (Eds), *Holistic learning and spirituality in education: Breaking new ground*. Albany, NY: SUNY Press.
Denton, D. & Ashton, W. (Eds) (2004). *Spirituality, action, and pedagogy: Teaching from the heart*. Bern: Peter Lang.
Einstein, A. (1918/2017). Preestablished harmony. Discovery. *Lapham's Quarterly, 17*(2). Retrieved from www.laphamsquarterly.org/discovery/preestablished-harmony.
Fox, M. (2014). *Meister Eckhart: A mystic–warrior for our times*. Novato, CA: New World Library.
Goleman, D. (2005). *Emotional intelligence: Why it can matter more than IQ* (2nd edn). New York: Bantam.
Hafiz (1999). *The gift: Poems by Hafiz, the great Sufi master*. Trans. D. Ladinsky. New York: Penguin.
Hafiz (2003). *The subject tonight is love: 60 wild and sweet poems of Hafiz*. Trans. D. Ladinsky. New York: Penguin.
Keith, J. (2016). Love in teaching ESL. Final paper in 'Adult Larning,' EESL 627, University of Alabama at Birmingham.
Kessler, R. (2000). *The soul of education: Helping students find connection, compassion, and character at school*. Alexandria, VA: Association for Supervision and Curriculum Development.
King, M. L., Jr. (1963). *Strength to love*. Minneapolis: Fortress Press. Quoted in Couch (2011).
Lewis, T., Amini, F., & Lannon, R. (2000). *A general theory of love*. New York: Random House.
Lin, J. (2006). *Love, peace and wisdom in education: Vision for education in the 21st century*. Lanham, MD: Rowman & Littlefield.
Lin, J. & Wang, Y. (2010). Confucius's teaching of virtues and peace education. In J. Lin, J. Miller, & E. J. Brantmeier (Eds), *Religion, spirituality and peace education* (pp. 3–17). Charlotte, NC: Information Age.
Mair, V. H. (1990). *Tao Te Ching: The classic book of integrity and the way*, by Lao Tzu; an entirely new translation based on the recently discovered Ma-wang-tui manuscripts. New York: Bantam Books.
Maslow, A. H. (1971). *The farther reaches of human nature*. New York: Penguin.
McCraty, R. (2004). The energetic heart: Bioelectromagnetic communication within and between people. In P. J. Rosch & M. S. Markov (Eds), *Bioelectromagnetic medicine* (pp. 541–562). New York: Marcel Dekker.

McCraty, R. (2015). *Science of the heart: Exploring the role of the heart in human performance.* Boulder Creek, CA: Heart Math Institute.

Merriam, S. B. & Bierema, L. (2014). *Adult learning: Linking theory and practice.* San Francisco, CA: Jossey-Bass.

Miller, J. P. (2009). Education and Eros. In M. de Souza, L. J. Francis, J. O'Higgins-Norman, & D. Scott (Eds.), *International handbook of education for spirituality, care and wellbeing* (pp. 581–592). *International handbooks of religion and education,* 3. New York: Springer Science+Business Media. DOI 10.1007/978-1-4020-9018-9 31

Miller, J. P. (2018). *Love and compassion: Exploring their role in education.* Toronto, ON: University of Toronto Press.

Oxford, R. L. (2014). *Understanding peace cultures.* Charlotte, NC: Information Age.

Oxford, R. L. (2016). Creation Spirituality as a spiritual research paradigm drawing on many faiths. In J. Lin, R. L. Oxford, & T. Culham (Eds), *Toward a spiritual research paradigm: Exploring new ways of knowing, researching and being* (pp. 199–232). Charlotte, NC: Information Age.

Palmer, P. J. (2003). Teaching with heart and soul: Reflections on spirituality in teacher education. *Journal of Teacher Education, 54*(5), 376–385.

Palmer, P. J. (2009, Mar/Apr). The broken-open heart: Living with faith and hope in the tragic gap. A PDF reprint from *Weavings: A Journal of the Christian Spiritual Life, 24*(2). Retrieved from www.couragerenewal.org/PDFs/PJP-WeavingsArticle-Broken-OpenHeart.pdf.

Palmer, P. J. with Scribner, M. (2017). *The courage to teach guide for reflection and renewal* (10th Anniversary edn). San Francisco, CA: Jossey-Bass.

Palmer, P. J., Zajonc, A., with Scribner, M. (2014). *The heart of higher education: A call to renewal – transforming the academy through collegial conversations.* San Francisco, CA: Jossey-Bass.

Rice, B. (2015). The need for caring environments for teaching adults in | ESL and EFL. Final paper in 'Adult Learning,' EESL 627, University of Alabama at Birmingham.

Roth, H. D. (1999). *Original Tao: Inward training (nei-yeh) and the foundations of Taoist mysticism.* New York: Columbia University Press.

Roth, H. D. (2006). Contemplative studies: Prospects for a new field. *Teachers College Record, 108*(9), 1787–1815.

Salovey, P., Mayer, J. D., Caruso, D., & Yoo, S. H. (2011). The positive psychology of emotional intelligence. In S. J. Lopez & C. R. Snyder (Eds), *The Oxford handbook of positive psychology* (pp. 237–248). New York: Oxford University Press.

Schwartz, G. E. (2007). *The energy healing experiments: Science reveals our natural power to heal.* New York: Atria Books.

Wang, Y. (2014). A teacher's journey: Integrating peace education in language classes. In R. L. Oxford (Ed.), *Understanding peace cultures* (pp. 87–104). Charlotte, NC: Information Age.

Zajonc, A. (2003). Spirituality in higher education: Overcoming the divide. *Liberal Education, 89*(1), 50–58.

Zajonc, A. (2006, Sept.) Love and knowledge: Recovering the heart of learning through contemplation. *Teachers College Record, 108*(9), 1742–1759.

Zhang, D. (1999). Love and the history of Chinese bioethics. *Eubios Journal of Asian and International Bioethics, 9,* 47–49. www.eubios.info/EJ92/ej92k.htm.

19

Lhomon Education
Teaching for Well-being in Bhutan

Jackie Mitchell and Yang Gyeltshen

A gong rings, and a wave of maroon flows in the direction of the classrooms. Fifty young monks, between the ages of seven and seventeen, assemble on the balcony outside their classrooms, waiting to be admitted for morning classes. They kick off their sandals and line them up along the wall, laughing and joking as they wait. The teacher invites them inside and they find their places, seated cross-legged on cushions on the floor in front of low tables. The chant leader strikes a small cymbal, indicating the start of the class. Class begins with a prayer of dedication to Manjushri, the bodhisattva of insight and intellect, chanted in English, and is followed by several minutes of meditation. The room is still and silent, the monks' hands folded in their laps, eyes cast down, until another strike on the cymbal. Then there is a flurry of activity and chatter, as they arrange their books, or get up to go to another classroom, until their teacher calls them to order and the lesson begins.

These monks are students at the Chokyi Gyatso Institute in southeastern Bhutan. They have entered the monastery to follow a nine-year course in Buddhist philosophy and practice, called Shedra. Their abbot, Dzongsar Khyentse, Rinpoche, has introduced a course of secular education that the monks follow alongside their Buddhist studies. This was prompted out of his concern that the monastic traditions in Bhutan are waning, as well as concern for the well-being of the monks in the twenty-first century who need to be literate and educated in order to function in the modern world. This school within the monastery, known as Lhomon Education (LME), has been created as a laboratory for an innovative approach to education in Bhutan, not only within the monastic setting, but also as a demonstration of how education could be approached differently in the public-school system. As it is not tied into the public-school system, there is freedom to take a different approach to learning and teaching at LME that impacts the curriculum, the pedagogy, and the philosophy behind it.

The Bhutanese Context

Bhutan is a small country with a population of approximately 750,000 people, nestled in the eastern end of the Himalayas. Bhutan is often compared with Switzerland, both in size and natural beauty. The far northern half of the country is adorned with majestic snowcapped peaks and the southern half with lush green subtropical mountains and foothills, with fertile river valleys in between. Despite its giant neighbors—India to its east, south, and west frontiers and the Autonomous Region of Tibet or China to the north, Bhutan has been independent throughout its history. However, until recently, Bhutan has not opened itself to the outside world, and global movements had little impact on Bhutan, partly due to the country's geography, making navigation of mountainous terrains difficult. Thus, topography shaped Bhutanese life, history, and culture, with little outside influence. Before any large-scale development activities took place, Bhutanese people largely lived on subsistence farming. As in other Himalayan countries, early settlers in Bhutan were semi-nomadic herdsmen, for whom the trees, lakes, and mountains were sacred. Bhutanese still regard the natural environment with great respect. Trade or commerce if any, existed only in the form of barter between the neighboring valleys. Literacy, either in *Dzongkha*[1] or *Choekey*,[2] received from monastic education was sufficient then. With the arrival of Buddhism in Bhutan in the eighth century, religion has played a significant role in the lives of Bhutanese people.

Bhutan has only recently become more open to the rest of the world. Television was introduced in Bhutan for the first time in 1999; satellite connections and internet services began after that. Thus, Bhutanese have only been exposed to the outside media in recent years, but its impact is already felt with the availability of Indian and American television and media, cellphones, and imported junk food gaining in popularity over traditional and locally produced foods and drinks.

A Thimphu [Capital City] high school student is more apt to choose a plastic bottle of artificial juice from Bangkok over a glass of locally pressed apple juice. The first cases of anorexia are surfacing in the country. Boys are beginning to model behavior they've seen in Korean gangster films. Villagers are selling their land or going into debt in order to buy flashy cars, or simply letting the land go fallow (LMS, 2012).

Lhomon Education and Gross National Happiness

In recognition of the impact of modernization, the LME program is founded on the belief that the goals of education for the twenty-first century must address the crisis of the environment and the social and economic consequences of a system that pursues growth at any cost. Education that focuses on material success and academic achievement by means of a homogenized curriculum, standardized testing, competition, and individual achievement does not address the human hardship and environmental devastation we are witnessing in the world at present. As mentioned, its impact is being felt in many ways in Bhutan. LME seeks to bring an awareness of the interconnection of all aspects of life to the students, and thus its goals are focused on cultivating an ecological consciousness in the students, through an understanding of the interconnected nature of our existence with others, wherever and however they manifest. It emphasises the attitude of sacredness with which the Bhutanese regard the environment. The curriculum is thus place-based, in that it values the existing ecological wisdom in the community that has been formulated over the centuries. It furthers an understanding of sustainable practices, both old and new, that support a harmonious way of living in accord with the environment. Taking an integrated approach to subject matter, the curriculum highlights the relationships within and between subject areas. The emphasis is on the process of learning, as opposed to learning as a product. LME is holistic in its pedagogical practice, seeking to educate and nurture the whole child, body, heart, mind, and spirit. Mindfulness and contemplative practices, together with experiential learning, anchors learning and makes it relevant and meaningful.

At the heart of the LME program is a commitment to the concept of Gross National Happiness (GNH), the inspiration for an alternative development policy for Bhutan as it entered the modern era in the 1960s. Soon after his enthronement in 1972, King Jigme Singye Wangchuck, father to the present king, declared that Gross National Happiness was more important than Gross National Product, thereby launching Bhutan on a path towards sustainable development. The four pillars of GNH assert the protection of the environment, equitable economic development, protection of Bhutan's cultural heritage, and good governance. They are interdependent aspects of an approach to development that puts sustainability and the well-being of the Bhutanese population at its heart, rather than one that is purely economic in its aims. The tiny Himalayan kingdom of Bhutan is drawing the attention of the world with its commitment to sustainable and equitable development and enlightened environmental policies (Global Vision International, n.d.). In 2008, a parliamentary democracy was established and elections were held for the first time. The king's authority was now limited to that of a constitutional monarch. The people of Bhutan, however, continue to regard the King with the highest respect and reverence.

In adopting the vision of Gross National Happiness (GNH), the King and his government made a commitment to promote development that valued the people and the environment, as well as upholding the Buddhist traditions of the country. GNH comes out of, and is an articulation of, Buddhist wisdom and the inseparability and interdependence of all aspects of existence, reflecting an attitude of sacredness towards the environment. GNH provides guidance to policy makers as Bhutan enters the modern world and is a reminder and, since it came from the King, a Royal Command, to keep human values at the heart of development and a sustainable future for the people of Bhutan. The current King, Jigme Khesar Namgyel Wangchuck restated the importance of GNH in the following way:

> Thus, for my nation, today GNH is the bridge between the fundamental values of Kindness, Equality and Humanity and the necessary pursuit of economic growth. It ensures that no matter what our nation may seek to achieve, the human dimension, the individual's place in the nation, is never forgotten. It is a constant reminder that we must strive for a caring leadership so that as the world and country changes, as our nation's goals change, our foremost priority will always remain the happiness and wellbeing of our people—including the generations to come after us.
> *(Wangchuk, as cited in Gordon, 2013, p. 287)*

Following the first election, the prime minister, Jigme Thinley, turned his attention to the education system and convened a conference in the capital, Thimphu, in 2009 to which educators from around the world were invited, along with Bhutanese educators, officials, students, and monastics. Called *Educating for GNH*, this conference laid out guidelines for instituting an approach to education that would be in line with the principles of GNH. Thinley recognised that for GNH to take hold in Bhutan, it would have to become implanted in the hearts and minds of the younger generation of Bhutanese. They would be the ones inheriting the task of making Bhutan a viable country in the twenty-first century, dedicated to sustainable practices and the well-being of its people. As it stood, he saw that the education system was not suited to the task. Its focus on standardized curriculum, rote learning, and exam results, geared towards competition and material success, was at odds with the vision of GNH. Following the conference, the definition of a literate population that could carry out the vision of GNH was expanded beyond that of basic literacy in language and mathematics, to include literacy in ecology, Indigenous knowledge, science and health, food and nutrition, civics and politics, multiculturalism, media, statistics, and the arts (Hayward, Pannozzo, & Colman, 2009).

Before Bhutan opened its doors to the outside world, the only education available was through the monasteries. Following the introduction of a modern education system, Bhutanese students could choose a traditional, monastic education or a secular, modern one. From a Bhutanese perspective, "traditional" would mean anything Indigenous passed on through the generations, while "modern" is viewed as ideas and concepts that come from outside the country, especially from the scientific, Western world. Bhutanese traditional learning is focused on spiritual content, the fundamental goal being the attainment of the Buddha wisdom, "the benevolent thought of seeking enlightenment for the sake of all sentient beings. Education is to be viewed as a process of edification and knowledge as a tool for benefiting the world" (Phuntsho, 2000, p. 100). Modern education, by contrast, is, among other goals, a means of acquiring knowledge and skills for a career. According to Hayward et al. (2009), most Western education initiatives today are driven by the belief that improvements in economic performance will lead to the enhancement of societal well-being. The key role of education, therefore, is to prepare students for their role and function in the economy. While preparing students for the job market to secure a livelihood is important, it is only one of the elements of what is needed for overall well-being and happiness. Hayward et al. (2009) write:

> GNH values define quality of life and wellbeing broadly to include physical and mental health, time balance, vital communities, a healthy environment, and good governance. From the GNH perspective, therefore, an effective education system is one that, as its outcome, enhances well-being in all these domains.
>
> *(p. 2)*

Lhomon Society (Bhutan Foundation, 2017)[3] a major civil society organization in Bhutan, is one proponent of holistic education that advances the vision of GNH. Its mission is to foster genuine GNH-based development, in collaboration with existing education institutions and in harmony with government goals. The impact of modern media on Bhutanese youth is one of Lhomon Society's main concerns. They believe that Bhutanese youth are being indoctrinated by powerful consumerist messages, which are not only contradictory to the Indigenous social and cultural values, but also undermine the very philosophy of Gross National Happiness. In the face of so-called "modern development," Lhomon Society worries that Bhutanese youth are losing their connection to the wealth of their own traditions and culture (Idealist, n.d.).

With the launch of development activities in Bhutan from the early 1960s, and changing socio-economic conditions, the meaning of "success" has changed; for many young Bhutanese people these days, "success" is determined not only by a college degree, but also by becoming a civil servant, and hopefully rising to the status of a *Dasho*,[4] with power, privilege, and respect in society. People began to view English medium education as the path to success (Ueda, 2004). Opportunities to climb the ladder of success are almost exclusively for those in English medium education.

It is one of the aims of Lhomon Society, and of LME, its education program, to reverse the value orientation that has overtaken the youth of Bhutan so that they gain a real appreciation for the traditional ways of their people, ways that go beyond wearing national dress and attending festivals. The wisdom and knowledge that has evolved through the centuries has allowed the people to survive through their understanding of the climate and the land on which they live. When enhanced with new techniques and ideas, this traditional knowledge has great potential to establish personal well-being and security which then extends to the security and well-being of Bhutan as a whole, through self-sufficiency in the rural areas, which is where the majority of the population still live. By extending entrepreneurial education and opportunities to the villagers, LME hopes to create a climate that attracts young people back to the villages. At the same time, it educates and promotes the values of GNH in an active and hands-on way, giving youth an understanding of the ideal that is not purely theoretical. There is an emphasis on the value of community, counteracting the increasing influence of individualism that comes out of a competitive education system and media that are focused on consumerism. The LME program integrates these values into its education program for the young monks. The highly respected status of monks in Bhutanese society means that they can be powerful proponents of these values in the future. Not only are they learning the skills with which to put these values into practice, but because the program is approached from a holistic and integrated standpoint, they are also developing a deeply felt appreciation for the interconnectedness of all aspects of being in the world.

Lho Mon Education (LME), developed by Lhomon Society, seeks to create education alternatives that reinforce ancient Bhutanese wisdom traditions while introducing the best of progressive sustainable development practices. The aim is to educate the whole person by engaging the heart and mind in a holistic and integrated curriculum [which draws] upon local resources and knowledge making it relevant to the local culture, and that of Bhutan in general . . . Taking the view that education is a process of lifelong learning, students will engage in exploration of the environment, ask big questions and find answers based on their experience . . . They will appreciate, not only intellectually but also in their hearts, that everything is connected and everything matters.

(Mitchell, 2017).

What is being practiced at LME has the potential for unification and harmonization of the two systems of education in Bhutan—one that is traditional, monastic, spiritual, and focused on students' affective development, and the other that is modern, school-based, secular, and focused on students' cognitive development. Educating for the GNH approach is holistic—incorporating mind, body, and spirit, hence *holistic education*—education with values.

The Lhomon Education Curriculum

The LME curriculum for the young monks, therefore, is founded on the need to bring education into a context of place and language that is relevant and ecologically coherent, one that brings the ideal of GNH into practical reality. It does this using a holistic and integrated pedagogy. The aim is to encourage students and their teachers to see themselves as part of an integrated whole, valuing the wealth of knowledge that exists in the traditions of the locality. It aspires to generate in the students a heartfelt respect and love for nature of which they see themselves a part, extending from the local context to the larger context of the world beyond their community and to the nation. This provides the rationale for the way the curriculum is constructed, that being: integration of subject matter, the inclusion of Indigenous and traditional knowledge and the language, customs, and practices associated with it, and bringing a contemplative and ecological perspective to the whole. Addressing the whole child within the context of the environment within which they live, work, and study, makes education meaningful and heartfelt.

The curriculum is structured around the four pillars of GNH. Referencing the 2009 conference materials (GPI Atlantic, 2009; Hayward, Pannozzo & Colman, 2009), thematic units concentrate on each of the four pillars as a starting point, covering most of the twelve literacies in the units. In the first year, for example, the environmental pillar is addressed by an in-depth examination of the monks' immediate environment and their place in it, that being the monastery and the local community, and the plant and animal life surrounding it. This is extended to an exploration of their own villages in the context of the district and of Bhutan as whole. It is also an opportunity for the teacher to get to know the students, their backgrounds, and their abilities. This includes extensive education on the idea of Zero Waste, which is actively practiced at the monastery and in the local town and villages. The cultural pillar is introduced through tracing the evolution of human culture from hunter-gatherers to farming, comparing the latter with present day agriculture in Bhutan, and integrating local customs and traditions. For the focus on sustainable development, the monks make an organic vegetable garden, with the help of local farmers, and all subject areas are related and integrated with that activity. For the governance unit, they learned about the Indian Buddhist king, Ashoka, in the third century BC, who has been dubbed "the first environmentalist" by some for his work planting trees, digging wells, and protecting wildlife. From a violent start in life, Ashoka had a change of heart and from then on worked to bring peace, prosperity, and equality to all his subjects, including women, prisoners, and animals. Buddhism and Buddhist values, as the root of Bhutanese culture, are addressed in all units throughout the curriculum, which also build upon and expand those that have preceded them, giving depth and scope to the program.

Given the integrated and interdependent nature of GNH as a philosophical standpoint, it soon becomes evident that one cannot talk about one pillar without referring to the others. Through activities, exploration, and field trips, the environmental, cultural, and policy issues around development and sustainability are addressed through the experience of the students and on the local level. This extends to an examination of how they are played out on the national and international level. The curriculum, while adaptable to other environments, strongly emphasises the importance of becoming familiar with the local environment and the traditional ecological knowledge of the local people. By starting at the point of students' experience, the context for future learning is established. Stories from Bhutan, as well as from other cultures that address the topic at hand, create the ground for understanding how ecological knowledge is rooted in the culture and is not just an abstract concept. During the topic on fire in the environmental pillar, students heard a story of how fire came to humans. This was followed by students' stories of fire that they had experienced. The story talks about making fire from friction so the students made bow drills from materials they found in the locality and had some success in using them to make fire. On a field trip, we took a bow drill and a local farmer and his wife, both old, whom we happened to meet on the way, told the students about how they had had to rub sticks to make fire in the olden days. A senior monk addressed the class on the significance of offering fire in Buddhist ritual. We made a sundial and solar cookers. We discussed forest fire prevention, and adopting solar technology on a grand scale and the impact it would have to reduce the dependence on fossil fuels. The interweaving of the aspects of environment, culture, sustainability, and national policy was achieved and presented as an integrated whole in order to ground the students' learning. Writing, drawing, and reading, speaking, and writing in English, as well as related math projects were part of the whole.

Indigenous Knowledge

The LME program and the curriculum strongly emphasises the wisdom and knowledge of the local Elders and community members. Wherever possible, the Elders and knowledge holders in the community are invited into the classroom, and the students are taken out to visit these people in their own settings. Local farmers instruct them on making compost for the garden they grow at the monastery, and on the care of an orchard and the young plants; they also teach the monks the signs in nature that have traditionally indicated when to sow and harvest. There are songs and rituals bound up with all these practices that the monks learn too. Breaking new ground is always determined by the astrological calendar and accompanied by prayers and offerings to the local deities. Besides the spiritual and contemplative benefits of practices in which people engage in the natural setting, being outdoors gives rise to an ecological understanding that is born of direct connection and engagement with the earth, the plants, and the animals. It also offers multiple opportunities for integrated learning. Plant biology, the symbiotic relationship of insects and animals to plants, chemical components of compost, the role of micro-organisms and decomposers, photosynthesis, the carbon cycle, measurement—the list of learning opportunities that arise out of creating a garden is extensive.

The monks manifest a keen awareness of their environment and what occurs within it. They demonstrate a knowledge of the way the animals and birds have adapted to their environment, as well as knowledge of their habits and habitats. These young monks, generally sheltered as they are from the pressures of media and modernity, have a relationship to the world as sacred which was not only born of their circumstances in the monastery, or even from their rural backgrounds. When teaching and learning is integrated and not piecemeal, the ability to see the relationships between and within phenomena is enhanced. This gives rise to wonder and delight in what they experience, whether in school, the garden, or community work in the monastery, and extends out into the environment.

Language

The Indigenous language group of Eastern Bhutan is known as Sharchop, or Tshangla.[5] As this language has never been written down, there is a rich oral culture, and a wealth of stories, customs, music, and dances, as well as agricultural, healing, and religious traditions that have been passed down through the generations. It is these that are in danger of being lost, and which LME program integrates into the educational program. Given the importance attributed to local and traditional wisdom in the LME program, Sharchop, which is the language of almost all the young monks, is actively encouraged. At the same time, English, with extensive Sharchop translation, is the language of instruction because the huge majority of materials, the internet, and much of the media is in English. On the premise that the knowledge that is bound up in a language will be lost if the language itself is lost, the program encourages the students to record words and phrases in Sharchop in their dictionary, gathering a record of the names of local plants, animals, and practices. These transcriptions are phonetic because there are no formal rules for transcription. Classes at LME are, therefore, conducted in a mixture of English and Sharchop.

Contemplative Practice

The ubiquitous relationship to the sacred in everyday life in Bhutan, combined with the fact that the setting is monastic, obviously impacts the students and the way that the curriculum unfolds. It is human, however, to become busy, distracted, goal oriented, and preoccupied, even within a monastery, and neither students nor teachers are immune to that. Mindfulness and contemplative practices are, therefore, an important aspect of the LME curriculum. What makes the learning of the LME program contemplative is the integration of body, heart, and mind in the teaching and learning process. When these three are synchronized and addressed in the curriculum in the context of an ecological approach to pedagogy that is culturally relevant and place-based, the interdependent nature of reality is less of a concept and more experiential.

Bringing body, heart, and mind into coherence creates the ground for a teaching and learning experience that works with and through the world as the source of all life. By taking this holistic approach to curriculum and pedagogy, LME takes a cautious view of modern education, while maintaining a connection to the social, cultural, and spiritual values of Bhutan's unique heritage. The long-term view of the LME program aspires to shift the paradigm in education from one that implicitly supports materialism, individualism, and human and environmental chaos to one that acts on behalf of community, ecological sustainability, and wisdom in whatever form that appears. Although LME is specific to the Bhutanese context, the principles upon which it is founded—contemplative practice, ecological perspectives, and compassionate action—are universally applicable. When applied with sensitivity to the culture and ecology of place, education can be relevant, joyful, and effective in addressing the problems of modernization in both East and West.

Notes

1 Bhutan's national language
2 *Choekey* literally means *dharma language*, the classical Tibetan language specified for expressing dharma [Buddhist] teachings as opposed to *Phalkey*, the language used for general communication in Bhutan.
3 *Lho* means south and *Mon* region. *Lhomon* therefore refers to the people of the region south of the Tibetan plateau, meaning Bhutan.
4 *Dasho* is the title of a high-ranking officer in the government. Traditionally, commoners wear white scarfs, Dashos wear red, Ministers wear orange, and the kings wear yellow. The coloured scarves are awarded only by the King. When a person gets the rank of Dasho, he or she is given the red scarf by the King, together with a sword.

5 There are about 24 languages spoken in Bhutan, besides Dzongkha and English, each with their own traditions and customs, which are enshrined in the different languages. There is an overall national culture that is expressed through dress, architecture, and adherence to Buddhist practice and principles, among other things. The advent of a broadcasting network and television has helped establish the uniformity of the national culture.

References

Bhutan Foundation (2017). *The Lhomon Society*. Retrieved from https://bhutanfound.org/partners/#the-lhomon-society.

Global Vision International (n.d.). *Bhutan becomes the world's first carbon negative country*. Retrieved October 12, 2017 from www.gvi.co.uk/blog/bhutan-carbon-negative-country-world/.

Gordon, J. (2013). Bhutan: Educational challenges in the land of the Thunder Dragon. *Ethnography and Education, 8*(3), 286–300.

GPI Atlantic (2009). *Educating for Gross National Happiness in Bhutan*. Conference Sourcebook, volume 3, part 1. GPI Atlantic, multiple authors. Retrieved from www.sji.bt/assets/LME/Sourcebook-Volume-3.Part-1.doc

Hayward, K., Pannozzo L., & Colman, R. (2009). *Educating for Gross National happiness in Bhutan: Developing curricula and indicators for an educated populace. A literature review*. Vols 1 and 2. GPI Atlantic. Retrieved from http://gpiatlantic.org/pdf/education/bhutaneduc_litrev_1.pdf.

Idealist (n.d.) Lhomon Society. Retrieved from www.idealist.org/en/nonprofit/91e28abeaedd43e0a5cd790a1f087549-lhomon-society-paro.

Lhomon Society (LMS) (2012). Lhomon education: Creating education alternatives for Bhutan. Lhomon Society. Retrieved from www.lhomon.bt/education/.

Lhomon Society (LMS). (n.d.). Lhomon education: Curriculum framework and map. Bhutan: The Lhomon Society.

Mitchell, J. (2017). Lhomon Education Gross National Happiness Curriculum Framework. Unpublished manuscript, Samdrup Jongkhar Initiative, Dewathang, Bhutan.

Phuntsho, K. (2000). On the two ways of learning in Bhutan. *Journal of Bhutan Studies, 3*, 96–126.

Ueda, A. (2004). Education system and the "ladder of success." In K. Ura & S. Kinga (Eds), *The spider and the piglet: Proceedings of the First International Seminar on Bhutan Studies* (pp. 327–349). Thimphu: The Centre for Bhutan Studies.

20

The School Forest Movement in South Korea From a Holistic Perspective

Bokyoung Kim

Introduction

Holistic education and the ecology movement are closely linked through the concept of interdependence. Both share the principle that interconnectedness is a fundamental reality of nature and should guide our awareness and actions. Earth connections, then, can reawaken us to the natural processes of life. The wind, the sun, the trees, and grasses can help us come alive and awaken us from the treadmill we find ourselves on. As much as possible, students should have direct experiences with the earth through such activities as gardening, caring for the animals, and outdoor education. As much as possible, ecological education should arise from a love and reverence for the earth rather than from a sense of guilt (Miller, 2012).

David Orr (1994), a renowned environmentalist, outlined that "all education is environmental education" (p. 12). He believes that we should educate students for ecological literacy. In other words, students would be able to see the connections that are inherent in the environment. Orr also argues that when students learn about their surroundings, they gain a sense of place.

In this context, one of the most influential figures in Japan is a former principal, Giichiro Yamanouchi, who developed the idea of planting small forests on school grounds. Miller (2008) recollects that one of my first trips in Japan was to Niigata prefecture to see these schools. Niigata lies on the northwest coast of Honshu, the largest island in Japan. Yamanouchi's vision has also spread to Korea. His vision is a powerful example of how holistic education and environmental education can be integrated into the school curriculum (Miller, 2008, p. 229).

In South Korea the Korean Society for Holistic Education was established in 1997 with the help of Dr. Hyunjae Kim, former professor of Kyeongin National University of Education and Dr. Minyoung Song who returned to her motherland after earning her doctorate in Japan. She introduced principal Yamanouchi's ideas to members of the Korean society. At that time, the Korean edition of *School with Forest and Meadow*, authored by Ikue Tezuka and John P. Miller, was published in 1995 followed by the Korean translation of *An Introduction to Holistic Education*, published by the Japanese Association for Holistic Education in 1999. In the next year, *The Holistic Curriculum*, authored by John P. Miller, was translated into Korean.

Study Tours to Japanese School Forests

From June 24 to 28 in 1999, members of the Korean Society for Holistic Education visited schools at the elementary and secondary levels in Niigata prefecture. The schools were well known for using school forests as curriculum content in Japan. The society members who visited the Japanese schools were composed of education and landscape professors and principals. The following describes the study tours to four Japanese schools. The description of these schools is based on short essays in the study tours by Lee (1999) and Cho (1999).

Kawasaki Elementary School

Kawasaki Elementary School, with more than 600 students enrolled and 126 years of history, is located in Nagaoka City in Niigata prefecture. This is a typical Japanese elementary school, but what distinguishes it from other schools is its emphasis on developing students' relationship with nature. Important to the school is a forest at the right side of the school gate. The forest, composed of deciduous and evergreen trees native to the area, was planted by students, teachers, parents, and community members.

Much of what has happened at Kawasaki Elementary School is based on the dedication of a former principal, Giichiro Yamanouchi. Meeting our party in the school, he was willing to explain the background philosophy of the forest and its integration into the school curriculum. Miller (2007, pp. 170–171) claimed that Yamanouchi's work is an excellent example of the subject–community connection. Yamanouchi is one of the most interesting and passionate educators I have ever met. Although retired, he is still very active and passionate. In a nutshell, he is a real game changer in environmental and holistic education at home and abroad.

The Kawasaki Elementary School's holistic approach to curriculum is characterized as follows: Grade 1, taking care of animals, Grade 2, vegetable gardening, Grade 3, activities in the stream, Grade 4, activities in the forest, Grade 5, learning welfare facilities, Grade 6, learning the history of Nagaoka City. Each grade publishes literary works on the forest that inspires students to love nature and revere life.

Sasaoka Elementary School

Sasaoka Elementary School is a small rural school located in Agano City in Niigata prefecture. Lee (1999) and Cho (1999) explain that while construction work to build a gymnasium is in full swing at the back of the school, a female teacher is gardening with 5th graders in a small plot. Also, an entrance ceremony was being held in the playground for a sheep donated by a parent to help develop a sense of community. As this sheep becomes a member of the school, students also learn to respect life by taking care of the animal.

Second grade students in a classroom sit around a grandmother telling a story originated from the local area. It is a good example of how oral tradition in the community can be integrated into the school curriculum. In another classroom, fifth grade students make *dango* (rice cake), which is a Japanese sweet dumpling made from *mochiko* (rice flour). This is also a good example of transmitting their traditional life wisdom to the young. After that we moved to the multi-purpose classroom and listened to a brief lecture on holistic curriculum by the principal. He explained that the Japanese school curriculum comprises subject matter, ethics, extra-curricular activities, and integrated learning. Through integrated learning, this school develops a holistic curriculum.

Imegasaki Elementary School

Imegasaki Elementary School is also a small rural school located in Uonuma City in Niigata prefecture. Because the Gosen River flows near the school, the school sits on marshes. Due to heavy snow in winter, school buildings are built on raised cement foundations. A cluster of trees is growing in the school forest. Unfortunately, there is no sign of utilizing the forest as a resource for the curriculum.

However, we learned that a manual for a school forest plan was there and literary works on the forest helped us in developing our school forest models in South Korea.

Minami Junior High School

Minami Junior High School is a co-ed school located in Tokamachi City in Niigata prefecture. Tokamachi is home to the Tokamachi Snow Festival, which takes place every February. Every winter, snow falls to an average depth of two meters. Important Indigenous products of this region are the kimono, the traditional Japanese garment, and rice. Because the school is located in the marshes like Imegasaki Elementary School, it is also built on a raised cement foundation. The principal presented the process of producing the forest through some slides. During the presentation, the presenter showed three principles: first, planting the forest together, second, enjoying each other in developing the forest, last, remembering 'Homeland Forest' indigenous to Tokamachi City.

Returning to South Korea, the Society members, with the help of the Forest for Life, one of the most important environmental associations, founded in 1998, produced the first school forest at Shingi Elementary School in Anyang near Seoul in 1999. The school is still recognized as a model for maintaining a holistic approach to teaching and learning. For instance, students enjoy hanging out, writing poems, and drawing pictures in the school forest, which leads to promoting students' eco-friendly attitude.

Expansion of the School Forest Movement

As I mentioned above, the history of the school forest movement in South Korea was derived from the Korean Society for Holistic Education. In 1999, the School Forest Movement Project was jointly initiated by the Forest for Life, the Korea Forest Service, an independent agency specializing in forestry that is overseen by the Ministry for Food, Agriculture, Forestry and Fisheries, and Yuhan–Kimberly, the joint venture between Korea's Yuhan Corporation and U.S. based Kimberly-Clark. In the same year, the city of Seoul started the School Park Project. A few projects followed suit, such as the School Forest Project by Gyeonggi Province surrounding Seoul in 2003, the Green School Project by the Ministry of Education, and the Green School Project by the city of Incheon in 2006.

After producing the first forest at Shingi Elementary School, the society was not able to be directly involved in school forest projects. However, the society was instrumental in expanding the school forest movement, since it inspired the school forest committee associated with the Forest for Life. While the school forest movement spread under the general supervision of civil groups, the Green School Project, conducted as part of a movement to plant 10 million trees, was initiated under the general supervision of the city of Seoul. These movements played an important role as being a catalyst for change in diffusing to other local governments, even if the supporting funds were not sufficient (Kim, Choi, & Lee, 2000).

The school forest movement conducted by Forest for Life, the school forest movement undertaken by the city of Seoul, the Korean Society for Holistic Education, the Green School, financially supported by the Ministry of Education, and Floral Land Cultivation Project, financed by the LG Evergreen Foundation have resulted in generating 762 school forests in South Korea as of 2017.

Key Issues in Implementing the School Forest Movement

Now is the time to reconsider the school forest movement from a holistic perspective. Previous studies suggest that we need to consider conducting a systematic review or meta-analysis (Hur et al., 2014; Kim, 2001). The key issues raised from the previous literature reviews can be articulated through the importance of focusing on process over product.

Most of the early forest projects were undertaken without the benefit of much planning and design, as the focus was on the process of involving students, parents, and community members in the creation of the school forest. In essence, one of the main processes of these forest projects can be viewed as community building (Hitchmough, 2001).

Community building is clearly a valuable dynamic to encourage in any school; however, it is also important to consider the outcomes resulting from the process, as it is unlikely that there will be sufficient time and energy available to engage every student cohort of every school in the creation of a forest. If the process does not lead to landscapes that can be seen as successful by the children, their parents, teachers, and education authorities, then the long-term future for the projects may be compromised. An alternative is to evaluate the projects in a holistic way.

Connection to the Environmental and Holistic Education Curriculum

The school forest movement emphasizes maximizing the potential of the space for environmental education by planting the trees on the playground and embracing a holistic perspective. The eco-friendly school-oriented policies adopted by the advanced countries, including the Organization for Economic Co-operation and Development (OECD) member countries, suggest that the direction to move should be towards holistic education.

The European Environment and School Initiative Program (EESIP), one of the programs supported by the Center for Educational Research and Innovation (CERI) under the OECD, is organized to develop a curriculum of environmental education. It reports that the sustainable strategies, related to the school environment and joined by 23 member countries, reinforce the teamwork between the local community and the school. Also a sense of accomplishment and self-esteem is enhanced if the students positively participate in the school forest project. For example, the School Biotope Program, as part of the eco-school program in Japan, has spread widely by being connected to an environmental and holistic curriculum and eco-friendly school-oriented projects such as EESIP and European eco-schools (Kim, 2001).

The school forest is the outdoor classroom where the teacher and students get together and study. It is the place where environmental and holistic education allow for a teachable moment. In summary, the utilization of the school forest as curriculum materials provides an excellent case for holistic education (Kim, 1999; Song, 2004).

Challenges with Developing School Forests

There has been considerable interest in generating the school forest in South Korea for environmental and holistic education. There is extensive published information available to schools on how to approach this project, and opportunities to develop partnerships at the civil and governmental levels. While this represents a positive step forward, there is still much to do and the problems of long-term projects are far from resolved. Many schools have developed wonderful school forests; however, many more have either not started the process or have made little progress.

The use of the school forest as curriculum content in environmental and holistic education is not always possible due to the transfer of principals in the public schools in South Korea and Japan. It depends on whether the educational philosophy of a new principal is congruent with the former principal's vision. The teacher in charge of the school forest can also be transferred to other schools on a regular basis. Another problem is that a school is designated as a model for only a couple of years in South Korea. This is too short a time span for the forest to be fully developed.

The funds to create the school forest can be made available through a process of school-based funding applications. However, there are often no funds available for the care of the school forest after it has been created. Increasingly, the emphasis on school forest development is where schools enter a partnership with non-governmental organizations (NGOs) or governmental institutions to apply for funding to redevelop the school forest. This process requires the development of a master-plan for the whole school grounds, undertaken by professional designer with continuous input from teachers and students.

Another challenge is that the South Korean government, with large funding, has begun to dominate the forest school projects. It follows that ensuing school forests begin to be standardized and lose their diversity. Finally, the school forest is popular with elementary students rather than secondary school students because of the college entrance examination. Those are the tasks facing educators in the process of developing the school forest.

We live in a time when the fourth Industrial Revolution, described as a range of new technologies that are fusing the physical, digital, and biological worlds, and impacting all disciplines, economies, and industries, is around the corner. Despite these challenges, our aim in South Korea is to instill what French philosopher Henri Bergson (1983) called *élan vital* translated as 'vital impetus' or 'vital force' that is continually developing and generating a new sense of awe and reverence for life.

References

Bergson, H. (1983). *Creative evolution* (*L'Évolution créatrice*, 1907). Lanham, MD: University Press of America.

Cho, K. (1999). A review of holistic forests in Niigata prefecture. *Journal of Holistic Education, 3*(2), 287–288.

Hitchmough, J. (2001). Enriching the landscape of schools through woodland and other naturalistic planting. The 4th International Symposium of KIYEE.

Hur, Y., Lee, S., Shim, Y., Kim, I., Han, K., Yoon, S., . . . Jung, Y. (2014). A study on the composition principles and the classification of school forest movement: Based on the performance in 15 years and value of school forest. *Journal of Environmental Education, 27*(2), 174–186.

Japanese Association for Holistic Education (1999). *An introduction to holistic education* (Korean trans.). Seongnam, Gyeonggi Prvince: Booksarang.

Kim, B. (1999). Forests as materials for social studies in ecological education: A holistic approach. *Social Studies Education, 33*, 37–47.

Kim, I. (2001). School forest movement developing process and project in Korea. International School Forest Movement Seminar Data, Forest for Life, pp.14–46.

Kim, I., Choi, S., & Lee, S. (2000). A study on the activation strategy and state of school forest movement. *Journal of Environmental Education, 13*(1), 111–121.

Lee, G. (1999). A reflection on my trip to Japanese school forests. *Journal of Holistic Education, 3*(2), 289–291.

Miller, J. P. (2000). *The holistic curriculum* (Korean trans.). Seongnam, Gyeonggi Prvince: Booksarang.

Miller, J. P. (2007). *The holistic curriculum* (2nd edn). Toronto, ON: OISE Press.

Miller, J. P. (2008). A journey of transformation of a Vietnam War resistor. In M. Gardner & U. Kelly (Eds), *Narrating transformative learning in education*. New York: Palgrave Macmillan.

Miller, J. P. (Ed.) (2012). *Transcendental learning: The educational legacy of Alcott, Emerson, Fuller, Peabody and Thoreau*. Charlotte, NC: Information Age.

Orr, D. W. (1994). *Earth in mind: On education, environment and the human prospect*. Washington, DC: Island Press.

Song, M. (2004). School forest generation and the management of extra-curricular activities and discretionary activity curriculum. *Journal of Holistic Education, 8*(1), 45–71.

Tezuka, I. & Miller, J. P. (1995). *School with forest and meadow* (Korean trans.). Gwangmyeong, Gyeonggi Province: Gwangmyeong.

21

Madrasa Schools in East Africa

An Islamic Perspective in Holistic Education

Antum Panjwani and Sarfaroz Niyozov

Whole Child Education, in our current time and context, holds the potential to mitigate fragmentation in economic, social, cultural, and personal contexts (Miller, 1988, p. 4). In spite of material wealth, many people today feel disconnected from spirituality, lacking a sense of awe, a connection to nature, or reverence for life. There are several educational frameworks, for example, Waldorf Schools (Carlgren, Rudel, & Rudell, 1976; Stacey, 1997), Montessori Education (Lillard, 1996) and Roots of Empathy in Canada (Gordon, 2005) that practice whole teaching approaches. These frameworks aim for connectedness by moving away from fragmented approaches to education and life, thereby facilitating connectedness in every sphere of learning (Miller, 2010). Education with a holistic perspective, leads to the development of creative and critical thinkers who experience connection both within themselves and with the world at large (Miller, 2010, p. 57).

The *Madrasa* schools in East Africa represent an early learning model rooted in a revitalised and reconceptualised understanding of the traditional *madrasa* framework in Islam. The *Madrasa* schools have changed from the colonial schools, having been turned into modern learning environments (Munir & Nanji, 2002, p. 235), as well as affirming local spaces and institutions. The *Madrasa* schools in East Africa embody a model of holistic learning for early years through an integrated and interdisciplinary curriculum, specifically designed for Muslim children (Panjwani, 2017). In this chapter, we describe *Madrasa* education in East Africa, not only because *Madrasa* schools promote holistic teaching and learning, but because the schools also serve as a developmental model for education in certain parts of the world, where access to education is a challenge. This particular example of holistic education offers learning to some of the poorest and most marginalised communities in the world. The goals of the *Madrasa* program are to increase students' access to, and retention in, primary school by improving their well-being through a child-friendly, supportive environment.

This chapter presents a conceptual framework, based on principles of Islam (Figure 21.1). It details an approach to holistic education rooted in Islamic spirituality (Panjwani, 2008), and connects this with Miller's framework of holistic education, which builds on a synthesis of many perspectives from around the world. The case of *Madrasa* Schools in East Africa and *Madrasa* Resource Centers (MRCs) demonstrates a blend of the two holistic frameworks: that of Miller (1988, 2010) and that of Islam. We begin by drawing a brief review of Miller's *Whole Child Education* and *Holistic Curriculum* perspectives (1988; 2010). This is followed by the corresponding understanding of the principles and values underlying Whole Child Education from an Islamic worldview. The latter is explored through a description of spirituality in Islam and a framework of ethical underpinnings that inform

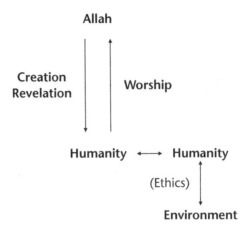

Figure 21.1   Framework describing Islamic and Ismaili Worldview

the work of the Aga Khan Development Network (Aga Khan Development, n.d.). Finally, the *Madrasa* schools are discussed, with an emphasis on the connections to both frameworks.

Holistic Education

Whole Child Education, according to Gandhi (1958) develops mind, body, and spirit in an integrated manner. It is based on the belief that each human being is endowed with a divine spark, or soul, that has life-nourishing energy. Maria Montessori's educational vision consists of cosmic education that nurtures children's sense of meaning and purpose in their lives through reading stories from different traditions. The wholeness, mentioned by Gandhi, can be achieved through understanding and engagement with whole teaching. According to Miller (2010), one of the ways of practicing whole teaching is through a combination of three approaches to teaching: transmission, transaction, and transformation. Holistic education is rooted in balance, inclusion, and connection. It integrates multiple spheres of learning, namely the intellectual, emotional, physical, social, and aesthetic, while also paying heed to the spiritual dimension (Miller, 2005). Engagement of the student as a whole, and the balance of the rational and the intuitive, are pillars of holistic learning.

The Whole Curriculum

Holistic education implies a Whole Curriculum that connects with the child. It is centered on relationships and an understanding of the interdependence of human life, society, and nature. Miller (2010, p. 60) examines six types of connections to support integrated learning: those of subject, community, earth, body–mind, thinking, and soul. Integrated curriculum focuses on personal and social issues (Beane, 1997). An ethic of love, as described by bell hooks (2001) is a pivotal value in the whole school and Whole Curriculum. hooks links love to spirituality, maintaining that love is our true destiny (Miller, 2010, p. 83). Different types of love, like *eros* and *philia*, are necessary to build a whole school community. The leadership of whole school community mitigates divisions in the school through love (Miller, 2010, p. 90).

Islamic Worldview and Spirituality in Islam

In Islam, spirituality is considered a state of mind that perceives life beyond its temporal/worldly nature and connects all of humanity with its divine origin. The religious belief system in Islam is harmonious with nature. Muslims perceive nature and Allah's creation as the first revelation, even before the initiation of divine revelations (Nasr, 2002, p. 12). Spirituality in Islam is a universal, holistic, all-pervading, benevolent, humanitarian spark, which enlightens the paths of humanity and is divinely guided (Panjwani, 2008).

Ethical Framework of Islam

The *Madrasa* schools are guided by the mandate of the Aga Khan Development Network (AKDN), which is derived from an ethical framework of Islam (The Institute of Ismaili Studies, 2004). Operating through this framework, the Aga Khan Development Network represents a contemporary endeavor of the Ismaili Imamat to realize the social conscience of Islam through institutional action.

The Ismaili Imamat

The message of Islam as revealed to Prophet Muhammad calls upon people to seek signs that point to the Creator and Sustainer of all creation in their daily life, to see the rhythm of nature and the order of the universe, in their own selves. While this requires worship of, and obedience to, God, it also suggests human responsibility towards God's creation, including nourishing the soul, not abusing the body, and refraining from indulging in excesses that create pain and diversion from God. Historically, the responses to these central messages of Islam have been expressed through two main perspectives within Islam: the Shia and the Sunni. The Ismailis are the second largest Shia Muslim community (Daftary, 1990). The leader of the Ismaili community is His Highness Prince Karim Aga Khan, also known as the Aga Khan IV, the 49th hereditary Imam of the Shia Imami Ismaili Muslims. According to the Aga Khan: "The Ismaili Imamat is a supra-national entity representing the succession of Imams since the time of the Prophet" (His Highness the Aga Khan, 2014).

The Ismaili Worldview

The Ismaili worldview constitutes a historically grounded perspective within the wider tapestry of Islamic worldviews (Panjwani, 2008). The Ismailis believe in a vertical relationship with God that is bi-directional. From Allah to humankind, this relationship is in the form of divine guidance received through the revelations to Prophet Muhammad. This guidance continued through Ismaili Imams, who are divinely guided to interpret the revelations with changing times and contexts. Muslims reciprocate their relationships with God, the Prophet, and those in authority through prayers, supplication, good deeds, and leading a life based on the Islamic tradition of ethical principles. Besides the vertical relationship, a horizontal link also exists with the divine in the form of human relationships and, finally, humankind's relationship with nature (Mitha, July 2006).[1] Understanding of this framework is foundational to Ismailis' daily actions and decision making. This vision (Figure 21.1) not only links the human with the divine and human beings with each other, but also positions every action within a divinely guided ethical framework.

Aga Khan Development Network

The Aga Khan Development Network (AKDN) is a network of private, non-denominational development agencies founded by the Aga Khan, which work primarily in the poorest parts of Asia and Africa. His Highness, the Aga Khan IV is the founder of the AKDN. He became the 49th hereditary Imam as spiritual leader of the Shia Ismaili Muslims in 1957. The network focuses on health, education, culture, rural development, institution building, and the promotion of economic development. The AKDN aims to improve living conditions and opportunities for the poor, without regard to their faith, origin, or gender. AKDN's annual budget for not-for-profit activities is approximately $600 million US—mainly for use in Africa, Asia, and the Middle East. The AKDN works in 30 countries around the world, and it employs over 80,000 paid staff, mostly in developing countries. While the agencies are secular, they are guided by Islamic ethics, which bridge faith and society (Aga Khan Development Network, n.d.). The institutions of the Network derive their impetus from the ethics of Islam, which bridge the two realms of the faith: *din* and *dunya*. *Din* is the spiritual/religious and *dunya* symbolizes the material and worldly. Islam's ethical ideal is the

> . . . enablement of each person to live up to his exalted status as vicegerent of God on earth, in whom God has breathed His own spirit and to whom He has made whatever is in the heavens and the earth, an object of trust and quest.
>
> *(The Institute of Ismaili Studies, 2004, p. 1)*

In this way, *dunya* is not a distraction leading the humans away from the true purpose of life, but a reminder that service to God is not only worship, but also service to humanity and the rest of creation.

According to the *Quran*, righteousness is not only fulfilling one's religious obligations. It is also accepting social responsibility. Without the latter, religiosity can become a show of conceit. Thus, in Islam, both *din* (spirit) and *dunya* (matter) are distinct but intertwined. Each of these aspects is critically important and neither are to be abandoned (The Institute of Ismaili Studies, 2004). In this way, Islam elevates the sense of public and social order to a transcendent level inspired by a spiritual, universal ethic of eliciting the noble (*ihsan*) that is inherent in each person. Islam's ethical ideals that inform the AKDN mandate are: Inclusiveness, Education, and Research, Compassion and Sharing, Self-Reliance, Respect for Life and Health Care, Sound Mind, Sustainable Environment—Physical, Social, and Cultural, and Governance. These ethical principles speak of the wholeness of humanity and the unity of the human race that is born from a single soul (Aga Khan, 2014). The *Quran* says: "Oh Mankind, fear your Lord, who created you of a single soul, and from it created its mate, and from the pair of them scattered abroad many men and women . . ." (4:1). In other words, this Islamic paradigm matches with the framework of Holistic Education premised on balance, inclusion, and connection. The relationship between *din* and *dunya* is akin to the presence of yin and yang in Chinese philosophy (Miller, 1988, p. 6), which are entwined with each other, providing inspiration and balance for living a holistic life.

The *Madrasa* Schools in East Africa

History and Tradition of Madrasa *Education in Islam*

Education has been vital in Islam since the time of its birth and has enjoyed a special status among Muslims. Prophet Muhammad laid great importance on learning and initiated the first school, called *kuttab*, during his lifetime. A famous *hadith* attributed to the Prophet calls upon Muslims to seek knowledge from cradle to grave, even if a person has to travel to far places, for example, China. Muslim communities around the world consider acquiring and sharing knowledge as important duties. *Madrasas*, meaning places of learning, also known by other names such as *hawza, maktab, kuttab,* and *jami'a* (Sakurai & Adelkhah, 2011) are part of this tradition, belief, and practice of Muslims' commitment to learning. The term *madrasa* derives its root from Arabic *darasa*, meaning 'to study' (Noor, Sikand, & Bruinessen, 2008). Since pursuit of knowledge is an important aspect of faith for Muslims, the original schools or learning centers were part of *Masjids*, or places of worship. Contrary to a common misunderstanding, *madrasas* do not merely impart religious education, they also teach other subjects, providing both religious/ethical and secular/professional education to students. In the modern-day context, these traditional places of learning have come under attack and suspicion for various reasons related to Islamic extremism (Noor et al., 2008, p. 9). While for some schools this perception might hold true, most of the *madrasas* do not fit into the generalized image created through the media (Park & Niyozov, 2008).

The *Madrasa* Early Childhood Program (MECP)

The *Madrasa* Early Childhood Development Program is an AKDN initiative to establish community-owned and managed preschools for disadvantaged Muslim communities in Mombasa (Kenya), Kampala (Uganda), and Zanzibar (Tanzania). It is a unique program systematically focused on Muslim identity development. In 1982, the leaders of the Muslim community in East Africa, along with representatives of the Aga Khan Foundation, met with His Highness the Aga Khan in Mombasa to address the educational needs of the Muslim community. Distress was expressed about the severe marginalization of Muslim children due to lack of access to primary schooling, which affected their future prospects (Aga Khan Foundation, 2008). A series of meetings spearheaded by the Aga Khan resulted in what is now the *Madrasa* project, emerging from a deep concern for acquiring and sharing knowledge in accordance with Islamic tradition. This creative vision guiding the *Madrasa* project aims to ". . . prepare young children for life itself – in all of its holistic dimensions" (Aga Khan, 2007, August 14).

A retired teacher, Bi Swafiya Said, initiated this educational model in 1986 as the first director, through a grant from the Aga Khan Foundation. She came from a family with a tradition of service to Muslim educational causes. Thus, she was able to convince the local community to broaden the reach of *madrasa* beyond religious teaching. She was also able to mobilize young Muslim women to come forward for training, as well as create resource centers promoting best practices drawn from international early childhood learning models.

For more than three decades now, the *Madrasa* project has been running successfully in a variety of East African contexts. Today, there are 203 preschools in East Africa under the *Madrasa* Program, serving over 54,000 students (Rashid, 2010). The *Madrasa* project operates under the *Madrasa* Resource Centers (MRCs) in the three countries. The Resource Centers assist marginalized communities to set up early childhood centers in the areas of need. The mandate of MRC also includes developing training methodologies, teaching programs, and manuals (Ismailimail, 2015). The *Madrasa* project is now a major educational movement in East Africa, joined by several other *madrasas* and community endeavors (Early Childhood Development Program, May 13, 2013). With the popularity and expansion of the program, other faith communities have also joined this educational venture, giving it a rich pluralist inclusivity. Local languages like Luganda in Uganda, and Swahili in Mombasa and Zanzibar are used as the medium of instruction. The program fosters "children's sense of cultural and religious identity" (Munir & Nanji, 2002, p. 234), through a balanced curriculum, resulting in a 'reimagining' of Muslim childhood. It utilizes child-centered pedagogy in learning, along with traditional forms of teaching such as reading and writing (Jaffer, 2009). The curriculum draws from global educational best practices, is modified to be culturally appropriate, and incorporates Islamic teaching and practices (Faizi, 2014). What Miller describes as 'Whole Curriculum' is termed as 'education for life' by the *Madrasa* project. It nurtures the children's religious and cultural identity while also ensuring that the ethical values drawn from Quranic education are not compromised.

The Kenyan *Madrasa* curriculum seeks to address and harmonize all three major spheres that influence the identity formation of Muslim children in Kenya: Islam, the tradition of Swahili culture, and the emergent values of the modern nation state of Kenya (Munir & Nanji, 2002, p. 234). It encompasses the wholeness of the spiritual vision of Islam integrated with community values and a national vision. The integration of religious formation and the learning of relevant skills are premised on a transformative-reproductive approach to teaching that enables these students to develop the skills, knowledge, and values while remaining Muslims, true to their faith. This transformative teaching is infused with religion and nurturing wisdom, compassion, and sense of purpose in one's life. Their Muslim faith is interpreted in terms of tolerance for each other and connecting the Muslim community with global humanity (Senge, Sharmer, Jaworski, & Flowers, 2005, p. 188, as quoted in Miller, 2010, p. 29). The connectedness between the outer world and inner world of lived experiences at a micro level, and the connectedness among people in the larger world, defines organic wholeness. The program also establishes linkages between preschool and local primary school teachers to ease children's transitions to primary schooling. Such a holistic approach ensures the non-compartmentalized development of a child, thus making the *Madrasa* a uniquely holistic model of education. The curriculum of the *Madrasa* project aims to cover six connections: community, earth, inner/soul, body–mind, subject, and intuition/inquiry at early learning and elementary levels. The *Madrasa* uses traditional spaces of learning, which help preserve the religious and cultural identity of the Muslim children.

Innovative approaches to the curriculum are utilized in the program. As Munir and Nanji (2002) write:

> Learning aids are developed out of local, low-cost materials such as sea-shells, seedpods, and coconuts. The curriculum includes Swahili stories and motifs from local culture as well as English, numeracy, and other interactive, child-centered forms of learning. Thus, the whole range of cosmopolitan learning – Muslim, local, and international – has found a place in the developing curriculum to inform the children's sense of self and preparation for the changing environment in which they will have to compete and function.
>
> *(Munir & Nanji, 2002, p. 234)*

The *Madrasa* education model promotes the view that cultural resources can be effectively used for educational, child, and community development. It is driven by local cultural values combined with Islamic religious and spiritual ideals. All these traits are successfully amalgamated within a secular educational setting, which makes it unique. The *Madrasas* also offer solutions for contemporary development challenges by developing human and material resources. As a visiting Canadian educator to a *Madrasa* school in Uganda observed:

> The teaching pedagogy in a Madrasa school can be compared with a preschool classroom in Canada. Having taught kindergarten in the Peel Board of Education in Ontario, I had fun immersing myself with the children at the various learning areas set up in each of the schools: a block area, book area, sand and water area, and shop and home areas.
>
> *(Murji, 2014, para. 8)*

The Community Connection: The Beloved Community and the *Ummah*

A caring community within and outside of the classroom is one of the essential tenets of nurturing the whole child. Miller (2010) cites Martin Luther King Jr.'s notion of The Beloved Community, which is a place of love and justice, to emphasize the role of community in developing the whole child. The Beloved Community is a human society based on interrelatedness, belonging, and inclusivity. King (as cited in Miller, 2010) maintains that each person is indebted to others for survival and for the existence of society. Thus, injustice done to one person is an injustice to all human beings. King's vision of The Beloved Community is inclusive of all races, classes, ethnic groups, nations, and religions (Miller, 2010). The whole school represents such a community, where teachers and students feel at home and look forward to being there. The leadership in such whole school communities plays a critical role in creating an enabling environment and actualizing the vision of The

Beloved Community. Miller (2010, p. 90) describes principles to be followed by the principal in building the Beloved Community: organic vision and focused plans with an understanding that change is not linear and that non-verbal dimensions are important. As Miller (1988) writes:

> The focus of holistic education is on relationships: the relationship between linear thinking and intuition, the relationship between mind and body, the relationships amongst various domains of knowledge, the relationship between the individual and community, the relationship to the earth, and our relationship to our souls.
>
> *(p. 13)*

The *Quran* enjoins a similar dictum signifying the connectedness between the common humanity:

> For that cause We decreed for the Children of Israel that whosoever killeth a human being for other than manslaughter or corruption in the earth, it shall be as if he had killed all mankind, and whoso saveth the life of one, it shall be as if he had saved the life of all mankind.
>
> *(5:32)*

The understanding of community in Islam has underpinnings similar to the Beloved Community of King. It is called *Ummah*. *Ummah* in Arabic means 'nation', 'community', or 'the people', denoting the collective community of Muslim peoples. The term is commonly used in Muslim countries to differentiate universal brotherhood of all men and women, as well as specific brotherhood shared by the commonality of the faith of Islam. For example, in the community of Medina at the time of Prophet, *Ummah* is believed to have included Jews, Christians, and Sabians (The *Quran*, 2:62). *The Charter of Medina*, drawn by Prophet Muhammad, also indicated this inclusive understanding (Firestone, 1999, p. 18; Serjeant, 1964; Watt, 1956).

In Islam, the interrelationship between God, individual, and human society can be presented graphically through a series of concentric circles (Nasr, 2002). The innermost circle stands for the relationship between an individual and God, followed by the circles of the family, the city or town where one lives, the nation, the Islamic community (*Ummah*), the entire humanity, and, finally, creation as a whole. Each circle has its center in the first circle, and all interactions in subsequent circles are based on the relationship between the individual and God. In conjunction with these interrelationships, there is a set of responsibilities each person is supposed to perform, starting with one's own self, followed by her/his duty towards the society and family. The individualistic Western perspective regarding the human body as entirely one's own and at one's disposal is not part of the Islamic belief system. Men and women in Islam are guided in personal morality by their faith, but Islam also envisions a social order that holds each person accountable through morally just conduct towards others. The foundation of Muslim *ummah* was drawn by Prophet Muhammad by the suffusion of daily life with religious morality and spirituality, which is a reminder of *din–dunya* balance described above. Further, in the traditional Islamic worldview, every necessity of life, including earning one's daily bread, is sanctified (Nasr, 2002).

Today, when technology and excessive materialism are diluting human connectedness, the *Madrasa* model presents the power of community endeavors in creating change and forging meaningful human relationships. It affirms *ubuntu*, a traditional African communal ethic of love that goes beyond the love of the family to include the tribe and humanity as a whole (Miller, 2010, p. 84). *Madrasa* schools are an integrated part of the community. The program's integrated dimensions of community values and national vision symbolize wholeness of the community (Miller, 2000), whereby people are able to relate to one another openly. Such community connections foster a sense of care. In these ways, the *Madrasa* schools embody relationship with faith, self, country, and earth.

Community empowerment and school-community connection are manifested in the ways in which community members come forward in constructing, raising funds, and managing the *Madrasa* schools. The development of community literacy enhances engagement of the community members with the program. Parents' literacy is also heightened as they learn from their children and participate in various school programs. The inclusive spirit can be witnessed from the participation of the members of the community and the girls having equal opportunity for education. These poor communities have the richness of unity, a spirit of sharing, kindness, generosity, forgiveness, and helping each other. These values help the community members harness resources and capacity. The shared values of these communities are an embodiment of community empowerment that has created a sense of pride, and empowerment, which will have a long-term impact on its education and development. The ethic of education and research in Islam inspires individuals to be lifelong learners with the realization that the journey to becoming whole human being is continuous. Seeking knowledge is getting closer to God. These ethics collectively lead the *Madrasa* teachers towards becoming Whole Teachers practicing, patience, presence, care, love, and humility.

Conclusion

The *Madrasa* project in East Africa, presents a faith–based model of holistic education. Holistic education as understood and practiced in the *Madrasa* model is an effort towards the vision of educating the whole child. As Miller (2010) writes:

> Educating the whole child needs whole teaching, a whole curriculum, whole schools, and whole teachers. Although whole child education challenges administrators and teachers, it can help create schools where students enjoy being and learning. The aim of the whole child education is the development of children and adolescents who can think, feel, and act and whose bodies and souls are nourished.
>
> *(p. 13)*

In providing education that involves parents, communities, and children, the *Madrasa* schools are civil societies that bring about change through community empowerment. They nullify the criticisms heaped on *madrasas* that we hear today. Instead, these schools enable Muslim children to thrive in a pluralistic and globalizing world, while nurturing their moral, spiritual, and cultural identity. The *Madrasa* schools offer development that is relevant to young children's local context. Together with an emphasis on continuous connection of the child with the indigenous ways of knowing, the *Madrasas* have the capacity to inspire different whole schools and faith communities to explore resources from their own sacred texts, religious values, and diverse histories in the process of developing whole children that are confident with their religious and cultural identities.

Significantly, these *madrasas* challenge the negative perceptions about *madrasa*, Islamic education, and Islam as a whole. They produce children who care for all beings and do not have to abandon their language, tradition, and culture to become cosmopolitans. They are empowered to transform these dimensions of their identity constructively and inclusively.

Note

1 Framework describing Islamic as well as Ismaili worldview from a presentation entitled "Authority and Community" given by Farouk Mitha at the International Human Resource Training programme in July 2006, London, UK.

References

Aga Khan, H. H. (2007, August 14). Commemoration of the 25th anniversary of the Madrasa programme. Retrieved July 27, 2017 from www.akdn.org/speech/his-highness-aga-khan/commemoration-of-25th-anniversary-of-madrasa-programme.

Aga Khan, H. H. (2014, February). Address to both Houses of the Parliament of Canada in the House of Commons Chamber. Retrieved July 8, 2017 from www.akdn.org/speech/his-highness-aga-khan/address-both-houses-parliament-canada-house-commons-chamber

Aga Khan Development Network. (n.d.). Retrieved December 15, 2017 from www.akdn.org/.

Aga Khan Development Network (n.d.). Ismaili Imamat. Retrieved July 04, 2017 from www.akdn.org/about-us/his-highness-aga-khan-1.

Aga Khan Foundation (2008). The Madrasa Early Childhood Programme: 25 years of experience. Retrieved July 27, 2017 from www.akdn.org/our-agencies/aga-khan-foundation/education/early-childhood-development-ecd.

Beane, J. A. (1997). *Curriculum integration: Designing the core of democratic education.* New York: Teachers College Press.

Carlgren, F., Rudel, J., & Rudel, S. (1976). *Education towards freedom: Rudolf Steiner education: A survey of the work of Waldorf schools throughout the world.* East Grinstead: Lanthorn Press.

Daftary, F. (1990). *The Ismāʿīlīs: Their history and doctrines.* Cambridge, UK: Cambridge University Press.

Faizi, Z. (2014, January 24). The Madrasa Early Childhood Program. Paper presented at A Conference for Presentation and Discussion of final projects of students in the course A801 Education Policy Analysis and Research in Comparative Perspective, Harvard Graduate School of Education, Gutman Conference Center.

Firestone, R. (1999). *Jihād: The Origin of Holy War in Islam.* New York: Oxford University Press.

Gandhi, M. (1958). *All men are brothers: Life and thoughts of Mahatma Gandhi.* Paris: UNESCO.

Gordon, M. (2005). *Roots of empathy: Changing the world, child by child.* Toronto, ON: Thomas Allen Publishers.

hooks, b. (2001). *All about love: New visions.* New York: Perennial.

Ismailimail (2015, December 27). Madrasa Resource Centre, Kenya – funded and supported by the Aga Khan Foundation. Retrieved November 19, 2017 from https://ismailimail.wordpress.com/2006/10/12/madrasa-resource-centre-kenya-funded-and-supported-by-the-aga-khan-foundation/.

Jaffer, S. (2009). The Madrasa Resource Centers, East Africa. Retrieved from http://www.cies.us/newsletter/sept%2009/Jaffer.html.

Lillard, P. P. (1996). *Montessori today: A comprehensive approach to education from birth to adulthood.* New York: Schocken Books.

Miller, J. P. (1988). *The holistic curriculum.* Toronto, ON: OISE Press, Ontario Institute for Studies in Education.

Miller, J. P. (2005). *Holistic learning and spirituality in education: Breaking new ground.* Albany, NY: State University of New York Press.

Miller, J. P. (2010). *Whole child education.* Toronto, ON: OISE Press, Ontario Institute for Studies in Education.

Miller, R. (2000). *Caring for new life: Essays on holistic education.* Brandon, VT: Foundation for Educational Renewal.

Mitha, F. (2006). Authority and community (PowerPoint slides). From lecture notes at the International Human Resource Training programme in July 2006, London, UK.

Munir, L. Z. & Nanji, A. (2002). Linking past and present educating Muslim children in diverse cultural contexts. In M. J. Bunge (Ed.), *Children, adults, and shared responsibilities Jewish, Christian and Muslim perspectives.* New York: Cambridge University Press.

Murji, S. (2014, August 29). Novel approach to early childhood education in Africa is creating a valuable legacy. Retrieved July 27, 2017 from www.theismaili.org/cms/924/Novel-approach-to-Early-Childhood-Education-in-Africa-is-creating-a-valuable-legacy.

Nasr, S. H. (2002). *The heart of Islam: Enduring values for humanity.* San Francisco, CA: Harper.

Noor, F. A., Sikand, Y., & Bruinessen, M. V. (Eds) (2008). *The Madrasa in Asia Political Activism and Transnational Linkages.* Amsterdam: Amsterdam University Press.

Panjwani, A. A. (2008). Conceptions of leadership and critical spirituality in ismailism (Order No. MR38982). Available from Dissertations & Theses @ University of Toronto; ProQuest Dissertations & Theses Global (304336928).

Panjwani, A. A. (2017). Representations of Muslim cultures and societies in children's literature as a curriculum resource for Ontario classrooms: Promises and prospects. (Doctoral Dissertation University of Toronto – Not yet published on Proquest Dissertations).

Park, J. & Niyozov, S. (2008). Madrasa education in South Asia and Southeast Asia: Current issues and debates. *Asia Pacific Journal of Education, 28*(4), 323–351. doi:10.1080/02188790802475372.

Rashid, N. (2010). Madrasa Early Childhood Development Program. Retrieved from http://blogs.tc.columbia.edu/transitions/files/2010/09/61.East-Africa-Madrasa-Program_profile.pdf.

Sakurai, K. & Adelkhah, F. (2011). *The moral economy of the madrasa: Islam and education today*. New York: Routledge.

Serjeant, R. B. (1964). The Constitution of Medina. *Islamic Quarterly*, *8*(4), 3–16.

Stacey, E. G. (1997). *The Waldorf promise*. Los Angeles, CA: Landfall Productions.

The Institute of Ismaili Studies (2004). Aga Khan Development Network (AKDN): An ethical framework. Retrieved July 04, 2017 from http://iis.ac.uk/search?query=ethical%2Bframework.

Vancouver Sun (2013, May 13). Early Childhood Development Program improves lives of kids in developing nations. *Vancouver Sun*. Retrieved from http://blogs.vancouversun.com/2013/05/13/early-childhood-development-program-improves-lives-of-kids-in-developing-nations/.

Watt, W. M. (1956). *Muhammad at Medina*. Oxford: Clarendon Press.

22

Queer Bodies and Holistic Imaginaries

Jamie Magnusson

What does holistic education mean for those of us with queer bodies, queer lives, and who identify with queer communities? I playfully spin out scenarios of my child self in a queer holistic education bliss, being encouraged to explore my potential to the fullest. I wonder who my teachers would be? Two spirited elders and transfolks? Would we do queer art? Would I be lovingly nurtured through puberty blocking therapy? Can we articulate a queer holistic education imaginary?

I teach a graduate course in a community development stream of an adult education program. The title is "Embodied Learning and Alternative Models of Community Development". In developing the course, I did not set out to create a "Queer Holistic Education" experience for graduate students. However, the course has become queerly popular. Each offering over the past three to four years has attracted many queer and queer positive graduate students, including a large number of trans students, as well as students negotiating 'trans' issues, such as having children or parents or partners who identify as trans. I also teach a course entitled Queer Interventions for Community Organizers, and while queer students seem to appreciate it, it is not nearly as popular as the embodied learning course. The attraction to the embodied learning course is its fierce commitment to holistic pedagogy and an opportunity to explore what a holistic approach to community organizing might look like. The course affords an opportunity to articulate 'embodiment' in ways that challenge western academic knowledge and to forge innovative spaces for personal and collective growth.

As a gender queer myself, in my community development practice I have worked with street level sex workers, youth who have been exploited in the domestic sex industry, and LGBTQ+ communities. There are significant overlaps among these three communities in that queer/trans youth are often beaten and thrown out of their family homes. They learn to make their way on the streets, sometimes turning to sex work and/or being exploited within the sex industry. In Canada, up to 40% of homeless youth are LGBTQ+, and similar statistics are reported for the U.S. I work within a community program that endorses harm reduction, and I do a considerable amount of harm reduction outreach. Practically speaking, this entails developing and encouraging strategies for safer sex work and safer illicit drug use. Harm reduction is in contrast with programs that insist that "clients" are drug free and not working the streets prior to accessing resources. After outreach and a hearty breakfast, and in the spirit of harm reduction, I offer qigong and self-defence training to whomever cares to join.

Qigong is a Daoist practice involving breath work and the set I teach is a martial qigong. The qigong teaches how to bring one's mind to the body-breath, and stay in the moment. The self-defence I teach flows from the qigong movements. It is a perfect practice for street warriors.

I also offer a similar kind of training to LGBTQ+ communities through a program I initiated called Fighting Out (Magnusson, 2018). Given my community, incorporating qigong and meditation into a course on 'alternative perspectives on community wellness' seemed natural. It felt 'real' to the kind of work I do.

Situating the Course, Situating Me

The course is taught in an Adult Education and Community Development graduate program in the faculty of education (Ontario Institute for Studies in Education, or OISE) at the University of Toronto in Canada. In its first offering it was entitled 'Qigong and Embodied Learning', but I redeveloped it, changing the title to "Embodied Learning and Alternative Approaches to Community Wellness" (see Magnusson, 2016). However, Daoist and Buddhist perspectives continued to be an organizing theme, as will be discussed later. I am a longtime practitioner of martial arts, and a Full Instructor in a Tai Chi and Meditation Centre.[1]

I present as gender queer and teach in a graduate program entitled Adult Education and Community Development. My graduate courses on community development lean heavily towards urban grassroots community organizing and activism. The students in my courses have different kinds of undergraduate experiences, but most of them have found themselves working for the non-profit sector as community organizers and activists. They may have backgrounds in social work, community health, nursing, medicine, or they may be artists who are community engaged. The kinds of agencies they work for include Women's Health in Women's Hands, Street Health, Rainbow Health, youth programs, Anishnawbe Health, centers for refugee and undocumented people, immigration centers, and so on. The kinds of community-engaged artists I have worked with include writers, dancers, visual artists, musicians, photographers, poets, videographers, et cetera. Most of the students live and work in the city of Toronto.

First Day of Class and Description of Assignments

The first session of "LHA1181: Embodied Learning: Alternative Approaches to Community Wellness" is about to begin. The large classroom is chaotic and overflowing. Students are chattering and laughing as if they're in a bar rather than a graduate seminar.

I bring the class to order by walking up to a device on a table beside the audiovisual equipment. It's a digital theramin. It looks like something from the Jetsons. I begin playing.

The chatter quiets and students watch as my hands wave through the air, creating ethereal sounds as only a theremin can. My playing is rough. I don't sound at all like young Gregoire Blanc playing *Claire de Lune* on a classical theremin. Students are nevertheless captivated.

"Why are my hand motions in the air creating music?" I ask.

Initially, no one answers. I am expecting them to speculate on bodies and energy interactions.

Kate, a beautiful trans woman who stands 6'2", is furiously googling the question. She hates any kind of references to "energy" that are not grounded in Western physics or evidence-based medicine. Intrigued by practices such as meditation, she is known to chase down evidence based neuroscience research linking meditation to plasticity of brain.

"Essentially the human body serves as a grounding conduit," she blurts out.

"According to Wikipedia", and she quotes from her iPad, '*The theremin is distinguished among musical instruments in that it is played without physical contact. The thereminist stands in front of the instrument and moves his or her hands in the proximity of two metal antennas. The distance from one antenna determines frequency (pitch), and the distance from the other controls amplitude (volume).*' So, it seems the hands serve as grounding plates, and the human body is a conduit connecting to the ground." That science rules victorious is written all over her face.

Oddly, her ultra-scientific explanation did not take away from the magic of the moment. Many of the students are 'millennials' and have never heard about theremins, an instrument whose existence is now a mere footnote in the history of contemporary music synthesizers. They loved witnessing the energetic interaction taking place between a body in motion and a musical experience connecting all of us.

I now turn on the projector, taking students via the internet to what I consider to be an astonishing video of a multi-media art installation developed by Jo Simalaya, a Toronto-based artist identifying as a member of the queer Filipino diaspora. The installation is entitled "Singing Plants Reconstruct Memory". The centerpiece to the installation is a "diasporic" banana plant brought over by Jo from the Phillipines.

The plant has been wired to function as a theremin. A small portion on each leaf of the plant has suffered an injury, and the hole sutured with a conductive thread. Through her research in the Phillipines, Jo has gathered digital recordings of Huhud chants of the Ifugao People, and other Indigenous music. When participants touch the plant, it "sings". Although the participant and plant create new music, the sound vocabulary is formed from the digitized Indigenous music. The singing tells "a story of Paalaal/Remembrance". As the plant sings, the sound is translated into moving colors that are projected onto a screen. Sound and colors reflect the moment-by-moment energetic interchange between a participant and the plant.

When I initially witnessed this installation in person, my young adult son interacted with the plant by hovering his hand over the leaves. The interchange between plant and this autistic young man produced music and images. Normally overwhelmed by human-to-human interaction, he was thrilled to be communing energetically with the plant. Jo explained to me that initially she touched the wire mesh to produce sounds, but discovered she could touch anywhere on the plant. Later, she realized, she need only hover her hands over the leaves to engage with the plant.

According to Jo's artist's statement:

Singing Plants Reconstruct Memory is an interactive installation in which living plants are keepers of story, cultural history and memory. The intent is to reconstruct what has been lost and repressed through trauma: the unspeakable.

Each Banana Leaf plant bears scars and soul wounds at different stages of healing. These physical wounds are sutured together with conductive thread. When participants touch the plants, they sing Hudhud chants of the Ifugao People, play instruments indigenous to the Philippines, and tell a story of Paalaala/Remembrance.

This project emerges from my personal experience of indirect witnessing. My great-grandparents lived in the Philippines when it was a Spanish colony, my grandparents experienced the shift to another colonial power during the Philippine–American War, my father grew up during the Japanese occupation of Manila, and my immediate family immigrated to Canada to escape Martial Law.

These events have different resonating points for each generation. As a child, I learned to be a silent witness to these stories of our family's roots of resistance. As I got older and started asking questions, I learned that adults have the prerogative to forget.

While doing research in the Philippines, I listened to our family stories unfold again. My Ninang (godmother) said she could hear the voices of our ancestors during those times, as those who reside in the spirit world are present when we include them in the telling. While these reconnections across time bring a deeper understanding of my family and homeland, they also bring a longing to make meaning from traumatic history.

The goal of Singing Plants Reconstruct Memory is to bring the story into the room. The participant acts as an indirect witness – one who did not experience the trauma, but whose engagement makes it possible to reconstruct the fragments left behind.

(SiMalaya Alcampo, n.d.)

This installation introduced students to the 'idea' of art-as-public-pedagogy and the potential of art as a community organizing tool to create politicized spaces for pedagogies of healing, solidarity building, and participatory action. It also primes and feeds the 'holistic imaginary'. The holistic imaginary consists of practices that academia is designed to 'gate', and even chase down, expulse, or destroy.

Holistic imaginaries encourage relational practices of mutual nourishment and a collective responsibility to develop life to the fullest. 'Life' here does not mean 'individual life', but planetary life in a relational sense. Holistic imaginaries can be fed by communities whose knowledges and life practices have been systematically devalued via cultural genocide enacted by the Western academy. Holistic imaginaries are not built on cultural appropriation of Indigenous knowledges, but rather are vested in decolonizing community spaces, and providing opportunities to explore the vast repertoire of life pedagogies afforded by these knowledges. In a queer friendly course filled with students from various diaspora, as well as students who are First Nations, this can mean acknowledging the radical implications of a term such as 'two spirited'. Specific holistic imaginaries do not necessarily need to be spiritual—there must be space for holistic secular humanism. Holistic imaginaries, secular or otherwise, can feed into community organizing, creating spaces of belonging and community life that is in stark contrast with, say, the global financialized imaginary.

Following the video presentation of the Singing Plant installation, I drew students' attention to the section in their course syllabi on "assignments". I explained that one of the major assignments for the course was to work in groups to produce an "art-as-public-pedagogy" installation to take place the final evening of class. The Singing Plant installation was an excellent model of how to engage themes emerging from queer diasporic experience, and produce decolonizing, interactive art-as-public-pedagogy. The installation emerges from a holistic, queer diasporic place.

The course assignments unfold in three stages. In the first assignment, students submit a proposal for using embodied art forms as vehicles for community organizing. Examples can include theatre-of-the-oppressed, slam poetry, dance, singing, drumming, dub poetry, experiential outdoor education, meditation, and so on. Students are asked to organize the proposal into three themes. First, they are to describe how their activity would build community. For example, some of the communities students worked in included an Iranian queer diasporic community, Muslim-identified women experiencing Islamophobic violence, South Asian women who had recently immigrated, men in a compulsory domestic violence program, Indigenous urban youth, Afghani refugee women, Asian queer diasporic youth, undocumented youth, and so on. Second, students were to think through how to organize activities such that the program they were proposing not only built community but "hooked into" social movements. For example, the person developing a program for Iranian queer diasporic youth thought through how to do theatre of the oppressed work such that queer youth would begin experiencing the excitement and safety of meeting up with one another, forming friendships, intergenerational mentoring relationships, and a sense of community. Hooking into social movements could involve having the youth initially meet to work on theatre, but later focusing on a collective project in conjunction with Pride Week. They could also spend an afternoon creating posters together, arranging to meet up as a contingent for one of the Pride marches (Trans, Dyke, Main Parade). Third, community proposals were to demonstrate how to organize pedagogies of solidarity building. For example, the queer Iranian community could support Black Lives Matter-Toronto (BLM-To) at a coalition-building rally organized by BLM-To. They could support a Missing and Murdered Indigenous Women (MMIW) event by showing up to a December 6 Anti-Violence Vigil with placards and posters that state their group is there in solidarity with MMIW. As will be discussed further on, time is set aside in each class for students to work through these discussions. Pedagogies of solidarity can be very exciting but is also a complex topic.

The second assignment, related to the first, is to work in groups to produce an 'art-as-public' pedagogy' installation. The first two years I ran the course, an M.A. fine arts student facilitated a session on 'art' as public pedagogy and community engagement.[2] We were very fortunate that during the first year she became excited about the ideas coming from the class, and she volunteered her time toward helping the class learn how to set up installations, from conceptualizing to advertising to the actual installation event. I learned much from her during those two years, and in the third year, when she was no longer available, I could apply my practical experience to helping students organize themselves.

The art-as-public-pedagogy project was connected to the first assignment in the following way. During the first few classes, a period was devoted to students sorting themselves into groups based on their community organizing interests as reflected in their proposals. There are no rules regarding group sizes, and so I've seen an assortment of sizes that seem to work for the participants. Although the timing, duration, and venue of the art installations have always been up for discussion and negotiation, the students have thus far opted to have one large, multi-installation event in a venue booked through our university, and it has been held on the last day of class. Without exception, the art installations produced by each group have been magnificent. Each one has had an interactive component, and has been transformative for participants. The event is advertised as a public installation, and it seems to draw a nice number of people.

The final written assignment is to produce a final document of the community organizing proposal. Throughout the term, class time is set aside to workshop ideas connected to these assignments. My experience has been that by the time students work up a proposal, receive my written feedback, and workshop their ideas in class, their final proposals are of exceptional quality. Moreover, they have something in hand that they can mobilize within their community spaces, and use as a funding proposal to submit to a non-profit organization. Over the past few years, several of the community organizing proposals from this class exercise have made their way into community spaces.

For example, the 'art-as-public-pedagogy' installation has sometimes had an inspiring life beyond the confines of the course. One installation pertaining to violence against women has been reproduced in at least one other community space, and contributed to a pedagogy of solidarity building. Hosted by communities of Indigenous women, the event was held in the Native Center of Toronto, and designed to foster solidarity across many groups of racialized women involved in anti-violence work. Violence experienced by transwomen was included in the installation, and helped consolidate the connections to be made across a diversity of women—from refugee to Indigenous women—in terms of multiple and interlocking systems such as white heteropatriarchy. The inclusion of transwomen was a significant historical redress in that a great deal of work in the feminist anti-violence movement had excluded transcommunities. The installation featured a video documentation of women's violence, and several stations where different modalities of holistic healing could be experienced. The holistic healing modalities were inspired by spiritually centered healing practices familiar to diasporic/Indigenous groups of women. For example, at one station, participants were given materials to create a sand art mandala, giving a feminist spin to a certain kind of spiritual practice familiar to the South Asian women who created the installation. Their idea was that healing from violence can borrow from some of the spiritual traditions they had grown up with as members of the queer South Asian diaspora (see Walcott, 2017).

To summarize, the course assignments were designed to nurture a holistic imaginary that could be useful in community organizing. The 'embodied learning' theme is especially interesting to students who embody difference in the context of community organizing, including queer diasporic students. The holistic approach creates room for a range of ways of thinking and working with the body. These include alternatives to Western academic ontology that presumes and encourages a schism between mind and body, and that refuses any kind of understanding of energetic, spiritual existence. One such alternative is the idea of 'two-spirited' existence, which simultaneously interrupts Western hegemonic gender binaries, heteronormativity, and introduces an integrative, relational understanding of mind, body, and spirit. South Asian students will often discuss the culture of hijras, and the spiritual and community organizing implications of understanding 'third gender' in a historically situated diasporic cultural context. Mati-ism is acknowledged throughout certain African, Caribbean, and other global South contexts, and is a culture wherein women have 'official' relationships with men, and raise children with them, but their most intimate relationships are with other women. In certain cultures, gender binaries are very fixed, but the communities are very accepting of 'trans' people. For example, one of my friends from a certain culture was accepted as a boy very early in his development, with the proclamation from the father "Oh good!! I'm so happy to have another boy!!" Now a young, fully transitioned and married man, the youngster was simply raised as a boy. This practice, culturally accepted within this particular diasporic community, is very controversial within the context I live and teach, and is only now receiving attention as a "new" development in the social spaces I inhabit. The controversy is framed as a question: at which age are children allowed to transition? These are only a few examples of what students bring to a class on community organizing based on leveraging the cultural richness of their queer diasporic lives (Walcott, 2012, 2017).

Qigong and Slam Poetry

The previous section explained how course assignments are used to nurture a holistic imaginary *vis-à-vis* community organizing. The other significant holistic feature to the course involves ongoing, class to class qigong practice and vipassana (or, mindfulness, or insight) meditation. As mentioned, these are practices that I have found extremely useful in various community organizing contexts, and which are an integral part of my own life. I have been training in martial arts for over 20 years, in recent years turning my attention fully to Daoist internal martial arts and vipassana meditation through the Toronto Tai Chi and Meditation Center (TCMC) where I am a Full Instructor.

Students' introduction to these practices are through my own teacher, who is the founder of the TCMC, and head instructor, Andy James (the Shifu, which means someone who has become adept in all these arts and who also teaches). He comes to one class session and does a wonderful workshop on qigong and vipassana mediation. Because he also writes on these topics, making connections between market driven society, environmental crises, and the benefits of more holistic 'ageless spiritualities', he is a welcomed guest in a course on community development. Students are assigned some of his writing prior to his class visit.

I then continue the qigong practices for the beginning portion of each class throughout the remainder of the term. We end class sessions with a relatively small session—five to ten minutes—of vipassana mediation. By the end of the term, students know how to perform the entire series of what is termed the 'Five Yin Organ' qigong exercise, and they gain a rudimentary understanding of vipassana practice. Each class is three hours, once a week. The qigong exercises take up about half an hour of each class. I cannot go into too much detail about the Five Yin Organ exercises, except to say that they are used in qigong as exercises to address stagnant or aberrant qi in the yin organs, which include the lungs, kidneys, heart, liver, and spleen. There is a great deal of Daoist theory, including yin–yang theory and five-element theory, that is relevant. For purpose of this chapter, it is very important to understand that bringing harmonious balance to this system of organs involves a profound emotional detoxification. Mind, body, emotions, and energy cannot be separated. Detoxing the liver will dissipate anger, improve the health of the liver, and promote overall physical, emotional, and spiritual well-being, for example.

In addition to the qigong exercises, I have students work on two different embodied arts, namely theatre of the oppressed and slam poetry. I assign several graduate level readings on how to use embodied arts in community organizing contexts, and, during the most recent course offering, we worked on these two embodied arts. These two arts were chosen based on previous course feedback where I initially tried a new art form each class, and students felt overwhelmed, preferring to concentrate on only two art forms in depth. For each of these classes I bring in guest instructors. For the theatre of the oppressed classes, various experienced instructors do workshops with the students. For the slam poetry classes, the guest instructor is a gifted drama coach who does an amazing workshop on connecting 'voice to body', but who also is an expert on holistic education. In fact, she is one of the editors of this volume . . . Kelli Nigh. Two class evenings are chosen as Slam Poetry Night. Before throwing down their 'Slams', Kelli's workshop helps students 'connect' in a profound way to the embodied spoken word aspect of the poetry. By the end of the workshop, they can truly embody their performed spoken word, and the Slam Poetry Evenings prove to be amazingly powerful events. By experiencing it themselves, students gain an understanding into why Slam Poetry is used extensively in community organizing contexts (e.g., Chepp, 2016).

Here is how the qigong aspect of the course works with the embodied arts aspect of the course, using slam poetry as the example I will work through. As soon as students know about Slam Poetry Night, they begin working on their poetry. I do not require students to participate as a performer, and there are always two or three students who choose to watch rather than perform. However, after the first Slam Poetry Evening, some of the watchers are inspired to become performers at the next Slam.

There is a noticeable queer theme to the classes, and this queer theme is part of what makes Slam Poetry Night fun and powerful. For example, one year a fairly large group that emerged to work together for their art assignment simply called themselves "The Queers". They were brimming with energy, making the classes fun for everyone. Not everyone in The Queers was queer. One student called herself "Queer Spawn", because she was raised by a lesbian couple. Another non-queer student had two mothers, one of whom was trans and the other a cis woman. Many of the students in this group explained to me that they have never in all their university experiences had such an affirming bonding experience in a course. I believe my own gender queer politics may have contributed to a certain extent.

In my experience, the non-queer students self-selected into equally affirming themes that reflected their life passions and activism. Some were working on environmental activism, anti-Black racism, or violence against women, for example. Non-queer students cheered The Queers on during various classes, including theatre of the oppressed workshops and Slam Poetry Nights. This kind of queer affirmation from non-queers was seldom experienced in other courses.

Students will have been working on the emotionally detoxifying Five Yin Organ exercises for several weeks prior to the first Slam Poetry Night, and will have bonded over pulling together their art-as-public-pedagogy installations in their themed groups. They will have had significant affirmation of their queer lives from within their own group, and from the other students who make their love and support for their queer course mates apparent in each class. They will have completed and processed several graduate readings on topics pertaining to critical pedagogy, politics of community organizing, and working with diverse communities, including queer diaspora. By the time drama coach and holistic educator Kelli Nigh comes in to run a workshop connecting 'voice to body', students are primed for a spectacular evening of Slam.

Without exception, each slam poetry performance to date has been some of the most powerful embodied art I have experienced anywhere. The poetry is skillful and intelligent. The delivery has been brilliant. Kelli and I have been thoroughly impressed by how emotionally deep the poetry reaches. The emotional depth is skilfully tempered by insight and wisdom. The Queers slam down innovative verse that bear witness to the diversity of queer lives: two-spirited, diasporic, trans, etc., and the intentional communities we seek to build—a queer holistic imaginary.

The rest of the narrative is a leap of faith. I do not expect all readers to follow me in making this leap. Nevertheless, I am very sincere in what I am about to write. I believe that the energy work we collectively undertake in the course is key to the transformative, collective healing and community building we all witness. The qigong and the slam poetry work together in a holistic interchange. The qigong opens students in an energetic sense, and provides them with tools for energetic emotional detoxification. Vipassana meditation cultivates loving wisdom. Personal healing and collective transformation nurtures powerful art that speaks from the heart and soul. In their course evaluations, almost all students have provided feedback that the course was one of the most powerful and transformational learning experiences in their extensive university experience. I have no doubt that the course inspires skillful and creative community organizing once students leave the classroom.

Notes

1 The course involves working through issues of cultural appropriation, and I follow guidelines to ensure that when incorporating practices from my internal martial arts teachings, I acknowledge and fully communicate the historical and spiritual context of these practices. In my community work, I offer my expertise free of charge to communities who would not otherwise have access. An example of an excellent discussion on cultural appropriation can be found here: http://everydayfeminism.com/2016/05/yoga-cultural-appropriation/
2 I am deeply indebted to Dr. Ana Jofre, a brilliant physicist, artist, and educator for her unsurpassed work on the art-as-public-pedagogy projects.

References

Chepp, V. (2016). Activating politics with spoken word. *Contexts*, *15*(4), 42–47.

Magnusson, J. (June, 2016). Let the Tao be present in your life and you will be genuine. Retrieved from www.torontotaichimeditationcentre.com/new/article/let-tao-present-life-will-become-genuine-2/.

Magnusson, J. (2018). Fighting out: Fractious bodies and rebel streets. In S. Batacharya and R. Wong (Eds), *Sharing breath: Embodied learning and decolonization*. Edmonton: Athabasca University Press.

SiMalaya Alcampo, J. (n.d.) Singing plants reconstruct memory. Retrieved from www.josimalaya.com/singing-plants.html.

Walcott, R. (2012). Outside in Black studies: Reading from a queer space in the diaspora. In M. FitzGerald & S. Rayter (Eds). *Queerly Canadian: An introductory reader in sexuality studies*. Toronto, ON: Canadian Scholars Press.

Walcott, R. (2017). *Queer returns: Essays on multiculturalism, diaspora and Black studies*. London, ON: Insomniac Press.

23

Holistic Features of Traditional Chinese Spiritual Practices for Personal Cultivation[1]

Wong Ping Ho

The Chinese literati-official Su Shi (1037–1101) wrote that Sicong, a monk,

> was good at playing the zither when he was seven. He . . . started practising calligraphy when he was twelve. After he excelled in calligraphy, at fifteen he . . . started studying poetry. . . . He proceeded to read *sūtras* . . . and entered the realm of dharma . . . If Sicong will progress daily without halt and reach the Way through hearing, reflecting and practising, then even *Avatamsaka Sūtra* with its oceanic wisdom in the realm of dharma will just become a guesthouse [to the Way], not to mention calligraphy, poetry and zither! Even so, no student of the Way . . . has ever entered its realm through emptiness. Just as the wheelwright Bian crafted wheels or the Old Hunchback caught cicadas – a thing is never too base if it inspires one's dexterity and intelligence! If Sicong would achieve the Way, then zither and calligraphy will both have helped, and poetry particularly so.
>
> *(Yang, 2015, pp. 37–38; square brackets in the original)*

A number of things are worth noting in this quote. First, the monk pursued the Way through various practices, including zither (*qin* in Chinese) playing, calligraphy, poetry, and reading Buddhist scriptures. In other words, these served as his spiritual practices. Second, the fact that "no student of the Way . . . has ever entered its realm through emptiness" means that spiritual practices are necessary if one is to pursue the Way. Third, although the monk's spiritual practices are artistic and intellectual in nature, actually anything whatsoever can serve as a spiritual conduit toward the Way. Fourth, however, to be effective as a spiritual conduit, a practice must be engaged in in the proper manner, as highlighted by Su's reference to the wheelwright Bian crafting wheels and the Old Hunchback catching cicadas, two among a number of characters described by the ancient Daoist sage Zhuangzi to exemplify the mindful way of conduct. This quote thus serves well as an introduction to the discussion below of the characteristics of traditional Chinese spiritual practices for personal cultivation.

Diversity of Skilful Means

Zen master and musicologist Lin Gufang observed that in Chinese culture, art and nature are both considered expressions of, and effective conduits toward, the Way, and that life in its totality is itself

art (Lin, 1998). In Buddhist parlance, there is a diversity of *upaya* (skilful means) for spiritual eleva-
tion. Chen (2008) remarked that *yangshen* (nourishing one's spirit) is achieved "through emotional
balance and intellectual engagement", and "Walking, sleeping, writing, painting, reading, playing
chess or musical instruments, meditation, or travelling, were all activities that could be turned to this
objective" (p. 31), typical spiritual practices that were popular among the literati. This echoes Hong
Yingming's (1572–1620) words:

> Wandering among mountains and forests, springs and rocks, cravings for fame and fortune are
> wafted from the mind. In poetry, calligraphy and painting one effortlessly finds contentment and
> worldly stirrings pass away unnoticed. Thus, the virtuous man, without indulging in sensuous
> pleasures and losing his lofty aspirations, often finds a place where he can foster both body and
> mind.
>
> *(Hong, 2003, p. 270)*

The implication of the last remark in this quote is that, provided they are indulged within proper
limits and in the right spirit, all sorts of hobbies can be spiritually uplifting. Even so, as this quote
hints, poetry, calligraphy, and painting were among the most common spiritual pursuits. Poetry, as
Fong (2008) said, "pervaded the quotidian life of literate women and men" (p. 364) in the Ming
(1368–1644) and Qing (1644–1911) dynasties, not least as a path of personal cultivation. According
to David Hinton, an expert on Chinese poetry,

> Buddhist monks use koans and meditation to get past the illusions of self; the poet tries to do
> the same thing by engaging with regular life. This makes the task messier and harder, but . . .
> the result is richer. It's based in everyday experience, not this special, cloistered environment.

To him, "The most spiritually engaged poems were a form of Ch'an [Zen] practice" (Tonino, 2015,
unpaginated).

However popular poetry was, it bore no comparison with calligraphy, which every literate
Chinese person needed to master, and which indeed was the prerequisite for all forms of writing,
poetry included. As such, calligraphy provided a spiritual–artistic practice in the form of an everyday
pragmatic activity (Wong, 2005).

The list of skilful means traditionally engaged in by the Chinese for personal cultivation is practically endless. They constitute diverse routes toward spiritual development; an individual can take the
most convenient one(s) given his/her circumstances. The whole enterprise can thus be said to be
holistic in this sense. Furthermore, as explained below, there are common, interconnecting threads
running through many of these skilful means, making them holistic in a second sense.

Unity in Diversity

Sicong was adept at a number of spiritual practices in the form (but not only in the form) of artistic
pursuits. This is a common phenomenon in Chinese culture, persisting until the twentieth century.
An example is the Sinologist Jao Tsung-i (1917–2018), whose "accomplishments in poetry, calligraphy and painting, as well as zither-playing, are well-known", and, thus, in whom "the essence of
traditional Chinese men of letters finds full expression" (*Chinese University Bulletin*, 1977, p. 8). Jao
specifically described calligraphy, painting, and zither playing as his means of self-cultivation. He has
also practised quiet sitting since adolescence (Shi, 2011).

The *grande dame* of zither, Tsar Teh-yun (1905–2007), belonged roughly to the same generation
as Jao. Besides zither playing, she was adept at poetry and calligraphy. During meetings with her
zither friends, "they tried out new pieces . . . played the old standard repertory, and practiced related

arts such as poetry, calligraphy, singing of qin [zither] songs and Kun Opera arias, and sword dance" (Yung, 2008, p. 63). Kun Opera (*kunqu*/k'un-ch'ü) is an elegant art. Numerous members of the literati class took it up as an amateur pursuit, one of whom was Chang Ch'ung-ho (1914–2015), who taught *kunqu*, calligraphy, and poetry (Chin, 2002).

It is tempting to ask how one could excel at various demanding artistic pursuits, which, as mentioned above, was common in traditional China. The consensus view is that these various pursuits follow similar principles, with transfer of learning among them. According to Barrass (2002),

> In the Chinese mind and the Chinese eye there is a close link between music, dance, opera and calligraphy. Some talk about calligraphy as an art in which "the brush dances and the ink sings", others refer to it as a form of "music without sound".
>
> *(p. 15)*

This is rather abstract. Let us go to the practitioners and connoisseurs for descriptions of how *kunqu*, say, is similar to calligraphy and poetry. For example, all forms of art Chang Ch'ung-ho loved are about, in her own words, *lingkong* (being suspended): "A good calligrapher has it in the wrist . . . A good k'un-ch'ü performer has it in her gesturing. And a good poet is able to express it in words" (Chin, 2002, p. xxiv). But what does "being suspended" mean? Here is the interpretation of Annping Chin, Chang's admirer:

> A calligrapher's wrist is suspended slightly above the table, his palm is empty, his fingers are strong, and his brush has freedom of movement: he can speed up without haste and linger without getting stuck. And when he has mastered speed and lingering and arrested "the bearing of phoenixes dancing" and "the grace of dragons leaping," he has suspended himself—"the mind has forgotten itself in the brush and the hand has forgotten itself in the writing." Performing k'un-ch'ü is no different. The best actor lets her singing and her gesturing play the part. She keeps herself distant—suspended—while letting her skills explore her character's motives and moods and manner. Ch'ung-ho feels that the most difficult skill in the k'un-ch'ü theater is to be able to represent all that is not shown. Just as a good playwright does not resort to sentimental colloquy, a good actor holds back what she could express. In other words, "she is able to move but does not move"; this is also a kind of suspending, between the apparent and the unapparent, and only strong acting can bring it off.
>
> *(Chin, 2002, p. 309)*

The reference to "the mind forgetting itself in the brush, and the hand forgetting itself in the writing" characterizes the state of *wuwei*, a Daoist notion "which literally means 'nothing doing', or more descriptively, 'selfless action': acting spontaneously as a selfless part of *tzu-jan* [*ziran*],[2] rather than with self-conscious intention" (Hinton, 2003, p. 215). Something similar was said by a twentieth-century grandfather while teaching his granddaughter calligraphy:

> the brush needs to be free. The brush could be a sword, it could be a hoe, and so on. . . . [C]alligraphy presents the form from the formless origin of one's mental consciousness, so the First thing to do is to understand who you are without asking who you are: just directly enter a kind of nothingness with no 'I', 'me', or no one 'up there' writing calligraphy. Then you can be totally free.
>
> *(Hsieh, 2010, p. 113)*

Pai Hsien-yung (1937–), novelist and *kunqu* promoter, added his take on the matter: Chinese art works such as calligraphy and painting "in essence bear resemblance to *kunqu* performance", in that "smooth lines are utilized not only in Chinese calligraphy and painting, but also in the graceful movements of *kunqu* performances" (Zhou, 2011, p. 215). Interpreting Pai's view in the light of Chang's description above, one sees that graceful lines are made possible precisely through the ample room for movement provided by the state "of finding oneself suspended in space between this and that" (Chin, 2002, p. xxiv).

Similar affinities between calligraphy (and painting) and Chinese music have been observed. As a zither player herself, Mingmei Yip likened both the movements of fingers across the strings over the zither board and the resultant melodic movements to movements of calligraphic brush strokes over the paper and the resultant ink traces of varying intensity, thickness, and direction (Yip, 1994). In addition to making this same point, Lin (1998) raised two further points. First, in calligraphy, "the soft brush meets soft paper" (p. 140), posing a problem for controlled execution of brush strokes, particularly as the writer's wrist must avoid touching the table. However, this also enables more pronounced variations and contrasts in the intensity, thickness, and direction of resultant ink traces. This reminds us of the state of "being suspended" stressed by Chang Ch'ung-ho. A similar situation pertains to the playing of a Chinese bowed instrument, with "the soft bow meeting soft strings" (p. 140), carrying pros and cons analogous to those of "the soft brush meeting soft paper". Second, in Chinese calligraphy and painting, importance is placed on delicate juxtaposition between filled and unfilled spaces on the paper, embodying the Daoist idea of *wu*, rendered as "non-presence" by Moeller (2006). As Moeller explains, the Daoist foundational text *Daodejing* contains numerous images of efficacy showing "how something works. In every case the efficacy is based on the combination of emptiness and fullness, of 'having' and 'not-having,' of 'presence' and 'non-presence'" (p. 11). Analogously, soundless moments occupy an important place in Chinese music.

Stillness

The *Daodejing* sets great store by *jing*, which is variously translated as "stillness" (Lao-tzu, 1996) and "quietude"[3] (Yang, 2015), among other possibilities: "Through stillness, being without desire, the world rights itself" (Moretz, 2009, p. 169). Stillness here refers to a state of mind, rather than necessarily the absence of motion, as various examples of this state found in *Zhuangzi* indicate. The following is the story of the hunchback catching cicadas mentioned by Su Shi, from the chapter "Mastering life".

> [Confucius] saw a hunchback catching cicadas with a sticky pole as easily as though he were grabbing them with his hand.
> Confucius said, "What skill you have! Is there a special way to this?"
> "I have a way," said the hunchback. ". . . I hold my body like a stiff tree trunk and use my arm like an old dry limb. No matter how huge heaven and earth or how numerous the ten thousand things, I'm aware of nothing but cicada wings. Not wavering, not tipping, not letting any of the other ten thousand things take the place of those cicada wings—how can I help but succeed?"
> Confucius [commented], "He keeps his will undivided and concentrates his spirit—that would serve to describe our hunchback gentleman here, would it not?"
> *(Zhuangzi, 2013, p. 147)*

This is far more than a matter of success in achieving task efficiency through keeping the will undivided and concentrating one's spirit. One can even say that success in this sense is beside the point, which is "mastering life".

Ouyang Xiu (1007–1072) explained the importance of stillness:

When something is reflected in water, if the water is agitated the image will be blurred. But if the water remains still then the smaller detail will be discernible. As for men, . . . [i]f a person can keep his senses from being dazzled and agitated by external things, then his mind will remain still, and if his mind remains still, then his understanding will be clear. Thereafter, as he praises what is right and finds fault with what is wrong, he will be correct in everything he does.

(Parker, 1999, p. 33)

It is unclear whether the terms "right", "wrong", and "correct" in the quote are to be understood not only in the factual sense, but also the ethical sense. But given the heavy ethical emphasis of personal cultivation in traditional China, the ethical sense is probably included, if not dominant. In other words, Ouyang Xiu held that a still mind is also an ethical mind. A remark by Tsar Teh-yun supports this interpretation. She advised that "in order to play qin, one should have a tranquil heart (*jingxin*) and an upstanding heart (*zhengxin*)" (Lin, cited in Yung, 2008, p. 138), putting "tranquil" and "upstanding" together.

Given its importance, stillness naturally forms the foundation of all self-cultivation practices in traditional China. As Moretz (2009) noted, all kinds of practices, whether internal alchemy, ritual, qigong, or taiji quan, "require a foundation of stillness to be safe and efficacious" (p. 170). For example, in calligraphy and painting, preparatory rituals play an important part in stilling the mind before the writing or painting begins, including:

flattening rice paper on a table, softening a brush with water, dripping water onto an ink stone, gripping the brush properly, maintaining a straight posture, and grinding the ink. Artists approach these steps as a ritualistic, spiritual, and meditative process.

(Chung, 2006, p. 35)

Although stillness does not necessarily mean absence of motion, or, for that matter, absence of sound, stillness as a mental state does often require silence. Musicologists have noted the importance of "silence" in *qin* music. (Recall the reference above to "non-presence", unfilled space in calligraphy and painting, and silent moments in Chinese music.) Silence includes "not only pauses and interruptions but also the dying away of audible sounds, supported by hand and finger movements that may continue for a while after any audible pitch has disappeared", suggesting "imaginary continuation of sounds beyond what the normal human ear can detect" (Kouwenhoven, cited in Tien, 2015, p. 42). This requires, and therefore cultivates, deep, spiritual listening.

A *qin* student of Tsar Teh-yun noted how the master's room exuded a spiritual aura with a miraculous soothing effect:

The calmness of the . . . apartment contrasted with the noise outside. . . . This situation reminded me of a line in Tao Yuanming's poem, "If your mind is distant, the place becomes remote." The calm of the Yinyin[4] Study not only reflected the inner state of Tsar laoshi [teacher], but was also felt by her students. This kind of association brought me into a different state of mind. Before beginning my lesson, I already felt that I had progressed.

(cited in Yung, 2008, p. 10)

The last remark matches Wang's (2012) observation that "Moral cultivation is already created via emotional moderation and regulation before any string is plucked" (p. 275), echoing the point above about preparatory rituals for calligraphy.

Another student recalled the impact of Tsar's playing: "I can still clearly remember the impression that this sound, although barely audible due to the traffic noise, made on me. It had a strength and subtle grace that attracted me at once" (cited in Yung, 2008, p. 11). So, to bring the argument full-circle, although it was stressed above that stillness as a mental state often requires silence, a strong enough state of stillness can, on the other hand, even overcome noise, and help others overcome noise too.

This state of stillness enables one to break out of one's ego and connect spiritually with both one's deep self and the world (and the deep self and the world are actually one). Practitioners of all sorts of Chinese arts often describe their experiences of learning from nature. It is not that nature offers a material model for the painter or musician to emulate. Learning from nature rather involves an intuitive grasp of the essence or spirit of what is observed, which the Chinese call *shen*. "In this state, the practitioner grasps, and is being grasped, by Dao. Hence in the practice of his art, he is not exactly himself" (Wong, 2005, p. 165). Arnheim (1997) illustrates this with a poem by Su Shi on the painter Wen Yuke: "When Yu-k'o painted bamboo, / He saw bamboo, not himself. / Nor was he simply unconscious of himself: / Trance-like, he left his body. / His body was transformed into bamboo" (p. 157).

Reverence

Respect and stillness are often mentioned together. For example, "respect and solemnity, along with serenity and peacefulness", both before and during musical engagements, are required of a *qin* player, who is expected to "play in awe as if facing an elder, whether or not there are listeners," and "to always be respectful and devoted as if facing one's teachers and friends" (Wang, 2012, p. 275).

Clearly, both stillness and respect have dual, inner and outer, aspects. While the Chinese traditionally recognize that in all types of dichotomies, the dichotomized elements mutually transform into each other, symbolized graphically by the *taiji* circle, when it comes to personal cultivation, the emphasis seems to be more on the inner elements. Take Confucius' attitude toward ritual practice. Peng (2009) showed that Confucius took all sorts of everyday rituals as occasions for bodily and spiritual exercise, and comported himself accordingly. This might sometimes be suspected of servile adherence to behavioral prescriptions. But Confucius was fully aware that the ultimate point of ritual is not the action itself, but the spirit animating it: "The Master said, A man who is not Good, what can he have to do with ritual? A man who is not Good, what can he have to do with music?" (Confucius, 2000, p. 86)

So one's state of mind is crucial. The Neo-Confucian Zhu Xi (1130–1200) considered reverence to be of the utmost importance (de Bary, Gluck, & Tiedemann, 2005), prioritizing it over stillness, thus setting the tone for personal cultivation for subsequent generations. Keenan (2011) noted that, "The Neo-Confucian program for lifelong self-cultivation in this world makes reverence indispensable at every step of moral development" (p. 111). Spiritual Master Nan Huai-Chin (1918–2012) explained the reason for the priority of reverence: "If there is nothing that arouses respect and reverence in your mind, then the mind of reverence cannot arise, and you will certainly not be able to concentrate your mind" (Nan, 1994, p. 210). This observation gains support from etymological study of the term *guan* (contemplation), which concludes that the kind of contemplation it connoted "is respectful and detached in the sense that it is not ego-driven" (Mattice, 2014, p. 92). Mindful reverence or reverential mindfulness thus underlies various Chinese spiritual practices.

The Dialectic of Stillness and Activity

Earlier on, an example from *Zhuangzi* was offered as an illustration of stillness, as a mental rather than physical state. From that, one may already surmise that stillness is pursued not for its own sake, but instead for effective action, among other things. Tsar Teh-yun's biography provides another example of action in stillness. When she played the *qin*, she was transformed into a different presence and seemed to be the embodiment of paradox, for her posture was calm and stately with hardly any overt movement, and her facial expression was neutral, betraying no emotion. In contrast, her hands were swift and flexible, darting this way and that, sliding, lifting, striking, or in repose. The music that emanated from the instrument, alive with excitement, rhythmic suppleness and subtlety, seemed to be an extension of the movements of her hands. In turn, her two hands, when she was playing the qin, seemed to become the essence of her existence, the manifestation of her energy and spirit.

(Yung, 2008, p. 12)

This is stillness engendering graceful action. Or is it actually the other way round, graceful action engendering stillness? Or mutual engendering at one and the same time? Or are stillness and action an inseparable one, without even the need to invoke the process of engendering, in whichever direction? Here analytical thinking breaks down, or, should we say, is transcended. This is the state of *wuwei* and *ziran*, of selfless and effortless action, mentioned some way back, which gives an immense sense of well-being to not only the actor but also the onlooker.

Even the seemingly most inactive practice of quiet sitting only gets its point in action. For example, for Zhu Xi, quiet sitting was meant to bring one's mind and spirit into calmness, ready for proper action and advancement in serious study. Thus, quietude and activity were complementary (Tsai, 2009).

Transtemporality

Chinese spiritual practices serve as conduits for communion with the ancients. Consider Zhu Xi's representative view on the proper way of reading classic texts: "One's reading is to get into the sage mind through one's mind. Eventually with repeated immersion, one's mind will then be the sage mind" (cited in Peng, 2007, p. 97). Such an approach did not begin with Zhu Xi; neither was it followed only in the reading of textual classics. The historian Sima Qian (c. 145–86 BCE) recorded:

Confucius practised playing the lute[5] for ten days without attempting anything new. Shi Xiang, his tutor said, "You can go ahead now."

"I have learned the tune but not the technique," said Confucius.

After some time Shi Xiang said, "You have mastered the measure now, you can go on."

But Confucius replied, "I have not yet caught the spirit."

Some time later the other said, "Now you have caught the spirit, you can go on."

"I cannot yet visualize the man behind it," answered Confucius. Later he observed, "This is the work of a man who thought deeply and seriously, one who saw far ahead and had a calm, lofty look." He continued, "I see him now. He is dark and tall, with far-seeing eyes that seem to command all the kingdoms around. No one but King Wen could have composed this music."

Shi Xiang rose from his seat and bowed as he rejoined, "Yes, this is the *Lute-song of King Wen*."

(Sima, 2008, pp. 245–247)

Confucius did not know who composed the lute-song, but after he had fully internalized it, he could literally see the composer and identify (and identify with) him. The implication is that a piece of work, whether textual, musical, calligraphic, or of some other domain, is an embodiment of its originator: the creation bears the mark of the creator, and hence provides a channel for an encounter with, and "appropriation" of, the creator. The creator "externalizes" himself/herself in a material creation; the reader (listener, learner, etc.) reverses the process, "penetrating" the external creation, reaching back to the creator.

That is why all kinds of learning in traditional Chinese culture involve imitation (Wong, 2005). Lin (1998) stressed that artistic imitation enables entry into past masters' souls, noting that sometimes a practitioner who has successfully established his or her own personal style would still continue imitation exercises for the sake of inspiration. And even without further imitation exercises, those carried out in the past may still provide fresh inspiration, as the following record illuminates:

> Listening to recordings spanning two decades of playing [the *qin*], I hear significant change and development taking place in the repertoire of my teacher, Zheng Chengwei . . . When I asked him about this, he told me that when he plays he feels as though his teacher is playing with him, that he can almost see his teacher out of the corner of his eye. (The idea that Zheng feels he can almost "see" his teacher further enhances the idea that he is experiencing some form of past-in-present as he practices because Zheng is legally blind. He is not only remembering the visual experience of his teacher, but also visual experience as a whole.) As he plays with his teacher, he remembers various movements his teacher would make, as if he were "suggesting" certain variations that he did not actually realize. Sometimes Zheng develops these suggestions and incorporates them into his playing. He . . . sometimes comes to understand things his teacher suggested years and even decades earlier. Other times, he plays "together" with his teacher, and at still other times, he discovers something different than what his teacher played and plays that. . . . Zheng's description of playing with—and sometimes against—his memories of his teacher suggests that the resonance this creates imbues his experience with that of past-in-present.
>
> *(Khalil, 2009, pp. 213–214; content in parentheses inserted from original footnote)*

This past-in-present is a kind of transtemporal spiritual encounter.

Holistic Efficacy

Although this chapter discusses traditional Chinese practices of personal cultivation as spiritual practices, their effects are actually holistic and global, encompassing also the physical, moral, and psychological domains. Indeed, they challenge the reification of these categories. For example, Chen (2012) noted that Chinese martial arts "was not just for combat, but also for illness prevention and self-cultivation" (p. 155). Similarly, *daoyin* gymnastics "deals with the issues of disease prevention, health maintenance and longevity, as well as physical beauty. Its ultimate goal is certainly to attain spiritual perfection" (p. 158).

While it is understandable that physical exercises like martial arts and *daoyin* can promote both physical and spiritual well-being, it is less obvious that sedentary spiritual practices can also contribute to physical health. The connection between personal cultivation and physical health has long been recognized in China. "Like Taiji Quan practitioners, Chinese artists are often said to live to an old age and 'return to the youthfulness'" (Wang, 2014, p.171). According to Zhu Xi, mindful reading requires proper posture, eye movement, and vocal deployment, and is, therefore, a form of body cultivation too (Wang, 2014). The wholesome effect of mindful reading as a spiritual-cum-physical practice is, thus, multi-faceted and global. Lu Shiyi (1611–1672), a follower of Zhu Xi, claimed that Confucian classics can cure minor illness (Peng, 2007). The painter Huang Binhong (1865–1955) also wrote this from his own experience: "Calligraphy and painting . . . can cure those with illness and prevent illness in those who are not ill" (Roberts, 2005, p. 269). Even quiet sitting, a most sedentary practice, has salutary effects on health, as Chinese medical practitioners have long stressed. *Phlegm-Fire Touching Snow*, a medical book published in 1630 covering the condition called "phlegm-fire", devoted its concluding section to quiet sitting (Gong, 1996). Of course, as pointed out above, quiet sitting, to be effective, requires the right mindset, viz., reverence, similar to other Chinese practices of personal cultivation.

Final Remarks

This chapter explored the holistic features of traditional Chinese spiritual practices, which represent different points of entry into mindful action. An individual can choose the one(s) he or she finds most congenial. The ultimate aim is that one naturally acts mindfully in all domains of life, which is most difficult, an unending, lifelong pursuit.

Notes

1 This chapter is an abridged version of a paper presented at the 2016 Mind Humanities International Conference, Republic of Korea, 11–13 April, 2016.
2 Hinton (2003) renders *ziran* as "self-so", "the of-itself" or "being such of itself" (p. 214).
3 *Jing*, as an adjective, may mean either "still" or "quiet", or both.
4 *Yinyin* means "quiet, serene".
5 This is the same instrument *qin* that is translated as "zither" in other sources quoted above.

References

Arnheim, R. (1997). Ancient Chinese aesthetics and its modernity. *British Journal of Aesthetics*, *37*(2), 155–157.
Barrass, G. S. (2002). *The art of calligraphy in modern China*. Berkeley, CA: University of California Press.
Chen, H. (2008). Nourishing life, cultivation and material culture in the late Ming: Some thoughts on Zunsheng bajian 遵生八牋 (Eight discourses on respecting life, 1591). *Asian Medicine*, *4*(1), 29–45.
Chen, H. (2012). Visual representation and oral transmission of *yangsheng* techniques in Ming China. *Asian Medicine*, *7*(1), 128–163.
Chin, A. (2002). *Four sisters of Hofei: A history*. New York: Scribner.
Chinese University Bulletin (1977). Interview with Professor Jao Tsung-i of Chinese Department. *Chinese University Bulletin, Summer*, 5–9.
Chung, S. K. (2006). Aesthetic practice and spirituality: Chi in traditional East Asian brushwork. *Art Education*, *59*(4), 33–38.
Confucius (2000). *The Analects* (A. Waley, Trans.). London: Everyman.
de Bary, W. T., Gluck, C., & Tiedemann, A. E. (Eds) (2005). *Sources of Japanese tradition, Vol. 2* (2nd edn). New York: Columbia University Press.
Fong, G. S. (2008). *Shi* Poetry of the Ming and Qing dynasties. In Z. Cai (Ed.), *How to read Chinese poetry: A guided anthology* (pp. 354–378). New York: Columbia University Press.
Gong, J. (1996). *Phlegm-fire touching snow*. Beijing: People's Medical Publishing House (in Chinese).
Hinton, D. (2003). On Po Chü-i. In E. Weinberger (Ed.), *The New Directions anthology of classical Chinese poetry* (pp. 213–216). New York: New Directions Books.
Hong, Y. (2003). *Tending the roots of wisdom* (P. White, Trans.). Beijing: New World Press.
Hsieh, S. (2010). Buddhist meditation as art practice: Art practice as Buddhist meditation (Doctoral thesis, Northumbria University, Newcastle, UK). Retrieved from http://nrl.northumbria.ac.uk/1942/1/hsieh.sulien_phd.pdf.
Keenan, B. C. (2011). *Neo-Confucian self-cultivation*. Honolulu, HI: University of Hawaii Press.
Khalil, A. K. (2009). Echoes of Constantinople: Oral and written tradition of the psaltes of the Ecumenical Patriarchate (PhD dissertation, University of California, San Diego, California, USA). Retrieved from https://cloudfront.escholarship.org/dist/prd/content/qt6r2794cz/qt6r2794cz.pdf?t=1q6wjq.
Lao-tzu (1996). *Taoteching: With selected commentaries of the past 2000 years* (Red Pine, Trans.). San Francisco, CA: Mercury Press.
Lin, G. (1998). *Contemplating the sentient world: Enduring classics of Chinese music*. Beijing: Kunlun (in Chinese).
Mattice, S. A. (2014). *Metaphor and metaphilosophy: Philosophy as combat, play, and aesthetic experience*. Lanham, MD: Lexington Books.
Moeller, H. (2006). *The philosophy of the Daodejing*. New York: Columbia University Press.
Moretz, H. (2009). The Dao is not for sale. *Journal of Daoist Studies*, *2*, 167–176.
Nan, H. (1994) *To realize enlightenment: practice of the cultivation path* (J. C. Cleary, Trans.). York Beach, ME: Samuel Weiser.
Parker, J. D. (1999). *Zen Buddhist landscape arts of early Muromachi Japan (1336–1573)*. Albany, NY: SUNY Press.
Peng, G. (2007). *Confucian tradition: Crossing religion and humanism*. Beijing: Peking University Press (in Chinese).
Peng, G. (2009). Ritual practice as a spiritual and bodily exercise: Focusing on "Xiangdang" in *Lunyu* as an example. *Taiwan Journal of East Asian Studies*, *6*(1), 1–27 (in Chinese).

Roberts, C. (2005). The dark side of the mountain: Huang Binhong (1865–1955) and artistic continuity in twentieth century China (PhD thesis, The Australian National University, Canberra, Australia). Retrieved from https://openresearch-repository.anu.edu.au/bitstream/1885/11334/23/23illustrationschapter8.pdf.

Shi, Y. (Ed.) (2011). *Literature and the divine: Interviews with Jao Tsung-i*. Beijing: SDX (in Chinese).

Sima, Q. (2008). *Selections from Records of the Historian I* (P. An, Ed.; X. Yang & G. Yang, Trans.). Beijing: Foreign Languages Press.

Tien, A. (2015). *The semantics of Chinese music: Analysing selected Chinese musical concepts*. Amsterdam: John Benjamins.

Tonino, L. (2015). The egret lifting from the river: David Hinton on the wisdom of ancient Chinese poets. *The Sun Magazine*, 469. Retrieved from www.davidhinton.net/#!interview/c10gw.

Tsai, Y. (2009). Preserving the One and residing in harmony: Daoist connections in Zhu Xi's instruction for breath regulation. In F. C Reiter (Ed.), *Foundations of Daoist ritual: A Berlin symposium* (pp. 1–12). Wiesbaden: Harrassowitz.

Wang, J. (2014). Chinese medicine: Health and balance for the whole person. In L. F. Johnston & W. Bauman (Eds.), *Science and religion: One planet, many possibilities* (pp. 159–173). New York: Routledge.

Wang, Y. (2012). Cultivating virtuous character: The Chinese traditional perspective of music education. In W. D. Bowman & A. L. Frega (Eds), *The Oxford handbook of philosophy in music education* (pp. 263–283). Oxford: Oxford University Press.

Wong, P. H. (2005). The Chinese approach to learning: The paradigmatic case of Chinese calligraphy. In O. Cathy & C. Erricker (Eds), *Spiritual education: Literary, empirical, and pedagogical approaches* (pp. 154–170). Brighton, UK: Sussex Academic Press.

Yang, Z. (2015). *Dialectics of spontaneity: The aesthetics and ethics of Su Shi (1037–1101) in poetry*. Leiden: Brill.

Yip, M. (1994). *Art of the Chinese zither and Chinese culture*. Hong Kong: Chung Hwa Book[s] (in Chinese).

Yung, B. (2008). *The last of China's literati: The music, poetry and life of Tsar Teh-yun*. Hong Kong: Hong Kong University Press.

Zhou, W. (2011). A *Peony* transplanted: Pai Hsien-yung and the preservation of Chinese kunqu (PhD dissertation, The University of Edinburgh, UK). Retrieved from www.era.lib.ed.ac.uk/bitstream/handle/1842/5994/Wei2011.pdf?sequence=2&isAllowed=y.

Zhuangzi (2013). *The complete works of Zhuangzi* (B. Watson, Trans.). New York: Columbia University Press.

PART IV
Research
Introduction

Kelli Nigh and Erica Killick

May my melody not be wanting to the season. May I gird myself to be a hunter of the beautiful,
that nought escape me.

(Thoreau)

Today the air is thick with fog and beads of water speckle the window yet it is still possible to see through the moisture to the tree outside; a willow stands with its darkened trunk, solid branches and gently moving golden fronds. The significance of the chapters in this research section correspond to the tree's interconnected branches which appear vivid and clear amidst the opaque atmosphere. Research within the field of holistic education introduces an intercommunion of theories and practices within the knowledge that all life is sacred.

The chapters in this section have been arranged according to various research methodologies, beginning with those that access and originate in personal experiences, and progress to those that can be applied to schools and communities. Methods from the fields of phenomenology, arts-based, poetic and narrative inquiry, action and participatory action research are engaged. Four of the chapters are qualitative in nature (Nigh, Snowber, Leggo, Beattie). Three chapters (Harris, Mayo, Niyom) convey findings from mixed method and action research studies. The final chapter (Spier, Leenknecht, & Osher) reports on a quantitative study, which proposes that holistic educators employ scientific methods to assess effective holistic classroom practices.

The phenomenological research methodology attends to ways in which consciousness is constituted. In "The Coexistence of Anxiety and Spirituality: Mothers and Daughters", Kelli Nigh applies Robert Romanyshyn's (2007) research method that keeps the "soul in mind" during the inquiry process. Some exploratory methods include the interpretation of dreams, imagery, and interviews in nature. Resonance is used as a way to draw soulful understandings from two women's life experiences into essential insight. To alleviate anxiety, both women talk about meditation, yoga, how to absorb life experience, and trust the quiet to encounter the deep self.

Wellness is also explored in Celeste Snowber's "Embodied Inquiry". A dancer and arts-based researcher, Snowber declares that embodied inquiry inspires educators and researchers to pursue questions that are guided by the body's way of knowing. The reader is invited into the curiosity and wonder of presence. Snowber captures the complexity and interconnectedness that sensual engagement offers: "We are designed as body and soul, heart and mind, veins and tissues, bellies and hips, hearts and limbs. The core value of holistic education is the ingredient of connection . . .".

Poetic inquiry is advancing as a legitimate research method, applicable to multiple disciplines (Sameshima, Fidyk, James, & Leggo, 2017). Poet Carl Leggo reflects on the "intersections of the mind, heart, imagination, and memory" in "The Curriculum of Character: Poetic Ruminations on Growing Old(er)." This collection of poems extends an arresting invitation to deep thought and feeling. While reading them, one cannot help but be touched by the painful beauty of relationships over time: "I have been attending poetically to the curriculum of growing old(er) for a long time". Connections are made between poetic discoveries and the reflections of Quaker Parker Palmer, transpersonal psychologist James Hillman, and humanist Jean Vanier. We are reminded, to "live with wellness".

Although narrative methods are often used in educational research, Mary Beattie skillfully explains how the soul, so enlivened by the stories we tell, is welcomed in holistic narrative research. An experienced teacher, scholar, and researcher, Beattie describes the power of narrative to ignite the passions of student researchers and act as a viable method for holistic inquiries. Her chapter "Conducting Narrative Inquiry Research from a Holistic Perspective: Honoring Story and Soul" reviews methods in three narrative projects. The research at Corktown Community High School features a brief overview of the methods used for a large-scale study in Canada. Beattie's second research project uses interacting narratives for a "five year project that focused on the aesthetic and spiritual dimensions in the lives of eight experienced holistic educators". Narratives represent a new method in medical research that help to forge the patient's "journey from illness to wellness".

Employing a narrative approach to interviews, musician Diana Harris reports on two research projects that question whether music, as it is performed and listened to, can be considered a spiritual experience. The chapter "Sound Escapes" draws from qualitative and quantitative data, and surveys over 45 respondents who reside throughout the UK and Europe. One of the strengths of this research is the diverse range of age groups, religions, and cultural contexts. Harris' thematic interpretation features participants' evocative insights on the relationship between spirituality and music. One example is a 13-year-old Sikh girl who sensitively explains that playing music is about precision, "but in assembly when everybody's singing to the harmonium and everybody joins in, that's like, that's when you get the feeling that . . . you've got a connection with God".

Action research is used in holistic education for its capacity to inspire transformative, socially engaged research. Its emphasis on praxis includes resolving educational problems. Like narrative research, action research continually enters into periods of reflection and analysis as new understandings and strategies are implemented. Action research in education engages individuals, classrooms, schools, and communities.

Aziza Mayo demonstrates the effectiveness of action research in resolving educational challenges in Waldorf schools. In the chapter "Research in, on, and with Waldorf education in the Netherlands", Mayo explains a brief history of Waldorf education and its current challenges in Holland. To address students' low math and literacy scores, she explains that Waldorf researchers and teachers form Knowledge Circles with the aim to develop theoretical frameworks and methodologies that support research on teaching and learning. The integration of both quantitative and qualitative methods, under the umbrella of academic collaboration and critical discourse, has been shown to influence curriculum development and the test scores of Waldorf students. It has been argued throughout this handbook that mainstream education should relax a singular focus on cognition and standardized testing. Waldorf curriculum is renowned for nurturing the spirit and emotions, yet now standardization is selectively introduced to ensure students' vocational prospects. These efforts have resulted in an increased number of parents who seek out Waldorf education in the Netherlands.

The potential for participatory action research (PAR) to lead to educational change in schools and communities is evidenced in Prapapat Niyom's chapter, "Thai Buddhist Schools". Niyom describes a research project that effectively integrates Buddhist values as a foundation for holistic teaching and learning:

Actually, the heart of the Buddha's teaching means "right practice" and is called the Eightfold Path. When applied to everyday life The Eightfold Path enables us to become enlightened. Imparting these principles into education encourages the student to engage in self-practice so that they understand their interconnectedness with the cosmos, thereby achieving the ultimate goal of enlightenment.

The project also critiques the current emphasis on cognition in Thai schools and balances students' learning experiences by grounding classroom teaching in value based learning. Resonant with the climate of responsible critical analysis that occurs within Knowledge Circles, the Buddhist Approach Schools project has, through the collaboration of all educational stakeholders, expanded its interests to the development and evaluation of whole child teaching methods.

Elizabeth Spier, Frederik Leenknecht, and David Osher are also concerned with effective holistic teaching and learning. In "Many Layers, Many Dimensions: Building a New Science of Holistic Education", these researchers report on a ten-country study that revealed "there is a substantial gap between what is known about the benefits of holistic education and its consistent and effective implementation in schools". Again, a common refrain amongst holistic educators is echoed in the authors' statement: "many schools focus on cognitive development as if it is the only target of interest". The authors provide a detailed framework for whole child development, and claim that it is embodied in kindergarten classrooms, but gradually disappears as students mature. Methods from neuroscience are proposed so that educators learn "more about what works and can help support holistic human development".

The field of holistic education is in the midst of a multidirectional shift from refining its conceptual understandings to deepening insights into wellness, examining classroom practices, enhancing professional collaborations, and expanding into large-scale research projects. It is a balance between wellness and cognition that resounds throughout the intercommunion of practices and findings as researchers situate the whole student at the base of their work.

References

Romanyshyn, R. D. (2007). *The wounded researcher: Research with soul in mind.* New Orleans, LA: Spring Journal Books.
Sameshima, P., Fidyk, A., James, K., & Leggo, C. (2017). *Poetic inquiry: Enchantment of place.* Delaware: Vernon Press.

24

The Coexistence of Spirituality and Anxiety

Mothers and Daughters

Kelli Nigh

This Inquiry and its Question

My mother: "When I was a child, your grandmother would become upset at the dinner table waiting for your grandfather to come home. I would get knots in my stomach watching her stew and fuss." Where was the grace in those moments, so palpable during that morning's hymn sing? Recently, I attended a meditation class with people who were lost in political turmoil and all of a sudden, for 20 minutes, a beautiful stillness fell over the group. Quiet. Gentle currents flowed through the room; a peace that surpassed understanding. Although holistic educators hope for this sustained calmness, edifying stillness is a rare occurrence.

In this chapter, I am proposing that spirituality and anxiety coexist together in the interconnected web that we wish could contain only beneficial experience. If spirituality is experienced as a fundamental connection to the cosmos, then it is possible that anxiety can be encountered while spiritual sensitivity is growing.

Anxiety, understood as the experience of fear while encountering life challenges, is not neatly contained within the closed self. Anxious energy floats through an atmosphere and escapes from the movements and words of the people we love. The realization of the coexistence between anxiety and spiritualty emerged in a research inquiry that focused on developing a vital connection with nature through contemplative practices (Nigh, in press). The underlying assumption for the nature inquiry was that the body–mind awareness that was acquired by six former drama students (who later became participants) would naturally lead to a deeper relationship with nature. Short-term studies on mindfulness and nature based therapies show that stress is reduced and cognition refreshed after meditation and also after spending time in nature (Murphy, 1992; Williams, 2017). Then why were young female members of the participant group in this yearlong nature inquiry falling apart, encountering anxiety and depression throughout the inquiry year and after its conclusion?

Angela, one of the participants, described her experience of anxiety as we sat talking in a parked car. Dreams in Angela's research journal showed that she was hiding in the basement while being chased by sexual predators. It was not my plan to make reference to Angela's dreams for this present inquiry, until the night of a mass shooting. On that night, I also dreamt that I was trapped in a locked car. A predator was circling the vehicle and pounding on the windows. In the early morning hours, details of the previous night's shooting unfolded in the news. The image I saw in that dream echoed two ways; in the direction of Angela's dreams and towards the accounts of people who hid in their cars during that terrible evening. Later in the day, I understood one implication behind these dream images. If we accept interconnectedness as a great invisible web, it is also true that anxiety resides within the collective field of consciousness and that it is not perhaps as easy as we think to stop it or disentangle from it.

Bob Kull (2009) lived in solitude for one year in the Patagonia wilderness. After experiencing degrees of anxiety upon his return, he wrote: "Nevertheless, although not aware of it at first, I fell into a depression" (p. 313). I was not aware of my own anxiety after years of deep attention in nature, neither was the depression that ensued expected after so many transcendent moments. As the nature study drew to a close, one of the phrases that I heard in meditation, was, "Follow experience". During the seven years that have passed, my mother, young and elderly women alike, began to reveal stories of their anxieties. From spiritual women's life experiences, I believed that no matter how deeply or profoundly spirituality is nurtured, anxiety is a part of our lived experience and it is time to be honest about it.

As early as ancient Egypt, women have been accused of being the anxious gender. Hippocrates first named anxiety, hysteria, claiming that the primary symptom was a "wandering uterus" from inadequate sex. Hysteria was the term for anxiety until Sigmund Freud developed his libido theory and later renamed it, anxiety (Tasca, Rapetti, Carta, & Fadda, 2012). In 2017, the World Health Organization (WHO) declared that: "Depression is the leading cause of ill health and disability worldwide. More than 300 million people are now living with depression, an increase of more than 18% between 2005 and 2015" (WHO, 2017). Although I am not addressing depression directly, anxiety is the precursor to depression. The WHO has encouraged people across the globe to talk openly about their feelings.

Doing Phenomenological Research

How does a researcher follow a holistic inquiry that focuses on the coexistence of spirituality and anxiety in women's lives? As a philosophical field of inquiry, phenomenology shares important concepts with holistic education; the pre-reflective body, unity, and relationship as primary to life experience. In *Researching Lived Experience*, Max van Manen (1997) explains that "we want to know that which is most essential to being" (p. 5). Edmund Husserl claimed that phenomenology involves the study of conscious experience and argued that consciousness "lifts up" dim moments from the pre-reflective body (van Manen, 2016).

Merleau-Ponty (2006) later refined the phenomenological discourse by grounding Husserl's transcendental theorizing in the body's experience. Ontological phenomenology focuses on being and shows how being is experienced in relation to an object or question. Through a situated presence in the pre-reflective body, it is possible to feel the currents of experience, for example, spatially, sensually, emotionally, and energetically. Sensations and feelings energize images, symbols, metaphors, and language. When we attend to an object or question, the phenomenon transforms us and, thus, in turn we transform it. Phenomenological research introduces unanticipated complexity, but Merleau-Ponty (2003) distills what it means to navigate through the web of existence:

> The Nature within us must have some relation to Nature outside us, indeed Nature outside us must be revealed to us by the Nature that we are. . . . By the nature in us, we can know Nature, and reciprocally it is from ourselves that living beings and even space speak to us . . . It is no longer a matter of constructing arguments, but of seeing how all this *hangs together.*
>
> *(p. 206)*

While observing how things hang together, it is necessary to see with feeling or with heart. With the intention to explain how it is possible to attend feelingly to lived experience, Darroch-Lozowski (2006) writes:

> Where we place our attention and to what we choose to respond properly for the sake of felt resonance with what is before us is the beginning of an awareness of resonances that allow us to sort ourselves through the world more feelingly.
>
> *(p. 3)*

How objects and questions resonate and how they are connected within life's matrix will call on the need to make meaning. Existential phenomenology "makes sense of what it means to 'be (human), that is to say, what it means to live as an embodied being in a (particular) physical and social world" (van Manen, 1997, p. 118). Phenomenology, no matter whether the study begins with a surrender to being, or a desire to make meaning, forges its pathways always through lived experience.

Given to the practices of holism, I learn to trust images that appear in my consciousness. These arise during walks in nature, dreams, imaginal inquiries, or meditations (Romanyshyn, 2007). One night, an image appeared in my dreams, revealing an archetypal dynamic between two opposites; the masculine and the feminine. Jung believed that the self was an archetype that encompassed the personal unconscious and the ego (Jung, 1977). In the dream, a masculine figure (the ego) raised a feminine figure (the unconscious) far above his head as she reclined in a posture of pleasure. As the inquiry progressed, I believed that this research would evolve through the wisdom of the self. Heschel claims that wisdom is "evoked" by "being in rapport with the mystery of reality" (cited in Miller, 2006, p. 72).

Sorting Through Life Experience Soulfully

Carl Jung (2009) wrote: "Hence, I had to speak to my soul as to something far off and unknown, which did not exist through me, but through whom I existed". Jung believed that he had to call upon "her as a living and self-existing being" (p. 129). In *The Wounded Researcher: Research with Soul in Mind*, Robert Romanyshyn (2007) claims that "feeling is a function of the feeling heart" (p. 287). The soul is a feeling being and will look into a personal wound with love, mourn and interpret experience within a metaphoric sensibility. The soul also integrates both the light and dark of human life.

The soul will guide the inquirer back to the beginning, not to where everything seems perfect and pristine, but to where life "speaks". As a child, I wandered through the apple orchards and carried my adopted brother Jim when our family went to the river to fish. As a teenager, our family of seven lived with six children with disabilities; a world of races and abilities gathered around our table. With everyone humming, laughing, and talking passionately, the sound of that table was holism and humanism. Each person was sounding out what it means to be included, as Jean Vanier (2008) explained to us when he visited. However, to challenge the idealism of everything our family thought was true about being human, one day my brother, who suffered from schizophrenia, was violently restrained and died. Jim was black and his life mattered to us. Imagining my anxiety as a giant harp, some of the strings still sound through memories of Jim, and my mother's dream of inclusion, which was both heavy and beautiful.

Methods

Writing is a research method. The research journal that provided an important data source for this study chronicled life experiences, dreams, and meditations since the year 2005. Definitions for terms such as the ego were achieved through exploring symbols in these journal entries. For example, the ego's shadow is understood as driven-ness. As van Manen (2016) has outlined, phenomenological research includes a variety of philological methods, namely heuristic, experiential, insight cultivation, vocative and interpretive writing approaches. In response to the World Health Organization's invitation to reach out and talk about anxiety, I interviewed two women who were given the pseudonyms Eliska and Aidya. The interviews took place at a table that overlooks Lake Ontario. I recorded and transcribed the interviews.

Aidya

Aidya talked with me on a cool summer's evening at dusk. The mosquitos were swarming and bats swooped through the night air. Aidya had just finished a long hot day caring for young children. She is married with two older children; one daughter and one son who has autism. She is a smart, socially engaged woman in her mid-fifties. She fondly recalled watching bats as she played as a young child.

Aidya began by explaining the anxiety she experiences as a black mother with a son who is nineteen. Throughout the conversation, her phone was turned on. She apologized, explaining that she needed to receive texts about where her son was going and how he would return home safely. Her husband was harassed by the police as a young teen. Twenty years ago, police would take young black teenage boys and rough them up down on the beach by forcing them to their knees and putting a gun to their head. The fear that her son will be subject to such violence is an anxiety Aidya lives with on a daily basis.

Aidya is also a day-care provider, a reflexologist, and an energy healer. She had recently finished tending to her daughter's serious illness. After many agonizing weeks, doctors discovered a rare but curable disease. Her daughter now gently accuses Aidya of being a hovering parent, but there is reason for her parenting vigilance. Aidya's life as a child and young adult was not simple. Her father was overwhelmed with her mother's mental illness and left his wife with eight young children. Social assistance would come in the mail in the form of a check, but no one from social services came to make sure that the children were safe:

> She did not have anyone to help her. They just left her with all these kids. I remember looking out the window and just crying as a little kid, staring out the window and just praying, "If you get me through this I will work hard and get my family through this." I was just 7 or 8. Just a little kid.

The image of a scared young girl, praying at a window inspired an unusual resonance with my originating dream. Never knowing that Aidya's mother suffered from schizophrenia, I was in awe listening to how she navigated her childhood and dedicated her adult years to strong family relationships.

Eliska

I talked with Eliska by the lake on a sunny summer afternoon. Eliska often enjoys nature by collecting herbs, gardening, and pursuing a passion for trees. A rabbit and a groundhog nibbled on grass nearby. Animal visitations such as this usually only happen when I am alone. Eliska is a white woman in her early sixties who lives in the suburbs and provides daycare for her grandson and support for her daughter's business. She has also cared for her parents for the past 44 years.

Eliska is married and has two daughters. She is a heartfelt woman, a talented artist and marvellously witty. It was moments into the conversation when she described how her mother and grandparents risked a treacherous escape from their home country: "They were wealthy business owners, with a large home, gardens, and servants". The family came to Canada from Czechoslovakia in 1950, escaping in the night "like the story of *The Sound of Music*". Her mother and grandmother walked away from the homeland they loved: "They came with nothing but the knapsacks on their back. All the money was gone".

In Canada, their life radically changed. Eliska's mother worked long hours to build a business while three generations of their family lived together and struggled to make ends meet. Eliska's grandmother was educated and fluent in seven languages: "My grandmother was a maid and cleaned other people's toilets. And she took any hand-me-down clothes that the rich ladies gave her". The family gathered every year to remember their escape.

Spirituality

Aidya has explored spirituality through various practices, naming yoga as a recent one. She explained: "This has been a crazy difficult year . . . When my daughter got sick I was meditating before that . . . then when she got sick I couldn't do it . . .". Aidya had to set aside her meditation classes to become a healer and advocate for her daughter. She explained an embodied perspective on spirituality:

When I do something, I do it from my heart. I think of how it is affecting somebody else. I think that is what spirituality is. Knowing that and being mindful about how you are affecting other people. So, when I was on the yoga journey, I realized that and it was confirming that I was doing the right thing. I was being very spiritual. I volunteered at the school. If my neighbors needed anything I would go to bat for them and do it. I did a lot of spiritual work.

The following comment is an important aspect of Aidya's interview and provides insight into the types of spiritual experience that are not yet accepted in normative discourses about spirituality and learning:

It was weird because I was astral travelling at an early age and I would not remember the journey. I'd pop back into my body with all the weird sounds and paralysis. I thought I was crazy. What's happening to me? What am I doing? Is someone holding me down? And I was just led down that path. All of a sudden, I was doing research into why I was feeling . . . or why I knew things before they happened.

One practical outlet for Aidya's desire to become a healer is reflexology. She applied pressure to her daughter's feet almost every day while her daughter was in the hospital. Smiling, Aidya admitted that she might have been anxious about her daughter's recovery, as there should be a period of time between each treatment.

Rejecting the idea that spirituality is dependent on a designated practice, Eliska explained that spirituality for her is a part of who she is:

It is not what I do but a part of who I am . . . And I have always known that. It has always been there. At times, I am much more connected to it than others, of course. Where there is stress and anxiety, you sort of get ripped from that place. I am not a church-goer. Never have been. Yet I am extremely deeply connected to . . . to everything . . . to people, to, to, to the plants, to the air I breathe, animals, everything, everything. The older I get I know it. I know it. When I get to my wits' end, I realize I am going there on a very superficial plane, which is not at all who I am. As soon as it hits me, I can reconnect. I can immediately reconnect. I don't have to be in a church or in meditation. It is a sudden and complete shift back—back to where I belong, back to where I need to be. I'll feel it when I'm driving because I'll feel my spirit singing.

I lamented that it is challenging to live openly in society; masks are needed to protect the deep self. Choosing a metaphor that does not mask the face, Eliska said:

I think we are spiritual beings, we are just so busy with the noise in our heads that we don't feel it. Everyone's at their own level and everyone's evolving . . . maybe we need to discover what level we can function at peacefully and harmoniously so we do not have to put on that hat . . . We all have to function as a whole. But everyone's at a different level.

Mothers and Daughters

I did not want either woman to feel as if they placed the blame for their anxieties on their mothers. There was tremendous emotion and passion in their voices as they talked about their mothers. For years Aidya carried the fear that she, too, would live with schizophrenia:

I used to worry "Okay, is this genetic and I am going to eventually come down with schizophrenia?" I asked my doctor and she said that it does run in people's families. I felt I was doing everything possible to keep myself healthy and that took away the fear of being unhealthy. My mom was healthy. Other than that, I wanted to be like her. I understood that her mind was ill, but I thought she was a very amazing human being inside this problem she had.

Yet, as a girl, Aidya kept the curtains closed so no one would see her mother staring or talking with her voices:

> You feel that the world did not understand . . . I did not want anyone to misunderstand her and treat her . . . She had no safety net. There was no one to catch her. She had eight kids and we were not old enough to handle it. And her siblings did not know what to do with someone who was that ill. There was nothing. She did not have parents that stepped in.

In Aidya's late teens, her mother became homeless. Aidya took time to nurture herself and focused on her health. However, one day she saw her mother on the street and decided to fulfill the promise she made as a young girl. She made space for her mother in her small, one bedroom apartment.

Eliska also admired and was devoted to her mother. Her voice trembled as she pointed out: "My mother's anxiety . . . touched me deeply, deeply, it completely rubbed off". It manifested daily:

> There was always a tension. For example, a meal. A dinner. As soon as the soup was served and as soon as the first person was finished my mother was hovering ready to lift that plate. There couldn't be a lull, a moment so we could speak and just have a moment . . . I used to say to my Mom, "Can't you just sit back and just enjoy it?" But it wasn't to be. Now I am worried about her and now I am jumping up. And by the time dinner was finished it was knots in my stomach. It was not enjoyable. It felt like an obligatory thing to have dinners . . .

As a teenager Eliska wanted to break free from the family's devotion to the old country, but the obligation to family values and language continued. Anxiety intensified at the age of 16 when her mother fell ill with breast cancer. Eliska's mother died at the age of 92, suffering from breast cancer and Hodgkin's lymphoma.

Heightened Anxiety

I asked both women to relay moments where their anxieties heightened and affected their perceptions. Just after Aidya's father passed away, she had a full-blown anxiety attack:

> I had a really bad anxiety attack in a furniture store. I was standing in line and all of a sudden it felt like the room moved in on me. It was like dodododo (hands move together in rhythm) my eyes were like this, tunnel. It wasn't like there was something wrong with me, but I knew that it was anxiety. I was having a panic attack. I calmed myself down by saying, "It's Okay, this is not really happening, close your eyes." I think that it was because I was not dealing with his death. That was my first bout of anxiety. I have had two . . . where you get that overwhelming fear.

Aiyda knew that the panic attack was because:

> I don't cry enough. I do not sit by the water . . . sit on the grass or lie under a tree to let those energies release. But I caught it: "Okay, breathe close your eyes, don't stare". I actually felt as if I was going to faint . . . I thought I would faint. If I stare at this happening, my mind would say there is something wrong with me. I was going to die . . . I knew that if I stared and panicked my brain would say there is something wrong and it would become a real thing.

Having the experience of knowing what she needs to do to care of herself, Aidya was able to coax herself out of the narrowing affect. Eliska talked about the toll that many dedicated years of serving her family had on her body:

It accumulates. The years all building of my mother's bad health and two years solid. I ended up in hospital. My heart started racing and I had to have surgery to have it stop. But I never stopped to have those moments. The anxiety kept building until it exploded.

I asked Eliska to describe what happens to her body:

I become disconnected to self. Completely disconnected at that moment. Overwhelmed. As if there is a boa constrictor wrapping around my whole being, my soul, choking my soul. I become that person on a different level. Because it all takes over. Suddenly that overwhelming-ness of . . . this and that and the other, has to be done and everyone wants a piece of me and somehow, I have to work it all out and it becomes a battle.

Carl Jung (2009) wrote that transformational growth occurs when our sense of self is not defined by events and thoughts. This wisdom is implicit in Eliska's statement:

Yeah, and it is probably myself that triggers it the most. I am starting to see at this age. It is not the situations. I can see where I had come by it honestly. However, I'm the one that's responsible for it. There wouldn't be anything if I did not put the pressure on myself. I am doing it to myself . . . That is my challenge now, trying to figure out how to navigate it. I am aware of it.

Pushing Through

Neuroscientist Iain McGilchrist (2010) writes about the detrimental effect of intransigent left-brain positivity. The left brain will "insist on its theory at the expense of getting things wrong" (p. 82). Although Aidya has facilitated healing for herself and her family, she admits that when life is really challenging she reverts back to her childhood conviction that she must push through alone:

"Watch me I can do it." It's just another bump in the road and . . . . nobody was there and I don't expect anyone to be there. Because I was focused on getting her well. I wasn't going to let Spirit take her. Because I was focused on getting her well. . . . If I lost focus how am I going to return to get that strength back? There was no adult that helped my mother . . .

Ironically, Aidya's family was offering support during her daughter's illness but she could not seem to bring herself to accept their help. When Eliska's mother was at the end of her life, Eliska found herself also enclosed in her own determination to fix her mother's failing health:

When my mom died . . . they put us in palliative care . . . I was so obsessed with making eve-rything better. To not make her better, that is what I had a horrible time with . . . [weeps]. I failed her . . . and um . . . and that affects the heart, it's the very heart, it's completely unre-alistic and completely ridiculous . . . anybody would say, are you out of your mind? All that time I wasn't connected.

Essential Insight: Loving the Self

In a recent holistic education conference keynote, John P. Miller (2017) proposed four core virtues for holistic education: trust, love, joy, and mystery. bell hooks (2016) also critiques ". . . misguided notions of self-love. We need to stop fearfully equating it with self-centredness: Self-love is the foundation for a loving practice" (p. 67). As an adult, Aidya turned to self-care to heal from her childhood:

I went on a journey of self-awareness to recover from not being taken care of. So, I went into fitness. That made me more spiritual because I was so fit. I would ride down by the beach and just sit by the water by myself and just absorb, and I never had any anxiety because I was healthy and connected to my body.

Eliska responded to a question about caring for the self:

I always felt like it was something selfish: "I've got this" . . . Even with kids, jump, jump, jump, do, do . . . that is where you lose yourself. I knew who my self was. I felt the anxiety up until the point where I got ill. It kept building up and building up.

In an embodied example of Miller's four virtues, Eliska described her insight into how to trust the quiet so that she can encounter the deep self:

I think that you can never know yourself or find yourself when you are looking. I think you find yourself when you can finally be quiet, long enough that it comes to you, it emerges . . . As things are going, going and you say, I need to find self. And I have to find time for the self. No, that it is on that same plane of putting another pressure on your list, another to do. No, you won't find it because that self is in that quiet place. Like even if you all of a sudden say, "Okay. I am going to meditate so my self is going to come." No, because the self did not come in that meditation. Because I kept waiting for it and it did not come. However, the quiet that brought me to that quiet place where I can quiet myself and stop with the noise in my head—and then the self is there. And when you are able to connect with it suddenly, then you can bump into it a little bit and feel it. And then when you start connecting with it you can have a conversation with it and you can say, "What would make the heart sing?"

A Letter to Our Daughters

To my stepdaughter, to Eliska's daughters, and Aidya's daughter. To Angela, who is now a successful singer. And to our future grandchildren; to all the young women I have taught and worked with. These are the wise words of two women to whom I am deeply grateful. I hope you remember this generation of women who were very much a part of this anxious time and this spiritual searching. Remember us with love and compassion. As we were trying to figure out how things hang together, perhaps we thought that our work and will would triumph. We were wrong. I know we taught you to achieve and to focus, to overcome, sometimes at all cost, but there are times, very rich times, where surrender to the deep self will nurture you more than a dream of success. Life experience must be accepted as a whole; both the light waves and the dark waves pass through you in the ocean of life's experience. Do not push your self all the time, neither your heart, your service, nor your intellect: take time to see how all things on this earth are connected and trust the mystery that holds this life.

Acknowledgement

I am grateful to Vivian Darroch-Lozowski for reviewing various drafts of this manuscript.

References

Darroch-Lozowski, V. (2006). Re-patterning global warming. *The Environmentalist, 26*(3), 195–200.
hooks, b. (2016). *All about love: New visions.* New York: Harper Perennial.

Jung, C. G. (1977). *Collected Works of C. G. Jung, Volume 18* (Sir H. Read & M. Fordham, Eds; R. Hull, Trans.). Princeton: Routledge & Kegan Paul.

Jung, C. G. (2009). *The red book*: Liber novus (S. Shamdasani, Ed.; M. Kyburz, J. Peck, & S. Shamdasani, Trans.). New York: W. W. Norton.

Kull, R. F. (2009). *Solitude: Seeking wisdom in extremes: A year alone in the Patagonia wilderness*. Novato: New World Library.

McGilchrist, I. (2010). *The master and his emissary: The divided brain and the making of the Western world*. New Haven, CT: Yale University Press.

Merleau-Ponty, M. (2003). *Nature: Course notes from the Collège de France*. Compiled by Séglard, M. (R. Vallier, Trans.) Evanston, IL: Northwestern University Press.

Merleau-Ponty, M. (2006). *Phenomenology of perception*. London: Routledge.

Miller, J. P. (2006). *Educating for wisdom and compassion: Creating conditions for timeless learning*. Thousand Oaks, CA: Corwin Press.

Miller, J. P. (2017, Nov. 25). Trust, love, joy, mystery: Keystones for holistic education. Paper presented at Asia Pacific Holistic Education Conference, Bangkok, Thailand.

Murphy, M. (1992). *The future of the body: Explorations into the further evolution of human nature*. New York: Tarcher/Perigee.

Nigh, K. (in press). *Nature and learning: A depth perspective*. NC: Information Age.

Romanyshyn, R. D. (2007). *The wounded researcher: research with soul in mind*. New Orleans, LA: Spring Journal Books.

Tasca, C., Rapetti, M., Carta, M. G., & Fadda, B. (2012). Women and hysteria in the history of mental health. *Clinical practice and epidemiology in Mental Health: CP & EMH, 8*, 110–119. DOI.org/10.2174/1745017901208010110

Vanier, J. (2008). *Becoming human*. ON: Anansi.

Van Manen, M. (1997). *Researching lived experience: Human science for an action sensitive pedagogy*. London: Routledge.

Van Manen, M. V. (2016). *Phenomenology of practice: Meaning-giving methods in phenomenological research and writing*. London: Routledge.

Williams, F. (2017). *Nature fix: Why nature makes us happier, healthier, and more creative*. New York: W. W. Norton.

World Health Organization (WHO) (2017). Depression: Let's Talk. Geneva, Switzerland. Retrieved from www.who.int/mental_health/management/depression/en/.

25

Embodied Inquiry in Holistic Education

Celeste Snowber

The fabric of human beings is deeply connected. We are designed as body and soul, heart and mind, veins and tissues, bellies and hips, hearts and limbs. The core value of holistic education is the ingredient of connection, and increasingly there is a longing to emphasize the relationship with our bodies to the art of living, teaching, and writing. My passion in my vocation and life has been to honor all the textures of the body; for the body is messy and wonderful, paradoxical and present, full of limitations and wonder. One cannot control when he or she weeps for grief or ecstasy, or dictate body language, which is as natural as breathing. Breath connects us all—too many absent breaths we suffer. And yet many of us are breathing from the neck up, even while reading this text. So, I invite you to take a deep breath, release your arms, sternum, and shoulders and release a huge sigh.

This chapter introduces the body as a place for embodied inquiry. I have recently written a more comprehensive book on embodied inquiry, but here is a taster for you to let your bodies wake up to their longing (Snowber, 2016). Embodied ways of inquiry are a place of deep listening to the pulses within our lives, the rumbling inside our cells and the sacred and mundane space where body knowledge and body wisdom can be honored. Here there is room to listen to each curve of the heart, nuance of the fingers, and lilt in your steps. I am after a visceral knowing and becoming, and am committed to writing that attends to the sensuous and embodied articulation of thought. Here there is rhythm and poetry, vulnerability and joy, and a return of writing from blood turning to ink. I invite you as a reader to take a journey with me in reclaiming your own body's wisdom and befriend what sometimes has been left behind. There is a lot of talk of no child left behind, yet what has often been left behind is the body.

There is ample research and data on areas of the body, whether it is from neuroscience, somatics, dance studies, phenomenology, feminist thought, or socio-cultural perspectives and a variety of philosophers, artists, and educators. The body has been informed and inscribed by many of these discourses, and the conversations in various fields continue to legitimize the body in its relationship to knowledge. This is in stark contrast to the many years of polarity rooted in Cartesian dualism that posited two distinct and mutually exclusive domains of the body and mind. The past few decades have exhibited a proliferation of scholarship that has made a mark in theorizing the connection of body to knowledge and understanding and shifted the way one conceptualizes the body (Bresler, 2004, Cancienne & Snowber, 2003; Fraleigh, 2004; Hanna, 1988, 2014; Lawrence, 2012; Lloyd, 2011, 2012; Sheets-Johnstone, 2009; Shusterman, 2008; Smith, 2012; Smith & Lloyd, 2006; Snowber, 2002, 2005, 2012; Springgay & Freedman, 2007; Stinson, 1995, 2004). And there has been amazing scholarship in the fields of somatics and spirituality, which has attended to the connections between physicality and spirituality (Halprin, 2000; Johnson, 1983, 1994; Lamothe, 2015; Snowber, 2004, 2014, 2016; Williamson, 2010; Williamson, Batson, Whatley, & Weber, 2014). However, this scholar and dancer still longed for an articulation of the body, which was compatible with the sensuous, visceral, and poetic way the body lives in the world. There has been a lack of attention to this area, so it has been my passion to develop a scholarly and artistic way to not only experience the phenomenological body, but also write from the body.

In this chapter, I draw upon arts-based ways of research, which have sprung from the field of curriculum theorists as I have developed a way of speaking and writing about the body, which is from the body (Aoki, 1993; Bickel, 2005; Cancienne, 2008; Leavy, 2015; Ricketts & Snowber, 2013; Snowber, 2005, 2007, 2012, 2013, 2016). Arts-based research grew out of curriculum studies and has burgeoned and informed many fields, including holistic education, where multiple forms of qualitative research have exploded. Areas of poetic inquiry, performative inquiry, artography, narrative inquiry, and embodied forms of inquiry are methodological streams that allow for holistic methods of investigating, discovering and uncovering research.

The various forms of arts-based research have the capacity to intersect with our own lived experiences, our relationship to the world and with ourselves. Here, the interconnections between the personal and professional, autobiographical and artistic are made apparent within research; taking on the endeavor of researching our own lives. The fields of arts-based research, curriculum theory, phenomenology, and holistic education gave me the wings to let my belly and hips be places of knowledge, discovery, and wisdom. In the field of Curriculum Theory, I was given the soil to conceptualize curriculum as lived, and the body as a place of inquiry. I wrote, taught, and performed these connections. My dance practice leaped from my own lived experience and took form in movement, the poetic, essay, voice and performance. I did not have to leave my artist at the door of the academy, but could let it inform all my work. The field of holistic education companioned many of these alternative areas of scholarship and provided the theoretical framework to honor epistemologies that connected body, mind, and spirit (Denton, 2005; Denton & Ashton, 2004; Margolin, 2013, 2014; Miller & Nigh, 2017; Miller, Karsten, Denton, Orr, & Kates, 2005; Richmond & Snowber, 2009/2011; Snowber, 2005, 2014; Snowber & Bickel, 2015). Both arts-based methodologies and holistic education have fostered a connection for the scholar, artist, and educator to connect mind, body, and heart and have informed one another. Integral to attending to the creative is a holistic emphasis of including all of who we are as humans in the inquiry process. Combining the areas of holistic education and arts-based methodologies was particularly salient for me in developing and articulating an embodied way of inquiry.

Inviting the Body into Presence

I often tell my students that we do not have bodies, but we are bodies. We came from the belly and hips and we must return there (Snowber, 2012). In Western culture, there is more concern about having a flat stomach, what our hair looks like, or the size of our nose, hips, and chest than how the body feels as it moves in space, or connects to the expanse in our limbs. Prominence has been placed on the outer body, rather than the *lived body*, which has the capacity to connect to emotional intelligence. The lived body is how one notices posture, sitting at the computer, or the breeze on a face, an ache in the small of the back, or the feeling of expanse in the torso when swimming in the lake. It is where tears and ecstasy lie and the sensations in the heart take root. Children can have less inhibition and skipping, tussling, and jumping are more natural forms of expression until they learn otherwise and there is the erroneous message that attending is equated with stillness. Some of us need to move to be still, or to enter a flow where listening calls us to attention. Therefore, in moving, one can have the capacity to be more present and awake. So, over time, many of us leave our bodies, even if we actually believe in connection or a holistic understanding. The wealth and depth available becomes distant, and unless there is a dedicated somatic practice of integrating body and mind, it is easy to leave the integrated body behind. One example of leaving the body behind is to see knowledge as distant, untouchable, and not allow for knowledge to be a place of intimacy. Here, knowledge and learning only focuses on the conceptual, and long lasting possibilities of transformation are more limited. If we just stop to remember what teachers or curricula had the most impact on our learning journey, it is often connected to an experiential component, which called forth all our senses.

I like to think of the body as a free global positioning satelite (GPS) system (Snowber, 2010). It tells us where we are located in space and time and where we need to go. The body waits as a patient lover to be reclaimed, honored, embraced, to be listened to and expressed through. We do not listen only through the mind, but through the body: imagination, neck, toes, pelvis, and shoulders. One of the greatest gifts as humans is to be able to listen to the bold proclamations and subtle sensations that the body is always revealing. Think of the time that you passed the ocean, or an apple tree, or heard the sounds of the river, calling you back to a place in childhood. Memories live and dwell through the senses and in fragrance there lies a storage house of lived experience.

Grammar of the Gut

A holistic approach to learning calls the body back to a place of being comfortable in our own skins. Here, one can let the difficulties and beauty live together in what I call a paradoxology, in praise of paradox (Snowber, 2002, p. 31). The body is like a lover, wanting to woo you back to a deeper embodied connection, where listening to the body is a breath away; a breath away from returning home to hearing what the body is speaking. I call this the grammar of the gut, where syllables are pronounced in the language of sweat and tears, gestures and postures, contractions and releases. Listening to the body is a valuable gift; in fact, it is not separate from spiritual, intellectual, or philo-sophical guidance. Embracing body knowledge honors a holistic and healthy path. But what does that truly mean for individuals and how does this connect to our personal, professional, scholarly, creative, and educative lives? And how can we call the body back as a holistic practice?

"The body has a pronouncement all to itself, which is felt in the lived experience of fingers and toes, shoulders and hips, through the heart of veins and on the breath of limbs" (Snowber, 2014, p. 119). Notice how often we can have a visceral feeling in our bellies when some event in the world can be imbued with horror or loss, or when our chest flutters when excited, or our shoulders relax and breath softens when relieved at hearing good news. There are times someone may say they are doing so wonderfully, but something inside our kinetic intelligence tells us otherwise. What if we actually brought all of our bodies to honoring a way of listening? Listening through our limbs and words. Here is the muscle of intuition giving voice.

Embodied ways of inquiry are an invitation to dwell more richly in the territory of the sensual life, where all of life is sensual, sacred, and whole. Our physicality and sensuality is a birthright con-nected to what it means to be human. Feeling the salt on our face, the freshness of water on flesh, the blood of life running through our cells, the sway of a bending willow, the taste of a wild strawberry, or the joy of skipping are all forms of embodied knowing. To cherish our bodies is a sacred and holistic art. We get information through our bodies in countless ways, and this is not just for pleasure but also for how to live more fully, compassionately, and truly in a wide-awake state, as philosopher Maxine Greene (1995) reminds us. There is much emphasis on mindfulness these days, but I'd like to stretch that concept to bodyfulness, or a mindfulness that emphasizes the body. The word choice utilized for articulation around mindfulness can inform the philosophical positioning of the emphasis of mind over body, or suggest the mind has the body in control, rather than a place of harmony. I continue to be conscious of the way our words inform the view of our bodies, as if the mind sees the body as the poor sister. Mind, body, and soul are deeply connected, interwoven and braided within our beings. It is time for us to let the braids out.

One strand of inquiry that continues to animate my own research, artistic practice of dance and poetry as well as teaching, is the question, "what would it look like to bring the body into places of scholarship and education?" Given the scope of this chapter, I would like to focus on three areas of how I see the body informing and being compatible with the field of holistic education. All three areas connect to what I call embodied ways of inquiry, for inquiry connects to all of our teaching, writing, living, being, and researching. These areas are, body pedagogy, body inquiry, and research practice and they are braided together as a three-strand chord. One cannot be fully separated from the other just as body, soul, mind, and heart are in a constant dance with each other.

Body Pedagogy: Teaching Through the Body

How can we embrace the complexity and paradox of being full-bodied humans? The body is messy and unpredictable, and doesn't give a plan when sick or has a spontaneous reaction of elation. The body cannot always be prescribed, controlled, or fit into the neatness of a curriculum. The body is the lived curriculum. I have been fortunate that over the past three decades I have had ample opportunity and freedom to teach in a university where I can explore what I call "body pedagogy" (Snowber, 2005). There is much emphasis on being a reflective practitioner in both teacher education and graduate class in education and many have been schooled in gifted writer Parker Palmer's words when he says "we teach who we are" (1998, p. 2). The question begs to be asked, where is our body in the process of teaching who we are? As soon as an educator enters a class, the students know if he or she is comfortable in his or her body. We teach with and through our full bodies. I work with student teachers and open up places to learn improvisation, movement, and body awareness as place to befriend their bodies and reflect with their bodies, minds, and hearts. This is not an area that one needs a cognitive shift in understanding the body, but it is necessary to feel the body from the inside out.

I open up spaces for my pre-service teachers to learn simple ways of moving their bodies that incorporate creative movement, contemporary dance, and a variety of somatic practices. Even simply breathing through our whole bodies, and stretching the muscles, loosening the joints, activating the voice, and moving out of the comfort zone of desks, chairs, and devices can be a radical act. At first it can be a leap, to dance in a community, tell stories with words and movement, create new gestures, but it doesn't take long for students to discover that there is a visceral creativity waiting within their bones to be unleashed. From these places of bodily awakening, we write poems, haikus, narratives, and begin to ignite our bodies as a place of deep listening. Our teacher education students write a credo—a belief in their philosophy of teaching. I invite them to dance and move some of their words, to get the words inside their skin. We can take our own students as far as we can also go in terms of creativity. Creativity is a birthright and bringing the body to the creative process has the capacity to birth new ideas, perceptions, and possibilities only a breath away.

My goal is to always have my students know that the most important thing they can do for their own students is show up for their own lives, completely. Here they can find ways to think on their feet, perceive with the eyes in the back of their heads, and listen to the knowing under the skin. The world is far too complex and difficult for every curriculum to address the rate of change. But if we connect to all of who we are—body, mind, soul, imagination, cognition, muscles—there is the opening to trust the brilliance within us. I have had teachers find ways to bring the body to teaching in ways that they may have never thought before, whether it is letting students find body shapes in geometry, or bringing their gestural emotions to a Shakespeare play, or understanding the lifecycle of bees through creative movement. But most of all, when the body is brought to pedagogy, more room is made for a full-bodied holistic approach to teaching in difficult times.

The gift of holistic ways of learning and teaching give rise to connecting to all the fabrics of our lives. Body pedagogy supports the reality that we teach through our bodies, and learning takes place through all the intelligences. Therefore, experiential, somatic, visceral, and embodied practices within teaching are imperative for including a holistic classroom. Movement has the possibility to reach us physically and emotionally at our core, and it is an invitation to reimagine ourselves and the worlds we are in (Snowber, 2012). It is important for me to take the classroom outside the confines of walls, allowing for experiential, visceral, and somatic ways of learning, particularly in the class I teach on Embodiment. This class is now offered in graduate cohorts in Arts Education, Health Education, and Contemplative Inquiry. Even though the context may differ, what is central is the connections to the world of our bodies, and the world outside. We walk around lakes and write from being in the natural world in silence, do inquiry in botanical gardens and feel and weave ourselves through the textures, colors, and scents; seeing through artistic, bodily, and scientific lenses. Hundreds of shades of green enter the visceral imagination. We go to galleries and performances, or leave the classroom and share our writings around within different architectural spaces in the building. Often, students in a university setting are attached to a device, and yet the most sensational and sensate device is within. The inner spirit is longing for attention, waiting patiently as a lover to bring the body to all one does, whether it is science or artmaking, the full body wants more real estate in our lives.

To attend with all of our bodies, hearts, minds, and spirits is a radical act and has a direct effect on living and teaching. Annie Dillard, an extraordinary writer says, "You were made and set here to give voice to this, your own astonishment" (1990, p. 68). Living through our bodies is a way to give voice to our own astonishment and opening up the steps to being fully alive.

Body Inquiry: Listening and Responding Through the Body

What would it mean for our bodies to be truly a place of listening and responding to ourselves and the world around us? What would our bodies say about climate change, or a shift in heart, or how someone performs power? As a dancer, writer, and scholar, I have always felt it is the questions that are more important than the answers. What does it mean to ask questions through my body? I will never forget the day I was doing an improvisation of dance and voice, and I said, "Whom did they kill first? – It was the artists, poets, and intellectuals." I hadn't significantly thought of the ramifications of my mother surviving genocide in years. That one line put me on a trajectory to rediscover my own Armenian heritage and not only go to Armenia, but to recover my identity through integrating dance and poetry as an inquiry to my own lineage. The strong movements of longing and lament rippled through my body as if the history was inside me, embedded in an ancient form, yet in my middle-aged body. Sometimes the questions, the chase of curiosity within us, needs to be opened up, as a flower, watered and fed by the literal loosening of moving the body. I often think of an archaeological dig; here stored within us, is the material to research lives for years to come. Many years ago, in our joint article, "Writing Rhythm: Movement as Method" (2003), Mary Beth Cancienne and I articulated how we are moving researchers and use movement method within the education research process to open up the questions and see the self as a place of discovery. The body has a huge capacity to open up places of knowledge and wisdom where the feet, hands, hips, and heart literally uncover multiple realities and perceptions weaving inquiry, research, and pedagogy together.

Research Practice: Writing from the Body

Much of the training around writing, particularly within academic circles, has been thought of as coming from the head, as if our body was detached from this process. Thinking of writing as having our fingers on the keyboard is everyday practice. Yet, at one time, there was more emphasis on words coming from oral culture. I am interested in getting our feet in our thinking and thinking on our feet. To let the breath in our hands and hips, throat and back to seep onto the page. How can one nourish a writing practice that connects to the body, where words become a place to sing and dance on the page? Words and sentences, syllables and grammar have a rhythm and tone and yearn to be an extension of the interior life, where the personal is political, the poetic has precision, and writing is a holistic act connecting to body, mind, and soul. Cognition and intuition become partners in this dance.

My own practice of writing, as well as what I introduce to my students, includes cultivating an ongoing relationship between physicality and writing. Attending to a flow in your body, whether a practice of yoga, walking, swimming, or dancing and then writing, allows for syllables to connect back to the belly. Even the simple act of letting your breath in your words can create space and rhythm in the stream of a writing practice. When I teach a class, we move, walk, dance, or breathe in connection to writing prompts. Students are encouraged to go on foot with the body, as philosopher Helene Cixous says, "Writing is not arriving; most of the time it's not arriving. One must go on foot with the body" (1993, p. 65). The connections between physicality and literacy allow for the sensate world to inhabit the writing process and bring body and mind together. Writing from the body opens up spaces for the vulnerabilities of our lives to be a place of honoring, listening, and expression. So, one might ask, what does this have to do with research? It is important to understand that research is also an endeavor in researching and listening to our own lives and the lives of others. Often, when writing, there is the tendency to go back to the head, and not have the capacity to caress the details in ways that bring the same kind of aliveness in which one experienced them. My task as an educator and researcher is to open up places for my students to write through all their senses. To see writing and research also as a place of art, so theses and dissertations can be places of writing that soar with poetry, narrative, prose, and scholarship which has the kind of writing that the writer and reader fall in love with. To fall into the beauty of words, where a word can hold a sky.

Everything is material for the holistic curriculum, whether it is transitions in life, grief, or joy, or living in uncertainty. There is a connection between the personal and universal as our narratives and stories are found within each other. Autobiographical approaches to research and inquiry continue to be present in a variety of qualitative methodologies and arts-based ways of research within qualitative inquiry has opened up connections between integrating narrative, poetic, performative, and embodied ways of articulating language, ideas, and split open the ways in which research can be construed. Holistic education has had an emphasis on the connections between heart, body, mind, and soul. The blending of these fields is deeply needed in a world thirsty for integration and reimagining scholarship.

Invitation

Much more resides in our bodies than we know. Passion is often an endangered species, yet lives in the cracks of our skin, in between the tissues. Integration is the place to honor even the inconsistencies and uncertainty in our lives, and often through our bodies. As I write this, I am reminded that breath connects us to our bodies, and that is very precious. The sky this week has been filled with smoke from fires in the interior of British Columbia, Canada. The earth is in lament, and there is no one who cannot witness this reality, when the air is threatened. I invite you to honor all the parts of your body as a place for the spiritual and intellectual to take root and become a place of inquiry. Be compassionate and let the body have its voice. Here, too, is a place to begin again.

References

Aoki, T. (1993). Legitimating lived curriculum: Towards a curricular landscape of multiplicity. *Journal of Curriculum and Supervision, 8*(3), 255–268.

Bickel, B. (2005). From artist to a/r/tographer: An autoethnographic ritual inquiry into writing on the body. *Journal of Curriculum and Pedagogy, 2*(2), 8–17.

Bresler, L. (Ed.) (2004). *Knowing bodies, moving minds: Towards embodied teaching and learning.* Dordrecht, The Netherlands: Kluwer Academic.

Cancienne, M. B. (2008). From research analysis to performance: The choreographic process. In J. G. Knowles & A. Cole (Eds), *The Handbook of the Arts in Qualitative Research: Perspectives, Methodologies, Examples, and Issues* (pp. 397–406). Thousand Oaks, CA: Sage.

Cancienne, M. B. & Snowber, C. (2003). Writing rhythm: Movement as method. *Qualitative Inquiry, 9*(2), 237–253.

Cixous, H. (1993). *Three steps on a ladder of writing.* New York: Columbia University Press.

Denton, D. (2005). Toward a sacred discourse: Reconceptualizing the heart through metaphor. *Qualitative Inquiry, 11*(5), 752–770.

Denton, D. & Ashton, W. (Eds) (2004). *Spirituality, action and pedagogy: Teaching from the heart*. New York: Peter Lang.

Dillard, A. (1990). *The writing life*. New York: HarperPerennial.

Fraleigh, S. (2004). *Dancing identity: Metaphysics in motion*. Pittsburgh, PA: University of Pittsburgh Press.

Greene, M. (1995). *Releasing the Imagination: Essays on Education, the Arts, and Social Change*. San Francisco, CA: Jossey-Bass

Halprin, A. (2000). *Dance as a healing art: Returning to health with movement and imagery*. Mendocino, CA: LifeRhythm.

Hanna, J. L. (1988). *To dance is human: A theory of nonverbal communication*. Chicago, IL: University of Chicago Press.

Hanna, J. L. (2014). *Dancing to learn: The brains cognition, emotion and movement*. Lanham, MD: Rowman & Littlefield.

Johnson, D. H. (1983). *Body: Recovering our sensual wisdom*. Boston, MA: Beacon Press.

Johnson, D. H. (1994). *Body, spirit and democracy*. Berkley, CA: North Atlantic Books.

Lamothe, K. L. (2015). *Why we dance: A philosophy of bodily becoming*. New York: Columbia University Press.

Lawrence, R. L. (Ed.) (2012). *Bodies of knowledge: Embodied learning in adult education: New directions for adult and continuing education, Number 134*. San Francisco, CA: Jossey-Bass.

Leavy, P. (2015). *Method meets art: Arts-based research practice* (2nd edn). New York: Guilford Press.

Lloyd, R. J. (2011). Running with and like my dog: An animate curriculum for living life beyond the track. *Journal of Curriculum Theorizing*, 27(3), 117–133.

Lloyd, R. J. (2012). Moving to learn and learning to move: A phenomenological exploration of children's climbing with an interdisciplinary movement consciousness. *The Humanistic Psychologist*, 40(1), 23–37.

Margolin, I. (2013). Expanding empathy through dance. In B. White & T. Costantino (Eds), *Aesthetics, Empathy, and Education* (pp. 83–98). New York: Lang.

Margolin, I. (2014). Bodyself: Linking dance and spirituality. *Journal of Dance and Somatic Practices*, 1(1), 1–20.

Miller, J. & Nigh, K. (Eds). (2017). *Holistic education and embodied learning*. Charlotte, NC: Information Age.

Miller, J., Karsten, S., Denton, D., Orr, D., & Kates, I. C. (Eds) (2005). *Holistic learning: Breaking new ground*. New York: SUNY Press.

Palmer, P. J. (1998). *The courage to teach: Exploring the inner landscape of a teacher's life*. San Francisco, CA: Jossey-Bass.

Richmond, S. & Snowber, C. (2009/2011). *Landscapes in Aesthetic Education*. Newcastle upon Tyne, UK: Cambridge Scholars.

Ricketts, K. & Snowber, C. (2013). Autobiographical footsteps: Tracing our stories within and through body, space and time. [Special Issue: A/r/tography and the Literary and the Performing Arts] *UNESCO Observatory Multi-Disciplinary Journal in the Arts*, 2(13), 1–17.

Sheets-Johnstone, M. (2009). *The Primacy of Movement: Expanded Second Edition*. Philadelphia, PA: John Benjamin.

Shusterman, R. (2008). *Body consciousness: A philosophy of mindfulness and somaesthetics*. New York: Cambridge University Press.

Smith, S. J. (2012). Caring caresses and the embodiment of good teaching. *Phenomenology & Practice*, 6(2), 65–83.

Smith, S. J. & Lloyd, R. J. (2006). Promoting vitality in health and physical education. *Qualitative Health Research: An International, Interdisciplinary Journal*, 16(2), 245–267.

Snowber, C. (2002). Bodydance: Fleshing soulful inquiry through improvisation. In C. Bagley & M. B. Cancienne (Eds), *Dancing the data* (pp. 20–33). New York: Peter Lang.

Snowber, C. (2004). *Embodied prayer: Towards wholeness of body mind soul*. Kelowna, BC: Wood Lake/Northstone.

Snowber, C. (2005). The eros of teaching. In J. Miller, S. Karsten, D. Denton, D. Orr, & I. C. Kates (Eds), *Holistic learning: Breaking new ground* (pp. 215–222). New York: SUNY Press.

Snowber, C. (2007). The soul moves: Dance and spirituality in educative practice. In L. Bresler (Ed.), *International handbook for research in the arts and education* (pp. 1449–1458). Dordrecht: Springer.

Snowber, C. (2010). Let the body out: A love letter to the academy from the body. In E. Malewski & N. Jaramillo (Eds), *Epistemologies of ignorance and the studies of limits in education* (pp. 187–198). Charlotte, NC: Information Age.

Snowber, C. (2012). Dance as a way of knowing. [Special Issue: Bodies of Knowledge: Embodied Learning in Adult Education] *New Directions for Adult and Continuing Education*, (134), 53–60.

Snowber, C. (2013). Visceral creativity: Organic creativity in teaching arts/dance education. In J. Piirto (Ed.), *Organic creativity in the classroom*. Waco, TX: Prufrock Press.

Snowber, C. (2014). Dancing on the breath of limbs: Embodied inquiry as a place of opening. In A. Williamson, G. Batson, S. Whatley, & R. Weber (Eds), *Dance, somatics and spiritualities: Contemporary sacred narratives*. Bristol, UK: Intellect.

Snowber, C. (2016). *Embodied inquiry: Writing, living and being through the body.* Rotterdam, The Netherlands: Sense.

Snowber, C. & Bickel, B. (2015). Companions with mystery: Art, spirit and the ecstatic. In S. Walsh, B. Bickel, & C. Leggo (Eds), *Arts-based and contemplative practices in research and teaching: Honoring presence.* New York: Routledge.

Springgay, S. & Freedman, D. (Eds) (2007). *Curriculum and the cultural body.* New York: Peter Lang.

Stinson, S. W. (1995). Body of knowledge. *Educational Theory, 45*(1), 43–54.

Stinson, S. W. (2004). My body/myself: Lessons from dance education. In L. Bresler (Ed.), *Knowing bodies, moving minds: Toward embodied teaching and learning* (pp. 153–167). Dordrecht, the Netherlands: Kluwer Academic.

Williamson, A. (2010). Reflections and theoretical approaches to the studies of spiritualities within the field of somatic movement dance education. *Journal of Dance and Somatic Practices, 2*(1), 35–61.

Williamson, A., Batson, G., Whatley, S., & Weber, R. (Eds) (2014). *Dance, somatics and spiritualities: Contemporary sacred narratives.* Bristol, UK: Intellect.

26

The Curriculum of Character
Poetic Ruminations on Growing Old(er)

Carl Leggo

George Elliott Clarke (2009) notes that "every life carries an expiration date" (p. 70), and Erín Moure (2009) writes that "it matters to be born. The rest, after this impossibility of birth, is sheer gift" (p. 251). I begin with a poem because a poem reminds us that life is a "sheer gift" with "an expiration date." When I turned fifty, now long ago, I wrote a poem. I have been attending poetically to the curriculum of growing old(er) for a long time.

Picnics

(November 14, 2003)

like an expiration date on bacon or bread,
I have one more day in the decade of my forties,
and while I confess the fiction of chronology
composed by clocks and calendars, the imposition
of time as linear like a ladder, I can't dispel
the relentless realization: in a day I will be old
at least much older than I am now, will wake up
on Saturday (for the first time I see weekend
as weakened) and notice how almost everyone
is young, younger than me, how, unless I am
a statistical anomaly, I will not live another
fifty years, perhaps another decade or two or three,
which today with the sun chasing shadows in early
winter light during a long run around the curve
of York Harbour will simply not be enough
I don't know what eternity holds, what aftertaste
of earth will linger at the back of the heart, but I am
in no hurry to find out, since on this day I am teased
to distraction with the light I see everywhere,
need nothing more than eager licks of the earth
always greedy for more picnics, even as a teen,

I used the resources of high school mathematics
to compute the irrefutable conclusion that eating up
an annual average of fifty picnics, I would still
devour only three and a half thousand in a typical
biblical lifetime, and knew with unassailable certainty,
even then, that wouldn't be enough, not nearly enough
like Emily Dickinson, I know for sure only,
Too few the mornings be, Too scant the nights,
and I wonder if Emily savoured many picnics,
probably not, since I don't think she went out
much, or was that Emily Bronte? oh the waste
of getting old! after a lifetime of rehearsing
for *Jeopardy* (cramming my cheeks with facts
like a neurotic squirrel), everything is now
jumbled up like jambalaya, and all the facts
are so much mouldy manna that will not sustain
me in the long winter without picnics
and writing this poem about growing old and longing
for picnics (even though every sensible husband knows
I should be helping Lana prepare for the birthday party
tomorrow) is a sign I sing to ward off the murky
monsters under my bed, including loss and lumbago,
congestion and indigestion, headaches and heartaches,
violet varicose veins like a map of violent places
I have travelled, grateful and glad Anna sent me
Walter the Farting Dog to remind me I am still loved

My main way of ruminating, investigating, and questioning is to write poetry. In the process of writing poetry I slow down and linger with memories, experiences, and emotions. In all my writing, I am seeking ways to live with wellness. We need poetry because poets engage with Ted Aoki's (1993/2005) "playful singing in the midst of life" (p. 282). Poets are always attending to the alphabet, grammar, spelling, music, and imagery, as well as the keen intersections of the mind, heart, imagination, and memory. As Jane Hirshfield (1997) claims, poetry brings "new spiritual and emotional and ethical understandings, new ways of seeing, new tools of knowledge" (p. 79). In poetry, I seek new ways of knowing and being and becoming.

James Hillman (1999) asks, "What does aging serve? What is its point?" (p. xiv). The question is poignant, especially since I now live daily the keen experience of aging as well as the experience of witnessing many friends who do not have the privilege of living long. Hillman suggests that "the last years confirm and fulfill character" (p. xiii). He understands aging as "an art form" (p. xv). He recommends that "the aesthetic imagination is the primary mode of knowing the cosmos, and aesthetic language the most fitting way to formulate the world" (p. 184). As a poet, I share Hillman's conviction. In my poetry, I engage in life writing and life review in order to seek patterns, themes, and interpretations that can hold the diaphanous, fluid, permeable understanding of life in a story or, more accurately, a sequence of stories: "Life review is really nothing other than rewriting—or writing for the first time—the story of your life, or writing your life into stories" (p. 91), explains Hillman. I am encouraged by Hillman's hope that "character is refined in the laboratory of aging" (p. 163). I have made many regrettable decisions in my life, and I have hurt some generous people in egregious ways, and I have failed to accomplish many of my goals on the journey, but I have never lost faith that I can continue to learn. Hillman provides the encouragement I need: "Each day brings another opportunity to strike the right mix, neither too malleable nor too rigid, neither too sweet nor too dry, giving the older character its power to bless with a tough-minded tenderness" (p. 163).

Now in my sixties, I read Carolyn G. Heilbrun's (1997) evocative memoir *The Last Gift of Time: Life Beyond Sixty* with poignant recognition. She writes that "the greatest oddity of one's sixties is that, if one dances for joy, one always supposes it is for the last time" (p. 55). She then adds: "Yet this supposition provides the rarest and most exquisite flavour to one's later years. The piercing sense of 'last time' adds intensity, while the possibility of 'again' is never quite effaced" (p. 55). Heilbrun evokes the tension at the heart of my daily living experience. On November 18, 2008, my father died. A few months earlier he was diagnosed with a brain tumor. When he died, he was seventy-eight years old. My father had always been a robust, energetic man, and I anticipated he would live for a long time. I have written many poems in an effort to understand my stories with my father, especially the memories of joy and grief.

Remains

after the surgery
    with only
a sickle of staples
to stitch your head
together,
the ambulance carried you
back home across the island
to autumn in palliative care,
the final quick slide down the church aisle,
the silent parade to Mt. Patricia Cemetery
near Wild Cove
(where we often spent summer Sundays
sitting in the sun, eating egg salad sandwiches,
glad for whatever the day might mean),
and the last slow slip
into the frost littered ground
like an elevator shaft
to somewhere we couldn't go,
and now I stand in the mirror,
naked, wrapped only
in your memory,
and I see more and more
of you each time I glimpse
like a ghost is writing me
from somewhere faraway
I know I don't
    want to know

I am learning with James Hillman (1999) that my "father's character . . . goes on unfolding" and I "go on learning about him, from him. He returns to mind in flashbacks and reveries" (p. 157). As I age, and "become more like him, he often feels nearer" (p. 157). I see him in the mirror often, and I catch echoes of his speech, especially in moments when I am humorous, critical, weary, glad, frustrated, and hopeful. My father is still teaching me; I am still learning from my father.

Brewed Awakening

Death is not about the dead. It's about the living.
(Brian Brett, 2009, p. 22)

1

Skipper shuffled
out of the hospital
in Wal-Mart slippers
like he never wore
for the first time ever
he held my arm
and we sidled
into his last October
my mother slipped
up a trail with KFC
and my father smiled
from lost places
when she sighed,
I got a haircut,
he whispered, nice,
like he always did

2

tomorrow is
my father's birthday
and he won't be
celebrating
with my mother
at Mary Brown's or
the Canton Chinese Restaurant
in Murphy Square

3

I don't need
to make up stories
except now
in February
I do
wish only
I could
get it right
write it down
be done

4

I am learning
slowly like a crocus

pushing its way
through spring ice
to value silence
the ways words
invite spaces
between sounds
I am alive not dead
all the difference

According to Mary Oliver (1994), "poetry is one of the ancient arts, and it began, as did all the fine arts, within the original wilderness of the earth" (p. 106). I write poetry because I need to know I am connected to the earth. As Oliver understands, poetry "began through the process of seeing, and feeling, and hearing, and smelling, and touching, and then remembering—I mean *remembering in words*—what these perceptual experiences were like" (p. 106). The poet's calling is "to describe the endless invisible fears and desires of our inner lives" (p. 106). As a poet, I am always attending to experiences and I am always seeking to translate and interpret the experiences in ways that help me live with wellness in the world. Gregory Orr (2002) understands the "enormous transformative power" of poetry and story-making (p. 6) because they help us "to live" (p. 21).

In *Writing at the End of the World*, Richard E. Miller (2005) asks: "Why go on teaching when everything seems to be falling apart? Why read when the world is overrun with books? Why write when there's no hope of ever gaining an audience?" (p. x). He recommends that we need to ask these kinds of tough questions in order to initiate an ongoing conversation about the value of reading and writing. Miller encourages us to confirm our commitment to education that is personal, transformative, and holistic. Miller notes that "schools currently provide extensive training in the fact that worlds end; what is missing is training in how to bring better worlds into being" (p. x). In all my research I focus on life writing. I write about the personal in order to understand how the personal is always connected to the public and universal. Miller asks, "Is it possible to produce writing that generates a greater sense of connection to the world and its inhabitants?" (p. 25). I agree with Miller that we begin with self-understanding, but our writing must move out from "the mundane, personal tragedies that mark any individual life into the history, the culture, and the lives of the institutions that surround us all" (p. 25). Miller understands "writing as a place where the personal and the academic, the private and the public, the individual and the institutional, are always inextricably interwoven" (p. 31). When I write about my personal experiences of growing old(er), including the death of my father, I am not writing about these experiences because I am eager for others to know my particular stories. I write in order to invite conversation about what it means to be human on the earth in the twenty-first century. I write with the hope that others will share their stories, too. I write with the anticipation that we will discover together how to make difficult and critical decisions for living, the kind of decisions that will sustain the ecology of our countless interconnections with all the sentient and non-sentient creation. As a teacher, I have always been committed to holistic education because we can only live well on the earth with one another if we are devoted to living well in our own bodies, spirits, hearts, imaginations, and minds. I write poetry and essays as a way to hold out my hands in both gratitude and invitation, always seeking to make connections.

Molasses

on a silver winter night
my brother threatened to pour molasses
on my homework (What kind of house
did Bunga the Pygmy live in?)
his grinning threat, my whining complaint

filling the kitchen air with purple
while my father in the living room
worked a crossword puzzle
(a five-letter word for regret,
unsolvable with sons, a four-letter word)
until he charged into the kitchen
and my brother shot out the door
speeding through the snow in his socks
with my father on the trail of hot footprints
like Bunga's father hunting a wild hog
up Lynch's Lane, over Mamie Jenkins'
picket fence through wind-swept drifts
riddled with tunnels and traps
after a weekend of boys' busy burrowing
and I was still listing Bunga's favourite foods
when my brother's head poked around the door
blowing poison darts from cinnamon eyes
but I only grinned, and my father tracked
wet footprints across the kitchen floor
into my brother's room while I waited
in the deep, still house, then leaving Bunga
digging yams, I sneaked toward my brother's door,
I'm sorry I chased you, my father's voice,
light blue, and the next day I couldn't
read my Bunga homework because the pages
were dark and soggy with molasses

Jean Vanier (1998) asks, "Are not all our lives a movement from order to disorder, which in turn evolves into a new order?" (p. 12). I have lived a long life with much re-searching of my past stories. Only now in old age can I re-cognize how little I understood as a young person, and how little I will ever understand. "To be human," Vanier advises, "is to create sufficient order so that we can move on into insecurity and seeming disorder. In this way, we discover the new" (p. 13). This is the heart of my understanding of curriculum. I will continue to journey in "seeming disorder" in order to know how everything is connected, how everything flows together, even if we cannot know the source or the destination. I have been a schoolteacher or university professor of education for more than 36 years. So much has changed in all these years. In the 1970s, when I began teaching, I heard little about holistic curriculum, or embodiment and education, or spirituality and social activism. Nevertheless, when I first read John P. Miller's writing in the 1980s as a graduate student, I recognized that I had always been committed to holistic education. Miller's explanation of transmission, transaction, and transformation as three approaches to curriculum and pedagogy impressed me as one of the most important conceptualizations of teaching I had ever read. For Miller (1996), "holistic education is an education of balance (for example, right relationship), inclusion, and connection" (p. 14). In all my teaching, I have sought to live holistically, always convinced that the whole creation, and all sentient and non-sentient parts of the creation, co-exist ecologically and organically. Everybody and everything is connected. Like a poem, we need to find the rhythms that hold us inclusively in balance. As Jane Hirshfield (1997) notes, the "central energies" of poetry are "the concentrations of music, rhetoric, image, emotion, story, and voice" (p. 7). Etymologically derived from the Greek *poiesis*, to make, a poem is composed—deliberately, conscientiously, and creatively. In writing a poem, the poet seeks balance among the central energies that infuse and transfuse the art of poetry. I seek this balance in my poetry and in my living.

Carl Leggo

Return

the return disappoints
(Ernst Bloch, 2006, p. 62)

1

another sluggish run on the dike
that guards the Fraser River
you've seen only a couple times
a flurry of cherry blossoms spring
into a thousand snow geese
startled from the slough
while I remember you huddled
over bits of caribou hair and feathers
tying flies for trout, always waiting
leaning into the crocus bold
purple in the last snow amidst
morning light in the harbour

2

we went fishing in your secret
sun-splashed pond, a hard trek
in good health, now quickly used
up, and on a day you later called
the best of summer, we caught
our last trout, casting a line
into the far past, not knowing
the past was so soon all we
had left, our fishing done
even if *the return* disappoints
I will return, over and over,
perhaps I missed something

3

you knelt to pray, leaned into
the back of the pew, fell
into contemplation and a nap
while snow falls in the streetlight
a shard of moon etches lost images
on an icy window, indecipherable
seven crows on the backyard fence
sing a persistent song of death
amidst winter like a stone, though
I think I see a path in the snow
where you passed by, one foot
shuffling alongside another

Joan Givner (2009) suggests that "perhaps gaining a little wisdom from a grievous loss is the most any of us can hope for" (p. 183). I am always seeking wisdom. A few days ago, my brother phoned to tell me he was recently diagnosed with liver cancer. He has lived all his life in Newfoundland while I have spent half my life elsewhere, especially British Columbia. We have lived most of our adult lives on opposite coasts of Canada. While we were always very close as children, we have not sustained close contact in the past few decades. When my brother phoned, I knew the news was not good. He never calls. The occasional email reminds each of us that we are still here and there, still connected by a web of history, memory, and blood. Following the phone call, I received a text message from my brother. He had seen the oncologist, and my brother's message was: "Not looking good." Now my imagination is primarily occupied with memories of my brother.

The Diver

In the gray-blue sky my brother hung,
long and lean, his body a line
lined with taut muscles, and Macky's
mouth was a gaping hole in a scream
or laugh because my brother was making
the death-defying dive never dared
from the concrete abutment at the end
of the dam where the water was no more
than a foot deep though it got deeper,
out and out (if only you could fly
and my brother loved to fly).
Earlier in the summer
my brother climbed the arch
of heavy timbers that hold
the dam in place, and golden
in the falling sun, high
above our heads, he flew
through the air and sliced
the water, and was gone,
and Frazer moaned, He's dead,
but my brother emerged
slowly like a submarine,
and though he was silent
I saw the quick smile.
In the still air my brother hung,
blonde and brown and blue, his head
tucked between his arms, hands clenched,
body a missile, toes pointed back
like jet engines, and Cec shouted, He's
doin' it, holy smoke, and my brother
needed to dive far out like shooting
off a rocket launch pad, out and out,
and since he knew he couldn't move fast
enough to reach orbit, knew he would come
down, he had to skip over the water
like a racing boat or run aground
on the rocky bottom.
Earlier in the summer

my brother chased his shadow
across the grass and leaped
off the rock, flying, shooting
just under the surface
like a torpedo, and Macky
grinned, He dives so shallow,
he hardly breaks the water,
but my brother just looked
at us with no smile
though I saw the purple sky
reflected in his eyes.
The gray-blue sky and still air broke
and my brother dropped, but he
didn't skip once, twice, three
times in quick smooth skips, and plunged
into the black water, and my eyes closed
but wouldn't stay closed, and my brother
stood in the water up to his knees.
I can't recall the dive
as a series of movements;
I remember only the still
moment when my brother hung
in the gray-blue sky
and that other moment
when he stood in the water
stained with his blood,
raw and bloody
like a skinned rabbit,
his eyes darting, searching,
as if he'd awaken
in a brightly lit room
he didn't know.

My brother is a year younger than me. We are very different people. My brother has always been shy and quiet, reserved and conservative. He is full of humour and humility. His heart is keen, but he is not demonstrative, never outgoing. When I began kindergarten, my brother insisted that he dress in the same uniform of white collared shirt and wool pants that I was required to wear. My brother often followed in my footsteps as if I was navigating a way he could safely pursue. As boys we enjoyed many adventures together, and I considered my brother the perfect companion for wrestling, ribbing, and imagining. Like Patrick Lane (2004), my brother and I lived childhood as "a strange paradise" (p. 39).

Chips

the morning my brother danced
out of the house, his first summer job,
    Got you a job, son, at George's Diner,
    work hard, job could last all summer,
    might even chop potatoes for chips,

Carrie, Nan, my sister, and I
all stood in the backdoor and waved
as Skipper and my brother eased
down Lynch's Lane under an opal sky,
Skipper's broad smile gleaming
like the grill on his Chevy II,
and at day's end we all stood
in the backdoor again to greet
George's new employee, the apprentice chef,
we called him, when the Chevy II crawled
up Lynch's Lane with Skipper's head
jutted out the side window,
his face a pickled beet, barking,
    Shit, up to his knees in shit,
echoes off the Blow-Me-Down Mountains,
my brother, his face shiny yellow-white
like a thin slice of potato, muttered,
    I shovelled out George's septic tank,
and long after midnight Skipper still sat
in the backyard, sipping Old Sam and Coke
while my brother soaked in Skin-So-Soft
for six or seven baths, sometimes shouting,
    Shovelling shit was fun

At sixteen, I began dating Lana, whom I married at twenty. Lana became the center of my life, and my brother began finding his own way. I realized I no longer understood my brother, at least not well. We slowly became strangers to one another.

Scribbled in Winter Light

After a semester at Memorial, I returned home with Lana in December, eager to introduce her to my family. They knew Lana from my letters but this was their first opportunity to meet her. Lana and I almost needed snowshoes to tramp through the deep snow from Eddy's Bus depot up Old Humber Road. When I introduced Lana to my brother, he just nodded and smiled. I knew my brother was shy but I expected a little more effort in his greeting . . . a story, a question, a little wit. Instead, my brother said nothing, just quickly slipped on his coat and left the house. My brother was a puzzle but Skipper compensated for him with an almost manic burst of stories, jokes, and opinions. When it was time for Lana to catch her bus back to Stephenville, we stepped outside to see my brother leaning on a snow shovel with a wide grin. Like Charlton Heston opening the Red Sea, he had shovelled a wide path through the deep snow in the yard. He still didn't say anything, but Lana kissed his hot face as she passed.

In our twenties I slipped further and further away from my brother, eventually living in Toronto, Fredericton, Edmonton, and Richmond. Distance rewrote our stories, or effectively did not write any more stories. There are now many blank pages between us.

Lottery Tickets

Like a seagull scavenging the shore for scraps
I turned again to my mother's house in search
of still more stories, though I long thought I'd written

all the stories of Lynch's Lane, learned instead stories
always end in et cetera, like rain in Vancouver.
My brother flew five hundred miles
to spend five days, the first in five years,
came I assumed with a store of memories.
I was eager to listen, to receive gifts of stories.
I called my brother my research assistant.
We drove the autumn circle of the Bay of Islands.
What do you recall? I asked. He was silent.
Finally he said, Nothing. Perhaps I was asleep.
I told him about playing cowboys, about how
he and Cec argued about who shot who.
He said, I think it was you who argued.
I poked, Recall how you mimicked Chanel No. 5 ads,
whispered with weary French worldliness,
It's not easy being Catherine Deneuve, left eyebrow
raised barely. I think I saw his eyebrow hover.
My brother sat in a corner of our mother's sofa,
watched the movie channel, scratched lottery tickets
without end, counted wins and losses, always zero.
While I seek a fictional past, he seeks a fictional future.
He flew back home, and phoned the next night,
perhaps scared by the stories I might write out of
silence, perhaps eager to set the record straight,
said, It was fun, still held his stories sacred.
Like tuckamore I cling to the granite edge of memory,
while my brother lets the past pass like gallstones,
his stories stored in an iron urn buried in his backyard.
I am a poet pushed off shore in a punt with no oars.

In *A Hidden Wholeness: The Journey toward an Undivided Life*, Parker J. Palmer (2004) writes about "the shape of an integral life" and "teaching and learning for transformation" (p. ix). He is especially concerned that "we hide our true identities from each other" by "living with illusions" (p. 4). According to Palmer, our culture "separates inner from outer, private from public, personal from professional" (p. 47), but Palmer claims that "we all live on the Möbius strip all the time" (p. 47) where "there is no 'inside' and 'outside'" (p. 47). We must learn to open up to others, to be present to others, to listen to the stories of others. Like Mary Oliver (1994), my poetry is "a confession of faith" (p. 122), and "a life-cherishing force" (p. 122). Since, as Oliver knows, "language is a vibrant, malleable, living material" (p. 91), I immerse myself in language as an artful way to understand my relationships with others, relationships that are not locked in chronology. I have learned many lessons from the stories I have lived with my father and my brother, especially how to live more joyfully in the new stories that are emerging in my life. I am attending to Linda Hogan's example (1995): "Walking, I am listening to a deeper way. Suddenly all my ancestors are behind me. Be still, they say. Watch and listen. You are the result of the love of thousands" (p. 159).

I am now a grandfather to four granddaughters, Madeleine, Mirabelle, Gwenoviere, and Alexandria. They are my best teachers. Recently, I considered buying a sporty convertible! I imagined driving down the highway in a Mazda Miata—tiny, compact, speedy! Then, one afternoon I was walking in the neighborhood with Mirabelle, who is 6. We saw a Mazda Miata with the convertible top down. Mirabelle looked at the car with its two seats, and asked, "Where do the children sit?" I knew in that moment I would never own a Mazda Miata. I need a Dodge Caravan!

Like Patrick Lane (2004), "it is the present I seek. Not to deny the past and not to ignore the future, but to have them live where they must, in memory and imagination" (p. 20). The stories I have lived with my father and my brother are integral parts of the texture of my living experiences. The stories are written in the heart's ink as well as in the gaps and silences that no language can compose. Mystery abounds, but I will continue to write poetry as a way to map a little of the journey, partial and fragmentary, as I learn to lean into the story, whole and hopeful.

References

Aoki, T. T. (1993/2005). The child-centered curriculum: Where is the social in pedocentricism? In W. F. Pinar & R. L. Irwin (Eds), *Curriculum in a new key: The collected works of Ted T. Aoki* (pp. 279–289). Mahwah, NJ: Lawrence Erlbaum.

Bloch, E. (2006). *Traces* (A. A. Nassar, Trans.). Stanford, CA: Stanford University Press.

Brett, B. (2009). Tasting my father. In G. Bowering & J. Baird (Eds), *The heart does break: Canadian writers on grief and mourning* (pp. 17–31). Toronto, ON: Random House Canada.

Clarke, G. E. (2009). The baggage handler. In G. Bowering & J. Baird (Eds), *The heart does break: Canadian writers on grief and mourning* (pp. 69–80). Toronto, ON: Random House Canada.

Givner, J. (2009). On preparing my daughter's fiction for posthumous publication. In G. Bowering & J. Baird (Eds), *The heart does break: Canadian writers on grief and mourning* (pp. 169–183). Toronto, ON: Random House Canada.

Heilbrun, C. G. (1997). *The last gift of time: Life beyond sixty*. New York: Ballantine.

Hillman, J. (1999). *The force of character and the lasting life*. New York: Ballantine Books.

Hirshfield, J. (1997). *Nine gates: Entering the mind of poetry*. New York: Harper Perennial.

Hogan, L. (1995). *Dwellings: A spiritual history of the living world*. New York: W. W. Norton.

Lane, P. (2004). *There is a season: A memoir*. Toronto, ON: McClelland & Stewart.

Miller, J. P. (1996). *The holistic curriculum* (2nd edn). Toronto, ON: OISE Press.

Miller, R. E. (2005). *Writing at the end of the world*. Pittsburgh, PA: University of Pittsburgh Press.

Moure, E. (2009). A year later, I am in lilac now. In G. Bowering & J. Baird (Eds.), *The heart does break: Canadian writers on grief and mourning* (pp. 243–260). Toronto, ON: Random House Canada.

Oliver, M. (1994). *A poetry handbook*. Boston, MA: Mariner Books.

Orr, G. (2002). *Poetry as survival*. Athens, GA: University of Georgia Press.

Palmer, P. J. (2004). *A hidden wholeness: The journey toward an undivided life*. San Francisco, CA: Jossey-Bass.

Vanier, J. (1998). *Becoming human*. Toronto, ON: House of Anansi Press.

27

Conducting Narrative Inquiry Research From a Holistic Perspective

Honoring Story and Soul

Mary Beattie

This chapter is focused on furthering the development and understanding of an orientation to narrative inquiry research from a holistic perspective. This kind of qualitative research is focused on the study of research participants' experiences from their own unique perspectives, and in the context of who they are as whole human beings. It is grounded in the understanding that we live storied lives, and that we can choose to tell and enact those stories that give our lives purpose and meaning. Collaborative research relationships provide an intimate context for reflecting on our stories, and for the recollection and reconstruction of the past in order to provide direction for the present and the future. When they are well researched and written, the stories that lives tell can stimulate readers' imaginations, promote empathy and compassion for others, change perspectives, and promote new ways of knowing and being.

In this chapter, I draw on over two decades of research, and a pedagogy that was developed in a graduate course in education, Narrative and Story in Research and Professional Practice, that I have taught to Masters' and Doctoral students at The Ontario Institute for Studies in Education at the University of Toronto (Beattie, 2009). I provide an overview of three research projects where I have intentionally focused on making deeper connections between narrative inquiry research and holistic education.

In the past three decades, narrative research has flourished, as researchers in the field of education have experimented with a variety of literary forms for the representation of their data (Barone, 2007). Here, I focus on a distinctive form of narrative inquiry research, pioneered by Connelly and Clandinin (1988), where narrative is understood both as the structure of the phenomenon being studied and as a set of methods for the study of experience. This orientation to research is grounded in the understanding that narrative is at the heart of our meaning-making structures, and that we understand the events of our lives in the context of stories that have beginnings, middles, and ends (Bruner, 1986). It provides a holistic and unified framework for the study of individuals' lived experience where it is acknowledged that meanings are human interpretations, that they have been created in a context, and that they can be reinterpreted and reconstructed.

Trusting and respectful research relationships where individuals are fully present to each other, have each others' interests and purposes at heart, and nurture each others' understandings, are at the heart of this approach to research. Through storytelling, dialogue, reflection, and a range of arts-based and mindfulness methods, individuals come to new understandings of how the stories they are telling and enacting enhance and constrain their lives. As they integrate these understandings into their future actions, change and transformation takes place "not as the monolithic imposition of ideas, beliefs and values by one person on another, but as the polyphonic reforming and reconstruction of understandings by all the persons involved" (Beattie, 1995a, p. 146).

This approach to research grew out of work in the social sciences and humanities, and fields such as history, philosophy, literary theory, psychotherapy, theology, and psychology. It also grew out of a postmodern constructivist approach to education, where it is understood that knowledge is embodied, relational, and socially constructed. It promotes practices that allow researchers and participants to learn from and with each other within research relationships where it is acknowledged that no two people have had the same life experiences, no two people perceive the world or interpret it in the same way; neither do they have the same purposes and goals for their future lives.

The Importance of Stories

> One way or another we are living the stories planted in us early on, knowingly or unknowingly, in ourselves. We live stories that either give our lives meaning or negate it with meaninglessness. If we change the stories we live by, quite possibly we change our lives.
>
> *(Okri, 1997, p. 46)*

When we reflect on our stories, we reveal the knowledge that is embedded in them, and in this way we can make our core beliefs, principles, perspectives, and worldviews explicit. When we find that these are no longer suitable to living authentically in accordance with our inner purposes and the future direction of our lives, we can choose to re-interpret, re-frame, and re-construct them. As the philosopher Charles Taylor (1989) explains:

> In order to have a sense of who we are, we have to have a notion of how we have become, and of where we are going . . . [and] because we cannot but orient ourselves to the good, and thus determine our place relative to it and hence determine the direction of our lives, we must inescapably understand our lives in narrative form, as a quest.
>
> *(pp. 49–52)*

Research methods that include open-ended interviews, conversations, and story prompts help participants to recall significant events in their lives, and to tell deeply felt stories of purpose, pleasure, and passion; of family and friends, of presence and pride of accomplishment; of disappointment, shame, oppression, anger, joy, inspiration, and transcendence. These methods are designed to stimulate participants' imaginations and memories, and to encourage them to inhabit events imaginatively before they categorized and named them; to draw insights into what has nurtured them in the past, and to identify that which could be valuable in the future. They can connect participants to the sources of their energy and inspiration, to their personal purposes, and to the wisdom that arises from the inner life; to what Thomas Merton (2005) calls "the hidden wholeness" of themselves.

When they are expanded to include methods such as reflective and creative writing, visualization, artifacts presentations, meditation, poetry, art, and music, they create spaces for mutually beneficial dialogue that allows participants and researchers alike to listen to our values, beliefs, and cultural structures, and to consider the perspectives and practices that will lead us to new ways of thinking and acting. They can allow us to access the cover stories (Crites, 1979) we all tell to the outside world to be accepted, invulnerable, and respectable, and to the suppressed, silenced, and frozen stories "[which] can become prisons of sorts when we forget that that are stories in which we are authors and characters at the same time" (Conle, 2003, p. 20). They can help us to more fully understand the extent to which our stories are repositories of our cultural ways of knowing and being, and can nurture the development of our fragile stories (Beattie & Conle, 1996)—those taken-for-granted stories that constrain us and prevent us from developing the wholeness of ourselves. These methods encourage us to use our feelings as a bridge, not only to what we know intellectually, but also to what we perceive visually, aurally, socially, intuitively, aesthetically, and spiritually, and because they also include written feedback in the form of interim narratives and shared interpretation, they provide rich opportunities for interacting narratives (Beattie, 1995a) where our lives meet in all their wholeness, inform and influence each other, and where both are changed through the co-creation of new insights and understandings. They can nurture the development of our insights into how all stories work—in our own lives, in the lives of others, in the world around us—and of the connections between them.

Connecting Narrative Inquiry Research and Holistic Education

> Our own existence cannot be separated from the account we can give of ourselves. It is in telling our own stories that we give ourselves an identity.
>
> *(Ricoeur, 1985, p. 214)*

As researchers, we need to tell and re-tell our stories continuously as we simultaneously develop our specialized knowledge, skills, and attitudes (Beattie, 1995b, 2009). A growing body of literature in philosophy and psychology acknowledges that narrative structure is at the core of the formation of the self, and recognizes the role of narrative in understanding one's identity and that of others in the context of the wholeness and unity of an individual's whole life (Brockelman, 1985; Carr, 1986; MacIntyre, 1981; Noddings, 1984; Polkinghorne, 1988). It is only when we know ourselves, and are conscious of what is going on internally and externally, that we can work from what Palmer (2004) calls "the undivided self", that we can align our inner purposes with our external actions, and learn to listen deeply to research participants' stories from these individuals' own perspectives.

My interest in the connection between story and soul goes back to my childhood, where I grew up in the traditions of Catholicism, and learned that soul is that immortal aspect of ourselves that lives on when we die. Simultaneously, I learned through the stories and legends of the ancient Celts that, like the Indigenous peoples of many lands, they found soul and divinity all around them—in themselves, in each other, in the rivers, mountains, the ocean, the sky, and the land. For the Celts, there was no separation between mind, body, and soul, or between themselves and others. This vibrant spiritual tradition existed for thousands of years in Ireland before the introduction of Christianity in the fifth century.

I use the terms soul and spirit interchangeably here, and understand them as describing that non-material, ineffable aspect of ourselves that animates us and gives our lives purpose. George Bernard Shaw (1970) refers to the soul as "the life force", and Dylan Thomas (1953) calls it "the green fuse that drives the flower". Thomas Moore (1992) explains that when we acknowledge soul in our lives, we are encouraging life [and the story we tell of ourselves], to blossom forth according to its own designs and with its own "unpredictable beauty" (p. xix). Through graduate studies in English literature, I pursued my interest in the connections between religions, spirituality, and story, and also learned the creative and critical reading of texts that has served me well as an educator and researcher. The study of literature teaches us imaginative empathy. It also teaches us how to listen closely to stories, and to use our critical thinking as well as our senses and our imaginations to interpret them in order to illuminate, edify, and "secure a true comprehension of the way things are" (Eisner, cited in Beattie, 1995a, p. ix)

In research and pedagogy, I draw on Connelly and Clandinin (1988) and Clandinin and Connelly's (2000) work in narrative inquiry, and also on Eisner's principles for qualitative research, namely his emphasis on the importance of the arts and aesthetic experiences on an individual's efforts to create a life that has authenticity, integrity, connectedness, and meaning (Eisner, 1991, 2002). Also important is Maxine Greene's (1978, 1995) work on the imagination, and Charles Taylor's (1989) work on the creation of identity. In my early research (Beattie, 1995a), these authors provided the pillars for explorations into the nature of professional knowledge, the interconnectedness of the personal and professional, and of professional practice as personalized accounts of a practitioner's knowing. In Connelly and Clandinin's (1988) conception of personal practical knowledge, theory and practice are intertwined in a knowledge that is personal because it is derived from a person's narrative, and it is practical because it is aimed at meeting the needs of a particular situation. In later work, I explored the aesthetic and spiritual dimensions of this knowledge (Beattie, 2008), and drew on the work of Miller (2000, 2007), Moore (1992), and O'Donohue (1997). This new focus helped me to become more intentional about creating deeper research relationships by searching for ways to be more attentive to the soul presence of research participants, by attending to their purposes and needs within the research processes, and by acknowledging all aspects of their being in the practices and products of the research.

A pedagogy for beginning researchers needs to provide them with a range of experiences in which to learn to conduct self-study research and collaborative research with others (Beattie, 2009). They need practice and feedback as they search for the themes, tensions, contradictions, resonances, and narrative unities (MacIntyre, 1981) in their own lives and in the lives of others. For these individuals, it is only when they create their own narratives that they come to see the events, interruptions, and discontinuities of their lives as a unified and coherent whole. It allows them to see that intelligence will allow them to pose and solve problems, but it is only when they connect it to intuition and imagination that they can create personal narratives that have the qualities of authenticity, coherence, and integrity, can create an authentic identity as a researcher, and align their proposed research with their internal purposes. These individuals need a range of opportunities for critical reflection and dialogue, and ongoing guidance as they address issues such as:

- Who am I?
- What are the connections between the personal, professional and scholarly aspects of my life?
- What do I learn by reflecting on a time when I was totally present in an event (personal, professional, or scholarly), and was fully engaged with purpose and passion, pleasure, and pride?
- What is my vision for the researcher I want to be? Working backwards, how will I develop the necessary ways of knowing and being to enact that vision?
- How will my research practices and its products contribute to research participants' lives, touch readers' hearts as well as their minds, inspire action, and make a positive difference in the world?

Creating Collaborative Soul-Friend Relationships

Narrative inquiry research from a holistic perspective is grounded in the kind of collaborative research relationships that O'Donohue (1997) describes as soul friendship, within which individuals acknowledge the presence of each other's souls, feel a sense of connection with each other, have one another's best interests at heart, and engage in dialogue as only the soul knows it. Soul friend-ship is necessary for the creation of research contexts where participants will be willing to tap into the life force that is within them, and to explore the intimacies of their inner lives. To create these kinds of relationships requires researchers to move beyond standardized research practices, which tend to be rational and managerial, and to use their creativity, imagination, intuition, and wisdom, as well as their intellects.

Hunt's (1987) New Three R's—reflexivity, responsiveness, and reciprocality—are valuable in the creation of meaningful soul friend research relationships. Reflexivity describes an attitude wherein researchers engage in ongoing reflective practice and become increasingly more aware of themselves as both researchers and practitioners. Responsiveness describes a way of being in relation with participants where the researcher listens and tries to understand practitioners' meanings as they understand them. Reciprocality describes the ability of the researcher to encourage and facilitate shared explorations, interpretations, and meaning making. Witherell and Noddings' (1991) concept of "interpersonal reasoning" is also valuable in that it describes the enactment of a reasoning that grows out of an attitude that values the relationship over any particular outcome. It is open, flex-ible, and responsive to others, is marked by attachment and connection rather than separation and abstraction, and it is in contrast to logico-scientific mathematical reasoning that proceeds step by step according to *a priori* rules (p. 158).

Conducting Narrative Inquiry Research: Three Research Projects

I have profiled three research projects spanning a decade where I have been intentional about making deeper connections between narrative inquiry research and holistic education. I begin with the research on Corktown, an alternative secondary school in Toronto that was one of 21 schools studied as part of a large-scale national research study in Canada in 1993–4. The research was led by a national team who developed the overall research questions into the meaning and recognition of success. As the principal researcher at Corktown, I designed the study, and, in collaboration with two other researchers, we conducted the study over the course of a full academic year. This government-funded project was the largest research project of its kind in the history of Canadian education.

The Research at Corktown

The purpose of the study was to explore the reasons for the school's success in meeting the needs of students, and enabling such a large percentage of them to graduate and to be successful in university and in their chosen lives and careers, from the perspectives of the teachers, students, administrators, alumni, and parents, as well as those of the researchers. The stated vision and daily practices at Corktown promoted "the education of the whole person, with an emphasis on the development of self-knowledge and responsiveness to others, on creative and critical thought, and on connectedness between self, school, community and society" (Beattie, 2004, p. 3). This stated vision and philosophy allowed for research questions and extended conversations that acknowledged the wholeness of students' and teachers' lives, and those aspects of the school relationships and community that helped students to develop according to their own interests, inner purposes, and future goals.

I began the research by observing in classrooms, and spent well in excess of the required twenty days in the school as well as attending many school events, and accompanying classes on field trips. As a research team, we conducted approximately forty hours of interviews with teachers, teacher/co-ordinators, students, community representatives, parents, alumni, school board personnel, and the off-site principal. We also conducted individual and focus group interviews with different groups of students and teachers. All interviews were taped and transcribed. We collaborated in the work of student shadowing and the analysis of documents and guidelines. In addition to this, I conducted in-depth semi-structured research interviews with three teachers and two students, and kept a reflective journal of my ongoing reflections throughout the research. The data were analysed and thematized by the members of the research team. I wrote the interim narratives for research participants' feedback, and received feedback from them, from the research team, and from two members of the national research team. The full explanation of this research is detailed in Beattie (2007a,b, 2004).

Narrative accounts, portraits, and other literary forms allowed me to illustrate the ways in which the founding principles of the school were enacted in its daily life, in the relationships between adults and students, and in helping students to make connections between the different aspects of themselves—mind, body, and soul. From the one-on-one mentoring and counselling, the Breakfast Program, the community building events, field trips, and the Outreach programme, these practices helped students to develop autonomy and responsibility, to develop their own voices and interests, and to make a commitment to themselves, to the community, and to their roles in the wider world.

Literary portraits of students and teachers allowed me to show how interacting narratives (Beattie, 1995a) worked in this context, as the wholeness of these individuals' lives were intertwined in pursuit of a shared purpose. Narrative accounts of classes also showed how this way of working together helped students deal with their difficulties rather than being defeated by them, and to pursue their goals with confidence and resilience. Using portraits of the teacher/co-ordinators, I presented insights into the challenges these individuals experienced as well as their achievements, and outlined a holistic approach to leadership based in empathy and connectedness (Beattie, 2007a).

The Aesthetic and Spiritual Dimensions of Holistic Educators' Ways of Knowing and Being

This five-year research project focused on exploring the meaning of long-standing mindfulness and arts practices in the lives of eight experienced holistic educators (Beattie, 2008). These practices included literary, visual, musical, mindfulness, and spiritual practices. The research was funded by the Social Science and Humanities Research Council of Canada (SSHRC).

My interest in this topic is long-standing, and it was intensified by reading writers such as Jung, Shakespeare, Blake, and Heaney over the years; writers who have all written about how these kinds of practices allow us to access the ocean of consciousness that lies within the layers of the conscious–subconscious–unconscious aspects of ourselves. In *The Spirit Level*, Heaney's (1996) poems address the connections between the practical and poetic, the visible and invisible, the mysterious aspects of consciousness, and the state of balance and measure suggested by the title.

In this research, I used an expanded concept of interacting narratives "to encompass the literary, aesthetic, and spiritual narratives chosen by research participants for their influence and shaping effects on their lives", and an expanded conception of personal practical knowledge "to encompass the aesthetic and spiritual aspects of their ways of knowing and being" (Beattie, 2008). Each of the final narratives shows how an individual's chosen practices provided them with contexts in which to access the creative and critical aspects of themselves, to create new connections and categories, imagine new perspectives and possibilities, and develop all aspects of who they are as human beings. Their practices affected the education of their hearts as well as their intellects, the stories they were telling and enacting, and their abilities to be intentional about choosing the narratives they would tell and enact in their future lives.

A surprising aspect of the research was the extent to which each of these individuals used their developing awareness and abilities to be of service to others in order to make a positive contribution to others' lives. As they did so, they developed new skill sets and abilities, became more aware of others' perspectives, more mindful of the quality of their relationships with them, and of ways to nurture their ways of knowing and being.

With each participant, I conducted three semi-structured interviews of three to four hours that were taped and transcribed. I also attended a range of events—choral concerts, art exhibitions, classes and symposia, conference presentations—and read participants' work in novels, academic articles, and books. I wrote field notes of all events, kept a research journal, and, in the third year of the research, I wrote interim narratives to which participants provided feedback.

Before the final interviews, I invited research participants to prepare a collection of artifacts that were significant to them in understanding the meaning of their chosen practices in their lives. This helped them to identify the intersecting and overlapping spirals and circles of connections and meanings, and to engage in deep reflection before and during the interviews. Some of these interviews lasted more than the allotted three hours, and, by agreement, we carried on the following day, in some cases for three or four more hours.

Owing to the research funding, I had a team of four former graduate students to read the transcripts with me, to discuss and analyse them, and to write and re-write the interim narratives. The interpretation of each individual's narrative can be described as taking place in layers, as the recursive processes of writing several drafts of these interim narratives led us to new levels of understanding and connections. We talked and wrote until we could agree on a satisfactory interpretation that each research participant would recognize as authentic, coherent, and true to their meanings. I wrote the final research narratives and used literary forms and language to be a witness to the complexities of the lived realities of participants' lives, to present new perspectives and understandings, and to inspire and stimulate future explorations. The book publication from this research is still a work in progress.

Narrative in Health Care Education

Patient narratives are becoming an important part of the medical literature and more prevalent in the education of medical and healthcare professionals. Narrative ways of knowing and arts and humanities activities are being introduced more fully to teach healthcare practitioners to hear and respond to patients' stories from the patients' perspective, to see beyond the illness, and to acknowledge the wholeness and humanity of the person (Charon, 2006). In my own life, the disruption caused by serious illness in the lives of two people I love led me to explore how I could use my knowledge and skills as a researcher to help them explore the lived experiences of a cancer diagnosis, its treatments, and the restorative practices they chose to try to restore well-being and to forge a new identity. My two patient participants were my husband, Jim, and my colleague and friend, Sheila.

Drawing on an innovative literary biography of Seamus Heaney by the poet Dennis O'Driscoll (2008), I designed a study where the participants wrote in response to a set of sequenced and iterative questions that encouraged them to reflect on how their experiences affected the emotional, social, moral, aesthetic, spiritual, and physical aspects of their lives and identities, and to tell and re-tell their stories. They wrote according to their own schedules, answered the questions in their preferred sequence, chose those they would answer and those they would decline, and re-worded them if necessary. I read and responded in writing to the first draft of each document, the participants responded to my comments and invitations to go deeper into the stories, and then they read and responded to each other's work.

The writing and re-writing of the various drafts was done over a period of 18 months. With some editing and sequencing, we co-created the final narratives (Beattie, Cook, & Beattie, 2016) which provide unique insights into the realities of these two individuals' journeys from illness to wellness, the different ways in which they used health-seeking behaviors, and the role of mindfulness, caring relationships, and community in helping each person to create a new narrative for their current and future lives.

Postscript

It is significant to note that, for the past two decades, the importance of narrative, storytelling, dialogue, and reciprocal conversations is being recognized across the disciplines and in professional programs in higher education (Beattie, 2018). Narrative inquiry research from a holistic perspective provides a framework for the exploration of the issues that concern us in our search for a better world, and in documenting the lived realities of people whose lives are affected by issues such as human suffering, social and gender inequity, oppression, the use and abuse of power, poverty, forced immigration, and war, and to do so with humility and respect for their humanity, and in ways that figures and literal prose can never do.

My hope for this chapter is that it will inspire and support researchers to conduct purposeful and meaningful research that will speak to readers' hearts as well as their minds, will contribute to our common quest for a better world, and will allow us "to be here for good in every sense" (Heaney, 1996). When they are well researched and artistically crafted, research narratives can be a spur to the development of imaginative empathy, to what Richard Rorty (1979) calls "edification", and to the education of the heart. Like literature, music, and art, they can speak to our conscious minds and senses in direct ways, and to our subconscious and unconscious minds in complex, circuitous, and indirect ways. They can evoke thoughts and feelings that invite us to wonder, to move across the boundaries between what we know and what we might yet know, and to change our actions. When they connect our hearts, souls, and minds to those of others, and allow our lives to interact in all their wholeness, they can be transformative. As Elliot Eisner once wrote: "The lives that stories tell cannot be told in other ways" (Eisner, in Beattie, 1995a p. ix).

References

Barone, T. (2007). A return to the gold standard? Questioning the future of narrative construction as educational research. *Qualitative Inquiry, 13*(4), 454–470.

Beattie, M. (1995a). *Constructing professional knowledge in teaching: A narrative of change and growth.* New York: Teachers' College Press.

Beattie, M. (1995b). New prospects for teacher education: Narrative ways of knowing, teaching and learning. *Educational Research, 36*(3), 53–70.

Beattie, M. (2004). *Narratives in the making: Teaching and learning at Corktown Community High School.* Toronto, ON: University of Toronto Press.

Beattie, M. (2007a). Educational leadership: Modeling, mentoring, making and re-making a learning community. *European Journal of Teacher Education, 25*(2 & 3), 199–221.

Beattie, M. (2007b). Creating a self: A narrative and holistic perspective. *International Journal of Education and the Arts, 8*(13), 1–25, http://ijea.asu.edu.

Beattie, M. (2008). Unpublished research report to Social Science and Humanities Council of Canada (SSHRC).

Beattie, M. (2009). *The quest for meaning: Narratives of teaching, learning and the arts.* Rotterdam, The Netherlands: Sense.

Beattie, M. (2018). Foreword. In Latham, G. & Ewing, R. *Generative conversations for creative learning: Reimagining literacy education and understanding.* Switzerland: Palgrave Macmillan.

Beattie, M. & Conle, C. (1996). Teacher narratives: Fragile stories and change. *Asia Pacific Journal of Teacher Education, 24*(3), 309–326.

Beattie, M., Cook, S., & Beattie, J. (2016). Paper presented at *Creating Space V Conference, Canadian Medical Association, Montreal, Quebec, Canada*, Patient stories: Caring for ourselves and each other. (Under review)

Brockelman, P. (1985). *Time and self: Phenomenological explorations.* New York: Crossroads.

Bruner, J. (1986). *Actual minds, possible worlds.* Cambridge, MA: Harvard University Press.

Carr, D. (1986). *Time, narrative and history.* Indianapolis, IN: Indiana University Press.

Charon, R. (2006). *Narrative medicine: Honoring the stories of illness.* Oxford: Oxford University Press.

Clandinin, D. J. & Connelly, M. (2000). *Narrative inquiry: Experience and story in qualitative research.* San Francisco, CA: Jossey-Bass.

Conle, C. (2003). An anatomy of narrative curricula. *Educational Researcher, 32*(3), 3–15.

Connelly, F. M. & Clandinin, D. J. (1988). *Teachers as curriculum planners, narratives of experience.* New York: Teachers College Press.

Crites, S. (1979). The aesthetics of self-deception. *Soundings, 62*, 107–129.

Eisner, E. (1991). *The enlightened eye.* New York: Macmillan.

Eisner, E. (2002). *Arts and the creation of mind.* New Haven, CT: Yale University Press.

Greene, M. (1978). *Landscapes of learning.* New York: Teachers College Press.

Greene, M. (1995). *Releasing the imagination.* San Francisco, CA: Jossey Bass.

Heaney, S. (1996). *The spirit level.* London, UK: Faber and Faber.

Hunt, D. (1987). *Beginning with ourselves in practice, theory, and human affairs.* Cambridge, MA: Brookline Books.

MacIntyre, A. (1981). *After virtue: A study in moral theory.* Notre Dame, IN: University of Notre Dame Press.

Merton, T. (2005). *In the dark before dawn: New selected poems of Thomas Merton.* New York: New Directions.

Miller, J. P. (2000). *Education and the soul: Towards a spiritual curriculum.* Albany, NY: SUNY Press.

Miller, J. P. (2007). *The holistic curriculum.* Toronto, ON: OISE Press.

Moore, T. (1992). *Care of the soul.* New York: HarperCollins.

Noddings, N. (1984). *Caring.* Berkeley, CA: University of California Press.

O'Donohue, J. (1997). *Anam cara: A book of Celtic wisdom.* London: Bantam Press.

O'Driscoll, D. (2008). *Stepping stones: Interviews with Seamus Heaney.* London: Faber and Faber.

Okri, B. (1997). *A way of being free.* London: Orion.

Palmer, P. (2004). *Hidden wholeness: The journey towards an undivided self.* San Francisco, CA: Jossey-Bass.

Polkinghorne, D. E. (1988). *Narrative knowing and the human sciences.* New York: SUNY Press.

Ricoeur, P. (1985). History as narrative and practice. In Kirby, A. P. (1991) *Narrative and the Self.* Bloomington, IN: Indiana University Press.

Rorty, R. (1979). *Philosophy and the mirror of nature.* Princeton, NJ: Princeton University Press.

Shaw, G. B. (1970–1974). *Bernard Shaw: Collected plays with their prefaces* (Dan Laurence, Ed.). London: The Bodley Head.

Taylor, C. (1989). *Sources of the self.* Cambridge, MA: Harvard University Press.

Thomas, D. (1953) *Collected poems, 1934–1952.* New York: New Directions.

Witherell, C. & Noddings, N. (1991). *Stories lives tell: Narrative and dialogue in education.* New York: Teachers College Press.

28

Sound Escapes

An Holistic Approach to Spirituality and Music Education

Diana Harris

To begin at the beginning, the title is courtesy of the sound research group at the London College of Communication, who explore art and sound in the natural environment. In this chapter, it is being used as a pun on sound: in one sense sound, by its transient nature, does indeed 'escape'; in another, I want to encourage pupils to be able to escape into sound, or maybe through sound; finally, in a third sense, I want the way they do this to be 'sound' in the epistemological and pedagogic sense.

While viewing education from a holistic standpoint it would seem to make sense to disregard the traditional dualism between mind and body in favor of a tripartite division between mind, body, and spirit. However, tripartite comprises three parts and this is still not the same as 'holistic', as the whole is known to be more than the sum of its parts. While these parts can be identified as three distinct aspects of an individual, the body, mind, and spirit are inseparably intertwined, and influence one another. The spirit, therefore, lives and acts in unison with the body and mind. As I show later in this chapter, one of the terms used most commonly to explain spiritual experience is 'connected', this being a precondition of holism.

It is not just in education where seeing students as whole human beings is important. Senge (2005), in his book *Presence: Exploring Change in People, Organisations and Society*, says that we need to understand everything in nature as a whole but also how parts and wholes are interrelated. He makes the distinction between machines and living systems saying, "They [people] are not mere assemblages of their parts but are continually growing and changing along with their elements" (p. 5). Csikszentmihalyi (1990) calls this same process "flow", which he describes as reaching a state of concentration and enjoyment which is effortless, an idea that has also been taken to heart in many enlightened fields of inquiry, such as medicine. This can be seen in a research report produced on behalf of Museums and Galleries at Leicester University (Dodd & Jones, 2014). They act as a public forum that can influence individual and community health and provide a space to help people make sense of their world. Surely education as a discipline should provide opportunities to influence wholeness, or flow, and I argue that it is through an understanding of spirituality that music education can do this.

Spirituality as a Stochastic Process

A light came on for me when I began to view spirituality as a stochastic process, a sequence of events that combines the random with what is known already in such a way as to only allow certain outcomes that are of use to either an individual or a community. I want to argue that feelings associated with spirituality can be seen as a stochastic process, and for spirituality to be a useful concept, it is necessary for both individuals and communities.

Stochastic process is an idea more commonly referred to in math or science, particularly evolution and genetic change, than music or spirituality. Stochastic comes from the Greek, meaning to aim at, or guess, but for a better understanding of how I could use the term, I went to Bateson. In his chapter dealing with the stochastic process he described it as:

> . . . a stream of events that is random in certain aspects and in each case there is a non-random selection process which causes certain of the random components to "survive" longer than others. Without the random there can be no new thing.
>
> *(Bateson, 1979, p. 163)*

Bateson relates this to the twin ideas of evolutionary and somatic change, somatic meaning "the characteristic was achieved by bodily change brought about during the lifetime of the individual by environmental impact or by practice" (Bateson, 1979, p. 252), which includes learning and thought. He argues that Darwin was right only up to a point and that it has come to be accepted that body and mind have evolved simultaneously and are both stochastic processes. What is important, and indeed necessary, is the unity of the combined system of mind and body and, I would argue, spirit.

Incorporating the random is, of course, not new in music; see, for example, the aleatoric music by John Cage and Iannis Xenakis, the Romanian-born, Greek–French composer, who used stochastic processes or elements in some of his work including probability, game theory, Boolean algebra, and computers to create his compositions (for example, his huge multimedia performances he called *Polytopes*). A happy consequence of the stochastic process being used to describe spirituality is Bateson's view that there is no creative process unless the random and the non-random are engaged together. However, I believe it might also be used as a model of understanding the notion of spirituality in music. For, as well as the prior knowledge gained from teachers, music books, fellow musicians, and our experience of a specific genre, we must also consider the random. The latter might include our non-musical experiences such as our upbringing, attitudes, ethnicity, beliefs, our imagining or dreaming, and the significant traumatic or joyous events in our life, which for each individual will be different, in other words our "funds of knowledge" (Moll, Amanti, Neff, & Gonzalez, 1992).

So, when a group of musicians meet to play or compose, it is a bringing together of individuals, a mix of both their common, shared, prior musical understandings that we call the 'knowns' (those things we might expect in terms of the musical understanding and experience of such players), but also the personal experiences, both musical and non-musical, and beliefs of each individual, the 'unknowns', or 'random'. In fact, without this random human element, compositions and performances would be less diverse and the creative process impoverished. This is not a new idea, nor is it limited to the arts. For example, Ashby (cited in Bateson, 1979) points out that: "no system (neither computer nor organism) can produce anything *new* unless the system contains some source of the random" (p. 174).

I would argue that the process of combining the known with the random is also in operation during listening. For listeners, whether they are trained musical performers or listeners with little or no musical training, bring with them this randomness of their prior knowledge and understanding each time they listen to music. It is this randomness that contributes to each music class, and each music lesson, being different in response to the same or similar learning experiences. Taking into account these variables, I would argue that it is understandable that we find it difficult to plan for a spiritual response in the music classroom.

As music teachers, the careful selection of music for children to listen to is unlikely to be a random process. It is the experiential influence of the music on pupils that is random and unpredictable. What teachers need to guide the process is an integration between knowledge and randomness in such a way as to ensure that the experience leads to something useful both for the individual and for society. The following is research into how the notion of spirituality in music education can fulfill this process. The report on this research is a fresh look at this question and may perhaps lead us towards an answer that holds practical implications for life and for the classroom.

Introduction to the Research

The research that I am about to describe emerged from the writing of *Music Education and Muslims* (Harris, 2006) and the critical insights that came from this study. The book explored pedagogical issues surrounding music and Islam and intended to answer why some Muslims found music lessons in school raised complex issues. I was asked by the editor of a series of books on music education if I could look at the relevance of music in relation to other religions. I did not feel I had the expertise to do this but did have experience with the concept of spirituality, and an interest in how it can be explored within music education. Although aspects of religion informed some of my ideas, spirituality arose as fundamentally a secular concept.

Research into the Notion of Spirituality and Music (1)

In a previous publication (Harris & Mackrill, 2013), data were presented from mainly qualitative research. Forty respondents and four focus groups of children (Harris) were included. Quantitative research from questionnaires completed by 38 trainee music teachers (Mackrill) also informed the research. Interviewees came from various contexts, cultures, and backgrounds and were all music students in tertiary education, teachers, performers, or composers. The children were from music classes in Christian, Jewish, and Sikh schools. Thematic data analysis (Miles & Huberman, 1994) was employed and from these data five themes were identified relating to the respondents' understanding of the term 'spirituality' in relation to music. The paradigm position is interpretive with the original interviews in a narrative format (Soler, 2012). Ideas about spirituality were first discussed in general terms, leading on more specifically to spirituality and music. Having analysed these data, subsequent interviews and questionnaires addressed these specific themes. The questionnaires arose from this thematic analysis and were developed specifically for a cohort of teacher training students at the University of Sussex, where Mackrill was director of music education. The ideas presented in this discussion constitute a summary of the key findings under each thematic heading.

Spirituality and Religion

A split emerged between those participants who associated spirituality with religion and those who did not. This split was fairly even. Of those who associated it with religion, the majority were from a traditional religious upbringing, who still considered themselves religious, and for whom all aspects of life were underpinned by their religious convictions. A significant group still linked the idea of spirituality with God, but not a specific organized religion. Those who did not consider either God or religion to be relevant to their lives still mostly expressed a belief that spirituality could be found in/through music. One performer, who had been brought up as a Christian, but no longer considered himself to be, admitted he was in an ambiguous situation by saying that he found music written for a religious context was still the most spiritual for him.

An Inner or Outer Experience

On the whole, spirituality was most often seen as a private affair and not one that was shared with other people. To some extent this changed when music was part of a specifically religious experience. However, for many, the response was on a continuum depending on the context of the music being played. One university lecturer, a member of the Salvation Army, said that he experienced spirituality only as part of a community, always in relation to other people.

The Relevance of Words

Overwhelmingly what emerged here was that words were not the most important factor. Some considered that words could lead them to a particular spiritual place, but more expressed the view that words tended to be a stumbling block that directed the listener/singer in a direction that was unhelpful. The reason given for this was that the music itself was communicating something more powerful than the words could express. The words then became a distraction because they guided you in what you should be feeling.

Knowledge and Emotion

It became clear during the data analysis that the knowledge being spoken about applied almost entirely to technical knowledge, the knowing 'how' (Philpott, 2001). It came as no surprise to us that the definitions of 'emotion' and 'spiritual' took some teasing out. The determining factor seemed to be the depth of the experience/feeling, spirituality seeming to encompass more depth than emotion. Another difference that emerged was that emotion was a more spontaneous reaction. For some, the knowledge of music allowed them to express themselves more spiritually or feel more spiritual. A student in Nepal believed his performances were made up of technical aspects influenced by his brain and a spirit guiding him as to how to make the performance musical. He defined this as thinking one thing and playing another.

Listening or Performing

As a musician, I find that I can 'lose' myself in music more readily as a listener and was perhaps surprised to realize that this is not the case for all musicians. One teacher talked of an "outer, other worldliness when performing" which he said came from the idea of communicating with other people, both those he was performing with and the audience. A cellist agreed, because she said that performing felt more immediate, especially playing an instrument that resonates like the cello. However, in a focus group in a Sikh school, a year 9 (age 13–14) girl said:

> When you're playing it it's more about trying to get all the notes right and get the sound right but when you listen to it it's a different . . . like in assembly when everybody's singing to the harmonium and everybody joins in, that's like, that's when you get the feeling that you're actually . . . you've got a connection with God.

Overall most people responded to the idea of the power of listening to music and being moved by it, sometimes without any understanding of how this happens. Perhaps we might have asked whether this response is random or if it can be predicted in some way. Might the same piece of music be powerful on one occasion but not another? As educators tasked with determining what music to play to children, this seems an important question.

As part of the same research project (but not reported in the 2013 paper) I asked the question of the 40 interviewees: How do you think the concept of spirituality could be relevant to class music? In looking at the term spirituality in general, it is perhaps not surprising that many people link it with peace and calmness. One School of Oriental and African Studies (SOAS) music student believed that to achieve this calmness the first step would be to become aware of the breath. He said: "everything we need is inside, so the peace that we look for is inside, so we need to find a way that we can find the peace". Monks from the Tashi Lhunpo Buddhist Monastery in Tibet use music and dance to bring an awareness of Buddhism to schools around the world. They start their workshops by coming in and sitting quietly with the children, then begin to chant a quiet prayer to still the mind as a preliminary to meditation. Their coordinator in the UK said:

We've found that we can get a roomful of 120 children, from the ages of 5 to 12 sitting silently and really entering into that and that's fantastic. After that the peace is shattered as they begin to play their instruments and dance.

They explain to the children that although the music and dance is loud and exciting, it is still a form of meditation because they are imagining themselves as wrathful deities who are ridding the world of evil, and it is all part of mind awareness, or getting into a particular mindset. When they play the long horns, in particular, the little children squeal with excitement. The children then learn about how the monks went into the monasteries when they were as young as 7 and the children get a chance to talk with the monks in order to try to relate to them, to understand that behind the costumes, music, and dance these are ordinary people.

When I visited a Jewish secondary school in London, I had the opportunity to talk to the head-teacher and the music teacher. To begin with, the conversation revolved around singing because women and girls are not allowed to sing in front of men, unless it is their own family (Summit, 2000). Since the music teacher was a woman, it meant she could not sing to her classes in the boys' part of the school. However, the boys themselves were very good at singing because it is so much a part of the Jewish tradition. Conversely, she could sing to the girls' classes, but found it difficult to get the girls to sing because it was alien to their life. This means that music classes in both parts of the school had an emphasis on instrumental work. In order to link Judaism with modern music, they have a project whereby they look at the history of Ashkenazic, Seraphic, and Hasidic Jews and how that has fed into pop music, especially in Israel.

For instance, if we play some rap and have it on the interactive whiteboard and it's all very cool, and so on, we then ask if this is Jewish music? They have endless debates about it, it's really quite fascinating. They get confused because the message is right but the style feels wrong to them.

(Head of Music, Jewish school)

As with many teachers, the Jewish music teacher questioned what spirituality really was in the context of teaching music, and whether it is really possible to promote it. Although she had been talking about Jewish music, she did not see spirituality as something that needed to be linked to religion. She spoke about a gamelan lesson that she teaches, which was observed by a school inspector who said it was "a spiritual experience". In mentioning this, she said: "I thought right, okay! But I think it was simply because everyone was completely focused and the whole expression was non-verbal". For this teacher, it was when the girls were composing for the General Certificate of Secondary Education (14–16) and Advanced Level (16–18) that she thought something approaching an expression of spirituality might be happening as she accessed their creative thoughts. Many of them chose to set a piece from the *Siddur* (Jewish religious texts) to music. The headteacher felt it was through this exercise that they identified the importance of their faith. However, I would want to emphasize at this point that looking at spirituality only from a religious point of view in a secular school would not be desirable or acceptable. A workable definition for spiritual education might be "any intended or unintended circumstance or effort that promotes the development and flourishing of spirituality, in particular, the capability of and the disposition to transcendence and raised awareness, including relational consciousness" (Wong Ping Ho, 2006, p. 77).

Research into Notions of Spirituality (2)

Research data from music educators at the Practice and Research in Integrated Music Education (PRIME) week-long symposium in Solothurn, Germany, were collected. All those who attended were interested in how music could be integrated within other subjects in the curriculum. The paper and workshop I presented examined the use of art to represent thoughts and feelings aroused by music. This kind of arousal was considered to be the beginning of a spiritual experience. A questionnaire was given to the 15 participants after the workshop. Having written their answers mainly in German, the text was then translated. There were only three open questions: How would you define spirituality? How do you see spirituality in terms of music? Have you any ideas about how spirituality might be included in the music classroom? Several people discussed their answers with me.

Throughout the participant responses, the word most used in relation to spiritual experience was 'connection'. Ten participants either used this actual term or it was implied. Many talked about connectedness in terms of the universe, the world, everything. Three specifically mentioned that spirituality has to do with connecting to other people. The second aspect most mentioned was directly in relation to personal experience. Of the nine who talked about themselves, only three did not refer to other people. As well, one participant was particularly interesting in saying that spirituality is a preoccupation with oneself, thus apparently denying a connection with others.

In view of the way spirituality has traditionally been associated with religion, it was perhaps surprising that only three of the 15 participants mentioned religion. One of the teachers wrote: "Spirituality involves the invisible, often also the transcendental. For me, it also involves the preoccupation with oneself, especially one's own emotions. But spirituality quickly becomes a subject of religion . . ."

Another wrote about how her ideas were changing:

> Having been raised in a Greek Orthodox Christian tradition spirituality was always connected to religion and I hadn't given much thought to it in another dimension. However, during the last [few] years, through my reading, I have started to think in a different way. I could not define spirituality only as part of a religion anymore, but I can't yet define it in a satisfying way . . .

And the third brought in the concept of the known and unknown, thus linking with my thoughts on the stochastic process, by saying:

> I see it as a state in which we feel a deep connection with the self, but this connection is also and always in relation to others – present and not present, known and not known, situated temporally in the 'now' and in the past. I see it as separate from religion, which can be a "choice".

A fourth used the term '*the* divine' which may, or may not, have been a religious concept, although I would contend that the use of the definite article suggests a more sacred meaning than the word divine *alone* would: "Spirituality is our search beyond our limitations, to understand – love – experience the other and other beings more deeply. We know the divine briefly; [we] are always going home."

Spirituality and Music

The answers to the question of how spirituality relates to music were equally diverse. Here, one person directly mentioned the link between music, spirituality and religion: "Music is strongly emotional. It promotes one's own expression of emotions and it can also evoke emotions. At the same time, music plays a major role in most religions, especially for connecting with the invisible world."

Another respondent listed a series of music he found spiritual, some of which is also religious: "Gregorian music, chorales within a religious context, Bach oratorio, and others; contemplative music. Compositions by Oliver Messiaen (Saint Francis of Assisi, Birds Awakening, and others)."

Continuing to look at spirituality more specifically in relation to music, some of the same themes exist as in defining spirituality more generally, for example, five of the respondents here mentioned being 'connected'. Another theme is in relation to whether people expressed personal feelings. This is difficult because, of course, to some extent everything is subjective, but here it feels as if there

Diana Harris

is a difference between those who talk about spirituality and music in direct relation to themselves and those who are talking in the third person. The third aspect I have drawn out here is in relation to energy, and, although this was mentioned by only two respondents, this feels like a powerful idea, which related back to Csikszentmihalyi's ideas about flow. For example, one wrote: "I find spirituality in music everywhere, I am touched within by the music and where I perceive vibrations that let flow the energy of my life."

Spirituality in the Music Classroom

When it comes to how music may be used to allow for spiritual development in a classroom, there were again many different ideas. This question produced the most diverse response and these responses could be divided into expected areas within the music curriculum, namely listening, performing, and composing/creating, and those that could be said to be more generic: for example, promoting respect and caring. One person wrote: "by creating opportunities for immersion in experiences that are 'musical' – which begs[*sic*] the question how do we define a musical experience . . ." Others were more specific about what musical experiences could include:

Listening to music and painting at the same time, dancing, moving;

Translating a poem into sounds;

Creating experiences for the senses: distinguishing sounds;

Painting mandalas/representing as a group/meanwhile humming, singing quietly;

Exploring symmetric forms (for example, snail-shells (sounds by blowing), singing bowl: observing the waves);

Representing scenes from fairy tales with music after concentrated journeys into the land of fantasy.

Integrating music with other subjects was hardly a surprise, in view of the nature of the conference. A more extended response highlighted the idea of integration:

By integration of actively doing something such as painting, creating, moving or other forms for example from mathematics from geography or cultural history. By this integration, the pupil becomes more 'whole' and develops a more connected and interlinked view of the world.

Another key concept was that of emotion, and it appeared that, for some, spirituality and emotion might be thought of interchangeably. One felt that spirituality could only be dealt with in the context of emotions. She wrote that creating music helped to express emotion, but also music was important for releasing emotions.

Finally, relaxation was a key term used. Making music or listening was thought to encourage relaxation and a time for play, especially important for younger children. This, then, might promote talking about experiences and listening to music from different cultures and religions to expand an awareness of a greater range of music. One person advocated relaxation, stillness, calm, and quietness, before giving performances as a way to help self-belief in herself as a performer.

Discussion

In this research, four key concepts have been identified in relation to music education: spirituality, stochastic process, creativity, and connection, which all relate to being 'whole'. Draper said:

"Spirituality is not about seeking some floaty state of disembodied reverie but being here more fully, more soulfully . . . bringing matter and spirit together to make something that is greater than the sum of its parts" (Draper, 2017, para. 8).

Bown (2015) discusses Simonton and Csikszentmihalyi in his paper on creativity, claiming that both call for heterogenous groups of participants when researching the creative process. It seems to me that heterogeneity is necessary for the stochastic process as well. It is the putting together of many different, perhaps random, ideas that create the ground necessary for spiritual development, and, by extension, ideas that will be of use to both the individual and society. Shah (2013) reminds us that creativity is different in every culture and acknowledges that context and experience influences creativity. Thus, myriad cultures will allow for a cornucopia of connections. The arts have the opportunity to embrace the awe and wonder that is so key to what Draper (2017, para. 12) calls "finding our place more fully".

Plater (2017), looking at evidence for spirituality across the curriculum, discusses the spirit in relation to the soul. He argues that we should be looking at the contemporary *Wholeness Movement*, which perceives the spirit as "that in us which seeks vision and transcendence", and soul as "that which seeks engagement, depth and rootedness", in looking for "personal and community maturity" in a "balance and wholeness of body, soul and spirit" (Plater, 2017, p. 14). This view from Plater mirrors the responses from the participants in the Solothurn research in connecting the personal and communal aspects of spirituality as the way forward in music education of the future.

In this chapter, I have offered a sample of the many thousands of words, and many hours of recordings, collected during these two research projects. I hope that I have convinced you, as readers, that a truly holistic approach to education must take into consideration the spiritual development of a child, and that music education may be a good place to begin this process. However, there may well be many of you who doubt whether spiritual is the right word, primarily because of its long association with religion. You may be happier with terms like presence (Senge, Scharmer, Jaworski, & Flowers, 2005) or mindfulness, as taught by the Paws b programme (developed in 2012 by the Mindfulness in Schools Project with Tabitha Sawyer and Rhian Roxburgh). Whatever you call this concept, it cannot be developed in any sense that can be measured; it cannot be interrogated in the classroom. With younger children, it may not even be relevant to focus on it directly. Spirituality blossoms at its own speed. This is only possible when the teacher recognizes it within her or his own life. As teachers, though, we can all make spaces, silent spaces and surprising spaces: spaces that may appear to contain random sounds but may provide opportunities to allow the connections so important to thinking about spirituality—maybe we should call them stochastic spaces . . . or sound escapes.

References

Bateson, G. (1979). *Mind and nature: A necessary unity*. New York: Bantam Books.

Bown, O. (2015). Are we doing it right? In H. Toivonen, S. Colton, M. Cook, & D. Ventura (Eds), *Proceedings of the Sixth International Conference on Computational Creativity (ICCC 2015). Park City, Utah, June 29– July 2, 2015*. Provo, UT: Brigham Young University.

Csikszentmihalyi, M. (1990). *Flow: The psychology of optimal experience*. New York: HarperCollins.

Dodd, J. & Jones, C. (2014). *Mind, body, spirit: How museums impact health and wellbeing*. Leicester: University Leicester Research Centre for Museums and Galleries (RCMG), University of Leicester.

Draper, B. (Contributor) (2017). Brian Draper: 14/10/2017 [Radio series episode]. In *Today's Thought for the Day*. London: BBC Radio 4. Retrieved from www.bbc.co.uk/programmes/p05k3wvj.

Harris, D. (2006). *Music education and Muslims*. Stoke on Trent, UK: Trentham Books.

Harris, D. & Mackrill, D. (2013). Sound escapes: Images of spirituality from music teachers and students. *International Journal of Children's Spirituality, 18*(2), 188–199.

Miles, M. B. & Huberman, A. M. (1994). *Qualitative data analysis*. London: Sage.

Moll, L. C., Amanti, C., Neff, D., & Gonzalez, N. (1992). Funds of knowledge for teaching: Using a qualitative approach to connect homes and classrooms: Theory into practice. *Qualitative Issues in Educational Research, 31*(2), 132–141.

Philpott, C. (2001). Musical learning and musical development. In C. Philpott & G. Spruce (Eds), *Learning to teach music in the secondary school*. London: Routledge.

Plater, M. (2017). Re-souling spirituality: redefining the spiritual dimension in schools. *International Journal of Children's Spirituality, 22*(1), 14–23.

Senge, P., Scharmer, O. C., Jaworski, J., & Flowers, B. S. (Eds) (2005). *Presence: Exploring profound change in people, organizations and society*. London: Nicholas Brealey.

Shah, S. (2013). Creativity across cultures: A comparison of cognitive creativity and creativity achievement between the United States and India. UNF Theses and Dissertations Paper 432.

Soler, J. (2012). Multiple lives, disparate voices, different educational experiences: The power of narrative enquiry to investigate diversity and inform pedagogical change. In S. Soler, C. S. Walsh, A. Craft, J. Rix, & K. Simmons (Eds), *Transforming practice: critical issues in equity, diversity and education*. Milton Keynes, UK: Open University/SAGE.

Summit, J. A. (2000). *The Lord's song in a strange land: Music and identity in contemporary Jewish worship*. Oxford: Oxford University Press.

Wong Ping Ho (2006). A conceptual investigation into the possibility of spiritual education. *International Journal of Children's Spirituality, 11*(1), 73–85.

29

Research In, On, and With Waldorf Education in The Netherlands

Aziza Mayo

Waldorf education has been part of the Dutch educational system for nearly a century. Major changes on the level of organization and practices within Waldorf schools and changes in society's perception of what constitutes good education have given rise to the need for an ongoing dialogue on the meaning and purposes of Waldorf education in contemporary society. The research program Values and Value of Waldorf Education was founded in 2014 as a joint initiative with the University of Applied Sciences, Leiden, and Waldorf education organizations throughout the Netherlands, to work towards this process. The program brings together researchers and practitioners engaged in collaborative research that aims to:

1. Build knowledge and understanding of purposes and practices in contemporary Waldorf education.
2. Explore and evaluate innovative practices in Waldorf education.
3. Contribute to the professional development of present and future educators in Waldorf schools.

This chapter provides a description of how teachers, teacher trainers, and trained researchers conduct mixed-method projects with an emphasis on qualitative action research. One of the studies is described in more detail to provide an example of how the research projects contribute towards each of the three program aims. The chapter starts by describing some of the developments in Dutch Waldorf schools in particular, and in Dutch society in general, that lead up to the program.

Transitions of Waldorf Education in the Netherlands

The initiative for the program Values and Value of Waldorf Education arose from two heartfelt wishes within the movement of Waldorf schools in the Netherlands. The first was to strengthen the quality of children's everyday educational experiences in Waldorf schools; the second was to strengthen the voice and position of Waldorf education in the ongoing national debate regarding purpose and quality of education in and for contemporary and future societies. Both wishes and the urgency that is felt to work on their realization in practice are related to substantial, perhaps even fundamental, changes that occurred in the practices and perceptions of Waldorf education in the Netherlands over the past two decades.

   Waldorf schools have been part of Dutch society for nearly a century. Over this time, these schools have experienced the freedom they need to offer the education they value. Waldorf schools are based on the educational philosophy developed by the Austrian founder of the anthroposophical movement, Rudolf Steiner (1861–1925). The development of individual children through pedagogical and educational experiences is approached from the assumption that this individual development is directly linked with the development of society and mankind as a whole. Waldorf pedagogy, didactics, and curriculum are aimed at helping students to develop into beings who are willing and able to contribute towards a just, peaceful, and sustainable society:

-   by intentionally shaping their participation in the economic realm of society from the perspective of fraternity;
-   by becoming knowledgeable and active in the social realm from the perspective of equality;
-   and by engaging in cultural and spiritual realms from the perspective of inner freedom.

(Steiner, 1996)

As such, Waldorf education is 'world-centered', in the sense that it is "focused on our worldly existence, that is our existence *in, with* and *for* the world" (Biesta, 2012, p. 94).

In Waldorf education, both learning and teaching are understood as creative processes in which intellectual, social, practical, and artistic development are integrated and balanced to afford children the opportunity to unfold their human potential and their humanity to its fullest. These processes are tailored to meet the natural receptivity and needs of children for them to choose and realize their individual paths through life as free, morally responsible beings. During early childhood, education focuses on physical and playful exploration of self and world. Elementary education has a strong focus on developing artistic expression and social capacities and children are encouraged to explore the world through conscious imagination. As the rational, abstract power of the intellect emerges, adolescents focus on ethics, social responsibility, and mastery of complex and rigorous subject matter (Pope Edwards, 2002).

In many respects, educational experiences in Dutch Waldorf schools throughout the twentieth century were similar to those in the initial years of Dutch Waldorf education. Principles for teaching, curriculum content, school traditions, and materials used in classes and furnishings underwent only a few changes. However, shared understandings, values, expectations, practices, and traditions in Dutch society where education was taking place were changing considerably due to, for instance, technological innovation and changing needs of children growing up in this society. These changes influenced society's definition of good education. Towards the end of the century, the quality of education was defined by the extent to which it contributed to the economic progress of society. From this perspective, good education coaches students in the process of obtaining specific knowledge, skills, and attitudes which allow them to qualify for participation in the economy as (young) adults (Dutch Educational Council, 2013). This includes qualifications for specific professions and more general qualifications such as literacy; both types of qualifications create a pathway to earning a decent salary and social status. Cognitive knowledge and skills play a lead role in this qualification process and standardized, quantifiable tests and exam results are used to evaluate educational quality.

While this perception of good education was far too limited for Waldorf educators, it did raise questions regarding the changes that might be needed to meet the evolving needs of children and society. After all, Waldorf schools fully intend to offer educational experiences that help children find and shape a meaningful way to participate in current and future societies; this implies that they need to be prepared appropriately for active participation in society's institutions, practices, and traditions. The question of change became even more urgent as government assessments showed that math and literacy development stayed behind in Waldorf schools and some schools were, albeit temporarily, placed under close supervision by the Dutch Inspectorate of Education. An analysis of a large cohort of students in Dutch high schools in 1999 showed that while Waldorf students overall were well developed in non-cognitive domains, they lagged behind their peers from mainstream education in math and literacy skills. It also showed these students performed poorer on tasks that required skills that were likely to serve them well in higher education or in jobs that require a person to perform under time pressure or take tests or successfully complete tests (Steenbergen, 2009).

In the year 2000, Dutch Waldorf schools made the transition into the official state system of exams and regulations. Although they still experience a high degree of freedom in *what* and *how* they teach, notable changes in these areas have taken place as a result. In primary education, the transition has resulted, for instance, in a much stronger emphasis on standardized teaching and assessment. Schools designated more time and resources to math and literacy; many schools introduced standardized teaching methods and materials for these subjects rather than have every teacher develop their own lesson plans, lesson content, and didactic methodology, and the use of standardized, government approved math and literacy assessments has become common practice in most primary schools. Math and literacy abilities of Waldorf pupils in the Netherlands are now on par with, or above, those of their peers. However, many parents, and teachers, too, worry that an important quality of Waldorf teaching—the artistic process through which teachers create their lessons—has been compromised in the process. Worries are also voiced about the reliance on standardized tests to evaluate different aspects of children's developmental process, rather than a teacher's holistic observations and understanding of the child.

The transition also held consequences for the educational experiences of high school students. Traditionally, all Waldorf students left school at the end of the twelfth grade with a descriptive assessment of their developmental process and resulting cognitive, artistic, social, and practical skills, knowledge and understandings on a broad range of subjects. Following the transition, students also obtain official qualifications through national examination, as an integrated part of their school trajectories. These qualifications provide entry into higher education institutes and, eventually, the labor market. Now Waldorf high school students no longer have heterogeneous year groups throughout, but are streamed into (cognitive) ability tiers, either from the start of high school or as they enter the higher grades. Furthermore, students who follow a pre-vocational track now leave high school after grade 10, while students in a general track do so after grade 11 or 12, depending on whether they aim to study at an applied or a research university. As a consequence, high school students now spend a greater amount of their time preparing for exams; typically working on narrowly defined topics and skills and strongly focused on cognitive aspects of learning. This comes at the expense of more traditional Waldorf lessons; these address broad topic fields, have an integrated approach to cognitive, artistic, and practical development, and are aimed to foster a gradual deepening of students' understanding of self, the world, and their inherent connectedness.

Within Waldorf schools, it is acknowledged that these developments have changed community interactions and have influenced individual student learning experiences in a range of developmental domains—cognitive, artistic, social, and practical. Whether these changes are perceived to be for better or for worse depends on whom you ask. The general understanding is that these changes effectively facilitate students' abilities to meet societal expectations. At the same time, it is also felt that these changes require educators to re-examine how their core values about children, learning, and teaching, can be ensured and brought to life within these changed learning environments. This need is felt even more strongly as an increasing number of Waldorf teachers have not been specifically trained in Waldorf pedagogics and didactics; these teachers generally have limited knowledge and understanding of the core principles of Waldorf education and of the particular image of a human being that forms its foundation (see, for instance, Pedagogical Section Council, 2017 for a description of these principles). This development is related to increased numbers of students enrolling in Waldorf schools. As Waldorf schools moved up on national rankings, more and more parents (and students) have come to see Waldorf education as a positive alternative to mainstream education.

Shifting Perspectives on Good Education

The second wish, which is to strengthen the voice and position of Waldorf education in the ongoing national debate regarding purpose, value, and quality of education, is relatively new. While the understanding within the Waldorf movement has always been that the educational experiences that are offered to children in their schools are of great value to child and society, Dutch society's perception of Waldorf education was often skeptical or even highly critical. These days, Waldorf education is recognized by parents, as well as by educational specialists and researchers, as an example of formative education that not just qualifies or 'schools' children to participate in society's institutions and practices, but that prepares them, in useful and valuable ways, for life in general. Didactical practices, such as the integrated use of rhythmic movement during math lessons that used to be regarded as outlandish and 'typical Waldorf', have now become regular features in many mainstream Dutch schools.

This new perception reflects a gradual shift in the way 'good' education is defined and regulated within our society. Over the past decade, parents, teachers, researchers, and even politicians are voicing their concerns regarding the 'narrow' perception of society's purpose for education. This partly arises from a growing awareness that the educational experiences we offer children in our current school system probably do little towards preparing them for the actual requirements of our future societies. Societies are changing so rapidly that we simply no longer know or can foresee which particular qualifications, or sets of knowledge, skills, and attitudes, will be required and useful for future work and life. In addition, a need is felt to interact with each other and with the natural world in a more respectful, sustainable way. As a result, what we, as a society, see as the purpose of education, and how we define good education accordingly, is shifting towards a more holistic and perhaps more 'human' orientation. Yes, becoming qualified for the economic domain is an important goal, but so is, for instance, internalizing the democratic values, traditions, and norms of our society; or developing identities that incorporate the fundamental values of our humanity, such as compassion, love, and a sense of connectedness with the world.

Furthermore, educational experiences are also seen as an important experimental setting for children to discover—and practice—mature ways of expressing their individual freedom; mature in the sense that they become willing and able to consider and relate their personal wishes and needs in the light of those of others and of the world around them (Biesta, 2012). In a way, society's perspective on education is becoming less narrowly focused on economic purposes, and, instead, becoming more broadly focused on human qualities; as such it might be seen as becoming more 'world-centered'.

These days, the Dutch Waldorf movement actively participates in national debates on the quality of education, schools participate in national innovative educational projects, and educational researchers turn to Waldorf schools in search of effective alternative curricula and teaching. From within the Waldorf movement in the Netherlands the need is felt to develop a more contemporary vocabulary to jointly examine, evaluate, and communicate Waldorf schools' understandings and practices in a meaningful way.

Values and Value of Waldorf Education: Research Program

At my appointment as program director, I was given the assignment to develop a program that will inspire, fuel, expand, and deepen the ongoing dialogue about what we consider 'good education' for present and future generations. This dialogue needs to be an ongoing and integrated part of the profession of the (Waldorf) educators and of their professional development. The same goes for other professionals within the field of education, such as school leaders, educational researchers, or governmental officials who develop educational policy and assess and enforce schools' compliance with state instituted educational goals, rules, and regulations.

To this purpose, we develop activities that 1) help build knowledge and understanding of purposes and practices in contemporary Waldorf education; 2) explore and evaluate innovative practices in

Waldorf education; and 3) contribute to professional development of (future) educators in Waldorf schools. Program activities include, for instance, lectures, workshops, (re)development of teacher training courses, dialogue sessions, and publications. However, the core of our program consists of collaborative research activities of what is known as the 'Knowledge Circle'. Such Knowledge Circles are a common practice at Dutch universities of applied sciences. Headed by a professor (e.g., program director), these circles bring together practitioners from within a particular work field and/or trained researchers to collaboratively explore emerging themes of interest through applied research activities.

As a program director, I have identified and positioned the current theme of the Knowledge Circle as the development of children's sense of autonomy, in communion with others and the world, as a core value of contemporary Dutch Waldorf education. I have developed theoretical frames and methodological approaches that integrated anthroposophical and scientific understandings from which the (practitioner) researchers have designed their individual research projects. Furthermore, I supervise the research projects and design the collaborative work sessions of the Knowledge Circle. These activities allow me to synthesize findings from different projects and to reflect on how these understandings and practices might transfer to other work settings within the respective work fields.

To form our Knowledge Circle, a call went out to practitioners who worked in Waldorf education or who had a special interest and/or expertise regarding Waldorf education. The call explained the theme, objectives, and the methodological orientation of the research program, and invited practitioners to formulate a research question regarding an issue they encountered during their work as educational practitioners related to the theme. Our circle currently includes a primary school teacher, two secondary school teachers, a school psychologist, two teacher trainers, and a former secondary teacher who now works for the national Waldorf movement in Flanders, Belgium. These circle members were selected from 70 applications; they have earned at least a relevant Masters degree from an applied or research university. They are relieved from regular (educational) assignments for one day a week in order to work on their research project. Every five weeks, our circle meets for a collaborative work session for a full afternoon. Depending on their needs, members can work either individually or in collaboration with the program director or with their fellow research practitioners on designated research days between these sessions.

Each circle member has developed a project regarding an issue or question he or she personally encountered in their educational practice, but that they understood to be relevant for other practitioners as well. Current projects focus on teaching intellectually gifted children; the value of main lessons for students and teachers; perceptions of artistic learning and teaching; purposeful and meaningful assessment of teaching and learning; aspired images of adulthood held by teachers and students in contemporary Waldorf schools; and realities of adulthood for former Waldorf students. Our circle members conduct most of their research projects within the schools and educational contexts in which they work as practitioners. We regard their research as action research, in the sense that "action research combines a substantive act with a research procedure; it is action disciplined by enquiry, a personal attempt at understanding, while engaged in a process of improvement and reform" (Hopkins, 2002, p. 42). In our projects, this 'substantive act' typically takes the form of a cumulative dialogue within an educational setting that is primed by a thoroughly thought-out set of interview questions, posed by the practitioner researcher, regarding specific practices or understandings within that educational community.

The Knowledge Circle is now moving into its third year. I explicitly set up our Knowledge Circle sessions as a learning opportunity through which we can develop a (shared) understanding of practical and conceptual issues that will help us to contribute to improvement and reform of educational practice. Circle members take on the role of critical friend in each other's projects. These sessions offer an opportunity to collaboratively explore theoretical, methodological, and process related questions that arise over the course of each project and to develop skills to tackle these. For instance, conducting in-depth semi-structured interviews was part of the methodology of every project. For some researchers, this was a new experience. During several sessions throughout the previous two years, we specifically worked on designing interview questions, conducting interviews, and analyzing interview data. During these sessions, we would use texts from research handbooks for preparatory reading; sometimes sessions would start with a short lecture; topics would then be explored through dialogue and in a more hands-on way, for instance by practicing interviews and offering each other feedback on skills and content.

As a part of each circle session, we also engage in dialogue to explore theoretical questions, interpretations, and understandings that arise over the course of the projects. During these dialogues, each participant contributes understandings from a range of sources. *Professional understandings* refer to the often implicit and intuitive practical knowledge that each of us has developed through our professional interactions in educational settings. We use them to give meaning to our professional actions in practice; sometimes these understandings have developed into a personal theory of practice. However, these understandings or theories have not been verified or evaluated in a methodologically sound and rigorous (scientific) way. *Personal understandings* refer to our individual values and our life experiences in general; they constitute our personal belief systems and shape the way we give meaning to life and our being in general. *Scientific understandings* are also included in these dialogues. For example, these scientific understandings are based on the best and most up-to-date empirical evidence, as well as established theoretical concepts, models, and theories that are not (yet) necessarily validated through empirical research; they present helpful perspectives or offer alternative explanations for what is observed and experienced in our research practice.

Finally, *anthroposophical understandings* are derived from the works of Rudolf Steiner, but also work from authors who reflect on Steiner's theories, concepts, and understandings, or interpret these from a contemporary perspective. During this process, we build on pre-existing knowledge, we readjust existing knowledge, and we give meaning to newly gained information and experiences. Through this process, each circle member develops a personal, unique understanding of the educational reality we participate in. As we move through multiple cycles in which we question, criticize, and put to the test new knowledge and understandings, we also develop 'co-owned' and 'co-authored' temporary shared bodies of knowledge and understanding.

Since the Knowledge Circle began, projects have proceeded through multiple cycles in which research questions and understandings are formulated, explored in theory and in practice, tested in practice, and evaluated with fellow researchers and practitioners. During the first year, researchers focused on designing their projects and collecting data. As part of this process they checked the perceived relevance of the issue among a broad group of educational practitioners. Primary stakeholders were identified and plans developed to ensure that project findings would eventually reach them. Researchers created overviews of existing knowledge, understandings, and practices from different perspectives (i.e., general scientific and Waldorf specific). They used these explorations to develop workable research questions, research plans, and instruments for data collection. Data were collected from (scientific) literature, school documents, (semi-) standardized questionnaires, in-depth interviews, and classroom observations.

During the second year, circle members focused on analyzing data, on checking validity of findings, descriptions, and understandings with stakeholders, and on developing 'products' that allowed them to share project findings with stakeholders. Quantitative data were analyzed using descriptive statistics. However, collected data were mostly qualitative and we used a grounded theory approach for analyses. In each project, we looked for themes that emerged from descriptions of practice and perceptions of the participants as they were expressed in the interviews (see, for instance, Birks & Mills, 2011 for a practical guide). In some projects, we applied an adaptation of grounded theory in which these data were also analyzed using a 'top-down' approach. Coding categories were created based on evidence, concepts, and theories derived from literature reviews and educational practices. Findings derived through both approaches were compared and differences explored, for instance through additional interviews, observations, or further literature reviews. Understandings that developed in each new phase of the project were used to re-evaluate previous understandings and to readjust plans for following steps and phases (for a more detailed description of this kind of mixed-method approach see, for instance, Siraj & Mayo, 2014).

During the second year, each circle session focused on a particular research project. The researcher of this project would provide in advance a written, up to date text describing the project, listing questions or topic s/he would like the group to focus their written and oral feedback on. During the sessions, the researcher presented the project and (initial) findings and understandings. They received detailed written feedback on the texts they provided; feedback on their presentation came by way of an image or metaphor describing qualities of the research process as observed by the critical friends—often these were images derived from the natural world. After this, all the questions, ideas, and suggestions that arose through the reading and the presentation were collected and the presenting researcher chose which of these the following dialogue session would focus on. Sometimes the dialogue was aimed at developing understanding of particular theoretical concepts; at other times its focus was more practical, such as solving methodological puzzles or the collaborative interpretation of data.

As we have now entered the third and final year of this particular Knowledge Circle, our meetings focus on formulating and communicating findings and practical implications for teachers and teacher training that follow from our research findings. We illustrate our recommendations with examples obtained through our research activities and with sets of questions that practitioners might use to explore how the findings and recommendations might be relevant and applied in their educational settings. By doing so, we aim to help educational practitioners to further develop their sense of agency regarding finding ways to transform theoretical understandings from research into actual practices.

An Example of Practitioner Research: Teaching Intellectually Gifted Children in Waldorf Schools

Saskia is a former Waldorf primary school teacher who now works as a school psychologist at a training and advisory institute for Waldorf schools. She found that over the past few years more and more schools started asking for advice and training on how to teach cognitively gifted children in kindergarten and primary Waldorf classrooms. Teachers indicate that they struggle to offer these children teaching experiences that are challenging enough to keep them fully engaged and to learn new things, without always having to separate them from class lessons and the communal learning experiences they offer. Traditionally, in Waldorf schools, literacy and numeracy skills are not taught explicitly until first grade. In kindergarten, children encounter numeracy and literacy concepts only implicitly as they participate in activities that are part of everyday life, such as baking bread or washing up activities, or through oral storytelling and singing.

However, as teachers find that increasing numbers of older kindergartners are highly motivated to develop, for instance, their reading and writing skills, kindergarten classes now typically offer one (half) day a week in which the elder children engage in explicit 'learning' activities. Once in first grade, many of these highly motivated children are well advanced in their math and literacy skills and show a seemingly insatiable thirst for knowledge; they engage with new learning tasks with strong task orientation and great creativity. Teachers face the task of finding ways to help these children develop a healthy and balanced way of engaging with cognitive, artistic, practical, and social aspects of learning and being. Designing learning experiences that allow these children to develop the will to work through difficulties and to become engaged in new processes is also a particular challenge. This not only requires specific understandings of how gifted children learn and develop, but also pedagogical sensitivity to unravel their individual developmental challenges, as well as inventiveness and creativity to develop appropriate practices, contents, and experiences for these individual children and the class they are part of. Despite their efforts to meet the needs of these children, teachers and parents find that, over time, many of these children seem to lose their intrinsic motivation for learning; they develop a negative attitude towards school and learning. Some develop performance anxiety, and many no longer develop and perform according to their (cognitive) abilities.

Saskia's aim for her research project is to provide class teachers and remedial teachers with tools and understandings that will help them to create wholesome educational experiences for gifted children that are in accordance with intentions and understandings of Waldorf education. Saskia approached her project from several angles. She conducted an ongoing literature review to develop an overview of what is known from empirical scientific studies about gifted children and their educational needs. She analyzed literature on Waldorf practices and theory in order to provide an overview of core teaching principles and understandings that might have specific implications for the understanding of, and teaching practices for, gifted children. Saskia also developed a questionnaire that was filled out by 52 out of the 70 Dutch Waldorf primary schools. Analysis of the data allowed her to develop an understanding 1) of how giftedness was generally perceived and approached in Dutch Waldorf schools; 2) of teaching practices aimed at gifted children; 3) the difficulties and challenges schools encountered in this process of teaching gifted children; 4) of successful factors in this process; 5) and of what schools perceived as 'good' practices. In the analyses, descriptive statistics were used and a grounded theory approach was applied in order to see what themes emerged from the open-ended questionnaire data. The collection of good practices was expanded during Saskia's observations in classrooms and during her training sessions with teachers. Examples were analyzed to understand to what extent they reflect scientific findings and Waldorf understandings of what constitutes appropriate practice in the teaching of gifted children. Examples of practices that were considered 'good' from both mainstream and Waldorf perspectives were further explored through in-depth interviews with teachers.

Saskia's research has given her a deeper understanding of what teachers need with regard to specific knowledge and skills to further develop their ability to create good practices in teaching gifted children. In the training courses for individual teachers or school teams, Saskia and her colleagues have incorporated the understandings she developed through the analyses of the literature, questionnaire data, observations, and interviews. Examples of good practices she encountered are now also part of the courses and are used to help teachers to design special projects or extended learning activities together with the gifted children, rather than for them. As a result, projects revolve around topics for which children show intrinsic motivation. However, rather than just using these projects to meet the child's need for cognitive challenge, projects also include activities that encourage children to engage and persevere in activities that they find more challenging or less interesting; they include opportunities to develop understanding, skills, and a relationship with the subjects through artistic and practical activities as well, and children are invited to share their projects with the class.

Saskia intends to explore the teaching and learning of gifted children more specifically from the point of view of these children themselves. Her encounters with gifted children have particularly sparked her interest to further investigate the need for autonomy of gifted children. Together with a remedial teacher from a Waldorf school, she is developing a self-assessment instrument for teachers to help them develop their understanding of how their classroom practices support the needs of gifted children.

Final remarks

Within the program Values and Value of Waldorf Education, research activities are conceived and practiced as a means to develop a shared, evolving body of understanding of educational processes, teaching, and child development in the context of Waldorf education. During the research process, Knowledge Circle members and program director collaboratively and individually explore, examine, and extend personal perceptions, experiences, pre-existing knowledge, and intuitions, as well as perceptions of other individuals or groups. Building this shared body of knowledge and practice is a cyclic and iterative process in which they move back and forth between abstract understandings and actual practice in schools and classrooms. Action research offers a way to treat abstract and practical knowledge, understandings, and experiences not as separate entities, but rather as different viewing points to observe children, ourselves, and our world. As it is, the program's practice of collaborative participation in educational action research contributes to the professional development of both educational practitioners and researchers. The collaborative research activities of the Knowledge Circle deepen both our shared and individual understanding of the educational realities we are part of. They also deepen our understanding of how each of us may further contribute towards educational realities that will help children find their way towards becoming "free human beings who are able of themselves to impart purpose and meaning to their lives" (Steiner, 1972, p. 23).

References

Biesta, G. J. J. (2012). The educational significance of the experience of resistance: Schooling and the dialogue between child and world. *Other Education: The Journal of Educational Alternatives, 1*(1), 92–103.

Birks, M. & Mills, J. (2011). *Grounded theory. A practical guide.* Los Angeles, CA: Sage.

Dutch Educational Council (2013). *A narrow view on education* [Onderwijs Raad (2013). Een smalle kijk op onderwijs]. The Hague: Dutch Educational Council.

Hopkins, D. (2002). *A teacher's guide to classroom research* (3rd edn). Philadelphia, PA: Open University Press.

Pedagogical Section Council (2017). The seven core principles of Waldorf education. In A. Leibner (Ed.), *The seven core principles of Waldorf education*. Chatham, NY: Waldorf.

Pope Edwards, C. (2002). Three approaches from Europe: Waldorf, Montessori, and Reggio Emilia. *Early Childhood Research & Practice: An Internet Journal on the Development, Care, and Education of Young Children, 4*(1).

Siraj, I. & Mayo, A. (2014). Methods and sample of the child and family case studies. In *Social class and educational inequality. The impact of parents and schools* (pp. 39–63). Cambridge: Cambridge University Press.

Steenbergen, H. (2009). *Waldorf and mainstream schools compared. A study on the effectiveness of Waldorf and mainstream high schools* [Vrije en reguliere scholen vergeleken. Een onderzoek naar de effectiviteit van Vrije scholen en reguliere scholen voor voortgezet onderwijs]. Groningen: Gion.

Steiner, M. (1972). Foreword by Marie Steiner to Rudolf Steiner's Ilkley lecture cycle. In R. Steiner, *A Modern Art of Education* (p. 23). Forest Row, UK: Rudolf Steiner Press.

Steiner, R. (1996). *Education as a force for social change. Lectures.* Hudson, NY: Anthroposophic Press.

30

Holistic Education in Thai Buddhist Schools

Prapapat Niyom

In this project in Thailand, Buddhist principles (BP) were integrated into schools as a way to support whole child education. The Roong Aroon School (RAS) research team provided leadership to Buddhist Approach Schools (BAS). The Buddhist principles serve as a key factor to encompass whole-child development and to engage active learners with values, mindfulness, and self-actualization.

Background

Over a century ago, prior to the establishment of the Ministry of Education, the first Thai schools were established in Buddhist temples, with monks teaching only Thai boys to read, write, solve mathematical problems, as well as study BP. Subsequently, the Ministry of Dhamma-Karn (Education) was established to launch a conventional school system that combined BP in the curriculum (Education Management Information System Centre (EMISC), n.d.). In 1941, the name of the ministry was changed to the Ministry of Education. Consequentially, Thai schools, public and private alike, have been required to teach ethics as one of the main subjects in their curricula (Chaiyaphon, 2011). These facts serve as evidence that Buddhism has been the foundation of Thai education for many years. Another fact that substantiates the importance of Buddhism as our national foundation is the high percentage of Buddhists in Thailand, 94.6%, according to the National Statistical Office, 2015. However, every Thai is free to choose his/her religion, as well as the type of school they attend. Recently, BP in the curriculum have declined and can only be found in the ethics section of social studies in the compulsory curriculum of the Thai education system.

During the first education reform period, 1997–2006, the BAS model was designated to be one of the five additional innovative programs proposed for schools to choose their approach to education reform. At present, 22,736 schools out of the 30,816 conventional public schools joined the project, incorporating traditional practices and extra activities in addition to the regular curriculum (Bureau of Educational Innovation Development, Ministry of Education, 2017).

Paradoxical Aspects in Thai Buddhist Schools

The Thai BAS agreed that adopting BP into the teaching and learning practices of their school systems could facilitate the ultimate goal of a well-rounded person in all dimensions, including psychomotor and cognitive skills, as well as building the students' character. However, the curriculum and pedagogy still depend on the existing curriculum, which focuses primarily on the cognitive domain. BAS, in a conventional schooling system could hardly achieve whole child development, especially with respect to helping students develop moral values. In order to manage two different directions in their schools, BAS decided to combine traditional and disciplined Buddhist activities with the conventional classroom teaching, in the hope that the students would improve their learning outcomes as well as their moral values.

Subsequently, during the fifth to the seventh years of the project, measures were established to evaluate the BAS program. A set of 29 indicators was formulated from the analyzed evidence of an earlier research study that focused on the status of BAS (Niyom, 2015). The indicators represented both the "input factors" and the "outputs and outcomes", and were then organized into five categories of best practice: 1) the seven elements of physical environments; 2) the four Buddhist holy day activities; 3) the five extra learning activities and contemplative practices; 4) the five general good behaviors, such as smiling, bowing nicely to pay respect, a healthy diet, saving or economizing, and learning with perseverance; 5) the eight supportive factors for the Buddhist way of living, such as:

- not selling junk food in school;
- not scolding students;
- appreciatively announcing good practices in front of the morning assembly;
- reflecting on those good deeds during home room;
- writing a journal of good deeds experienced by teachers and students;
- and passing the minimum standard test of Dharmma Sueksa;
- meditating at the beginning of each meeting and regularly having monks teach in the school.

(Bureau of Educational Innovation Development, Ministry of Education, n.d.).

Unfortunately, these 29 indicators themselves led to an increased concentration on extracurricular activities and attained only some specific outcomes while continuing to separate ethics from classroom learning.

In order to nurture the human core values of self-awareness and interconnectedness in oneself and the cosmos, BAS was compelled to respond to those indicators and the national examination test scores. The BAS program then faced a serious dilemma. Could this innovation positively impact educational reform? During 2010–2012, there was evidence of decreased budget support, from over 200 million baht to less than 20 million baht. The number of registered schools in this program dropped from over 20,000 to 12,000 schools, due to the promotion of more challenging education reform innovations than the BAS initiative (Bureau of Educational Innovation Development, Ministry of Education, n.d.).

These challenges were noticed by Roong Aroon School Foundation (RASF), which had been experimenting with its own holistic integration of Thai BAS into its school curriculum and pedagogy, from its inception 20 years earlier. From 2007 to 2008, the RASF has been involved with the public BAS program by providing training for the BAS coaching team. The training is for almost 1,200 personnel in all parts of the country (Niyom, 2008). The RASF also launched an additional follow-up program by arranging peer coaching to those BAS schools. Subsequently, RASF was invited to join the advisory committee on the screening and nominating of awards for best practices of the BAS in 2014.

Upon increased involvement, the RASF became more convinced that it should propose research that would be more conducive to sharing its knowledge with the BAS. The research proposal titled, "The Transformation of Buddhist Oriented Schools as the Basic Bovorn Community" was submitted to the Thailand Research Fund. The proposal was written to promote a holistic perspective in the integration of BP and the 27 best practices in the BAS in 2014. A three-year participatory action research and development project was granted for the period of January 2015 to March 2017.

Research Focus

The RASF had 20 years' experience with implementing holistic approaches. Thus it became one of the most important contributing elements in the BP objective to introduce human core values that can be developed and integrated into the school curriculum and pedagogy. The establishment of the required BP into the school's organization were analyzed and developed as tools and indicators for the selected schools. Basically, those implementation tools were only guidelines, which could be adjusted according to each school's local context. The research revealed just how much these target schools were able to achieve whole school development as they applied the BP core concepts to the school curriculum.

Analyzing the BP Essence: Application to Schooling

Considering the meaning of education in terms of BP, Somdej Phra Buddhakosajarn[1] (Payutto, 1988/2012) suggested, in his distinguished text of *Buddha Dharma*, that we use a synonym for the Buddha's teaching in the term, Sikhaboth, while calling those who practice Buddha's teaching a Sekkha person. It was widely known that this Pali word Sikha, or Sekkha, or Sueksa in Sanskrit represents the original meaning of education in the Thai language. Actually, the heart of the Buddha's teaching means "right practice" and is called the Noble Eightfold Path. When applied to everyday life The Eightfold Path enables us to become enlightened. Imparting these principles into education encourages the student to engage in self-practice so that they understand their interconnectedness with the cosmos, thereby achieving the ultimate goal of enlightenment.

However, when the modern schooling system adopted the term of education, the previous Buddhist interpretation was diluted from its original meaning. Instead of maintaining the holistic dimension, the conventional education system increasingly depended on a standard curriculum that led to content-coverage and test-score based outcomes.

In contrast, throughout RASF's 20 years, there has been continuous experimentation with how much the school could benefit from the original interpretation of Sikha and from accommodating such a holistic perspective. Roong Aroon School (RAS) was one of the pioneers in launching this concept into its school. Founded in 1997, RAS, a privately owned and not-for-profit organization, set out to be a BAS, with the aim to foster whole child development. Following the Buddha's teaching, decoded by Somdej Phra Buddhakosajarn (Payutto, 1988/2012) in his eminent text of *Buddha Dharma*, Tri-Sikha was one of the major principles of Buddhism that was then applied to the BAS program. Actually, the Tri-Sikha: Sila–Smadhi–Panna is the concise trifold pattern of the Noble Eightfold Path, which means the single way of nurturing and achieving the highest state of mind or enlightenment. This core principle focuses on self-practice or one's inner learning to nurture self-actualization, which is a central goal of BAS. RAS applied the Tri-Sikha principle into the school system curriculum to clearly state the ultimate goal for student learning.

Generally, the learning objectives are well defined in the three domains: knowledge, skills, and attitude. However, in the case of RAS, the attitude domain provides an opportunity to connect the value and wisdom based learning outcomes to the first two domains. This emphasis is appropriately placed as an objective of the school curriculum to adhere to the holistic mission of the school. The school, therefore, can become a place where students learn to nourish their inner life along with learning to acquire knowledge and skills.

Furthermore, RAS formulated a special template called, "One Page Lesson Plan" in order to integrate the value based objectives into the content, the learning process, and the evaluation plan. This template (Table 30.1) was the basic guideline for each teacher so that they could guide their classroom learning towards the development of the whole student. Accordingly, it became one of the practical tools for this action research.

Table 30.1 One-Page Lesson Plan: an integrated value objectives based lesson plan

Scope of content	Value based objectives			Process of learning	Evaluation
Subject Matter	Knowledge (Head)	Learning Skills (Hands)	Value (Heart)	Learning by doing & reflective share & learn	Process/tools Formative assessment & summative evaluation

Research Tools

In launching holistic concepts within the 27 target schools in this research, the three core Buddhist principles: the Tri-Sikha, the Galayanamitre–Yonisomanasigarn and Satipattathan, have been the foundation for tools and mechanisms incorporated into the school practices for research.

First principle: Tri-Sikha; Sila–Smadhi–Panna (self-discipline–mindfulness concentration—wisdom), is the first key element in the value based goal of BAS for whole child development. RAS described this first core principle as a holistic learning goal: Life is Learning or Learning is Life (Somdet Phra Buddhakosajarn) (Payutto, 1995).

Second principle: Galayanamitre to Yonisomanasigarn is interpreted by Steve Weissman (2011) as friendly guidance to wise reflection. This principle is derived from an initiative by Somdej Phra Buddhakosajarn in his book, *The Dawn of Education* (Payutto, 2002). This principle can be summarized in the golden phrase: "When the first glimpse of sunlight appears at dawn, it means that the sun will rise towards its highest peak". Similarly, when all the aspects of Galayanamitre to Yonisomanasigarn are promptly integrated into a student's learning process, then it is possible to reach their highest capacity to learn: "In RAS, the two principles were stated as the second core principle in a 'Value oriented academic system'" (Mohjhaw, Tubsree, & Chomdokmai, 2013).

Third principle: Satipattathan means mindful meditation. These are specific self-practices for developing the quality of mind into a state of wisdom where there is liberation from the two extremes of satisfaction and dissatisfaction. From RAS experience, it was found that the community of practice was the key success of BAS when the spiritual leadership among parents, school leaders, and teachers was cultivated. These adults changed their roles from being supervisors to learning partners of the students. This principle was stated as the third core principle, "Contemplative Community of Practices".

Buddhism in Schools: The Core Principles Framework

These three Buddhist Principles and their applications are presented in an interconnected cycle as shown in Figure 30.1.

The three principles were applied and presented to the target schools, together with each set of indicators for implementation. The following is the three sets of criteria and indicators used for implementing and evaluating tools in the 27 BAS target schools:

First Core Principle: Tri-Sikha

Criteria: Value oriented school curriculum and lesson plan with holistic learning goals.

Indicator: 11 sub-indicators covered the value oriented curriculum, integrated value objective lesson plan (See Table 30.1), mindful active learning processes and an embedded formative assessment system.

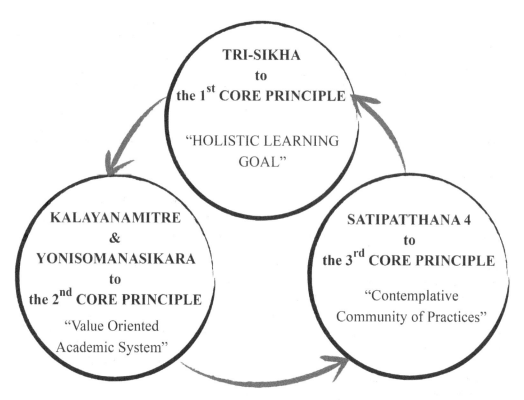

Figure 30.1   RAS's three core principles as a conceptual framework in applying Buddhism into the academic school system

Second Core Principle: Galayanamitre to Yonisomanasigarn

Criteria: Value oriented academic system.

Indicator: Four sub-indicators including being a mindful academic leader and a compassionate coach, nine sub-indicators for teachers being students' learning partners and creative value learning designers, and providing critical active learning opportunities in their classrooms.

Third Core Principle: Satipatthan 4

Criteria: Contemplative community of practices.

Indicator: Three sub-indicators for school leaders, teachers, students, and parents, including ongoing mindful meditation practice. Two sub-indicators of providing Buddhist voluntary activities for all, two sub-indicators for teachers and parents sharing and learning with the students.

The Research Process

The principles were designed to be a tangible operating system which the 27 target BAS could easily incorporate as regular ongoing practices in their planning, implementation and evaluation. The seven stages of action research for whole school development were launched with the following actions:

(1) The implementation of shared vision workshops where school leaders and teachers worked together in the application of Tri-Sikha so that each school's goals for education could be reached.

(2) The formulation of each school's goals and target achievements, including academic and student characteristics were used as guiding principles, instead of content-based curriculum.

(3) Several single lesson plan designs were created by the school's director and teacher teams in accordance with BAS goals that concentrate on value-based learning objectives.

(4) Coaching for active learning and formative assessment were introduced by applying Galayanamitre-Yonisomanasigarn practices that help teachers become more inspiring and connected with each student during classroom learning.

(5) Micro teaching from a selected lesson plan is performed in a real classroom setting in each school, along with the observations by teacher teams to help participate in the following After Action Review (AAR) meeting.

(6) A Professional Learning Community is established through researching conditions that support mindful reflection and dialogue. Before and After Action Review (BAR-AAR) involves regularly applying Galayanamitre–Yonisomanasigarn practices to provide the platform for friendly and constructive feedback and dialogue.

(7) A school reflective report, which includes scenes of school life and classroom performances, was delivered as a short VDO clip and prepared by the research team to include classroom implementations, BAR-AAR meetings as well as interviews with students, teachers, and the school director.

After launching the first stage of sharing visions with those 27 school leaders and teachers, the interactions and responses were active and enthusiastic. They were eager to move to the next stage of whole school curriculum and pedagogy development. Unfortunately, after reviewing the existing infrastructure and the facilities of each school, some schools were overwhelmed by the other special innovation projects, which had been adopted by the Ministry of Education. These schools could not bridge the gap between their existing program and a value-oriented approach. However, these difficulties were considered an opportunity to find alternatives for transformative change and the research team started to develop more and more practical tools. Still, seven schools were omitted from the project as they were unable to adjust their curriculum and institutional practices to accommodate these processes.

The research team had to work closely with the 20 remaining target schools and focus more on the single lesson plan design, classroom implementation, and on the AAR platform for the whole school project. They also developed and adjusted the simpler indicators for evaluation. For example, finally, all agreed to accept the VDO clip reports from the real classroom micro teaching and the BAR-AAR platform activities. During the experimental stages, some schoolteacher teams arranged a study visit to RAS to see how the value attitude emerges in a real classroom situation. They became even more eager to participate in the BAR-AAR platform right after the study of classroom observation. Some schools asked our research team to coach them at their schools, which really inspired most of the school directors and teachers. Eventually, the schools began to experiment with the tools themselves and gradually developed a whole-school direction with a clearer view of value- oriented curriculum and pedagogy.

Developing and Implementing Holistic Core Practices

Once the existing practices following the 29 factors were accepted, the RAS research team extended the implementation to include more meaningful activities linking the research tools to the whole school teaching and learning system. All 20 schools that shared in this research agreed that an appropriate operating system should be created and constructively implemented within the school timetable to transition to the crucial practices. After a few workshops of vision sharing and discussion among these schools and the RAS study visit, the "Value Oriented Curriculum and Learning" was selected as a tool for study and experimentation. The micro process of lesson plan design was undertaken and shared among the teacher teams. The lesson plan design process clarified how to articulate value achievement as one of the three main objectives (knowledge–skill–value) in each lesson plan.

Pilot micro teaching provided the opportunity to apply the designed lesson plan into the classroom. This was a tremendous opportunity for both the performing teacher and the observers to experience how the value oriented lesson plan could facilitate active learning. The students had more opportunity to play their roles as active learners. The observers were surprised that both teacher and students were more active and happy to learn; teachers were able to design lesson plans with their own objectives, instead of using the instant, ready-made ones. Accordingly, they could organize more active learning and let their students demonstrate their capability to not only understand the content, but also interpret the value of what they had learned. The result was a happier classroom of active learners, a significant improvement on the one-way, or transmission, teaching approach.

It was relevant to these 20 BAS that participated in the process of this action research that the BAS mission in education is to educate the students not only in the subject content (cognitive development), but also in the process of thinking and intellectual development. Some directors started the school change after bringing their teachers to observe the learning atmosphere in RAS. From their visit, they received a clear picture regarding how the teachers planned the lessons with three objectives; knowledge, skills, and values, and how all three were integrated into the classroom learning process. Observations also involved how the students connect the importance of the curriculum content to their day-to-day lives, which represents value learning.

For example, while visiting RAS, one of the BAS teams had an opportunity to join the field study of RAS students at a nearby village beside the mangrove area. The BAS team realized that in providing a learning activity between students and the villagers in their daily lives, the teachers can support the students in their understanding of the interconnectedness of people and nature. The students also learned gratitude and respect for the valuable contribution the villagers made to the community. This value aspect inspired the BAS team when they returned to their school, so they created the new integrated learning unit with a field study—a visit to a nearby fisherman's village. The whole school learning process contributed to the deeper appreciation of values from real life experiences. Moreover, the students mentioned how the villagers were also very happy and proud of themselves in guiding the students to understand their community's heritage.

In addition, the second tangible tool was the BAR-AAR (Before–After Reflection) platform of sharing values from the experimental value oriented classrooms. During the observation at RAS in the After Action Review (AAR) meeting, the BAS director and group of teachers noticed how the teachers and observing coaches reflected on the teaching and learning process, specifically in terms of how students met the objectives as well as how the teachers could improve their teaching in order to facilitate the students' knowledge and understanding. This compassionate feedback was inspiring for the teams in such a way that it focused more on the students' learning experiences rather than on the teachers' performance. Some directors returned to their schools with the idea that teachers should plan their lessons with three objectives, based on content, skills, and values. They also began to hold some AAR meetings. Incredibly, one school's director was able to help every teacher of every subject to design their own lesson plans.

The researchers visited each school twice to follow up by observing their classroom activities and participating in the AAR sessions. In the AAR, the researchers gave feedback based on the evidence of how much the students had achieved the learning objectives, which was related to their teaching. The teachers understood and accepted feedback that explained how to improve teaching approaches that foster whole child development. The researchers also gave suggestions on how to change their teaching approaches so that the students would come to learn the fundamental value of their lives. Some of the teachers stated that they had never experienced this kind of constructive feedback before; they appreciated it and promised to try their best to continue to elicit the benefits behind connecting curriculum content to real life experience.

The Findings and Lessons Learned

Right after the seven schools left the project, the research team had a good opportunity to reconsider and closely investigate central issues in the project. The research tools were the ones directly affecting the active change process. Once they were simplified and focused on classroom activities, the schools then let go of the tensions associated with the previous value lesson plan design. After the school visits, both to and from RAS and their schools, the situation has since improved. The research team realized that the most crucial tools handed to the BAS were those of the Galayanamitre–Yonisomanasigarn through our own Galayanamitre coaching role (a good guidance team for teachers and the school director). This finding revealed the most important key factor, even more so than the role of the research tools: the partnership between the research team and target schools. The experimental process provided the potential to move beyond the limitations of BAS while improving the learning community and moving forward to reach their ultimate objectives. On the other hand, this is also the platform of Galayanamitre and Yonisomanasigarn, to develop more awareness of Buddhist values in each teacher through real classroom situations. Teachers grew to be Galayanamitre to each other and themselves and created a nourishing and effective collaborative working environment. The effect of Galayanamitre and Yonisomanasigarn can arise within each teacher's mind, which affects the working environment and nurtures the teachers' souls.

It can be concluded that this research was using holistic sharing and learning experiences created from micro teaching within a whole school approach. Further findings from the project include three aspects. First, the design of a school-based curriculum was integrated into each lesson plan, which states the clear vision and ultimate goal of student achievement. Second, the important pair elements are the Galayanamitre and Yonisomanasigarn which develop a special skill for wise reflection and applies to group learning at every level, with students, teachers, and school leaders. The third element is the individual practice of mindfulness meditation to develop self-reflection and actualization. These practices were already established in the schools.

Notices and Expectations

In addition to school directors and teachers developing their programs and including learning activities that allow the value oriented curriculum and pedagogy to be established holistically, the students in the 20 schools also benefited immensely from this research. Since the research team had less involvement with the parents and community temples, the contemplative community of practice could not be fully evaluated. Last, in order to strengthen these schools to sustain and maintain their expertise, the research team planned to arrange a follow-up symposium for the 20 target schools to present and share their experiences, resulting from the research in the subsequent months. The researchers anticipate that the schools will possess the confidence to extend these experiences to coach the nearby schools or the schools in their networks.

Note

1 Prayudh Payutto is a well-known Thai Buddhist monk, an intellectual, and a prolific writer.

References

Bureau of Educational Innovation Development (n.d.). *Indicators for quality Buddhist schools.* Retrieved from www.vitheebuddha.com/main.php?url=about&id=34.

Chaiyaphon, C. (2011). *A vision towards education of the Chakri Monarch; His Majesty the King Rama 1–9.* Bangkok: Education Council of Thailand.

Education Management Information System Centre (EMISC) (n.d.). *History of Thai education.* Retrieved from www.moe.go.th/main2/article/e-hist01.htm.

Mohjhaw, A., Tubsree, C., & Chomdokmai, M. (2013). *Integration of the Buddhist Yonisomanasikara thinking framework with the problem solving cycle: Phenomenological research at Roong Aroon School.* Chonburi: Burapa University.

National Statistical Office (2015). *Statistical Yearbook Thailand.*

Niyom, P. (2008). *Coaching team development and pair participatory action research.* Bangkok: Roong Aroon School Foundation.

Niyom, P. (2015). *The transforming of the Buddhist approach schools as the basic Bovorn community.* Bangkok: The Thailand Research Fund.

Payutto, P. (Somdet Phra Buddhakosajarn) (1988, 2012). *Buddha Dhamma.* Bangkok. Retrieved from www.buddhistteachings.org.

Payutto, P. (Somdet Phra Buddhakosajarn) (1995). *Dhamma and Thai education.* Bangkok: Sahathammik.

Payutto, P. (Somdet Phra Buddhakosajarn) (2002). *The dawn of education.* Bangkok: Sahathammik.

Weissman, S. (2011). *Wise reflection: The importance of wise reflection in meditation.* Sri Lanka: BPS Transcription Project.

31

Many Layers, Many Dimensions
Building a New Science of Holistic Education

Elizabeth Spier, Frederik Leenknecht, and David Osher

A holistic (or "whole child") educational approach has been defined as attending to the cognitive, social, emotional, physical, and talent development of children and youth from diverse backgrounds (ASCD, 2012). A holistic education framework embodies relational and bioecological principles of child development.[1] Despite the promise of holistic education for improving educational outcomes and reducing disparities, a recent ten-country study suggests that there is a substantial gap between what is known about the benefits of holistic education and its consistent and effective implementation in schools. Fortunately, innovations in the science of learning and development can build our understanding of which holistic educational approaches are most effective for children of different ages and backgrounds, and innovations in implementation science can tell us how to make these approaches work in classrooms.

Children Develop Holistically, Within an Ecological Context

Children and youth develop and experience the world through cultural and linguistic lenses as well as through the webs of relationships and contexts in which they participate. Their individual attributes, which interact dynamically, include their genetic make-up; neurobiology; social, emotional, cognitive, physical, and ethical characteristics and competencies; temperament and personality; attitudes, values and mindsets; cultural and linguistic background; accumulated experience and knowledge; and how they perceive and make sense of world (Cantor, Osher, Berg, Steyer, & Rose, 2018). Although these factors interact to influence child and youth development, so do the qualities of the social and physical environments that children and youth experience, particularly those that they experience repeatedly over time, such as their family, their school, and the other organizational settings in which they participate regularly. These settings can be characterized by the extent to which they provide developmentally appropriate and culturally responsive conditions and opportunities for learning and development (Osher, Kendziora, Spier, & Garibaldi, 2014). These kinds of conditions are characterized by a positive social and emotional climate; sensitivity to trauma; emotional, intellectual, and physical safety; social, emotional, and cognitive support; challenge and engagement; meaningful learning opportunities; and interactions with adults and peers who are socially and emotionally competent and intellectually engaged (Osher, Kidron, DeCandia, Kendziora, & Weissberg, 2016). Opportunities provided by these settings include chances to develop healthy relationships with adults and peers; creativity, self-expression; social, emotional, and cognitive competencies; engagement, recognition, and leadership roles (Osher & Berg, 2018; Osher, Cantor, Berg, Steyer, & Rose, 2018).

Although many schools focus on cognitive development as if it were the only target of interest, such an approach is problematic for three reasons. First, there is an inextricable relationship between social, emotional, cognitive, and physical development; growth in one area is best facilitated by growth in all three (Cantor et al., 2018; Jones, Barnes, Bailey, & Doolittle, 2017; Osher, Kidron, Brackett, et al., 2016). Second, both context in general and the social and emotional conditions for learning mediate and moderate learning outcomes (Cantor et al., 2018; Osher et al., 2018). Third, schools do more than produce learners and workers; they also develop future parents and citizens. Although a focus on learning is important, learning is more than cognitive development and academic performance, and a whole child approach maximizes learning. This is particularly important for children who struggle with the impacts of adversity or who come from a background that lacks warmth, compassion, and strong, supportive relationships. For example, schools and early childhood educational settings can heighten human development and buffer the effects of poverty-related stress and other adversity on development through positive relationships and by direct targeting of self-regulation, executive function, and social and behavioral skills (Jones & Bouffard, 2012; Osher et al., 2018).

A whole child development framework promotes all dimensions of development from early childhood to young adulthood, including physical, social, emotional, cognitive, spiritual, and values-based learning. At their best, whole child settings integrate these components while supporting engagement, creativity, and the development of intrapersonal and interpersonal skills and related attitudes.

Holistic Education is Underrealized in Formal Education Systems

Education systems are largely unprepared to provide holistic education at scale. A recent study (Spier et al., 2017) mapped the extent to which formal education systems valued and provided education that supported the whole child (or at least some aspects beyond simply academic learning) in Western Europe (Belgium, France, Germany, Ireland, the Netherlands, Portugal, Spain, and the United Kingdom) and in North America (the United States and Ontario, Canada). The study found that holistic education is both highly valued and consistently provided in the pre-primary grades (kindergarten). However, as children enter primary school, most education systems rapidly narrow their focus to academic instruction that does not explicitly or intentionally address social, emotional, physical, expressive, and, in many cases, ethical needs. Non-cognitive aspects of children's development—social, physical, artistic, and so on—are increasingly seen as distinct from academic learning and not essential to core educational (i.e., academic) content. When these aspects of holistic development are addressed, it is often through a "menu" approach rather than an integrated, holistic approach, supporting only some areas of children's development, for some children, and at some ages. For example, in most of the countries in the study, arts education was universally provided to children in primary grades but tended to vanish from the curriculum once children entered secondary school—especially for those not on a "university track." Supports for physical development, social and emotional learning, and play-based learning and creative thinking faced a similar fate. Yet, adolescence is an extremely important period of development. In fact, adolescent brains show greater malleability of non-cognitive skills than of cognitive skills (Kautz, Heckman, Diris, ter Weel, & Borghans, 2008).

When educators feel strong pressure to boost academic achievement, other aspects of holistic education are not prioritized. Change toward addressing these aspects of learning can be costly, takes time, and involves a certain degree of uncertainty. Educators and policy makers are unlikely to make substantial changes in how classrooms and schools operate without a clear understanding of both why *and* how to do so. We know that within formal education systems, it is possible to provide holistic education to all children because that is what we do already at the pre-primary level. We now need to better understand how to make effective holistic education a reality from early childhood to young adulthood.

We Need to Know More About What Works to Support Holistic Development

Empirical evidence lends support for a holistic view of child development. There is an existing body of evidence for what works to support social and emotional learning, and some other aspects of children's holistic development. Yet, as is the case with much intervention research, there is a lack of ecologically valid empirical evidence for what works, in what contexts, with which children, and with what effects. This issue may not stop the scaling of holistic education in general but may compromise the scaling of *the right* supports in effective ways.

For example, studies conducted in France, Canada, and the United States have shown that musical training improves preschool children's cognitive skills in areas related to literacy (Anvari, Trainor, Woodside, & Levy, 2002; Chobert, François, Velay, & Besson, 2014; François, Chobert, Besson, & Schön, 2013; Moreno, Friesen, & Bialystok, 2011). A recent study of children attending Head Start preschools in the United States found that participation in arts activities (music, dance, and visual arts) over several months significantly reduced children's levels of a stress hormone (cortisol), relative to children who spent the time in typical homeroom activities (Brown, Garnett, Anderson, & Laurenceau, 2017). There is also evidence from Germany that music lessons improve preschool children's stress regulation (Kranefeld, 2015). We are left with a strong suggestion that the arts, or at least some aspects of the arts, may be beneficial for children's development and psychosocial well-being. Most of this evidence comes from preschools, and we also know that in formal education systems, the availability of arts programming is typically at its highest for younger children (Spier et al., 2017). Would older children also receive these same benefits from arts programming? Do children receive benefits from the arts if they are integrated into other learning activities, or only if they receive direct instruction in the arts? Without this information, it would be difficult to know how best to develop beneficial educational programming that integrates the arts in ways that are beneficial to children of a specific age and in a specific context. There are similar questions around other kinds of holistic educational supports—questions that we can increasingly answer using innovations in neurobiological sciences.

New and Innovative Research Tools Can Help Us Learn More

Although the science of learning and development demonstrates how tightly interrelated a child's developmental processes are and how they jointly produce the outcomes for which educators are responsible (Darling-Hammond, Cook-Harvey, Flook, Barron, & Osher, under review), many linkages of this "constructive web" (Fischer & Bidell, 2006) have not been fully explored, demonstrated, or translated into actionable strategies or results. We need information about how different children's skills develop across different situations and time. Teachers are still unclear exactly what works, and how they can implement it, particularly in a context with pressure on producing students with high academic learning outcomes, along pre-decided lines, and in a limited time.

In recent years, the integration of the fields of education and social neuroscience have produced promising insights to bridge the gap between academic knowledge and student learning on the one hand and effective teaching for whole child development on the other. The next sections look at neurological findings that have shown preliminary yet promising results for holistic education, and issues that have surrounded the implementation of these findings.

Neuroscience

Neurological techniques look at the structure and function of the brain. Brain structures that are not used decrease in size ("use it or lose it") while new experiences can shape the structure of the brain, so functionality and structure are closely interlinked. Neuroscience research makes use of technological devices that scan the cerebral blood flow or electrical activity of the brain. Two methods that track changes in cerebral blood flow, functional magnetic resonance imaging (fMRI) and functional near-infrared spectroscopy (fNIRS), provide high-resolution *spatial information*. They show which areas of the brain are activated upon the execution of certain (cognitive or manual) tasks or through various experiences. For example, fMRI has been used to examine how emotions are processed in the brain, with comparisons across cultural groups (Immordino-Yang, Yang, & Damasio, 2016). This type of brain imaging has shown the great extent to which cognition, emotion, and social learning are all interrelated (Immordino-Yang, 2011).

A second group of brain imaging techniques, such as electroencephalography (EEG) and event-related potentials (ERPs), assess changes in the electrical activity of the brain. They provide high-resolution *temporal information* and show us *when* information is processed and how children are engaged. For example, while engaging children in an activity such as sleeping, exercising, playing the violin, or solving a mathematical problem, researchers can monitor which brain areas are activated, in which sequence. They have the potential to explore and uncover the interconnection between different development areas.

Neuroscientists have recently begun exploring the integrated uses of both techniques (Antonenko, van Gog, & Paas, 2014), each of which comes with its advantages and limitations. Near-infrared spectroscopy has gained significant popularity among researchers because the devices are more compact, cost-effective, and allow for more ecologically valid research than other functional neuro-imaging techniques (Antonenko et al., 2014). Similarly, EEGs that traditionally require the wearing of an electrode skull cap that is connected to a machine, have currently been developed as wireless headsets (see products of *Advanced Brain Monitoring* or *NeuroSky*).[2]

Many studies have been conducted regarding the links between training or experience and brain structures or functions. For example, in 2008, Limb and Braun (2008) found through an fMRI scan that jazz musicians who improvise while playing showed increased activation of brain areas related to self-knowledge and a decrease in the self-inhibitory regions. Other research at Stanford University has used fNIRS to examine the association between humor and creativity in young children, as well as the effect of physical exercise on thoughts and feelings.[3] Neuroimaging studies have also shown that the prefrontal cortex in adolescents' brains is not yet fully developed, which provides a neurobiological explanation for the impulsivity and poor judgment often seen during adolescence (Kautz et al., 2008). In turn, these insights provide real input that can be valuable to strengthen holistic teaching and learning. For example, viewing mathematics education from this perspective leads to the suggestion of meditation to improve students' concentration and focus on material presented in a classroom (Vaninsky, 2017). Other counter-intuitive findings of neuroscience that are relevant for education include the idea that play is the best way for children to learn self-control, that rote memorization can be a stepping stone to using higher-order critical thinking and problem-solving skills, and that integrating arts into the curriculum can improve students' long-term memory of what is taught (Carey & Hardiman, 2014).

Multimedia

Like neurological research, multimedia technology continues to develop innovative techniques that enable us to better research holistic development processes. One method that has recently gained importance for education research is eye tracking (Holmqvist et al., 2011; Rodrigues & Rosa, 2017), because students take in most information through their eyes, and rely on their vision to execute tasks. For example, students' visual attention allocation data can be used to identify and analyze students' learning strategies, the interaction between students and teachers in the classroom, or the use of the teaching environment (Jarodzka, Holmqvist, & Gruber, 2017). These can then lead to improvements in students' learning, teachers' instructions or classroom design, and ultimately to increased holistic development.

Taken together, these and other emerging innovations in neuroscience and multimedia can and should be used to provide a more comprehensive and coherent picture of children's holistic development—a picture that can inform what needs to happen in classrooms.

We Need to Know More About How to Effectively Provide Holistic Education

There are innovations in technology that can provide us with a direct window into children's brain activity during classroom experiences. For example, the Australian Science of Learning Research Center hosts two experimental classrooms which allow for studying students' social behavior and cognitive learning in a natural setting. The educational neuroscience classroom, based at the University of Queensland, allows for precise measurement of brain activity, eye movements, and physiological responses that occur while individuals engage in learning. The Learning Interaction Classroom at the University of Melbourne is equipped with audio and video recording technology and has a one-way mirrored window through which classroom action can be observed by a team of scientists. By taking this kind of information and using dynamic, non-linear statistical modeling, we can learn how an individual child is affected by a specific experience at a specific time and in a specific place (the "Specificity Principle"), rather than just focusing on what is "typical" (Bornstein, 2018; Singer & Willett, 2003).

There is also a new impetus in the field to move away from solely relying on very lengthy and costly impact studies to learn whether innovations work in classrooms. For example, rapid-cycle evaluations (RCE), or micro-randomized trials, consist of series of low-cost and quick-turnaround evaluations that help researchers understand whether their interventions are having intended effects, when and for whom they are effective, and what factors moderate the interventions' effects (e.g., see Nesselroade, 2018; Klasnja et al., 2015). RCEs typically rely upon administrative data (such as student attendance) to track outcomes, so there are currently some limitations in terms of what kinds of interventions and outcomes can be studied using this methodology.

Evidence is necessary, but not sufficient. For innovations to work in schools, educators need to implement the innovations with fidelity to the key drivers and principles that underlie the interventions. This must be done *in a sustainable, scalable, but also nuanced manner* if we are to reach and address the needs of diverse learners in diverse contexts (Blase, Fixsen, & Duda, 2011; Dymnicki, Wandersman, Osher, & Pakstis, 2016). We need to not only find out what works, but also invest the time and resources required to bring innovations in neuroscience into all schools and classrooms, in ways that teachers can provide holistic education.

We need to develop the readiness and capacity of teachers and schools to implement fluently, efficiently, and with quality and understanding (Coburn, 2003). Building readiness and capacity entails addressing the affective, social, emotional, and cognitive barriers to change (Dymnicki et al., in press). We can build and enhance capacity by addressing both the affective and skills issues that undermine readiness and capacity (Hall, Dymnicki, Coffey & Brodowski, 2014) and through continuous quality improvement (CQI). CQI should be done in a manner that addresses the individuality of learning as well as variation of impact among individuals and environments. Implementation is a process, not an event, and readiness is not a moment in time. Both unfold in dynamic environments and diverse contexts (Chambers, Glasgow, & Stange, 2013). Quality implementation is not just an individual phenomenon; it depends upon the conditions for implementation, which include a leadership environment and school climate that support good implementation (Education Endowment Foundation, 2018).

In Conclusion

The promise of holistic education has been only partially fulfilled. We know that it is possible to support holistic development for all children, in typical education systems. However, more information is needed to help us understand exactly what types of support work best for children of different ages, backgrounds, and needs, and living and going to school in different contexts. Fortunately, new innovations in biological and behavioral research can help us fill in the gaps. There is also a great need to understand how to make holistic education work well in practice. Here, new innovations in implementation science can help us to identify more efficiently how to make holistic education a reality for all children and youth.

Elizabeth Spier, Frederik Leenknecht, and David Osher

Notes

1 "Bioecological" refers to the interaction between a child's genetic predispositions or potentialities and his or her environment.
2 For example, see www.advancedbrainmonitoring.com or http://neurosky.com
3 See https://nirs.stanford.edu/research

References

Antonenko, P. D., van Gog, T., & Paas, F. (2014). Implications of neuroimaging for educational research. In M. Spector, M. D. Merrill, J. Elen, & M. J. Bishop (Eds), *Handbook of research on educational communications and technology* (pp. 51–63). New York: Springer.

Anvari, S., Trainor, L., Woodside, J., & Levy, B. (2002). Relations among musical skills, phonological processing, and early reading ability in preschool children. *Journal of Experimental Child Psychology*, *83*, 111–130.

ASCD (2012). Making the case for educating the whole child. *Washington, DC: ASCD*. Retrieved from www.wholechildeducation.org/assets/content/mx-resources/WholeChild-MakingTheCase.pdf.

Blase, K. A., Fixsen, D. L., & Duda, M. (2011). *Implementation science: Building the bridge between science and practice*. Washington, DC: National Implementation Sciences Network.

Bornstein, M. H. (2018). Fostering optimal development and averting detrimental development: Prescriptions, proscriptions, and specificity, *Applied Developmental Science*, DOI: 10.1080/10888691.2017.1421424

Brown, E. D., Garnett, M. L., Anderson, K. E., & Laurenceau, J.-P. (2017). Can the arts get under the skin? Arts and cortisol for economically disadvantaged children. *Child Development*, *88*, 1368–1381.

Cantor, P., Osher, D., Berg, J., Steyer, L., & Rose, T. (2018). Malleability, plasticity, and individuality: How children learn and develop in context. *Applied Developmental Science*, DOI: 10.1080/10888691.2017.1398649

Carey, B. & Hardiman, M. (2014). *The cognitive science revolution: How brain research can improve teaching and make learning more fun*. Retrieved from www.americanprogress.org/events/2014/10/22/99531/the-cognitive-science-revolution/?elq=~~eloqua..type--emailfield..syntax--recipientid~~&elqCampaignId=~~eloqua..type--campaign..campaignid--0..fieldname--id.

Chambers, D. A., Glasgow, R. E., & Stange, K. C. (2013). The dynamic sustainability framework: Addressing the paradox of sustainment amid ongoing change. *Implementation Science*, *8*(117), 1–11.

Chobert, J., François, C., Velay, J., & Besson, M. (2014). Twelve months of active musical training in 8- to 10-year-old children enhances the preattentive processing of syllabic duration and voice onset time. *Cerebral Cortex*, *24*(4), 956–967.

Coburn, C. E. (2003). Rethinking scale: Moving beyond numbers to deep and lasting change. *Educational Researcher*, *32*(6), 3–12.

Darling-Hammond, L., Cook-Harvey, C., Flook, L., Barron, B., & Osher, D. (under review). *Science of learning and development: Implications for educational practice*.

Dymnicki, A., Wandersman, A., Osher, D., & Pakstis, A. (2016). Bringing interventions to scale: Implications and challenges for the field of community psychology. In M. Bond, I. Serrano-Garcia, & C. B. Keys (Eds), *APA handbook of school psychology* (pp. 297–310). Washington, DC: American Psychological Association.

Education Endowment Foundation (2018). *Putting evidence to work: A school's guide to implementation*. London: Education Endowment Foundation.

Fischer, K. W. & Bidell, T. R. (2006). Dynamic development of action, thought, and emotion. In W. Damon & R. M. Learner (Eds), *Theoretical models of human development. Handbook of child psychology Volume 1* (6th edn) (pp. 313–399). New York: Wiley.

François, C., Chobert, J., Besson, M., & Schön, D. (2013). Music training for the development of speech segmentation. *Cerebral Cortex*, *23*(9), 2038–2043.

Hall, G., Dymnicki, A., Coffey, J., & Brodowski, M. (2014, September). Using evidence-based constructs to assess extent of implementation of evidence-based interventions. *ASPE Issue Brief*. Washington, DC: Office of the Assistant Secretary for Planning and Evaluation, U.S. Department of Health and Human Services.

Holmqvist, K., Nystrom, M., Andersson, R., Dewhurst, R., Jarodzka, H., & van de Weijer, J. (2011). *Eye tracking: A comprehensive guide to methods and measures*. Oxford, UK: Oxford University Press.

Immordino-Yang, M. H. (2011). Implications of social and affective neuroscience for educational theory. *Educational Philosophy and Theory*, *43*, 98–103.

Immordino-Yang, M. H., Yang, X.-F., & Damasio, H. (2016, June 6). Cultural modes of expressing emotions influence how emotions are experienced. *Emotion*. Advance online publication. http://dx.doi.org/10.1037/emo0000201

Jarodzka, H., Holmqvist, K., & Gruber, H. (2017). Eye tracking in educational science: Theoretical frameworks and research agendas. *Journal of Eye Movement Research*, *10*(1), 1–18.

Jones, S. M. & Bouffard, S. M. (2012). Social and emotional learning in schools: From programs to strategies. *Social Policy Report, 26,* 4.

Jones, S. M., Barnes, S. P., Bailey, R., & Doolittle, E. J. (2017). Promoting social and emotional competencies in elementary school. *The Future of Children, 27,* 49–72.

Kautz, T., Heckman, J. J., Diris, R., ter Weel, B., & Borghans, L. (2008). *Fostering and measuring skills: Improving cognitive and non-cognitive skills to promote lifetime success.* Paris: OECD.

Klasnja, P., Hekler, E. B., Shiffman, S., Boruvka, A., Almirall, D., Tewari, A., & Murphy, S. A. (2015). Microrandomized trials: An experimental design for developing just-in-time adaptive interventions. *Health Psychology, 34*(S), 1220–1228.

Kranefeld, U. (2015). *Instrumentalunterricht in der Grundschule. Prozess- und Wirkungsanalysen zum Programm Jedem Kind ein Instrument.* Berlin: BMBF: Bildungsforschung. Retrieved from www.bmbf.de/pub/ Instrumentalunterricht_in_der_Grundschule.pdf.

Limb, C. J. & Braun, A. R. (2008). Neural substrates of spontaneous musical performance: An FMRI study of jazz improvisation. *PLoS One, 3*(2).

Moreno, S., Friesen D., & Bialystok, E. (2011). Effect of musical training on preliteracy skills: Preliminary causal evidence. *Music Perception, 29,* 165–172.

Nesselroade, J. R. (2018). Developments in developmental research and theory. *Applied Developmental Science,* DOI: 10.1080/10888691.2017.1421426

Osher, D. & Berg, J. (2018). *School climate and social and emotional development: The integration of two approaches.* Princeton, NJ: Robert Wood Johnson Foundation.

Osher, D., Cantor, P., Berg, J., Steyer, L., & Rose, T. (2018). Drivers of human development: How relationships and context shape learning. *Applied Developmental Science.* DOI: 10.1080/10888691.2017.1398650

Osher, D., Kendziora, K., Spier E., & Garibaldi, M. L. (2014). School influences on child and youth development. In Z. Sloboda & H. Petras (Eds), *Advances in Prevention Science Series: Volume 1. Defining prevention science* (pp. 151–169). Boston, MA: Springer.

Osher, D., Kidron, Y., Brackett, M., Dymnicki, A., Jones, S., & Weissberg, R. P. (2016). Advancing the science and practice of social and emotional learning: Looking back and moving forward. *Review of Research in Education, 40,* 644–681.

Osher, D., Kidron, Y., DeCandia, C. J., Kendziora, K., & Weissberg, R. P. (2016). *Handbook of social influences in school contexts: Social-emotional, motivation and cognitive outcomes.* New York: Routledge.

Rodrigues, P. & Rosa, P. J. (2017). Eye tracking as a research methodology in educational context: A spanning framework. In C. Was, F. Sansosti, & B. Morris (Eds), *Eye tracking technology applications in educational research.* Hershey, PA: IGI Global.

Singer, J. D. & Willett, J. B. (2003). *Applied longitudinal data analysis: Modeling change and event occurrence.* Oxford, UK: Oxford University Press.

Spier, E., Osher, D., Pulizzi, S., Wayne, A., García-Piriz, D., . . . Kendziora, K. (2017). *Mapping of whole child development pedagogies and models: Western Europe and North America.* Washington, DC: American Institutes for Research.

Vaninsky, A. (2017). Educational neuroscience, educational psychology, and classroom pedagogy as a system. *American Journal of Educational Research, 5,* 384–391.

Part V
Future Directions
Introduction

Sam Crowell

A quotation attributed to Antonio Machado (in Thompson, 2007, p. 13) states "Wanderer the road is your footsteps, nothing else; you lay down a path in walking." This feels like an apt metaphor for this final section that points to some possible future directions of holistic education and potential areas of development and research. There is no template or standardized elaboration on what holistic education must be, but this volume provides glimpses that can guide the imagination and creativity of all educators.

As Jack Miller commented in his introduction, the field of holistic education is "unfolding" and "emergent." Teaching for meaning, purpose, and integrated understanding is supported by much of today's traditional research. But holistic education is more than new methodologies, it is a shift in how we view the world. This shift is grounded in consciousness and has implications for personal and societal transformation. It is a creative project that re-enchants not only learning but also the relationship with oneself, one another, nature, and spirit. The authors in this section deepen our understanding of what this means and how we may "wander" ourselves into the future.

Susan Schiller, using a literary form of a manifesto, beautifully synthesizes some of the key attributes of holistic education. Schiller exhorts us to seek the constancy of a holistic perspective. She uses unity and personal choice as a working framework that integrates the social, political, and communal agenda of education with nurturance, engagement, and creativity grounded in personal freedom. The spiritual development that leads to compassion, caring, and respect in a diverse and complex world is also a foundation for emotional engagement in one's learning and creative thinking that leads to transformative potential and possibility.

Schiller suggests that the future of holistic education is essentially a creative task where new and original work opens our minds and hearts, where the joy and pleasure of learning can be reclaimed. As holistic education continues to become more than just an educational alternative, it must remain true to its mission to "awaken learners to their highest potential. . . ."

The future development of holistic education, however, must also find ways to address the current complexities and issues of the societies in which we live. De Souza looks at the contemporary context of education and the growing influence of technology and communication on young people. Specifically addressing multicultural and multi-religious diversity in countries like Australia, she confronts the harmful effects of "non-conscious" education that perpetuates cultural racism and fosters religious, ethnic, and racial stereotypes.

Importantly, holistic education rejects mindless and unreflective learning. It moves the educational vision towards cognitive, emotional, and spiritual intelligence. But how can educators find a meaningful way to integrate spirituality in highly pluralistic contexts? De Souza suggests that the heart of spirituality is "living in relationship" and the exploration of what this means can lead to powerful understandings of one's sense of belonging, identity, meaning, and purpose. It creates the potential for a different kind of citizen for tomorrow's world. The challenges of the future need a more holistic perspective and a more integrated approach to learning.

Two contributions in this section provide unique insights from Latin America and the continent of Africa. We learn that holistic education can positively disrupt attitudes and hegemonic systems of separation. Both of these selections focus on higher education – one in Costa Rica, the other in Kenya.

These chapters expose the lingering effects of colonialism that continue to influence the thinking and policies of these regions. The program in Costa Rica seeks to create a harmony between the holism of science and an emerging Latino aesthetic, while the Kenyan project looks to African Indigenous expressions that go to the heart of a cultural identity that has been masked and diluted by Western models and epistemologies. Both affirm a holistic perspective that underlies these efforts while honoring the stories, place, and cultural expressions of a people.

Prado, Robert, Hurwitch, and Crowell describe a doctoral program in education at La Universidad de La Salle in Costa Rica. The program builds upon the scientific and humanistic understandings emerging from the "new holonomic sciences" and from a more ecological view of the world. The program at La Salle is constructed around the concept of pedagogical mediation. It is a participatory model that places an emphasis on feeling, the subjective experience of the individual, the pedagogical relationship where each is a teacher and a student, and creative expression as a vehicle for dialogue and sharing. The program combines circles of culture and collaboration with one's personal *chifladura*. This is the passionate commitment that involves "understanding and feeling life as a permanent and holistic search for meaning . . . in who we are and in who we wish to be."

Wane and Munene offer a compelling historical analysis of higher education in Kenya that illuminates the possibilities of an African Indigenous education and the persistent obstacles that deny the celebration of a cultural legacy that has the potential to revive a rich diversity of ideas and expressions that are part of the African experience. This history builds upon the relational qualities and wholeness of body, mind, and spirit and has the potential to re-imagine African education outside the confinement of Western educational thought.

The chapter by Bruce Novak illustrates that the future development of holistic models must take into account the diversity of human experience, honoring cultural identities and multiple forms of expression. We are also reminded that holism has deep roots in the history of our cultures. There are common threads of relationship, connection, wholeness, embodied experience, and spirituality that seem to transcend particularities and diversities. We also find that while holistic learning is bound within the individual experience of a learner, it has implications for collective and even political action.

Novak searches for universals within the particularity of his own Hellenic strand of Western culture and his rediscovered Jewish faith. His chapter represents a deeply existential and phenomenological quest that illustrates how the human qualities of love and relationship undergird our multiple efforts to walk this path. By sharing his own story of self-discovery, Novak shows by example that holistic learning will always remain deeply personal and related to one's lived experience of the world.

The final chapter of this section by Tobin Hart returns us to a key understanding that holistic education represents a fundamental shift in human consciousness and culture. This is an essential insight that brings the current episteme of our time into question. Holistic education is not just a better way of educating. According to Hart, it is a "recalibration of the process of knowing." He provides five gateways for holistic educators to explore and develop. Each of these points the way "toward a more holistic, integrated consciousness with the power to bridge the divides we have created in our world." They are contemplation, empathy, imagination, beauty, and embodiment.

As we consider the future of holistic education, may we be guided by Hart's closing vision to make "deep knowing and deep loving the new standard for education and for human existence on earth." So, in the process of imagining and creating a holistic perspective of education, may we walk our path with a true and sincere heart; and may we walk the path true to our hearts, living in harmony with love and wholeness.

References

Thompson, E. (2007). *Mind in life: Biology, phenomenology, and the sciences of mind.* London: Belknap Press of Harvard University Press.

32

A Manifesto of Holistic Education
A Declaration for Unity and Personal Choice

Susan A. Schiller

This manifesto places unity and personal choice at the foundation of a holistic philosophy to ground program development and pedagogical practice. Unity is seen as *a political communal endeavor* while personal choice is seen as an *intellectual and/or emotional decision*. Since the overlap of unity and personal choice inevitably occurs, separation of these two is paradoxical and persuades us to witness and accept the holistic nature of life. Furthermore, as life is holistic, it follows that learning is, as well, since all life stages are founded on learning and growth, even at the end of life when we engage death and dying. Human-ness exists because we learn. We learn *from* others who have learned before us and then share with us; we learn *with* others when we are together in the same stage experiencing responses to specific exigencies. We learn *from* ourselves when we contemplatively reflect on our thoughts, emotions, and actions. As we become members of any community, whether that is small and momentary, or larger and longer lasting, we experience unity with others who are like-minded. Our choices to belong, reject, speak out, or remain silent are initiated by a societal hegemony that exerts energy on our actions. Such societal exigence tends to be more universal across life than we generally admit. It is experienced by all cultures around the globe albeit its form may manifest differently. It also occurs in varying degrees across and within differing venues, that is to say, for example, that the medical field varies from the educational field, both vary from the culinary field, and so it occurs on and on across all venues. Yet, in all venues, unity and personal choice exert a holistic nature into each.

While my personal and public growth as a professional educator is deeply influenced by like-minded colleagues, I explore ideas and make declarations below which I believe, even as I recognize that they may or may not be shared by others. These declarations reflect a conjoining of mind, body, and spirit that happens when we elicit our whole being. They are not presented as a "comprehensive" treatise; they are presented as a complex instantiation of knowledge that has grown out of association and practice. As an educator, employed in a traditional state university, I push against isolation, coercion, competition, and privilege that reigns in the majority of schools now existing. I use holistic education to push. From within a traditional educational system, a holistic approach is a political counter-cultural action that I choose, but it is also a philosophy to live by. I choose it, because teacher and learner are one, because learning is reciprocal, and because limitations imposed by societal roles that have historically assigned power to teachers while withholding it from students must be resisted, if not eradicated. I choose holistic approaches, because they are quicker to bring forth happiness and joy, and they can form a more peaceful cooperative learning environment that evokes the best each and every person can give and receive.

Unity

Holistic education is essential to an international populace seeking peace, social justice, and sustainability. To promote an international paradigm shift into holism, various tenets, now espoused and promoted by holistic educators, should lead curricular change in all schools.

First: We need to recognize and proclaim that spiritual approaches to learning, as well as living in wholeness, naturally promote the development of compassion. When we function from a platform of compassion, much follows: for instance, respect for each other and for life; caring for the planet and for nature; recognition of knowledge and wisdom; embracing human growth as an innate condition; and a strong value for peace and justice.

Second: We need to recognize that the public and the personal each impose discrete conditions of exigency that control choice and either invite or restrict unity. Since we are thinking human beings, differences exist in ways we solve problems, the values we use as the basis to justify decisions, and the goals we set in any given situation. The cultures from within which we live also apply pressures that turn our activities in the directions they move. For example, if we aim to teach a certain style or amount of writing within a determined timeframe, these conditions will shape decisions to do so.

Third: We have to open our eyes and see, now! The framework used to set boundaries for any pedagogical activity is a result of societal pressure, whether that framework is set by others or by ourselves. We never are free from such pressure, so it is more efficacious to see why, how, where, and when that pressure influences our decisions. If we see it, then we can make choices about ways to create within it or, if possible, to make changes to it that are aligned with holism. To see such complexity requires reflection, dialogue, and time to consider what we learn. Of course, this means we have to make time for discernment and then more time to set goals, take actions, and experience the outcomes. Often, our goals, actions, and experiences flow pleasantly along, leading to greater levels of holism and unity. But then, during other occasions, great courage is necessary, especially if we are prompting change in the status quo. Community support for our goals and actions have a direct influence on our experiences. If holistic education is to flourish and unite us more strongly than currently is the case, we have to see what works "on" us so that we can promote the necessary paradigm shift that reshapes coercive and restrictive frameworks.

Fourth: We have to keep talking to one another and encouraging each other to activate and sustain our energy as we create holistic approaches in education. We must work against isolation and create opportunities for like-minded people to be supported by one another. This is vital, not only between individuals, but also between groups. The international holistic education community is growing, but it needs to be stronger and we need to be more unified. Such unity arises out of contact with one another. This is why we need to sustain our holistic education conferences and support those leaders who organize them. We need to continue and build support for written and electronic publications that forward holism. We should accept invitations to join dialogue groups whether they meet face-to-face or on the Web. *We* should *start* these groups. In this way, hope and activism is inspired in each of us and we are strengthened.

Fifth: The most challenging goal we share is to change the way we think of and use time. To do this, we must be attentive to time and understand how it drives us as we work alone or in community. We also must be willing to consistently resist habits formed by societal conditioning. Almost everyone is "strapped for time" or, at least, we frequently tell ourselves and others this. Yet, time is mostly an illusion that we are taught to believe has power. As children, we had little awareness of time. A day, a week, a month seemed endless. Years appeared even longer. Then time shrunk as we were conditioned to more and more personal responsibility brought on by societal expectations identified in developmental (st)ages. We learned not to "waste" time. Daydreaming became taboo. Relaxation or pleasure was regulated to "down time". We learned to slot pleasure into non-work events. We learned to "relax" only *after* "work" was finished. Before we knew what was happening to us, we completely believed that we only had a specific time allotted to get that something done, say in 30 minutes, even if 30 minutes did not fit. In other words, we learned how to block out time. The greater the amount we accomplished the more "productive" we believed we were. This perception of time is a controlling force in education and learning for joy and happiness as a "human right" was replaced with learning for productivity, grades, and job preparation. Holistic educators attempt to offset this view, or to soften its effects, for example through age-mixing in schools or cooperative project based learning agreements chosen by learners. Holistic educators attempt to reclaim learning for joy and pleasure. We aim to bring learners back to a "time-less" frame of reference so that learning can be experienced as a "natural" human activity that lies outside the societal constraints of time-management. This means most of us have to slow down and reset our internal clocks or, even better, throw them out. Personal choice empowers us to do so.

Personal Choice

Personal choice sustains and promotes unity when we accept certain fundamental ideas to support the advancement of personal choice. The ideas listed below are far from comprehensive, but they form a platform from which to grow.

First: We seek to excite others into self-selected learning activities that evoke small and/or large improvements in the world. How do we do this? We do it through unity with others and personal choice. We recognize that the whole person is in relationship with: the emotional or affective; the physical; the intellectual; the social; the aesthetic (love of beauty); the spiritual. We understand that wholeness is fully experienced only in the soul, and we build new programs on these precepts. Ron Miller has said that "Holistic education is founded upon a deep reverence for life and for the unknown (and never fully knowable) source of life: whether this great mystery is described in religious, psychological, ecological or philosophical terms, a holistic approach tries to answer its call, rather than shape it to cultural or ideological specifications" (Miller, 1997, p. 221). With this in mind, holistic programs rely less on measurement, as they rely heavily on responding to human needs such as compassion, justice, equality, sustainability, happiness, and well-being.

Second: Holistic educators promote humanistic skills, not only job skills, because we believe that humanistic skills apply in all life challenges, which include the personal *and* the professional venues. We suggest that life (and thus learning) be seen through a spiritual lens that scopes out the whole person as a being of extreme potential and possibility--a person who is a life-long learner and a creative decision maker for positive action to support the greater good within any situation. We seek to elicit awe and wonder, joy and pleasure, knowledge and skill, connections between all people, and a pedagogical base that promotes human justice and equality across the globe.

Third: As stated in the introduction of this manifesto, personal choice is an *intellectual and/or emotional decision*. It is also activated by circumstance, opportunity, and desire. Obviously, personal choice, rather than coercion, stimulates self-initiated learning and motivates the greatness within each person. As educators, we design frameworks with space that inculcates the development of selection skills. We engage spirit and rely on multiple ways of knowing: verbal, visual, emotional, physical, intellectual, social, environmental, and spiritual. Students learn to discern what constitutes a negative or positive choice given the set of circumstances they face. Personal choice leads to positive and penetrating experiences that further enhance an individual's love for learning as well as a willingness to self-initiate learning in school *and* out of school. We learn that our choices activate emotional and cognitive responses. We learn to analyze, speculate, question, imagine, wonder, and create. Creative thinking followed by selected action can lead to wonder and awe; on this path spirits soar and skills are honed. We are energized with a joy and happiness that fuels our willingness to shout "bravo", and/or to face challenge, hardship, even failure. When failure or hardship do arrive, we reflect and inspect it to select where we can revise our choices in order to be strengthened, to move forward, and to do what we had determined to do. This is basic to human nature, but pedagogical practice, and even program development generally, are shaped by coercion instead of personal choice. This happens because those who think they know more move within a top to bottom hierarchy (which they sustain) that privileges them through their status, position, authority, or advanced training. Most traditional educators are in this camp. I am, and I know it; but, I resist it. I want a new camp, a holistic camp that helps me find freedom and helps me bring such freedom to students. A holistic pedagogy based on personal choice and creativity works for me; it has worked for my students, too.

Fourth: Personal choice is inherently a creative act. As a creative act, we can see choice as a process as well. When we are faced with choosing anything, we automatically size up the situation, weigh the pros and cons that face us, and speculate about the ramifications of one direction or another. We might talk to others for advice. We might look to the past to compare or contrast similar events. We might reflect on our expectations to determine if they are reasonable, plausible, or too risky. In any instance of personal choice we "weigh in" to make a decision. If the choice is small, inconsequential even, we do not spend a lot of energy on it. But, if the choice is important, vital even, then our energy is heavily and carefully invested. The same process occurs in program development, albeit usually in a communal way. Most new programs in the developing stages are shaped in committees, by groups of people who have interest in the endeavor. They come together to "create" something new, something worthwhile which will be recognized and valued by others. Of course, interests greatly vary, but they are always driven with an eye to the future and with an eye to "improve" quality of life for those people whom the program engages.

Fifth: Future program development should be grounded in creativity. Creativity, as a self-motivated action that connects the individual's inner life with exterior social and environmental exigencies, is a process. We know this from all the current findings in the field of Creativity Studies. Processes are "learned". We can teach creativity once we understand an easy approach to it. George Ainsworth-Land claims that creativity proceeds in steps:

1. It arises out of physical need.
2. Analysis and evaluation are activated.
3. Synthesis for new knowledge occurs
4. One's whole being comes into play with the conscious and unconscious minds.
5. Reason and intuition, (inner and outer) are subsumed into a kind of meta-consciousness.
6. The self is part of a larger reality.
7. Finally, we build a new perceptual order (Zohar & Marshall, quoted in Lantieri, 2001, p. 17).

Those who "create" strive to bring about something new and original into the world. Creative acts from poets, artists, musicians, architects, writers, chefs, carpenters, and others are easy to spot. Unfortunately, we generally do not assign the label "creative" to an analytic decision or a product not associated with the arts.

Seventh: *All decisions are creative acts.* If we accept this truth, then we automatically broaden the usage of creativity to *any* area of life. Moreover, since all decisions are creative acts, it means that all people are creative beings. We can expand our capacity for using creativity so that it is a daily gift that fuels our actions. Creativity can function as the avenue that renders greater unity between our inner and outer life. As a source of strength and inspiration, it can become our cornerstone and well of sustenance.

Eighth: A foundation in creativity automatically links us to transcendence and transformation. This means we must teach students to recognize the powerful moments that show them deeper dimensions in life. As we develop new programs, we must create conditions for students wherein transcendence is invited and may occur. Holistic educators know that spiritual experiences may happen in the classroom and that learners need them. As we come to a meaningful understanding of our spirit, our inner and outer lives are no longer isolated, but integrated into a wholeness that fosters full awareness of our decisions and actions. This leads to wisdom and optimal community involvement. We seek wisdom, not just increased knowledge. We advocate for global equality and sustainability, not just momentary gratification. We root practice in happiness and well-being for all.

Conclusion: New programs should rely on a variety of practices that foster choice and unity. For example: meditation, loving kindness, environmental respect and stewardship, compassion, silence, collaborative learning, community building, social activism, problem solving, and multiple ways of knowing serve this goal. But practices have to be carefully selected to meet the teacher's strengths *and* the students' needs. As in any other developmental endeavors, objectives, goals, and principles must be articulated and accepted by those responsible for implementation. Processes of review and evaluation for the purpose of refinement and improvement should be ongoing. Education at its best is always dynamic, heartfelt, and true to its mission to awaken leaners to their highest potential as well as to their highest level of self-motivation. When we focus on choice and unity, we can both activate and protect such dynamism. We can learn; we can grow. We can keep spirit at the core of education.

References

Lantieri, L. (Ed.) (2001). *Schools with spirit: Nurturing the inner lives of children and teachers*. Boston, MA: Beacon.

Miller, R. (1997). *What are schools for? Holistic education in American culture* (3rd revised edn). Brandon, VT: Holistic Education Press.

33

Belonging, Identity, and Meaning Making—the Essence of Spirituality

Implications for Holistic Educational Programs in Plural Societies

Marian de Souza

Introduction

Much has been written about holistic education in the past few decades and yet, mainstream education systems in much of the Western world, and in Eastern countries where Western educational thinking and practice has influenced programs, still do not often reflect the basic principles that aim to address the whole child. Instead, there is much concentration on cognitive learning and an equal neglect of emotional and spiritual learning in schools today. As well, the intention that stems from nineteenth century schooling, that education should prepare children for the workplace, continues to underlie curriculum policies and programs, undeterred by the very obvious fact that the workplace of the future remains relatively unknown. Such uncertainty, alongside the plurality that is symptomatic of both the global and local contexts within which most people live today, have distinct implications for educators at all levels, policy and curriculum writers as well as classroom practitioners. Preparing our students to live in a world of uncertainty requires more than just preparation for the workplace. Children need to learn how to develop as well rounded, resilient people who can engage comfortably with the different Other.[1] As such, children need an education that will address the cognitive, emotional, and spiritual dimensions of learning so as to provide them with skills to manage their thinking and feelings, to access their intuitive, imaginative, and creative abilities by drawing on their inner lives, and which will help them develop wholly, with all their intrinsic gifts, qualities, and dispositions, into the people they are meant to be.

As well, media and communications technology have impact on the lifestyles of children and young people. On the one hand, these factors have enriched and expanded their learning programs and environments and created means for connecting with others that were inconceivable in the recent past. As teachers and parents have found, when used with care and wisdom, media and technology provide superb and stimulating ways to open up new worlds to children and young people. On the other hand, recent and ongoing research into the effects of social media usage does suggest that there are quite serious problems that need to be acknowledged (for instance, Australian Media and Communications Authority, 2013; Donath, 1999; Pitman, 2008). Some are related to mental and physical health linked to cyber bullying and extensive screen time where children retreat into the world of virtual reality to avoid facing problems in the real world (for a more detailed discussion of these factors see de Souza, 2014, 2016a; de Souza & McLean, 2012). Other experiences with social media can lead to feelings of dissatisfaction with their lives or being somewhat depressed (Kross et al., 2013). More important is the fact that we need to remain aware that some of the long-term negative effects of the use of technology and social media are yet to be discovered.

These factors have created a complex situation where, at one level, efforts to address the more obvious signs of plurality are undertaken by communities and governments but equally, at another level, the less intrusive, more subtle, and elusive elements of cultural and religious plurality pose quite substantial problems for teachers in classrooms who have not always been trained adequately to recognize or address them. Further, it is almost impossible for schools and teachers to control the duration and content of screen time of their students. Therefore, it comes down to individual teachers or school teams to identify and find ways to employ innovative and creative ways to use technology to promote learning.

As well, given the global context that now exerts some influence on different aspects of people's everyday lives, teachers need to address problems associated with plurality such as identity, prejudice, and racism, which can also involve bullying. These are some of the issues that have relevance for developing and maintaining a holistic approach to learning that I address in this chapter.

The Significance of Contemporary Contexts for Educational Policy and Practice

A particular aspect that has relevance for any education system is the fabric of the society from which it gets life. I have discussed in detail, elsewhere, the changes that have taken place in the fabric of Australian society in the past 40 years (for instance, de Souza, 2006, 2016a,b) and their relevance for education. While I will focus on Australia, it is important to consider that this discussion is relevant and applicable to other Western societies where the political, technological, cultural, and religious elements have changed dramatically in the past 50 years. Many communities that were, once, largely homogenous are visibly pluralistic in culture, religion, and language today and, in general, many classrooms reflect this plurality. It is inevitable, then, that the racial and cultural tensions that emanate from within the broader social community also arise in the classroom and need to be attended to.

With the speed of travel today assisted by new developments in technology, the world has rapidly become a much smaller area to traverse. This has meant that, over the past few decades, large numbers of people have moved across the globe, for all kinds of reasons, where they find themselves engaging with people who are quite different from themselves in terms of religious and cultural worldviews and practices. Given the tribal nature implicit in human beings (Law, 2006), it is not surprising that the otherness of Other can become a confronting force. To be sure, these are aspects that present a certain challenge in societies such as Australia, where, for a few generations, people only engaged with others like themselves—European and Christian. When people suddenly encounter different worldviews and belief systems, which sometimes appear to conflict with their own, the safety of their own world feels threatened so that the Other who is different becomes 'them' who is not one of 'us'. Experiences of 'them and us' are common for people who live in societies where the social fabric has changed significantly from mono-cultural and mono-religious to multicultural and multireligious.

It is also important to note that there may be quite significant challenges when educators who have little engagement with different cultures and religions teach about other worldviews and belief systems. Erricker (2008 identified a situation pertinent to this situation that occurred in the UK where "the emerging teacher graduates did not reflect the new ethnic and religious population of England and Wales in their number, but often sought to represent them in the curriculum" (p. 6) and argued that, "there is always a tendency to understand the other in terms of your own cultural 'grammar' and its conceptual base" (p. 50). Echoing a similar issue from a Canadian context, Van Arragon and Beaman (2015) argue that any discussion about belief systems or worldviews in public schools cannot be undertaken in isolation, since schools are social structures which are designed to mirror the attitudes and ideals of the wider society in which they operate and serve. Moreover, their contention is that such structures are weakened when the societies become fractured by cultural and religious plurality. As they observe, this is particularly the case where the opinions and values of majority stakeholders, usually the state, claim precedence while the voices of religious minorities are neglected. Generally, teacher training programs do not prepare teachers effectively to address such problems. Therefore, teachers who have to deal with issues related to such tensions very often rely on their own personal and professional experiences, which result in varying degrees of success.

Returning to the Australian situation, it is quite probable that knowledge and understanding of other religious and cultural belief systems and practices among educators may be reduced to an understanding contextualized by a marginalized Anglo-Australian perspective. Further, they could have particular views about certain religious or cultural groups generated by nonconscious assumptions about the superiority of their own religious and cultural practices. Indeed, over the years, I have heard colleagues at the Australian Catholic University who are of Anglo Australian origin refer to newly arrived Indian Australian Catholics as being very 'devout'. I was interested that each time, the person added that they did not mean to be derogatory or cause any offence by using that word. It is quite possible that the additional statement showed their awareness that their initial statement may have betrayed their feelings of superiority towards the Other who was different so that they hastened to correct it. This is a clear example of how nonconscious learning may show attitudes through a spontaneous response before the conscious mind is activated to display a politically correct one. Thus, we may see instances of cultural racism (Helms, 1993) and religious racism (de Souza 2016b) in societies divided by plurality. Helms' (1993) conceptualization of cultural racism alluded to those groups who felt that their beliefs, customs and traditions were superior to other cultures. He stated that "Cultural racism exists when there is widespread acceptance of stereotypes concerning different ethnic or racial groups" (accessed May 16, 2014).

It could be argued that the concept of cultural racism may be extended to include a concept of religious racism where an assumption about the superiority of one's own religious beliefs and practices lead to attitudes that marginalize other belief systems or, indeed, other religious practices that exist within a particular tradition because of different regional histories and influences (de Souza, 2016b). This was evident in the earliest days of Christianity in Australia, when British and Irish people brought over their differences from the old world. In fact, Australian Catholics were marginalized people for most of the first two hundred years (for instance, see Hughes, 2003; Kenneally, 2011).

The sobering fact is that cultural and religious marginalization exist even in societies that appear to be homogenous, as in Australia's past (Hughes, 2003; Kenneally, 2011) and the potential for divisiveness is heightened when religious and cultural plurality become the norm. When the pressures of such situations are compounded by acts of terror, which are committed by extremists belonging to a particular religious group, sharp divisions arise between all members of that particular religious group and the rest of society. This has been the case in Australia for Australian Muslims, and for Muslims who have settled in other Western countries. Many of them share the same condemnation of terrorists that non-Muslims have, but have suffered prejudice and racism because they share the same religion as the terrorists. The rise in Islamophobia is one consequence and its life is renewed constantly by non-Muslim fundamentalists and extremists who live within the mainstream community (Pratt, 2015). Some relevant research, here, comes from scholars from the University of Western Sydney, Charles Sturt University, and the Islamic Sciences Research Academy. They undertook a collaborative research project and reported their findings in November 2015. Their study included nearly 600 Muslim participants and they discovered that most Muslims still experience verbal and, sometimes, physical abuse as they go about their everyday lives. Further, while 86% believed relations between Australian Muslims and non-Muslims were friendly:

- 57% had experienced racism;
- 62% had experienced racism in the workplace or when seeking employment;
- 1 in 10 Sydney Muslims had "very high" rates of exposure to racism (*Sydney Muslims experience discrimination at three times the rate of other Australians: Study*. Retrieved August 8, 2017, www. abc.net.au/news/2015-11-30/muslims-discrimination-three-times-more-than-other-austral ians/6985138).

Other statistics which indicate levels of discrimination towards Muslims are revealed in the annual Scanlon Surveys into social cohesion in Australia which have been conducted between 2010 and 2016:

> The Scanlon Foundation surveys find a relatively high level of negative opinion towards Muslims, similar to the findings of VicHealth. Over the course of six surveys between 2010 and 2016 negative opinion has been in the range 22%–25% (11%–14% very negative), at an average of 24.2%. This compares to 4%–5% negative option towards Christians (average 4.2%) and Buddhists (average 4.6%). However, in an important finding of relevance to contemporary commentary, while concern over national security and the threat of terrorism has significantly increased, there has been no statistically significant shift in negative opinion towards Muslims over the course of the six surveys.
>
> *(Markus, 2016, p. 43)*

Moreover, the 2016 Scanlon survey indicated the levels of discrimination reported by different racial groups: 11%–15% for a number of European countries, 39% for those born in India, 39% China, 55% South Korea, 67% Kenya, 75% Zimbabwe, and 77% South Sudan (Markus, 2016, p. 62). These statistics serve to indicate the subtle or obvious divisiveness in Australian communities today that can be linked to racial, cultural, and religious plurality and it is possible that such statistics may be reflected in other countries with similar multicultural and multireligious populations. Since school populations mirror the society in which they function, anxieties and stresses related to plurality are also found in classrooms and need to be addressed.

Impact on Young Australians

What is important here is that many young Australians were confronted with these conflicting and tension-generating attitudes from their infancy, particularly since September 11, 2001 and the subsequent wars in Iraq and Afghanistan. Through the early years of their childhood, they witnessed their parents' reactions to news items on television about the atrocities committed in the name of Islam. Such experiences through their vulnerable years were bound to affect their sense of self and identity as well as belonging to a community that was being vilified in the media. There is little doubt that their nonconscious minds (de Souza, 2008, 2009) have taken on these images along with the emotions or the reactions of the adults around them. It may, indeed, be the nonconscious learning that took place during those vital early years that has prompted Muslim adolescents as young as 14 or 15 years of age to react to the hostile attitudes towards their communities, thereby becoming involved in some of the recent terror activities that have been witnessed both here in Australia[2] and elsewhere (de Souza, 2016a).

As always, there is another side to this situation, which relates to the nonconscious learning of non-Muslim adolescents. The reaction in children from mainstream communities who have also been exposed to media reports about Muslims and terrorists may, in fact, have been instrumental in their developing attitudes steeped in fear and hostility towards their Muslim neighbours, thereby presenting a collective face of Islamophobia. And while their formal education may teach them that not all Muslims are terrorists and they learn at a conscious level to display a more inclusive attitude, when faced with a fearful or threatening situation, their nonconscious learning will determine the attitude or stance they display. Timothy Wilson (2002) refers to this as the "adaptive unconscious":

> The adaptive unconscious might have learned to respond in prejudiced ways, on the basis of thousands of exposures to racist views in the media or exposure to role models such as one's parents. Some people learn to reject such attitudes at a conscious level, and egalitarian views become a central part of their self-stories. They will act on their conscious non-prejudiced views when they are monitoring and controlling their behaviour, but will act on the more racist disposition of their adaptive unconscious when they are not monitoring or cannot control their actions.
>
> *(p. 190)*

In this discussion, I have focused on religious tensions because this has been a dominating factor in the rise in prejudice and hostility for some years now. Nonetheless, it is important to note that there are several other minority communities in Australia who have also experienced cultural and racial abuse, as shown in the Scanlon surveys mentioned earlier. Accordingly, when a child experiences anger or hostility just for being who they are, their sense of belonging and identity may become damaged and they may suffer withdrawal symptoms and alienation.

Essentially, both teachers and students need to become aware of their nonconscious learning in order to make wise and informed decisions about their attitudes and relational behaviour in the classroom. They need to take steps to creating an inclusive environment of openness towards and acceptance of the otherness of Other. As long as they remain unaware of any nonconscious learning that underlies their own prejudicial opinions and stances, they will be unable to take the crucial steps to connect sincerely with people different from themselves. These are some reasons why holistic approaches to learning which include addressing the spiritual dimension is a worthy and extremely relevant proposition for the twenty-first century, since spirituality is about relationships and connectedness. But first, I examine the ambiguity that often surrounds the concept of spirituality and the changed understandings of spirituality that have occurred over the past few decades.

The Spiritual Dimension in Life and Learning

In a recent project (de Souza, Bone, & Watson, 2016), which investigated reasons for the uncertainty that appears to be implicit in understandings of spirituality today, we identified two concepts—traditional and contemporary spirituality. The first was linked to religious practice and was, therefore, God-related, and it had been the common understanding of spirituality for most of the twentieth century. However, we also discovered that contemporary notions of spirituality pertained to the relational dimension of being which did not always include a relationship with a Higher Being or Divine Power (see de Souza & Watson, 2016) but was grounded in the physical spheres of human relationality. We discovered that any ambiguity surrounding the concept of spirituality was a relatively new entity and it was restricted to contemporary spirituality. However, in analyzing the views of over 20 academics who came from a range of disciplines, we detected an element that was shared among them all. It was a sense that one's spirituality was about living in relationship. This confirmed an aspect of my own early research where, along with others, I identified spirituality as pertaining to the relational dimension of being.[3] My findings led me to conceptualize a relational (or spiritual) continuum where, at one end, the individual is quite separate from the Other. However, as s/he moves along the continuum, the boundaries between self and the Other become blurred until the end point is reached, a point of Ultimate Unity, where self blends with the Other. I was able to find parallels in many worldviews and belief systems where the notion of being part of the Whole and a journey to unity persist (see for instance, Armstrong, 2009; Griffiths, 1976, 1989; Laszlo, 2008; Newberg, D'Aquili, & Rause, 2001; Teasdale, 1999). As well, I was able to align my notion of Ultimate Unity with the sense of oneness as described by many mystics from different religious traditions (de Souza, 2016a).

To summarize, the human person lives in relationship with their families and communities, with the world and, for some, with a Divine mystery that stretches beyond the physical realm. Human spirituality, then, is an essential element in being human, that is, the sense that one is part of something bigger than oneself. It may be perceived as the sense and expressions of connectedness that individuals feel to the Other in their communities and the wider world, and also, for some, to a Supreme Being or Transcendent Other. More importantly, the connectedness that a person feels gives them a sense of identity and belonging and also a sense of self-worth, although this latter may sometime be a negative one.[4] Nevertheless, a sense of belonging to a group or community provides a person with a place and sense of purpose—for instance s/he may feel some responsibility to the group. As well, the shared beliefs and values may help them shape and interpret their daily experiences into meaningful patterns and encounters.

If we accept that spirituality is a vital human element because people live their lives in relationship, and that it is a critical factor in helping young people develop a sense of belonging and identity, which, in turn, brings meaning and purpose to their lives, we should accept that it needs to be addressed in education. In the next section, I revisit a learning approach that explores the spiritual dimension of learning.

The Complementarity of Cognitive, Affective, and Spiritual Learning

It is many years since I developed an approach to learning that recognized the complementarity of the cognitive, affective, and spiritual dimensions of learning.[5] I examined the elements of thinking, feeling, intuiting, and imagination in the learning process, which I aligned with three intelligences—intellectual, emotional, and spiritual. In particular, Danah Zohar and Ian Marshall's (2000) thesis on spiritual intelligence influenced my research when they argued that spiritual intelligence "unifies, integrates and has the potential to transform material" (p. 7) arising from the processes of thinking and feeling linked to rational and emotional intelligences. Spiritual Intelligence, they claimed, facilitated "a dialogue between reason and emotion, between mind and body. It provides a fulcrum for growth and transformation. It provides the self with an active, unifying, meaning-giving centre" (p. 7).

As well, I highlighted the importance of multisensory learning, which implemented the use of multisensory stimuli to engage different senses in the learning process. This is central to the learning approach, since different kinds of information may be absorbed by the different senses, which helps the mind to develop a holistic understanding of a situation and/or topic. Thus, the learning approach attempts to address the fact that the child is a multidimensional being; an individual with a rational mind that thinks, an emotional mind that feels, and a spiritual mind that intuits, imagines, wonders, and creates. And this multidimensional mind is encased in a physical body, which allows the child to engage, mediate, and interact with the world around them through their perceptions and senses. Therefore, it was expected that learning activities, environments, and resources would be designed with the aim that they:

- were multidimensional and involved a process that allowed each child to draw on his/her individual gifts, abilities and resources, whatever they were, so as to reach his/her potential to become a well-rounded, whole person;
- would equip each child to engage positively with the world in all aspects of his/her life as each of them experienced it;
- would develop innate strengths and capabilities that would empower each child to make effective and beneficial contributions to the well-being of future communities which, in turn, would promote their own sense of self, place, and well-being.

A quick overview of these aims will reveal that many mission statements and educational goals would have similar statements. However, in general, programs and practices still reflect the scientific, dualist, objectivist, and reductionist mindset of a past era. Such a system compartmentalizes learning, focuses on competition and assessment, and gives weight to some gifts and skills over others, thus dehumanizing some students and creating divisive elements within the class and school community. As Ken Robinson (2001) states: "academic ability has been conflated with intelligence" (p. 7) and schools are structured on the assumption that there are only two types of people in the world, academic and non-academic, which leads to the rather discriminating attitude that labels them: "The able and the less able" (p. 7). In addition, the aim for children to be constantly exposed to learning environments that recognize the role of their feelings, or that stimulate their thinking beyond comprehension and memorizing facts is too often relegated to the idealist's basket. Ventures into areas of wonderment, imagination, compassion, feelings of liberation and self-transcendence, and, finally, a holistic approach to problem solving are usually perceived as generally unobtainable in the current system, requiring too much time, expense, and resources. The result may lead to classroom practice dissolving into the tedium of mind-numbing and uninspiring learning activities.

Indeed, there are many teachers who strive to improve the learning experiences of their students so that everyday classrooms may be enlivened by thinking outside traditional frameworks. These are occasions when children find that they enjoy their learning; it is relevant to their interests and needs, they are encouraged to cooperate and respect one another, and they are more likely to maintain a happy and hopeful outlook in the process. However, maintaining this visionary approach within the restrictions of existing educational systems can lead to stressful and oppressive states, thereby diluting the enthusiasm of classroom practitioners.

To conclude, if teachers aim to nurture children in their wholeness and provide them with learning experiences that help them to develop their potential, attention needs to be given to a holistic approach where cognitive, affective, and spiritual learning interact with one another. More activities that draw on the inner self and involve creativity, imagination, storytelling, and reflection should be explored and trialled to evaluate their effectiveness in addressing the three dimensions. The use of the arts as a resource to teach various topics across the curriculum is an effective way forward. The arts promote learning through different senses leading to a plethora of perceptions that generate different thoughts and feelings. When students share these varied thought patterns and the feelings associated with them, their respective horizons may be enlarged to stimulate further creativity and imaginative thinking. This is equally the case with the use of other visually and aurally stimulating resources and activities, which connect and resonate with students' stories and lives, so that they become more relevant and meaningful. Such activities, conceivably, may reduce the otherness of the Other and connect children from different cultural backgrounds and belief systems.

Also, daily timetables and classroom structures can be designed to promote communication, connectedness, and an integration of learning across different subject areas. Further, attention needs to be given to incorporating periods of stillness, silence, and contemplation into the everyday. These are all ways in which this learning approach can be implemented effectively. Such learning, then, has the potential to be transformative and have a more lasting impact, something that the children may be able to revisit throughout their lives. As well, the learning experiences may help children develop a raised awareness of their connectedness to themselves and to the Other in their worlds. Such experiences provide those moments that both teachers and students remember as enjoyable and meaningful.

If educators develop holistic learning programs and environments that provide space and time for an integrative learning approach where the interplay of cognitive, affective, and spiritual learning is enabled, they will be creating the potential for today's students to become balanced, insightful, inclusive, and concerned citizens for tomorrow's world. Surely this is the goal of every educator.

Notes

1 I use Other as a collective noun for all others.
2 See the news report on the shooting in Paramatta, NSW in 2015 on the following website: www.abc.net.au/news/2015-10-03/nsw-police-headquarters-gunman-was-radicalised-youth/6825028.
3 I have discussed this in detail in Chapter 1 in de Souza. (2016a).
4 I have discussed this at length when examining the shadow side of spirituality. See de Souza (2012, 2016a).
5 For instance, see de Souza, 2004, 2005, 2006 for a more extensive discussion.

References

Armstrong, K. (2009). *The case for God: What religion really means.* London: The Bodley Head.

Australian Communication and Media Authority (ACMA). (2013). Like, post, share: Young Australian's experiences of social media. *Quantitative research report prepared for the Australian Communication and Media Authority.* Newspoll Market and Social Research. Retrieved from www.cybersmart.gov.au/About%20Cybersmart/Research/~/media/Cybersmart/About%20Cybersmart/Documents/Newspoll%20Quantitative%20Like%20Post%20Share%20%20%20final%20PDF.pdf.

de Souza, M. (2004). Teaching for effective learning in religious education: A discussion of the perceiving, thinking, feeling and intuiting elements in the learning process. *Journal of Religious Education, 52*(3), 22–30.

de Souza, M. (2005). Engaging the mind, heart and soul of the student in religious education: Teaching for meaning and connection. *Journal of Religious Education, 53*(4), 40–47.

de Souza, M. (2006). Educating for hope, compassion and meaning in a divisive and intolerant world. *International Journal of Children's Spirituality. Special Issue: Spiritual Education in a divided world: Social, environment and pedagogical perspectives on the spirituality of children and young people, 11*(1), 165–175.

de Souza, M. (2008). Spirituality in education: Addressing the inner and outer lives of students to promote meaning and connectedness in learning. *Children, Adolescents and Spirituality Interface. A Forum for Theology in the World, 10*(2), 98–118.

de Souza, M. (2009). Promoting wholeness and wellbeing in education: Exploring aspects of the spiritual dimension. In M. de Souza, L. Francis, J. O'Higgins-Norman, & D. Scott (Eds), *International handbook of education for spirituality, care and wellbeing* (pp. 677–692). Dordrecht, The Netherlands: Springer Academic.

de Souza, M. (2012). Connectedness and *connectedness.* The dark side of spirituality: Implications for education. *International Journal of Children's Spirituality, 17*(3), 291–304.

de Souza, M. (2014). The empathetic mind: The essence of human spirituality. *International Journal of Children's Spirituality, 19*(1), 45–54.

de Souza, M. (2016a) *Spirituality in education in a global pluralized world.* Abingdon, UK: Routledge.

de Souza, M. (2016b). The spiritual dimension of education in addressing issues of identity and belonging. *Discourse and Communication for Sustainable Education, 7*(1), 125–138.

de Souza, M. & McLean, K. (2012). Bullying and violence: changing an act of disconnectedness into an act of kindness. *Pastoral Care in Education, 30*(2), 165–180.

de Souza, M. & Watson, J. (2016). Understandings and applications of contemporary spirituality – Analysing the voices. In M. de Souza, J. Bone, & J. Watson (Eds), *Spirituality across disciplines – Research and practice: Perspectives from mysticism and secular cultures, education, health and social care, business, social and cultural studies* (pp. 331–347). Switzerland: Springer International.

de Souza, M., Bone, J., & Watson, J. (Eds) (2016). *Spirituality across disciplines - Research and practice: Perspectives from mysticism and secular cultures, education, health and social care, business, social and cultural studies.* Switzerland: Springer International.

Donath, J. S. (1999). Identity and deception in the virtual community. In M. A. Smith & P. Kollack (Eds), *Communities in cyberspace* (pp. 27–58). London: Routledge.

Erricker, C. (2008). In fifty years, who will be here? Reflections on globalisation, migration and spiritual identity. *International Journal of Children's Spirituality, 13*(1), 15–26.

Griffiths, B. (1976). *Return to the centre*. Springfield, IL: Templegate.

Griffiths, B. (1989). *A new vision of reality: Western science, Eastern mysticism and Christian faith*. London: Fount Paperbacks.

Helms, J. E. (1990/1993). Cultural racism: Conceptualization. *American Psychology Association Division 38*. Retrieved from www.health-psych.org/Cultural.cfm.

Hughes, R. (2003). *The fatal shore*. London: Vintage Books.

Kenneally, T. (2011). *Australians: Eureka to the diggers*. Crow's Nest, NSW: Allen & Unwin.

Kross, E., Verduyn, P., Demiralp, E., Park, J., Lee, D. S., Liu, N., . . . & Ybarra, O. (2013). Facebook use predicts declines in subjective well-being in young adults. *PloS one, 8*(8), e69841.

Laszlo, E. (2008). *Quantum shift in the global brain: How the new scientific reality can change us and our world*. Rochester, VT: Inner Traditions.

Law, S. (2006). *The war for children's minds*. Abingdon, UK: Routledge.

Markus, A. (2016). Mapping social cohesion. The Scanlon surveys. Retrieved from http://scanlonfoundation. org.au/wp-content/uploads/2016/11/2016-Mapping-Social-Cohesion-Report-FINAL-with-covers.pdf on November 2, 2016.

Newberg, A., D'Aquili, E., & Rause, V. (2001). *Why God won't go away*. New York: Ballantine Books.

Pitman, S. (2008). The impact of media technologies on child development and wellbeing. Ozchild. Retrieved from www.pdc.org.au/scarf/res/file/Resources%20and%20Useful%20Links/ImpactOfElectronicMedia.pdf.

Pratt, D. (2015). Islamophobia as reactive co-radicalization. *Islam and Christian-Muslim Relations, 26*(2), 205–218. DOI: 10.1080/09596410.2014.1000025

Robinson, K. (2001). *Out of our minds: Learning to be creative*. Chichester, UK: Capstone.

Teasdale, W. (1999). *The mystic heart: Discovering a universal spirituality in the world's religions*. Novato, CA: New World Library.

Van Arragon, L. & Beaman, L. G. (2015). Introduction. In L. Beaman & L. Van Arragon (Eds), *Issues in Religion and Education: Whose religion?* Leiden, The Netherlands: Brill.

Wilson, T. (2002). *Strangers to ourselves: Discovering the adaptive unconscious*. Cambridge, MA: Belknap Press of Harvard University Press.

Zohar, D. & Marshall, I. (2000). *SQ: Ssiritual intelligence, The ultimate intelligence*. US: Bloomsbury.

34

Pedagogical Mediation as a Foundation for Doctoral Study at the Universidad De La Salle in Costa Rica

Cruz Prado, Anne Robert, Jan Hurwitch, with Sam Crowell

The death of Paulo Freire interrupted the development of a new educational focus in Latin America that would bring together understandings emerging from new scientific paradigms, the humanities, and a growing commitment to reestablish a more visceral connection with the Earth. Freire, Francisco Gutierrez, and Moacir Gadotti were founding directors of the Paulo Freire Institute in Brazil and collaborators in this endeavor. Freire's last book, *Pedagogy of the Heart* (1997) was originally entitled *In the Shadow of the Mango Tree.* That tree is in the garden of Francisco's small cottage in Costa Rica, where he and Paulo outlined the major ideas of a new pedagogical focus for the future. Those conversations would become the foundation for eco-pedagogy and for a new and innovative doctoral program that applies these ideas to educational practice.

Francisco Gutierrez, who passed away in 2016, developed those ideas in his book with Cruz Prado (1999) entitled *Eco-Pedagogy and Planetary Citizenship*, and in the creation of an innovative doctoral program at LaSalle University. His ideas on pedagogical mediation became the foundation for an innovative approach to instruction that embodied a more holistic paradigm of education. Pedagogical mediation focuses not only on the relationship between teacher and student but also among the learners themselves, both reflexively and interactively. With this decidedly holistic perspective and using the Freirean notion of "circles of culture," a unique and forward-thinking doctoral program that has a growing influence in Latin America was developed. The program demonstrates how important new ideas with a holistic perspective can be applied in academic settings. Moreover, it points the way toward future possibilities and new understandings of wholeness and integration. This chapter describes this program.

The Need for a New Educational Scenario

The doctoral program at LaSalle University embraces a holistic perspective that is common among other holistic educators. It recognizes that the mechanistic paradigm that characterized a classical scientific view of the world is no longer an adequate epistemology for our time. The Cartesian/ Newtonian separation of the world into isolated and unrelated parts is no longer relevant as a curriculum or pedagogy.

Let us imagine that a teacher and a doctor who died at the end of the past century should come back today, and each was to practice their profession as they did 100 years ago. The doctor enters the operating theatre and with astonishment contemplates an absolutely unimaginable scene. He looks around him, at his colleagues and at the sophisticated instruments, and without much hesitation decides to withdraw from the operating theatre.

The teacher, on the other hand, walks into the classroom and feels completely comfortable. The changes are minimal and insignificant. She can easily begin her class with the well-known phrase, "As we were saying yesterday". . . In other words, while the medical profession over the years has transitioned into increasingly sophisticated means and processes of surgery, the education profession largely remains unchanged and still mired in early twentieth century concepts and practices.

A new educational vision and scenario is both necessary and possible if we pay attention to the extraordinary advances in the new understandings in the sciences and humanities. These are characterized by the emergence of a new scientific vision that resists being inserted within the exclusively mechanistic, Newtonian scheme. In some sense, we have passed from a "clockwork paradigm" wherein everything was mechanically predetermined, rigid, and linear, to a much more open, flexible, holistic, and ecological one that requires a fundamental transformation of our thoughts, our perceptions, and our values. This emerging paradigm brings with it a change in mentality and, consequently, a profound modification of most of our social relationships, as well as of our organizations.

The profound global changes make clear that humanity has entered a stage without precedent and with unpredictable repercussions for the societies of the twenty-first century. There is a great need for an education that addresses these historical challenges.

Towards the Education that We Need

The education that we need is so much broader than the narrow view of education that we have, which is centered on the logic of competition and accumulation and the incessant production of wealth without consideration of the limits of nature and the true requirements of human beings. We cannot continue to deny our most essential human nature, the understanding and meaning of life.

To rethink education is to propose a paradigmatic reform that obliges us to change profoundly our vision of the world while inviting us to see and analyze reality from new categories of interpretation. Within the doctoral program at Universidad De La Salle in Costa Rica, this rethinking includes an emphasis on the *decolonial*. The decolonial perspective is an academic trend in Latin America that continues to be developed. While Latin America has managed to decolonize itself politically, it has not freed itself from a colonial culture that continues to pervade individuals thinking and belief systems, particularly in academia. Part of the La Salle experience is to explore these issues and in the process begin to identify and define a uniquely Latin American epistemology and aesthetic. This cultural and educational project is situated within an emerging worldview that contains a more holistic and ecological vision.

The La Salle University Doctorate in Education Using Pedagogic Mediation

In mid-2000, a trans-disciplinary group began to think about education from a new perspective. Their frame of reference was the basis, assumptions, principles, and values of the new scientific paradigm. Two years later, the group self-organized as a doctoral program within the Universidad de La Salle in Costa Rica.

The doctoral program in education at Universidad de La Salle in Costa Rica is nurtured by the transformational processes our societies are currently experiencing, due to technological, social, economic, ethical, political, and ecological changes, as well as changes in health and lifestyles. These include new forms of reflection and new ways to self-organize and exchange knowledge, while fomenting self-realization as well as a dynamic social construction. Francisco Gutierrez called this *pedagogical mediation*.

In pedagogical mediation there is a "horizontalizing" of the teacher–student relationship, as well as the student–student responsibilities. Self-organization and conviviality in the group leads to a group-defined process of working together, with freedom to select the spaces, places, schedule, and modus operandi. Assuming responsibility for their own learning, group members are accompanied by their teachers, who advise the process and assist in creating the culture of a unique learning community.

Staffed by professors, both in person and virtually, devoid of traditional evaluations, with self-organized and interrelated study groups, there is a complex methodology of readings and dialogues. The learning community comprises 4–10 persons. The groups are linked together within a larger group of 30–40 persons interacting virtually or in person on a bi-monthly basis. A team of three teachers facilitates continuous learning over the year.

Importantly, the doctoral program at the Universidad de La Salle in Costa Rica is founded on the principles of self-organization, interconnectivity, and complexity, based on quantum physics and chaos theory, as well as on a search for a universal ethos which can illuminate new fields of action offered by the digital world, the biosciences, humanistic economics, the arts, and emerging cultural dimensions. Early in the development of the program, the International Earth Charter provided a cogent articulation for many of these values.

These programmatic elements are organized into three thematic cycles woven into the curriculum: Cycle 1 emphasizes new epistemological foundations; Cycle 2 explores emerging pedagogical theory and curricula; Cycle 3 delves into trans-disciplinary implications and meanings.

The program also has a strong focus on research, reflection, production, and exchange. These are contained throughout the doctoral experience. There are four foundational keys that are woven holistically throughout the program. Each is reflected in the concept of *pedagogical mediation*: (a) Feeling as the basis for educational process; (b) The human being as the subject for the educational process; (c) Pedagogical relationship as the essence of the pedagogical process; and (d) Creative expression as an appropriate environment for the learning process.

Feeling as the Basis for the Educational Process

From the beginning of the 1990s, together with Daniel Prieto, we promoted "Pedagogic Mediation", defining pedagogy as promoting learning through deep feeling. Subjective experience is grounded in felt meaning. This is not transferable, nor is it taught; feeling is constructed, it is made and remade within a process. Meaning is not in study plans, nor in objectives, nor in the transfer of content. Felt meaning is interwoven through immediate relationships, through each being, through successive contexts in which we live, and through significant relationships.

If meaning is made and remade in daily activity, it is clear that meaning, within educational practice, has to be pedagogic because it requires a method and, consequently, pedagogical strategies and procedures. Either we promote learning with meaning, or we impose learning without meaning. Learning with meaning creates protagonists, beings for whom every concept means something in their own lives.

The Human Being as the Subject of the Educational Process

The subject of the process, as underscored by Paulo Freire, is the human being. The human subject always learns as long as he/she is in a learning mode, constantly searching and receptive to the vast amount of information that saturates today's world. To achieve this attitude, the learner must feel hope, interest, and love. In other words, the learner must be in a state of well-being that leads to learning. This attitude of searching, of openness; this questioning the reality of every day, is to live a very rich educational process. For this reason, our essential objective should lead us to develop a learning aimed at:

- Sensing, intuiting, vibrating emotionally.
- Imagining, inventing, creating new scenarios.
- Knowing how to move from one horizon of comprehension to another.
- Relating to and capturing interconnections between phenomena.
- Expressing oneself, communicating.
- Locating, processing and utilizing the immense information in today's world.
- Seeking causes and foreseeing consequences.
- Critiquing, evaluating and making decisions.
- Thinking holistically.

What does developing one's own capabilities imply? It implies breaking stereotypical and unproductive molds and opening an educational process directed towards horizons that seek to develop the human being, not just filling one's head with a lot of information, however current and important it may be. It implies that the educator, without relinquishing being a teacher—and a good teacher—has to be concerned above all with promoting a learning centered on developing the human being, not so much on completing a study plan.

Pedagogic Relationships as the Essence of the Educational Process

Pedagogical relationships constitute one of the keys to understanding whether teachers continue to cling to the old school or whether they are open to the new school. In these relationships, the teacher may be authoritarian and coercive, or on the contrary, may promote:

- Dialogue.
- Interlocution.
- Empathic relationships.

A frank, sincere, and real dialogue implies the transformation of teaching into a process of:

- Exchange.
- Interaction.
- Communication.

In a process thus conceived as emitter–receiver, the educator is—or should be—sending and receiving messages, just as the student sends and receives them as perceiver–emitter. This means that educator and student develop and promote processes of communication that affirm co-participation, co-production, co-understanding, and communion. Improving the quality of education presupposes the creation of open dialogue, through a wealth of intersubjective, rich, dynamic, and significant relationships.

In pedagogical mediation, developed by Francisco Gutierrez (Gutierrez & Prieto, 1996), we affirm that a pedagogic discourse centered on the experience of the participants becomes much richer than one centered only on concepts. This is why one of the central bases of all educational processes is dialogical. Gutierrez used the term *interlocution*. For him, without interlocution, there is no educational act. The word interlocution is akin to an ongoing intimate conversation or discourse, whereby evolving meanings and purposes transform both the conversation and the participants. It signifies an authentic coming together within horizontal dialogue, always having the other present because we lead from their experiences, expectations, beliefs, dreams, wishes, and, thus, implies respect, tolerance, and recognition of the ideas and contributions of the other; it implies interaction and communication.

So that interlocution can take place in the educational process, teachers must be very careful with their language, their style, and their presence. Kind, familiar, fluid, transparent, simple, and clear conversation is the key to achieving this interlocution. The student should not feel invaded, forced, violated. Violence can occur not only in what is said, but in the way it is said: one's voice, gestures, and look should all invite peace, harmony, and agreement. For this reason, simple, clear, friendly, and humble forms of expression are all important and obligatory ingredients for interlocution.

To achieve interlocution, empathy plays an essential role. It requires the capacity to reach the other and to open and promote paths of expression. Interlocution provides a space for the joy of working together with the aim of creating relationship and facilitating learning.

Creative Expression as an Appropriate Environment for the Learning Process

Education begins when the student becomes the owner of his or her own expression. The student who is unable to achieve expression remains repressed. Giving and finding meaning are not only a matter of comprehension; they are also, above all, a matter of expression.

The capacity to express means that s/he who studies masters not only the topic studied, but also its different languages and modes of expression. It means that s/he has mastered the clarity, coherence, security, richness, and beauty of managing the forms of the different epistemological languages. The new educational scenario for our time is unthinkable if it does not generate the appropriate climate for this type of experiential expression, which brings with it a great liberation from extremely coercive norms and controls.

Frequent exercise of expression and communication permits the development of positive attitudes in students such as commitment, initiative, personal choice, and self-confidence. Creative expression permits a playful environment that provides security and helps develop creative talent and respect for others. In summary, we could say that creative expression permits the student to move from information receptor to creator, thus breaking the dichotomy of mere spectator to re-creator of the world.

Innovative Features

The La Salle University program looks and feels different to conventional doctoral programs in education. The first difference with other doctoral programs is that of group production of knowledge; the second, conditioned on the first, is that the individual production of knowledge is based on a *chifladura* or personal passion, in other words, on desire, passion, emotion, feeling, because without feeling we cannot seek meaning. Essentially, this involves understanding and feeling life as a permanent and holistic search for meaning; in our family and professional relationships; in what we do and in what we do not do; in who we are and in who we wish to be.

Significantly, the group itself is the privileged arena for learning. The key is precisely in the dynamism and the richness supplied by the confrontation of ideas and opinions that put into play previous experiences and the constructive tension between achieving consensus and dissension within a process of expression and reflection. The forms of expression require, without a doubt, training processes which lead to the knowledge and practice of different expressive resources that make possible both personal and group expression. Every act of knowledge requires forms of expression. This program places emphasis on textual forms and dialogue.

Among the innovative aspects of the doctorate, aside from the articulation of different topics, personal and collective questioning, and its rhizomatic topology, is the process of written production. Perhaps the best way to describe this experience is through the ecology of writing. This emerges from a person's ideas, memories, arguments, purposes, and dreams, interacting in a complex way with their social, cultural, familiar, academic, and natural environment. The rational, emotional, intuitive, and aesthetic merge organically as each topic is addressed.

This experience is neither linear nor summative, but, rather, non-linear and associative. This process is focused around the changing of perceptions and views that occur continuously throughout the program. The individual and group products continually refine and re-define new ways of looking at and being in the world. It gives permission for textual production to be subject to advances, setbacks, apparent dead-ends, errors, randomness, and uncertainty.

This means that the textual production is a privileged cognitive strategy, yet is also the basis for communicating ideas among the doctoral participants. This ultimately leads to two final products. The first is a group thesis that encapsulates the unique perspectives and dialogues of the group. The second is an individual thesis constructed around one's personal *chifladura*. There is a natural praxis that envelops one's research and how one combines this with the expression of new modes of thinking, being, and doing in the world.

Bearing in mind that the essence of the doctoral program is the group production of knowledge, we have defined the program as a pedagogical adventure that takes place in self-organized groups by means of:

- Exchange of selves.
- Exchange of knowledge.
- Exchange of powers.
- Exchange of pleasures.

The La Salle doctorate is conceived as a living organism that evolves in order to maintain its sustainability. This entails a network structure of self-organized nodes that enable horizontal interaction and coordination. Such a way of operating, in turn, fosters a culture that should sustain an ongoing change with a focus on the future.

Ultimately, finding meaning is a permanent process that should never be interrupted. Meaning is neither transferred nor taught; meaning is lived, is constructed, is made and remade by living this doctoral process fully and consciously. The doctorate in education at Universidad de La Salle in Costa Rica has extended its influence to programs in Panama, Spain, Colombia, Italy, Guatemala, Brazil, Honduras, Venezuela, Mexico, and Argentina. The holistic perspective contained in Pedagogical Mediation is contributing to a culture of hope and possibility for a new kind of education in Latin America.

Acknowledgment

The authors wish to acknowledge the seminal thinking of Dr. Francisco Gutierrez (d.), which has comprised the conceptual foundation of this doctoral program. We also wish to thank Deny Dyer and Jim Molloy for their work on the final editing of this chapter.

References

Freire, P. (1997). *Pedagogy of the heart*. New York: Continuum.
Gutierrez, F. & Prado, C. (1999). *Eco-Pedagogy and planetary citizenship*. Sao Paulo, Brazil: Cortez.
Gutierrez, F. & Prieto, D. (1996). *Pedagogic mediation*. Guatemala: IIME Universidad San Carlos.

35

African Indigenous Education in Kenyan Universities

A Decolonizing and Transformational Tool

Njoki N. Wane and Ishmael I. Munene

Introduction

Since 1963, when Kenya attained her political independence, the government took seriously the question of education for all. The effort to provide education for all Kenyans is evidenced in the various policy documents and development plans commissioned by the government during the past fifty years (see reports on The Development Plans and commissions from 1964–2018). Some of the commissions called for complete restructuring and overhaul of education (GoK, 1964). One document even suggested that education should also take into account African Indigenous education—its philosophy and pedagogy. Unfortunately, several decades later, there is no trace of African Indigenous knowledge at any level of education in Kenya.

Although some people might argue that we have made great strides since our colonial independence, our emphasis is that the process of recolonization persists, particularly through Eurocentric education. Using a historical trajectory, this chapter examines the evolution of the university mission from the colonial epoch, the post-independence period era, along with the contemporary period to argue that university education as it stands now is bereft of attributes pertaining to African Indigenous knowledges. In our discussion, we acknowledge that people of African Descent are not homogenous and there is cultural diversity, and that African Indigenous systems have been subjected to different forms of colonialism and distortion. We situate our arguments on anti-colonial thought and indigenous theoretical framework.

Anti-colonial and African Indigenous Knowledge (IK) and Education

Anti-colonial thought is a form of intellectual and philosophical response to colonial ways that were imposed on colonized peoples. Anti-colonial thought is a complex ideology that takes different forms to resist colonial indoctrination. It is an undertaking that forces the colonized subjects to question their subjectivity and the subordination of their knowledge (Nkomo, 2011). The colonizers goal was to make the colonized subjects view and experience themselves as the 'Other' and to see themselves as an inferior race. Wane argues (2009) that the colonizers knew any form of seduction would keep the African people interested in the European lifestyle, and many fell for formal Western education. Many Africans acquiring literacy in English or French were quick to realize that university education opened up prospects for economic and individual advancement (Wane, 2014).

The discourse of anti-colonial nationalism, then, reveals the complex and slippery slope for those who attempted to forge a means of resisting the hegemonic effects of European colonialism on the subjectivities and representations of colonial African subjects. However, at the same time, it demonstrates why anti-colonialism is essential to understanding the particular form of colonialism in Africa and the means of resisting it.

Indigenous Knowledge

Indigenous is a loaded terminology with its coinage inextricably linked to colonialism. Semali and Kincheloe (1999) explain that the term Indigenous and the concept of IK has often been associated in the Western context with the primitive, the wild, and the natural. According to Wane (2009), making reference to Maurial (1999), Indigenous knowledge (IK) is an outcome of interactions that occur among families and communities. IK is holistic, and all forms of learning and teaching are intertwined with everyday interactions. Members of the community generate this form of knowledge, then this knowledge is passed on to the next generation through storytelling, observation, songs, ceremonies, or traditional rituals. There are many definitions of what constitutes indigeneity, but most agree that Indigenous people have a common group history of traditions, culture, and language and continue to depend on the environment and land of their ancestors (Wane, 2014). This is not to imply that Indigenous people are homogenous. Quite the contrary, Indigenous people are spread throughout the world, and are often dispersed over large segments of land.

Growing up in Kenya, our teaching was anchored on our ancestors' knowledge. It was not an unusual phenomenon for our parents to use proverbs, idioms, or myths. As educators teaching at various universities, we feel it is our responsibility to revisit our African Indigenous ways of knowing and demonstrate its scholarly benefits for young scholars. How would this type of education look? The Indigenous education would entail the core values of African people as set out in the section below.

Fafunwa (1974) described African Indigenous education (AIE) as an integrated experience that combined physical training with character building and intellectual training. The goal of AIE was to develop the whole person and emphasized social responsibility, job orientation, political participation, and spiritual and moral values (Fafunwa, 1974), in addition to the importance of generosity, hospitality, respect for self, family, community, and environment (Adeyemi & Adeyinka, 2003). AIE is based on philosophical foundations and principles that include preparationism, functionalism, communalism, perennialism, holisticism, and social politics (Adeyemi & Adeyinka, 2003; Futhwa, 2011). For instance, the principle of preparationism prepared children to develop a sense of obligation to the community, while functionalism prepared them for their life. This was done through participation in work, plays, and oral literature. The principle of communalism referred to the communal spirit, while perennialism was a vehicle for maintaining and preserving the cultural heritage and traditional societies. Holisticism was viewed as multiple learning, and, spirituality was taught to ensure that children were aware of the Supreme Being and other spiritual beings that were the immediate receivers of prayers, sacrifices, and active religious worship (Futhwa, 2011). The principle of apprenticeship included participation in all family and community activities (Adeyemi & Adeyinka, 2003). Included in apprenticeship was participation in religious ceremonies for traditional priesthood or divination (Kingsley, 2010). The principle of social politics was essential, and the elders felt the importance of the children being equipped with good knowledge and understanding of traditional institutions, which included kingship, chieftaincy, and the family unit. This is the type of education we do not find in our universities today.

The dilemma is this: Why should educators and governments who shunted aside IK for five decades, embrace it now? As Nkomo (2011) states, colonization was not just about a scramble for markets, labour, and other resources. It also meant the newly acquired colonies had to be reinscribed in European discourse. The colonizers' goals were to ensure that anything African or Native was represented as negative while everything positive was European (Nkomo, 2011). The colonizers succeeded in making sure that Eurocentric knowledge would reproduce itself at every level of education in Africa.

Universities in Kenya

An appreciation of the extenuating factors that impede Kenya's universities from incorporating IK systems in their pedagogy and curriculum content requires that we take a historical look at the development of the contemporary university. A historical analysis provides an opportunity to critically account for a developmental context that made it impossible to incorporate African-centered approaches into university development. It also allows us to ponder where we need to go from here if we are to reform the university sector in order to make it holistic and relevant to the new dispensation that calls for a higher education system that is in consonance with Africa's needs. The four historical epochs that are worthy of this introspection are: (a) the medieval university, (b) the colonial university, (c) the developmental university, and (d) the multiversity. As we undertake the analysis, two key questions remain at the back of our minds: For whom was the university developed? How relevant is the university to the prevailing needs of the Indigenous people?

(a) The Medieval University

Truth be told, universities had their origins in Africa. The medieval universities, the precursors to the modern Western universities, had their roots in Africa. The similarities between the two have led skeptics to deny the existence of higher education in Africa before the conquest by European invaders, as Lulat (2003) has rightly observed:

> Given the high degree of resemblance between African and Western higher education today, there is often the assumption that higher education in Africa is a Western colonial invention . . . one must begin a historical survey of African higher education by asking whether or not higher education existed in pre-Colonial Africa. . . . Ashby (1966) states that they did but emphasizes they are of no relevance to the development of modern higher education in Africa today.
>
> (p. 15)

Though there is no documentary evidence that Kenya had any of the medieval universities, it makes sense to critically examine their existence in North and West Africa in order to understand how well they were connected with the prevailing IK systems. The medieval university archetype that existed included a research library at Alexandria and Egypt founded in third century BC (Munene, 2015a).

The Medieval era also includes religious universities that appeared in Africa around the eleventh century AD, such as the Al-hazar in Egypt, Sankore at Timbuktu in Mali, Quaraouiyine in Morocco, and Ez-Zitouna in Tunisia. The most prestigious of this group was the university of Timbuktu, which had more than 100,000 manuscripts stretching from pre-Islamic times to the twelfth century AD, and it covered such diverse subject areas as astronomy, botany, history, law, science, and music. In terms of knowledge development, these universities pioneered the systematic advancement of scholastic traditions involving the collection and preservation of academic information through research and dissemination of knowledge.

In the context of Indigenous education, medieval institutions exhibited a close nexus with the socio-cultural, political, and religious environment and knowledge systems. The modes of knowledge production, preservation, and transmission were congruent with the prevailing epistemological traditions. Local religion, culture, customs, and natural environment provided the raw materials upon which knowledge was constructed. The universities permitted academics to experiment with local knowledge and resources uninhibited by social hierarchies, obligations, and highly regimented social roles (Munene, 2010).

Assie-Lumumba (2006) and Lulat (2003) aver that even though Africans did not set up institutions of higher learning that were akin to what we have as universities today, they had systems that fulfilled missions that were not radically different. They note that the Nile Valley civilization, for instance, was a great beneficiary of the existence of early universities and other centers of higher learning in Egypt. It is in this context that questions of educational relevance arise when colonial universities were established in the continent once Africa was colonized by European powers. The origins and nature of colonial universities, along with their relationship to African IK systems is the subject of our next section.

(b) The Colonial University

The contemporary Kenyan universities, like the rest of Africa, have their beginnings in the colonial period. If the medieval university represented the best synergy between IK and higher education in the continent, the colonial university epitomized the first intellectual assault on this synergistic engagement. The colonial university was never meant to empower the Indigenous people and address challenges confronting their lives. Rather, it was incorporated to serve the interests of the colonial masters. In Kenya, the colonial university's footprints were marked by the establishment of the Royal Technical College, Nairobi in 1956, the precursor to the current University of Nairobi. In 1964, it was renamed University College Nairobi, which was part of the federal University of East Africa.

The establishment of colonial universities in Africa was a by-product of the colonial economic development. As colonies grew in complexities, they required skilled manpower to run them: State bureaucracy had to be managed, the native populations had to be controlled administratively, social services had to be planned and delivered, and economic growth had to be sustained. The maintenance and sustenance of colonies was henceforth to be a process of acculturation, and higher education was used to acculturate the local population.

As is evident from the foregoing, the colonial university in Kenya, and Africa for that matter, was in no position to incorporate IK systems in the teaching approach as well as in the content. The university was subsumed within the entire colonial architecture, whose prime motive was the cultural and economic conquest of the Indigenous people of Kenya rather than empowering them through the harnessing of their knowledge base. The university functioned as a powerful instrument of cultural conquest through instruction in English (and other European languages), university culture, and organizational forms which were imported from the University of London. Colonial universities were, on the whole, cultural tools at the disposal of the colonial state to perpetuate their dominance over the territories they occupied. Their programmatic focus on occupational training for the management of the colonies accentuated their inability to harness local knowledge that had long enabled Indigenous people to exist harmoniously with the prevailing reality.

(c) The National Development University

Kenya attained independence in 1963. How was the colonial university going to fit in the new dispensation? This question confronted many newly independent African nations, due to the foreignness of their higher education institutions. Their establishment and continued existence was inimical to the aspirations and development goals of the newly emergent nations. The national liberation movements that championed independence sought to reclaim African values, political autonomy, and economic empowerment, which the colonial universities sought to suppress. It is in this context that Kenya opted to pursue a development strategy focused on eradicating hunger, illiteracy and diseases, as encapsulated in the 1965 Sessional paper No. 1 (Go K, 1965).

In this post-independence period of optimism, Kenya, like many African countries, transformed the colonial university into a national development university in order to assist the government in fulfilling its development agenda. These invigorated universities were ". . . to train and develop the skills and high-level manpower to replace the erstwhile colonial officials . . . [and] to staff the new and expanded political, administrative, social, and economic institutions" (Yessufu, 1973, p. 4). To provide a framework for steering universities into the development path, the United Nations Education, Scientific and Cultural Organization (UNESCO), helped establish the Association of African Universities (AAU), which was founded in Rabat, Morocco, during the 1967 conference on African Education.

The transformation of the colonial universities required that they fit the role of a modernization program of nation building. From the late 1960s to the mid-1980s, Kenya had only three universities, namely: University of Nairobi, Kenyatta University, and Moi University (Alperovitz, Dubb, & Howard, 2009; Weerts & Sandmann, 2010).

In spite of the optimism accorded to national universities, the institutions largely failed to deliver on the promise. A decade after independence, serious questions arose as to their viability in transforming society and inculcating African values. The universities still continued to espouse European values. The universities had simply mutated into elite institutions that catered to a small number of state-sponsored students mesmerized by Western lifestyles and consumption habits. The universities retreated to their pre-independence role of perpetuating Western cultural dependency (Mazrui, 1992).

This description of the national development university model in Kenya reveals certain salient reasons why the universities never embraced African IK systems in their programs. First, the university did not aspire to radically alter the Western epistemology and methodological approach to knowledge. Rather, it sought to build upon the approach as an instrument of turning Kenya (and Africa, for that matter) into a European-like country in all spheres of human development. There was no attempt to capture or recreate in the academic programs those aspects of African spirituality and knowledge that enabled the Indigenous people to survive and prosper for centuries. In the words of Dani Nabudere (2003):

> [Universities] have continued to reproduce dependent Eurocentric knowledge, a knowledge that is dependent on its actualization in centers that exploit the African people and utilize African resources freely . . . The models of Western Universities, which Africa adopted, have proved completely unsuitable for Africa's needs.
>
> *(p. 5–6)*

Second, rather than conceptualizing development as a holistic attribute that encompasses social and economic transformation based on complex cultural and environmental factors, it was viewed as merely extending the process of economic development that had been initiated by the colonial authorities (Assie-Lumumba, 2006; Munene, 2010). With university education expected to reinforce this skewed view of development, state universities were hamstrung in any attempt to redefine their role and activities to tap the rich repertoire of African knowledge systems. An African-based epistemology ought to have been the foundation upon which a truly transformative African university should have been founded.

The alienation effect of the national development universities has been documented widely. Mazrui (1975) has argued that the universities are akin to multinational corporations; they are channels through which Western culture, attitudes, and dispositions are transmitted to the young generation, leading to cultural dependency. Okot p'Bitek (1967) captured similar effects in the following terms:

> We blame colonialists and imperialists and neo-colonialists; we blame Communists both from Moscow and Peking, and sent their representatives packing. We blame the Americans and the CIA. . . . Another, but contradictory phenomenon is the belief that the solution to our social ills can be imported. Foreign 'experts' and peace-corps swarm the country like white ants. Economic 'advisers,' military 'advisers' and security 'advisers' surround our leaders.
>
> *(1967, p. 47)*

Therefore, expecting the rebranded colonial universities to operate as national development universities to resuscitate Indigenous African knowledge systems was to be widely optimistic. Hope turned into despair, as African nations, including Kenya, looked to the outside to rebrand the failed national universities into market institutions.

(d) The New Multiversity

To ameliorate the failure of the development university, Kenya, since the early 1990s to the present, has embraced neo-liberalism as the policy to guide the development of universities in order to make them more responsive to the needs of the society. Under neo-liberalism, the state role in higher education development will be largely restricted to policy development, accreditation, regulation, and access. The market will shape the growth and direction of university development, since the institutions will be expected to generate resources from the marketplace. Academic programming and related activities will be a response to the market needs rather than state policy. Within this neo-liberal policy, privatization will be central, as some aspects of public universities will be privatized as private universities are encouraged and promoted (Munene, 2015b). Under neo-liberalism, public universities would be state-owned but largely privately financed. This neo-liberal policy, which was adopted across the length and breadth of the African continent, had a dual impetus: (a) pressure by multilateral donor agencies such as the World Bank and the International Monetary Fund as part of the broad structural economic reforms, and (b) perceived failure of state universities in terms of providing market-relevant education (Munene, 2015b).

The government's position on the neo-liberal policy in university development was articulated by the minister for education, Hon Prof. George Saitoti, when he asserted the following:

> This is a turning point in the development of our public universities, where they are being called upon to adopt business-like financial management styles. It is also a point in time when universities have to plan well ahead about resources expected to be coming from sources other than the exchequer . . . Time has come to seriously take account of the universities potential to generate income internally . . . Income from such sources should be exploited and treated as definite sources of university revenue.
>
> *(cited in Kiamba, 2004, p. 55)*

Put simply, the state expects the universities, public and private, to be entrepreneurial in their academic programming and other activities. The results of this policy has been the massification of higher education in the country, as seen in the surge in the number of universities and in student enrollment. From a paltry three state universities in 1985, the country now boasts 32 (2018) accredited public universities, a growth of around 966% in 32 years. Equally, the number of private universities has grown, with 13 of them authorized to operate while awaiting accreditation (Commission for University Education, 2018).

The move towards increased marketization of universities has inspired "academic capitalism", efforts to develop, market, and sell research products, educational services, and consumer goods in the private marketplace (Slaughter & Leslie, 1997). In terms of knowledge production and transmission, we have witnessed an increased commodification of knowledge. This is epitomized by the vocationalization of the curricula, which involves offering more academic programs as opposed to basic and fundamental programs and short-term training courses, applied and contract research as opposed to basic and fundamental research, and more teaching and less research. The new market regime has not only altered the nature of academic work but has also led to institutional identity crises. Kenyan universities are in a dilemma as to how they define themselves and their role as vanguards of knowledge creation and dissemination.

It goes without saying that the market university is a bad candidate for incorporating African IK in the curricula. Increasing African knowledge and developing rural areas as centers of African knowledge does not feature prominently in the vocationalization agenda of the neo-liberal university. Codifying science and technology in epistemological and linguistic terms that are in tandem with rural communities, where the majority of Kenyans live, have not been prioritized nor articulated as central objectives of university development in the current era. Without significant attention to basic and fundamental knowledge in the curricula, it is difficult, if not impossible, to tap into the rich repertoire of African IK to re-orient university education towards African culture and values.

Furthermore, in the neo-liberal era of higher education development, we continue to see footprints of earlier university developments which made it impossible to inculcate African IK in academics. The continued reliance on Western models of development, along with Western paradigms of understanding society, has meant that Kenyan universities hardly question Western epistemologies and methodologies of knowledge production. Universities do not problematize Western theoretical constructs but, rather, elevate them and use them to critique and analyze African societies. This has become more pervasive now that internationalization and globalization shape the development of universities in the market era. For Kenyan universities, becoming a global and international university means becoming more and more like a Western university and less and less of an African one.

Like the three previous eras of university development that we have analyzed, the neo-liberal epoch is foreign-initiated. Transforming a higher education system that had foreign roots with additional foreign concepts in order to make it more relevant appears to miss the point about the maladies affecting the university sector. The failure of the university in national development is rooted in its foreignness, or foreign origin. Treating this illness requires a reconceptualization of the university with an African IK system being the center and focus of the emergent institution. It requires a consideration of the following pertinent questions: Where is the country moving? What is the role of university education in the context? By doing this, or by considering these questions, we can begin the process of harnessing African IK to advance a university education that develops the *whole person*, fully integrated with the spiritual and moral forces that have bound African societies for centuries.

Implications

This chapter is advocating mastery and understanding of Africa's education from within. We argue that this becomes possible only when the teachers are empowered through Indigenous ways of knowing to re-imagine African education as existing outside of Western educational thought. We argue that, ultimately, Africa's development should be measured by African peoples' ability to articulate their philosophical thought from an Afrocentric standpoint. This can only happen when African people conceptualize who they are and what they stand for, from a 100% African-centered position; when their education priorities and implementation tools are not regulated from outside, but from within; when the African people are proud of their Blackness and embodiment of everything that comes with it and they do not make excuses for being African. Of course, we do know, as educators, that there is no one way of achieving this; it is a process, it is a journey, that might not happen even within our lifetime. What we are advocating here is an entry point for an ongoing discussion of Africanness and all that it entails. We do not want to provide a list of do's and don'ts, because this will close the door to dialogue (Sium, 2014).

A critical dialogical engagement with educators, activists, and learners involves a process of transformation, unlearning, learning, and decolonizing one's way of seeing and being in the world and, in particular, in the world of education. Our aim, therefore, is to move the transformative learning debates beyond the goals of bringing African Indigenous education, that focuses on integration to an emphasis on critical self-reflections and re-examinations that would allow for the interrogation of individual's beliefs, values, biases, and, hence, work towards decolonizing the mind. The implication in this kind of engagement is to ensure that the dialogues take into account the social, political, and cultural changes that impede inclusion of African Indigenous education and to rethink and re-imagine a renewed vision and tools for analyzing the dominant seductive ideologies that serve to marginalize African ways of knowing. This chapter is therefore pointing to different ways to conceptualize and engage with the education process that do not negate African people's core values and beliefs. We want to rupture the normative thinking that has been embedded in the African education system and challenge the status quo, in addition to offering alternative ideas and interpretations that would allow for dismantling the persistent ambiguous relationships between African Indigenous education and Western education; known and the unknown; the self and the constructed other.

Conclusion

In this chapter, we have provided the reader with an overview of why African Indigenous education is not taught in African universities and, in particular, in Kenya. This is despite the fact that Africa is known to have had the earliest universities in the world that had emphasized a holistic form of knowing. These earlier institutions exhibited a close nexus with the socio-cultural, political, and religious environments and the modes of knowledge production and transmission were congruent with the prevailing cultural traditions of the people. We situated our arguments in anti-colonial and Indigenous frameworks as a way of decentering Eurocentrism. In addition, we have also provided some aspects of how African Indigenous education would look like. Employing a historical analysis, we were able to reflect on where we were before colonization. During the process of writing this chapter, we had more questions than answers because, challenging the current status quo requires more than writing a paper. We need to engage in a dialogue with all stakeholders involved with issues of education.

References

Adeyemi. M. B. & Adeyinka, A. A. (2003). The principles and content of African traditional education. *Journal of Educational Philosophy and Theory*, 35(4), 425–440.
Alperovitz, G., Dubb, S., & Howard, T. (2009). The next wave: Building university engagement for the 21st century. *Good Society*, 17, 69–75.
Ashby, E. (1966). *Universities: British, Indian, African—A study in the ecology of higher education.* Cambridge, MA: Harvard University Press.
Assie-Lumumba, T. (2006). *Higher education in Africa: Crisis, reforms, and transformations.* Dakar, Senegal: Codesria Books.
Commission for University Education (2018). Accredited universities in Kenya. Retrieved from www.cue.or.ke/images/phocadownload/Accredited_Universities_in_Kenya_November_2017.pdf on 1/4/2018.
Fafunwa, A. B. (1974). *History of education in Nigeria.* London: Macmillian.
Futhwa, F. (2011). *Setho: Afrikan thought and belief system.* Alberton: Nalane ka Fexekile Futhwa.
GoK (1964). Kenya Education Commission Report, part I. *Presidential committee on unemployment* (1982/1983). Nairobi: Government Press.
GoK (1965). *Kenya Education Commission report.* Nairobi: Government Press.
Kiamba, C. (2004). The experience of privately sponsored studentship and other income generating activities at the University of Nairobi. *Journal of Higher Education in Africa*, 2(2), 53–73.

Kingsley, O. (2010). African traditional education: A viable alternative for peace building process in modern Africa. *Journal of Alternative Perspectives in the Social Sciences*, 2, 136–159.

Lulat, Y. G.-M. (2003). The development of higher education: A historical survey. In D. Teferra & P. G. Altbach (Eds), *Africa higher education: An international reference handbook* (pp. 15–31). Bloomington, IN: Indiana University Press.

Maurial, M. (1999). Indigenous knowledge and schooling: A continuum between conflict and dialogue. In L. Semali & J. L. Kincheloe (Eds), *What is indigenous knowledge: Voices from the academy* (pp. 60–77). New York: Falmer Press.

Mazrui, A. (1975). The African university as a multinational corporation: Problems of penetration and dependency. *Harvard Educational Review*, 45, 191–210.

Mazrui, A. (1992). Towards diagnosing and treating cultural dependency: The case of the African university. *International Journal of Educational Development*, 12, 95–111.

Munene, I. (2010). Universities and centers of learning. In F. Abiola Irele & Biodun Jeyifo (Eds), *The Oxford Encyclopedia of African Thought Vol. 2* (pp. 309–402). New York: Oxford University Press.

*Munene, I. (2015a). *Multi-campus university systems: Africa and the Kenyan experience*. New York: Routledge.

Munene, I. (2015b). Profits and pragmatism: The commercial lives of market universities in Kenya and Uganda. *Sage Open*, October–November, 1–14. Retrieved from http://journals.sagepub.com/doi/pdf/10.1177/2158244015612519 on 1/4/2018.

Nabudere, D. (2003). Towards the establishment of a pan-African university: A strategic concept paper. *African Journal of Political Science*, 8(1), 1–30.

Nkomo, S. M. (2011). A postcolonial and anti-colonial reading of 'African' leadership and management in organization studies: Tensions, contradictions and possibilities. *Organization*, 18(3), 365–386.

Okot, p'B. (1967). Indigenous ills. *Transition*, 7, 32, 47.

Semali, L., & Kincheloe, J. L. (1999). *What is Indigenous knowledge? Voices from the academy*. New York: Falmer Press.

Sium, A. (2014). Dreaming beyond the state: Centering Indigenous governance as a framework for African development. In G. Dei & P. Adje (Eds), *Emerging perspectives on 'African Development' speaking differently* (pp. 63–82). Peter Lang.

Slaughter, S. & Leslie, L. L(1997). *Academic capitalism: Politics, policies, and the entrepreneurial university*. Baltimore, MD: Johns Hopkins University Press.

Wane, N. N. (2009). Black Canadian feminism thought: Perspectives on equity and diversity in the academy. *Journal Race Ethnicity and Education*, 12(1), 65–77.

Wane, N. N. (2014). *African women's voices on Indigenous knowledge of food processing practices among Kenyan rural women: A Kenyan perspective*. Toronto, ON: University of Toronto Press.

Weerts, D. J. & Sandmann, L. R. (2010). Community engagement and boundary-spanning roles at research universities. *Journal of Higher Education*, 18, 702–727.

Yessufu, T. (1973). *Creating the African university: Emerging issues of the 1970s*. Ibadan, Nigeria: Oxford University Press.

36

Hebraism, Hellenism, and Holism

Finding Sources of Life in
Western Culture

Bruce Novak

This handbook is being compiled in a time in which Western culture is in crisis. Yet, unfortunately, the people who seem to see this most clearly, and are acting most decisively to face this crisis, are the various forms of fundamentalists—religionists, free marketeers, and, most recently, political nationalists—who believe the only coherent road to the future is a decisive return to a somehow "great," but isolated past, rather than seeing in these times the opportunity to creatively forge a greater vision to newly and more deeply unite the world.

A large question that holistic educators need to find some kind of coherent answer to in these times is, thus, How can we thoroughly reclaim the *good* in Western culture, in ways that promote not its dominance over other cultures and the earth, but human and planetary wholeness?

Quite a lot may come to hinge on whether we can find a coherent answer to this.

Of course, there is no way that a definitive answer can be found in a short essay. What I *can* do in a *somewhat* thorough and coherent way, though, is to testify how the two main traditional strands of Western culture, stemming from Athens and Jerusalem—alliteratively named "Hebraism and Hellenism" by the nineteenth century poet and educational theorist Matthew Arnold—have helped me find a holistic coherence to my own life, and have helped me help others find similar coherence.

Since the central concern of holistic education has traditionally been with the development of wholeness in the human person, I hope that you will find an account of the finding of such personal wholeness through a long search for the *potential* wholeness of a powerful and dominant culture—oft-disparaged for its vaingloriousness and fragmentation—to be meaningful and significant in envisioning how a world now dominated by that culture can eventually also be helped to be holistically transformed by it.

My experience of Hebraism and Hellenism has been in some ways the inverse of Arnold's, who found "Hebraism" to be fundamentally characterized by a "strictness of conscience" that tended to be overbearing upon the Victorian culture from which he stemmed, and found "Hellenism" to be fundamentally characterized by a "spontaneity of consciousness" he thought could much ameliorate the strictness of that culture if education were to be thoroughly imbued by it. He was seeking a kind of golden mean between two countervailing influences.

What *I* have found, by contrast, is an attraction, on the one hand, to what might be called the "strictness of epistemic consciousness" in the Hellenic strand of Western culture. And, on the other hand, especially in recent years, I have found a deep attraction to the "spontaneity of *feeling*—personally and interpersonally meaningful—or moral conscience" that has been opened up to me by a newfound Jewish faith that is not in any way in conflict with the interests of universal philosophy, but rather comes as a direct existential consequence of its epistemic principles: manifesting, moment by living moment, the personal moral intutions that are the direct consequence and living fulfillment of its universal concepts.

A "*real* teacher," says Robert Inchausti in his *Spitwad Sutras: Classroom Teaching as Sublime Vocation* (1993), "takes [his or her] very life into speech, so that others may do the same" (p. 141) What I have personally found to lie at the heart of Western culture, and the fully holistic interweaving of its two main strands, is not the root of all the evil in the world—though certainly it has spawned more than its share of such evil—but precisely the search for a definitive and permanent educative and life-giving cure for the worst kinds of evils that our species has perennially, and across most all cultures (Harari, 2015), inflicted upon one another and the earth.

Thus, what I try to do in what follows is to show, first, that there is a coherent holistic philosophical method that can be discerned behind what Inchausti calls "real teaching": a method that has been more and more precisely and caringly developed over millennia of patient philosophical thought. Then, second, I will show how I have learned to apply this method to the concrete particulars of my own life, focusing on how it has entailed the personal appropriation over time of my Jewish heritage: using the meaning I have found in my own life so as to enrich my capacity to evoke life in others, to personally extend the love of personal wisdom so to help it eventually become the *prevailing* mode of love in human life, overcoming the love of wealth and power that is now overtaking the globe in unprecedented ways.

Hellenism and Holism: The Search for More and More Holistic Conceptions of Life, and More and More Empathic Conceptions of Intelligence[1]

How to sum up over 2,000 years of trenchant thinking in a few pages? Perhaps the best place to start is with Plato's prognosis in the *Republic* that "unless there is a conjunction of these two things, political power and philosophical intelligence, there can be no cessation of troubles . . . for the human race" (1961, 473d). What I want to suggest is that this is, in a certain way, the central hypothesis of Western culture, and the central gift of that culture to the human world, but that it has taken over two millennia of experiments in thought and action to properly test it, and to refine it in a way that it is readily realizable in the world. And that a philosophically conceived and democratically implemented holistic pedagogy is the key to its realization, and can, once and for all, unlock the bars of insane violence that have long thwarted its emergence in most all large civilizations, not just the West.

In the *Republic*, of course, Plato concocted both a political utopia ruled by a few philosopher *kings* and the first sketch of a metaphysical philosophical system, positing the basic principles of the universe as the pure Ideas of the Beautiful, the True, and the Good. But the *Republic* ends with the admission that this *particular* utopia could probably never become anything more than a "city of words" (592b, cited in Cavell, 2004, p. xii) set up as a model for the right constitution of the rare personal soul strong enough to seek wisdom in a crazed world, but not for any feasible political state on earth. In the end, Plato himself sanctioned the divorce of "political power and philosophical intelligence" whose marriage, he said, was essential to the salvation of our species.

Modern philosophy has sought to improve on Plato by making "philosophical intelligence" more practical, and thus has given rise to a good number of political revolutions, the most successful of which has been the current—though newly tenuous—world prevalence of representative democracy. But its success came at the cost of a *divorce within* "philosophical intelligence" that bought it "political power" at the cost of its integrity.

The most powerful strands of modern philosophy, which came eventually to be known as "science," knowingly cast aside the pursuit of the beautiful and the good for the exclusive pursuit of "knowledge" in the *sole interest* of "power," in Francis Bacon's famous phrase. Baconian "mind over matter" "empiricism" *has* given a limited form of "philosophical intelligence"—the outward human empire over nature through technology—shallow outward rule over the whole earth. However, it was apparent to some very early on that humanity was being led down a potentially fatal blind alley by this *unwise* version of philosophy centered on mere *outward* power, as the root of *empire* at the heart of *empiricism* indicates. And that new patterns of "philosophical intelligence" embracing "the beautiful" and "the good" in more concrete ways than Plato and other idealists had been able to envision would need to be perceived and broadly implemented for a definitive end to be found for the "assault on humanity" (Sloan, 2005) initiated by a "science" that has eclipsed—and broadly and brutally usurped—the human orientation to the good and the whole.

The person generally agreed to be the first modern holistic educator, Jean-Jacques Rousseau, began his career in 1749, through a sudden epiphany that the scientific and technological "improvements" of modern life were having a drastically corruptive effect on human morals and human wholeness. His *Emile, or On Education*, in particular, initiated what one writer has called a "*Platonic* Enlightenment" (Williams, 2007), seeking to combine the best of ancient and modern philosophy, that has extended to today. This was furthered particularly through the philosophical system of Immanuel Kant, which generated the deeply influential educational thought of the American Transcendentalists. And from them stemmed the newly *moral* democratic politics of Lincoln, Tolstoy, Gandhi, and Martin Luther King, among others, through whom a morally "philosophical intelligence" has gained many footholds in the mostly thoroughly *im*moral modern political world.

Yet, essential to a fuller political instantiation of morally democratic "philosophical intelligence" is a better basic mode of thinking than Kant's, who believed in a quasi-Platonic, dualistic "metaphysics of morals," and thus left physical empiricism's *truth* claims about the workings of the material world relatively untouched, calling himself an "empirical realist, and a moral idealist." While recognizing humanity's fundamental orientation toward moral wholeness, he, at the same time, famously remarked on "the crooked timber of humanity that never could be made straight." He believed in a set of rational moral intuitions that was the common possession of humanity, and believed at the same time that we were possessed of selfish inclinations that could never be eliminated, never brought fully and wholly under rein by "philosophical intelligence." Where mind over matter empiricism eclipsed and occluded the beautiful and the good in the name of an all-powerful knowledge, *Kantian* transcendentalism exalted them over knowledge, but didn't have a consistent way of connecting what we feel as beautiful and know as good to *all* of what we know to be true. That became the task of a mode of philosophy that came to be known as "phenomenology," also called "*transcendental* empiricism" by its founder and greatest exponent, Edmund Husserl.

Where the motto of "mind over matter" empiricism is "knowledge is power," showing it is based on the untested presumption that life is fundamentally about the acquisition of power *for* oneself and one's tribe *over* others and things *not* oneself, the founding idea of phenomenology is that the very boundary between self and world is artificial and untrue. The world in which we *oppose* "I" and "it" is an illusion. Only the holistically *relational* world of "I" and "thou" is true. This deeper, grounding understanding, which Husserl called the *correlational apriori*, reveals that "The world and the world-experiencing [person] are dancing—at all times, on all levels, in all forms and shapes—a tango" (Luft, 2011, p. 15).

This fundamental understanding of life as a dance of all with all, not as a war of all against all, provides a philosophical *para*physics and a natural *para*psychology that generates an *eductive logic* of empathy, an educative *ethic* of care, and a *co*-educative *politics* of meaning to replace the *meta*physical oppositions between duty and inclination and between power and goodness plaguing even the sublime thinking of Plato and Kant (Novak, in progress).

Phenomenology thus methodically opens up an empathic and ecological vision of community and political life that can be constituted in such a way that *everyone* can become what Inchausti calls a "real teacher" of others. And the more that everyone seeks for and attains empathy, care, and meaning, the more the world *itself* becomes alive with and imbued with meaning. The mutual cultivation of empathic lifeforce results in the creation of a *real* lifeworld that is the *full, living, intentionally created* correlative of relational awareness.

The magical re-enchantment of life that we see in so many holistic schools is, thus, an image of how we can holistically re-create the world as a whole.

And holistic education becomes the means of awakening ourselves from the nightmare of what has hitherto constituted human history: the envisionment of a universal human awakeness to life and the gradual accomplishment of each person's facility in dancing with it constitute the definitive end of the wars amongst ourselves and against nature that the West has certainly egregiously exacerbated, but did not initiate.

In his 1935 Vienna Lecture, Husserl declared that out of the ashes of what we now *call* "civilization"—but has become patently uncivil in Fascist states and is latently so in the fascination with technology and the resultant eclipse of humanity that the West had unleashed on the world—can arise a new humanism and a new humanity, arising like a phoenix out of those very ashes.

This is no less true today. And for it we will probably need *both* the methodical strictness of consciousness of philosophical phenomenology to encompass the dehumanizing aspects of an objective science falsely exalted as the supreme human accomplishment *and* the assiduous cultivation of the diverse lifeforce of a host of "real teachers," in schools and beyond them. To produce the tremendous spontaneity of conscience now sorely needed to heal the many different wounds our species has come to inflict on the world through its newfound power over it. And so, to teach us not to dominate the world, but to dance with it.

Hebraism and Holism: The Story of Judaism Retold as the Search for More and More Holistic Intuitions of Life, through the Cultivation of the Seeing of Holy Meaning in Each Event of Personal Life

It is actually even more difficult for me to sum up the storied meaning of my own life in a few pages than it was to sum up the story of Western philosophy. The best way to begin, though, is with a cross-culturally historic moment occurring decades before my life began: the moment when the scion of Hebraic Hasidism, Abraham Joshua Heschel, became enamored with the Hellenic philosophy of Edmund Husserl. For those of you for whom the name of Heschel does not ring an immediate bell, you may be familiar with (or you can google) the picture of him, with his majestic white hair and beard, crossing the Selma bridge arm in arm with Martin Luther King. Heschel's fascination with Husserlian phenomenology as a student in Berlin in the 1920s helped him come to see, a few decades later, that the wholeness of his *own* being and personal voice could be an essential force for the renewal of the holistic community of Judaism—whose central prayer, the Sh'ma (Deuteronomy 6:4), invokes a people's careful attention to the hidden divine wholeness of creation—after its devastation in the Nazi Holocaust.

And out of Heschel's vibrant voice eventually grew a global religious movement called Jewish Renewal, with which, over the past 20 years, I have become more and more closely affiliated, and which I have come to see as an historic source of life both for myself and for the world. It seems in no way an accident that the founder of this movement, the neo-Hasidic Rabbi Zalman Schachter-Shalomi, became deep friends with the Dalai Lama, and occupied the World Wisdom Chair of Buddhist Naropa University for the last two decades of his long life.

From their first receiving of the commandments, the Jews have called themselves "a people of priests" (Exodus 19:6), a spiritual democracy. And Jewish Renewal, in my experience, has given a pedagogical tilt to this, seeking to create a people of "real teachers" (and the Hebrew word "rabbi," or "reb," means nothing more than "teacher"): who, in Inchausti's words, take their very lives—both as individual persons and as living members of this special people—up into transcendent speech and action, which helps others do precisely the same, both as individual persons and as members of whatever larger historical peoples they happen to belong to. Many are familiar with the Jewish toast "l'chaim!"—"to life!"—through the song of that title in *Fiddler on the Roof*. Jewish Renewal has, in a way, interpreted that toast as the utmost of ethical categorical imperatives: that the cultivation of empathically meaningful speech and action that brings transcendent life to an otherwise mundane world—the life that *adds* "to life" and blesses it (and the Hebrew word for "blessing" is *baruch*, which translates literally as "more life," as Tony Kushner notes at the end of his epic play *Angels in America*)—is the fundamental manifestation of the divine, whether literally "Jewish" or not.

So, Inchaustian "real teaching" has come to be *my* Judaism. And, in some ways, it has been one of the great gifts of life in my life that it took most of the course of my life for me to be able to understand this.

I was raised Jewish in the "enlightened" Reform tradition. But my history with my heritage was a spotty one. When I was 14, I asked my dad, in typical 14-year-old fashion, if he thought he was God. And when he said, "Yes, I *am* the God of *this* house!" I immediately, intuitively and unthinkingly, became an atheist. In my late thirties I first became interested in, and then became deeply involved in, a political movement called the Politics of Meaning, led by Rabbi Michael Lerner, one of Heschel's strongest disciples. But I didn't really start on a path to claiming Judaism as my own until—at a Jewish retreat I mostly chose to attend to study with Rabbi Lerner—I encountered the gentler personhoods of two other rabbis, one of them a woman, who had been influenced more by Reb Zalman than by Heschel.

What it took in the end to solidify my relationship to my heritage, though, was a phenomenal epiphany that directly healed the wound that had long ago severed my relationship with it.

In the summer of 2015, nearly 60, I happened to put on a holistic education conference not far from Boulder, where Zalman had settled at the end of his life to teach at Naropa. And one of the attendees who was a friend of mine, and had also been a friend of his, knew that there was going to be a celebration of his yahrzeit there, the one-year anniversary of his death. This took the form mostly of two hours of extended Islamic Sufi dancing in a Boulder synagogue. That one friend and I, along with a female friend of mine with whom I was going through some personal difficulties, drove down to Boulder. Beyond being regaled with wondrous tales of Reb Zalman's wondrous life, we encountered the sparkling eyes and moving bodies of person after person after person in the deep and transcendent ecumenicism of those circle dances—and in this seeing of and moving with one another we seemed to dance with the whole circle of life.

Once the dancing was done, I was able to make the acquaintance of many souls who since have grown to be of deep importance in my life. But, more importantly, this evening turned into the gateway for an ongoing series of transformative events that have increasingly bound the whole of my own soul to my Jewish heritage. Three such events, in particular, bear relating here. Through the first, occurring the very next night, Reb Zalman became my spiritual father. Through the second, a few weeks after, I came to feelingly reconcile with my birth father. And through the third, later that year, I came to be a kind of father, rabbi, and teacher to a group of fellow Jews to whom I could relate the process of my own healing as a kind of symbol for the historic healing of our people, and as a revelation of the deepest gifts it has to offer the world.

In 1988, when I was 31, my father who thought he was God, after a series of mishaps and bad choices, chose to leave life: becoming the God who killed himself. I, in turn, chose not to attend his funeral, and had never had a desire to visit his grave, which lay outside a small town in Nebraska. In 2014, though, a good friend, who had reminded me a lot of the best parts of my dad, happened to visit that town, and went of his own choice to the gravesite. He phoned me as he approached it, and read to me the inscription. It read "You were loved!" But I heard him say "You *are* loved!" And suddenly all the deep and lavish emotions I had felt for my dad as a child rushed over my being, and went out to my living friend at the same time as to my dead father.

By the time I attended Reb Zalman's yahrzeit, I was not, for various reasons, consciously looking for that kind of intensely deep male bonding any longer. And when my female friend and I visited Zalman's grave the night after the yahrzeit, at the invitation of a new friend we had met there, I made no conscious connection with my dad. But at one point, with many of the Rebbe's closest friends and relatives gathered around the grave, this new friend began to sing a niggun—a Jewish spiritual nonsense song—that he had earlier written for and sung for Zalman. Magically, the friend with whom I had once been romantically involved, but now was experiencing some personal difficulties with, took my arm and put it around her waist. And something huge clicked deep inside me, opening the whole world in new ways. I suddenly felt deeply united both with the spirit of this sacred man—through these living gestures of these friends—and with the entire people whose goodness he sought both to represent and to cultivate. In a way, for the first time in my life, I had a *human* father, in Reb Zalman, and through him became a Jew who suddenly saw the whole of my humanity through the perspective of the life of this ancient people who had waveringly sought life over millennia, and been taught to do so a lot less waveringly by this wonderful man, this rebbe of rebbes, this real teacher of real teachers.

Not long afterward, I wrote to the friend who had gone to my dad's grave, to commemorate the anniversary of that event, though even then not consciously connecting the meaning of the two events at the two gravesites. But when he told me he had been to Nebraska again and had considered putting a stone on the grave—as is the Jewish custom—but in the end saw that was for me to do, it at once became blazingly clear that I *literally* had a God-given mission: to take a pink granite stone I had been given at my conference and had placed on the blessed Zalman's grave, and place it on the grave of the cursed man who had given me birth: precisely as a way of giving life again to a man who had chosen to remove himself from it in many ways, and not just through his suicide. So that I did. And I wept as I knelt and kissed the low gravestone.

Months later, I was able to sum up the meaning of this event at a Jewish men's retreat I was attending thanks to the encouragement of the male rabbi who had helped me initially reclaim my Judaism back in 1998. After telling my story around the campfire on the last night, this was the moral to it I came up with: "Our people went through another holocaust than the one the Nazis delivered to us. This was a holocaust to which we delivered ourselves: the holocaust of pursuing worldly 'success' at all costs, the self-inflicted holocaust of the soul of which my dad was a victim. This was largely a holocaust of men who, like him, chose to pretend to be Gods in the limited domains of their businesses and homes, and so unthinkingly forsook the living God always urging us *to life* and its *infinite* wholeness. Had my dad and I been able to attend an event like this together, he might have chosen differently. And when I see fathers and sons praying together here, I also see my dad and me, and all the lifegiving experiences we might have had together had we had *this* kind of Jewish framework for our relationship."

At that moment, a man who had become a great new friend—the night before he had, in fact, helped me write a letter to Reb Zalman on a Hebrew typewriter once belonging to him—came up and gave me a huge bear hug. And one of the founders of the event said that his hearing these words was a kind of capstone to the quarter century of work he had undertaken to create and build it, and through it to seek to build new kinds of Jewish men, more dedicated to life.

As I was preparing to leave the retreat, I realized I had another mission. My new friend had spoken around the campfire of the deep happiness he had discovered in his relatively new family. And I asked if I could make a quick visit to them on my way to visit other friends. We met at a park in the small town he lived in and then walked a few blocks to meet his wife and three very young children who were coming from a class they had all gone to. As soon as the children saw their father, there came the most joyous squeal simultaneously from all three: "Abba! Abba! Abba! Abba!" they called to him in Hebrew. And these cries were yet another way of waking my dad from the dead, and of bringing new life to my world.

A Clash of Fragmented Civilizations? Or a Cosmopolitan Tango?

The presidency of Donald Trump, for me, has been something of an image of my dad's coming back from the dead in quite another way: the mentality of pretended omnipotence and omniscience that killed him suddenly installed at the pinnacle of world power.

At this writing, we know not what holocausts may be in store.

But I think I can leave you with an image indicating that the lifegiving power of holism—if enough of humanity is educatively brought under its sway through real learning from real teachers—may eventually surmount the death-dealing power of holocausts brought about by humans vaunting themselves, and the differing cultures to which they belong, to be gods rather than vessels of divine life.

One of my new Jewish friends from Boulder is named Gabriella. After I had come to know her well, she confided in me that she had asked Reb Zalman to give her a new name to help her inaugurate a new spiritual emergence after a period of paralyzing depression she had recently experienced. "Gabriella" in Hebrew means, "she who is empowered by God." And I felt it as a very deep honor when she later said that our new friendship has been a decisive factor in making that power a reality in her life, as she has learned to turn many of the challenges of mental *dis*ability into new spiritual *a*bility, and has helped others do the same, in Inchaustian fashion, through a project she has called "Diagnosis: Human."

This friendship also provided me with a deeply teachable moment I experienced not long ago with a young African-American man I am helping to mentor, named Gabe. The university identifies this young man. And, though we haven't yet met in person as of this writing, we have had many conversations over the phone about his educational past, present, and future. From sixth grade through high school, he'd experienced challenge after challenge in the largely nonholistic schools he'd attended. But by the time we first conversed he had gotten solidly on his feet, attending a fine community college in California where he had found a fresh start. And he had developed strong aspirations to be a personal force for the healing of the many holocausts visited upon his own people—in many ways far worse than anything ever visited upon mine.

One day a few months ago, I was helping Gabe talk through some new challenges he was facing, and was searching for a hopeful way to end our conversation. Knowing he was an evangelical Christian, I asked him if he happened to know the Hebrew meaning of his given name, Gabriel. My new knowledge that it meant "the strength of God"—which in fact he did *not* know—was a holistic gift of meaning passed directly from Zalman, to Gabriella, to me, and finally to Gabe as he audibly choked up on hearing those words as a divine opening through the crisis he was then experiencing.

Since that time Gabe has been accepted as a transfer student to one of the top liberal arts colleges in the States. And the boost of confidence given by that, at the same time, accidental and intentional gift, and our pedagogical relationship which that gift encapsulated, were perhaps critical factors in his confidence to present himself in such a way that *others* had confidence in his ability to make that enormous educational leap.

Gabe's leap was also a leap of meaning *across* cultures, and thus can serve as a symbol for the many more such leaps that need to be made in the new global world in which we all now live, which so many are finding personally and culturally threatening.

When asked why he refrained from obeying so many of the customs of his city, the philosopher Diogenes replied, "Before I am a citizen of Athens, I am a citizen of the universe, *kosmos polites*, and my main object in life is to make myself one with the ultimate power of the universe, not just the limited power of my people." This was the historic origin of the term "cosmopolitan."

This word today has in some contexts become equilibrated with the morally lax, with the idea that freeing ourselves from traditional moral strictures frees us to wallow in hedonism—an object of *legitimate* fear by those with ties to tradition if that is the kind of cosmopolitanism the world actually chooses to follow.

But this was *not* Diogenes' idea. He believed in *higher* meanings, not in the loss of meaning, when bridges beyond our particular cultures are made.[2]

My conversation with Gabe was a lot easier than the conversations that need to be held between, and within, the many fragmented nations, and other factions, of our global world. But I hope, none-theless, that it can serve as an image for you of the great, divine power that can course through the world, as each of us learns holistically "to take our very lives up into speech so that others may do the same." A hope that we can one day transform the many battles in which we are now engaged into what the Kantians Schiller and Beethoven called "*diesen Kuss der ganzen Welt*"—"this kiss of the *whole* world"—that we might now phenomenologically rename "the cosmopolitan tango"! And that the gifts of Western culture will supply their share of the genuinely divine music of that tango—dispelling at long last the deafening drumbeats of the march of mere human power, vaunting false divinity, with which that culture, over most of the course of modernity until now, has sought to dominate the earth.

Notes

1 The two central sections of the paper build on a famous saying of the philosopher Immanuel Kant--"Concepts without intuitions are empty; intuitions without concepts are blind."
2 See Hansen, 2011 for a full educational treatment of practices of cosmopolitanism in today's schools.

References

Cavell, S. (2004). *Cities of words: Pedagogical letters on a register of the moral life*. Cambridge, MA: Harvard University Press.
Hansen, D. T. (2011). *The teacher and the world: A study of cosmopolitanism as education*. New York: Routledge.
Harari, Y. N. (2015). *Sapiens: A brief history of humankind*. New York: HarperCollins.
Inchausti, R. (1993). *Spitwad sutras: Classroom teaching as sublime vocation*. Westport, CT: Bergin & Garvey.
Luft, S. (2011). *Subjectivity and lifeworld in transcendental phenomenology*. Evanston: Northwestern University Press.
Novak, B. (in progress). *The opening of the American heart: The great educational awakening on the horizon of democratic life*.
Plato (1961). *Dialogues* (E. Hamilton & H. Cairns, Eds). Princeton, NJ: Bollingen.
Sloan, D. (2005). Education and the modern assault on being human: Nurturing body, soul, and spirit. In J. P. Miller, S. Karsten, D. Denton, D. Orr, & I. C. Kates (Eds), *Holistic learning and spirituality in education: Breaking new ground* (pp. 26–47). Albany, NY: SUNY Press.
Williams, D. L. (2007). *Rousseau's Platonic Enlightenment*. University Park: Pennsylvania State University Press.

37

Toward an Integrative Mind

Tobin Hart

What kind of mind do we need for these days and the days to come? Lightening fast change, global interdependence, technological wizardry, political bifurcation, shuddering danger, and remarkable possibility are the norm. The U.S. military has an acronym, VUCA–volatility, uncertainly, change, ambiguity–that captures this sheer intensity.

Our current emphasis on information acquisition and on basic literacy and numeracy is simply insufficient to prepare our charges for even the near horizon. It seems increasingly clear that our largely nineteenth century-based model of learning is in desperate need of an upgrade. The simplistic and continuing emphasis built around basic information acquisition, truncated and instantiated through standardized test scores, misses a genuine consideration of the kind of depth, creativity, and transformative flexibility of mind that seems so essential for the real concerns of today's world. This fixation has distracted us from the big questions: What kind of person and populace do we want and need for the world of today and tomorrow? Without a big enough view, we end up at best with improved means to an unimproved end. Central to holding a more holistic vision of education and fostering consciousness that is adequate to this age is understanding not simply *what* we know that matters, but far more *how* and *why* we know.

The Good Life

There is a place where developing the mind and serving society was the central mission of education: the original Liberal Arts. The Liberal Arts have a 2,500-year history originating from the ancient Greeks. This was the original schooling for the free man and the means to preserve such freedom. These were disciplines to help one develop through reflection, study, and practice.

These original seven arts were divided into two categories that should seem familiar: the trivium, consisting of the verbal arts of logic, grammar, and rhetoric, and the quadrivium, consisting of the numerical arts of mathematics, geometry, music, and astronomy. Music, and then the language arts, were taught earliest, as they were essential for everything that followed; music especially for its evocation and training of direct feeling. Mathematics blended in soon thereafter. We do almost the same thing 2,500 years later, with the unfortunate exception of the early centrality of music.

This ancient approach is the very literal foundation for formal education in the West. But the central organizing principles and practices of the Liberal Arts are something we might not recognize. It was not acquisition of content that was the key, although information was and must remain the *currency* of learning.

Liberal, as in Liberal Arts, is often understood to mean broad, as in broadly educated. But the root of the word liberal is the same as liberty and liberation; it is about freedom, not merely knowing lots of different bits. These were the arts of liberty (although mostly available only for the elite at that time). The goal was freedom from ignorance, from prejudice, and from out of control "passions" such as lust or greed. The learning was about cultivating the freedom to choose wisely, to develop reason, grow in virtue, to create our work and our life in a way that serves and satisfies. This genuinely holistic view was the meaning of *The Good Life.*

The ultimate function of the Liberal Arts was to secure the liberation of the mind. The integrative principle is *humanitas.* The fullness of our humanity is revealed and may flourish through this inner growth; our human potential for the good of self and society was to be liberated in this way. Historian Pierre Hadot (1995) described the high end of these original liberal arts as "a method for training people to live and look at the world in a new way. It is an attempt to transform humankind" (p. 107). The roots of our education are about preparing us for a life of flourishing and fulfillment by developing our humanity, our human consciousness, our mind and soul.

The Renaissance found much of its inspiration through the rediscovery of ancient Greek ideas. This period profoundly opened human horizons in ways that we still celebrate, even revere, including greater freedom for far more people. However, these visions and values that are often associated with the ancient Greek and early Renaissance eras have undergone significant changes that have been shaping our consciousness and culture ever since.

From the sixteenth to the seventeenth centuries there was a particular turning away from earlier Renaissance values. Toulmin (1992) contends that the intellectual fashion became more rigid and dogmatic and reason itself became narrower, no longer respecting context or appreciating diversity to the same degree.

This narrowing of knowing is hinged on separating the object we are perceiving from us—objectification—and by reducing it to parts—reductionism. Objectification and reductionism, alongside assumptions of materialism, dualism, mechanism, and determinism, are the primary tools of the modernist way of knowing and tend to engender knowing by detachment, reduction, and domination. Whether the atom or our neighboring state or a competing ideology, we might say the work is to capture and tame it to our will and then we celebrate our victory, our greatness.

Sir Francis Bacon, instrumental in the formation of this worldview and method of inquiry through his articulation of inductive reasoning, understood just what this knowing implied for education: "Mastery of nature for the relief of man's estate begins to become the governing objective of education" (Bacon, 1900, p. 315). The aim was now to "enlarge the power and empire of mankind in general over the universe" (p. 366). It looks as if we have succeeded remarkably well in expanding our powers. In Rene Descartes' (1994) words, "[We have rendered] ourselves the lords and possessor of nature" (p. 46).

As powerful and valuable as this is—and there is absolutely no denying its worth—we are recognizing the limits and unintended consequences of this as an exclusive way of knowing.

One hundred years before Bacon and Descartes, Leonardo da Vinci understood the limits and danger of this emerging perspective; he referred to it as the *abbreviators'* approach. His words seem stunningly prophetic now, 500 years later.

> The abbreviators of works do injury to knowledge and to love . . . Of what value is he who, in order to abbreviate the parts of those things of which he professes to give complete knowledge, leaves out the greater part of the things of which the whole is composed? . . . . You don't see that you are falling into the same error as one who strips the tree of its adornment of branches full of leaves, intermingled with fragrant flowers or fruit, in order to demonstrate that the tree is good for making planks.
>
> *(cited in Capra, 2007, p. 12)*

Da Vinci's approach was an integrated science, philosophy, and art of quality and wholeness, an exploration of patterns and the interrelatedness of things, more complete than the mechanistic and reductionistic understanding that was to emerge and dominate our worldview and education.

His keen sensibilities and intimate style of knowing engendered reverence for natural creations and recognition of patterns and interconnecting phenomena that provided a more integrated way of seeing the world. Without this way of knowing, as he says, we "do injury to knowledge and to love." Herein lies our current educational predicament. We have invested nearly everything in an abbreviators' approach. To what extent does our leaving out key ways of knowing foster the same kind of injury?

Episteme

Confusion arises in education today particularly because we are at the end of an era and we cannot quite make out the near horizon and, thus, how education should best prepare for it.

Civilization appears to move through various eras or epochs of knowing, that is, the grounds on which we constitute truth and knowledge. Philosopher Michel Foucault (2002) referred to this as the *episteme* of an era. Thomas Kuhn (1962) spoke of scientific *paradigms* in a fairly similar way. Basically, the episteme is made up of the assumptions, rules, roles, standards, and methods of knowing that guide and constrain how we think and know. This serves as a kind of epistemic unconscious that we operate within. Such an epoch of knowing is thought to last a few centuries and emerges from, overlaps with, and then eclipses the previous episteme. For example, in the West, the enlightenment saw the rise of the individual and the application of a particular scientific, materialist knowing as the ultimate standard for truth, bit by bit overturning the ultimate authority of religion to shape worldview.

More recently, the postmodern turn has opened cracks in the modernist episteme. It helps us recognize that our nature and knowing is more socially embedded and historically shaped. It helps us unpack "facts," unearth assumptions, and ask critical questions about the backstory of knowledge. For example, knowledge is often tied to power. When we ask, "Who funded that research?" we are recognizing the mutability of "objective fact." Truth is mediated by our intent, expectations, social status, language, race, history, spin, and more.

This in no way whatsoever diminishes the importance of science or facts or measurement, but instead helps us go behind the curtain of so-called "objective" knowledge, recognizing that "truth," to one degree or another, is historically situated and socially constructed.

Today, after 400 years of a modernist backdrop challenged by the postmodern turn, it appears that we are on the cusp of a new episteme, able for the first time to see not just the cracks in the modernist paradigm, but how it can be expanded, deepened, and enriched to form a new whole, a more definitive, and, above all, a more *human*, worldview. The challenge involves not just exposing the flaws in the abbreviators' approach as the postmodernists do, but finding a way to bring together the bits and the bytes in the living of an integrated life in a world of global technical interconnection but human disconnect. Goethe (2008) said it this way: "To find yourself in the infinite you must distinguish and then combine" (p. 48).

Both the modern and the postmodern have helped us to distinguish, dissect, define, and deconstruct in so many domains. We have focused on the function of mind that takes things apart and meets the world at arm's length.

We also need to connect, meeting the world up close and in person, to feel it in our bodies, to be moved, to find context, meaning, and beauty so that the bits and bytes make sense. We do not want or need to just catalogue our life; we need to enter it. In so doing, we are transformed.

This shift is not a romanticized return to a simpler time, turning back the clock to the pre-modern immersion in the forces of the world. It is, instead, about moving beneath the surface of a value-less, materialist, reductionist worldview to recognize our emergent, co-constituted, interdependent, integrated existence.

After centuries of increasingly one-sided knowing, we are called to find a balance between subjective and objective, participative and detached, meaning and "fact," unseen and seen, rhizomatic and viral development beside linear and sequential, intuition and logic, resonance and rationality, systems and components, compassion and calculation, feeling and reason, forest and tree, mystery and certainty.

This integration requires a fundamental recalibration in knowing.

Two Ways of Knowing

There are two ways of knowing. That is, two basic ways that the mind works to know the world. Of course, knowing is complex and multifaceted. There are myriad variations, to be sure, and certainly plenty of other ways to slice this rhetorically, but essentially most knowing comes down to this.

One way we could call *categorical*. This knows the world through abstraction, through labeling, separating it from us, through taking apart to understand. Categorical awareness narrows focus, seeks precision, detail, and objectivity. It simplifies and represents, proceeds linearly and sequentially. As we dig deeper with this tool, things are reduced to parts, to lowest units that are differentiated and catalogued. It reaches its current apex in the metaphor of computer zeros and ones. Schooling has been emphasizing categorical knowing.

The other knowing is through *contact*. It is direct, embodied, recognizes wholes and connections. It is intimate, holistic, relational, and dynamic. Awareness through contact enables a broader view, one connected with the world and the body. This knowing seeks novelty, picks up implicit meaning and metaphor.

Drawing from a vast body of neuroscientific and phenomenological data, McGilchrist (2009) contends that these ways of knowing have neurological substrates roughly corresponding to the anatomically distinct hemispheres of the brain.

Today, we are recognizing that left and right hemispheres of the brain help to provide two different ways of relating to the world. Left brings that categorical, narrowed, discriminative focus, while the attention of the right is broad and flexible, connects directly, and recognizes connected wholes as opposed to the left's individual parts. These seem perfectly designed to complement one another and both ways of knowing are essential to human understanding. The problem is that their partnership has come unhinged.

One of McGilchrist's primary insights is that the left does not have the capacity to integrate the right. By its very nature, the left cannot process or value in wholes or draw material from the body and senses so readily. On the other hand, the right is largely integrative and naturally incorporates the data from the left, and is, thus, positioned to serve as the driver of consciousness.

However, because of the current domination of categorical consciousness activated and amplified by objectivism and reductionism and the education that both derives from and reinforces it, the right has lost its primacy; the left is running the show. Inevitably, the view it can see is limited, an abstracted or virtual view of the world—a simulacrum—but one thought to be real and assumed to be complete, encouraging a particularly fixed view of "truth."

Both ways of knowing are critical. Both impact how we see, what we see, and, ultimately, how we treat what we see. But in human culture and classrooms, the past several centuries have increasingly emphasized one aspect of mind—da Vinci's abbreviators' approach—and the consequences have been monumental to both how we know and how we love.

It is not hard to see that the power of technology has overrun our wisdom to use it, that despite great advances in knowledge across every discipline and instantaneous access to information and one another, we are not treating one another better or more fairly. The Greeks' notion of liberation gets mistaken for buying power; we take advantage of unprecedented opportunities for indulgence; The Good Life comes to mean stuff and celebrity. In gaining the possession of the world, we seem to have lost possession of our very minds, and certainly to have lost our way.

Gateways Toward the New Good Life

How do we balance the powerful precision of categorical consciousness with the open-ended view and intimate touch of contact? Is it even possible or practical to go about this in our daily life and in contemporary education?

In the middle of this moment, this day, or a school assignment, there are certain orienting activities that help open the aperture of consciousness, welcoming contact and engendering a more integrated knowing. These have largely been absent from contemporary consideration as they fall outside the modernist–abbreviators' approach that guides educational enterprise. There are, of course, wonderful exceptions in which other means and directions of inquiry have been included. Historically, more intimate knowing has found some harbor in the humanities, where subjectivity, meaning, and beauty have retained some cache. A host of "progressive" educational orientations (e.g., Holistic, Humanistic, Contemplative, Democratic, Critical, etc.), although having plenty of variability, share a larger view of the learner and of learning. And recent initiatives, ranging from character education to social–emotional learning, demonstrate the acknowledgment of education's role in fostering civility and interiority. But it is hard to sustain such initiatives in the unstable winds of political, economic, or social conditions and implemented through an out-of-date operating system. A more fundamental recalibration and revaluation of our ways of knowing is required at the edge of this new episteme.

There is certainly a wide array of conditions, approaches, and practices that engender the kind of deep understanding that is called for. But a very brief thumbnail sketch of five gateways—approaches to knowing or inquiry—may give some sense of the general kind of emphases that may move us toward a more holistic, integrated consciousness with the power to bridge the divides we have created in our world. These are elaborated in detail with practical classroom examples elsewhere (see Hart, 2014).

Contemplation

"Pay attention" is perhaps the instruction we implore most often in education. Yet, we rarely help students to do this, we just insist that they do. To deploy, shift, sustain, and open awareness gives us power to use the mind intentionally. The most basic and universal practices of contemplation do just this, developing the strength and flexibility of the muscle of attention. In addition, the contemplative mind allows us to do more. With just a little practice we can turn our gaze inward, witness the content (sensations, thoughts, feelings) and the process of one's own consciousness, helping to clean and even regrind the lens of perception.

This reflection leads to metacognition, which allows us not only to inquire into the question at hand, but also toward the asker of the question. We can become the object of inquiry as well as the instrument, as we look into self and subject. Ultimately, the contemplative allows us to interrupt habitual patterns and reactions and stay awake to new ways of thinking and being, to the immediate flow of consciousness inside and out. In a contemplative moment, there is fresh chance to awake to the taste of the food, the sound of the bird, a fresh inspiration that arrives out of the blue, or notice the pattern of thought that has kept me stuck. This opening of consciousness can bring vitality, depth, and meaning to existence.

In addition, the attention to attention has a variety of related effects. This inner technology allows us to steady the mind and modulate emotional reaction, reduce stress response in the body, and foster executive function, especially important at a time when outer technology is pushing so much, so fast, at us. We discover that this way of knowing has the potential to alter the function and even the structure of the brain and, with it, shift long-term traits such as compassion and emotional balance (see Hart, 2008). The simplest of activities, such as a moment of silence, mindful attention, or quiet reflection, can help to open this gateway in a moment, in or outside of the classroom (see Hart, 2004).

Empathy

While science claims a detached, objective gaze, the way some great scientists do science is often quite different from the way we teach it. Specifically, that difference involves a less detached empiricism where the gap between knower and the object of study is reduced. Nobel Laureate in genetics Barbara McClintock says it this way, "You have to have a feeling for the organism, you have to have an openness to let it come to you" (Keller, 1983, p. 198).

Not only in science, but in all domains, a capacity to put oneself in another's shoes provides a multiplicity of perspectives, helping us understand how a terrorist might, from another point of view, be a freedom fighter or vice versa. This allows us to reconsider our own assumptions, the other's vantage point, and see the impact of social context on worldview and one's choices.

As we close the distance between self and object, something else happens. We become less willing to do violence to the other, whether a tree or our neighbor. In fact, empathy has been described as the trait that makes us most human (Azar, 1997) and the foundation for morality (Hoffman, 1990). Thus, a more intimate empiricism has profound implications for values and virtue, caring and civility, domains that education has been tasked to develop. When we open to this level of understanding, we find the mind most often naturally includes the heart.

Empathy is about a way of meeting the world, a participative way of knowing. We begin to resonate with the other, experiencing intimately our interconnection, our *interbeing* (Nhat Hanh, 1995). When the frustrated teacher comes to really meet and understand the "frustrating" student, the world changes for both. When a student has "a feeling for the organism", appreciation, awe, wonder, and understanding follow. This quality of meeting engenders the possibility for collaboration, community, and communion and, with it, a more vibrant sense of interdependence.

Imagination

In general, there has been a tendency in the modern West not to take imagination seriously. The non-observable, non-logical nature of imagination renders it difficult to pin down and, thus, awkward in a rational, materialist backdrop. Imagination has been mistaken as merely a colorful accent to life, and largely dismissed in an educational age anxious about meeting standards and status. However, we do not outgrow imagination individually or culturally, as this process is fundamental to our knowing at every level of development and across every significant domain. We hear, for example, that imagination is the source of insight from scientific discovery to artistic innovation to practical problem solving. Improvisation, divergent thinking, play, fantasy, myth, spontaneity, irony, metaphor, and design are at home here as we imagine possibility beyond the information given, so essential in this dynamic age. Leonard and Willis (2008) make explicit the role of imagination in teaching and learning.

We might imagine ourselves as a cancer cell or bacterium, as did the inventor of the polio vaccine, Jonas Salk (1983), or conduct thought experiments, such as Einstein imagining, for example, what would happen if we traveled at the speed of light. The moral imagination of Mother Theresa or the "dream" of Martin Luther King, Jr. opens new possibilities, changing both consciousness and culture. Essentially, imagination builds a bridge between the known and the unknown. It enables us to work through problems in the laboratory of our minds and perhaps reach into hidden realms, the *mundus imaginals*, as Henri Corbin (1972) named it, from where we may draw inspiration.

Beauty[1]

The ancients knew that somehow the goal of life was not only about the good and the true; it was also about the beautiful. Whitehead (1967) claimed that the "teleology of the universe is the production of beauty" (p. 324). Somehow, beauty embodies something both immanent and transcendent that resonates deep within us. It awakens emotion and we know emotion is central to deep learning and motivation. We recognize it, we seek it, we base decisions on it; we might call it "quality." Even in science we discover beauty may be the prime mover: "The scientist . . . studies [nature] because he takes pleasure in it; and he takes pleasure in it because it is beautiful" (Poincaré, 2003, p. 22).

One of the primary sources of beauty is nature: a spectacular sunset, the redness of a rose, the majestic flight of a hawk. Nature serves as wonder for the mind. We know that most descriptions of transcendent ecstasy are triggered by nature (Laski, 1968) and ecstasy reflects a profound opening of consciousness, hinting at a move from category to contact. In intimate encounter with the natural world, we so often come to recognize that we are part of nature rather than detached from it and, as such, our sense of belonging and responsibility is radically amplified.

Attention to beauty, quality, or an aesthetic is not ancillary, but instead central to an integrated mind. In this day or this assignment, we may lead with appreciation instead of categorization, try to behold rather than just label, encounter first hand the tension of contrast and harmony (Whitehead, 1967) in an assignment or any moment, and work to manifest our own beautiful expression in the world.

Embodiment

From Plato to Augustine to Descartes, the body has been understood as primitive or mechanistic. But contemporary cognitive science and our lived experience paints a picture of a body—feeling, sensation, movement, physiological processes—that is not separate from, or inferior to, thinking, but is instead unified with it. For example, the discovery of neuropeptides and their receptor sites, assumed to exist only in the brain and associated with thinking, have been discovered in the gut (Pert, 1986). This enteric nervous system alongside other body-based systems, such as the heart, appear to be central to knowing. Thinking is a more embodied process than assumed.

From this expanded understanding, education is dramatically catalyzed by attention to the body, developing an embodied mind, we might say. The mind–body unity helps put our parts back together and with it comes a richer, sensual, more robust way of knowing cultivated by attunement to the body. Asking simple questions such as "Where am I now? "What do I notice in my body?" turns us toward the felt sense (Gendlin, 1988) that incorporates a more immediate and integrated knowing.

In addition to this most direct understanding of embodiment, we can recognize that we are embodied and embedded in a locale, a culture, and the natural world. A front edge in the study of human cognition is referred to as 4E cognition (enacted, embodied, extended, embedded). Rather than passively receiving the world, there is constant interaction between mind, body, and environment. Enacted implies that we shape and activate the world we see. Embodied tells us we know through our bodies. Extended suggests that consciousness extends beyond the body–mind into the environment. Embedded recognizes that we exist within a context, embedded in culture and locale. This is too superficial a depiction, of course, but it does give a sketch of a theory of mind that challenges the prevailing Cartesian dualism and the detached, self-generating consciousness that remains a dominant superstructure for educational theory and practice. As such, it helps to understand and make space for the return of the body to education.

Knowing and Loving

Recalibrating knowing in teaching and learning gives us a better shot at a consciousness in which transformative flexibility is the norm. Consciousness stands on content, but is not reduced to it. An integrated, holistic approach returns information and basic skills to their rightful place as the currency of education and returns the development of mind (knower and knowing) in its relationship to the world to being the primary agent and the target for teaching.

In every moment we stand poised between moving on and moving into our experience, between differentiation and integration, between categorizing or making contact with our world. The opening of a more intimate knowing in balance with the powerful analytic mind gives us a chance, in the words of Thomas Berry (2000), to view the world not as a collection of objects, but to experience it instead as a communion of subjects. When we do so, we not only lessen the chance of doing injury to knowledge and to love, we heighten the possibility of making deep knowing and deep loving the new standard for education and for human existence on earth.

Note

1 See also Hart, this volume
This chapter has been partially excerpted with permission from: Hart, T. (2014). *The integrated mind: Transformative education for a world on fire.* Lanham, MD: Rowman and Littlefield.

References

Azar, B. (1997). Defining the trait that makes us most human. *APA Monitor, 28*(11), 1–15.

Bacon, F. (1900). Novum Organum, I. 3; I. 129. In *Advancement of learning and Novum Organum.* New York: Wiley.

Berry, T. (2000). *The great work: Our way into the future.* New York: Random House.

Capra, F. (2007). *The science of Leonardo: Inside the mind of the great genius of the renaissance.* New York: Doubleday.

Corbin, H. (1972). *Mundus imaginalis, or the imaginary and the imaginal.* Ashuelot, NH: Golgonooza Press.

Descartes, R. (1994). *A discourse on method: meditations and principles.* New York: J. M. Dent.

Foucault, M. (2002). *The archeology of knowledge* (A. M. Sheridan Smith, Trans.) London: Routledge (original work published 1969).

Gendlin, E. T. (1988). *Focusing* (2nd edn). New York: Bantam Books.

Goethe, J. W. (2008). Excerpt from Atmosphäre. In P. Bishop, *Analytical psychology and German classical aesthetics: Goethe, Schiller, and Jung Vol. 1.* New York: Routledge.

Hadot, P. (1995). *Philosophy as a way of life: Spiritual exercises from Socrates to Foucault* (A. Davidson, Ed.). Oxford, UK: Blackwell.

Hart, T. (2004). Opening the contemplative mind in the classroom. *Journal of Transformative Education, 2*(1), 28–46.

Hart, T. (2008). Interiority and education: Exploring the neurophenomenology of contemplation and its potential role in learning. *Journal of Transformative Education, 6*(4), 235–250.

Hart, T. (2014). *The integrated mind: Transformative education for a world on fire.* Lanham, MD: Rowman and Littlefield.

Hoffman, M. L. (1990). Empathy and justice motivation. *Motivation and Emotion, 14*(2), 151–172.

Keller, E. (1983). *A feeling for the organism: The life and work of Barbara McClintock.* New York: Freeman.

Kuhn, T. S. (1962). *The structure of scientific revolutions.* Chicago, IL: University of Chicago Press.

Laski, M. (1968). *Ecstasy: A study of some secular and religious experiences.* London: Cresset Press.

Leonard, T. & Willis, P. (Eds) (2008). *Pedagogies of the imagination: Mythopoetic curriculum in educational practice.* Dordrecht: The Netherlands: Springer.

McGilchrist, I. (2009). *The master and his emissary: The divided brain and the making of the western world.* New Haven: Yale University Press.

Nhat Hanh, T. (1995). *The Heart of understanding: Commentaries on the Prajna-paramita heart sutra.* Berkeley, CA: Parallax Press.

Pert, C. B. (1986). The wisdom of the receptors: Neuropeptides, the emotions, and bodymind. *Advance, 3*(3), 8–16.

Poincaré, H. (2003). *Science and method.* Mineola, NY: Dover (original work published 1914).

Salk, J. (1983). *Anatomy of reality: Merging of intuition and reason.* New York: Columbia University Press.

Toulmin, S. (1992). *Cosmopolis: The hidden agenda of modernity.* Chicago, IL: University of Chicago Press.

Whitehead, A. N. (1967). *Adventures of ideas.* New York: Penguin.

Index

Locators in *italics* refer to figures and those in **bold** to tables.